Advances
in Forensic
Taphonomy

Method, Theory, and
Archaeological
Perspectives

Advances in Forensic Taphonomy

Method, Theory, and Archaeological Perspectives

Edited by
William D. Haglund
Marcella H. Sorg

CRC Press
Boca Raton London New York Washington, D.C.

Library of Congress Cataloging-in-Publication Data

Advances in forensic taphonomy : method, theory, and archaeological perspectives /
edited by William D. Haglund and Marcella Sorg.
   p. cm.
Includes bibliographical references and index.
ISBN 0-8493-1189-6 (alk. paper)
   1. Forensic taphonomy. I. Haglund, William D. II. Sorg, Marcella H.

RA1063.47 .A37 2001
614'.1--dc21

2001029514

No claim to original U.S. Government works
International Standard Book Number 0-8493-1189-6
Library of Congress Card Number 2001029514
Printed in the United States of America 1 2 3 4 5 6 7 8 9 0
Printed on acid-free paper

Table of Contents

Section 4: Modification of Bone, Soft Tissue, and Associated Materials

Preface

It is only when viewed through the interdisciplinary lens that the full value of forensic taphonomy can be realized. Thus, we began the volume with a tri-partite foreword that is meant to be an integral part of this volume. These three contributions convey the perspectives of eminent spokespersons from pathology, anthropology/archaeology, and paleontology: the primary disciplines upon which taphonomy is based. Each author underscores the interdisciplinary nature of the field and, in the case of Hunter, presents a timely international perspective.

Forensic pathologist Donald Reay speaks to the compatibility of collecting taphonomic data in the context of contemporary death investigations, its non-intrusiveness to the investigation process, and its potential contribution of broader-based data sets. He spreads a welcome mat to taphonomic approaches that is founded on personal experience and an enlightened vision.

Lee Lyman, archaeologist and a leader in articulating taphonomic theory, points to what we believe is the seminal contribution that contemporary death investigation can repay to archaeology and paleontology. That is, a high-resolution perspective provided by actualistic experience in the time period spanning the "realms of flesh," from the time of death through decomposition, and the flesh's disappearance. Lyman further suggests a deeper, theoretical contribution of forensic taphonomy: its emphasis on positive findings (taphonomic data as evidence) as opposed to the more usual approach in paleontology of viewing taphonomic characteristics as a bias one must strip away to get to the truth.

John Hunter offers a refreshing historical view of the recognition and growing pains of "forensic archaeology" in Great Britain. He also touches on the paradigm difference between the United Kingdom and the United States in the teaching of archaeology/anthropology. We would hope this makes more salient our sometimes provincial tendencies, characteristics we must confront more and more as we meet on the international stage to ply our professions.

In addition to the bedrock disciplines of taphonomy, contributions to these pages also come from molecular biology, entomology, oceanography, criminal investigation, and philosophy — and from several authors outside the United States. Thus, it is in the spirit of interdisciplinary and international collaboration that we offer this volume.

William D. Haglund, Ph.D.
Marcella H. Sorg, Ph.D., D.A.B.F.A.

The Editors

William D. Haglund, Ph.D., received his B.A. degree in biology from the University of California, Irvine, and his Ph.D. in physical anthropology from the University of Washington, Seattle. He served as Chief Medical Investigator of the King County Medical Examiner's Office, Seattle, Washington, for 14 years. In December 1995 he became the United Nations' Senior Forensic Advisor for the International Criminal Tribunals for Rwanda and the former Yugoslavia. He is presently Director of the International forensic Program for Physicians for Human Rights, a Boston-based non-governmental organization. He has conducted forensic missions in numerous countries, including Guatemala, Honduras, Rwanda, Somaliland, Georgia/Abkhazia, the former Yugoslavia, Cyprus, Sri Lanka, Indonesia and East Timor.

Dr. Haglund teaches medicolegal death investigation through the Washington State Criminal Justice Training Commission. He also conducts international workshops, seminars and training in international forensic investigations.

Dr. Haglund's numerous publications have addressed issues such as outdoor scene processing for human remains, taphonomy, and human identification. Among these are two books, *Taphonomy: the Postmortem Fate of Human Remains* and the *Medicolegal Death Investigator Training Manual*. He has been an affiliate member of the Board of Directors of the National Association of Medical Examiners, is a past, three-time president of the Washington State Coroner/Medical Examiner's Association, and is a fellow of the American Academy of Forensic Sciences.

Marcella Harnish Sorg, Ph.D., D.A.B.F.A., is the consulting forensic anthropologist for the states of Maine and New Hampshire and an associated faculty member of the Department of Anthropology, University of Maine, since 1977. She served at the University of Maine as Associate Director of the Center for the Study of the First Americans, Institute for Quaternary Studies, from 1983 to 1988, and in private business from 1988 to 1996. She is currently Research Associate at the Margaret Chase Smith Center for Public Policy and on the faculty of both the School of Nursing and Department of Anthropology.

Dr. Sorg received her R.N. from Fairview Park General Hospital in 1969, her B.A. in psychology from Bowling Green State University in 1972, and her Ph.D. in physical anthropology from The Ohio State University in 1979, and she was certified by the American Board of Forensic Anthropology in 1984. She has served as Secretary and as President of the American Board of Forensic Anthropology, and has returned recently to serve as a Director. Dr. Sorg is a Fellow of the American Academy of Forensic Sciences, a Member of the American Association of Physical Anthropologists, and the Maine Medico-Legal Society, and co-founder of the Northeast Forensic Anthropology Association.

Dr. Sorg has authored many publications in forensic anthropology, taphonomy, and genetic demography. She was co-editor of the book *Bone Modification* in 1987, of *Forensic Taphonomy* in 1997, and co-authored *The Cadaver Dog Handbook* in 2000. She has done forensic research on scavenger modification of human remains as well as on the timing of epiphyseal union in the female medial clavicle. Her current forensic research focuses on taphonomic approaches to remains exposed in both marine and terrestrial environments, the estimation of postmortem interval, and the use of cadaver dogs, particularly for scattered remains.

The Contributors

Gail S. Anderson, Ph.D.
School of Criminology
Simon Fraser University
Burnaby, British Columbia
Canada

Owen B. Beattie, Ph.D.
Department of Anthropology
University of Alberta
Edmonton, Alberta
Canada

Hugh E. Berryman, Ph.D.
Berryman Consulting
228 Bluegrass Circle
Lebanon, Tennessee

D. R. Brothwell, Ph.D.
Department of Archaeology
University of York
York, England
United Kingdom

Valerie J. Cervenka, M.Sc.
Department of Entomology
University of Minnesota
St. Paul, Minnesota

Melissa Connor, M.A.
Forensic and Archaeological Services
Lincoln, Nebraska

Pamela M. Mayne Correia, M.A.
Department of Anthropology
University of Alberta
Edmonton, Alberta
Canada

Christyann M. Darwent, M.A.
Department of Anthropology
University of Missouri
Columbia, Missouri

Dennis C. Dirkmaat, Ph.D.
Department of Anthropology
Mercyhurst Archaeological Institute
Mercyhurst College
Erie, Pennsylvania

Curtis C. Ebbesmeyer, Ph.D.
Evans-Hamilton, Inc.
Seattle, Washington

Heather Gill-Robinson, M.A.
Department of Archaeology
University of York
York, England
United Kingdom

Sally Graver, B.A.
Smithsonian Institution
Washington, D.C.

William D. Haglund, Ph.D.
International Forensic Program
Physicians for Human Rights
Seattle, Washington

Michele Harvey, Ph.D.
Division of Medical Genetics
School of Medicine
University of Washington
Seattle, Washington

Michael J. Hochrein, B.A.
Federal Bureau of Investigation
St. Louis, Missouri

Michael J. Hoffman, Ph.D.
Department of Anthropology
Colorado College
Colorado Springs, Colorado

Thomas D. Holland, Ph.D.
U.S. Army Central Identification Laboratory
Hickam AFB, Hawaii

J.R. Hunter, Ph.D.
University of Birmingham
Birmingham, England
United Kingdom

R.C. Janaway, M.Sc.
Department of Archaeological Sciences
University of Bradford
Bradford, England
United Kingdom

Mary-Claire King, Ph.D.
Division of Medical Genetics
School of Medicine
University of Washington
Seattle, Washington

Wayne D. Lord, Ph.D.
National Center for the Analysis of Violent Crime
FBI Academy
Quantico, Virginia

R. Lee Lyman, Ph.D.
Department of Anthropology
University of Missouri
Columbia, Missouri

Robert J. Morton, B.A.
National Center for the Analysis of Violent Crime
FBI Academy
Quantico, Virginia

Elizabeth A. Murray, Ph.D.
Department of Biology
College of Mount St. Joseph
Cincinnati, Ohio

Jon J. Nordby, Ph.D.
Final Analysis Forensics
Tacoma, Washington

Elayne J. Pope, M.A.
Department of Anthropology
University of Tennessee
Knoxville, Tennessee

Donald T. Reay, M.D.
Oak Harbor, Washington

William C. Rodriguez III, Ph.D.
Office of the Armed Forces Medical Examiner
Armed Forces Institute of Pathology
Washington, D.C.

Mirjana Roksandic, Ph.D.
Max Planck Institute for Demographic Research
Rostock, Germany

Frank P. Saul, Ph.D.
DMORT V Regional Command
Lucas County Coroner's Office
Toledo, Ohio

Julie Mather Saul, B.A.
Forensic Anthropology Laboratory
Lucas County Coroner's Office
Toledo, Ohio

Stefan Schmitt, M.S.
School of Criminology and Criminal Justice
Florida State University, and
Florida Department of Law Enforcement
Tallahassee, Florida

Douglas D. Scott, Ph.D.
Midwest Archaeological Center
National Park Service
Lincoln, Nebraska

Tal Simmons, Ph.D.
Department of Anthropology
Western Michigan University
Kalamazoo, Michigan

Mark Skinner, Ph.D.
Department of Archaeology
Simon Fraser University
Burnaby, British Columbia
Canada

Paul Sledzik, M.S.
National Museum of Health and Medicine
Armed Forces Institute of Pathology
Washington, D.C.

Kristin O. Sobolik, Ph.D.
Department of Anthropology, and
Institute of Quaternary and Climate Studies
University of Maine
Orono, Maine

Marcella H. Sorg, Ph.D.
Margaret Chase Smith Center of Public Policy,
School of Nursing, and
Department of Anthropology
University of Maine
Orono, Maine

Steven A. Symes, Ph.D.
Department of Pathology
University of Tennessee, and
Regional Forensic Center
Memphis, Tennessee

Douglas H. Ubelaker, Ph.D.
Department of Anthropology
National Museum of Natural History
Smithsonian Institution
Washington, D.C.

John Whittaker, Ph.D.
Department of Anthropology
Grinnell College
Grinnell, Iowa

John A. Williams, Ph.D.
Department of Anthropology
University of North Dakota
Grand Forks, North Dakota

Heather P. York, M.A.
Department of Anthropology
Kent State University
Kent, Ohio

Acknowledgments

As always in our endeavors, we thank those closest to us for their support and patience, especially Claudia and Ed. We also thank Joy Sorg, Noah Haglund, C.J. Bidwell, Juliet Fernandez, Boyd Brown III, Judith Cooper, Karen Turnmire, Bill and Kathy Cook, Amy Clifford, and Barbara Harrity. And, we offer our eternal gratitude to Becky McEldowney of CRC Press for her saintly forbearance during the birthing of this volume. We extend our gratitude to the Physicians for Human Rights of Boston, whose commitment to forensic issues in international human rights is an inspiration. We also thank colleagues at the Margaret Chase Smith Center for Public Policy and the School of Nursing, University of Maine, for their encouragement.

Foreword

R. LEE LYMAN

Russian paleontologist I.A. Efremov (1940) coined the term *taphonomy* and defined it as the study of the transition, in all its details, of organic remains from the biosphere to the lithosphere. My dictionary defines *forensic* as pertaining to argument, debate, or public discussion suitable for courts of justice. Contributors to this volume and its precursor (Haglund and Sorg, 1997) would define *forensic taphonomy* as the study of the transition of humans from living organisms to mortal remains, including causes of death, for judicial or legal purposes. I find the extension of taphonomic research into forensics to be critical for one simple reason.

What can readily be categorized as taphonomic research has a deep history in paleontology, one of my two personal choices for the most exciting field of scientific inquiry, the other being archaeology. In the early nineteenth century, William Buckland (1823) observed how a hyena gnawed and thereby destroyed animal bones. Buckland used his observations to conclude that ancient bones with similar damage recovered from ancient cave deposits had been chewed by ancient hyenas. Archaeologist Edouard Lartet (1860) used precisely the same sort of reasoning to conclude that prehistoric humans had butchered extinct animals and, thus, humans and those beasts had been contemporaries. What Buckland, Lartet, and others in the nineteenth century were doing was *actualistic research* in an effort to gain insight to the processes that created particular taphonomic patterns among modern bones.

Actualistic research — documentation of modern processes and the visible effects and patterns they produce — formed the basis for their inferences that the same processes had created the patterns among both the modern and the prehistoric materials.

More than a century later, taphonomists have microscopes, including scanning electronic microscopes, instead of magnifying glasses, and they have computers to crunch all kinds of data of which Buckland and Lartet never dreamed. They also have radiocarbon dating laboratories to tell them exactly how old the bones are; biologists who can tell them the most intimate details about the physiology and life ways of the animals whose remains they are studying; chemists and geneticists to study dietary and genetic variation, respectively, as reflected in preserved tissues; and a host of other specialists, laboratories, and machines to help them decipher the fossil and subfossil records and thereby write taphonomic histories. Books and journal articles abound on each topic, indicating we know a great deal more about taphonomy than our intellectual predecessors of the nineteenth century. Yet the fundamental epistemology of actualism pioneered by Buckland, Lartet, and others remains the centerpiece of taphonomic and forensic research.

Taphonomy and forensics are identical fields of investigation. Both seek an answer to the question "What are these bones doing here?" as taphonomist Pat Shipman put it 20 years ago. True, forensic scientists want an answer they can take to court, whereas a taphonomist's answer is usually judged only by other taphonomists and perhaps a few paleontologists or zooarchaeologists. Otherwise, there is absolutely no reason why the methods and techniques of one field of inquiry cannot overlap virtually completely those of the other, and this brings us to the point of my brief history of taphonomy, the reason I find the extension of the definition of taphonomy to include forensics and human remains to be significant.

That point is simply this. Forensic scientists, on the one hand, are always looking for evidence that tells them what I think of as something positive about the bones and teeth they examine. Who was the represented individual? How and why did he or she die? Why are the mortal remains of the individual in the condition they are when found? Does anything about that condition imply a felonious act or help identify a perpetrator of the act? On the other hand, paleontologists and, particularly, zooarchaeologists are typically looking for what I think of as negative evidence, which I do not mean is the notion captured by the phrase "the absence of evidence is not necessarily evidence of absence," sometimes referred to with the shorthand "negative evidence." Rather, what I mean is that taphonomy is too often construed by taphonomists to merely comprise biasing processes.

Most of the time in the zooarchaeological literature of the 1980s and 1990s we find the phrase "strip away the taphonomy cover print" or some variant thereof (see Lyman [1994] for an introduction to the relevant literature). Much less frequently do we see the evidence a taphonomist examines construed as somehow contributing in a positive way to our understanding of and knowledge about the past. And that, I think, is an important lesson that taphonomists can learn from forensic scientists. What do those gnawing marks apparently generated by carnivores represent with respect to the paleoecological setting in which the bones were deposited? Certainly more than that some bones or bone parts might be missing not because ancient hominids didn't deposit them in the site sediments but because carnivores removed them. Those gnawing marks clearly mean that carnivores were part of the paleoecological setting, just as butchering marks on other bones in the collection signify that hominids were another part of the setting, had tools, and were extracting resources from animal carcasses; this was Lartet's inference of 1860 and that same inference can be made today.

Perhaps I am a bit too pessimistic with respect to my taphonomically inclined colleagues. Regardless of that, I think it is clear that we need to think about taphonomic histories in the same way that forensic scientists think about the human remains that they study — as revealing aspects of those histories that could be important for both analysis and interpretation. But by the same token, forensic scientists need to think, at least sometimes, like taphonomists; that is, to think of the negative aspects of taphonomic histories, the possible biases. For example, they need to be able to distinguish damage to bones that resulted from rodent gnawing from damage that resulted from felonious assault on the individual. They also must recognize that the former, if sufficiently extensive, may well remove all traces of the latter; that is, taphonomic history can bias — be negative — forensic evidence.

I have argued that taphonomy and forensic science are, in a very practical way, sister disciplines. But they are also a bit different and some of us occasionally forget that fact. That these disciplines are different can be made clear by posing a question and telling a brief story to answer. Why are human feet sometimes so much better preserved than other parts of the body? A taphonomist would argue that it may be the result of the greater structural density of foot bones than other bones of the human skeleton. But as my colleague Sam Stout, who oversees the Human Skeletal Identification Laboratory at the University of Missouri, Columbia, pointed out to me, humans wear shoes, and footwear protects and shields human feet from the ravages of various sorts of taphonomic agents. On one occasion, Stout was out of town and two deputy sheriffs seeking his counsel showed up at my office near the forensic lab. They handed me a tightly sealed plastic bag and asked that I make sure that Dr. Stout be given the bag as its contents comprised important forensic evidence for a legal case.

I glanced at the bag and asked the deputies why Stout would want the wing tip shoe the bag contained. The deputies replied, "Because of the foot inside the shoe." Stout was glad to have such a complete portion of the human anatomy; I nearly lost my lunch. Looking back at that example, I *did* learn something from the forensic perspective. Forensic scientists can no doubt learn similar lessons from taphonomists, and probably without any feeling of nausea.

The chapters in this volume are important contributions. In my view they reveal many of the parallels between taphonomy and forensic science, and in many ways other than the most fundamental shared aspect — actualism. Those of us in the taphonomy business can learn much about the earliest stages of taphonomic histories by reading this book. Forensic scientists can learn an equal amount by close study of the research undertaken by taphonomists that is described here. There is no shortage of paleontologically and archaeologically related studies focusing on single and multiple body or carcass sets of remains. Taphonomists often perform various types of actualistic research that forensic scientists would no doubt find of some utility were they to examine it. Recently, I've heard more and more regarding the benefits of interdisciplinary research — more funding, more solidly founded results, more relevant and pertinent conclusions, more marketable graduate students with interdisciplinary training. Forensic scientists and taphonomists would be well advised to pay heed and to interact much more frequently. This book is an important step in that direction.

References

Buckland, W.
   1823   *Reliquiae Diluvianae, or Observations on the Organic Remains Contained in Caves, Fissures and Diluvial Gravel and on Other Phenomena, Attesting to the Action of a Universal Deluge.* Murray, London.

Efremov, I.A.
   1940   Taphonomy: a new branch of paleontology, *Pan-American Geologist* 74:81–93.

Haglund, W.D. and M.H. Sorg, Editors
   1997   *Forensic Taphonomy: The Postmortem Fate of Human Remains*, CRC Press, Boca Raton, FL.

Lartet, E.
   1860   On the coexistence of man with certain extinct quadrupeds proved by fossil bones, from various Pleistocene deposits bearing incisions made by sharp instruments, *M.G.S. Quarterly Journal of the Geological Society of London* 16:471–479.

Lyman, R.L.
   1994   *Vertebrate Taphonomy*, Cambridge University Press, Cambridge, U.K.

Foreword

DONALD T. REAY

This second volume on forensic taphonomy adds to the available information about the postmortem fate of human remains. It is necessary to review the objectives first laid out by the editors in their first volume, *Forensic Taphonomy: the Postmortem Fate of Human Remains* (1997). In its introduction, the editors stated, "Data can be collected routinely in the normal course of the forensic investigation without interfering with the medical legal process. And if data collection strategies are shared among practitioners, the data sets will be more comparable and broader-based." In their first volume, the editors made a major contribution to our understanding of how bodies decompose in different environmental conditions, the effects on the body of human and non-human activities including animal scavenging, the effects of aqueous dispersion of bodies and body parts, and the effects of immediate postmortem transfer. Although the first volume is multi-authored, each chapter provides the reader with new data and observations, frequently about individual cases, but nicely synthesized and discussed for the reader to ponder their significance. This second volume brings new data and observations extending from the initial volume, and again gives us insight into the discipline of forensic taphonomy.

I would be remiss not to comment on what I consider the major achievement that the editors have attained by publishing on this subject. In 1991, I had the distinct privilege of reviewing the doctoral thesis of Dr. Haglund (Haglund, 1991). This was my first exposure to an organized body of information which dealt with the subject of taphonomy. Much of this work was the result of some 10 years of investigation into the deaths of a number of women who were the composite of the Green River murder investigation. During that investigation the bodies of young women were discovered in varying states of decomposition including skeletonization. At that time, our emphasis was on establishing identity and cause of death, the typical obligation and expectation of any agency responsible for examining human remains in a death investigation. Through the efforts of Dr. Haglund other information began to emerge. The manner and sequence of the disarticulation of the skeleton were noted and the way in which bodies were scavenged by predators was observed. Additionally, the environmental milieu in which human remains were found took on new significance. Although the ambient conditions have always been recognized as playing a major role in establishing time of death, as it unfolds and manifests itself in decomposition, assessing these observations for answers took on considerable urgency because of the nature of this serial murder investigation.

In attempting to answer some questions concerning the nature of the decomposition and the dispersal of skeletal remains by predators, standard references in anthropology and forensic pathology were consulted. Sources from both these fields were found wanting in providing specific useful information. It was clear that anthropology and forensic pathology had not progressed to the point where useful information and observations had been recorded to aid our investigation. It was also clear that archeologists and paleontologists had much to say regarding the handling and processing of a scene where ancient human remains had been discovered.

Recognizing the limitations of the information that was available, we attempted to answer questions about the postmortem fate of human remains during our death investigation. This was a new and exciting area of exploration which stimulated Dr. Haglund to organize the observations that later formed the central theme of his doctoral thesis. In my view, a new discipline of forensic taphonomy emerged for use by the forensic community.

Why "taphonomy?" The use of the word has been generally restricted to the archeological recovery of burial sites and, to some authors (Olsen, 1980), the study of dead organisms from the biosphere to the lithosphere, i.e., fossilized organisms and their death assemblages. Taphonomy comes from the Greek *taphe*, which means grave. Since it has an archeological meaning for the study of gravesites, the subject material under examination from a forensic point of view is the study of the site of discovery of a body, which can be a shallow or deep grave or a surface deposit. The immediate concerns of the death investigator are the disintegration of flesh and bone in different environmental conditions and how it relates to the time of death. Other concerns include the modifications and disbursement of body parts caused by animal scavengers and the effects of standing and running water on a body; and the effects on a body of postmortem trauma whether inflicted by another human, animal, or the environment.

It is fitting to make available whatever information exists on the subject of forensic taphonomy to enhance any death investigation where a body has been exposed to a variety of forces of man and nature. Volume 1 succeeded in accomplishing its goal of presenting data and information from a variety of sources in a very readable and scholarly fashion. This second volume amplifies the success of the first. The editors are to be commended for assembling the contributors to present information for use by the forensic community.

References

Haglund, W.D.
    1991   Applications of Taphonomic Models to Forensic Investigations. Ph.D. dissertation, Department of Anthropology, University of Washington, Seattle, University Microfilms, Ann Arbor, MI.

Haglund W.D. and M.H. Sorg, Editors
    1997   *Forensic Taphonomy: The Postmortem Fate of Human Remains*, CRC Press, Boca Raton, FL.

Olsen, E.C.
    1980   Taphonomy: its history and role in community evolution. In *Fossils in the Making: Vertebrate Taphonomy and Paleoecology*, edited by A.K. Behrensmeyer and A.P. Hill, pp. 5–19. University of Chicago Press, Chicago, IL.

Foreword: A Pilgrim in Forensic Archaeology — A Personal View

J.R. HUNTER

Forensic archaeology is a relatively well-recognized area of study in the United States where it is a component of physical anthropology in medico-legal matters. However, in the United Kingdom, where archaeology evolved as an independent discipline concerned purely with excavation and field skills, and in which human skeletal analysis was incidental rather than focal, forensic archaeology developed somewhat later and with a different character. Differences between the two "archaeologies" become compounded at scenes of crime: in Britain, for example, post-mortem study is normally the legal responsibility of the forensic pathologist, the role of the forensic archaeologist being one of providing supporting data through fieldwork.

Forensic archaeology probably took its first public bow on a U.K. stage in 1988 with the discovery and excavation of a 3-year-old boy called Stephen Jennings, murdered by his father some 26 years earlier. There may have been instances of archaeologists assisting in other cases before then, but there are no informal, or even folk records of such, nor are there any more formal reports of archaeologists being called upon to give evidence in court. For this archaeologist, one of those involved in the recovery of Stephen Jennings, the event set in motion an unwitting divergence from an otherwise innocent career in historical archaeology.

Since that time the smooth and predictable cycle of academic life has been disrupted by visits to distant parts of the country at short notice, by lengthy briefing meetings about hitherto unknown nefarious individuals and their activities, and by unpredictable late night telephone calls. The number of homicide cases involved over the years has never been counted; some merely reared their heads as requests for advice, or as visits by officers bearing a bag of bones, but every year a consistent number developed into scene visits and into deeper, practical involvement. These have occurred as complete burials, dismemberments and cremations; they have involved adults, children, ex-lovers, and spouses, and prostitutes; they have been brought about by drugs, accident, cultural incompatibility, or by sheer hatred; and the victims have been buried deeply, shallowly, or simply dumped on the surface and concealed. Taphonomically, some have decayed beyond recognition, some show differential decay, some still hung together articulately thanks to the resilience of synthetic fibers, and others had been scavenged by creatures of the wild. No two cases have ever been the same, or even remotely similar. They testify to unpleasant sub-cultures normally concealed from the gaze of much of society, and are viewed uncomfortably by many middle-class undergraduates who wrongly considered forensic archaeology to be a more glamorous subject for study.

Forensic archaeology has evolved rather than flourished, and this somewhat personal view touches upon, inter alia, matters of professional and ethical responsibility encountered by its practitioners working in a novel arena. Conveniently, it follows an earlier paper that sought to market forensic archaeology to an unwary U.K. archaeological community (Hunter 1994).

Background

There used to be the naive view, certainly held by this practitioner, that to trot across a suspect's garden with a twin-probe geophysics array would undoubtedly detect the buried remains of some unfaithful spouse allegedly buried there and, equally, that to apply skilled archaeological methodology at a scene of crime was all that was necessary to ensure recovery in the best professional way. Such simplicity was soon dashed. It became manifestly apparent that forensic archaeology would never be a straightforward transference of methodology, but rather the application of archaeological theory to forensic circumstance. The time frame, the protocols, the processes, the chains of evidence, the working parameters, the ancillary disciplines, and the judicial constraints were all distinctive. More pertinently, the way in which the buried data were interrogated was different, and this alone effectively created a divergence between forensic archaeology and research-driven archaeology.

In a recent paper entitled "The Excavation of Modern Murder" there was an attempt to flag some of the questioning that guided the excavation of a homicide victim; it also highlighted the differences between those questions and those designs which underlie the research-driven excavation of, for example, a Romano-British burial (Hunter, 1999). Pathological examination of a murder victim normally requires responses on at least three fronts: identity, interval since death, and cause/manner of death. Archaeological intervention can, directly or indirectly, aid all three, but the questions are already diverging from those normally asked under typical archaeological circumstances. Most significant is the issue of individuality: the homicide remains become personalized, they have a name, and they may have a grieving family. The life, activities, and last movement of the victim become a focus of necessary interest, and thus the ethical issues and professional responsibilities take on a different character from those of the traditional archaeological norm.

Ultimately the forensic inquiry is geared to resolving the question, "Who killed this person?" In helping to achieve that answer the forensic archaeologist asks questions not normally voiced under purely archaeological conditions, and these questions frame the methodology of inquiry accordingly. Recovery is not simply the recording of buried evidence. It involves an understanding of how a grave might have been dug, the transfer of material between offender and grave, the nature of that material, how it can be sampled, how it can be contaminated, and often the degree of conclusiveness it can offer as evidence within the strict definitions imposed by forensic science.

The archaeologist not only needs to be sure of his or her role within the investigating team, but must also be confident about how other members of the team operate, the nature of their evidence, and their respective methodologies. Other team members — the forensic scientist, entomologist, pathologist, and scene of crime examiners, etc. — have different evidentiary requirements based on diverse knowledge, background, and training. There are also new areas of study, including taphonomy, which lie in no-man's land. Taphonomy covers more than simple decay process. Often perceived incorrectly as the exclusive remit of the forensic pathologist, it requires a diversity of knowledge from animal behavior and bacteriological activity to climatic and botanical effects (see Haglund and Sorg, 1997).

Mission and Morality

Forensic archaeology requires team playing within a broad panorama of the different groups and disciplines involved. The archaeologist needs not only to understand the respective roles, but also to ensure that the different groups understand the nature of archaeological inquiry. Sigler Eisenberg's early (1985) identification of a mission factor was especially perspicacious in this respect, but mission also seems equally relevant within the archaeological community itself. In a well-worded article, Cox (1998) criticized a number of operators for calling themselves forensic archaeologists when they were unlikely to appreciate the nature of criminal inquiry, the archaeologist's role within it, or the extent of subject areas involved from psychology to taphonomy. There are also, sadly, archaeological purists who have failed to grasp what forensic archaeology is really about simply because they have been unable to recognize that the questioning of the buried data and the goals are distinctive from traditional archaeology.

The end point of the forensic process is the conviction of the offender. In the recovery and autopsy of the victim, there is a strong argument to suggest that the end justifies whatever means are necessary to achieve it. In human terms, the recovered buried remains possess a name, a history, and a set of familial relationships. In cold, clinical, terms, they constitute potential evidence that requires investigation, analysis, or dissection to answer specific questions. It may be that the need to achieve those answers requires the dominance of one technique over another, that the need to collect one type of evidence overrules the loss of other evidence. Decisions are made through collaboration between scene specialists, not through a process of ethical and moral dilemmas, nor through the exactitudes of archaeological purism. What matters most are the underlying principles of the various techniques involved and the ability of all concerned to understand them. This is a process in which the archaeologist has to respond to a given situation: what may be professional best practice in one archaeological context is not necessarily best practice in a forensic one, and vice versa.

It is perhaps opportune that the levels of competence and ability required in a forensic archaeologist are now being defined more precisely. The U.K. is moving inexorably toward the registration of forensic practitioners in all fields, from archaeologists to entomologists and from fingerprint specialists to toxicologists. Experience suggests that key requirements for a forensic archaeologist will be a long and varied experience in archaeological fieldwork, a working knowledge of skeletal remains, and the ability to operate independently within a crime scene, to make rapid decisions, and to be confident. Over-arching, however, is the need to understand crime scene protocols and the evidentiary requirements of others involved at the scene itself.

The fragmented police structure in Britain means that disseminating information of any type or spreading mission is extremely difficult. The evidence from the relatively low number of burials in the U.K. each year (there is no precise figure but information suggests probably less than around 15 per year out of a total of some 700 homicides), based on word of mouth and anecdote, suggests that around half of these utilize proper archaeological techniques. Most involve instances where the burial site is known, the operation is fully briefed, and the forensic archaeologist is brought in at an early stage. The others (again, based on word of mouth and anecdote) are dug up rapidly without archaeological support through the necessity for speed (custody law in Scotland, for example, is only 6 hours), because they were found in an existing operation, or because of the perceived costs of bringing in specialists when the case is already cut and dried (i.e., when the necessary questions had already been answered without specialist support).

Some police forces are more than happy to use archaeologists, and draw them in frequently at the earliest opportunity, whereas others are clearly not interested. Ignorance is no longer an excuse: several archaeologists have expended much energy and effort over the last decade in presentations on search and recovery to various groups involved, e.g., detectives, scene of crime officers, forensic scientists, coroners, etc. Homicide convictions have used archaeological evidence, and hence exhumation without archaeological assistance now lays itself open to more exacting cross-examination in court. One recent case was based entirely on taphonomic criteria. Was the victim's state of decay commensurate with the interval since death and with active local carnivore activity, or had the body been moved? And who is competent to give opinion? To what extent is this "archaeology" by either U.K. or U.S. definitions?

In retrospect, some 12 years since Stephen Jennings was excavated by archaeologists, there has been substantial progress, but not wholesale practical acceptance by either police forces or even archaeologists themselves. Stephen Jennings was a landmark. Whatever brutality and abuse he suffered in his 3.5 years of life are in some small way balanced by a growing string of life sentences that have occurred since, for which the recovery of his body was an archaeological precedent. However, even after these same 12 years, those few archaeologists who practiced forensic archaeology on their own time then, as some form of conviction, are still doing it today, still on their own time as an extra to their "day" jobs. More significant progress might perhaps have been made from a single high-profile case with national media interest.

Breadth

At a conference in 1995 I made the throwaway comment that forensic investigation was one of the most frightening exercises for an archaeologist to undertake (see Cox, 1995). It was, however, a comment restricted to an experience of the occasional scene of crime, of helping to resolve some clandestine event by pitting wits against an unknown adversary. The rewards lie in achieving a sense of altruism from applying skills to society's darker side, while being protected from the full reality by a cushion of scene protocols and a buffer of judicial machinery. These mixed sensations will be familiar to those who have undertaken the same or something similar, but the experience did not embrace the horrors of genocide and mass graves, where the motivation of inquiry and the questioning of evidence differ even further from research-led archaeology. Nor was it anticipated that Mant's early work on taphonomic processes might be called upon to explain or predict the state of decay in multiple burials (see Mant, 1987). Those archaeologists who have gone to the killing fields of Rwanda, Bosnia, or Kosovo will be more acutely aware of these various issues as well as the emotional factors involved.

The word "forensic" is not to be taken lightly. Unlike other specialist archaeological epithets — "environmental," "underwater," or "Aegean" — it involves a gravitas and a more distinctive knowledge base than is generally recognized by many other archaeologists. Like its research parent, forensic archaeology has no well-defined limits: it branches into fairly obvious areas such as biological anthropology; and it covers other taphonomic phenomena, although both the timescales and the materials are novel (cardboard, paper, cigarette butts, plastics and synthetic fibers, and human decay in the short term). Forensic archaeology also feeds off other intelligences of which the pure archaeologist might be better aware, notably offender profiling and dump site analysis. It also merges, uncomfortably, into matters of human rights.

Until about 5 years ago, the concept of human rights had no place in the emerging forensic archaeology of Europe, or even in its vocabulary. From the United States physical anthropologists spread their expertise into South and Central America, and then into Africa, initially to recover and assess the mass graves of victims of genocide and political killings, and subsequently to recognize evidence of torture and human rights violations on human remains. Belief that such atrocity could never occur within the civilized western world was overly optimistic. Bosnia put an end to that, as later did Kosovo.

Pessimism suggests that it is in human nature for there to be more killings, and that there is some urgency to improve on our expertise for the next time. Forensic archaeology's first 12 years in the U.K., if nothing else, have been a learning curve; no two scenes of crime, big or small are ever the same and the emergence of human rights issues has become a fact of life in forensic archaeology whether we like it or not. Torture, for example, both psychological and physical, can occur in many ways: beatings, suspension, electric shock, burns, asphyxiation, nail torture, dental torture, pressure, strapping, forced positions, sexual abuse, etc., and any of these can leave traces on the hard as well as the soft tissue (Henneberg, 1999). It is important that the archaeologist knows about them during the recovery process, and that the anthropologist knows what to look for in the autopsy. Once again it is the nature of the questions that drives the method of recovery, not the direct application of field archaeology.

The excavation of mass graves in Bosnia and Kosovo has also provided a much needed focus for the energies and convictions of forensic archaeologists and forensic anthropologists from many parts of Europe, notably Scandinavia and the United Kingdom. This is understandable given that the skills and knowledge these people learn (many of them students) from a growing range of university courses are largely unpracticed in what we might call normal criminal circumstances, and are likely to remain so. For some this is probably the only way of getting forensic archaeology experience.

Archaeologists tend to be noted for the values they hold, their concern for the environment, and for their contribution to society's knowledge base. To many archaeologists, working within mass graves is to exercise archaeological skills in an unusually meaningful way, and one more suited to satisfying personal missions under the disguise of altruism. It fits well, too, with a profession based on short-term employment contracts, and which in the United Kingdom at least has seen the prescriptive processing of developer-led archaeology sap much of the creative spirit from the discipline. Bosnia also gives some scope for physical anthropologists to practice in a real scenario, not just with the bones from an Iron Age cemetery and the odd Romano-British family. This is particularly relevant for those practitioners from countries where, unlike the United States, physical anthropologists have no traditional role in the forensic process. These may be some of the reasons why Bosnia and Kosovo seem so attractive.

Forensic archaeology can also act as a postbox to a rich variety of skills that may be used on an occasional basis — zoological and botanical reference sets, total station recording or conservation skills, palynology, soils science etc. — all of which supplement the existing bread-and-butter techniques of the established forensic science service. This is a new and largely untapped forensic science resource. Sadly, it can become embarrassing when the archaeological proponents of these skills profess minimal or nil interest in support. They are reluctant to drop everything at a few hours' notice, to be distracted, or be inconvenienced after hours. While quite content to bask in the heat of being an expert in beetles, grasses, teeth, cremations, or snails, they are not prepared to be inconvenienced where their contribution might matter most.

Forensic archaeology feeds off other intelligences of which the traditional archaeologist might be aware, notably offender profiling, site disposal statistics, witness veracity, etc. All these have to be slotted into an equation in a forensic search before site targeting can take place. Not only does the archaeologist begin to know the victim, but there is also a real need to know about the offender, because knowing about the offender helps to locate the grave. How can objectivity possibly be retained under such circumstances? How is it possible to balance the need to remain clinical, and at a mental distance? And what happens when, despite all efforts to prevent it, there is involvement with the family of a victim, a victim who has not been found, and whose case the police may have wound down? Is it still possible to remain detached from the event? The longer and more detailed the case, the more familiar the victim becomes to the searcher. There are some victims I have never met, but I know them better than I know some of my friends. Where do ethics and responsibility fit into that context, and is it something that should now be reflected in our archaeology degree programs?

Search

Recovery is only one part of the forensic archaeological spectrum. Another important aspect, and probably the one used most frequently is search. Several archaeologists, working independently for any of the 40 or so separate police forces which constitute the United Kingdom's law enforcement system, noticed the lack of awareness among police forces regarding the range of search techniques available (technical, human, and canine) for finding clandestine graves. They also noted that the advantages and limitations of the respective techniques were largely unrecognized, and the extent to which the decay processes of the individual were being ignored in the detection equation. There was little conception, for example, of using complementary methods, or even sequences, depending on the situation. There was, by contrast, a tendency for police forces to use ground-penetrating radar (GPR) irrespective of whether it would work within the environment in question, its cost, and whether the operator was familiar with the responses given by GRP to human remains as opposed to the more customary civil engineering application. There was a similar tendency to consider geological search techniques with little in the way of regard for the scale of the task in hand, the nature of the local environment, or of the required sensitivity of response.

The clear need for a central advice forum was eventually satisfied by the setting up in 1996 of the Forensic Search Advisory Group (FSAG) which incorporated personnel in academic life, commerce, police, and the military, covering a range of skills including geophysics, aerial interpretation, archaeology, decay chemistry, and body-scent dog training. Although the group has no formal status, it enjoys the recognition of ACPO (Association of Chief Police Officers) and is used frequently by the Home Office and the National Crime

Faculty to put any police force requiring support in touch with the group by means of a 24-hour pager system. The group receives requests approximately 30 times per year on average, of which about two thirds result in operational support. The FSAG is broadly modeled on NecroSearch International, a similar but larger group in the United States. Elsewhere in Europe a similar organization has emerged in Sweden and a new group is forming in The Netherlands. There are embryonic noises emanating from other countries, but in general there is little awareness elsewhere of the opportunities and potential available from harnessing and centralizing resources in this way.

Experience of this centralized search facility suggests that search usually follows one of two broadly defined routes (although there are always exceptions): (1) cases where a person is missing and a homicide and disposal are thought to have occurred, and where a number of locations need identifying and targeting; and (2) instances where information is received that an alleged clandestine burial has occurred in a particular vicinity, usually in a place that can be closely defined.

The first of these involves a protracted analysis, initially desktop, of landscape, geology, and photographic evidence, together with psychological profiling, dump analysis, and the use of other intelligence. This includes targeting possible locations and utilizing certain techniques and sequences of techniques in order to maximize recovery potential. In these investigations the body of a known victim is being actively pursued. The second, and undoubtedly the more common, requires the elimination of sites. The information that promotes them is often hearsay, nostalgic, and warped through passage of time and drug or alcohol abuse. Despite this, the information often seems to contain some elements of truth and has to be verified, but in these investigations the onus is on eliminating the site from a potential inquiry and the methodology differs accordingly. These two broad types constitute the majority of scenarios. It could be argued that the methods for determining that a burial is not there are not necessarily the same as those implemented for proving that it is there.

The importance of the archaeological pedigree in forensic search, and in forensic geophysics in particular, is simply that the requirements of archaeology bear much closer resemblance to those of operational taphonomic phenomena, etc. Many of us would also like to see a situation in which some practitioners are able to operate in a manner that is more than a hurried addition to their own livelihoods and careers. Highest on the list, however, is the need to fund, coordinate and develop the discipline to a level of more universal respectability, not just in the United Kingdom but also throughout Europe. Forensic archaeology, a victim of structure and perception, still has a long, long way to go.

References

Cox, M.

1995　Crime scene archaeology is one of the most frightening areas of archaeology in which to operate, *The Field Archaeologist* 23:14–16.

1998　Criminal concerns: a plethora of forensic archaeologists, *The Archaeologist* 33:21–22.

Haglund, W.D. and M.H. Sorg, Editors

1997　*Forensic Taphonomy: The Postmortem Fate of Human Remains*, CRC Press, Boca Raton, FL.

Henneberg, M.

1999　Forensic Evidence of Torture: Investigations into Human Rights Violations, unpublished M.Phil. thesis, University of Birmingham.

Hunter, J.R.
  1994   Forensic archaeology in Britain, *Antiquity* 68:758–69.

  1999   The excavation of modern murder. In *The Loved Body's Corruption: Archaeological Contributions to the Study of Human Mortality*, edited by J. Downes and T. Pollard, pp. 209–223. Cruithne Press, Glasgow.

Mant, A.K.
  1987   Knowledge acquired from post-war exhumations. In *Death, Decay and Reconstruction: Approaches to Archaeology and Forensic Science*, edited by A. Boddington, A.N. Garland, and R.C. Janaway, pp. 65–78. Manchester University Press, Manchester, U.K.

Sigler Eisenberg, B.
  1985   Forensic research: expanding the concept of applied archaeology, *American Antiquity* 50(3):650–655.

Section 1

Theoretical Perspectives

Advancing Forensic Taphonomy: Purpose, Theory, and Process

1

MARCELLA H. SORG
WILLIAM D. HAGLUND

Contents

0-8493-1189-6/02/$0.00+$1.50
© 2002 by CRC Press LLC

Background

Since work began on the first volume *Forensic Taphonomy* in 1993 (Haglund and Sorg, 1997a), traditional taphonomy and forensic research has undergone significant change. Additionally, despite the wide range of topics covered in the first volume, there remained significant topics not covered and those that should be covered in more depth. This volume attempts to extend coverage to include recent advances in the allied taphonomic and forensic fields as well as to explore a number of topics more fully or from a different perspective. The continuing effort is to articulate the interface among the paleontological, archaeological, and forensic sciences, placing it under one interdisciplinary umbrella (Haglund, 1991; Haglund and Sorg, 1997b,c).

In many ways forensic taphonomy contrasts with and complements paleotaphonomy. Martin (1999) describes the purview of paleotaphonomy as an environmental and historical science, along with paleontology and geology. He argues that it is this very long timescale that is uniquely valuable in terms of its suitability for studying global environmental problems. With this long, time-averaged view, "The surface mixed layer or taphonomically active zone (TAZ) of sediment acts as a low pass filter, primarily through bioturbation and dissolution, that dumps high frequency signals before their incorporation into the historical record… (and) short-term noise is damped" (Martin, 1999b:vii). In fact, forensic taphonomy has just the opposite focus on the recent time frame (including the TAZ so contaminated by bioturbation) and particularly upon the anthropogenic 'noise' that Martin would seek to silence.

In our own evaluation of the first volume, we felt that, although we had brought many disparate topics together and had focused a taphonomic perspective on forensic work, there were shortcomings that we continue to face. The relevance of forensic case material and research to paleontology and archaeology needs to be demonstrated. More effort needs to be given to a systematic approach to forensic recovery and interpretation which incorporates archaeological methods, and some attention needs to be focused on understanding (and precisely describing) the early decomposition process and its consequences for diagenesis and paleontological or archaeological interpretation. In this volume, we have chosen an explicitly bioenvironmental and idioecological approach. By bioenvironmental, we mean the incorporation of biological and environmental data using interpretive frameworks, models, and theory from allied disciplines. By idioecological, we mean the explicit focus on the idiosyncratic synchronic and diachronic (so-called context-specific) features of the case microenvironment, including the ecology and the particular historic sequence of taphonomic events. This is not new within archaeology and paleontology (Donovan, 1991; Gifford-Gonzolez, 1981; Haynes, 1980; Klein and Cruz-Uribe, 1984; Lyman, 1994; Martin, 1999a; Morse et al., 1983; Schafer, 1972; Shipman, 1981; Voorhies, 1969). But forensic efforts suffer from either too narrow disciplinary efforts or, conversely, models that are too general to offer much explanatory value for forensic practice. There is much progress to be made along these lines; this is only a beginning.

The practice of forensic taphonomy is often an international endeavor. Although our closest connections have been with the Canada and the United Kingdom, recent work with mass fatalities, mass graves, and human rights offenses has involved problems worldwide with international teams of pathologists, archaeologists, and physical anthropologists (Haglund et al., 2001; Scott, 2001; Stover and Ryan, 2001). In fact, anthropologists have had to come to terms with human rights issues that rise to a level that dwarfs cultural relativism (An-Naím, 1992; Cohen, 1989; Fluehr-Lobban, 1995; Messer, 1993; Washburn, 1987). It is our purpose to increase visibility and understanding of the emerging issues, not only in terms of taphonomy and site interpretation, but also of variations across cultures and nations in how forensic taphonomy is practiced and how professionals are qualified (see, for example, Steyn and Meiring, 1997). To that end we have devoted a major section of the book to these topics.

Conceptual Framework of Forensic Taphonomy

The Unit of Analysis

From both taphonomic and ecological perspectives, the carcass can be considered the centerpiece of a newly emerging microenvironment (Kormondy and Brown, 1998; Krebs, 1994). It provides a serendipitous food source, setting off a complex set of trophic phases of consumption, decomposition, assimilation, and dispersal (Haglund, 1988a; Haynes, 1982; Hill, 1979; Mann et al., 1990). It also initiates particular changes in the chemistry and temperature of the immediate surroundings (Coe, 1978). Many of these changes are themselves catalytic, initiating or facilitating further processes.

These processes are dependent on whatever unique patterns or sequences characterized the environment prior to deposition of the body: local features of the biosphere, lithosphere, and atmosphere (Behrensmeyer and Hill, 1980; Lyman, 1994). These factors continually interact and impact whatever taphonomic activity is occurring, having a differential effect depending on their own cycles of variation (e.g., ecological community, geological processes, weather/season), the interplay of those cycles, and the phases of decomposition of the index set of remains.

As time passes and the body decomposes (in many outdoor settings), body and context tend to merge. The boundaries of the body diverge as decomposing materials penetrate the ground, are carried away by moving water, are digested by insect, mammalian, crustacean, or fish scavengers, or are volatilized to the air or water. Likewise, the environment penetrates the body as minerals from groundwater or sediment are incorporated into bone, plant roots and soil microbes penetrate soft tissue and bone, and sediment accumulates to surround and potentially bury the body.

The particular decomposing human body becomes our unit of analysis at some point in its postmortem processes (Table 1.1). This is an extremely arbitrary aspect of taphonomic analysis, i.e., that this particular decomposing organism should be singled out for our analytical attention from the myriad other organisms whose remains are currently present and also decomposing at a given location. This bias persists as we select pertinent models for understanding the index organism. The shorter postmortem timeframe of a forensic taphonomy investigation (compared with traditional paleotaphonomy) dictates that particular attention be paid to data accumulating from periodic changes (e.g., seasonal, diurnal) with a cycle wavelength shorter than the postmortem interval (Martin, 1999); these data constitute the relevant diachronic context. All other data can be grouped as the background, the synchronic context, for the purpose of a particular analysis.

Diachronic context data about other currently operating biotic process in the microenvironment, i.e., processes with a relevant periodicity (e.g., necrophagous insect succession associated with the body under consideration) provide useable taphonomic data. But diachronic data at the macroenvironmental level, such as faunal extinctions, probably

Table 1.1   Environmental Frameworks and Relevant Contexts

Macroenvironment [Synchronic Context]	Macroenvironment Periodicity, within the Postmortem Interval [Diachronic Context]	Microenvironment, Site Specific, at the Point of Recovery (Actual) or Point of Death (Reconstructed) [Synchronic Context]	Microenvironment Periodicity, Site Specific, within the Postmortem Interval [Diachronic Context]
Atmosphere	• Point within long-term climate change cycles	• Current temperature • Current precipitation • Current distribution of water • Oxygenation	• Accumulated degree days • Precipitation pattern
Lithosphere	• Point within long-term geological change, such as continental drift, rising sea levels	• Surface relief, terrain • Minerals present • Salinity • Alkalinity • Water vs. land distribution • Soil type	• Recent changes in landscape • Seasonal changes in landscape at that location
Biosphere	• Point within long-term faunal and floral changes, extinctions	• Producer, consumer, and decomposer presence • Primary productivity • Scavenger home ranges and territories	• Seasonal changes in plant and animal presence, activity • Necrophagous insect succession • Necrotic bacteria and fungal succession • Nitrogen cycle associated with remains

would not. Thus, the necessary interdisciplinary mix, the relevant biological models, and the data collection methods will differ somewhat between paleo- and forensic taphonomy, and will depend on the problem to be solved and the postmortem interval involved. Taphonomic data may provide clues to an ancient environment or may be extraneous or artifactual to the temporal or topical research focus (see Lyman Foreword, this volume).

Nevertheless, as the body makes its way from the biosphere to the lithosphere, both earlier and later diachronic data are potentially relevant no matter whether the postmortem interval is centuries or days. The consequences of local scavenger activity, for example, or deposition during a dry spell, or flash flood, while the remains are still articulated, or while the skeleton is still fresh, or some other set of variables, will theoretically affect any subsequent analysis.

The time during which soft tissue persists is a critical period taphonomically. The probability is enhanced for a wide range of dramatic alterations prior to decomposition, consumption, or preservation by, e.g., mummification, freezing, or adipocere formation (Haglund and Sorg, 1997a; Micozzi, 1991). The speed and attendant consequences of the taphonomic processes are great during this early period.

From a forensic point of view, correct interpretation of the events surrounding a death is dependent on knowing both the sequence and character of the taphonomic processes.

Taphonomic artifact may need to be stripped away to reveal forensic information, e.g., to discriminate scavenger modification from perimortem trauma. Conversely, taphonomic data may itself constitute forensic evidence, e.g., of the original place of death and transport, the behavior of the perpetrator (humans may be taphonomic agents), or the postmortem interval (cf. Lyman, 1994; Foreword this volume).

No longer is skeletal morphology the only primary data derived directly from the skeleton itself. DNA extraction and analysis have rapidly risen to assume a partnership role, even when remains are decomposed or skeletonized. Harvey and King (Chapter 24, this volume) provide an update on DNA techniques along with a number of case examples. The body's interface with its surroundings is not entirely discrete; it does not stop at the skeleton or the skin. Cells are lost constantly to the environment; some sources estimate thousands of dead or dying skin cells are lost each minute by a living individual. As our technical capacity increases, these tiny data sources will increase as well. Olfactory cues are used in forensic work (Hunt, 1999; Rebmann et al., 2000; Sorg et al., 1998) and may be a future potential source of taphonomic data. It is known that olfactory cues attract scavengers, including insects (see Hall, 1995); thus olfaction is an important aspect of scavenger patterning. As more is learned about decomposition, chemical signatures (Voss et al., 1992) and bacterial signatures (Pfeiffer et al., 1998) may become more important.

Taphonomic Time and Context

From the point of view of the forensic investigator, there are at least three events in taphonomic time: (1) the time of death; (2) the time of deposition in the recovery location; and (3) the time of recovery. But usually these events are not chronologically precise or even discoverable as actual points in time. Viewed in a more processual way, the taphonomic reconstruction is concerned with the ecological, biological, and physical context and processes impacting a particular set of remains during four temporal contexts: (1) the antemortem taphonomic period just prior to death and/or deposition; (2) the perimortem taphonomic period around the time of death and deposition; (3) the postmortem taphonomic period from deposition to recovery; and (4) the postrecovery taphonomic period from recovery to analysis. In some cases, there is also an archival period following analysis. Additionally, there may be a multiple, sequential taphonomic contexts due to transport or sequential modification agents.

We have added the qualifier taphonomic to the temporal context designations for several reasons. First, the taphonomic perspective differs, although not completely, from the traditional medical usage, which generally focuses on fleshed remains with a rather short postmortem interval and on chronological reconstructions. *Taphonomic time* is a form of the archaeological concept *relative time* as opposed to time expressed in hours, days, and years, i.e., *chronological time*. It may be expressed as a function of the condition of the remains, for example, a stage of decomposition or stage of disarticulation.

In medical parlance antemortem (*sensu stricto*, before death) can refer to the entirety of an individual's biological and medical history prior to the relatively precise moment of brain death (see also Symes et al., Chapter 21, this volume), although it is usually used more narrowly. Perimortem generally refers to a fairly narrow time interval encompassing the death event. By contrast, the antemortem taphonomic period is characterized by the condition of the organism just prior to death (location, position, covering, size, shape, stage of development, presence of non-fatal wounding), inferred from or based on characteristics that can be discovered at recovery or analysis. The perimortem taphonomic period is not an actual time period, but a designation that infers the investigator's inability to discriminate ante- and postmortem modifications, i.e., the remains have characteristics of being antemortem, but could possibly also be early postmortem. These determinations cannot be based on vital/non-vital reactions but rather must be based on biochemical and/or biomechanical conditions that are only indirectly related to the passage of time.

Thus, to the extent that remains are decomposed, fragmented, or skeletonized, taphonomic time designations (of wounding, for example) usually cannot be precise à propos the medically defined moment of death. By way of illustration, impacts upon living or freshly postmortem long bone shafts tend to create defects that are curvilinear or spiraled, so long as the bone tissue retains sufficient fat and moisture; these are related to the taphonomic perimortem period. Such fractures might have happened while the person was living, but died before healing took place, or they might have happened after death, while the bone was still behaving biomechanically as if it were fresh. The same impacts applied to more decomposed or dried bone tissue tend to be more rectilinear, may be frayed, or may expose unstained fracture margins; these occur in the taphonomic postmortem period.

Similarly, concepts and terms of taphonomic time may be applied to the scene or deposition site. This is conceptually useful in understanding and reconstructing the microenvironment that comes to house the remains, and in differentiating agents of modification. Predepositional period refers to the nature of the microenvironment just prior to deposition of the remains. Depositional period refers to the time in which alterations in the microenvironment were connected with the depositional event. Postdepositional period comprises the time after deposition and before recovery and refers to the characteristics and changes in the microenvironment due to the presence of the remains. Recovery period is the time during which the remains identifiable as such are removed from the context. Postrecovery period is the time following removal of the remains and refers to changes in the microenvironment due to removal of the remains.

Table 1.1 outlines these taphonomic periods with respect to the data sets and analytical foci potentially involved in handling a forensic case. The efforts itemized in individual cells may, however, be combined, abbreviated, or eliminated altogether depending on unique aspects of the case, budget, and time constraints. For conceptual clarity, a generic and simple forensic model is used to create Table 1.2: a homicide at one location and transported to a single outdoor deposition site where the remains are deposited and ultimately recovered. It assumes that both the death and the deposition at the place recovered occur in the perimortem time frame; obviously, this is not always so. Additionally, it assumes that recovery is done at the place of deposition; in reality, remains are sometimes moved more than once in the postmortem period.

A Brief History of Taphonomic Data Collection in Forensic Anthropology

Early comments regarding taphonomic data-gathering by physical anthropologists in forensic investigations are found in Krogman (1962:7) when discussing estimation of time since death, although he does not use the term taphonomy:

> The problem of time-elapse since death is so complex that I'm not attempting to tackle it in this book. There are often too many unknowns, not the least of which may be careless or inexperienced exhumation. The soil may tell of primary or secondary inhumation; it

Table 1.2 Taphonomic Time Periods, Analytical Foci, and Datasets for an Exemplar Homicide Victim Transported after Death to an Outdoor Site and Recovered after Skeletonization and Significant Weathering of the Remains

| Taphonomic Periods Being Reconstructed | Analytical Foci | | |
	Reconstruction of Taphonomic Context: (Sequences, and Nonhuman Taphonomic Agents)	Reconstruction of Taphonomic Events: (Particularly Human Perpetrator as Taphonomic Agent)	Reconstruction of Victim
Scene: Predepositional Remains: Antemortem	Context prior to arrival of human remains (learned through research): • Geological • Biological • Ecological • Climatological	Events leading up to deposition (due to human as taphonomic agent): • Antemortem trauma (with vital response) • Trace evidence connected with a previous location or with perpetrator identity • Human as taphonomic transport agent	Discriminate taphonomic changes from indicators of: • Antemortem history • Biological profile • Individual identity
Scene: Depositional Remains: Perimortem	Context at the time of deposition (inferred or extrapolated): • Time of day • Season • Presence of scavenger species	Events at the time of deposition: • Perimortem trauma • Postmortem modification of remains by perpetrator • Trace evidence of trauma (e.g., weapon) or deposition process (e.g., shovel marks)	Identify modifications which suggest: • Cause of death • Manner of death
Scene: Postdepositional Remains: Postmortem	Context changes between deposition and recovery (inferred or extrapolated): • Effect of remains on environment • Taphonomic agents of modification, both the processes and sequences	Events after deposition and before recovery: • Intentional postdepositional disturbance by perpetrator or other humans • Accidental disturbance by humans • Modifications or transport by humans at the time of discovery	Analyze condition of remains to indicate: • Postmortem interval • Transport history • Postmortem modification by nonhuman agents • Postmortem modification by humans at recovery or at autopsy
Scene: Postrecovery Remains: Postrecovery	Context at time of recovery (observed): • Ecological characteristics • Evidence of scavenger species	Events following recovery: • Modifications due to recovery, examination, or storage	Document process of data collection to ensure: • Associations at the scene • Chain of custody

may yield chemical (acid or base) evidence of rate of decomposition; it may tell of flora and fauna (vegetation and insect action); it may tell of the mechanical factors of movement of [sic] water-seepage (a homogeneous tightly-packed soil as in clays or glacial tills, or a heterogeneous soil as in gravels); depth of interment is very important; the swing of seasons and the amplitude of temperature change play their roles (in water deaths temperature and factors of stasis vs. current-movement are basic). The bones themselves give an idea of time-elapse in the presence or absence of ligamentous attachments and the rates of leaching out of fats and other organic content; surface erosions on bones are important, as well as changes in inner architecture (changes in cancellous tissue, in trabeculation seen radiographically). I don't think the physical anthropologist should tackle cause of death.

Although they do not address taphonomic issues in any systematic fashion, El-Najjar and McWilliams (1978) do recommend graves be excavated by an archaeologist with a physical anthropologist there to excavate the remains themselves.* We underscore the value. El-Najjar and McWilliams also propose a standard narrative report format (1978:9–11) to be used by the physical anthropologist in forensic investigations. Included in the format is a section for Condition in which patterns of decomposition are described. In a section proposed for Time of Death, they discuss the necessity of knowing circumstances of deposition, and their sample report mentions scavenger modification. The report format also includes sections for Trauma and one for Death in which possible evidence of the cause of death is discussed.

Stewart (1981) agrees that the physical anthropologist should assess evidence of the cause of death, i.e., the presence of trauma. He also devotes an entire chapter to "Judging Time and Cause of Death," and proposes a list of attributes regarding time of death to be scored, he says, as present or absent: (1) odor, and its intensity; (2) soft parts, and their location; (3) adherent earth (clay, loam, or sand); (4) adherent vegetation (twigs, leaves, grass, or moss); (5) adherent insects, living or dead, including immature stages; (6) tooth marks; (7) stains and/or bleaching; and (8) adipocere. In the subsequent pages he devotes complete sections to necrophagous insects, minimum time of skeltonization, varying frequency of carnivores, shielded remains, adipocere formation, effect of a shallow burial, residual bone nitrogen, root penetration, and staining and bleaching.

Stewart (1981:74) provides strong cautions against estimating time of death on the basis of skeletal appearance, citing the possible fresh appearance of long but deeply buried bone. He notes that the skeletons from the Korean war recovered "from the shallow graves of the American soldiers who had been held for varying lengths of time in prisoner-of-war camps were virtually indistinguishable in appearance from prehistoric skeletons recovered archeologically; that is, they gave little if any visible evidence of containing organic matter and were beginning to show breakdown of the cortical surfaces."

Buikstra and Ubelaker (1994) include a chapter "Postmortem Changes: Human Taphonomy" in their handbook of data collection standards for human skeletons. This contribution systematizes observations of *archaeological* bone with regard to basic alterations of color, surface, and shape. They recommend routinely collecting data on weathering, discoloration, polish, cutmarks, evidence of rodent and carnivore gnawing, and

---

* This issue has been a topic of conversation in recent meetings of the American Academy of Forensic Science, Physical Anthropology Section, and is a theme in a special, upcoming volume of the *Historical Archaeology* (Crist, 2001; Haglund, 2001; Haglund et al., 2001; Owsley, 2001; Scott and Connor, 2001; Stover and Ryan, 2001).

other forms of cultural modification including creation of artifacts. These characteristics are also applicable in forensic taphonomy. In contrast to our approach here, Buikstra and Ubelaker place "premortem and perimortem fractures, wounds, and abrasions" (p. 106) in the chapter on paleopathology, thus separating perimortem trauma from taphonomy. However, cutmarks and burning remain in the taphonomy chapter because they are assumed to be connected with mortuary ritual.

The taphonomic data collection protocols recommended in Buikstra and Ubelaker (1994) are fairly straightforward. All modifications are noted with the element and location. Munsell Color Charts are to be used for color observations; they offer a nominal scale for surface texture of burned bone. Weathering changes are to be recorded using Behrensmeyer's (1978) categories. Other taphonomic changes (rodent gnawing, carnivore chewing, artifact creation) are recorded with drawings and/or photographs. Cutmarks are described by the number, length (mean and range), and a cast of a representative example (optional).

The Perimortem Problem

Forensic reconstructions frequently focus on discriminating trauma that occurred at or immediately prior to the time of death (and which, therefore, provide evidence about cause and manner of death) from those occurring after that. But the definition of death is a medicolegal one, based on medical soft tissue observations of the absence of heart and brain activity. Aside from the vital reaction of bleeding or bone remodeling with healing, we have no proxy for demonstrating that a traumatic event preceded death. The morphology of perimortem wounding to bone cannot, by that alone, be differentiated from postmortem damage to fresh or nearly fresh bone.

As mentioned above, during the early postmortem period, before bone loses its moisture and organic components, it tends to respond to modification agents as if it were fresh. However, these patterns are not invariable or always diagnostic. The loss of organics and water is gradual and dependent on the microenvironment.

As bone elements are exposed to their surroundings, their composition changes. There may be staining of outer layers, or weathering, or mineral uptake/loss into soil or water. Once bone surface color is altered, or significant weathering has occurred, it becomes easier to differentiate perimortem from postmortem modifications, as the latter will tend to disrupt the outer layer and expose unstained or unweathered bone. Certainly, more research is needed to establish descriptive standards of bone condition using chemical and physical properties in addition to visual characteristics to measure 'freshness'. Sauer (1998) has offered a brief protocol for assessing the timing of a particular element or defect.

Humans Are Taphonomic Agents

One topic that has been an important issue in both forensic and archaeological investigation is that of humans as modifiers of remains, human or nonhuman. We believe the identification of common patterns of human modification of humans, whether due to homicide, dismemberment, warfare, scavenging, cannibalism, or burial ritual, should be included as an essential dimension of taphonomy. The differentiation of human from other agents causing long bone breakage has been debated for early hominid sites, in the controversy surrounding the peopling of the Americas (Bonnichsen and Sorg, 1987), and with respect to cannibalism (Graver et al., Chapter 16, this volume; Turner and Turner, 1999; White, 1992).

A key concept here is the equifinality of some taphonomic processes (Bunn, 1991), i.e., more than one agent producing the same or similar taphonomic signature. Is it possible, for example, to identify diagnostic features or signatures of particular taphonomic agents (e.g., see Haglund et al. (1988a,b) regarding canids)? In a useful review of literature, Bunn points to the need for more research, but comments on the importance of looking at complete patterns, and in context, as well as the importance (echoed by many others) of microscopic observation. He particularly notes the need for more research on cutmarks, bone fracture biomechanics, carnivore modification patterns, faunal ecology, and actualistic studies of site formation. During the last decade these topics have indeed received more attention.

Not only is human agency an issue, but the discrimination of peri- and postmortem can become the key issue in identifying human agency. Diez et al. (1999) describe the Atapuerca site in Spain, which dates to the Lower and Middle Pleistocene. They conclude that the array of butchered mammalian food includes humans, and they group humans with other mammals of similar weight. They list characteristics of the butchered bones, focusing on the identification of perimortem defects. The butchered remains are highly fragmented with few elements intact apart from teeth and articular bones. The fragments have a mixed representation of right-angled breaks (attributed to diagenesis) and oblique breaks (interpreted as perimortem). They note "curved, V-shaped fractures" as a "good discriminatory trait between fresh and old fractures" (1999:631). They find that smooth fracture edges, proposed by many as a characteristic of fresh breaks, do not discriminate; these are attributed more to a dynamic (vs. static) force impacting the bone. Jagged edges, they assert, are more likely related to the porosity due to loss of organic matter, low crystallinity, and non-mineralized tissue. Smooth edges are related to "compact structures, such as green bones with organic material still preserved in the Haversian and osteon canals, or fossil bones where mineralization and crystallization have occurred in the Haversian and osteon canals" (1999:631–632). They comment that a high frequency of bone fragments in which bone circumference is only half represented is more characteristic of scavenging or butchering; many complete shaft diameters, on the other hand, more likely represent postdepositional breaks. They also include observations of surface modifications related to fracture by humans, including impact points, flakes or notched fractures (conchoidal scars), commenting that most have associated hackle and rib marks which characterize green bone breaks according to Johnson (1985). Finally, they identify and extensively describe the cutmarks differentiating sawing from scraping, as well as skinning, viscera/periosteum extraction, dismembering, and filleting.

Human agency is critical in the resolution of human rights abuses, including mass fatalities or mass burials as addressed by many in this volume. Haglund provides a conceptual framework for mass graves and Schmitt discusses some of the taphonomic implications of human rights abuses. Skinner addresses a frequently overlooked human taphonomic activity, postmortem alteration of burials, sometimes long after the original event. In a parallel, but prehistorically focused, analysis, Darwent and Lyman address the discrimination of postdepositional modification of nonhuman bones (limited to small, dense tarsals, carpals, and phalanges). Darwent and Lyman seek to quantify the rather complex relationships among shape, size, food value, and diagenesis pertaining to these selected elements. They test hypotheses proposed by Marean regarding the detection of postdepositional damage using small, dense faunal remains which are less likely to be broken (see discussion below), as opposed to the patterns of human food utilization patterns.

Of course, modern forensic cases incorporate a varied array of human tool use, and tend to include relatively deviant behaviors. The forensic research is perhaps the clearest record of human conspecific predation. Symes et al. (Chapter 21, this volume) focus attention on several cases illustrating particular types of sharp trauma from tools. And Saul and Saul demonstrate the use of very small or subtle modifications to identify sharp trauma evidence. A parallel archaeological study described the patterning of ritual Mayan decapitation.

The differentiation of human-induced trauma from nonhuman predation or scavenging is based on familiarity with taxon-specific patterns of bone and soft tissue modification. Berryman (Chapter 25, this volume), for example, provides an unusual case of pig scavenging of human remains, documenting and illustrating the modifications due to dental morphology, mastication, and feeding patterns (see also, Kerbis et al., 1993, for examples involving chimpanzee remains). Taxon-specific patterns have been shown to have a large range of variability, however (Saavedra and Simonetti, 1998), and much more research needs to be done to document and analyze such signatures.

In an important example of the potential crossover between forensic and archaeological research, Gargett (1999) addresses the issue of identifying human agency in buried human remains (intentional burials), particularly for a number of so-called Middle Palaeoloithic burials. He concerns himself with the decomposition process, citing research by Haglund (1997), Micozzi (1997), and Galloway (1989), discussing the possible impact of decomposition sequence, rigor mortis, and rapid drying on evaluating burial position. The issue for these archaeological sites is whether burial (e.g., due to rapid sedimentation or cave roof falls) might occur prior to decomposition and disarticulation, thus imitating intentional burial. Another issue is the extent of disarticulation. For this author bones can remain "articulated"* following loss of flesh, assuming burial protects them from movement; it is important, therefore, to assess how close they are (at recovery) to anatomical position. He suggests focusing on three key processes: decomposition, disarticulation, and likelihood of disturbance. Gargett concludes with a set of factors to assess in evaluating whether a burial was purposeful; these include stratification, completeness of remains, articulation pattern, unequal preservation of parts, peri- vs. postmortem fragmentation patterns, position of remains, evidence of disturbance, characteristics of associated bedrock or cave, sedimentation pattern, and evidence of bioturbation.

A related debate about human agency is going on regarding the Klasies River Mouth site in South Africa, dating to the Last Interglacial. These hominids are anatomically near-modern, but did not use Upper Paleolithic tools. The question regarding their associated faunal remains is whether the hominids had hunted them or merely scavenged them, and much of the debate centers on which body parts are represented (scavenging should result in disproportionately more limb bones) (Binford, 1984; Blumenschine, 1986). Milo (1998) uses a wide range of analytical techniques to evaluate the array of faunal bones and the butchering marks, including assessment of minimum numbers, large carnivore scavenging signatures, and experimental butchering. In research very much applicable to the types of case studies in Symes et al., (Chapter 21, this volume) he outlines the morphology of cuts vs. stabs, the absolute necessity of microscopic examination (only 32% of marks he made in his experiments were macroscopically visible on fresh bone), and the mediation by

---

* The terms *disarticulation* and *articulation* will be discussed more fully in the section Taphonomic Observations and Terminology.

postdepositional deterioration (he estimates 30% of marks become undetectable). The conclusion is that the hominids were hunting, not scavenging.

In a related article about this site, Bartram and Marean (1999) examine the importance of recovering, identifying, and analyzing midshaft bone fragments in the differentiation of hunting and scavenging. They also discuss the ongoing debate in archaezoological and taphonomic research regarding the applicability of actualistic studies and uniformatarian theory. Their conclusion, aided by ethnographic examples, is that scavengers raid human sites after hunted animal bones have been processed for marrow (with heavy fragmentation of midshafts), differentially removing the epiphyseal portions. Bias is introduced when archaeozoologists subsequently exclude these midshaft fragments from their analysis because they are coded as nonidentifiable during the analysis.

Building Models and Data Sets

Experimental taphonomic research, also called *actualistic research*, is an important common ground between traditional, paleontological taphonomy and forensic taphonomy (Gifford-Gonzolez, 1981). In actualistic experiments a particular taphonomic process is the focus for model building; key independent variables are controlled, and observation of the dependent variables can be systematized, e.g., the now-classic studies of fluvial transport of human remains in the paleoanthropological literature (Behrensmeyer, 1982; Boaz and Behrensmeyer, 1976; Hanson, 1980) or of the decomposition process by human cadavers in the forensic literature (Bass, 1984, 1997).

In other actualistic approaches, the investigator studies a process seen in the fossil (or forensic) record by observing the same process in a natural setting, e.g., the studies of mammalian scavenging in the archaeological literature (Haynes, 1980, 1982; Brain, 1981; Hill, 1979). The forensic counterpart of these studies is the systematic analysis of a series of cases that bear certain structural similarities, such as the study of cases of canid scavenging of human remains by Haglund et al. (1988a,b) in order to construct a stage model of this process, or the study of cases of terrestrial decomposition (Galloway, 1997; Rhine and Dawson, 1998; Sorg et al., 1998) or marine decomposition (Boyle et al., 1997; Haglund, 1993; Sorg et al., 1997) in order to model the decomposition process regionally. The control in these case series is that time since death is known and a single investigator with a consistent and systematic approach to his or her cases is present. Data collection must be comparable across cases and, ideally, the data themselves are reported as part of the presentation of the model, enhancing the opportunity of replication or comparison by other scientists.

A third type of actualistic research is the case study. Although some forensic cases are never solved with respect to victim identity, time, or cause and manner of death, many are. Thus, investigators have a luxury (or challenge) not afforded to colleagues doing traditional archaeology or paleontology: to learn whether hypotheses about the case were correct. That is, inferences and estimates proposed in the analysis are tested as further details of the case are revealed. It is this aspect of forensic taphonomy that offers a new type of data to the field of taphonomy generally. The variables are not under investigator control, as they are in experimental design or even systematic naturalistic observation. Case studies offer the opportunity to enrich explanation through enhanced observation and analysis, particularly in terms of learning about the range of variation. In Symes et al. (Chapter 21, this volume) two of the cases presented include confessional statements by perpetrators describing the sharp force trauma they used, corroborating the hypotheses of the investigators

Forensic scientists have been constructing actualistic models of taphonomic change using nonhuman animal proxies for decades, with pigs being the most common choice due to their comparable mass, lack of fur, and availability (Anderson and Cervenka, Chapter 9, this volume; France et al., 1992, 1997; Haskell, 1989; Janaway, Chapter 20, this volume; Komar, 1999; Morton and Lord, Chapter 8, this volume; Payne, 1965; Payne and King, 1972). Others have done longitudinal studies with donated human cadavers under very controlled conditions (Bass, 1984, 1997; Rodriguez and Bass, 1985; Voss et al., 1992). A naturalistic study of rainforest taphonomy has recently been published utilizing the recovery of the remains of chimpanzees who died of natural causes, predation, or poaching (Peterhans et al., 1993). The purpose was to test the hypothesis that the primate fossil gap around the Pliocene might be due to the bone-destroying taphonomy of tropical forests. Chimpanzees are also potential models of human remains in forest settings. They conclude that some remains are undamaged even after several years, as long as the soil is not acid, permitting the accumulation of remains.

Taphonomic Observations and Terminology

The use of terms differs from one discipline to another. While a term may be well understood and functionally adequate, when it is applied in a new disciplinary context, its use may lead to misunderstanding or dwindle to meaninglessness. The lack of interdisciplinary term conventions may exacerbate misunderstanding, create error of assumption, and alter the inferences themselves. For example, the use of the terms articulated and disarticulated has different meanings when applied by forensic pathologists than by some forensic anthropologists.

Articulation is the state of having parts connected by joints. The word is derived from the Latin term for joint: articulus. Variations of the definition of articulate are (1) to join together so as to allow motion between the parts, or (2) united by means of a joint, or (3) to make of parts united (*Webster's Collegiate Dictionary*). With regard to anatomy specifically, an articulation is a place of union or junction between two or more bones of the skeleton (*Dorland's Illustrated Medical Dictionary*).

Contrarily, disarticulation is defined as the separation or amputation of a bone at a joint; to disarticulate is to become disjoined by flexible joints (*Webster's Collegiate Dictionary, Stedman's Medical Dictionary*).

With these definitions in mind, the medical use of articulation is generally related to anatomical relationships or associations between bones *maintained by soft tissue connections at joints*. When soft tissue is absent at the joint, bones are in fact disarticulated, even though they remain in relative anatomical position. Occasionally, remains may actually be held in complete anatomical relationship by the soil matrix, but generally elements will have moved slightly out of position. Hence, the forensic pathologist describing a fully skeletonized remains, arrayed carefully in anatomical position (but not joined by soft tissue), would characterize such a skeleton as disarticulated and in anatomical relationship. This same set of skeletal remains might be described as articulated by some forensic anthropologists (Bass, 1962; Ubelaker, 1974, 1989; and numerous others), a usage connoting soft tissue presence with which we disagree. Such terminology confuses connectedness with relative anatomical relationship or approximation of bones at a joint. A more precise application would separate descriptions of anatomical relationship *in situ* from inferences of the condition of remains when buried.

The foregoing misapplication of "articulation" has a range of consequences. First is the potential to introduce an erroneous assumption. When bones are connected at the joint by soft tissue, one can correctly assume they belong to a single individual. When bones rest in anatomical relationship, but are not physically connected, they may likely but not necessarily belong to the same individual (see Saul and Saul, Chapter 4, this volume). One must look to other contextual factors, such as the number of individuals and their relative positions.

A second problem introduced by misapplying this or other terms is the potential loss of that term's inferential power. For example, an important inference that can be drawn from the proper use of the term disarticulation is that the bone elements are now independent units, and are likely to be moved independently. This is of utmost significance in a taphonomic context, when dealing with issues of scavenged or otherwise transported remains. Transport units can be inferred to be (or to have been) joined and moved as a single entity, and therefore articulated.

In Chapter 5, this volume, Roksandic pays particular attention to the interaction of decomposition processes and burial contexts. She builds on research by Duday (1978, 1981, 1987a,b and Duday et al. (1990) that considers types of articular anatomy, their behavior during the postmortem period when buried, and inferences regarding burial practices. She shows that with careful excavation in certain context types, one can infer the condition of the remains when buried. Saul and Saul explore the mutual benefits of archaeological and forensic case experience in differentiating taphonomic agents and contexts. In one archaeological case inferences about articulation become critical in the sorting of commingled remains.

Biogeographic Context

To more fully understand issues, dynamics, and consequences of taphonomic processes, it is vital to collect higher resolution data on the ecological context from which individual cases are recovered. The goal of gathering these data, not generally part of forensic investigations, is to make forensic taphonomic research more systematic, comparative, and empirically based. This is a similar approach to that suggested by Potts (1998) in his treatment of an environmental hypothesis of hominin evolution. Conventionally, even when taphonomic issues are broached in the pursuit of death investigation data, environmental variables are poorly observed and little examined.

The corpse becomes part of an ecological setting (see Behrensmeyer, 1975, and Behrensmeyer et al., 1979, for early examples linking paleoanthropology, taphonomy, and paleoecology), in some sense even creating a new ecological community delimited by physical and biotic parameters, and having a particular history. (Complications may be introduced if the place of death, place of deposition, and the place the modifications occurred are different.) For each location, questions must be asked about the emerging ecological community centered on the remains, and about the climatological, physical, and biological parameters that may have influenced the modification process. Then, based on a knowledge of generalized taphonomic processes combined with information about the specific location, decisions should be made concerning at what levels these should be documented (Haglund, 1998). Following these decisions regarding context, choices should be made about methods and approaches to data gathering and analysis of the remains themselves. This two-step process will lend power to the theory building that may result.

For example, a variable as elemental as temperature, in routine death investigations, is usually documented by recording ambient atmospheric temperatures at the scene, including known maximum/minimum temperatures for the area along with seasonal and diurnal fluctuations. However, when considering putrefaction processes, air temperature is less important than temperatures on or near the surface. Coe (1978) pointed this out in his study of decomposition in elephant carcasses. In any local setting there are a host of temperature-driven microenvironments dependent on absorption of radiant energy. For a 3-day period, Coe found temperatures on open ground and scrub were between 25 and 28°C, but maximum surface open-ground temperature was 45 to 50°C in mid-afternoon. On rock surfaces, temperature approached 60°C, and for forest-shaded areas, the maximum surface temperature was only 28°C with a daily range of only 8°C. Among forensic entomologists, for example, the critical nature of temperature is already realized. Hence, more refined temperature observations are being demanded and more routinely made, increasing the resolution of their interpretations. In this volume, Anderson and Cervenka (Chapter 9) explore regional intra-species variation in the interpretation particularly of time since death for the Canadian northwest. Species-specific regional variation has been implicated in several taxas, including, for example, predation by owls (Fernandez-Janvo et al., 1999; Saavedra and Simonetti, 1998) and distribution of plant pollens (Horrocks et al., 1998). It is critical to take such potential variation into account by developing regional databases and comparing them.

Marine settings offer an important testing ground for taphonomic studies. The literature on marine taphonomy is rich (Donovan, 1991; Martin, 1999; Parsons and Brett, 1991). Research on mollusks and foraminifera provides interesting models for the decomposition and dissolution of the (also calcium-based) human skeleton (Walker and Goldstein, 1999) within the Taphonomically Active Zone (TAZ) or bioturbation zone (Davies, et al., 1989). Walker and Goldstein (1999) propose a model for preservation of hardparts which may be applicable to skeletal remains. They comment that, for mollusks, time spent on the surface prior to burial is much more likely to drive the condition of the remains than is time since death. They have also concluded that burial may not be so much of a preservative as has been thought. They use a concept which may be useful in guiding recoveries in forensic settings: dominant taphonomic processes, which may be regionally specific, but discoverable, in terms of their applicability to common forensic problems.

Bogs and Aquatic Contexts

Human bodies have been recovered from an enormous variety of climatological, geographic, and physical contexts. Many forensic cases, with little archaeological comparison, are recovered from marine, riverine, or lacustrine environments. These cases tend to create considerable taphonomic difficulties due to the effects of extensive transport and/or the problems identifying and describing a meaningful, essentially 3-dimensional, taphonomic context. Haglund and Sorg provide in Chapter 10 in this volume a brief overview of taphonomic issues in aquatic settings. Ebbesmeyer and Haglund (Chapter 11) expand on particular circumstances and contextual issues: shipwrecks and ocean currents.

In some contexts such as bogs, long-term preservation of human remains is possible. Brothwell and Gill-Robinson (Chapter 6) compare the condition and contexts of an impressive series of bodies found in bog settings. A number of these cases are suspicious deaths. The bog microenvironment is a highly acid, moist, and anaerobic environment with well-known characteristics. Yet the variation is remarkable.

Mass Fatalities and Mass Graves

Mass Graves and Human Rights

The reach of forensic inquiry and research has recently been extended in a prominent way beyond the purview of state and federal legal systems to international and pan-national contexts. That death investigations are done in international circumstances is certainly not new, but the explicit application of taphonomic approaches in these contexts is. In particular, this includes the exhumation and interpretation of traumatic deaths and mass graves due to war crimes and human rights violations, as well as the recovery of remains and the investigation of deaths in mass disasters.

Haglund's introduction (Chapter 12) in this volume to some of the terminology and conceptual issues regarding mass graves leads a series of chapters focused on case examples of larger-scale human death due to disasters and human rights abuses (see also, Burns, 1998). Simmons (Chapter 13) describes a cave context, comparing it to a similar karstic cave australopithecine site, and discusses the recovery and interpretation issues. Sledzik and Rodriquez (Chapter 17) discuss mass fatalities such as plane crashes and the effects of these events on remains: burning, fragmentation, and scattering, in particular, and the resulting taphonomic implications (see Lyman, 1987, for a faunal analysis of a mass disaster, the Mount St. Helens volcanic eruption). Schmitt (Chapter 14) focuses on some of the legal issues and the resulting taphonomic implications for search and recovery methods for clandestine graves. Skinner et al. (Chapter 15) review instances of postburial disturbance by humans, a problem that frequently impacts interpretations in these cases.

Scattered or Commingled Remains

Many taphonomic agents scatter remains. Some situations provide significant challenges for archaeological techniques and interpretation. Haglund et al. (Chapter 7) provide a discussion of plow-zone contexts and the recovery of human remains, describing modern equipment and its effects on buried remains. Ubelaker (Chapter 18), on the other hand, provides a comprehensive review of the types of issues that emerge in identifying and sorting commingled remains; he provides a literature review as well as case studies to illustrate several common situations.

Reconstructing Taphonomic Context vs. Taphonomic History of the Remains

One advantage of this interdisciplinary field is the possibility for independent observations of the same data sets by different investigators. This can become more important when considering the problem of analytical focus. On the one hand, the condition of the remains constitutes evidence for a particular taphonomic context. On the other hand, one needs to reconstruct the taphonomic history of the remains using data about the taphonomic context. To minimize circularity, it is best to focus first on the context, using the perspective of several disciplines if possible, then focus attention on the condition of the remains as dependent variables.

Ethics and Standards of Practice

Important ethical questions arise when the processes of forensic case investigation and data collection for research overlap, not only with regard to actualistic studies but also data collection incidental to case investigation. A delicate balance must be struck between potential benefit to the public and potential costs regarding how bodies are treated.

The use of donated human bodies requires care and sensitivity. States, nations, and cultures differ in their tolerances, restrictions, and laws with regard to the treatment of human corpses for educational or research purposes. In most U.S. states, the collection and retention of any body part for study must be done only for legitimate inquiries in the case, unless the body has been donated for research. The use of nonhuman animal proxies also raises issues concerning humane treatment as well as levels of necessity for the research use.

Since most forensic investigations are funded by public (governmental) or quasi-public (nonprofit organization) dollars, and since these investigations are by their nature conducted in a humanitarian or judicial role, resources are generally limited and investigator conduct is in the public domain. Regardless, the sensitive nature of the situation demands discretion. Thus, for example, resources must be appropriated on the basis of the needs of the particular case rather than any research agenda, minimizing damage to the body, and maximizing investigative potential.

Nevertheless, investigatory quality (precision, thoroughness, accuracy, effectiveness) is enhanced by the use of basic standards and protocols, the use of which leads to routine collection of comparable sets of data (Buikstra and Ubelaker, 1994; Moore-Jansen et al., 1994). Whereas not all of these data may be seen as critical or even necessary in a particular case, the process of systematic coverage tends to reduce omissions and makes it more likely that data will be available in the event there are subsequent investigations.

Although forensic taphonomy has emerged as a significant focus for research since our earlier efforts to link the two fields (Haglund, 1991; Haglund and Sorg, 1997a; Sorg, 1985), there is still much to do. The challenge continues in constructing well-documented series of cases, and in making the data available across investigators for comparative research. Additionally, we feel it is time for setting some standards in forensic taphonomic data collection, particularly for outdoor scenes, including systematic collection of minimal region-specific and site-specific, comparative information about temperature (current, nearest weather station, seasonality; see Anderson and Cervenka, Chapter 9, this volume), climate (particularly humidity and precipitation), soil, scavengers (mammalian, crustacean, avian, and arthropod), plants, and site history, as well as case-specific details about the condition of the remains and details of the deposition.

Recommended Forensic Taphonomy Report Protocol

Most forensic anthropologists use some variation of the report format recommended by El-Najjar and McWilliams (1978). During the last decade, however, the scope of practice has broadened somewhat to include scene visits and the recovery of remains, mass fatality incidents, and human rights investigations involving excavation. Although the use of archaeological techniques in forensic recoveries was pioneered much earlier (Brooks, 1975; Morse et al., 1983), it is only recently that anthropologists have been asked routinely to recover remains (Haglund, 1993; Reichs, 1998). This signals a broadening of the scope of practice for forensic anthropology in the United States to more closely resemble forensic archaeology practice in the United Kingdom (see Hunter's Foreword, this volume). There has been a parallel

Table 1.3   Updated Forensic Anthropology Report Format

Part 1: Introduction	• Background and chain of custody
Part 2: Taphonomy	• Document microenvironment at scene • Document remains *in situ* • Document recovery process • Inventory remains • Describe condition, including an assessment of taphonomic modifications due to transport, burial, decomposition, scavenging, weathering • Incorporate reports from other disciplines such as entomology, botany, and geology • Estimate postmortem interval
Part 3: Biological Profile	Develop biological profile (individual and population characteristics) • Age • Sex • Stature • Discrete traits and anomalies (inherited and acquired) • Population ancestry • Pathology and evidence of medical history
Part 4: Individuation and Identification	• Combined pattern of anomalies, pathological conditions, or other traits known or documented for this individual • Compare remains and antemortem records of possible matches • Dental records • Radiographs • Medical history • Photographs • Facial imaging • DNA analysis
Part 5: Reconstruction of Death Event	• Trauma: types, location and patterning, trajectories, sequences, potential weapon classes • Document process of differentiating perimortem trauma from postmortem changes • Apply additional specialty analyses from other sources, e.g., tool marks, fracture biomechanics, trace evidence, histology, radiography

development of forensic taphonomy as a theoretical umbrella for interpreting postmortem processes in context. As a result, we recommend altering the basic forensic anthropology report format to include four parts, one of which focuses explicitly on taphonomy (see Table 1.3). Even when the formal report format must be abbreviated by request of the jurisdiction or function, the data collection and analysis that lie behind it should be thorough.

Broader Professional Issues

The forensic sciences are a fast-evolving cluster of applied disciplines that operate independently as well as in interdisciplinary teams. As these forensic fields mature and develop, they expand to incorporate new methods and theories (often borrowed or adapted from allied fields) and contract to exclude outmoded ones. As a result, the boundaries between disciplines can become blurred and even changed.

A distinction sometimes made in health care practice between the terms "interdisciplinary" and "multidisciplinary" highlights this complication. Multidisciplinary teams operate by applying multiple fields of learning to a problem in a parallel fashion, each discipline offering its own paradigm. Interdisciplinary teams operate by joining at the edges, often purposefully overlapping fields of knowledge and sharing competencies. The distinction between multidisciplinary and interdisciplinary is usually, however, not very clear in practice. The reality is that, at least within any group of allied fields, there is some shared knowledge or skills as a result of either common origins or shared experience.

For example, many physical anthropologists have training and experience in archaeological techniques and many archaeologists have training and experience in the analysis of human remains. This is due to the structures in the United States, Canada, and elsewhere of degree-granting programs in anthropology. Yet these structures are not universal (either in the United States and Canada or internationally) and the auxiliary skills are not always present in a given individual. The consequence is that coverage of these competencies will differ for a particular jurisdiction or case. Similarly, training and skills in gathering forensic entomological evidence may be present in non-entomologists, and forensic entomologists may possess skills in excavation techniques. Nevertheless, the competencies for both archaeological techniques and forensic entomology data collection should be present within the team. The careful, 3-dimensional documentation of artifact provenience in a surface recovery or excavation of a clandestine burial is a skill and role often shared by criminalists, police, physical anthropologists, and occasionally medical examiner/coroners or death investigators, although it is probably best done by a forensic archaeologist.

Thus, the case manager of a particular jurisdiction must evaluate both expertise and auxiliary competencies in team members. Budgets and circumstances limit both. It is not always possible to know, in advance, which knowledge bases will be critical for a particular case. First, in general and at a minimum, competencies for all basic areas of data collection should be represented on the team (for outdoor scenes in the northeast United States, for example, these would include scene context data, human remains collection, archaeological excavation or surface recovery, entomology, plant and fiber, DNA, and trace evidence). The development and maintenance of the knowledge base regarding data collection should be encouraged and ideally managed at an administrative level. Second, to the extent it is anticipated to be critical in a particular case, expertise (as opposed to just competence) should be present at the recovery and for the analysis. Teams comprised of individuals with basic competencies and frequently used expertise should be maintained and mobilizable. The bar has been raised in the United States during the last decade due to increased public awareness; unfortunately, budgets have not always followed.

Forensic taphonomy, introduced within the past 15 years or so (Haglund et al., 1988a,b; Haglund, 1991; Haglund and Sorg, 1997; Micozzi, 1991; Sorg, 1985, 1986; Ubelaker, 1989), and mirroring paleotaphonomy, has been explicitly interdisciplinary. The result is increased ambiguity regarding professional or disciplinary roles. With its focus on postmortem changes and the incorporation of contextual data associated with human remains, forensic taphonomy embraces all disciplines charged with collecting and interpreting death and/or crime scene evidence. Competencies or skills in evidence collection and interpretation are partly shared, interdisciplinary, and may vary across jurisdictions according to expertise, local statutes, budgets, and customs.

As in health care, procedural and knowledge-based skills in forensic sciences often cross-cut professional status, competence, certification, and/or licensure. Each jurisdiction is faced with the task of assembling a competent interdisciplinary team, utilizing the disciplines and skills (i.e., people) available for an often-limited set of resources. At another level, certification or licensing bodies are faced with continual pressures to evaluate incorporating more competencies or different types. Occasional turf battles are unavoidable.

Potentially desirable consequences of the focus on interdisciplinary teams and shared competencies in forensic sciences include (paradoxically) a compensatory sharpening of professional distinctions through the adoption of certification processes and practice standards, lower (often public) cost of operation, or better articulation and clarification of the relationship between the knowledge base and the skills. Potentially undesirable consequences or costs include the weakening or extinction of certain disciplines, and/or the loss of quality.

The challenge is to keep costs low and quality high. The value of taphonomic data is undeniable, but the cost of involving multiple disciplines is potentially high. A full range of taphonomic experts will normally not be on the staff. Pragmatic solutions will, we believe, include (1) cross-training of team members across disciplines in best practices for systematically *collecting* a multidisciplinary range of datasets; (2) avoiding attempts at cross-training or using less qualified persons for the *interpretation* of those data; (3) identifying within each jurisdiction one or more competent case managers or team leaders who can coordinate multidisciplinary data collections and make decisions about requesting expert consult for difficult data collections and for all interpretations; (4) cultivating a strong relationship with a basic team of experts, regularly requesting their interpretive input in both medium and high level cases (thus developing expertise for forensic applications through regular experience); (5) working in a team structure outside of the pressure of a particular case to set data collection standards and protocols for the group; and (6) encouraging team members to develop professional associations with forensic colleagues and to conduct research in their areas of expertise.

References

An-Naím, A.A.
  1992 *Human Rights in Cross-Cultural Perspective: A Quest for Consensus,* University of Pennsylvania Press, Philadelphia, PA.

Bartram, L.E., Jr. and C.W. Marean
  1999 Explaining the "Klasies Pattern": Kua Ethnoarchaeology, the Die Kelders Middle Stone Age archaeofauna, long bone fragmentation and carnivore ravaging, *Journal of Archaeological Science* 26:9–29.

Bass, W.M.
  1962 The excavation of human skeletal remains. In *Field Handbook on Human Skeleton,* R.F. G. Spier, pp. 39–51. Missouri Archaeological Society, Colombia.

  1984 Time interval since death. In *Human Identification: Case Studies in Forensic Anthropology,* edited by T.A. Rathbun and J.E. Buikstra, pp. 136–147. Charles C Thomas, Springfield, IL.

1997 Outdoor decomposition rates in Tennessee. In *Forensic Taphonomy: The Postmortem Fate of Human Remains*, edited by W.D. Haglund and M.H. Sorg, pp 181–186. CRC Press, Boca Raton, FL.

Behrensmeyer, A.K.

1975 Taphonomy and paleoecology of the Plio-Pleistocene vertebrate assemblages east of Lake Rudolf, Kenya, *Museum of Comparative Zoology Bulletin* 146:473–578.

1978 Taphonomic and ecologic information from bone weathering, *Paleobiology* 4:150–162.

1982 Time resolution in fluvial vertebrate assemblages, *Paleobiology* 8:211–227.

Behrensmeyer, A.K. and A. Hill

1980 *Fossils in the Making: Vertebrate Taphonomy and Paleoecology*, University of Chicago Press, Chicago, IL.

Behrensmeyer, A.K. and S.M. Kidwell

1985 Taphonomy's contributions to paleobiology, *Paleobiology* 11:105–119.

Behrensmeyer, A.K., D. Western, and D. Dechant-Boaz

1979 New perspectives in vertebrate Paleoecology from a recent bone assemblage, *Paleobiology* 5:12–21.

Binford, L. R.

1984 *Faunal Remains from Klasies River Mouth*, Academic Press, New York.

Blumenschine, R.J.

1986 Carcass consumption and the archaeological distinction of scavenging and hunting, *Journal of Human Evolution* 15:639–59.

Boaz, N.J. and A.K. Behrensmeyer

1976 Hominid taphonomy: Transport of human skeletal parts in an artificial fluvial environment, *American Journal of Physical Anthropology* 45:53–60.

Bonnichsen, R. and M.H. Sorg

1987 *Bone Modification*, Center for the Study of the First Americans, Orono, ME.

Boyle, S., A. Galloway, and R.T. Mason

1997 Human aquatic taphonomy in the Monterey Bay area. In *Forensic Taphonomy: The Postmortem Fate of Human Remains*, edited by W.D. Haglund and M.H. Sorg, pp. 605–614. CRC Press, Boca Raton, FL.

Brain, C.K

1981 *The Hunters or the Hunted? An Introduction to African Cave Taphonomy*, University of Chicago Press, Chicago, IL.

Brooks, S.T.

1975 Human or not? A problem in skeletal identification, *Journal of Forensic Sciences* 20:149–153.

Buikstra, J. and D. Ubelaker

1994 *Standards for Data Collection from Human Skeletal Remains*, Arkansas Archeological Survey Research Series No. 44.

Bunn, H.T.

1991 A taphonomic perspective on the archaeology of human origins, *Annual Review of Anthropology* 20:433–467.

Burns, K.R.

1998 Forensic anthropology and human rights issues. In *Forensic Osteology: Advances in the Identification of Human Remains*, 2nd edition, edited by K.J. Reichs, pp. 63–85. Charles C Thomas, Springfield, IL.

Coe, M.
  1978   The decomposition of elephant carcasses in the Tsavo (East) National Park, Kenya, *Journal of the Arid Environments* 1:71–86.

Cohen, R.
  1989   Human rights and cultural relativism: The need for a new approach, *American Anthropologist* 91:1014–1017.

Connor, M. and D.D. Scott
  2001   Paradigms and perpetrators, *Historical Archaeology* 35(1):1–6.

Crist, T.A.
  2001   Bad to the bone?: Historical archaeologists in the practice of forensic science, *Journal of Historical Archaeology* 35(1):39–56.

Davies, D.J., F.N. Powell, and R.J. Stanton, Jr.
  1989   Relative rates of shell dissolution and net sediment accumulation — a commentary: Can shell beds form by the gradual accumulation of biogenic debris on the sea floor? *Lethaia* 22:207–212.

Diez, J.D., Y. Fernandez-Janvo, J. Rosell, and I. Caceres
  1999   Zooarchaeology and taphonomy of Aurora Stratus (Gran Dolina, Sierra de Atapuerca, Spain), *Journal of Human Evolution* 37:623–652.

Donovan, S.K.
  1991   *The Processes of Fossilization*, Columbia University Press, New York.

Duday, H.
  1978   Archaeologie funeraire et anthroplogie, *Cahiers d'Anthropologie*, 1: 55–101.

  1981   Le place de l'anthropologie dans l'etude des sepultures anciennes, *Cahiers d'Anthropologie*, (1):27–42.

  1985   Nouvelles observations sur la décomposition des corps dans un espace libre. In *Méthode d'étude des sépultures*, pp. 6–13. Saint-Germain en Laye: Saint-Germain en Laye, France.

  1987a Contribution des observations osteologiques a la chronologie interne des sepultures collectives. In *Anthropologie Physique et Archéologie*, edited by H. Duday and C. Masset, pp. 51–61, C.N.R.S., Paris.

  1987b Organisation et fonctionnement d'une sepulture collective neolithique. L'aven de la Boucle a Corconne (Gard). In *Anthropologie Physique et Archéologie*, edited by H. Duday and C. Masset, pp. 105–111. C.N.R.S., Paris.

Duday, H., P. Courtaud, E. Crubezy, P. Sellier, and A.M. Tillier
  1990   L'anthropologie de "terrain": reconnaissance et interpretation des gestes funeraires, *Bulletins et Memoires de la Societe d'Anthropologie de Paris* 2(3–4):26–49.

Duday, H., and Masset, C.
  1987   *Anthropologie Physique et Archaéologie*, C.N.R.S., Paris.

El-Najjar, M.Y. and K.R. McWilliams
  1978   *Forensic Anthropology: The Structure, Morphology, and Variation of Human Bone and Dentition*, Charles C Thomas, Springfield, IL.

Fernandez-Jalvo, Y., L. Scott, and C. Denys
  1999   Taphonomy of pollen associated with predation, *Paleogeography, Paleoclimatology, Paleoecology* 149:271–282.

Fluehr-Lobban, C.
  1995   Cultural relativism and universal rights, *The Chronicle of Higher Education* June 9:B1–B2.

France, D.L. et al.

1992 A multidisciplinary approach to the detection of clandestine graves, *Journal of Forensic Sciences* 37:1445–1458.

1997 NecroSearch revisited: Further multidisciplinary approaches to the detection of clandestine graves. In *Forensic Taphonomy: The Postmortem Fate of Human Remains,* edited by W.D. Haglund and M.H. Sorg, pp. 497–510. CRC Press, Boca Raton, FL.

Galloway, A.

1989 Decay rates of human remains in an arid environment. *Journal of Forensic Sciences* 34:607–616.

1997 The process of decomposition: A model from the Arizona-Sonoran Desert. In *Forensic Taphonomy: The Postmortem Fate of Human Remains,* edited by W.D. Haglund and M.H. Sorg, pp. 139–150. CRC Press, Boca Raton, FL.

Gargett, R.H.

1999 Middle Palaeolithic burial is not a dead issue: The view from Qafzeh, Saint-Césaire, Kebara, Amud, and Dederiyeh, *Journal of Human Evolution* 37:27–90.

Gifford-Gonzolez, D.P.

1981 Taphonomy and paleoecology: A critical review of archaeology's sister disciplines. In *Advances in Archaeological Method and Theory,* edited by M.B. Schiffer, pp. 365–438. Academic Press, New York.

1987 Modern analogues: Developing an interpretive framework. In *Bone Modification,* edited by R. Bonnichsen and M.H. Sorg, pp. 43–52. Center for the Study of the First Americans, Orono, ME.

Haglund, W.D.

1991 *Applications of Taphonomic Models to Forensic Investigations,* Ph.D. dissertation, Department of Anthropology, University of Washington, Seattle, University Microfilms, Ann Arbor, MI.

1993a Disappearance of soft tissue and the disarticulation of human remains from aqueous environments, *Journal of Forensic Sciences* 38(4):806–815.

1993b Beyond bare bones: From consultation to authority, *Practicing Anthropology* 15(3):17–19.

1998 The scene and context: Contributions of the forensic anthropologist, In *Forensic Osteology: Advances in the Identification of Human Remains,* 2nd edition, edited by K.J. Reichs, pp. 41–62. Charles C Thomas, Springfield, IL

2001 Archeology and forensic death investigations, *Journal of Historical Archaeology* 35(1):26–34.

Haglund, W.D. and D.T. Reay

1993 Problems of recovering partial human remains at different times and locations: Concerns for death investigators, *Journal of Forensic Sciences* 38:69–80.

Haglund, W.D., M. Connor, and D.D. Scott

2001 The archeology of contemporary mass graves, *Journal of Historical Archaeology* 35(1):57–69.

Haglund, W.D., D.T. Reay, and D.R. Swindler

1988a Canid scavenging/disarticulation sequence of human remains in the Pacific northwest, *Journal of Forensic Sciences* 34:587–606.

1988b Tooth artifacts and survival of bones in animal-scavenged human skeletons, *Journal of Forensic Sciences* 33(4):985–997.

Haglund, W.D. and M.H. Sorg

1997a *Forensic Taphonomy: The Postmortem Fate of Human Remains,* CRC Press, Boca Raton, FL.

1997b Introduction. In *Forensic Taphonomy: The Postmortem Fate of Human Remains*, edited by W.D. Haglund and M.H. Sorg, pp. 1–9. CRC Press, Boca Raton, FL.

1997c Method and theory of forensic taphonomy research. In *Forensic Taphonomy: The Postmortem Fate of Human Remains*, edited by W.D. Haglund and M.H. Sorg, pp. 13–26. CRC Press, Boca Raton, FL.

Hall, M.J.R.
1995 Trapping the flies that cause myiasis: Their reponses to host-stimuli, *Annals of Tropical Medicine and Parisitology* 89(4):333–357.

Hanson, B.C.
1980 Fluvial taphonomic processes: Models and experiments. In *Fossils in the Making: Vertebrate Taphonomy and Paleoecology,* edited by A.K. Behrensmeyer and A. Hill, University of Chicago Press, Chicago, IL.

Haskell, N.H.
1989 *Calliphoridae of Pig Carrion in Northwest Indiana: A Seasonal Comparative Study,* Master's thesis, Purdue University, West Lafayette, IN.

Haynes, G.
1980 Prey bones and predators: Potential ecologic information from analysis of bone sites, *Ossa* 7:75–97.

1982 Utilization and skeletal disturbances of North American prey carcasses, *Arctic* 35(2):226–281.

Hill, A.P.
1979 Disarticulation and scattering of mammal skeletons, *Paleobiology* 5(3):261–274.

Horrocks, M., S.A. Coulson, and K.A.J. Walsh
1998 Forensic palynology: Variation in the pollen content of soil surface samples, *Journal of Forensic Sciences* 43(2):320–323.

Hunt, R.
1999 The benefits of scent evidence, *FBI Law Enforcement Bulletin* 68(11):15–19.

Johnson, E.
1985 Current developments in bone technology. In *Advances in Archaeological Method and Theory,* edited by M.B. Schiffer, pp. 157–235. Academic Press, Orlando, FL.

Klein, R.G. and K. Cruz-Uribe
1984 *The Analysis of Animal Bones from Archaeological Sites,* University of Chicago Press, Chicago, IL.

Komar, D.
1999 The use of cadaver dogs in locating scattered, scavenged human remains: Preliminary field test results, *Journal of Forensic Sciences* 44(2):405–408.

Kormondy, E.J. and D.E. Brown
1998 *Fundamentals of Human Ecology,* Prentice Hall, Upper Saddle River, NJ.

Krebs, C.J.
1994 *Ecology: The Experimental Analysis of Distribution and Abundance,* Harper Collins, New York.

Krogman, W.M.
1962 *The Human Skeleton in Forensic Medicine,* Charles C Thomas, Springfield, IL.

Lyman, R.L.
1987 Taphonomy of cervids killed in the May 18, 1980 volcanic eruption of Mount St. Helens, Washington, U.S.A. In *Bone Modification,* edited by R. Bonnichsen and M.H. Sorg, pp. 149–168. Center for the Study of the First Americans, Orono, ME.

1994 *Vertebrate Taphonomy*, Cambridge University Press, New York.

Mann, R.W., W.M. Bass, and L. Meadows
1990 Time since death and decomposition of the human body: Variables and observations in case and experimental field studies, *Journal of Forensic Sciences* 35(11):103–111.

Martin, R.E.
1999 *Taphonomy: A Process Approach*, Cambridge University Press, New York.

Martin, R.E., S.T. Goldstein, R. Timothy Patterson
1999 Taphonomy as an environmental science, *Paleogeography, Paleoclimatology, Paleoecology* 149:vii–viii.

Messer, E.
1993 Anthropology and human rights, *Annual Review of Anthropology* 22:221–49.

Micozzi, M.
1991 *Postmortem Change in Human and Animal Remains: A Systematic Approach*, Charles C Thomas, Springfield, IL.

1997 Frozen environments and soft tissue preservation. In *The Postmortem Fate of Human Remains*, edited by W.D. Haglund and M.H. Sorg, pp. 171–180. CRC Press, Boca Raton, FL.

Milo, R.G.
1998 Evidence for hominid predation at Klasies River mouth, South Africa, and its implications for the behaviour of early modern humans, *Journal of Archaeological Science* 25:99–133.

Moore-Jansen, P., S. Ousley, and R. Jantz
1994 *Data Collection Procedure for Forensic Skeletal Material Report*, 3rd edition, Investigations No. 48, Department of Anthropology, The University of Tennessee, Knoxville.

Morse, D., J. Duncan, and J. Stoutamire
1983 *Handbook of Forensic Archaeology and Anthropology*, Rose Printing, Tallahassee, FL.

Owsley, D.W.
2001 Why the forensic anthropologist needs the archaeologist, *Journal of Historical Archaeology* 35(1):35–38.

Parsons, K.M. and C.E. Brett
1991 Taphonomic processes and biases in modern marine environments: An actualistic perspective of fossil assemblage preservation. In *The Processes of Fossilization*, edited by S.K. Donovan, pp. 22–65. Columbia University Press, New York.

Payne, J.A.
1965 A summer carrion study of the baby pig, *Sus scrofa*. Linnaeus, *Ecology* 46:592–602.

Payne, J.A. and E.W. King
1972 Insect succession and decomposition of pig carcasses in water, *Journal of the Georgia Entomological Society* 7:153–162.

Peterhans, J.C.K., R.W. Wrangham, M.L. Carter, and M.D. Hauser
1993 A contribution to tropical rain forest taphonomy: Retrieval and documentation of chimpanzee remains from Kibale Forest, Uganda, *Journal of Human Evolution* 25:485–514.

Pfeiffer, S., S. Milne, and R. M. Stevenson
1998 The natural decomposition of adipocere, *Journal of Forensic Science* 43(2):368–370.

Potts, R.
1998 Environmental hypotheses of hominin evolution, *Yearbook of Physical Anthropology* 41: 93–136.

Rebmann, A.J., E. David, and M.H. Sorg
2000 *Cadaver Dog Handbook: Forensic Training and Tactics for the Recovery of Human Remains*, CRC Press, Boca Raton, FL.

Reichs, K.J.
    1998   A decade of forensic anthropology practice. In *Forensic Osteology: Advances in the Identi-fication of Human Remains,* 2nd edition, edited by K.J. Reichs, Charles C Thomas, Springfield, IL.

Rhine, S. and J.E. Dawson
    1998   Estimation of time since death in the southwestern United States. In *Forensic Osteology: Advances in the Identification of Human Remains,* 2nd edition, edited by K.J. Reichs, pp. 145–160. Charles C Thomas, Springfield, IL.

Rodriguez, W.C., III and W.M. Bass
    1985   Decomposition of buried bodies and methods that may aid in their location, *Journal of Forensic Sciences* 30(3):836–852.

Saavedra, B. and J.A. Simonetti
    1998   Small mammal taphonomy: Intraspecific bone assemblage comparison between South and North American barn owl, *Tyto alba,* populations, *Journal of Archaeological Science* 25:165–170.

Sauer, N.J.
    1998   The timing of injuries and manner of death: Distinguishing among antemortem, peri-mortem and postmortem trauma. In *Forensic Osteology: Advances in the Identification of Human Remains,* 2nd edition, edited by K.J. Reichs, pp. 321–332. Charles C Thomas, Springfield, IL.

Schäfer, W.
    1972   *Ecology and Paleoecology of Marine Environments,* edited by G. Craig and translated by I. Ortel, University of Chicago Press, Chicago, IL.

Scott, D.D.
    2001   Firearms identification in support of identifying a mass execution at El Mosote, El Salva-dor, *Journal of Historical Archaeology* 35(1):79–86.

Scott, D. D. and M. Connor
    2001   The role and future of archaeology in forensic science, *Journal of Historical Archaeology* 35(1):101–104.

Shipman, P.
    1981   *Life History of a Fossil: An Introduction to Taphonomy and Paleoecology,* Harvard University Press, Boston, MA.

Sonderman, R.C.
    2001   Looking for a needle in a haystack: Developing closer relationships between law enforce-ment specialists and archaeology, *Journal of Historical Archaeology* 35(1):70–78.

Sorg, M.H.
    1985   Scavenger modification of human remains, *Current Research in the Pleistocene* 2:37–38.

    1986   Scavenger modifications of human skeletal remains in forensic anthropology. Paper pre-sented at the 38th Annual Meeting of the American Academy of Forensic Sciences, New Orleans, LA.

Sorg, M.H., E. David, and A.J. Rebmann
    1998   Cadaver dogs, taphonomy, and postmortem interval in the northeast. In *Forensic Osteol-ogy: Advances in the Identification of Human Remains,* 2nd edition, edited by K.J. Reichs, pp. 120–144. Charles C Thomas, Springfield, IL.

Sorg, M.H., J.H. Dearborn, E.I. Monahan, H.F. Ryan, K.G. Sweeney, and E. David
    1997   Forensic taphonomy in marine contexts. In *Forensic Taphonomy: The Postmortem Fate of Human Remains,* edited by W.D. Haglund and M.H. Sorg, pp. 567–604, CRC Press, Boca Raton, FL.

Stewart, T.D.
   1981   *Essentials of Forensic Anthropology: Especially as Developed in the United States,* Charles C
   Thomas, Springfield, IL

Steyn, M. and J.H. Meiring
   1997   Forensic anthropology in South Africa: A profile of cases from 1993 to 1995 at the
   Department of Anatomy, University of Pretoria, *South African Journal of Ethnology* 20(1):23–27.

Stover, E. and M. Ryan
   2001   Breaking bread with the dead, *Journal of Historical Archaeology* 35(1):7–25.

Turner, C.G., II and J.A. Turner
   1999   *Man Corn: Cannibalism and Violence in the Prehistoric American Southwest,* The University
   of Utah Press, Salt Lake City, UT.

Ubelaker, D.H.
   1974   *Reconstruction of Demographic Profiles from Ossuary Skeletal Samples: A Case Study from
   the Tidewater Potomac,* Smithsonian Contributions to Anthropology 18, Smithsonian Institution Press, Washington, D.C.

   1989   *Human Skeletal Remains: Excavation, Analysis, Interpretation,* Taraxacum, Washington,
   D.C.

Voorhies, M.
   1969   *Taphonomy and Population Dynamics of an Early Pliocene Vertebrate Fauna. Knox County,
   Nebraska,* Contributions in Geology: Special Paper, No. 1, University of Wyoming Press,
   Laramie, WY.

Voss, A.A. et al.
   1992   Time since death determination of human cadaver using soil solution, *Journal of Forensic
   Sciences* 37(5):1236–1252.

Walker, S.E. and S.T. Goldstein
   1999   Taphonomic tiering: Experimental field taphonomy of mollusks and *Foraminifera* above
   and below the sediment-water interface, *Paleogeography, Paleoclimatology, Paleoecology*
   149:227–244.

Washburn, W.E.
   1987   Cultural relativism, human rights, and the AAA, *American Anthropologist* 89:939–943.

White, T.D.
   1992   *Prehistoric Cannibalism at Mancos 5MTUMR-2346,* Princeton University Press, Princeton,
   NJ.

Is Forensic Taphonomy Scientific?

2

Diagnosing death is more than accumulating evidence against the hypothesis that no one is dead.

JON J. NORDBY

Contents

Introduction

Distinctions between real science and mere collections of technical artistry, today politely referred to as multidisciplinary efforts, often appear arbitrary and unprincipled (Nordby, 1995). Many theoretical physicists, for example, enjoy disparaging mere applications of science, much as many sequestered academics eschew applications of pure science to practical problems, dismissing such efforts as mere technology unworthy of scholarly assessment (Cartwright and Nordby, 1983).

The forensic sciences along with medicine, squarely lumped within this merely applied camp, seem to provide paradigm examples of applied science (Nordby, 1995). It is difficult for traditional theoretical scientists, or classical philosophers of science, to appreciate just how such technical artistry, with its many case-specific correctives and seat-of the-pants techniques, may contribute to the development of robust general theories. Such theories must, after all, inform us about the physical nature of our universe, and allow supportable predictions from models wholly entailed by theory alone.

Much like medicine, the forensic sciences unite diverse scientific disciplines to unearth, construct, and justify the best explanations allowed by science for specific, concrete processes and events. For example, forensic anthropologists strive to explain specific human death scenes rather than simply testing and confirming the results predicted by models derived from some general anthropological theory. As such, forensic anthropology, and its relatively recent spin off, forensic taphonomy, supply no neat way for localizing the cluster of sciences to produce and defend these specific, concrete explanations of complex multivariate processes.

Multivariate contextual settings such as variations in location, climate, flora, and fauna, *appear* to make robust theory building in forensic taphonomy at best useless, and at worst, impossible. Without robust scientific theories and the theoretical models fully entailed by them, understanding the explanatory processes in forensic taphonomy appears to remain politely multidisciplinary and impolitely not science (Nordby, 1989).

Forensic taphonomy may at this time exist as a collection of hodge-podge theories, pasted together from many sciences, mixed with archaeological practices, and loosely accumulated to defend case-specific explanations and guide the discovery, investigation, and eventual explanation of specific decomposing human (or other) remains. However, to establish a scientific gauntlet for forensic taphonomy as punishment for its currently undeveloped theoretical perspectives ignores the theoretical growth of gradually maturing natural sciences for the last 2000 years (Neugerbauer, 1957).

To develop theoretical perspectives to "improve the interpretation of individual biology and history within the context of depositional environment" (Haglund and Sorg, 1997b:16–18) theoretical models, explanatory narratives of case-specific phenomena, and the relation of theory development with explanatory processes must be more clearly understood. To ask if forensic taphonomy is a science, however, is to ask the wrong question. Given this multidisciplinary concatenation of theory with practice from many different scientific disciplines, just as one sees in medical research, the more important prior question becomes: Is forensic taphonomy scientific?

If its methods are currently unscientific and no theoretical foundations can be developed, then at the very least, forensic taphonomy must refine its methods to be considered a natural science in the distant future. Can forensic taphonomy develop beyond its alleged war-story status, which thus far supplies a rather limited base for theory building? (See

Haglund and Sorg, 1997b.) Developing a theoretical basis for forensic taphonomy invokes the logical process of theory development familiar to students of the history, philosophy, and methodology of both theoretical science and research medicine. Paucity of theory building is not a phenomenon unique to forensic taphonomy; it's one component in the long story of all scientific progress.

Theories, Models, and Data

The practice of natural science involves recognizing, developing, and applying many different concepts collected under the same name. Scientific theory provides a well-discussed example (Cartwright, 1980a,b; Duhem, 1962; Hempel, 1965; and Van Frassen, 1980). Rather than seeing scientific theory as one distinct thing, it appears that "scientific theory" captures a whole family of different makes and models, much as "product of General Motors" encompasses many related, yet distinct, divisions and vehicles. While there may be many differences, certain similarities exist, otherwise the categories "scientific theory" and "product of General Motors" would lose their members completely (Weil and Nordby, 1989). The similarity rests with method (Nordby, 1995).

"Scientific model" also involves a whole family of concepts with significant practical and conceptual differences (Hanson, 1971; Weil and Nordby, 1989). A typical model presents an analogy — a relation between or among objects, supporting inferences about one based on manipulations with the other. Systematic western studies of the logical root of analogy began with Aristotle (384–322 B.C.). Archimedes (287–212 B.C.) also explains and defends the use of models in crafting the systematic explanations presented by natural philosophers (natural philosophers were first called scientists by William Whewell in 1840).

William Whewell (1794–1866) further refined the modern concept in *The Philosophy of the Inductive Sciences* (Whewell, 1847). In his account, Whewell conceived induction to be a logical pattern for discovery, rather than a dubious mode of justification through mere enumeration. [For the latter account, see Hume (1777) and Carnap (1950); against the notions developed by Hume and Carnap, Whewell's ideas were refined and developed by the American Pragmatist Charles Sanders Pierce (1839–1914) (Tursman, 1987).] A model represents, describes, exemplifies, or predicts some underlying phenomenon or process in terms of some other — it does not suffice as an explanation. Some brief examples illustrate.

Posing questions about the observed world in a mathematical way has been the scientific norm in the West at least since Galileo (1564–1642). This mathematical modeling process selects specific characteristics to be represented mathematically, usually at the expense of other characteristics not so captured, allowing predictions of the modeled phenomena from mathematical manipulations alone. Accordingly, such predictions are then either confirmed or refuted by observation or experiment with data made relevant by theory.

A model's accuracy and predictive power depend on the relevance of the abstraction it captures for the process under investigation. For example, using geometric figures like triangles as models to calculate the distance from the earth to the sun revolutionized both physics and cosmology. Atomic, pendulum, equilibrium, and countless other mathematical models infuse theories of physics (Nordby, 1989). In fact, in physics, merely calculating with these models has become almost synonymous with 'doing physics.'

Modeling, as an important element of scientific theory, is also evident in many examples from biology. William Harvey (1578–1657) pioneered the use of mathematics to resolve biological conundrums. The evidence supporting his theory of blood circulation included a quantitative analysis measuring the volume of blood the heart pumped in an hour. (In his experiment, he measured the amount of blood moved in each systole and multiplied by the number of heartbeats per hour). The amounts vary with the measured volume and the number of beats. The predictive power of his model rests with its generality and universality among differing organisms sharing relevantly similar physiological characteristics detailed in his theory.

Predator–prey, pollution, evolution, and countless statistical models abound in biology and medicine. For example, Gregor Mendel (1822–1884) modeled relationships among parental properties, breeding, and the properties of successive generations by using garden peas. Selecting snow peas from among the many garden pea varieties in order to investigate a developing genetic theory occurred through trial and error, mixed with critical scientific assessments distinguishing relevant from coincidental properties in the process they model.

Models of fundamental natural processes are chosen for many different reasons, including unashamedly practical considerations. Selecting humans as subjects, for example, to investigate dominant and recessive genes would pose insurmountable investigative problems — succeeding generations are too far apart in time. Mendel himself would not have lived long enough to make his observations and develop his conclusions. He chose snow peas over other pea varieties to model the relevant features of genes because they have a much faster generation turn-around time. Others then applied the power of what later became the genetic theory to predict the process in humans.

Choices among laboratory animals for medical research are often based upon developing an analogy — a systemic isomorphism or homomorphism — with humans; monkeys, rats, dogs, etc. each models some human systems and processes better than others do. The famous Bohr model of the atom, using planet-like subatomic orbits to model atomic structure, still has great heuristic value, although the model does not literally or accurately represent the atom. Instead, as with some medical models, it captures specific relationships among the particles thought essential for prediction and useful for understanding.

This universality and predictive power characterize both theoretical models and the developing theories supporting their application. Identifying the exact processes to model, however, requires the scientific sagacity, luck, and patience associated with scientific discoveries. According to Whewell's inductive logic and later, Peirce's abductive logic, these logical processes of discovery rest at the heart of scientific method (Tursman, 1987).

No model captures every element in a complex process under investigation. In real phenomena such as disease processes, factors covered by different theories and their models interact in ways not covered by any general umbrella theory. We pay a price for standing on the shoulders of past scientists, applying and investigating their theoretical constructs in relatively novel situations. For example, individuals appear to react differently to the HIV virus as well as to various medications developed to combat full-blown AIDS. The identification and explanation of these differences, however, allow medical researchers to identify and test alternative components of the general disease process, searching for the mechanisms that account for the differences while finding relevant similarities. Our successes or failures are measured by developing predictive and explanatory power.

Models in forensic taphonomy are not all based simply on mathematical equations, nor are they fully entailed by paleontological, paleoanthropological, or archeological theory alone. Taphonomy appears to focus on processes more like those of disease, with all their individuating circumstances embodied in seemingly unique investigative data.

One obstacle to classifying a theory, or a model of the theory, as scientific involves the need to make case specific correctives when applying the model. The presence of apparently *ad hoc* corrective procedures, without some logical rules for their application, appears to exclude certain theories and their models from being scientific.

Consider the early caloric theory of heat, which theoretically explained combustion through the release of a theoretical entity called phlogiston. [Compare explaining combustion theoretically with explaining the Chicago fire by citing Mrs. O'Leary's cow.] Combustion logically entailed phlogiston's release when objects such as human bodies transform by fire. According to a simple model of this theory, phlogiston, as an element in everything combustible, is physically released during combustion. This release explained the production of heat. This simple model appeared to be consistent with the observed combustion of many materials.

Of course, when Lavoisier roasted sheets of copper, the mass of the copper before combustion was less than its mass after combustion. If phlogiston, as a substance, was released during combustion, as caloric theory predicted through its theoretical model, then the mass of pre-roasted copper [copper plus phlogiston] would be greater than the mass of post-roasted copper [copper minus phlogiston]. Lavoisier's actual measurements of copper, however, showed just the opposite.

Caloric theorists first attempted to save the theory and explain the apparently contradictory result for copper by making copper a special case not captured in the model, or covered by the theory. Caloric theorists hypothesized that phlogiston, when a substance in copper, had a negative mass.

This bold stroke to save the caloric theory's theoretical model and the phenomenon, if not dignified with the status of corrective procedure, was certainly *ad hoc* and ultimately contradictory: the concept of negative mass was incoherent. This represents scientific progress: developing and investigating the caloric theory cannot be called unscientific simply because its model collapsed, and the theory turned out to be false.

Forensic taphonomists appear to make logically similar correctives when specific depositions of human remains seem to have absolutely unique properties, apparently inconsistent with empirically investigated decomposition models built with work from various chemical, physiological, and medical theories. Unique combinations of climate, location, weather, circumstance, etc., appear haphazardly to amend theoretically imprecise time interval-relating properties of the so-called stages of decomposition. The scientific challenge involves remodeling decomposition models that come up short by analyzing the specific mechanism at hand. This remodeling casts a scientific eye toward theoretically robust accounts of the decomposition process that move beyond case-specific explanations. Remodeling becomes a logical mechanism for scientific discovery.

If forensic taphonomy is to build a genuine theoretical basis from apparently anecdotal origins, the logical relations among different kinds of theories, and their differing models, must be systematically clarified and developed. Certainly not every corrective applied to a scientific model derived from theory must resort to *ad hoc* amendments to save the phenomena. If it did, no confirmed predictions demonstrating increased scientific understanding would be possible.

The relationship of anecdotal experiences with specific phenomena, the development of rather specific models, and the incorporation of corrective procedures to build, apply, and remodel them remains an essential part of theory-building in any maturing science. Persisting uniqueness, faced with overly general and contextually vague models from various scientific disciplines, need not defoliate the theoretical landscape of any natural science. In fact, they're necessary for sound theoretical development.

Methodological Mischief?

When a suspect was told that a witness had seen him commit murder, he calmly replied that he could bring forward a hundred witnesses who had not seen him commit it.

G.K. Chesterton

One common argument against the methods of any forensic science being scientific involves the forensic focus on investigations of single, unique events, usually crimes, which do not lend themselves to generalizations on a par with those of the natural sciences (Nordby, 1995). For example, crime assessment or profiling appears at first blush, at best, to be on a par with forecasting the weather, or with predicting the financial behavior of Wall Street investors.

When resident psychological, meteorological, or financial theories make inaccurate predictions through their models, particular amendments may appear to cover errant predictions, and to smooth over inconsistencies. Such additions appear to save both the fundamental theory and the actual phenomenon. Rather than admitting that the underlying theory has some defect, or that the model exhibits a fatal weakness, the theory and its model become particularized to account for the *now-expected* inaccuracy in this special case.

Such moves lead many who wash cars, invest money, or explain crimes to conclude that these areas simply lack an adequate theoretical basis altogether, much as shown by the caloric theory's collapse. But why theories collapse is critical for understanding their scientific status. The caloric theory was scientific, but stock market projections are not. Without defending crime assessment against such charges here, let's ask, "Does a similar charge *legitimately* apply to the corrective methods of forensic taphonomy?" Are the forensic taphonomic cases before us so particular, with conditions so unique to specific circumstance that no general bodies of theory, or no specific theoretical models, can even apply?"

Fortunately, taphonomy shares at least one legitimizing tool with caloric theory that stock market behavioral explanation lacks: the complex logic of scientific method. Challenging theory construction and model development as a necessary component of scientific method rests on the idea that independent investigators should be able to apply the same methods to the same data and get the same, or at least similar, results (Lynch, 1995). Individual stockbrokers, brokerage houses, and mutual fund managers market unique, individual abilities, like the psychic, rather than offering independently applicable principles open to community testing.

Unfortunately, scientists seldom agree on relevant bodies of experience, the accuracy or scope of a proposed or developing theory, or the bias introduced by the presence or absence of specialized training. Real conflicts about the same operation occur in medicine, chemistry, and physics; they are certainly familiar in expert disagreements among forensic scientists in courtrooms (Nordby, 1992). The independent reproducibility of complex events or experiments may remain more myth than fact, but this is not due to an inherently fatal, investigator-dependent uniqueness blocking any possible objective demonstrations of fact. The difficulty arises from differences among general theories and applicable predictive models, in principle open to independent analysis and critical investigation (see Hempel, 1965).

The particular details reported and developed from the specific work of various forensic anthropologists engaged in taphonomic research are often found among apparently subjective impressions, or sampling bias (Szibor, 1998). They appear to be both investigator and context dependent, seemingly in conflict with the development of well-rehearsed theories in the natural sciences (Cartwright, 1980a,b). Forensic taphonomy relies on investigator judgment, and investigator-dependent approximating procedures regarding sample recovery, collection methods, curation, and analysis (Haglund and Sorg, 1997b).

Given this dependence upon individually ordered procedures, imprecise theoretical terms, and as yet absent general theories with associated predictive models, forensic taphonomy has been referred to as more art than science. This may, according to some, capture the current status of forensic taphonomy.

However, the view reducing taphonomy to anecdote rests on a radically inadequate understanding of the nature and development of theoretical science, and on viciously misleading notions about the logics of discovery and explanation (Hanson, 1965; Nordby, 1992, 1995). Attributing mere artistry to forensic taphonomy rests specifically on a flawed view of the legitimate relations among theory, models, approximations, and investigator-dependent observations, or biases introduced by observers to the particularizing details.

In this artistic view, any variations from theoretically predicted results are explained by investigator bias, errors in measurement, flaws in practice, or shortcuts in procedure. Following this position, to say that forensic taphonomy is a science is to say that it rests on a foundation of fully developed, or at least developing, true theories and their models that cover all the processes involved in changing human remains from life to dust. This position carries all the arrogance of the politicians at the start of the 20th century who demanded that the U.S. Patent Office be eliminated "since everything has already been discovered."

On this assumption, when field determinations fail to match theoretical predictions, we conclude that either the theory needs refinement, or the theory remains true, while our application of it in practice falls short of theory. Just how a theory or its model falls short in a particular set of circumstances reveals more about the development of the theory and its models than about alleged flaws introduced by bias, measurement error, or shortcuts. It also suggests how theories and theoretical models are built in the first place.

Unlikely Bedfellows

Theory discovery and theory development differ from unique-event reconstruction and case-specific explanation. The absence of any umbrella theories in forensic taphonomy does not mean that we have no idea how to approach questions concerning the postmortem interval in individual cases, or where to look for teeth to help identify a body (Haglund, 1997). We do. But so far, this ability depends upon compilations of anecdotal experiences shared among death investigators practicing in the field from many different scientific

points of view [anthropologists, archeologists, pathologists, entomologists, botanists, geol-
ogists, meteorologists, and many others]. Unfortunately, precious few such anecdotes exist
to be compiled.

However, the logical status of this investigator-specific data, somehow relevant in
forensic taphonomy, parallels the logical status of data from any developing natural science
in its infancy (Cartwright, 1983). We may not yet be in a position to build the necessary
theoretical bridges. Forensic taphonomy, after all, only recently became a subject for formal
study (as compared with chemistry). We may be guilty of common contemporary impa-
tience for rigorous theoretical development, or we may not all be equipped scientifically
to develop existing data in more theoretical directions. We may even make quick, partisan
decisions between ill-chosen alternatives: Is taphonomy a mature science, or is it a waste
of scientific time? Patience gleaned from the history of medicine counsels that these options
remain profoundly incomplete.

The practical urgency to prevent patient deaths from "childbed fever" at Vienna General Hospital in 1844 supplies a useful lesson. The situation faced by Ignaz Semmelweis,
a Hungarian physician, loosely parallels the practical urgency of taphonomic analysis when
facing criminal cases.

As a staff member of the First Maternity Division, Semmelweis noted that many
patients who delivered babies contracted an often-fatal disease called puerperal fever, or
childbed fever. About 260 of the 3157 mothers, or 8.2 %, died from the disease. In 1845,
the rate in the First Division fell to 6.8%, but in 1846 it jumped to over 11% (Sinclair,
1909; Kruif, 1909). He also noted that the hospital's Second Maternity Division, over the
same period, enjoyed a much lower death rate from the disease — about 2 to 3%. Well-
qualified physicians, who taught in the medical school, treated patients in the First Division.
Those in the Second Division saw only midwives, adding further professional chagrin to
the otherwise intolerable situation.

Semmelweis followed and tested many avenues to solve the puzzle. In 1847, a colleague,
nicked by a student scalpel during an instructional autopsy, died a similar death. Semmelweis supposed that cadaveric matter from the dead body, introduced into the professor's
blood through the nick, had caused the fatal illness. He reasoned that washing with
chlorinated lime would destroy the cadaveric matter introduced to patients in the First
Division by physicians and medical students who routinely performed cadaver dissections.
In 1848, after this cleaning practice became routine, the death rate for the First Division
fell to a little over 1%, about the same as the Second Division, which followed the same
practice.

Additional data presented a new puzzle. After washing with chlorinated lime, Semmelweis examined an expectant mother suffering from a festering cervical cancer. The
following 12 healthy women he examined all developed childbed fever: 11 died. Semmelweis concluded that childbed fever was caused by both cadaveric matter and "putrid matter
derived from living organisms" (Sinclair, 1909).

While Semmelweis may have solved the practical puzzle, he did not even broach the
theoretical puzzle. He developed no theory to explain why cadaveric or putrid matter
caused childbed fever, nor why washing with chlorinated lime arrested its spread and
development. His practical success remained unexplained until the germ theory of disease
showcased just what it was in cadaveric and putrid matter that provided the mechanism
for what we now know as infections.

A similar paucity of theory exists among case-specific research in forensic taphonomy. We may successfully distinguish antemortem, perimortem, and postmortem intervals in a specific case without understanding the underlying explanatory mechanisms that serve to distinguish them. This leaves theoretical development outside the action. Many successful specific case analyses share the scientific status of a Viennese bath in chlorinated lime.

Facing multivariate, apparently unique factors, familiar in death assemblages and disease processes alike, remains the rule rather than the exception in the development of a scientifically solid theoretical structure. Eventually, forensic taphonomy may develop a theory to parallel the germ theory of disease through a more formal approach to current case experience. We may not yet have firmly established the science of forensic taphonomy, but it does not follow that it is unscientific — its developing methods and history parallel those of now recognized and trivially accepted theories of disease.

For inspiration, we may consider examining logical relations among theories of the HIV virus, the common effects of full-blown AIDS, and practical patient therapies. We see the logical interaction of each as a key to developing a scientific theory, with model application and revision, given apparently unique, concatenated phenomena. Theory development in forensic taphonomy (Haglund and Sorg, 1997b and Chapter 1, this volume) broadly parallels that in medicine. Somehow, like the scientific pioneers following Semmelweis, we learn to move from anecdote to theory by seeking and unraveling the common threads that unite apparently dissimilar phenomena.

Conclusion

Recognizing how a developing explanation or a proposed model falls short in a particular set of circumstances supplies insight into needed theory and model development. In fact, the history of medicine suggests how to build theories and theoretical models from specific case experiences.

Current case-specific research virtually ensures that forensic taphonomy will remain *scientific* as it develops and broadens its theoretical base (see Table 2.1). The nature of these insights may initially appear to be anecdotal, but in the discussion and analysis of anecdote rests the beginning of robust theory. After all, that's where theories come from in the first place: from the need to *explain the explanations* (Achinstein, 1983). Such theories in forensic taphonomy, developed through making particular corrections and tinkering with tentative models borrowed from intersecting sciences, may eventually change the theoretical faces of sciences such as paleoanthropology, physical anthropology, entomology, ecology, as well as taphonomy, forever.

Table 2.1 Characteristics of Scientific Theories

- Natural scientists do not always work with theories; they work with unexpected data and struggle to explain it. Particular explanations of unexpected or surprising phenomena lead to the development of general theories.

- Scientific theories are much more than simple generalizations — they capture law-like generalizations that are true anywhere their boundary conditions have been satisfied. Promising theories withstand specific challenge, and fit together with other developing theories, observations, and recognized law-like statements about natural processes.

- Scientific theories are a special kind of generalizing explanation. They systematize specific relationships to the exclusion of others in order to understand a complex phenomenon.

- Promising theories allow predictions that, at least in principle, can be confirmed or refuted. For example, in the developing theory of blood circulation, Harvey postulated minute channels between the arteries and veins. Such structures were logically necessary for the theory to work. This feature of his theory was not confirmed until 1661, when Marcello Malpighi observed capillaries microscopically.

- Scientific theories do not function to explain every, one could argue, any, unique event falling under their umbrella. Most unique events of forensic or other scientific interest fall under more than one theoretical umbrella, e.g., decomposition processes include putrefaction, a microbial process, as well as autolysis, a chemical process. But in a unique gravesite, a body decomposes among many other independent conditions, that are in turn covered by other theories, e.g., environmental factors

- Individually corrected explanatory stories must be consistent with scientific theories that cover the event, or the theory must supply good reasons why they are inconsistent. Otherwise the theory may be defective in its present form.

- Theories in a discipline must capture *systematic* regularities. When generalizations merely coexist with recognized exceptions, the generalizations retain the status of "rules of thumb," eschewing the status of scientific theory.

- Scientific theories, unlike causal or explanatory narratives, must not contain unspecified *ceteris paribus* clauses (all things being equal, or more clearly, all things being right). In specific forensic events, nothing is equal, and nothing is right as far as the rigid application of an umbrella theory goes.

- Scientific theories must logically comprise a well-defined set of counterfactual conditionals (what would happen if) when applied to hypothetical phenomena, e.g., What would happen to a human body which suffered blunt-force trauma to the head when it is buried in 10 feet of snow at 12,000 feet for 30 days? Theories of putrefaction, and autolysis as well as theories of thermal interaction, and environmental agency, may cover and yield predictions that would then give relevance to certain measured data in the event the hypothetical became actual. Any deviation from theoretical prediction then, would itself need explanation — ranging from charges of defective theory to modifications in materials, the presence or absence of specific features such as alcohol consumption, or disease processes, or other intervening events, etc. Note that these particularizing modifications would NOT involve modifications to scientific theory itself — they would involve modifications to developing explanations of specific, concrete events. This is a different intellectual task (Cartwright, 1980)

- In the absence of robust scientific theories, their construction proceeds through distinguishing corrective procedures that merely work in a specific case from those that inherently take us toward a true explanation. Systematic general theory building can begin with the systematic analysis of these specific corrections, keeping in mind that scientific theories do not assume the role of explaining all features of uniquely particular concrete events, but must retain the logical features listed above.

Note: "Theory" covers many differing conceptual structures, some unique to natural science, some not, but there are some general features that uniquely scientific theories of many different sorts must contain.

References

Achinstein, P.
  1983 *The Nature of Explanation*, Oxford University Press, New York.
Carnap, R.
  1950 *The Logical Foundations of Probability*, University of Chicago Press, Chicago.
Cartwright, N.
  1980a The truth doesn't explain much, *American Philosophical Quarterly* 17(2):184–189.
  1980b Do the laws of physics state the facts? *Pacific Philosophical Quarterly* 61:216–227.
  1983 *Do the Laws of Physics Lie?* Oxford University Press, New York.
Cartwright, N. and J. Nordby
  1983 How approximations take us from theory and toward truth, *Pacific Philosophical Quarterly* 64:273–280.
de Kruif, P.
  1932 *Men Against Death*, Harcourt Brace & World, New York.
Duhem, P.
  1962 *The Aim and Structure of Physical Theory*, trans. by Philip P. Wiener. Athenaeum, New York.
Haglund, W.D.
  1997 Scattered skeletal human remains: search strategy considerations for locating missing teeth. In *Forensic Taphonomy: The Postmortem Fate of Human Remains*, edited by W.D. Haglund and M.H. Sorg, pp. 383–394. CRC Press, Boca Raton, FL.
Haglund, W.D. and M.H. Sorg
  1997a *Forensic Taphonomy: The Postmortem Fate of Human Remains*, CRC Press, Boca Raton, FL.
  1997b Method and theory of forensic taphonomic research. In *Forensic Taphonomy: The Postmortem Fate of Human Remains*, edited by W.D. Haglund and M.H. Sorg, pp. 13–26. CRC Press, Boca Raton, FL.
Hanson, N.R.
  1965 *Patterns of Discovery: An Enquiry into the Conceptual Foundations of Science*, Cambridge University Press, New York.
  1971 *Observation and Explanation: A Guide to Philosophy of Science*, Harper & Row, New York.
Hempel, C. G.
  1965 *Aspects of Scientific Explanation and other Essays in the Philosophy of Science*, The Free Press, New York.
Hume, D.
  1777 *Enquiries Concerning the Human Understanding and the Principles of Morals.* Oxford University Press, Oxford, 1968.
Lynch, J.
  1995 *The Race To Catch a Bucky Ball*, WGBH TV Boston, BBC TV Service, WGBH video, Burlington, VT.
Neugerbauer, O.
  1957 *The Exact Sciences in Antiquity*, 2nd ed. Brown University Press, Providence.
Nordby, J.
  1989 Bootstrapping while barefoot [crime models vs. theoretical models in the hunt for serial killers], *Synthese* 81:373–389.
  1992 Can we believe what we see if we see what we believe? Expert disagreement, *Journal of Forensic Sciences* 37(4):1115–1124.
  1995 Science is as science does: the question of reliable methodologies in "real science," *Shepard's Expert and Scientific Evidence Quarterly* 2(3):701–710.

Sinclair, W.J.
   1909 *Semmelweis: His Life and His Doctrine*, Manchester University Press, Manchester, England.
Szibor, R., C. Schubert, and V. Wendt
   1998 Pollen analysis reveals murder season, *Nature* 395(6701):449.
Tursman, R.
   1987 *Peirce's Theory of Scientific Discovery: A System of Logic Conceived as Semiotic*, Indiana University Press, Bloomington, IN.
Van Frassen, B.
   1980 *The Scientific Image*, Clarendon Press, Oxford.
Weil, V. and J. Nordby
   1989 Introduction. In *Synthese: Philosophy of Applied Science,* Vol. 81, Kluwer Academic Publishers, The Netherlands.
Whewell, W.
   1847 *The Philosophical Foundations of the Inductive Sciences, Founded on Their History*, Vol. I-2, 2nd ed. Cambridge University Press, London.

Section 2

The Biogeographic Context

An Autopsy of the Grave: Recognizing, Collecting, and Preserving Forensic Geotaphonomic Evidence

3

MICHAEL J. HOCHREIN

Contents

Introduction

The use of archaeological methods on buried body crime scenes is not new to forensic science. Boddington et al. (1987), Brothwell (1981), Heizer and Graham (1967), Morse et al. (1983), Roberts et al. (1989), Skinner and Lazenby (1983), Ubelaker (1989), and others have become standard references in crime scene training; however, the actual application of formal archaeological techniques is too often ignored or shortcut to the point of absence at many crime scenes. At other sites, archaeology may be used without considering the recent, and forensic, contexts of scenes and the artifacts they include.

The ability to consult professional archaeologists is often not recognized by many police departments, or is thought to be outside their fiscal means. When archaeology consultants are called into crime scenes, investigators may be at the mercy of their expertise level. Not all archaeologists are trained with emphases in physical anthropology or osteology, nor do all physical anthropologists have adequate archaeological field experience to direct excavations for, and interpret, subtle subterranean clues left at burial sites. Very few anthropologists, in general, have any practical experience in processing forensically significant sites. From the homicide or death investigator's perspective, the need has been recognized (Horvarth and Meesig, 1998) for additional and appropriate training of law enforcement personnel who constitute first responders in the discovery, documentation, and collection of physical evidence. This also applies to those investigators tasked with interpreting the context of such evidence. For the non-anthropologist investigator, training in forensic anthropology is one of the least common areas of police instruction. When courses are available in forensic anthropology, they may concentrate on search techniques or the laboratory analyses of recovered evidence rather than collection methods. The end result may be the well-intended processing of crime scenes that appear to have been systematically excavated, but where subtle, important clues have been overlooked. In worse case scenarios, the excavations damage or destroy evidence. Consider the following descriptions of archaeological excavations:

> He stuck a small shovel several inches into the muck and struck something solid. "I pulled it up and it's a bone, a arm bone," (He) endured a week of ten hour days digging his gloved hand through decomposing flesh into rib cages and finding his fingers stuck in eye sockets.
>
> **Anonymous, 1994**

or this account:

> While digging in freshly turned dirt at the southeast corner of the property, (he) turned up some items that looked like pieces of cloth and beef jerky… when a lot of "whacking" and "banging away" on something that looked like a tree root failed to dislodge it, (he) wrapped (his) hand around it, braced (his) feet and started pulling on it… (He) pulled so hard that it broke loose, and when (he) pulled it up (he) could see the joint. It was a bone!
>
> **Wilson, 1993**

To the formally trained contemporary archaeologist, these accounts might conjure images of an Indiana Jones episode, or early classical archaeology and its emphasis on gathering artifacts for personal and museum collections, taking little care of their archaeological contexts. Unfortunately, these excerpts are not from movie scripts or of earlier eras. They describe more recent accounts of the recoveries of homicide victims.

Archaeological approaches to buried evidence crime scenes should be similar to that of a thorough forensic autopsy. The use of protocol in excavations must be combined with an understanding of the dynamics of the matrices (tissues) being excavated (dissected). Just as the forensic pathologist is well versed in postmortem changes to muscle, organs, and wounds, the forensic archaeologist is expected to be well versed in intrinsic characteristics and environmental factors which can affect soil horizons and interfaces through which clandestine pits are dug.

The concept of geotaphonomy was proposed to address the recognition and collection of specific types of evidence, which can be recovered only via appropriate archaeological techniques. Geotaphonomy has been defined as "The study of the geophysical characteristics of, and changes in, subterranean features associated with the interment of buried evidence." (Hochrein, 1997a). This study of the dynamics behind the creation, closing, and postdepositional history of burial features differs from taphonomy by recognizing, collecting, and interpreting cultural and environmental factors affecting the burial feature, including its contents. Where taphonomy broadly utilizes the condition of or modifications to, and context of deposited remains for interpretation of peri- and postburial environments, geotaphonomy focuses such forensic examinations on the grave context itself. The focus of geotaphonomy is on the pit, grave, or concealing matrices whether or not the evidence buried includes human remains. Geotaphonomy encompasses six areas or aspects of the burial environment: stratification; tool marks; bioturbation; sedimentation; compression-depression and internal compaction.

Stratification

The geological principles of stratification, including axioms of superposition, original horizontality, and original continuity, were conceptualized as early as the seventeenth century by individuals such as Nils Steensen (Steno), William Smith, and Sir Charles Lyell. Those principles have been further developed, or applied, in more recent works (Donovan, 1966; Drucker, 1972; Dunbar and Rodgers, 1957; Harris et al., 1993; Pydokke, 1961; Schiffer, 1987; Spennemann and Franke, 1995, and others) as tenets of archaeology and paleontology. Stratigraphy is the primary basis for understanding buried crime scene evidence. The excavation of graves or pits cannot take place without permanently interrupting and mixing soil horizons. These layers can be naturally or artificially formed. Since the digging of a feature is chronologically and spatially relative to the soil layers in which it intrudes, changes to the stratification of manmade fill are as apparent as those of natural horizons.

In the search for clandestine burials, e.g., Case Histories 1 to 3, interruptions to stratification is one basis for intensifying pedestrian, geophysical, and remote search techniques. Pedestrian searchers look for surface indications that subsoil horizons have been displaced to the top and mixed with superseding and underlying layers during the process of digging and then infilling a pit. These indications may be as obvious as differences between the color of the pit fill, backdirt remnants, and surface layer; however, they are often subtle textural differences. Geophysical prospection uses technically refined measurements of naturally or induced signals to identify areas in which a site's stratification has been disturbed (Davenport, 1996; Killam, 1990; and Wynn, 1986).

Stratification is also evident in trash dump deposits. The archaeology of commercial landfills is well documented, and has been refined, through the research of Rathje et al. (1992). The systematic excavation of refuse underlying and covering primary evidence can provide some of the clearest means of dating that evidence. Layers of garbage above, below, and contemporaneous with the primary object being sought contain artifacts that may be dated by marks, serial numbers, or calendar dates. At a minimum, such associated items offer a *terminus post quem* for when the primary evidence could have been deposited (Noël Hüme, 1970). When dating evidence on the basis of associated debris, investigators must take care to rely on the chronology of depositional layers rather than relying on individual pieces of garbage. Individual items may be curated for varying lengths of time resulting in a manufacture-deposition lag (Hill, 1982). For example, resealable items such as jars typically demonstrate datable labels or maker's marks but are more subject to reuse than non-collectable beverage cans. Disadvantages associated with landfill searches are logistical in nature and relate to the size of the dumpsite and the length of time since the evidence was disposed. Laska (1996) describes the extent and cost such problems posed in the search for remains of a missing child. In that case, approximately three weeks and $100,000 were expended before the search concluded without the discovery of a body.

Stratigraphy is even more forensically significant when applied within the burial feature. Often, a subject's intent toward further concealment of buried evidence is reflected in introduced additives, which constitute layers of the clandestine pit's stratification. It is not uncommon to discover graves into which lime, or related chemicals, were poured to mask the odor of decomposition or hasten the process. Subjects often confuse the properties of calcium oxide with similarly named but less caustic products such as calcium carbonate or calcium hydroxide. Inadvertently, their mistakes help to preserve the remains. Whatever the intent or outcome (Figure 3.1), the continuity of that stratum can be utilized to clearly document postburial tampering.

Once an anomaly is identified as a burial feature, its examination is limited to the contents or stratification within the grave or pit. Internal interruption to the strata may represent a subject's return to remove or alter grave contents. Likewise, multiple burials separated by time will be reflected by interruptions visible in horizontal and vertical stratifications. The forensic archaeologist must remember that each shovelful theoretically represents a separate stratigraphic event. To ignore stratification is to ignore some of the most direct information of how the evidence came to be interred.

Case History #1

During a homicide investigation in which the author assisted, the establishment and maintenance of a vertical profile or section within a clandestine grave allowed the interpretation of grave construction and later intrusion. The case involved the sudden disappearance of an elderly couple. Foul play was immediately suspected and an investigation was initiated. Approximately 1 year later, accomplices confessed and told investigators where both victims were interred in a common grave. Evidence team members were able to document the sequence of deposits (Hochrein, 1997a) within the grave beginning with the wrapped bodies of both victims, followed by a layer of soil, a thin layer of concrete, additional soil, and finally horse manure. During excavation, a series of profiles or sections

Figure 3.1 (a) Bisection and partial excavation of a burial feature. (b) Stratum of calcium carbonate exposed in a vertical profile during archaeological excavation.

were established across the grave and perpendicular to the buried remains. The profiles revealed that stratification was interrupted by a pit dug through layers in the southern half of the grave. This confirmed witness accounts of an abandoned attempt to remove and relocate the bodies. Archaeological techniques also allowed the discovery and precise recording of trace evidence, single synthetic fibers recovered *in situ*. The trace, associated, and stratigraphic evidence ultimately supported witness accounts of the double homicide, burial, and attempt to remove the bodies. These geotaphonomic clues would have gone unrecognized had large tools or heavy machinery been used in the exhumation.

Case History #2

In a second case, the victim, murdered by a business associate, lay concealed for 9 months until an accomplice led investigators to a farm on which the remains were buried. Cadaver dogs pinpointed the location. The subject, familiar with a particular sinkhole historically used as the farm's dump, disposed of the body in the sinkhole and covered it with layers of hay, trash, and lime (calcium hydroxide). During the exhumation, investigators asked if it appeared as if the lime-like substance was poured into the sinkhole prior to the deposition of the body. Such evidence might suggest additional planning and preparation for the homicide. The sandwiching of the remains between layers of lime would have called for some preparation of the burial site and procurement of a large quantity of lime. The information also would be valuable in future interrogations of subjects and witnesses.

Excavation first required the establishment of a 3-dimensional grid system. Following the systematic documentation and removal of debris from above the sinkhole, the grid was projected down into it. Evidence and geotaphonomic artifacts of postdeposition environmental events were documented. The excavation revealed that heavy rains during the 9-month burial caused the northwestern edge of the sinkhole to erode down and over a portion of the remains. Attention to stratigraphy allowed the archaeologist to identify this depositional event as natural and not the result of dirt being shoveled onto the remains.

To answer the investigator's initial question, what appeared to be a thin layer of lime beneath the victim's remains was, again, an artifact of natural erosion. The geotaphonomic examination demonstrated that the lime had washed down the southern facing side of the body and seeped beneath the victim's right side. It did not constitute a pre-deposited layer on which the remains were placed.

Case History #3

The principles of landfill archaeology were put in practice in a case in which the forensic archaeologist was asked to search for the neonate remains allegedly taken from an incest victim and disposed of in the family's garbage. Approximately 20 months after the incident, the mother told authorities. She recollected being taken by her father, the morning after a forced delivery, to a gully that had been historically used as the farm's refuse site. Because she was asked to pay her last respects at the site, she suspected the baby's remains were buried within the dump.

The forensic search of the site began with the use of cadaver dogs to narrow the focus of the search. The dogs identified multiple sites (not unexpected in a dump context) requiring the entire dump be searched. With the assistance of anthropology students, a physical anthropologist, and a vertebrate taphonomist, the evidence team systematically dismantled the site. After the establishment of a 10 × 10 m grid system suspended over the gully, and the collection of topographic readings, a parallel grid was established on either side of the drainage. The grid was set so that its center line, or transect, bisected the dump lengthwise. Debris, including appliances, newspaper, cans, bottles, food items, etc., were then removed per grid square and placed in paralleling units in reverse stratification. In this manner, the human remains, if discovered, could be dated on the basis of datable debris situated above, below, and around them. Although the search uncovered numerous nonhuman bones, none of a human neonate were revealed.

Tool Marks

Tool mark evidence at crime scenes is a primary consideration in burglaries, home invasions, and other crimes involving mechanical means of prying or cutting. At scenes of buried evidence, however, there is often a misconception that tool marks do not survive the elements. Invalid assumptions may be made that all holes are dug with shovels, or that identifying the digging implement used by the subject is not important. Whatever the rationale, marks left during the construction of clandestine graves are routinely overlooked even though they may be preserved below and above ground surface. If tool marks are preserved in buried settings, recognition and collection depends on a systematic removal of the pit's fill from the original walls of the feature. The author has found one technique, known as profiling, sectioning, or partexing, the most expedient.

Understanding how a grave was dug may offer insight into the amount of planning and intent a subject had in dispatching a victim. Tool marks from atypical implements like tree branches or cups may be more consistent with hurried, unplanned disposals. On the other hand, deep pits exhibiting marks from one or more types of shovels may imply a more planned crime and the involvement of an accomplice. Geotaphonomic experiments (Hochrein, 1997b), as well as case experience, have demonstrated how the use of various digging implements introduces unique marks to the walls of burials. Media accounts of buried body cases have documented subjects' uses of a variety of digging implements from tire irons to clam shells (Anon., 1981a,b, 1984; Ross, 1994). Curwen and Curwen (1926), in discussing the use of a scapula as a tool, imply an even more interesting relationship between taphonomic and geotaphonomic agents.

The geotaphonomic experiments mentioned above showed that the act of backfilling, compressing, or stomping the fill and exposing each test feature to approximately 2 weeks of ambient weather did not impede the clear recognition of tool marks upon archaeological excavation.* Subterranean tool marks have been observed in empirical studies, training exercises, and crime scene settings ranging in age from 2 days (Figure 3.2) to 4 years (Figure 3.3). In two experiments (Hochrein, 1997b; Hochrein, [in preparation]), multiple heavy rainfalls in excess of 2.54 cm were recorded at test sites; the buried tool marks remained intact in spite of the precipitation. These findings support assumptions that ambient conditions do not completely obliterate tool marks.

Not all soil matrices are conducive to retaining the compression and friction details of digging marks. More plastic soils, with higher percentages of clays or silts, better hold

---

* An ongoing review of media accounts of buried body cases (Hochrein et al., 1999) supports the applicability of such short-duration empirical experiments. To date, of 881 victims, the remains of 607 (68.9%) were found within a year of their disappearances or abductions. Of the same 881, 328 (37.2%) were found within a month of their disappearances.

Figure 3.2 Claw hammer marks revealed in the walls of a burial (postdeposition period, 2 days).

Figure 3.3 Round-point shovel tool marks revealed in the walls of a burial (postdeposition period, 4 years).

striae and impression details. The least conducive matrices are those consisting of gravels or dry, sandy soils. The dynamics of digging a pit in rocky soil usually necessitate two digging implements: one, such as a pick or mattock to loosen soil and rock; and a shovel to removed the loosened matrix. Although compression-friction marks from the shovel may not be visible, the occurrence of large quantities of cracked or spalled rock in the remaining backdirt, or halo around a pit, can be the first indication of damage caused by a pick type tool. As with soils adhering to shovels, particles of rock impressed into the pick or mattock blade, as well as marks left on rock fragments and tool, might match when scrutinized under magnification. Hochrein (1997b) mentions specific characteristics associated with particular types of digging implements. These extend beyond the friction and compression details left by their blades, to the degree to which excavation with certain tools sever root networks, or require the excavator to stand or kneel in certain positions.

When examining subterranean features for tool marks, it is important to avoid contamination of forensically significant marks. The excavator may be aided by textural differences between the fill and the more compact sides of a pit. As the fill is archaeologically sectioned, it tends to spall from tool-marked surfaces. The void created between the arbitrary wall constituting an established vertical profile and the original wall of the grave can be filled with dental gypsum to produce a cast of the mark. At deeper depths, the same void can be created by inserting a rigid board in place of the archaeological profile excavated within the feature.

The instruments used examining tool mark evidence should include only small, handheld tools. Less refined instruments (such as spades) could allow the excavation to cause marks misattributed to the subject's excavation. There is also less tactile sensation and control when using larger tools. The author recommends a combination of handheld tools and a vacuum to remove fill from tool marks. The vacuum removes the excavated material without touching the tool marks and their striae. In several experimental and training incidents, casts made after such preparation demonstrated detailed striae. Preserving this level of detail could result in positive identification of specific digging implements, although it is more often only possible to determine the class of tool. Knowing at least the tool class can confirm witness accounts, as well as pertinent information for search warrants.

At, or near, the surface of a hand-dug pit, tool marks may be represented by handle impressions along the edge of the grave. As a feature is dug to greater depths using a shovel or long handled implement like a posthole digger, more of the handle, with greater force, is impressed into the top edge of the pit to lever dirt out of the hole; the pit's edge being used as the fulcrum. A concentration of handle marks, together with the position of the backdirt around the feature, may indicate position while digging. The backdirt should also be examined for potential tool marks (Figure 3.4). The process of digging a hole repeatedly creates tool marks in the last surface receiving the impression of the tool. As a result, each shovelful, or clod, of dirt removed from the pit potentially contains a compression-friction mark. This is particularly apparent in clods, or clumps of sod, where the root network tends to hold the dirt and mark together until destroyed by erosion or crushing actions.

Case History #4

In a missing person's investigation, information was provided to investigators, 2 years after the victim's disappearance, that a subject had been observed digging in his backyard. The subject lived near the victim and was known to have threatened him. Within days of the victim's disappearance, the subject was observed digging in a grave previously constructed for one of his pets buried 2 years before. The subject then sold his property and moved from the area. Investigators thought the subject might have used the pet grave to hide the victim's remains.

During a search of the property, examination of the pet grave first delineated its boundaries. Then, its fill was systematically removed in 10-cm levels. The original walls of the grave were preserved behind vertical profiles. When exposed, those walls demonstrated

Figure 3.4 Clods of soil, among backdirt from a burial feature, bearing shovel tool marks and striae.

pristine curvilinear tool marks with striae contemporaneous with the buried pet, approximately 4 years old. The excavation, removal of the animal remains, and soil core sampling at the base of the pit revealed no additional burials. The profiles did, however, offer an explanation of the subject's digging activities. The stratification above the original ground surface, and observations of plant growth over the burial indicated the subject was merely tending his pet's grave by planting grass.

Bioturbation

Micozzi (1991) mentions a number of environmental factors which can turbate, or naturally churn, mix, displace, or otherwise modify, the position and nature of remains. Those same agents act upon the grave or pit created to conceal the remains. Plant (floral turbation) and animal (faunal turbation) activities, in particular, are very recognizable. For example, experienced field archaeologists have spent many seasons excavating and distinguishing prehistoric, or historic, post molds from rodent burrows. Searches for clandestine burials may entail a spectrum of techniques ranging from low tech uses of probes or soil core samplers, (Imaizumi, 1974; Owsley, 1995; Whalen, 1990), to state-of-the-art techniques as sophisticated as infrared thermography (Weil and Graf, 1992) or ground penetrating radar (Conyers and Goodman, 1997), but there is no technique that can, in effect, X-ray soil matrices and conclusively determine the contents of a feature. Furthermore, subterranean anomalies may be produced by faunal turbation rather than burials. Burrowing animals will create chambers or networks of tunnels, open and infilled (krotovinas [Paton et al., 1995]), which appear as anomalies. If an experienced operator is unable to exclude such faunal-turbated areas as natural, limited test excavations may be required.

Burrows may also confound, or facilitate, searches using cadaver dogs. Their tunnels act as routes through which scents can travel. Search teams may be led to a grave through which, or near which, burrowing fauna have traveled. The author has also found that small burrowing animals, in taking paths of least resistance, tend to follow the upper edge of backfilled test pits. This could aid in identifying original grave outlines. The age of the internment might also be narrowed by determining the season(s) during which particular species of burrowing animals could have made runs. Recognizing faunal turbation also reveals possible routes taken by scavenging fauna, which may have carried off skeletal elements, associated evidence, or trace evidence.

In experiments conducted by the author (Hochrein, 1997b) the condition of root networks within some test excavations offered indications of the type of instruments used to dig the pits. Thin profile instruments such as crowbars, pitchforks, and screwdrivers were found to preserve root networks which appear as lattice across the interior of the burial feature but predominately beneath the remains. Broad-bladed instruments such as shovels tended to slice, or tear, roots at the interface of the pit fill and pit wall leaving root segments in the fill and a larger percentage of severed roots at the interface. As discussed in Bock and Norris (1997), Hall (1988, 1997), and Willey and Heilman (1997), this botanical evidence is collected for further interpretation of the crime scene environment.

Case History #5

In a case that demonstrated the degree to which burrowing animals could interfere in geotaphonomic interpretation, the victim was hurriedly interred in a shallow grave after his relationship with a friend turned deadly. The homicide and burial occurred in January. In March of the same year, a walker discovered the partially uncovered and scavenged body. Authorities carefully processed the scene in a conventional manner. Five months later, a forensic archaeologist was asked to examine the scene for geotaphonomic indications of how the grave was constructed.

Investigators explained how the body was exhumed by clearing soil from above the remains and lifting the corpse out of the shallow grave. The soils around the upper torso and head were dug out and screened for bullets and other evidence. The site was then backfilled. In the reexamination, the remnant of the foot end of the grave was relocated using archaeological techniques. Although the orientation and horizontal dimensions of the pit could be reconstructed, the identification of 3-dimensional tool marks was hindered by numerous krotovinas created during and after the depositional period. The faunal turbation destroyed diagnostic portions of the feature (Figure 3.5) that could have allowed a class determination of the tool used to dig the grave. Burrowing pocket gophers (*Geomys burarius*) eliminated the areas of the grave edge where the appearance of acute or nearly acute corners would have indicated that a flat-sided digging implement was used; the geotaphonomic examination was inconclusive. When the scene was originally processed, a qualified archaeologist might have been able to recover forensically significant tool marks.

Sedimentation

A third agent affecting geotaphonomic interpretations of burial features involves the effects of water within and on the feature. The pooling, evaporation, and drying of water and fine sediments within an open pit, as well as on the surface of an infilled pit, create patterns of cracking. These patterns offer information about the pit's spatial and temporal characteristics.

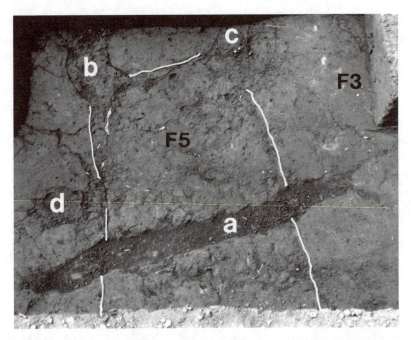

Figure 3.5 Close-up of the foot end of a grave (F5) and undisturbed soils (F3) at a depth of approximately 10 cm below ground surface. Note the intrusion of krotovinas, marked a–d.

McLaughlin (1974) and Morse et al. (1983) mention the identification of surface cracks as a means of locating the grave's edge during exhumation. Experiments designed to examine the effects of sedimentation on buried crime scenes (Hochrein, in preparation) have included the observation and monitoring of cracks that form along the infilled surface edge of test and control pits (Figure 3.6). In experimental and field school practical exercises, cracks formed as a result of desiccation and settling within 24 hours after rainfall. (Cracks will also form without rainfall, if the ambient moisture content of the fill and surrounding soils is sufficient.) The cracks reappeared after subsequent rainfalls obliterated those previously formed. The cracking will reoccur as long as the fill in the test and control features continues to settle. The cycle of moisture, reconstitution, and desiccation may continue for months after the interment. It has been observed to consistently reoccur along the same margins or boundary of the infilled feature. By comparison, sedimentation over very shallow or relatively flat surfaces, (i.e., puddles), will tend to crack in irregular, spider web-like fashion as the sediments dry.

Geotaphonomic research on surface sedimentation and cracking must examine the regularity of the desiccation cycle. In the aforementioned experiments, the width of surface cracks were measured daily for a period of 1 month, monitoring weather conditions. When plotted in relation to each other, an obvious correlation between the amount of precipitation and the width of surface cracks appeared. Moistening of the surface by minor rain showers caused the surface area to expand, closing previously formed cracks. More significant rainfall caused sediment to flow in the cracks in addition to swelling surface areas. In either case, the cracks returned in the same positions within 24 hours following the last rainfall. This pattern continued for the entire 30 days of the experiment. When reexamined 2 months after the end of the experiment, the test pits could still be distinguished by the position of surface cracks.

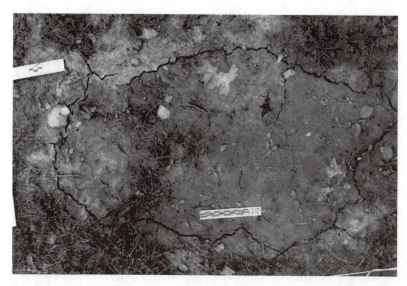

Figure 3.6 Surface desiccation and cracks formed around the edge of an infilled test pit.

The second pattern observed was crack width compared to the length of periods without precipitation. It appeared that the cracks would reach maximum widths during lengthy dry periods at a rate of approximately 1 mm per day. Closure during heavy rainfalls, however, could be rapid, going from as much as 7 mm to 0 mm within minutes. The preliminary implications of these observations are that it might be possible, through surface crack widths, to determine the time between the infilling of a clandestine pit and its discovery. With knowledge of the soil types and historical weather information, it may be feasible to determine the post-deposition interval to the last rainfall.

In recent cases when that rainfall occurred on or as the only rainfall since the burial date, it might be possible to determine the date of the burial. Surface cracking around the edges of the clandestine graves is often observed but rarely recorded in a standardized manner. Obviously, further experimentation and study are needed in this area.

Subsurface cracks, because they form within sedimentation at the bottom of the grave or pit, have an irregular spider's web appearance. As described above, this occurs because of the shallow, relatively uniform, nature of the underlying surface.

The abovementioned experiments, as well as field school observations, demonstrated that it was possible to excavate this desiccated stratum. The subterranean stratum formed from the settlement of sediments in water that accumulated and then drained at the base of the pit. (As with surface desiccation, cracks will form in exposed subsurfaces, without rainfall, when the ambient moisture in the soils evaporates, causing the surface area to shrink [Figure 3.7].) In the case of rainfall events, surface and subsurface sedimentation occurs primarily as the result of sediment going into solution with raindrops and pooling water. Little of the sediment comes from the erosion of backdirt piled near the pit. The experiments were conducted in two phases, wet and dry. The wet phase involved the accumulation of 4.36 cm of rainfall in a test pit followed by its drainage/evaporation. Once cracks formed in the remaining sediments the pit was infilled. The dry phase of the experiment repeated the wet phase protocol but allowed the sediment layer to dry more thoroughly before the pit was infilled. In both the wet- and dry-phase experiments archaeological excavation

Figure 3.7 Subsurface desiccation and cracks formed in the walls of an open pit 1 day after excavation.

of the test pits 23 to 30 days after they were backfilled revealed evidence of the desiccated strata's surfaces including the original cracks (Figures 3.8a and 3.8b).

Another indication of the interface between the buried strata and pit fill included vegetation, which settled upon the layer's surface when the water drained from the pit. In actual case situations, the longer the post-deposition interval, the more likely subsurface cracks will be affected by decompositus, or purge. In areas where the remains are buried below high water-table levels the marks may be obliterated.

The sedimentation experiments began with a hypothesis: Subsurface cracks that formed, and were covered after the sediments dried thoroughly, would be easier to identify through archaeological excavation than those covered while the sediments were still saturated. The hypothesis was based on observations that cracks reached a maximum width when lenses of sediment were allowed to dry more completely. Cracks that formed in, and were backfilled while the sediments were semisolid, almost gelatinous, tended to be less numerous and exhibited smaller widths.

The experiments did not support the hypothesis, however. Wet sediment cracks, although less numerous, were easier to identify. They retained their widths and depths because the sediments were already saturated. The sediments were apparently less able to absorb additional moisture from rainfall or the backfilled dirt. As a result, the saturated stratum could not swell and close the cracks. In sediment lenses allowed to dry more thoroughly, the subsurface cracks tended to close after the pit was backfilled. Even though the cracks were wider and deeper in dried sediments, the lenses in which they occurred apparently absorbed moisture after backfilling. Like a sponge, the layer of dried sediment swelled, leaving some cracks to begin to, or completely, close. In both the wet and dry phases of the experiment, it was extremely difficult, and in some areas not possible, to distinguish the subsurface stratum, or lenses, by color. This was partially due to the shallow nature of the test pits and subtle color differences between the naturally occurring soil horizons. Another reason for the lack of color difference lies in the dynamics of sediment formation. Since most of the sediment formed from raindrops pulverizing soils at the

(b)

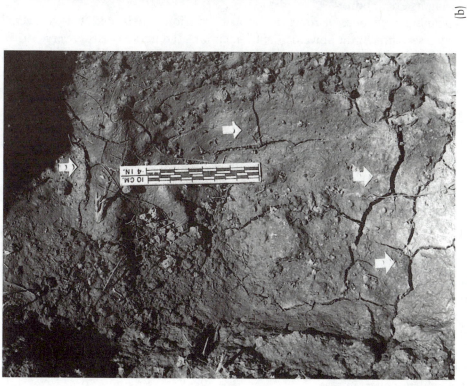

(a)

Figure 3.8 Subsurface cracks (arrowed) formed at the base of a test pit prior to backfilling (a) and upon partial excavation (b), or sectioning, 30 days after the pit was backfilled.

base of the pit, throwing them into suspension in pooled water, the color remained uniform.

The ability to recognize and record geotaphonomic artifacts of subsurface sedimentation may aid in determining whether a pit was dug and laid open in anticipation of a burial or a more spontaneous event occurring contemporaneously with the homicide. Several reference cases include subject or witness accounts of how clandestine graves were dug in preparation for homicides (Hays, 1995; Jackman, 1996; and Stuckey, 1981), but no research has been published identifying geotaphonomic characteristics of prepared graves. From the homicide investigator's standpoint, indications of intent and planning may be reflected in the physical circumstances of the burial and types of tools used. Evidence that a grave was dug a day or more before the homicide would have significant investigative and prosecutorial impact, e.g., for those who had been told that the crime was not planned.

Compression/Depression

Changes to surface contours in and around burial features fall into one of two categories: compression or depression. These geotaphonomic artifacts include the more traditional observations of primary and secondary depressions over clandestine inhumations as discussed in Hunter et al. (1996), Killam (1990), McLaughlin (1974), and Morse et al. (1983). Alternatively, they may include impressions left during the intentional compression of fill in a pit, or combinations of shoe and fabric impressions left in and around the burial feature during its excavation.

Geotaphonomic evidence of compression or depression may be detected with aerial and pedestrian searches for the grave. The abovementioned sources as well as Avery (1977), Bewley (1993), Riley (1987), Stanjek and Fassbinder (1995), and others address the use of aerial photography in archaeology. Of key importance is the time of day during which such surveys are conducted. Multiple fly-overs in the morning and late afternoon take advantage of shadows created by low angle, i.e., oblique, sunlight across typically depressed graves. Every advantage may be needed in spotting a single 2 m × 0.8 m depression among acres of undulating terrain. Primary depressions occur as freshly dug fill settles into a grave; secondary depression, when distinguishable, occurs as a result of the bloating from putrefaction followed by the release of gases and collapse of the cadaver's abdominal region. Although primary depressions may be discovered during pedestrian reconnaissance, observation of a secondary depression requires more specific conditions. These include a face-up corpse position, shallow burial, and a postdeposition interval sufficient for bloating and collapse of the abdomen. Secondary depressions may occur after containers holding human remains deteriorate.

Geotaphonomic artifacts may be misinterpreted as secondary depressions. The eroded remnants of holes dug into a grave by scavenging animals take on the appearance of secondary depressions. In most cases, a cross section of the feature, as well as documentation of the orientation of the body, will support or discount such an interpretation. Both primary and secondary surface depressions become subtler as time passes. Sedimentation, bioturbation, and cultural modifications to the landscape may obliterate compression and depression evidence over time.

McLaughlin (1974) presents what might be considered early examples of empirical work in forensic geotaphonomy. In addition to offering a table of (estimated or observed) widths of disturbed areas associated with burials, McLaughlin (1974) contains a chart entitled "Depression Depth In Inches." This chart presented depression depths in relation to soil types and burial feature depths. The ratios presented showed a precise association between depression depth and hole depth,* suggesting continued research on depression patterns is justified. Unfortunately, McLaughlin did not give the sources of his data. If based on experimentation, compression/depression studies should be replicated in a variety of soil, climate, and vegetation settings. The ability to predict or gauge clandestine pit depths from the measurement of surface depressions would be of obvious logistical value; for example, it might provide early information useful to confirm or deny subject or witness statements.

Criminalists routinely recognize, preserve, and collect tire, shoe, or foot impressions left at crime scenes (Bodziak, 1986, 1995; Brennan, 1993; Hildebrand, 1995; Jasvja, 1993; and McDonald, 1993). These types of evidence constitute compressed soils within and around burial features. Hochrein (1997b, and subsequent unpublished experiments) documents the unavoidable creation of shoeprints and knee impressions as a result of the digger's attempts to pack fill into the pit by stomping or tamping. Smaller, handheld digging implements require subjects to kneel or sit around the feature. Morse et al. (1983) note the recovery of a footprint at the base of a mock grave after 1 year of burial. As with subsurface sedimentation and desiccation, shoeprints and tool marks beneath remains may be blurred or destroyed as decomposition fluids and/or groundwater tables fill the interface between the burial feature and underlying substrate.

Occasionally, compression evidence in the form of shoe heel prints may become commingled with tool marks, and may be confusing. In shovel use, one foot is used to force the tool's blade into the soil. During such an operation, the heel of the shoe protrudes beyond the blade. If the shovel slips, the heel might slide down the newly exposed area of the grave wall leaving a curvilinear mark to the left or right of the shovel blade mark. In such instances, what might appear as two tools used in the construction of a burial feature would, in fact, be a combination of shoe print and tool mark.

There are aspects of tool marks that consist solely of compression detail. Handle impressions left along the surface edge of pits result from that point on the handle used against the pit's edge as a fulcrum to lever dirt out of the hole. Tools such as posthole diggers will tend to leave similar compression detail in deeper, straight-walled pits. Less apparent compression detail is impressed on the surface of the infilled pit if the shovel blade was slapped against the surface in an attempt to compress fill into the feature.

Case History #6

A case that included the discovery of perhaps the most fragile example of compression detail involved the search of a victim's basement. Four years after the reported disappearance of the victim, tenants happened upon some suspicious items in a basement once shared with the victim. The tenant's cat, while scratching in an area it adopted as its litter area, unearthed bedding, bones, tape, and miscellaneous debris thought to be associated with the victim. With this discovery local authorities were summoned.

The site was a half-walled, bin area in one corner of the basement. The area behind the wall was filled with landfill, and may once have been used to store coal. Large pieces

---

* 14 mm of settlement were noted for each foot that holes were dug in packed sand or gravel. Holes dug into adobe clay exhibited 16 mm settlement for each foot in depth. Holes in loam soils settled at a rate of 33 mm for every foot of depth.

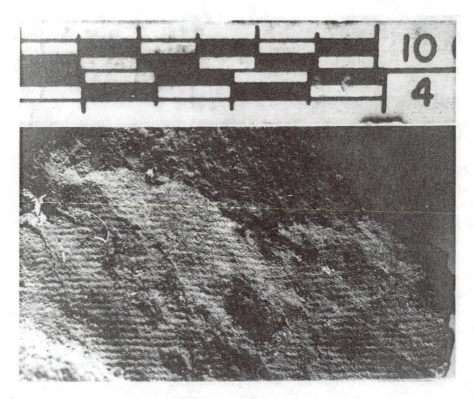

Figure 3.9 Close-up of fabric impression detail left in a dirt floor.

of metal, building material, and other debris were first systematically removed from the surface of the site. An examination of the exposed surface revealed fabric impressions consistent with an individual kneeling near the spot at which the cat had unearthed the artifacts. Debris removed from above this compression detail suggested the marks were not created by the tenants. Since the soil holding the impressions was reasonably hard, the impressions were removed en bloc, packaged so they would not shift during transport, and taken to the laboratory for further examination (Figure 3.9).

Excavation of the area continued with the creation of a 50 cm × 50 cm × 60 cm test pit and 90-cm deep soil cores sampled at 30-cm intervals across the adjacent area. The consistent, uninterrupted stratification of the fill outside the test area established there were no other burials. Bioturbation was limited to one corner exhibiting a rodent burrow. The skeletal elements unearthed by the tenant's cat were determined by a forensic anthropologist to be nonhuman. To date, the victim has not been located. The processing of that scene did not resolve the case but did demonstrate the existence and resilience of fabric impressions in a sheltered environment.

Internal Compaction

The sixth area of geotaphonomy involves internal compaction, or compressed areas of grave fill caused by movement of victims buried alive. Wood (1994) describes the possibility of such evidence in the Sacramento Boarding House Murders of the late 1980s:

... he and the anthropologist saw an unusual compaction of dirt on either side of the victim's wrapped legs, and a mound-like effect above the knees, as if the soil had been forced upward. A tunnel had been created between the victim's wrapped legs, caused by the packing of the dirt on either side ... it was possible, that (the victim) had awakened from her drugged stupor and begun jerking her wrapped legs... .

Unfortunately, the subterranean clues were not noticed until crime scene photographs were being reviewed after the exhumation of the bodies.

Empirical studies of archaeological techniques for uncovering evidence of internal compaction are needed. Often victims are wrapped and/or exhibit such advanced decomposition that it is impossible to determine whether soil may have been inhaled. In cases where the potential exists that a victim was buried alive, the excavation methodology should involve the creation of sections perpendicular to the direction of any potential movement (side to side and bottom to top in the areas of the shoulders and knees, or back to front at the heel of the foot). This may reveal and define compaction indicative of post-deposition movement.

Excavation Techniques

A wide variety of texts and empirical research on archaeological field techniques have been published (Barker, 1993; Connah, 1984; Dillon, 1993; Dirkmaat and Adovasio, 1997; Fladmark, 1978; Joukowsky, 1980; and others). Few, however, address forensically significant settings and none address the examination routines for all six types of geotaphonomic evidence. Given the unique nature of each buried crime scene, it would be impossible to assign one particular protocol to the excavation of all sites. Archaeology is a science that must be applied, not forced, upon sites (Hoshower, 1998). Forensic archaeology does, however, have two immutable requirements: excavations must be systematic and must consider the environment or context of the burial.

Much like an autopsy, the body, or in this case the grave, must first be examined for superficial defects as well as trace and transfer evidence. The immediate establishment of a coordinate-based grid tied to a primary datum and elevation is one method to reconstruct the position and context of those defects and evidence. This 3-dimensional system of recording points throughout a site also assists in documenting the position of the body in relation to the site's immediate topography. This may be crucial information for pathologists explaining the taphonomy of remains otherwise assumed to have been recovered from a level and unobstructed situation. Groundwater flow, surface erosion, and biota are all influenced by topography and, in turn, are part of the taphonomic process.

The initial examination of the grave should include documentation of surface evidence of sedimentation and cracking, compression/depression artifacts, bioturbation, and tool marks. It is also at this phase that botanical and entomological sampling takes place in concert with defoliation across the grave, collecting and cataloging representative plant samples over and near the burial. Much like the pathologist cleans the areas around wounds to better see and document the underlying trauma, the removal of vegetation over a gravesite reveals the color, texture, and contour of the ground surface. This also provides a view of the ground surface more similar to that affected by the subject and victim. All environmental samples including core and column samples, as well as thermometer positions, associated evidence, and the remains themselves, are photographed and mapped in relation to the grid system and in relation to a primary or secondary datum situated outside the burial feature.

To begin the systematic excavation of the grave, a technique found most expeditious by the author involves the creation of the archaeologist's Y-incision, a small rectangular window near the center of the burial. The window is excavated down to the top of the remains. It allows a quick assessment of the burial depth and preliminary view of stratification. The clean, plumb sides of the box are then incrementally expanded toward the margins of the pit, leaving one or two sides of the box intact to maintain a section or profile above and across the remains (Figure 3.1a and b). In effect, this method of excavation, known as partial excavation or partexing results in a series of photographic and diagrammatic thin sections across the grave. As evidence or stratigraphic changes are encountered in the exposed profiles, they are photographed and mapped. Alexandrowicz (1985) offers an expeditious method of mapping profiles by placing transparent plastic sheets against the sections and tracing artifacts and strata onto individual sheets.

Although the partexing method does not allow for the complete horizontal exposure of individual stratum as preferred by most archaeologists in traditional excavations, the same information can be diagrammed because both methods record data in 3 dimensions. Partexing does not involve the pedestaling of artifacts within the grave, i.e., preserving *in situ* on columns of fill. Pedestaling allows for dynamic photographs but is very time consuming. Pedestaled artifacts are also prone to be knocked off their columns during excavation. This inconvenience in traditional excavations has far greater implications in forensic examinations; the appearance of repositioned evidence, albeit slight or innocent should be questioned during deposition or trial.

Archaeological excavation is so much a tactile experience that anything less precise than small hand tools reduces the excavator's ability to sense horizontal and vertical changes in texture; however, specific archaeological protocols will be dictated by the nature of the crime scene or deposit site (Hoshower, 1998; Levine et al., 1984). Some scenes will require machinery or shovels to remove overburden to the original surface into which a pit or grave was dug (Bass, 1963). When utilizing heavy equipment, the investigator must consider whether the method will alter the appearance of the site from that which a subject might remember. The simple act of peeling off thin layers of soil with a backhoe or bulldozer in search of a grave outline may tear and drag root systems or uproot adjacent trees and rocks. Those same features may have been landmarks a subject or witness needs to remember the location of a burial. The use of heavy equipment must be a last resort, applied with surgical precision, and always involve the pulling of dirt toward a stationary machine with a smooth-edged blade or bucket.

The forensic excavator should not use tools that might typically be used by a subject to create the clandestine grave (i.e., spades or military style entrenchment tools), and the forensic excavator's tools must be clean and honed.

Once the burial feature is located and defined, there is no excuse for continued use of large mechanical excavators. The clandestine pit or grave is the focus of the excavation. The undisturbed subsoils into which the pit was dug need not be excavated since they were not altered by the subject's actions. To excavate the undisturbed areas may confound the interpretation of the site and creates unnecessary work for scene investigators.

Vacuum equipment is appropriate and necessary to evacuate fill from the burial feature (Figure 3.10). The use of a wet/dry vacuum should not constitute excavation. The vacuum is employed in a cleaning technique to remove excavated fill which otherwise might be

Figure 3.10 The application of crime scene vacuuming to aid in the archaeological excavation.

scraped or brushed into fine detail like desiccation cracks or tool mark striae. As with all excavated fill, vacuumed material must be screened.

Most commercially available wet/dry vacuums do not have blades or other internal workings which might damage inadvertently suctioned evidence; however, care should still be taken in its use and it must be treated with the same attention to security and avoidance of cross-contamination as traditional evidence vacuums, and avoid decompositus or purge as well as heavy ground water. In such examinations, use of the vacuum is generally limited to debris from the walls of the grave. Another advantage in utilizing vacuums is to avoid arguments that the forensic investigator's tool created tool marks attributed to the subject.

The systematic and clean excavation of burial features includes the establishment and maintenance of a clean, vertical, and plumb profile, (or section) within the pit. This method most clearly reveals depositional and intrusive episodes above and below the primary evidence (Figure 3.1) and has the following advantages:

1. The excavation is forced to proceed in a controlled, systematic manner and pace.
2. Contamination between strata is less likely.
3. The excavator is constantly presented with a clear picture of stratigraphic events.
4. At any time in the process, the excavator can compare stratification within the burial feature to that of undisturbed soils.
5. Stratification within the feature is more easily mapped and photographed as a series of slices, or thin sections.
6. Documents the *in situ* position of associated evidence, relationships between artifacts and the interfaces between depositional layers.

7. Postburial intrusions into the feature, as well as bioturbation, are efficiently depicted.
8. Soil samples and soil columns are easily obtained and recorded.

Conclusions

For forensic scientists, profilers, jurists, and jurors, the ideal crime scene evidence is submitted in as pristine a state as possible with its context recorded in as much detail as available. The integrity of forensic evidence and the conclusions drawn from that evidence remain contingent upon the manner in which the evidence was handled at its source. In cases of buried evidence, greater emphasis needs to be placed on recognizing and recording the burial environments. All too often forensic first responders recognize the value of the primary piece of evidence, the body, and direct their efforts at its extraction. In fact, the grave itself represents a second body of evidence, which deserves equal consideration because it was created or affected by witnesses to the burial.

The application of the techniques briefly described above will inevitably extend the amount of time required to process crime scenes. The author would argue, from personal experience, that such investments of time are cost effective and necessary given the nature of the crimes under investigation. At a minimum, it is incumbent upon law enforcement to liaison with departments of anthropology or agencies which maintain qualified archaeologists versed in geotaphonomy and the special requirements of crime scene management, i.e., logistical constraints and procedures for handling evidence. Forensic anthropology courses for the investigator and criminalist need to concentrate more on aspects of archaeological photography, 3-dimensional mapping, basic principles of stratigraphy, botanical and entomological collection procedures and exhumation–conservation techniques. Law enforcement's first responders frequently also have or share responsibility for the collection, documentation, and preservation of primary, associated, and trace evidence. The common denominator between the crime scene technician, forensic anthropologist, and forensic pathologist should be their systematic and holistic approaches toward the recovery and documentation of artifacts via methodologies, which are inherently site destructive.

Acknowledgments

The author extends special thanks to the FBI's St. Louis Evidence Response Team, Lincoln Police Department, Iowa Division of Criminal Investigation, and local Missouri law enforcement for their assistance in conducting training exercises which have proven invaluable toward empirical observations and the application of methodologies.

References

Alexandrowicz, J.S.
    1985 Rapid projected mapping: an alternative mapping technique for the Archaeologist, *Historical Archaeology* 19:79–85.
Anon.
    1981a Regional News, Texas. United Press International, Dateline: Galveston, TX, January 30.

1981b Regional News, New York. United Press International, Dateline: Johnston, NY, February 18.

1984 Court Upholds Murder Convictions. United Press International, Dateline: Austin, TX, February 29.

1994 John Wayne Gacy runs out of time 15 years after bodies discovered, *Rocky Mountain News*, May 10, Section F:26A.

Avery, T.E.
1977 *Interpretation of Aerial Photographs*, Burgess, Minneapolis, MN.

Barker, P.
1993 *Techniques of Archaeological Excavation*, B.T. Batsford, London.

Bass, W.H.
1963 The use of heavy power equipment in the excavation of human skeletal material, *Plains Anthropologist* 8(20):122–123.

Bevan, B.W.
1991 The search for graves, *Geophysics* 56(9): 1310–1319.

Bewley, R.H.
1993 Aerial photography for archaeology. In *Archaeological Resource Management in the U.K.: An Introduction*, edited by J.R. Hunter and I.B.M. Ralston, pp. 197–204. Stroud, Sutton Pub., Gloustershire, U.K.

Bock, J.H. and D.O. Norris
1997 Forensic botany: an under-utilized resource. *Journal of Forensic Sciences* 42(3):364–367.

Boddington, A., A.N. Garland, and R.C. Janaway
1987 *Death, Decay, and Reconstruction: Approaches to Archaeology and Forensic Science*, Manchester University Press, Manchester, U.K.

Bodziak, W.J.
1986 Shoe and tire impression evidence, *FBI Law Enforcement Bulletin* July.

1995 *Footwear Impression Evidence*, CRC Press, Boca Raton, FL.

Brennan, J.S.
1993 Dental stone for casting depressed shoemarks and tyremarks, *Journal of the Forensic Science Society* 23:275–286.

Brothwell, D.R.
1981 *Digging up Bones: The Excavation, Treatment, and Study of Human Skeletal Remains*, Cornell University Press, Ithaca, NY.

Connah, G.
1984 *Australian Field Archaeology: A Guide to Techniques*, Humanities Press, Atlantic Highlands, NJ.

Conyers, L.B. and D. Goodman
1997 *Ground Penetrating Radar: An Introduction for Archaeologists*, Altamira Press, Thousand Oaks, CA.

Curwen, E. and E.C. Curwen
1926 The efficiency of the scapula as a shovel, *Sussex Archaeological Collections* 67:139–145.

Davenport, G.C.
1996 *Geophysical Surveying, A Handbook for Criminal Investigators*, NecroSearch International, Lakewood, CO.

Dillon, B.D.
1993 *Practical Archaeology: Field and Laboratory Techniques and Archaeological Logistics*, University Museum Publications, Philadelphia, PA.

Dirkmaat, D.C. and J.M. Adovasio
  1997   The role of archaeology in the recovery and interpretation of human remains from an outdoor setting. In *Forensic Taphonomy: The Postmortem Fate of Human Remains*, edited by W.D. Haglund and M.H. Sorg, pp. 39–64. CRC Press, Boca Raton, FL.

Donovan, D.T.
  1966   *Stratigraphy: An Introduction to Principles*, George Allen and Unwin, London, U.K.

Drucker, P.
  1972   *Stratigraphy in Archaeology: An Introduction*, Modules in Anthropology 30, Addison-Wesley, Reading, MA.

Dunbar, C.O. and J. Rodgers
  1957   *Principles in Stratigraphy*, John Wiley, London, U.K.

Fladmark, K.R.
  1978   *A Guide to Basic Archaeological Field Methods*, Simon Fraser University, Burnaby, B.C., Canada.

Hall, D.W.
  1988   Contribution of the forensic botanist in crime scene investigations, *The Prosecutor*, Summer: 35–38.

  1997   Forensic botany. In *Forensic Taphonomy: The Postmortem Fate of Human Remains*, edited by W.D. Haglund and M.H. Sorg, pp. 353–366. CRC Press, Boca Raton, FL.

Harris, E.C., M.R. Brown III, and G.J. Brown (editors)
  1993   *Practices of Archaeological Stratigraphy*, Academic Press, San Diego, CA.

Hays, T.
  1995   Man Charged with Murder, Mutilation of Robbery Witness. The Associated Press, Dateline: New York, February 2.

Heizer, R.F. and J.A. Graham
  1967   *A Guide to Field Methods in Archaeology: Approaches to the Anthropology of the Dead*, National Press, Palo Alto, CA.

Hildebrand, D.S.
  1995   Footwear, the missing evidence, *Minutiae*, November–December: 2–11.

Hill, S.H.
  1982   An examination of manufacture-deposition lag for glass bottles from late historic sites. In *Archaeology of Urban America The Search for Pattern and Process*, edited by R.S. Dickens, Jr., pp. 291–327. Academic Press, New York.

Hochrein, M.J.
  In preparation. Sedimentation as a Geotaphonomic Agent (unpublished manuscript).

  1997a Buried crime scene evidence: the application of geotaphonomy in forensic archaeology. In *Forensic Dentistry*, edited by P. Stimson and C. Mertz, pp. 83–99. CRC Press, Boca Raton, FL.

  1997b The dirty dozen: the recognition and collection of toolmarks in the forensic geotaphonomic record, *Journal of Forensic Identification* 47(2):171–198.

  1998   An Autopsy of the Grave: The Preservation of Forensic Geotaphonomic Evidence. A Paper Presented at the 50th Annual Meeting of the American Academy of Forensic Sciences, February 14, 1998, San Francisco, CA.

Hochrein, M.J., J. Gabra, and S. Nawrocki
  1999   The Buried Body Cases Content Analyses Project: Patterns in Buried Body Investigations. A Paper Presented at the 51st Annual Meeting of the American Academy of Forensic Sciences, February 18, 1999, Orlando, FL.

Horvath, F. and R. Meesig
  1998 A content analysis of textbooks on criminal investigation: an evaluative comparison to empirical research findings on the investigative process and the role of forensic evidence, *Journal of Forensic Sciences* 43(1):133–140.

Hoshower, L.M.
  1998 Forensic archaeology and the need for flexible excavation strategies: a case study, *Journal of Forensic Sciences* 43(1):53–56.

Hunter, J., C. Roberts, and A. Martin
  1996 *Studies in Crime: An Introduction to Forensic Archaeology*, B.T. Batsford, London.

Imaizumi, M.
  1974 Locating buried bodies, *FBI Law Enforcement Bulletin* 43(8):2–5.

Jackman, T.
  1996 Brother Admits Guilt in Deaths; James Vest Agrees to Testify on Slaying of Two Cocaine Couriers, *The Kansas City Star*, January 3, C1.

Jasvja, M.
  1993 Estimation of stature from footstep length, *Forensic Science International* 61(1):1–5.

Joukowsky, M.
  1980 *A Complete Manual of Field Archaeology*, Prentice-Hall, Englewood Cliffs, NJ.

Killam, E.W.
  1990 *The Detection of Human Remains*, Charles C Thomas, Springfield, IL.

Laska, P.R.
  1996 Forensic search of a landfill, *Journal of Forensic Identification* 46(1):7–12.

Levine, L.J., H. Campbell, Jr., and S. Rhine
  1984 Perpendicular forensic archaeology. In *Human Identification: Case Studies in Forensic Anthropology*, edited by T.A. Rathbun and J.E. Buikstra, pp. 87–95. Charles C Thomas, Springfield, IL.

McDonald, P.
  1993 *Tire Imprint Evidence*, CRC Press, Boca Raton, FL.

McLaughlin, J.E.
  1974 *The Detection of Buried Bodies*, Andermac, Yuba City, CA.

Micozzi, M.S.
  1991 *Postmortem Change in Human and Animal Remains, A Systematic Approach*, Charles C Thomas, Springfield, IL.

Morse, D., J. Duncan, and J.W. Stoutamire (editors)
  1983 *Handbook of Forensic Archaeology and Anthropology*, Rose Printing, Tallahassee, FL.

Noël Hüme, I.
  1970 *A Guide to Artifacts of Colonial America*, Knopf, New York.

Owsley, D.W.
  1995 Techniques for locating burials with emphasis on the probe, *Journal of Forensic Sciences* 40(5):735–740.

Paton, T.R., G.S. Humphreys, and P.B. Mitchell
  1995 *Soils: A New Global View*, Yale University Press, New Haven, CT.

Pydokke, E.
  1961 *Stratification for the Archaeologist*, Phoenix House, London, U.K.

Rathje, W.L. et al.
  1992 The archaeology of contemporary landfills, *American Antiquity* 57(3):437–447.

Riley, D.N.
    1987   *Aerial Photos and Their Applications*, University of Pennsylvania Press, Philadelphia, PA.

Roberts, C.A., F. Lee, and J. Bintliff
    1989   *Burial Archaeology: Current Research, Methods, and Developments*, British Archaeological Series International Reports 211, Oxford, U.K.

Ross, B.
    1994   Two Pairs of Sneakers Found Near Bodies: Overpass Searched Slowly, *The Times-Picayune*, May 29:B1.

Schiffer, M.B.
    1987   *Formation Processes of the Archaeological Record*, University of New Mexico Press, Albuquerque, NM.

Skinner, M. and R.A. Lazenby
    1983   *Found! Human Remains: A Field Manual for the Recovery of the Recent Human Skeleton*, Archaeology Press, Simon Fraser University, Burnaby, B.C., Canada.

Spennemann, D.H.R. and B. Franke
    1995   Archaeological techniques for exhumation: a unique data source for crime scene investigators, *Forensic Science International* 74(1, 2):5–15.

Stanjek, H. and J.W.E. Fassbinder
    1995   Soil aspects affecting archaeological details in aerial photographs, *Archaeological Prospection* 2:91–101.

Stuckey, T.
    1981   White Teenager Sentenced to 10 Years in Killing of Black Classmate. The Associated Press, Dateline: Denton, MD, September 9.

Ubelaker, D.H.
    1989   *Human Skeletal Remains: Excavation, Analysis, Interpretation*, Taraxacum, Washington, D.C.

Weil, G.J. and R.J. Graf
    1992   Infrared Thermographic Detection of Buried Grave Sites. Manuscript on File, Entech Engineering, St. Louis, MO.

Whalen, M.E.
    1990   Defining buried features before excavation: a case from the American southwest, *Journal of Field Archaeology* 17:323–331.

Willey, P., and A. Heilman
    1987   Estimating time since death using plant roots and stems, *Journal of Forensic Sciences* 32(5):1264–1270.

Wilson, W.
    1993   Puente "Acted Shocked" by First Body. *Sacramento Bee*, February 25, B:1.

Wood, W.P.
    1994   *The Bone Garden*, Pocket Books, New York.

Wynn, J.C.
    1986   Review of geophysical methods used in archaeology, *Geoarchaeology* 1(3):245–257.

Forensics, Archaeology, and Taphonomy: The Symbiotic Relationship

4

JULIE MATHER SAUL
FRANK P. SAUL

Contents

0-8493-1189-6/02/$0.00+$1.50
© 2002 by CRC Press LLC

Introduction

Physical anthropologists who work only with ancient remains may be lulled into a sense of false security regarding their ability to designate individual skeletal remains as being of a certain sex and a specific age and perhaps to diagnose a lesion and associate it with a degree of disability. Such pronouncements on ancient remains are unlikely to be questioned, except rarely by rising graduate students or rival colleagues in need of a controversy. Unfortunately, the pronouncer cannot be proven right or wrong, as the next of kin are long dead. Forensic anthropologists, however, quickly learn that an error in assigning sex or a too narrow or inaccurate assessment of age will be discovered when the unknown remains are identified, unless, of course, the error results in non-identification.

Access to identified cases as well as known individuals on our autopsy tables provides forensic anthropologists with continuing education and testing in regard to sex determination, age estimation, evaluation of ancestry, functional health status assessment, indications of skeletal trauma, etc. They also give us an opportunity to check the standards themselves. Metric sex and ancestry formulae based on ancient populations (therefore unidentified individuals) are potentially inaccurate, and formulae based on dissecting room populations are potentially out of date. Even modern forensic case-based formulae can result in misclassifications. In short, the data forming the basis of decision-making require continuing refinement. In essence, forensic anthropology practice serves as a "reality check" for academic assumptions and all physical anthropologists need to proceed with caution (Saul and Saul, 1994).

The interaction between studies of ancient and modern skeletal remains should be a two-way street. Working with the poorly preserved remains of the ancient Maya has enhanced our ability to recognize, interpret and reconstruct very fragmentary forensic remains (Hammond et al., 1975; Saul, 1972, 1973, 1975, 1977, 1982; Saul and Saul, 1989, 1991, 1997a,b; Saul et al., 1995). This has been helpful in both identification analyses and interpretation of trauma and "weapon signatures" in support of determining cause of death. The latter activity in turn provides perspective for the interpretation of trauma in ancient remains. We also have the opportunity to see what happens in ancient cases of injury or disease in the absence of modern medical intervention. Familiarity with modern clinical cases then cautions us not to over-interpret or over-emphasize the physical disability that might have resulted. Finally, modern taphonomic research concerning decomposition, disarticulation, and postmortem disposition of remains in general supplies a basic framework for the recovery and interpretation of the human remains encountered in both ancient and modern contexts (Haglund and Sorg, 1997).

Working in both areas is symbiotic and even synergistic, as we hope to demonstrate in the following examples.

The Recreation of Past Events

"Forensic Science is used to predict not the future but the past."
Henry Lee, 1998

An archaeologic excavation and a crime scene are similar in many ways. The goal of investigators working at each is to recreate a past event — in the case of archaeology, many past events going back over hundreds, even thousands, of years. Each endeavor can reach its goal only through preserving the scene by limiting access and then documenting, gathering, preserving, and interpreting physical evidence. In both cases, this is best done by a team of specialists. Techniques used to excavate archaeologic burials (Ubelaker, 1978), with careful measurements and documentation (photos, sketches, and written notes) of the exact location of all items *in situ*, can provide the basis for recreating the scene whether it be a recent crime scene (Lee, 1994, Dirkmaat and Adovasio, 1997) or an ancient one (Scott and Connor, 1997). In the former, of course, law enforcement personnel — evidence specialists in particular — should be present to maintain the chain of custody.

Physical evidence from any burial is best gathered by a team that includes physical anthropologists and archaeologists. Although these two areas of expertise may overlap, each has specialized skills and knowledge. Experience in the Maya area has shown that much more information can be gathered if a physical anthropologist is present for burial removal. Typically, ancient Maya skeletal remains are extremely poorly preserved and incomplete due to the tropical climate with its intense rainy and dry seasons and rapidly growing vegetation. In many instances, basic information regarding who the individual was (sex, age, stature, cultural modification, pathology, etc.) may be lost upon removal unless the fragmentary bones can be examined and measured while still in the ground. Sorting out what happened to the individual during life, at death (perimortem trauma), and postmortem (taphonomic events) can be difficult if clues are lost. Inasmuch as subsequent analysis is based on the *in situ* diagram, accurate determinations should be made as to what bone is present in a specific location and whether or not it is in appropriate anatomic position.

Maya Mountains: Decapitation and Dismemberment?

As indicated above, both forensic and archaeologic scenes mandate knowing the exact orientation of bones in order to differentiate death events from postmortem events, and to interpret these events. A rock shelter excavation in the Maya Mountains of Belize illustrates this point. Unlike most Maya burial sites, preservation in the rock shelters seems to be excellent. The soil in rock shelters remains fairly dry, and due to locations near the tops of steep hillsides and cliffs, remains free of flooding from run-off. Additionally, there are few intrusions of the plant roots that in most other Maya burials produce major bone damage.

In this case, what at first appeared to be two separate burials became a confusing, intimate arrangement of three individuals. Uppermost was a fully articulated adult female (based on pelvic characteristics) in a tightly flexed, knee-to-chest position, face down, with her head to the north and her arms crossed at her waist (left forearm closest to the body). Her left cheek rested on large stones that had been placed on the chest of an articulated adult male (also based on pelvic characteristics). He lay in an extended supine position (head to south) with his right arm at his side and the left arm bent slightly at the elbow, allowing his left hand to rest near his right hand. His upper torso was covered by the flexed or kneeling female. Across the knees and upper legs of the male were arranged the postcranial bones of a child approximately 9 to 11 years old (Figure 4.1). (The child's age was determined using standard dental development and bone growth parameters.) Removal of the female's torso revealed the articulated skull and mandible of the child resting on the right shoulder of the male, beside the male's own skull and mandible. The right knee of

Figure 4.1 Possible family burial in the Maya Mountains, Belize, rock shelter. Fragments of the flexed female's skull (arrow) rest on rocks and dirt over the thorax of the adult male, whose lower body extends to the south. Bones of the child are scattered over the legs of the adult male.

the female rested directly on the skull of the child. Her left knee rested directly on the skull of the male.

Attempts to figure out the position of the child could not reconcile what appeared to be articulated portions with any conceivable body position. The child's pelvic bones were against the male's right femur and ribs were scattered over both femora and tibiae (especially the right), with lumbar vertebrae tumbled between. The left scapula and humerus were lying, anterior surface upward, beside the male's left femur. They appeared to be articulated and in a north–south orientation. The right humerus and scapula were east of this arrangement. However, the distal end of the humerus was closest to the glenoid cavity. The first two cervical vertebrae were tucked in under the left ilium of the male, with what appeared to be the rest of the cervical and thoracic vertebrae roughly lined up (north–south) about 2 in. north of C1 and C2. Whether these remaining vertebrae were

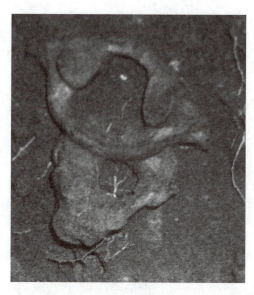

Figure 4.2 Cervical vertebrae of child in the rock shelter. Placement of C1 (upside down) on top of C2 (also upside down) indicates vertebrae were defleshed when interred.

in exact anatomic order could not be determined. Had the child been decapitated and dismembered before being placed in the ground?

We closely examined the child's left radius and ulna *in situ*, lying in a north-south orientation east of the male's right leg, some distance from the left humerus. They were lying close together, parallel, as one would expect in fleshed remains — except one of them had been flipped end for end, distal radius pointing south and distal ulna pointing north. An impossible situation if held together by soft tissue when buried. We turned our attention to the first two cervical vertebrae. C1 was sitting on top of C2, as one might expect in life; however, each individual vertebra was turned upside down (Figure 4.2). Again, impossible if fleshed. Upon closer examination we saw none of the incised or chopping marks indicative of possible decapitation, dismemberment, or defleshing. No signs of carnivore or rodent feeding or other such manipulation were evident.

The separation of skull and mandible could have taken place early on, as these two skeletal elements are generally the first to become disarticulated during decomposition, an event that should have taken place fairly quickly in the extreme heat and humidity of the tropics. The disarticulation of cervical vertebrae will also occur well before complete skeletonization of the rest of the body. However, the disarticulation of shoulder, elbow, wrist, ribs, lower back, and pelvis suggest that the child was probably skeletonized and disarticulated when placed in the grave with the male as a secondary burial (Bass, 1997; Micozzi, 1991; Rodriguez and Bass, 1983, 1985).

We conjectured that the child was probably the first to die. We have no way of knowing whether or not the child was initially buried following its death. Some time later, after the child had become skeletonized and disarticulated, the male died. When he was buried, the child was removed from his/her original resting place and interred with the male (the father?). The child's skull and mandible were put on the right shoulder of the male, beside the male's own head. The careful arrangement of the rest of the child's bones told us that an attempt had been made to maintain the relationships in which these bones had been originally found. When the female (the mother?) died, either at the same time or some time later, she was placed in the same grave, kneeling over them, perhaps in a protective manner. We hope to determine whether the three are indeed related through DNA studies.

This was a far cry from the decapitation and dismemberment that a less careful examination *in situ* might have suggested. Additionally, forensic experience and research reported in forensic literature enabled better understanding of the postmortem events involved.

Cuello: What Happened Here? Where Is the Rest of the Body?

Not only is good visual and written documentation important to interpreting burial information, but continuity of investigators can also play a part. A full year passed, until the next excavation season, before we understood the taphonomy of the following burial.

The skeleton that we were excavating at the Preclassic Maya site of Cuello (Saul and Saul, 1991, 1997b) in northern Belize appeared at first to be a simple extended supine burial. The pelvis and lower extremities were present and articulated, although poorly preserved. The position of the skull (face turned to the right) and clavicles seemed normal enough. But there was no sign of arm bones where they should have been, and no ribs or vertebrae.

Eventually, we discovered the right arm was indeed present, positioned with a slight bend at the elbow, hand and wrist missing, laid along the long axis of the burial to the right of center. The distal radius had an unusual clubbed shape. A few ribs were stacked on the humerus, forming a semicircle opening to the right (laterally). At the upper end of the curve formed by the ribs were the first two cervical vertebrae, one atop the other, with the odontoid process of C2 pointing to the sky. The left arm, scapulae, vertebrae, and remaining ribs were absent (Figure 4.3).

The skull appeared to be that of a female. There were no obvious signs of decapitation, defleshing, or disarticulation on the skull, mandible, cervical vertebrae, or left arm, although poor preservation could have masked them.

We examined the pelvis *in situ*, as it seemed to be too fragile to survive excavation in good enough condition to yield information later in the lab. Pelvis morphology was definitely that of a female. Bone fragments from the right wrist and hand were near the right hipbone and those of the left at the left hipbone. This suggested that she had originally been buried with her arms extended at her sides. But where was the rest of her skeleton, and why had it been removed? And why the odd arrangement of right arm, ribs, and cervical vertebrae?

The Maya, when engaged in remodeling and construction projects or in digging graves, often accidentally cut into and through previously existing burials. (We have excavated one individual whose grave cut passed through and disrupted five earlier burials.) Bones thus encountered were apparently usually tossed into the fill or put in with the subsequent burial. Bones and teeth of others were also often used as grave goods — placed in with the dead as offerings. But the arrangement here was unusual. Perhaps the burial was inadvertently disturbed by a later grave cut, removing thorax and arms. This would have to have been after decomposition had progressed to disarticulation and skeletonization, and perhaps after the grave location, and even its existence, had been forgotten. For unknown reasons some of her bones were laid back into her resting place and the intruding grave cut, unused, was filled in. Possibly the unique placement of the bones had some significance to the Maya. But where were the rest of her bones? The excavation season soon ended with that question still unanswered.

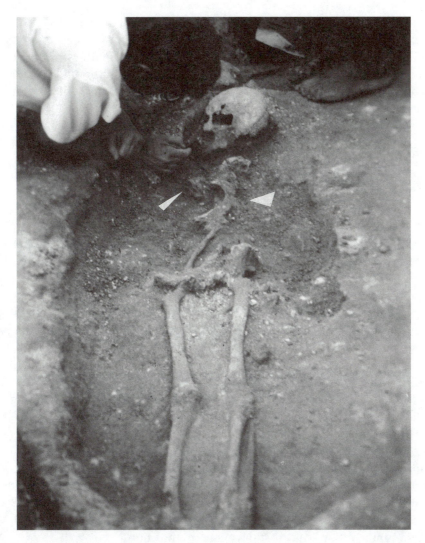

Figure 4.3 Disturbed and then rearranged extended burial, Cuello, Belize. Although skull, pelvis, and legs are in appropriate positions, only the right arm is present, laid out along the midline of the torso. Several stacked ribs (wide arrow) form a "C" on top of the humerus and cervical vertebrae (narrow arrow) are piled at the top of the "C."

Next season, we were excavating another confusing arrangement of bone, trying to figure out if it was a secondary or primary burial, and if primary, how the body was positioned. (The ancient Maya buried their dead in many positions, including flexed, seated, face down, prone, supine, and with various arrangements of head, arms, and legs. One of the challenges of Maya burials is trying to figure all this out for each burial.) What we were uncovering appeared to be pieces of humerus, radius, ulna, ribs, scapulae, and vertebrae all jumbled together, in the same part of the excavation site that had produced the incomplete female, but at a lower level.

Further excavation revealed bones of a left arm, with the distinctive clubbed shape of the left distal radius matching that of the right radius from the year before. The other bone fragments filled in the gaps — completing her skeleton with no duplications. Examination of excavation maps from the previous season revealed that this cluster of bone was located near where her left shoulder would have been and several inches deeper. Perhaps after intruding on her grave some bone was retrieved and replaced with care while the rest of it was dumped in with the fill. Careful excavation beneath and around a primary grave may uncover important information that might otherwise be missed and proper documentation can demonstrate relationships.

Chan Chich Tomb: Just a Scatter of Fragments, Offerings, or a Primary Burial?

We could not be present during the excavation of a tomb at Chan Chich (Robichaux, 1998), a Maya site in northern Belize. Small fragments of bone were found scattered around and within 11 vessels found on the tomb floor. There were two separate groups of teeth. Perhaps this represented a secondary burial? Or was it a primary burial? In any event, the bone fragments within the vessels could be offerings, as could the teeth — neither possibility uncommon in the Maya area.

The excavators were careful and followed our guidelines for recording the locations of bone fragments and teeth. They did this by measuring and recording the positions of bone fragments relative to individual vessels, after mapping in the vessels. With a diagram of the tomb and its vessels, we recreated the original relationships between vessels, bones, and teeth. Then we examined the fragments.

Cranial fragments were at the south end, vertebral and rib fragments scattered down the middle to the north, fragments of arm bones on each side, pelvic fragments lay north of the vertebrae and leg fragments further north and to the sides. There were no apparent duplications. The fragments represented a large male with his head to the south. Locations of two identifiable scapula fragments indicated a supine position. The group of teeth furthest south, found among cranial fragments, were all maxillary teeth, while the group of teeth north of them, found mixed in with cervical vertebra fragments, were all mandibular teeth. These are logical locations for the dentition of a single individual, with the mandible dropping toward the chest during decomposition.

The fragments of bone found within the vessels were from the bones found nearest these vessels on the tomb floor. Some fragments from within the vessels could even be joined to fragments from outside the vessels. This suggested that the body of the individual was placed on some sort of organic platform, and at least some of the vessels were placed beneath this platform. When the platform decayed and disintegrated, the skeletal remains dropped down onto and into the vessels. A small fragment of what is thought to be wood was found on the tomb floor.

Without careful recording and documentation during excavation, this information would never have been obtained. However, even this detailed recording might have been insufficient for understanding the subtleties of the individually flipped cervical vertebrae in the previously discussed rock shelter burials. It is still important to have a physical anthropologist participate in the excavation, if possible.

Forensic Applications

These and other excavations of ancient Maya skeletal remains provide lessons that apply to the forensic arena. Receiving an inadequately documented bag of bones in the lab, whether forensic or ancient, means that we have already lost information. This information loss is most critical in forensic cases, where a small detail can be crucial in the resolution of a case and thereby can profoundly affect the lives of others. Having a physical anthropologist experienced in excavation involved in recovery/excavation of remains is also crucial. As seen in the Maya examples above, knowing the exact location and orientation of bones and bone fragments relative to each other and objects in the ground, and being able to retrieve information from the bones while still in the ground, may make all the difference in distinguishing trauma from postmortem process and in understanding what the sequence of events may have been. Knowledge of the normal decomposition and disarticulation process, based on our own forensic work and the forensic literature, helps to make this understanding possible (Bass, 1997; Micozzi, 1991; Rodriguez and Bass, 1983, 1985).

Taphonomy, Pseudopathology, and Pseudotrauma: Roots vs. Blood Vessels

In 1954 the junior author was asked to evaluate skeletal remains encountered at a construction site. The coroner had announced to the media that the remains were those of several individuals who had come to a violent end (indicated by multiple fractures) in recent times (indicated by the presence of blood vessels). Unfortunately, the multiple fractures were postmortem and probably due to the excavation process (broken edges were rough, jagged, and unstained by soil), and the blood vessels were plant roots. Skeletal and dental features indicated that the individuals were of ancient Native American origin.

We have subsequently encountered many instances of misinterpretation of pathology and trauma, both in person and in the literature. Our presentations to forensic and academic groups stress the importance of ruling out taphonomy and normal variation as explanations before judging a lesion or defect to be pathologic or traumatic in origin.

As a consequence of working in the Maya area where thirsty living roots extend to depths of at least 4.7 m below the surface of the ground, we have developed great respect for the ability of acid-secreting roots to modify bone and even dental enamel, thereby mimicking abnormality.

Roots vs. Cannibalism

Pencil-sized roots may travel through medullary canals and split sturdy long bone shafts while various size roots disintegrate the spongy articulations (Figure 4.4). The unwary might wonder if they were dealing with the aftermath of cannibalism or some aspect of secondary burial procedures if they had not seen the roots *in situ*.

When seen in context, fragments of long bones split lengthwise by roots traversing the medullary canal will generally remain in proper relation to each other (Figure 4.5). Occasionally, roots can be seen on the external surface as they pass through the cortex, but often they are inside the medullary canal, producing the fractures by expansion from within. Such fractures may not even be visible initially, but the bone may come apart when recovery is attempted. Sometimes the bone will be tied down by rootlets passing on into the soil.

If not seen in context, cannibalism can still be ruled out. Long bone fragments produced by root action will not show those characteristics suggested by White (1992) and Turner and Turner (1999) as indicative of cannibalism. These include cut marks at muscle attachments (defleshing) and near articulations (disarticulation/dismemberment), percussion marks produced by tools used to break shafts open to get at marrow, and pot polish on bone ends from cooking and burning, seen preferably, although not always, in combination.

Figure 4.4 Root-damaged proximal tibia with roots still in place (Ancient Maya, Belize).

Figure 4.5 Flexed burial (Ancient Maya, Belize). Long bone shafts have been split by small roots that can be seen in and around the burial. Articular ends have been completely destroyed.

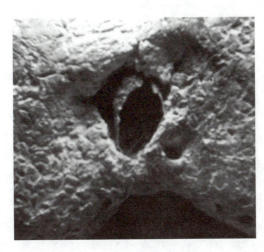

Figure 4.6 Occipital bone penetrated by root visible within opening. Note lace-like pattern on cortex due to fine root action. Edge of foramen magnum can be seen at bottom of photo (Ancient Maya, Belize).

Roots vs. Projectiles

Roots may also create openings that might be misinterpreted as due to a bullet or some other kind of projectile or piercing device (Figure 4.6).

Entrance openings produced by projectiles during the perimortem interval will normally bevel inward (inner dimensions of the defect will be larger than the outer dimensions) while the exit will show some outward beveling. Such openings often are accompanied by radiating and sometimes concentric fractures. Openings caused by roots will show none of these characteristics, although bone weakened by root intrusions is more likely to fracture. These fractures, however, will be more jagged and random and not show the characteristics of perimortem fractures (curved or straight lines, beveling, tapering, radiating and concentric fractures).

Roots vs. Incised Defects

Changes to bone surfaces due to root erosion might be misinterpreted as incised defects or the caries sicca of treponemal infection and the scouring of dental enamel might confuse those interested in dental pathology.

Incised defects, however, are usually straight and often involve multiple parallel grooves (see Symes, this volume). In cross section they are often V-shaped, whereas grooves caused by roots will have rounded floors (Figures 4.6, 4.8, 4.9). Roots also tend to meander over the surface, creating wavy lines or even a lace-like pattern (Figure 4.6).

Other Possible Sources of Confusion

Animals and insects also help create some pseudopathology and pseudotrauma (Haglund, 1997a,b; Haskell et al., 1997; Merbs, 1997; Murad, 1997; Rodriguez, 1997; Symes, this volume; Ubelaker, 1997).

In addition, roots may displace bones, teeth, and artifacts, as do animals, insects, and other processes of bioturbation. These processes should always be considered when analyzing body orientation, possible dismemberment, etc. within the grave. The common Maya practice of burying their dead within rubble fill, often below floors, adds another factor. These burials are literally floating in the rubble (made up of cobbles and other stones of various sizes plus ceramic fragments and other bits and pieces). As the rubble shifts over time the bones are broken up and teeth, in particular, disappear downward into crevices between the stones.

Blood Vessel Impressions
Misinterpreted as Cut Marks

Although forensic anthropology was not initially involved, the approaches and materials we used to clarify the origin of certain temporal region grooves overlap those of forensic anthropology. In 1981, Zimmerman et al., describing the paleopathology of a Peruvian mummy, listed the presence on the mummy's skull cap of "…a slightly curved, incised wound 20 mm long, 2 mm wide and less than 1 mm deep" (p. 498) and also referred to it as "an old incised wound" (p. 499).

The location and configuration of the "curving incised wound" as shown in their Figure 1 suggested to us that it was actually the impression that is sometimes produced by the pulsation of the frontal (or anterior) branch of the superficial temporal artery. This artery, which is a terminal branch of the external carotid artery, is used by anesthetists and others when they check the temporal pulse (Goss, 1973).

Illustrations from several anatomy texts show how the placement of the superficial temporal artery may vary in regard to its superimposition on bone or frontalis muscle. Goss (1973), for instance shows the artery upon frontalis whereas Lockhart et al. (1959) show a portion of it lying lateral to frontalis. We assume that the groove on bone is created when the frontalis muscle does not intervene.

We had previously seen similar impressions and assumed that they were vascular impressions of the sort that T. Dale Stewart had long ago indicated had been "erroneously interpreted as results of cauterizations of long bones" (1937, 1966). Wells (1963a,b) reviewed some of the same materials (without referencing Stewart) together with several other instances that were previously attributed to tight bandaging or healed wounds associated with cuts, fractures, postmortem root erosion, or worm action. Wells, like Stewart, ascribed these grooves to vascular impressions based on their anatomical context, together with some insights from surgical practices.

Campillo (1977) also suggested a vascular origin for temporal area frontal bone grooves. Campillo's work noted that this groove was listed earlier by Testut (1911) who considered it a non-constant, but frequently found (20–25%) vascular groove related to the superficial temporal artery.

It is obvious that the vascular origin of this feature has been accepted for some time, but the feature continues to be misinterpreted in both paleopathologic and forensic contexts (personal communications from Suchey and many others). In 1983, in response to the Zimmerman et al. article, we began to gather information on this apparently controversial subject. We were able to demonstrate the vascular relationship using a cadaver from the Medical College of Ohio dissecting room that shows the scalp (which is loosely attached in this area) peeled back to demonstrate a direct relationship on both sides between the frontal branch of the superficial temporal artery (embedded in the scalp) and the groove in the frontal bone (Figure 4.7).

Figure 4.7 Left frontotemporal region of adult white male cadaver. The scalp has been peeled superiorly to demonstrate the direct relationship between the superficial temporal artery embedded in the scalp tissue (above) and its groove in the frontal bone (below). (The temporalis muscle is to the right of the groove.)

We also surveyed a small sample (the first 10 males and first 10 females) from the Hamann-Todd Collection, a well-documented and studied dissecting room population obtained by the former Western Reserve University Medical School (now located at the Cleveland Museum of Natural History). The frequency is even higher (50%) than that previously indicated by Testut and it occurs in different frequencies in males (40%) and females (60%) in this sample. Our sample included 14 white individuals, of whom 5 (36%) exhibited the groove, with its presence noted in 2 of the 8 males (25%) and 3 of the 6 females (50%). Of the 6 black individuals, 5 manifest the groove (83%). It was present in both of the males (100%) and 3 of the 4 females (75%).

Only 2 out of the 10 who show the feature also demonstrate pathology (of uncertain origin) in the vicinity of the marking and the listed cause of death offers no obvious association with presence of the marking.

These blood vessel impressions do not appear to be age related inasmuch as they are present in both the oldest (age 70) and the youngest (age 19) of the individuals in this sample, and we have also found them in a commercially prepared neonate skull.

The Hamann-Todd specimens and other modern and ancient specimens show grooves that vary in size, shape, and number of branches and often show marked variation from the left to the right side in the same individual.

In 1984, with Dr. Delmas J. Allen (electron microscopist) and Dr. R.A. Burns (oral pathologist), we conducted a scanning electron microscopic evaluation of the previously mentioned Peruvian specimen. The scanning electron micrographs revealed the smooth channels and pores for branching vessels that are associated with blood vessel morphology rather than the striae associated with incised defects (Shipman and Rose, 1984). In fact, when we presented our findings at the 1984 Paleopathology Association meetings in Philadelphia (Allen et al., 1984; Saul and Saul, 1984), the late Dr. Walter Putschar called our attention to the presence of smooth muscle impressions.

Examination of the unprepared specimen with lower magnification or even the naked eye is usually sufficient to make the diagnosis. Knowledge of normal anatomical variation is the key (Saul and Saul, 1993). Similar blood vessel impressions may be found on other bones.

Trauma Assessment Based on Known Trauma

Archaeologists and bioarchaeologists delight in theorizing violent and bloody deaths when describing ancient remains. Skulls crushed by blunt force, decapitations, dismemberments, and human sacrifices make for much more interesting reading. Familiarity with coroner/medical examiner cases of known trauma can be essential to interpreting and indeed recognizing perimortem trauma, and differentiating it from taphonomic processes.

Lack of bony signs of a violent end, however, do not necessarily prove that the individual died a natural death. People may be murdered by sharp force and gunshot as well as with other equally lethal means (e.g., poison, suffocation, hanging) with no apparent bone defects (Saul and Saul, 1999).

Nonetheless, with archaeological remains it is best to follow the old adage that the simplest answer is usually the best, and violence and mayhem should not be suggested until taphonomic changes have been ruled out and specific signs of perimortem trauma are present. In forensic cases we also rule out taphonomic changes and then recognize conclusive indications of perimortem trauma. But then we must go one step further by demonstrating to the coroner/medical examiner, and eventually the court, that recognition and interpretation of such trauma are based on known cases (Saul, 1998; Saul and Scala-Barnett, 1992).

In trauma assessment and in development of the biographic profile, each forensic case teaches something. What we learn from each case enables us to do a better job with each succeeding case — whether archaeologic or forensic.

Sharp-Force Injury Examples

The subtleties of sharp-force injury illustrate the above concerns — in particular, the defects produced on cervical vertebrae by sharp-force injury to the neck. These defects are such that many would be overlooked and/or misinterpreted without having seen them in known situations. We have found that some defense cuts can also be exceedingly subtle.

Turnpike Case

Our interest in sharp-force injury to the neck began with skeletonized and mummified remains found by hunters in early November, 1992 in a ditch beside an overpass for a major interstate in rural Ohio (Saul et al., 1997). The soft tissue on the upper surface of the body (where the sun could shine on it) had mummified and was dark brown to black, while the underside of the body (more shaded and damp) had become skeletonized. Some dark blonde hair was present on the preserved partial scalp. The remains brought to us at the Lucas County Coroner's Office were essentially complete, lacking only 6 teeth, the right cornu of the unfused hyoid, and several phalanges from the right foot.

Our examination indicated that the deceased was definitely a white male, based on pelvic and cranial morphology. We suggested that this young man was in his mid to late

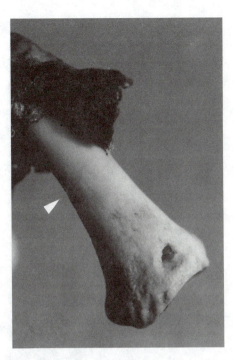

Figure 4.8 Dorsal view, proximal phalanx of the fifth digit of right hand. Two fine intersecting cuts forming a "V" on the medial edge (arrow) plus probable puncture near proximal end are defense wounds. (Photograph courtesy of Bud Weaver.)

teens, basing our age estimation on dental and skeletal developmental findings. We estimated a living stature range of between 6 ft and 6 ft 2 in. based on maximum lengths of femora and tibiae.

He was eventually identified as a 6 ft 1 in., 18-year-old white male whose physical description matched our person. Mummified fingers from the left hand yielded usable prints and he was identified by fingerprint comparison. (The right hand was almost completely skeletonized, with only a small amount of very dry mummified skin remaining at the tips of the fingers.) He had been missing for about 2.5 months, since late August.

The next question was cause and manner of death. The remains were too far (65 feet) from the interstate overpass for him to have jumped, or been thrown, from above. In the absence of appropriate soft tissue and obvious cause of death, we began the task of examining his bones using direct and cross lighting, the naked eye, and magnification.

The only sign of possible carnivore or rodent damage was a puncture on the dorsal surface of the proximal phalanx of the right fifth finger (Figure 4.8). Although the cone-shaped puncture was similar to carnivore tooth marks, there was none of the typical crushing of bone around it and no signs of carnivore activity on any other bones. We found no sign of rodent activity anywhere. On the medial edge of the same phalanx, and distal to the puncture, were two fine intersecting cut marks (Figure 4.8). The dorsal surface of the proximal phalanx of the right fourth finger bore two fine parallel cuts (Figure 4.9). These defects were so subtle that we discovered them by touch as we ran a fingernail gently along the shaft. Then, knowing that they were indeed there, we saw them with cross lighting and magnification. These were probable defense cuts. Due to the lack of any other signs

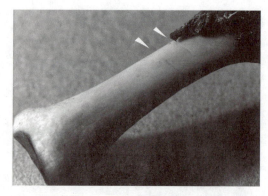

Figure 4.9 Two parallel defense cuts (arrows) across the dorsal surface of proximal phalanx, fourth digit of right hand. (Photograph courtesy of Bud Weaver.)

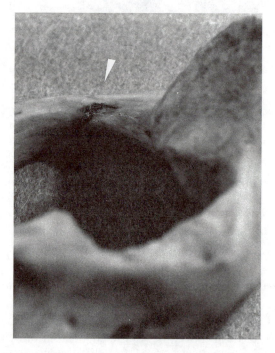

Figure 4.10 First cervical vertebra, inferior aspect upward. Sharp-force defect on interior surface of posterior arch (arrow) angles upward from right to left, originating from the right side of the space between the neural arches of C1 and C2. No defects are present on the second vertebra. (Photograph courtesy of Bud Weaver.)

of animal manipulation and the presence of these defense cuts, we suspected that the puncture might actually be another defense wound, perhaps from the point of a knife.

We examined the rest of his skeleton and found small defects on two cervical vertebrae. The location of the first was surprising. It was a 4-mm cut on the interior and inferior aspect of the right side of the posterior arch of the first cervical vertebra (Figure 4.10). The cut angled into the bone in such a way as to lift up a sliver of bone at the edge, a sign of perimortem injury (Ubelaker, 1978). This small cut angled upward from the right, thus

Figure 4.11 Anterior body of seventh cervical vertebra. Hinged flake (2.5 mm) of bone lifted from the left on the anterior/superior border of vertebral body. Small cut (7 mm) on anterior aspect of body with inward bending edges indicating an anterior-posterior direction. (Photograph courtesy of Bud Weaver.)

originating from the right side of the space between the neural arches of C1 and C2. The second cervical vertebra showed no damage, leading to the hypothesis that the sharp instrument involved had a fairly long, thin blade.

On the seventh cervical vertebra a hinged flake of bone (2.5 mm) was lifted from the left on the anterior/superior border of the vertebral body. A 7-mm cut on the anterior aspect of the body had edges that bent into the vertebral body, indicating an anterior-to-posterior thrust. The hinged aspect of both defects suggested that they also occurred during the perimortem interval (Figure 4.11).

The defect on the first cervical vertebra suggested the immediate cause of death was injury to the spinal cord and/or brain stem. Anecdotal information from military colleagues also confirmed this; such techniques may be taught in hand-to-hand combat. A sharp instrument, whether from the left or from the front, would also probably need to pass through other vital structures to arrive at the anterior surface of the seventh cervical body.

We did a literature search in an attempt to base our analysis on known cases. The search indicated an absence of information on the impact of sharp-force trauma on cervical vertebrae. This is understandable, inasmuch as autopsy evaluation of sharp-force injury to the neck focuses on tracking wounds through soft tissue and documenting damage to vital structures. The impact on cervical vertebrae is a peripheral issue. In addition, the cervical region of the spine is difficult to visualize radiographically and such minute defects cannot be seen easily.

Although the available literature failed to provide information about the recognition and interpretation of these defects, we felt certain that we were on the right track. In our opinion, the young man had suffered sharp-force injury to the neck originating from his left, right, and front. During the struggle, he had sustained defense cuts to his right hand.

The perpetrator was arrested for a second murder, and at that time confessed to the above killing. He used a "kris," an Oriental knife with a wavy blade. Surprisingly, the blade of the knife used reached a width of 1.5 cm just 4 cm from the tip and was 2.25 cm at the widest point, making it wider than hypothesized. In his confession he told of the struggle and said that he stabbed him in the neck "…three times … first in the left side, then in the right side, then through the middle."

We were surprised that the kris could create the incised defect on the interior of the posterior arch of C1 without damaging C2. Later, we were able to hold C1 and C2 in normal anatomic position and attempt to insert the kris between them from the right, lining the edge up with the incised defect. We found that if the knife angle is just right, it can be done with no difficulty. In fact, the width of the blade would probably have resulted in the severing of the right vertebral artery.

This experience convinced us that we needed to know more about sharp force and cervical vertebrae. We began to work with the pathologists in our office to learn more, by tracking wounds through soft tissue to locate the site of impact on bone, and then examining the bone itself. The two cases that follow illustrate this process. In the first case, stab wounds to the neck were tracked through the soft tissue to the cervical vertebrae, which were then cleaned, examined, and the resultant bony defects noted. In the second case, cervical vertebrae were examined in the absence of soft tissue and the recognition and interpretation of defects were based on the previous known case.

A Known Sharp-Force Injury Case

A young woman was stabbed multiple times in the neck. One stab wound was visible just below and behind her left ear. This was tracked back to the first cervical vertebra, where we could see that a small oval of periosteum had been lifted on the exterior surface of the left side of the posterior arch. Another stab wound entered the front of the neck just to the right of center, traveling back to impact on the right transverse process of the seventh cervical vertebra. All cervical vertebrae were cleaned and examined for defects. Defects were found only on C1 and C7.

First cervical vertebra: At the spot noted at autopsy, a small thin oval flake of bone, 6 mm × 2 mm, had been shaved from the outer cortex just medial to the groove for the vertebral artery (Figure 4.12). The flake of bone was not recovered. This defect was so subtle that we might have overlooked or ignored it if we hadn't known that the blade of the knife had hit that spot.

Seventh cervical vertebra: The tip of the transverse process had been broken off and the cancellous bone within was exposed. Edges of this break were rough (almost scalloped), with no straight edges or other signs of having been cut (Figure 4.13). A small fragment (7 mm × 4 mm) that had been broken from the tip, however, bore one straight edge, more consistent with sharp force (Figure 4.14). A fragment as tiny as this one would probably not be recovered if the remains had not been "fresh." This defect intrigued us. If we had been confronted earlier with such a defect (minus the fragment) in skeletal or decomposed remains, we would have been unlikely to think of sharp force as the origin, and more apt to postulate the possibility of blunt force or strangulation as the cause.

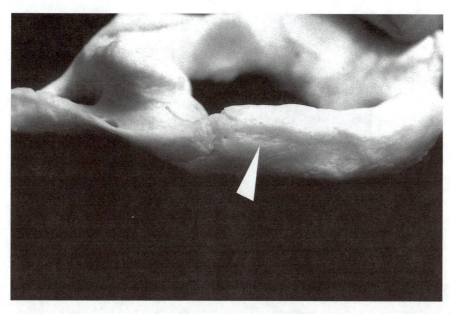

Figure 4.12 Left side of posterior arch of C1. Small oval defect (arrow) marks location where flake of bone was shaved off when individual was stabbed behind and below the left ear. Vertical cut to the left of oval was produced accidentally during removal of vertebra during autopsy. (Photograph courtesy of M.J. Naujock.)

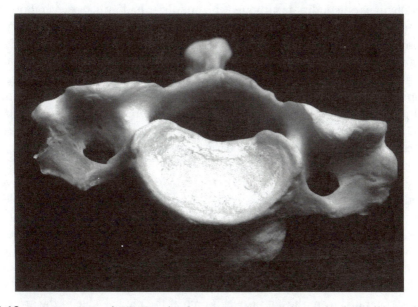

Figure 4.13 Superior view of C7. Tip of right transverse process was broken off by stab to front of neck just right of victim's midline. Note (far left of photo) the irregularity of edges and barely visible cancellous bone within. (Photograph courtesy of M.J. Naujock.)

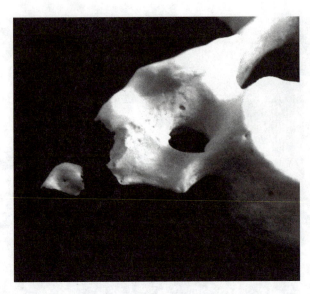

Figure 4.14 Broken tip of right transverse process of C7 plus fragment of bone broken from the tip. Note straight edge on fragment. (Photograph courtesy of M.J. Naujock.)

This case then provided a known case on which to base recognition and interpretation of perimortem trauma in the following unknown case.

A Probable Sharp-Force Injury Case

The body of a woman was discovered by a bulldozer (and its operator) in a quarry in mid-August. It was identified as a woman who had last been seen 2 weeks earlier. The body was generally in good condition, although the bulldozer had inflicted several postmortem soft tissue gashes and long bone fractures. There was no bleeding or bruising at the site of these injuries. There were no signs of carnivore or rodent activity.

Decomposition had progressed only slightly, except for the left side of her neck. This region contained a large quantity of insect remains and other signs of heavy insect activity and advanced decomposition and virtually all of the soft tissue was gone. Since this is not the usual progression of decomposition (Rodriguez and Bass, 1983, 1985; Micozzi, 1991; Bass, 1997), we suspected that this was the site of perimortem injury that had breached the protective covering of skin, allowing early entry to insects and bacteria.

The examining pathologist found no evidence of cause of death or perimortem trauma at autopsy, other than a cracked thyroid cartilage. We agreed that the cervical vertebrae, hyoid, and left clavicle should be removed, cleaned, and examined for possible defects, based on the disproportionately advanced amount of decomposition and insect activity in that area. We found defects on only the first and seventh cervical vertebrae. (Interestingly, in our limited experience so far we have found C1 and C7 to be the cervical vertebrae most often involved in perimortem sharp-force trauma.)

First cervical vertebra: An approximately 6-mm long, thin, elongated fragment (sliver) of bone was separated from the left posterior arch at the medial edge of the groove for the left vertebral artery. This fragment was still attached by its medial end to the posterior arch. The edges of this defect were fairly straight (Figure 4.15).

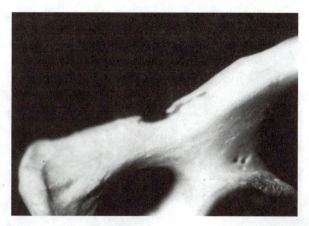

Figure 4.15 Left side of posterior arch of C1. Note cut extending medially from medial edge of the groove for the vertebral artery, producing a separate thin sliver of bone attached to C1 at its medial end.

Figure 4.16 Left transverse process of C7. Cancellous bone is visible where tip has been broken off (slightly to right and below center of photo).

Seventh cervical vertebra: (1) The tip of the left transverse process was broken off, revealing the cancellous bone within (Figure 4.16). The fragment was not recovered. (2) An approximately 4-mm long, narrow portion (again a sliver) of the inferior edge of the left costal process was separated from the rest of the process, but still attached to it at the lateral end. The edges of this defect were straight (see Figure 4.17).

The location and nature of two of these defects were surprisingly similar to those of the defects in the known case described earlier. Although the specifics of the defects on the first cervical vertebra differed (a sliver of detached bone vs. an oval flake shaved off), the location was essentially the same. Both of these defects were typical of sharp-force injury to bone. The broken tips of the transverse processes of the seventh cervical vertebrae

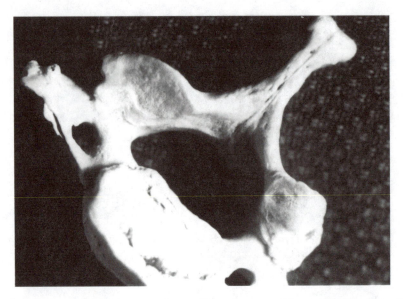

Figure 4.17 Inferior view of C7. Note sliver of bone separated from inferior edge of left costal process (far left).

were virtually identical. The straight-edged sliver of bone raised from the inferior edge of the costal process, close to the broken tip of the transverse process, suggested the possibility of an additional stab or other movement of the sharp instrument responsible.

These vertebral defects were too delicate to have been produced by the bulldozer. Based on experience with known cases of sharp-force injury to the neck, and especially the case described above, the defects were strongly suggestive of perimortem sharp-force injury to the neck.

Although the woman's estranged husband was the prime suspect, there were no witnesses and no weapon had been found. Only circumstantial evidence linked him to the crime. Although they were not living together and he said that he had not seen her for some time, the clothes she had worn to work on the last day she was seen were found in his house. Her stomach contents at autopsy were foods that were in his refrigerator when she was first reported to be missing. Bath mats and several towels had just been laundered and luminol revealed minute traces of blood in the bathroom (too little for DNA or other testing).

In spite of the lack of direct evidence or witnesses, the estranged husband was charged. A video deposition was scheduled due to non-availability of the anthropologist at the proposed date of the trial.

The deposition was taken in the courtroom, with the defendant present. It was conducted as expert witness testimony would be during a trial, but without judge and jury. The defects were demonstrated using photographs, diagrams, and the bones themselves to explain the difference between perimortem and postmortem injury and the similarities in this case to known cases of perimortem sharp-force injury to the neck. The interpretation was linked in particular to the case described above which was judged to be the result of sharp-force trauma to the neck. The defendant listened and watched with apparent great interest.

When the deposition was over and the defendant was leaving the room, he stopped and quietly told the anthropologist, "You done good."

Unfortunately, his comment confirming the trauma analysis could not be used in the trial. The case depended heavily on circumstantial evidence, and he was subsequently acquitted. A day or two later, the forewoman of the jury asked the prosecuting attorney if they could "do it over again" as she felt that they "didn't do the right thing."

In spite of the acquittal, we felt confident that our interpretation of the skeletal trauma, based on known cases, had been confirmed informally by the alleged perpetrator (Saul, 1994).

Conclusion

Although we strongly encourage physical anthropologists who work in the archaeologic arena and those who work in the forensic arena to learn from each other, the ramifications of forensic work are such that we worry about occasional dabbling by the academic physical anthropologist who has no real experience in forensics and does not keep up with the literature or the exchange of ideas and techniques that takes place at professional forensic meetings. There is too much at stake.

Errors in the excavation and recovery of forensic remains may mean the loss of evidence vital to the solution of the case, as well as damage to the human remains themselves. Damage to the remains may result in non-identification or misidentification of the individual and confounds perimortem trauma analysis.

Each case is a new and different puzzle to solve as well as an opportunity to learn. Solved puzzles (or known cases) help us to solve the new puzzles that come our way. Our academic techniques for determining sex and ancestry, and estimating age and stature are tested in each forensic case that we do. If our analysis is wrong we fail, and the individual may go unidentified. If the individual is identified in spite of our error, our credibility suffers, but we can re-examine our work and learn from the error. If our analysis is right and the individual is identified, our credibility is intact, proper techniques are reinforced, and we know we are on the right track. Knowledge of known cases comes from our own cases, the forensic literature, case and technique presentations at professional meetings, and informal discussions as well as from working with and/or observing the work of our colleagues, including those in other areas of specialization.

Perimortem trauma recognition and analysis also need to be based on a working knowledge of known forensic cases for interpretation. In addition, knowledge of the skeletal consequences of taphonomic forces is essential to recognition and interpretation of perimortem skeletal trauma.

The time frames may differ, but the goals (and some of the techniques) of forensic science and archaeology are similar — to recreate past events. Forensic science itself encompasses many specializations, as does archaeology. However, we are basically, each one of us, intrigued by the challenge of solving a puzzle. We will solve more puzzles correctly by collaboration, sharing and learning from each other than by isolation. And solving the puzzle is our goal.

Acknowledgments

We thank James R. Patrick, M.D., Lucas County Coroner; Diane Scala-Barnett, M.D., Deputy Lucas County Coroner; and Cynthia Beisser, M.D., Deputy Lucas County Coroner for their continuing support in the forensic arena. We are indebted to archaeologists R.E.W. Adams, Ph.D.; Norman Hammond, Ph.D.; Fred Valdez, Ph.D.; and Peter Dunham, Ph.D. for their continuing support in Maya bioarchaeology. Thanks also to M.J. Naujock and the late Bud Weaver for their technical and photographic assistance.

References

Allen, D.J. et al.
   1984   Old incised wound or vascular impression? Diagnosis by scanning electron microscopy. In *Abstracts of the Eleventh Annual Meeting of the Paleopathology Society*, Philadelphia, PA.

Bass, W.M.
   1997   Outdoor decomposition rates in Tennessee. In *Forensic Taphonomy: The Postmortem Fate of Human Remains*, edited by W.D. Haglund and M.H. Sorg, pp 181–186. CRC Press, Boca Raton, FL.

Campillo, D.
   1977   *Paleopatología del Craneo en Cataluña, Valencia y Baleares.* Editorial Montblanc-Martín, Barcelona, Spain.

Dirkmaat, D.D. and J.M. Adovasio
   1997   The role of archaeology in the recovery and interpretation of human remains from an outdoor forensic setting. In *Forensic Taphonomy: The Postmortem Fate of Human Remains*, edited by W.D. Haglund and M.H. Sorg, pp. 39–64. CRC Press, Boca Raton, FL.

Goss, C.M.
   1973   *Gray's Anatomy of the Human Body,* Lea & Febiger, Philadelphia, PA.

Haglund, W.D.
   1997a Dogs and coyotes: postmortem involvement with human remains. In *Forensic Taphonomy: The Postmortem Fate of Human Remains*, edited by W.D. Haglund and M.H. Sorg, pp. 367–381. CRC Press, Boca Raton, FL.

   1997b Rodents and human remains. In *Forensic Taphonomy: The Postmortem Fate of Human Remains*, edited by W.D. Haglund and M.H. Sorg, pp. 405–414. CRC Press, Boca Raton, FL.

Haglund, W.D. and M.H. Sorg (editors)
   1997   *Forensic Taphonomy: The Postmortem Fate of Human Remains*, CRC Press, Boca Raton, FL.

Hammond, N., K. Pretty, and F.P. Saul
   1975   A classic Maya family tomb, *World Archaeology* 7(1):57–78

Haskell, N.H. et al.
   1997   On the body: insects' life stage presence, their postmortem artifacts. In *Forensic Taphonomy: The Postmortem Fate of Human Remains,* edited by W.D. Haglund and M.H. Sorg, pp. 415–448. CRC Press, Boca Raton, FL.

Lee, H.C.
   1994   *Crime Scene Investigation,* Central Police University Press, Republic of China.

   1998   Quotation. In *Forensic Radiology*, B.G. Brogdon, p. 280, CRC Press, Boca Raton, FL.

Lockhart, R.D., G.F. Hamilton, and F.W. Fyfe
   1959   *Anatomy of the Human Body,* J.B. Lippincott Company, Philadelphia.

Merbs, C.F.
   1997   Eskimo skeleton taphonomy with identification of possible polar bear victims, In *Forensic Taphonomy: The Postmortem Fate of Human Remains*, edited by W.D. Haglund and M.H. Sorg, pp. 249–262. CRC Press, Boca Raton, FL.

Micozzi, M.S.

   1991   *Postmortem Change in Human and Animal Remains: A Systematic Approach,* Charles C
   Thomas, Springfield, IL.

Murad, T.A.

   1997   The utilization of faunal evidence in the recovery of human remains. In *Forensic Taphonomy: The Postmortem Fate of Human Remains,* edited by W.D. Haglund and M.H. Sorg, pp.
   395–404. CRC Press, Boca Raton, FL.

Robichaux, H.R.

   1998   Excavations at the Upper Plaza. In *The 1997 Season of the Chan Chich Archaeological Project,*
   edited by B.A. Houk, Papers of the Chan Chich Archaeological Project, Number 3, pp. 31–52.
   Center for Maya Studies, San Antonio, TX.

Rodriguez, W.C., III

   1997   Decomposition of buried and submerged bodies. In *Forensic Taphonomy: The Postmortem
   Fate of Human Remains,* edited by W.D. Haglund and M.H. Sorg, pp. 459–467. CRC Press,
   Boca Raton, FL.

Rodriguez, W.C., III and W.M. Bass

   1983   Insect activity and its relationship to decay rates of human cadavers in east Tennessee,
   Journal of Forensic Sciences 28:423–432.

   1985   Decomposition of buried bodies and methods that may aid in their location, *Journal of
   Forensic Sciences* 30:836–852.

Saul, F.P.

   1972   *The Human Skeletal Remains from Altar de Sacrificios, Guatemala: An Osteobiographic
   Analysis,* Papers of the Peabody Museum, Harvard 63:2:1–123, Peabody Museum of Harvard
   Press, Cambridge.

   1973 Disease in the Maya Area: the pre-Columbian evidence. In *The Classic Maya Collapse,* edited
   by T.P. Culbert, pp. 301–324. University of New Mexico Press, Albuquerque.

   1975   The human remains from Lubaantun. In *Lubaantun,* by N. Hammond, Appendix
   8:389–410. Cambridge, Peabody Museum Monographs, Harvard No. 2.

   1977   The paleopathology of anemia in Mexico and Guatemala. In *Porotic Hyperostosis: An
   Enquiry,* edited by E. Cockburn, Paleopathology Association Monograph, No. 2:10–15, 18 (plus
   cover photo), Detroit.

   1982   The human skeletal remains from Tancah, Mexico. In *On the Edge of the Sea: Mural
   Painting at Tancah-Tulum,* by Arthur G. Miller, Dumbarton Oaks Trustees for Harvard University, Washington, D.C., Appendix II, pp. 115–128.

Saul, F.P. and J.M. Saul

   1984   Pseudopathology and Vascular Impressions: Clues from Anatomy. Abstracts of the Eleventh Annual Meeting of the Paleopathology Society, Philadelphia, PA.

   1989   Osteobiography: a Maya example. In *Reconstruction of Life from the Skeleton,* edited by
   M.Y. Iscan and K.A.R. Kennedy, pp. 287–302. A.R. Liss, New York.

   1991   The preclassic population of Cuello. In *Cuello: An Early Maya Community in Belize,* edited
   by N. Hammond, pp.134–158. Cambridge University Press, Cambridge, England.

   1993   Cut marks or vascular impressions? Clues from paleopathology and anatomy (poster). In
   Abstracts of the 45th Annual Meeting of the Academy of Forensic Sciences, Boston, MA.

   1994   Forensic anthropology: a "reality check" for physical anthropology. In *Abstracts of the 1st
   Annual Midwest Bioarchaeology and Forensic Anthropology Conference,* Madison, WI.

Saul, J.M.

1994 "You done good": cervical nicks and an unusual confirmation of probable cause of death. In *Abstracts of the 1st Annual Midwest Bioarcharchaeology and Forensic Anthropology Conference,* Madison, WI.

1998 "This is what happened to me:" allowing the dead to speak for themselves in court. In *Proceedings of the American Academy of Forensic Sciences,* 4:184, San Francisco, CA.

Saul, J.M. and F.P. Saul

1997a The skeletal remains from a Maya royal tomb at La Milpa, northwest Belize. In *Abstracts of the 62nd Annual Meeting of the Society for American Archaeology,* Nashville, TN.

1997b The preclassic skeletons from Cuello. In *Bones of the Maya: Recent Studies of Ancient Skeletons,* edited by S.L. Whittington and D.M. Reed, pp. 28–50. Smithsonian Press, Washington, D.C.

1999 Biker's bones: an avocational syndrome. In *Forensic Osteological Analysis: A Book of Case studies,* edited by S.I. Fairgrieve, pp. 237–250. Charles C Thomas, Springfield, IL.

Saul, J.M. and D. Scala-Barnett

1992 A good fit: skull reconstruction fits the weapon to the wound (poster). In *Abstracts of the 44th Annual Meeting of the American Academy of Forensic Sciences,* New Orleans, LA.

Saul, J.M., C.S. Beisser, and F.P. Saul

1997 The unkindest cuts of all: sharp-force injury to the neck and its impact on underlying bone (a case study) (poster). In *Proceedings of the American Academy of Forensic Sciences,* 3:149.

Saul, J.M., F.P. Saul, and A.R. Muñoz

1995 Osteological analysis of burials from a small, non-elite site (RB-11, Programme for Belize). In *Abstracts of the 60th Annual Meeting of the Society for American Archaeology,* Minneapolis, MN.

Scott, D.D. and M. Connor

1997 Context delicti: archaeological context in forensic work. In *Forensic Taphonomy: The Postmortem Fate of Human Remains,* edited by W.D. Haglund and M.H. Sorg, pp. 27–38. CRC Press, Boca Raton, FL.

Shipman, P. and J.J. Rose

1984 Cutmark mimics on modern and fossil bovid bones, *Current Anthropology* 23(1):116–117.

Stewart, T.D

1937 Did the American Indians use the cautery in bone surgery? *American Journal of Physical Anthropology* 23(1)(O.S.):83–89.

1966 Some problems in human paleopathology. In *Human Paleopathology,* edited by S. Jarco, Yale University Press, New Haven, CT.

Testut, L.

1911 *Traite d'Anatomie Humaine,* 6th ed., Octave Doin et Fils, Paris.

Turner, C.G. and J.A. Turner

1999 *Man Corn: Cannibalism and Violence in the Prehistoric American Southwest,* University of Utah Press, Salt Lake City, UT.

Ubelaker, D.H.

1978 *Human Skeletal Remains: Excavation, Analysis, Interpretation,* Taraxacom, Washington, D.C.

1997 Taphonomic applications in forensic anthropology. In *Forensic Taphonomy: The Postmortem Fate of Human Remains,* edited by W.D. Haglund and M.H. Sorg, pp. 77–90. CRC Press, Boca Raton, FL.

Wells, C.

    1963a Cortical grooves on the tibia, *MAN* July, pp. 112–114.

    1963b Cortical grooves on the tibia, *MAN* Nov., p. 180.

White, T.D.

    1992 *Prehistoric Cannibalism at Mancos 5MTUMR-2346*, Princeton University Press, Princeton, NJ

Zimmerman, M.R. et al.

    1981 Trauma and trephination in a Peruvian mummy, *American Journal of Physical Anthropology* 55:497–501.

Position of Skeletal Remains as a Key to Understanding Mortuary Behavior

5

MIRJANA ROKSANDIC

Contents

Introduction

The key to understanding archeological mortuary behavior is to reconstruct the ritual context in which burial data are created. It is this intention that represents the greatest problem for the interpretation, but is also an opportunity to infer elements of conceptual life. In order to infer intentional behaviors related to understanding ideologies of past populations, it is necessary to incorporate information that pertains to periburial mortuary activity as well as mortuary and ancestral ritual (*sensu* Kinnes, 1975). At times this can be deduced from the relative position of the skeletal elements in the grave. However, simple correlation of the position of skeletal elements may not only prove insufficient but may also be misleading. Research methods and approaches borrowed from forensic anthropology can contribute to this analysis. Hence, the goals of this chapter are (1) to show that disposition of skeletal elements is a relevant source of information about mortuary behavior; (2) to argue that skeletons, as bearers of this information, must be excavated by experts trained in human osteology; (3) to call for a systematic investigation of taphonomic phenomena that affect disposition of remains; and (4) to suggest ways in which forensic experts can contribute to advancing this type of analysis.

Taphonomy in Human Remains Research

Because human skeletal remains — with the exclusion of early hominid material — are found in archaeological contexts primarily as a consequence of human cultural, and more specifically, ritual activity, both natural and cultural agents should be regarded as taphonomic (Bonnichsen and Sorg, 1987). Human behavior involved in mortuary practices can leave potentially recognizable taphonomic signatures (Boddington et al., 1987; Duday and Masset, 1987).

Modeling of the processes of decomposition and decay of the cadaver has been recognized as a relevant source of information on periburial activity. In France the interest arose from methodological approaches to excavating Neolithic group burials first developed by Andre Leroi-Gourhan et al. (1962), and promoted further in studies by Masset (1972a,b, 1973, 1987) and Duday (1978, 1987a,b; Duday et al., 1990). In French literature, concern for interpretation of mortuary ritual is evidenced by the focus on the disposition of skeletal elements as a primary goal of taphonomic studies. In England, studies such as those by Mant (1987) on war dead, although forensic in nature and scope, were recognized as relevant to the archaeological community. Regardless of their differences, Boddington et al. (1987) and Duday and Masset (1987) attempted to systematize current knowledge on the sequence of decomposition and the influence of the burial environment and other cultural factors on the position of bones within a grave. These texts are key for this type of archaeological inference.

In the North American literature, most of the research on decomposition and decay centers on questions of exclusive interest to forensic anthropology in the medicolegal context. It should be emphasized that the forensic context offers potential resolution of taphonomic issues relevant to the sequence of decomposition and position of individual bones and bone fragments within burials that have to be deduced in archaeological contexts (Haglund and Sorg, 1997a). The subsequent systematization and publication of such data greatly advance our understanding and provide well-grounded explanations of some of these phenomena for the field of archaeology (Haglund and Sorg, 1997b).

The taphonomic behavior of a cadaver is influenced by a large number of factors. Factors internal to the body include cause of death, state of the body at death, age, sex, body mass, and pathology. External factors such as the time elapsed between death and burial, the treatment of the body prior to burial, and the burial environment (Garland and Janaway, 1987) are all primarily cultural. Noncultural taphonomic factors are important in determining disturbance (bias) that in turn can be relevant for differentiation of culturally determined activity. For example, the extent of damage by burrowing animals can be relevant in inferring the presence and type of burial architecture (Mordant, 1987).

Human skeletal remains found in archeological contexts are most often the consequence of human cultural activity. From the perspective of understanding mortuary patterns, nonhuman taphonomic agents need to be identified and understood in order to eliminate their effect and the possible misinterpretations they can cause. For this reason, to pursue an understanding of mortuary ritual, physical anthropologists must be actively involved in the excavation and documentation of the site. Duday (1978) rightfully insists that knowledge of human osteology and anatomy should be an imperative for anyone excavating human burials. Knowledge of forensic contexts can also be critical (Haglund and Sorg, 1997b).

Utilizing Taphonomy To Understand Mortuary Practice

The original intent of human cultural activity in archeological contexts can be masked by the dynamics of decomposition and possible disturbance. Two phenomena of primary significance for funerary archaeology are the differential preservation of individual bones and differential disposition of human skeletal remains. Preservation is mitigated by cultural modes of disposal and by postdispositional agents. Understanding this interplay can assist in inferring burial circumstances. Cultural factors affecting preservation are numerous: Humans through their cultural norms decide who gets buried, where, when, and how the burial takes place. The place and mode of disposition will not only influence the position of the skeleton in the grave, but ultimately its preservation.

General Consequences of Soft Tissue Decomposition and Disarticulation

To understand the post-dispositional movements of bones, it is necessary to understand: (1) consequences of soft tissue decomposition, (2) the sequences of disarticulation or disintegration of connective tissue between bones, and (3) the potential amplitude of movement of skeletal elements.

Consequences of Decomposition

Decomposition is the general term used to refer to its two major processes, putrefaction (involving bacteria) and autolysis (involving autolytic enzymes). Disarticulation is defined as complete reduction of the soft tissues that hold bones together within a joint in living organisms. Therefore, even if every bone is in its correct anatomical position relative to the other bones, the skeleton is considered disarticulated as long as no soft tissue connects them.

Sequences of Disarticulation or Disintegration
of Connective Tissue between Joints

Most research on skeletonization deals with exposed human remains from forensic contexts, or are experimental studies based on nonhuman carcasses (Toots, 1965; Hill, 1979; Haynes, 1982; Weigelt, 1989). Forensic experience with buried remains is relatively limited (Rodriguez and Bass, 1985; Manhein, 1997) and more information is needed to come to meaningful conclusions about the rate and sequence of skeletonization. The time it takes a carcass to skeletonize is highly variable and context (microenvironment) specific. When a body is exposed to scavengers and insects on the surface, or in shallow burials, decay is more rapid (Micozzi, 1986, 1991; Janssen, 1984; Polson et al., 1985; Haglund et al., 1989; Garland and Janaway, 1987; Janaway, 1997).

Dirkmaat and Sienicki's 1995 skeletonization sequence based on observations of human remains decomposed in open space is presented here for illustration, rather than a set of generally applicable rules:

1. The cranium is first to skeletonize primarily due to the accessibility of facial cavities to flies. If exposed to sun it will desiccate rather than decompose, and preserve skin and hair tissue for longer periods.
2. Clavicles and sternum are exposed early in the sequence.
3. Cervical vertebrae, even when exposed, will remain articulated for longer periods due to strong ligaments and complex interlocking bony surfaces.
4. Arms are usually at an enhanced state of decomposition compared to lower limbs. As with the cranium, limb surfaces exposed to the sunlight desiccate rather than decompose.
5. Pelvis is reduced later than the thoracic/abdominal region, while the vertebral column remains intact and articulated, and ribs present differing degrees of disarticulation.
6. Legs, especially if clothed, are preserved much longer than arms. Feet, often protected by socks and shoes, will preserve their shape longer than any other part of the body. Clothing in general seems to postpone decomposition significantly (Dirkmaat and Sienicki, 1995:7).

Other disarticulation sequences suggested for human remains, such as Haglund's (1993) for water environments and for canid-assisted surface remains (Haglund et al., 1989) underscore departures in disarticulation sequences that are due to different environments and circumstances.

Comparison with archaeological observation demonstrates that disarticulation of the first and second cervical vertebrae is observed early in the sequence in both animals (Micozzi, 1991) and humans (Masset, 1987). This may have as much to do with the weight and shape of the cranium, allowing it to roll or rock, as with the joint. Mandible and cranium are frequently the first to separate from the rest of the skeleton. Hands and unprotected feet are also early to disarticulate, sometimes prior to disarticulation of head from the neck. Ubelaker (1974) suggests that the lower leg articulations can persist over longer periods of time. In archaeological contexts, the hip joint and the knee joint can become dislocated, whereas the foot retains perfect anatomical connections. The observed differences between forensic and experimental findings further underline the need to gather and systemize data on disarticulation rate and sequence in different burial environments. Some of the apparent differences may be due to the fact that the forensic cases Dirkmaat and Sienicki studied decomposed above ground. Forensic cases in which the deceased are interred might clarify these issues, provided relevant data are collected on a regular basis. The project by Rodriguez and Bass (1983, 1985) that deals with inhumated rather than exposed individuals over longer periods of time, although centered on forensic questions, could be an excellent source of information on sequence and pace of disarticulation not influenced by animal activity and weathering.

Potential Amplitude of Postdepositional Movement of Skeletal Elements

The potential for postdepositional position changes in human remains must be kept in mind. Empty space around the body leaves the potential for slight changes of body position due to buildup of gases during the decomposition process or collapse of joint connections. Examples of this type of movement might involve fingers spreading within the abdomen or splaying arms or legs.

Postdepositional movement of remains buried with soft tissue depends on the shape of the joint and its associated degree of freedom (Duday, personal communication) coupled with the amplitude of possible movement in any of the given directions and the strength of associated ligaments.

Amplitude of movement, i.e., displacement *in situ* from the original position, will depend upon the position of the remains, as deposited, and the available space in which the movement takes place. Potential for postdepositional movement of individual skeletal elements will differ for burials of fleshed, decomposing, and fully skeletonized remains. The amplitude of movement, or mobility, represents the extent to which a bone can move in any of the possible directions. Movement is, for example, only theoretical in adult cranial sutures, whereas it can be pronounced in the adult shoulder articulation. Potential for mobility and amplitude of mobility are crucial concepts, as they describe movement of any of the bones in the living individual. In the context of skeletonized remains, they serve to distinguish movements of bone that cannot be regarded as expected and thus require alternative explanations.

The presence of an anatomically correct position of bones in the skeleton as a whole, which is referred to as *anatomical relationship,* should be regarded in light of the resistance of certain articulations to decomposition and disarticulation. In that respect, the table that Ubelaker (1974:31) presents for Ossuary II from Tidewater Potomac on the relative frequencies of anatomical relationships in secondary burials is most instructive. However, in order to develop a set of rules, we need more comparative data from both forensic cases and other archaeological contexts. Dastugue (referenced in Duday and Masset, 1987:129) pointed out that classifying ligaments as strong or weak is not consistent with anatomical knowledge. Masset (1987:131) argues that in cases where archaeological experiences conflict with medical explanations, archaeological observations should be regarded as more relevant. For example, the fact that costo-vertebral ligaments are difficult to separate in medical praxis does not put them in the category of persistent articulations, as the costo-vertebral joints are rarely found preserved in archaeological context. Duday (Duday, 1985:12) draws attention to variation in the volume of soft tissue that is attached to joints as a possible explanation for these inconsistencies. He notes three types of articulations: weak articulations with a small volume of soft tissue attached to them (extremities), weak with an important volume of soft tissue attached (trunk), and persistent articulations. However, it has been argued that although the articulations might be weak, the ligaments accompanying them can be numerous or strong, which in turn affects the disarticulation sequence. Furthermore, not only the soft tissue of the joint, but also the mass of soft tissue surrounding the joint will substantially influence the sequence of disarticulation. No simplistic scheme can be envisaged for ligament resistance as it depends on a number of factors. One cannot talk only of ligament strength; the relationship of joints to portals of entry for insects, accessibility and feeding behavior of scavengers, the position of the body and types of surfaces the remains rest on (inclines for example) have to be included as well. Again, as with decomposition rate, disarticulation sequences are highly environmentally and micro environmentally specific (Haglund, pers. commun.).

Influence of Gravity and the Space in Which Decomposition Takes Place

The principles of gravity and space provide the basis for interpreting the disposal space allocated to the individual, type of disposition, perishable grave architecture, and internal chronology of the necropolis (Crubezy and Helas, 1989:34–42; Duday, 1987b). Gravity and space also affect interpretations of different ritual functions served by the grave (*sensu* Kinnes, 1975).

Most often, primary dispositions (especially burials) involve bodies and not skeletons (Garland and Janaway, 1987; Haglund and Sorg, 1997a). Given time, buried remains are usually reduced to a skeleton. If the mode of deposition puts bones in a stable position, little or no movement of bone will ensue following loss of soft tissue (other than collapsing). If disposition places bones in an unstable position, once soft tissue disappears, they will move in accordance with gravity and the architecture of the burial space. Clothing and wrappings will also affect potential movement. Additional space in a grave can be created from space previously occupied by the body volume. For example, if a hand is positioned flat on the substrate no movement will ensue, whereas, if it is positioned over the abdomen, as soft tissue of the abdomen disappears, disarticulated bones of the hand are subject to collapse into the pelvic area. Thus, bones of hands positioned in other than anterior palmer presentation are subject to relatively more displacement with decomposition. Interpretation of such postdispositional movement is dependent on the original position of the hand and requires expert knowledge of osteology and anatomy. Duday (1978:97) makes an excellent argument to illustrate this. By observing an uncommon *in situ* position of finger elements he was able to infer the paralysis of left ulna as a consequence of trauma. Had the position of the fingers not been noted during the excavation, even though the trauma was recorded, paralysis could not have been inferred.

The space assigned to the deposition of the body is an integral part of the ritual. The changes through which a cadaver goes in the disposition context, while following general rules of decomposition, will have a significantly different outcome if the individual is deposited on "plain earth" and covered with sediment compared with a grave which (*sensu lato*) forms empty space around the body that eventually fills with earth (Duday, 1985:6). Archaeological observation can be sufficient when the architecture is made of non-perishable materials (Figure 5.1). However, when the architectural elements are no longer preserved, the position of skeletal elements (Figures 5.2 and 5.3) carries important information (Mordant, 1987; Brothwell, 1987).

Figure 5.1 Non-perishable architectural elements (large rocks) account for (a) constriction at the level of left shoulder and lack of splaying of the left part of the rib cage. However, (b) shows that the other ribs on the same side tend to move in a predictable manner, as in (c), where there is no architecture limit. Normal movement (splaying) of the right side of the rib cage is shown at (c). (Photograph courtesy of B. Jovanovic, © STARINAR, Arheloŝki, Institut, Beograd.)

Figure 5.2 Perishable architecture elements (wrappings) are evidenced by constriction at the shoulder girdle (a–c) and wall effect (a–b). Slumping of the thoracic cage is only toward the coxal and not lateral (i.e., not splayed). The left radius and ulna migrated within the initial volume of the body itself. (Photograph courtesy of B. Jovanovic, © STARINAR, Arheloŝki, Institut, Beograd.)

The manner of burial can provide insight into chronology and function of the gravesite as well as the associated ritual (Duday, 1985). The type of articulation (strong or weak) and the decomposition environment (covered vs. empty) influence the sequence of events and amplitude of movement. The original position of bones with weak articulations and a small volume of surrounding soft tissue will be preserved in the case of progressive infilling even in an unstable position because the soft tissue is immediately replaced by sediment. If the infilling is differential, weak articulations will be preserved only if the part

Figure 5.3 The same wall effect that acts to preserve the position of the scapula and humerus in Figure 5.1a can be recognized here at (a). The right radius-ulna articulation persists (b), while the left radius migrates into the abdomen together with the hand (that had been displaced during excavation). At the same time, the unstable position of the left coxal and femur persists (c). (Photograph courtesy of B. Jovanovic, © STARINAR, Arheloški, Institut, Beograd.)

of the body is in a stable position, otherwise bones migrate within the initial volume of the cadaver. Persistent connections can be preserved in their anatomical position, on the other hand, even if the burial is secondary, depending on the time lapse between initial and secondary burial. The value any of these factors will have in determining the mode of disposition will depend upon site formation processes, disposition-specific parameters and the quality of excavation and the extent of documentation. Each case presents a set of specific problems, and because we often are dealing with equifinality, there are no simple space parameters; rather, a number of relevant observations have to be taken into consideration. Duday (1978:61–62, 1985:10) insists on the importance of discerning and documenting the amplitude of the displacement of bones relative to their expected anatomical position following decomposition.

The following special terms are essential to understanding these issues.

- *Empty space*, in the context of this discussion, refers to airspace between the body and surrounding sediment at the time or shortly after burial. Such space could be created by architectural elements of the burial, or by decomposition and disappearance of soft tissue. Empty space would allow limited movement of disarticulated skeletal elements, and might subsequently be vulnerable to infilling by sediment.
- *Wall effect* results from architectural limits that enclose the remains and may prevent movement that would otherwise be expected. An example would be constriction of the shoulder or pelvic girdle if a body is placed in a confined space (Figures 5.2 and 5.3). Alignment of bones where there is no anatomical necessity for it is a good indicator of wall effects (Masset, 1993:125).
- *Nondelineated empty space* refers to architectural or natural environments that do not involve burial, such as crypts, caves (Masset, 1993), and Bella-bella burial houses

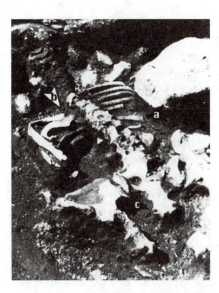

Figure 5.4 Decomposition in an empty space includes (a) slumping and splaying of the rib cage, (b) severing of the costo-transverse joints, and (c) splaying and flattening of the pelvic girdle. (Photograph courtesy of B. Jovanovic, © STARINAR, Arheloški, Institut, Beograd.)

(Hester and Nelson, 1978). If the remains are not disturbed by external agents, such as scavengers, the processes of decomposition and disarticulation will result in slumping of various elements. Dislocations of skeletal elements that might result are collapse of the thoracic cage (Figure 5.4a), rotation of vertebral segments relative to each other, or disjunction of the coxo-sacral articulation (Figure 5.4c).

- *Empty space with later infilling* presents a complex situation where it is necessary to demonstrate that infilling occurred long after cadaver decomposition and disarticulation. While decomposition occurred in a delineated empty space without any sediment, indicated by rearrangements of skulls, handfuls of ribs, and long bones, the sediment that covered them was brought in long after the last skeleton decomposed as a final event in the series of ritual actions (Leclerc, 1987). Duday (1978, 1987a,b) proposes a number of indicators of group burials within an empty space at the sites of Corconne and Villedubert: rearrangement of bones against walls, regrouping of long bones in a nonanatomical position, etc. Deposition in empty space was proposed for skeletons from Villedubert on the basis of following disposition: the left arm (elbow joint) of an adult (no. 1) lying against the fourth and fifth lumbar vertebrae of another (no. 2). The lumber vertebrae were rotated by 90 degrees with respect to sacrum, which itself was not in the anatomical position with coxal bones. The fact that the elbow (no. 1) was in correct anatomical relationship, although it is a far less persistent connection than the sacro-iliac joint, suggests that when subject no. 1 was deposited, disarticulation of subject no. 2 was already advanced and the individual was not covered with sediment.
- *Delineated empty space* refers to architectural elements that create space around the decomposing body and prevent direct contact between sediment and individuals, such as a coffin, sarcophagus, planks over the top of the burial pit, skins, etc. Architecture can maintain a very delimited empty space around the corpse, which cannot always be distinguished from the initial volume of the body (wrapping in

textile, skins, very narrow coffin). A good indicator of this constricted architecture is the wall effect, easily recognized in the perseverance of very unstable anatomical relationships and the rigid, unnatural position of the skeleton. Constriction of pelvic and shoulder girdle (Figures 5.2a–c and 5.3a–c), because it is in contradiction with the initial volume of the cadaver, is a very good indicator. The ability to determine these instances will depend on the relative rate of decomposition between the body and its associated architecture. If the architecture decomposes prior to the body, the effect will be the same as in covered space. Some damage to the bones from collapsing sediment is to be expected in the pubic region or at the sternal ends of the ribs, but only if there is a lapse of time between the decomposition of the body and the perishable architecture in which it is buried. If the two happen simultaneously, it is impossible to distinguish the interment "in plain ground" from interment in a coffin of very poor quality. If it decomposes well after the decomposition of the body, as in the case of wooden coffins, some displacement will occur outside the initial volume of the cadaver. The movements that ensue could be due to gravity, collapse of architectural elements, or human reintervention, such as reopening the grave to take out skulls or long bones. Note that these skeletons have to retain enough anatomical connections to group them into primary and not secondary burials. Other, nonritual factors of possible disturbance, such as burrowing animals, roots, movements of the terrain, grave robbers, etc. should always be considered.

- *Covered space* refers to immediate contact of the body with sediments throughout the process of decomposition. Decomposition in a covered space corresponds to inhumation *sensu stricto*: the grave is dug in the ground and the fossa is immediately refilled, the body is posed in the soil and covered by the earth (Duday, 1985:8). The filling of body cavities by sediment in a simple burial pit can be progressive or differential (Duday, 1985). When the body is surrounded by sediment, as soon as decomposition sets in the sediment may fill body cavities. However, depending on the integrity, compaction, and moisture of the sediment, a different effect may be produced. For example, some clays can leave the original space that was occupied by the body as empty space rather than infilling it (Haglund, pers. comm.). Some movement of bones is expected within the initial volume of the cadaver. Variability is caused by the volume of soft tissue that each individual has. A person with greater volume of the abdominal and pelvic region will create more initial space than a slim individual. In extreme cases, it can produce the same effect as architecture. However, examination of the skeletal parts subject to movement can provide reliable information.

- *Progressive infilling* occurs when the sediment is dry or fine-grained (sand or loess), and the filling of body cavities proceeds with decomposition and disappearance of soft tissue. No movement of bones is observable. However, the perseverance of the proper anatomical position of articulations is indicative only in those situations where the part of the body in question is in an unstable position. The left hand of the granolithic skeleton from Boniface (Corsica) was found on its side, positioned against the left hip, which makes the preservation of anatomical connection unlikely except in the case of continual filling (Duday, 1985:9). As was noted earlier, the hand articulations can be retained even when the body has not been covered with sediment, if they are in a stable position against the floor of the burial. However, proper anatomical position of the hyoid bone can be taken as a tell-tale sign of progressive sedimentation.

- *Differential filling* refers to covered space where sediments are less fine grained. The space created by the decomposition of the thorax and abdomen will allow bones to move within that initial volume of the cadaver for a short time before the sediment collapses and fills in the remaining cavity. Slumping* (Figure 5.1) of the thoracic cage with disjunction of costotransverse articulation, dislocation of sternum, rotation of the segments of the vertebral column relative to each other, and splaying (Figure 5.4) of the pelvic girdle with minor displacement of the femoral head in the case of dorsal decubitus (when the individual is laid on the back) are all very common. Movements of the hand ensue (Figure 5.3), if placed on either abdomen or thorax. The fact that bones never migrate outside the initial volume of the cadaver is important in arguing against architectural elements.

Inference about Ritual: Primary vs. Secondary Disposition

Disposition refers to the mode of disposing of the dead. *Primary disposition* concerns the initial location in which the body is placed. If the initial location is the same as final disposition, it is a primary burial. *Secondary dispositions* occur when remains are removed from the primary disposition; they are implied when the locus of soft tissue decomposition (or destruction in case of cremations) is different from the place of the final disposition.

Inference that recovered remains are a primary or secondary disposition is not necessarily straightforward (Masset, 1987). For example, one cannot necessarily infer primary disposition just because all skeletal elements are present in relative anatomical order. Bodies may be removed while still fleshed and in stages of decomposition without disarticulation. Bodies may also be moved from a primary disposition enveloped in wrappings or some sort of enclosure such as a coffin or casket. When most of the articulations, even the least persistent, are present at the site, and virtually all bones present, we can infer primary disposition. While small carpal and tarsal bones preserve remarkably well, in secondary burials they may not be collected and placed in the ultimate burial area (Duday, 1978). If the initial position of the deceased is stable with respect to gravity, reconstruction of the original position in which the individual was buried is relatively straightforward. However, with positions that contribute to instability of skeletal elements, as for example in the case of seated individuals (Audouze, 1987), the inference becomes more complicated and demands more detailed and expert analysis.

Caution should be used in deducing a secondary disposition simply because skeletal elements are in disarray or when complete skeletons are not present. Such disturbances can be caused by a variety of agents. Although secondary dispositions are traditionally described as containing complete skeletons, or having elements in anatomic disarray, such generalizations are useful only in cases of good preservation. A valuable indicator of secondary dispositions is the underrepresentation of normally well-preserved elements (see Darwent and Lyman, Chapter 19, this volume). When analyzing osteological collections, careful comparison of the found percentage of bones to the expected percentage is necessary (Mays, 1992). In case of good preservation where ribs, vertebral bodies, and sternum (for example) are present, lack of bones that preserve well can be indicative of secondary disposal. However, if skeletal material was collected earlier in the century, excavation and collection bias cannot be excluded.

---

* T. Rogers helped translate the term "mis à plât" used by French authors (Masset and Duday, 1987).

Secondary dispositions resulting from relocation of partly decomposing, relatively artic-ulated cadavers allow for the most complete skeletal representation (Ubelaker, 1974; Duday, 1985). When remains are skeletonized, even if a full skeleton is represented, often not all the bones will be collected to be removed to a secondary disposition site. In some incinerations, representation of the body can be anywhere between 2 and 3000 grams (Antunovic, 1991).

Completeness of dentition recovery has been discussed by Haglund as an indication of transport (1997a). If the number of teeth — especially incisors — is much smaller than expected, it can indicate secondary disposition, since teeth are susceptible to falling out of the alveoli after decay of the peridontal ligament, and thus may be overlooked when the individual is reburied. If the cranium is the object of an ancestral cult and is removed from the necropolis after decomposition, this argument is even more valid: the teeth will remain with the skeleton (primary disposition) while the cranium (or its fragments) will be missing. If the anatomical connections are lost due to successive rearrangements within the necropolis, the number of teeth in comparison with the number of skull fragments becomes a crucial argument (Gallay, 1987).

Quality excavation and documentation are necessary to provide insights into secondary dispositions (Duday, 1978). At the site of Saint-Michael-du Touch (Toulouse, France), Simmone was able to show irrefutably that a body of an adult had been schematically reassembled from bone pieces but with obvious anatomical errors: an arm was recon-structed by placing two humeri so that their distal ends met at the "elbow". In this case, if the position of bone fragments had not been noted during the excavation, the secondary disposition would have escaped the attention of the researchers (Duday, 1978:65–66).

Sellier (1985) notes that while certain partial skeletons are secondary dispositions, others are definitively primary dispositions from which certain bones have been removed. Removal of the skull or its displacement is well-known at a number of sites in epochs as different as PPNA and PPNB in Jericho, the Mesolithic of the Lepenski Vir culture, and the Late Iron Age of the La Tene type (Srejovic, 1969; Rozoy, 1987). In the abovementioned site of Benon, by plotting the teeth Jousseaume was able to determine the exact position of the skulls that had been removed from the skeleton after decomposition (referenced in Masset, 1993:110). Impli-cations of this practice go beyond mere funerary act; ancestral rituals can be implied.

In rare instances it is even possible to suggest the original corpse position from its array in the secondary grave. Ambroise and Perlès (1972) were able to suggest, after detailed analyses of the preserved anatomical position and the presence of bones in a pile excavated at Chaussee-Tirancourt (Neolithic, France), that the individual was primarily buried in a seated position. A similar, although somewhat easier to discern, situation is presented in Figure 5.5: vertical position of the humeri, inferior rather than lateral slumping of the rib cage, and migration of the mandible within the initial volume of the thorax, all point toward a burial in a seated position within a delineated empty space.

Group Burials: The Study of Function

Group burials are found in a number of cultural contexts. Depending on time of interment of individuals within the burial, group burials can be categorized as synchronous and diachronous. Synchronous burials can further be divided into primary, as in the case of mass burials, or secondary, as in the case of ossuaries. In the case of undisturbed tombs containing a number of buried individuals, we can presume catastrophic events: epidemics,

Figure 5.5 Probable burial in a seated position within a delineated empty space suggested by vertical position of humeri, inferior slumping of the rib cage, and migration of the mandible within the initial volume of the thorax. (Photograph courtesy of B. Jovanovic, © STARINAR, Arheloški, Institut, Beograd.)

massacre, or ritual suicides of the household at the death of the master or mistress (Masset, 1993:13). Synchronous dispositions in ossuaries require that all the decedents decomposed elsewhere and were redeposited at the same prescribed time regardless of the state of decomposition. This would cause quite a variety of patterns: some of the bones may be neatly, but artificially, arranged while others may exhibit fully preserved anatomical connections as in primary burials (Ubelaker, 1974).

Diachronic group burials are much more common and can be divided into primary and secondary as well. In the case of successive inhumations, it is necessary to have open access to the grave. These burials can be termed *collective burials*. In the case of secondary burials, the synchrony of the final interment does not imply the synchrony of death (Ubelaker, 1974, 1981; Masset, 1993), as the individuals interred might be brought in after a prescribed interval, rather than at a prescribed date. The diachronous ossuaries would differ from synchronous ones by greater uniformity of the degree of decomposition, as the skeleton would be brought in after a prescribed interval in the luminal phase of putrefaction (Metcalf and Huntington, 1991).

Various aspects of mortuary ritual and functioning of the cemetery can be discerned from different accumulations of bones: space for the deposition of the corpse, evidence of rearranging, space assigned (or used) for later circulation of the members of the group. (Duday, 1981; Duday et al., 1990; Sauzade and Duday, 1979). Duday notes that at Villedubert only 40 assemblages displaying anatomical connections were found in over 53,000 recorded human bones and bone fragments. Some of the articulations, being of a very persistent nature, did not provide insight into the functions of the cemetery; others, nonpersistent in nature (interphalangial, cervical spine, vertebral), were found in place as a positive indicator of primary burials. Although animal activities could be inferred in a number of cases of nonarticulated fragments, they could not explain excessive fragmentation and disturbance. There is a strong likelihood that prehistoric humans themselves were the source of disturbance by rearranging graves for successive burials. This was shown through careful examination of the data: ribs gathered together as in a handful, whole skulls regrouped in limited spaces within the tomb in contrast to the presence of cervical vertebrae that were distributed over the extent of the burial, etc. Further, the fact that the atlas usually accompanied the skull points toward the rearrangement of the skulls after decomposition. Other indices discussed above also show that the bodies were deposited at different times (Duday, 1987a:53). If the totality of the information human bones carry is recorded, a number of inferences can be made. Excessive fragmentation and lack of complete bones at certain areas indicate post-burial disturbance by humans creating new burials or ancestral cults. Careful examination of skeletal elements helped determine the time and the mode of abandonment of a burial site in Corconne (Leclerc, 1987).

Conclusions

Understanding taphonomic processes such as decomposition and disarticulation is crucial to understanding the function of a burial site in both its funerary and its ancestral ritual context. Ideally, presence, orientation, and association (levels of observation not traditionally documented) are crucial to such understanding. Needless to say, such observations should be made by experts knowledgeable about human osteology and anatomy. This requirement can be met only if the excavations of the burial are conducted by either a physical anthropologist or an archaeologist with extensive knowledge of anatomy and osteology. While it might be impossible to record every bone and bone fragment in the Cartesian system according to its anatomical position within the burial, the decision about the most efficient and relevant documentation should be made by an anthropologist well acquainted with the archaeological issues. In cases where efficiency is a must, photographic documentation has to be abundant. A number of careful, *in situ* observations are possible if the excavator is fully acquainted with osteology and can in certain cases substitute for excessive documentation.

Further, taphonomy should not remain limited to the study of natural postdepositional processes affecting individual bones, although their thorough understanding is essential in avoiding misinterpretation. As taphonomy incorporates the study of the evolution of a cadaver within a burial, it has to place stronger emphasis on the context of the skeleton, the disposition of its elements, and possible explanations for the observed phenomena. All of this has to be done from the perspective of understanding cultural agents affecting the dead body. All of the inferences taken together, accompanied by data about grave architecture, bone element mobility, and temporal trends can provide insight into the ritual meaning of the burial structures. Such detailed knowledge can make possible comparisons between sites and insight about between-site similarities and variations that can be applied cross-culturally.

By the nature of their study subjects, forensic experts often excavate human remains in different stages of decomposition and in different decomposition environments. These are, aside from conditions of exceptional preservation, unlikely occurrences in the archaeological record. By recording the stages of decomposition of individuals in different micro- and macrodecomposition environments and (even more importantly) sequences of disarticulation of joints, and systematizing this kind of information, forensic anthropologists can provide invaluable information that can be used to refine the interpretation of mortuary ritual.

Acknowledgments

My gratitude goes to Prof. Duday (University of Bordeaux I) whose course in taphonomy made this chapter possible, to Prof. Driver and Dr. Rogers (Simon Fraser University) for struggling through the first draft, Profs. Boyd (Radford University) and La Mota (University of Arizona) for their excellent criticism and encouragement, and to Dr. Sorg and Dr. Haglund for reviewing innumerable versions.

References

Ambroise, D. and C. Perlès
  1972   Étude de la position des ossements d'un squelette néolithique (sépulture collective de la Chausée-Tirancourt, Somme), *L'Anthropologie* 76(5–6):535–544.

Andrews, P. and J. Cook
  1985   Natural modifications to bones in a temperate setting, *Man* 20:675–691.

Antunovic, M.
  1991   Recherches preliminaires sur les restes humains incineres du site archaeologique de Konopiste (Mala Vrbica, Kladovo, Yugoslavie). D.E.A., Bordeaux I.

Audouze, F.
  1987   La sépulture d'enfant du Buisson Campin à Verberie (Oise). In *Anthropologie Physique et Archaeologie,* edited by H. Duday and C. Masset, pp. 147–155. C.N.R.S., Paris.

Baden, M.M.
  1982   *Medical-Legal Aspects of Microbiology,* New York Academy of Sciences, Section on Microbiology (February 17).

Baud, C.A. and M. Gossi
  1980   Degree of mineralization of bone tissue as determined by quantitative microradiography: effect of age, sex and pathological conditions. In *Proceedings of the Fourth International Conference on Bone Measurement,* pp. 345–351. U.S. Dept. of Health, Washington, D.C.

Boddington, A.
  1987   Chaos, disturbance and decay in an Anglo-Saxon cemetery. In *Death, Decay and Reconstruction. Approaches to Archaeology and Forensic Science,* edited by A. Boddington, A.N. Garland, and R.C. Janaway, pp. 27–42. Manchester University Press, Manchester.

Boddington, A., A.N. Garland, and R.C. Janaway (Eds.)
  1987   *Death, Decay and Reconstruction. Approaches to Archaeology and Forensic Science.* Manchester University Press, Manchester.

Bonnichsen, R. and M.H. Sorg (Eds.)
  1987   *Bone Modification,* Center for the Study of the First Americans, Orono, ME.

Boyd, D.C.
  1996   Skeletal correlates of human behavior in the Americas, *Journal of Archaeological Method and Theory* 3(3):189–251.

Brothwell, D.
  1987   Decay and disorder in the York Jewbury skeletons. In *Death, Decay and Reconstruction. Approaches to Archaeology and Forensic Science,* edited by A. Boddington, N.A. Garland, and R.C. Janaway, pp. 22–26. Manchester University Press, Manchester.

Crubezy, E. and J.-C. Helas

1989   Archéologie funéraire et anthropologie: application de l'étude ostéologique in situ a l'inter-
prétation de tombs rupestres adjacentes du cimetière médiéval de Saint-Come et Damien
(Montpellier, Hérault). In *La Matériel Anthropologique Provenant des Édifices Religieux,* edited
by L. Buchet, C.N.R.S., Paris.

Dirkmaat, D.C. and L.A. Sienicki

1995   Taphonomy in the northeast woodlands: four cases from western Pennsylvania. *Proceedings of the 47th Annual Meeting of the American Academy of Forensic Sciences* 1:10. Seattle.

Duday, H.

1978   Archaeologie funeraire et anthropologie, *Cahiers d'Anthropologie* 1:55–101.

1981   Le place de l'anthropologie dans l'etude des sépultures anciennes, *Cahiers d'Anthropologie*
(1):27–42.

1985   Nouvelles observations sur la décomposition des corps dans un espace libre. In *Méthode
d'Étude des Sépultures,* pp. 6–13. Saint-Germain en Laye, Saint-Germain en Laye, France.

1987a Contribution des observations osteologiques a la chronologie interne des sépultures collectives. In *Anthropologie Physique et Archaeologie,* edited by H. Duday and C. Masset, pp. 51–61.
C.N.R.S., Paris.

1987b Organisation et fonctionnement d'une sépulture collective néolithique. L'aven de la Boucle
a Corconne (Gard). In *Anthropologie Physique et Archaéologie,* edited by H. Duday and C.
Masset, pp. 105–111. C.N.R.S., Paris.

Duday, H. and C. Masset (Eds.)

1987   *Anthropologie Physique et Archaeologie,* C.N.R.S., Paris.

Duday, H. et al.

1990   L'anthropologie de "terrain": reconnaissance et interpretation des gestes funeraires, *Bulletins et Memoires de la Societe d'Anthropologie de Paris,* t.2(3–4):26–49.

Gallay, A.

1987   Analyse de la necropole néolithique du Petit-Chasseur (Valais, Suisse). Vers un bilan
méthodologique. In *Anthropologie Physique et Archaeologie,* edited by H. Duday and C. Masset,
pp. 19–47. C.N.R.S., Paris.

Garland, A.N. and R.C. Janaway

1987   The taphonomy of inhumation burials. In *Burial Archaeology Current Research, Methods
and Developments,* edited by C.A. Roberts, F. Lee, and J. Bintliff, pp. 14–38. University of
London, British Archaeological Reports International, Series 211, Oxford.

Haglund, W.D.

1991   Applications of Taphonomic Models to Forensic Investigation, Ph.D. dissertation, University of Washington, Seattle.

1993   Disappearance of soft tissue and the disarticulation of human remains from aqueous
environments, *Journal of Forensic Sciences* 38(4):806–815.

1997   Method and theory in forensic taphonomy research. In *Forensic Taphonomy: The Postmortem Fate of Human Remains,* edited by W.D. Haglund and M.H. Sorg, pp. 13–26. CRC Press,
Boca Raton, FL.

Haglund, W.D. and M.H. Sorg

1997   Introduction to forensic taphonomy. In *Forensic Taphonomy: The Postmortem Fate of
Human Remains,* edited by W.D. Haglund and M.H. Sorg, pp. 1–9. CRC Press, Boca Raton, FL.

Haglund, W.D., D.T. Reay, and D.R. Swindler

1989   Canid scavenging/disarticulation sequence of humans in the Pacific Northwest, *Journal
Forensic Sciences* 34(3):587–606.

Härke, H.
    1997 The nature of burial data. In *Burial and Society. The Chronological and Social Analysis of Archaeological Burial Data*, edited by C.K. Jensen and K.H. Nielsen, pp. 19–29. Aarhus University Press, Aarhus.

Haynes, G.
    1982 Utilization and skeletal disturbances of North American prey carcasses, *Arctic* 35(2):226–281.

Henderson, J.
    1987 Factors determining the state of preservation of human remains. In *Death, Decay and Reconstruction. Approaches to Archaeology and Forensic Science*, edited by A. Boddington, A.N. Garland and R.C. Janaway, pp. 43–54. Manchester University Press, Manchester.

Hester, J.J. and S.M. Nelson (Eds.)
    1978 *Studies in Bella Bella Prehistory*, Department of Archaeology, Simon Fraser University, Burnaby, B.C.

Hill, A.P.
    1979 Disarticulation and scattering of mammal skeletons, *Paleobiology* 5(3):261–274.

Janaway, R.C.
    1997 The decay of buried human remains and their associated materials. In *Studies in Crime: An Introduction to Forensic Archaeology*, edited by J. Hunter, C. Roberts, and A. Martin, pp. 58–85. Routledge, London.

Janssen, W.
    1984 *Forensic Histopathology*, Springer–Verlag, Berlin.

Kinnes, I.
    1975 Monumental function in British neolithic burial practices, *World Archaeology* 7:16–29.

Leclerc, J.
    1987 Procedures de condamnation dans les sepultures collectives Sein-Oise-Marne. In *Anthropologie Physique et Archaeologie*, edited by H. Duday and C. Masset, pp. 73–88. C.N.R.S., Paris.

Leroi-Gourhan, A. et al.
    1962 L'hypogée II des Mournouards (Mesnil-sur-Oger, Marne), *Gallia Prehistoire*, 5(1):23–133.

Lyman, R. L.
    1994 *Vertebrate Taphonomy*, Cambridge University Press, Cambridge, U.K.

Manhein, M.H.
    1997 Decomposition rates of deliberate burials: a case study of preservation. In *Forensic Taphonomy: The Postmortem Fate of Human Remains*, edited by W.D. Haglund and M.H. Sorg, pp. 469–482. CRC Press, Boca Raton, FL.

Mant, A.K.
    1987 Knowledge acquired from post-war exhumations. In *Death, Decay and Reconstruction. Approaches to Archaeology and Forensic Science*, edited by A. Boddington, A.N. Garland, and R.C. Janaway, pp. 65–78. Manchester University Press, Manchester.

Masset, C.
    1972a Influence du sexe et de l'âge sur la conservation des os humains. In *L'Homme hier et aujourd'hui*, pp. 334–343. Cujas, Paris.

    1972b The megalithic tomb of La Chassée Tirancourt, *Antiquity* 46:297–300 + pl. 47.

    1973 La démographie des populations inhumées. Essai de paléodemographie. *L'Homme* 13(4):95–131.

    1976 Sur des anomalies d'ordre demographique observees dans quelques sepultures neolithiques. IX Congress de l'UISPP (Nice) pretirages, vol. Themes Specializes, pp. 78–107.

1987 Le "Recrutement" d'un ensamble funéraire. In *Anthropologie Physique et Archaeologie*, edited by H. Duday and C. Masset, pp. 111–134. C.N.R.S., Paris.

1993 *Les Dolmens: Societes Neolithiques et Pratiques Funeraires: Les Sepultures Collectives d'Europe Occidentale*, Editions Errance, Paris.

Mays, S.
1992 Taphonomic factors in a human skeletal assemblage, *Circaea* 9(2):54–58.

Metcalf, P. and R. Huntington
1991 *Celebrations of Death: The Anthropology of Mortuary Ritual*, 2nd ed., Cambridge University Press, Cambridge, U.K.

Micozzi, M.S.
1986 Experimental study of postmortem change under field conditions: effects of freezing, thawing and mechanical injury, *Journal of Forensic Sciences* 31:953–961.

1991 *Postmortem Change in Human and Animal Remains: A Systematic Approach*, Charles C Thomas, Springfield, IL.

Mordant, D.
1987 Des inhumations en "pleine terre"? L'example dela Petite-Seine. In *Anthropologie Physique et Archaeologie*, edited by H. Duday and C. Masset, pp. 155–166. C.N.R.S., Paris.

Nawrocki, S.P.
1995 Taphonomic processes in historic cemeteries. In *Bodies of Evidence: Reconstructing History through Skeletal Remains*, edited by A.L. Grauer, pp. 49–68. Wiley-Liss, New York.

Polson, C.J., D.J. Gee, and B. Knight
1985 *The Essentials of Forensic Medicine*, 4th ed., Pergamon Press, Oxford.

Rodriguez, W.C. and W.M. Bass
1983 Insect activity and its relationship to decay rates of human cadavers in east Tennessee, *Journal of Forensic Sciences* 28:423–432.

1985 Decomposition of buried bodies and methods that may aid in their location, *Journal of Forensic Sciences* 30:836–852.

Rozoy, J.G.
1987 Manipulations celtiques dans les tombs au La Tène I. In *Méthode d'Étude des Sépultures*, pp. 59–63. Saint-Germain en Laye, France.

Sauzade, G. and H. Duday
1979 L'abri de Sanguinouse, tombe collective du Chalcolithique ancien (commune de la Roque-sur-Pernes, Vaucluse), 280–297.

Sellier, P.
1985 Observations sur la position des corps dans les cimetières de Mehrgarh (Pakistan). In *Méthode d'Étude des Sépultures*, pp. 39–43. Saint-Germain en Laye, France.

Skinner, M. and R.A. Lazenby
1983 *Found! Human Remains: A Field Manual for the Recovery of Recent Human Skeletons*, Archaeology Press, Simon Fraser University, Burnaby, B.C.

Srejovic, D.
1969 *Lepenski Vir. Nova Praistorijska Kultura u Podunavlju*, SKZ, Beograd.

Toots, H.
1965 Sequence of disarticulation in mammalian skeletons, *University of Wyoming Contributions in Geology* 4(1):37–39.

Ubelaker, D.H.

   1974   *Reconstruction of Demographic Profiles from Ossuary Skeletal Samples,* Smithonian Institution Press, Washington, D.C.

   1981   *The Ayalán Cemetery: A Late Integration Period Burial Site on the South Coast of Ecuador,* Smithsonian Institution Press, Washington D.C.

Weigelt, J.

   1989   *Recent Vertebrate Carcasses and their Paleobiological Implications,* translated by J. Schaefer, University of Chicago Press, Chicago, IL.

Willey, P. and L.M. Snyder

   1989   Canid modification of human remains: implications for time-since-death estimations, *Journal of Forensic Sciences* 34(4):894–910.

Taphonomic and Forensic Aspects of Bog Bodies

DON BROTHWELL
HEATHER GILL-ROBINSON

Contents

0-8493-1189-6/02/$0.00+$1.50

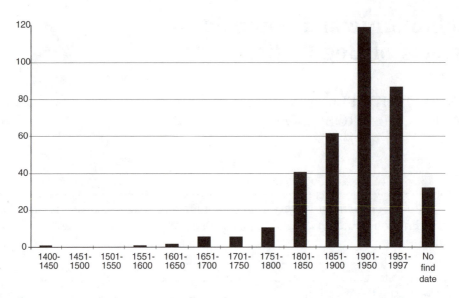

Figure 6.1 Dates at which there are recorded discoveries of bog bodies.

Introduction

During the conflicts this century in Ireland numerous deaths have resulted. Some of these bodies have been placed in bogs and are identifiable to recent events by their clothing or other associated objects, but many bodies from these wetland sites have origins further in the past. Some are even of prehistoric date and have relevance beyond archaeology, in that they provide further information on the long-term taphonomy of bodies in bogs, and of a range of trauma and pathology in a series of individuals showing much variation in preservation. In some cases, preservation looks remarkably good, yet survival of DNA in these acid wetlands is known to be very poor.

History, Dating, and General Preservation of the Finds

Because peat has been cut for fuel for many centuries, it seems likely that human remains have appeared in bogs over a long period of time. But it is only in the past two centuries (Figure 6.1) that literacy and interest in such finds have resulted in a growing number of written records about them. The total number of recorded finds probably is now in the order of 2000, but many of these are brief references, and there are relatively few well-preserved bodies.

Radiocarbon dating and associated cultural objects have enabled many of the bodies to be placed in a time sequence. Few of the prehistoric finds are earlier than 1000 BC, although the 160 bodies (mainly skeletons) from Windover in Florida are 7000 years old. Most of the earlier European bodies are in the time range 800 BC to 100 AD, and there is still much debate as to the reason for the bodies in the bogs. Was it the result of ritual, murder, punishment, or accident? Most of the more recent bodies are of post-medieval date and tend to display a better state of preservation. This may be because many of the prehistoric bodies are unclothed (or were superficially covered), whereas the more recent

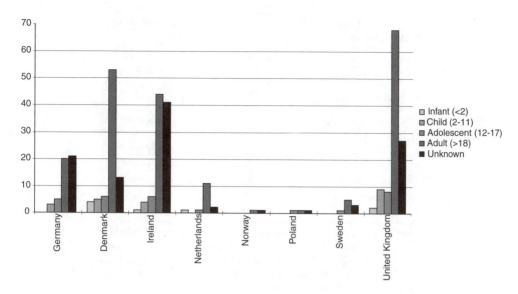

Figure 6.2 Estimated ages of the bog bodies at death (by country).

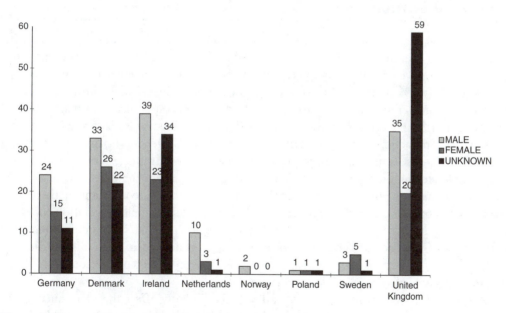

Figure 6.3 Sexes of the bog bodies by country of origin.

group were usually clothed. Immature individuals, which are not numerous (Figure 6.2), are not as well preserved as adults. No significant difference occurs between males and females (Figure 6.3), although there may be more evidence of adipocere in the females. Overall, it was possible from the data available to tentatively score the degree of preservation of the bog bodies in Europe, and this is summarized in Table 6.1. The score was based on the degree of preservation (bone, flesh, skin, etc.) in different regions of the body. Where information was limited, it was recorded as "unknown".

Table 6.1   European Bog Body Preservation, Scored into Eight Divisions

Score	Number of bodies (N = 369)	% Total Bodies
1. Very poor	107	29.00
2. Poor	11	2.98
3. Poor to fair	85	23.04
4. Fair	2	0.54
5. Fair to good	7	1.90
6. Good	9	2.44
7. Good to excellent	73	19.78
8. Excellent	5	1.36
9. Unknown	70	18.97

Note: Based on a simple point scoring system. Points for skin (1), flesh (1), and bone (1) were given separately for the head, torso, arms (L and R), hands (L and R), legs (L and R), feet (L and R), hair, heart, liver, lungs, brain, intestinal tract, etc. Very poor preservation rated a score of between 35 and 41.

The Burial Environment

The term *bog body* usually refers to human remains found in wetland peat deposits, although other mammals have been discovered occasionally. Depth of peat may vary from 30 cm to over 5 m. Waterlogged peatlands are common environments, perhaps covering nearly 5% of the earth's surface (Brown, 1995). Surprisingly, however, human remains have been found in only parts of northern Europe, especially Britain and Ireland, Denmark, northern Germany, and the north of The Netherlands. Peat is formed at varying rates by the compaction and accumulation of plant biomass. Depending on the underlying geology, nutrients available, topography, water table level, drainage, and precipitation, raised or blanket bogs may be formed. These may be restricted or extend over a considerable area. Although about 50% of wetlands in the world are concentrated in Canada, there have been no bog bodies found in this vast territory. This is not due to major vegetation contrasts between Canada and Europe, as typical bogs in both regions are likely to contain *Sphagnum* moss species in particular. The different species are influenced in their distribution by moisture levels and nutrient availability (Archibold, 1995). Bogs of the southern hemisphere also have *Sphagnum* species well represented.

A stagnant water source is critical and will significantly affect the plant succession. Bacteria are also essential in the modification of plant debris, attacking cellulose and polyphenols. It also would seem likely that microbial activity plays an important part in the differential decay of human bog bodies. Surprisingly, microbial decay is not well understood in relation to human corpses in bogs. Indeed, there is an urgent need for experimentation in order to understand the effects of such organisms on bone derived from contrasting environments (Child and Pollard, 1990).

The Body Surface

Although the epidermis appears to be shed from bodies in all wetland environments, there are in fact no good records of this outer layer of skin having been separately identified. In

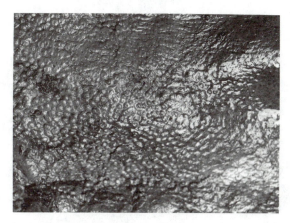

Figure 6.4 Blistering of the dermis of the lower back of Lindow Man (pseudopathology).

the careful extraction of the Lindow II body, nothing of the epidermis was identified, but the dermis was for the most part well preserved. In some peat environments, it is clear that the last identifiable part of the bog body is the dermis, nails, and hair. For instance, in the case of the two Weerdingerveen bodies from northern Holland (Landweer, 1906; van der Sanden, 1995) and the Damendorf body from north Germany (Glob, 1969), it is the outer integument and keratin structures which alone have survived to any noticeable extent.

Even in this advanced state of decay, the body surface can still reveal evidence of trauma, especially perforations through the skin as in the Lindow II scalp. Potentially, it may be possible to detect body surface pathology, although the blistering on the surface of the Lindow II body was in fact pseudopathology (Figure 6.4), the result of postmortem changes. Fingerprints can occasionally be well preserved, as in the male Grauballe corpse from Denmark. In the case of this individual, it was concluded that the undamaged nature of the dermal surface of the hands suggested that the individual did not undertake hard manual labor. Similar evidence has also been gleaned from the fingernails, and in the case of Lindow II, the smooth nail ends argue against hard manual labor in the individual's life for some time before death.

Hair has been found to be well preserved. In males, facial hair may be shaved off, or stubble as in Tollund man, or form a beard. In the case of the Huldremose woman and Lindow II man, there is clear evidence of cut hair ends, and in the latter case, the stepped form of some of the ends suggested cutting by scissors. Head hair of the Huldremose woman had been cut off and thrown down near the body (Figure 6.5).

Hair color is usually modified as a result of burial and early decomposition. In particular, the melanin appears to oxidize to a lighter color, and in archaeological hair in general, there is a tendency to change to more ginger-tinted shades. In some, but not all bodies, early changes within the hair follicle may significantly loosen the hair from the dermis, and this may cause conservation problems when attempting to clean away peat from the head region or body surface in general.

The chemistry of skin from wetland sites has been considered to a limited extent. Variation may be found even within one site, and in the Lindow II and III bodies, 12 and 10 elements, respectively, were noted (Pyatt et al., 1991a). Tests were also carried out to check for body decoration. Indigotin, which is the color in woad, was found to be negative in Lindow II. However, further skin tests using electron probe X-ray microanalysis revealed

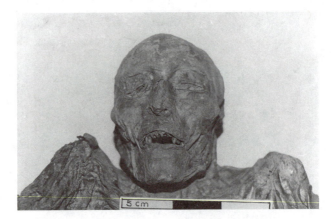

Figure 6.5 Frontal view of the head and shoulders of the Huldremose woman, showing hair cut off close to the scalp.

significant aluminium, silica, and copper, plus traces of titanium and zinc, and these were interpreted as residues of clay-based copper and other pigments that had been applied to the body (Pyatt et al., 1991b).

The Digestive Tract

Perhaps one of the most puzzling questions associated with the preservation of bog body tissues is concerned with the occasional survival of the gut. While the intestinal tract is formed of separate layers of varying thickness and of epithelial membrane, connective tissue, smooth muscle, and mucous membrane, its function and microbial ecology would argue against its chances of survival. Nevertheless, in the case of the Danish Tollund body, much of the intestinal tract remained (Figure 6.6), although the quality of the histology is not known. We can say, however, that in the case of the restricted preservation of the Lindow II gut, the segment of small intestine did not display the contrasting tissues, but simply residual collagen tissue.

The Nervous System

Because of the soft and delicate nature of nervous tissue, it would seem even less likely that any of this would survive. As yet, there seems to be no good evidence of nerves in general being identified, but the ultimate enigma is that tissue of the brain may retain its shape and quantity, although changes at a chemical and histological level have yet to be assessed. The whole brain remained a relatively normal size and shape in the Windeby girl, and indeed, the convolutions could be clearly seen (Glob, 1969). In some contrast, radiographic detail showed that the brains of the Lindow II and Huldremose bodies were partly changed and reduced in size (Figure 6.7). But why did they preserve better than stronger tissue such as muscle, ligament, and tendon? Experience by one of us (DRB) of the autopsy detail of Bosnian mass grave victims, where the bodies had been placed in deep pits about 4 years prior to excavation, again revealed well-preserved brain tissue as the common

Figure 6.6 Part of the intestinal tract of Tollund Man.

finding. Most of these individuals had been shot through the head, allowing direct microbial access to nervous tissue, yet the brain remained visibly intact. From this evidence, it clearly cannot be argued that the brain had the double sealing effect of the endocranial tissues surrounding it and rapid burial into anaerobic conditions. Clearly, other factors are involved, but what could they be?

Connective Tissue Preservation

Of the various forms of connective tissue, collagen fibers are one of the most important tissues to remain in bog bodies, maintaining the form of decalcified bones, the general structure of any remaining part of the intestinal tract, and defining the body surface, deprived of the epidermal layer.

Evidence of adipose tissue occurs less commonly and has not been well studied in bog bodies. Masses of adipocere were present on the thighs, trunk, arms, and face in the Irish Meenybraddan and Danish Huldremose bodies (Delaney and O'Floinn, 1995; Brothwell, Liversage, and Gottlieb, 1990). While not confirmed, it is likely that the Windeby girl and Borre Fen III female also had some adipocere, but it seems unlikely that any noticeable deposits were present in Lindow II or III, Rendswühren man, Borre Fen I, Grauballe man, or the Tollund body.

In the case of Lindow II, while adipocere was not evident, Evershed and Connolly (1988:144) point out that the fatty acid composition of the muscle tissue "suggests that processes of microbial alteration, analogous to these involved in adipocere formation, were in evidence in Lindow Man at some stage of submergence and burial" (in the bog). Could it be that where brain tissue is preserved in a recognizable state, it is due to environmental factors (waterlogging or significant dampness in particular), which initiate the rapid degradation of brain lipids that are then responsible for the maintenance of brain form (even if there are significant histological changes)? There is clearly a need for experimental burial specifically to investigate the interesting enigma of brain preservation.

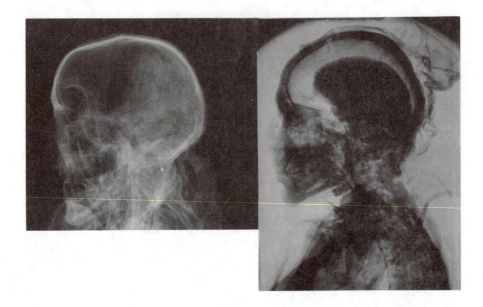

Figure 6.7 Lateral head X-rays of the Huldremose woman (left) and Tollund Man, showing brain preservation toward the back of the skull.

The Musculoskeletal System

The main frame of the body, the skeleton together with muscles and ligaments, is surprisingly variable in preservation. While soft tissues generally are most likely to be destroyed, bones may be relatively well preserved, as in the Zweeloo, Tollund, and Meenybraddan bodies (van der Sanden, 1995; Delaney and O'Floinn, 1995). In contrast, the Lindow II body had greatly reduced muscle and ligaments, modified cartilage, and bones which ranged from well-shaped (vertebrae) to collapsed and fragmenting (ulna and radius). In the majority of skeletons, bones and teeth are severely decalcified by the acid bog environment, and because most have been allowed to dry naturally, they display considerable shrinkage (as in the Zweeloo body and the Lindow I skull). Some, such as the Gallagh man (O'Floinn, 1995) and Huldremose woman (Brothwell, Liversage, and Gottlieb, 1990) appear to have retained much of their body size and proportions, or at least not display evidence of shrinkage.

In a number of instances the musculoskeletal system has largely decomposed, as in the Damendorf male (Glob, 1969), where only skin remained. Destruction of bone was mainly in terms of decalcification and collapse of the collagen infrastructure. Thus, although it has been well argued that *Sphagnum* peat has important preservative powers due to the tanning and antibiotic qualities of the polysaccharide sphagnan (Painter, 1991, 1995), there is some evidence that microbial damage does occur at times. In particular, bones of the hand of Lindow III (Figure 6.8) and part of a femur of Lindow II show punched-out lesions (Brothwell and Bourke, 1995). This could be the sequel to invasive microbial tunneling as studied by Bell, Skinner, and Jones (1996), and indeed they describe experimental work which included bacterial damage to bone from a waterlogged muskeg bog in British Columbia. Clearly, there is a need for further studies on microbial attack of bone and collagen (Child and Pollard, 1990) in bog bodies.

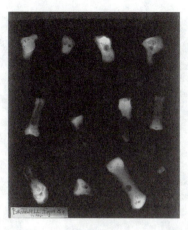

Figure 6.8 X-ray of Lindow III hand bones, showing the punched-out holes of postmortem origin.

Other Soft Tissues

As very few bog bodies have been submitted to CT scanning, our current knowledge of the survival of the lungs, heart, liver, blood vessels, kidneys, and reproductive systems is extremely limited. In the case of the Lindow II body, little intrathoracic or intra-abdominal soft tissue could be identified (Reznek, Hallett, and Charlesworth, 1986). In some contrast, in the Meenybraddan body, although individual organs had collapsed, shrunk, or been squashed during burial, nevertheless liver, and possibly lung, heart, and blood vessels were tentatively identified (Delaney and O'Floinn, 1995). Within the trunk, the evidence so far suggests that the intestinal tract, or part of it, is the most likely to survive. In one respect, this is fortunate, because food debris may remain — especially as fecal material — thus enabling some reconstruction of the food eaten before death (Helbaek, 1958; Holden, 1986, 1995).

Evidence of Trauma and Pathology

While establishing cause of death may be problematic in the case of recent deaths, it becomes far more so when the body has been immersed in water or buried for a substantial period of time. Nevertheless, there is, at times, evidence even in partially decomposed bodies of some trauma and pathology. Data available on peat-preserved bodies indicate that 20 males and 11 females display trauma (with 4 of unknown gender). This includes possible cuts and stab wounds, fractures, decapitation, furrows in the neck (linked to cords or rope for garroting or hanging), and other wounds. Much of the evidence is in the form of cuts or fractures, and in the case of the Huldremose woman, there are multiple wounds as well as an arm clearly cut off (Brothwell, Liversage, and Gottlieb, 1990). In contrast, the Grauballe male had his throat cut and the Borre Fen III (Figure 6.9) woman was severely beaten on the head and had a fractured right leg below the knee (Glob, 1969). Tollund man (Figure 6.10) and Borre Fen male were found with ropes still around their necks. The Lindow II man was struck twice on the head (Figure 6.11), had sinew twisted around the neck, received a deep cut on the right side of the neck, and suffered a fracture dislocation at the middle cervicals of the neck (West, 1986).

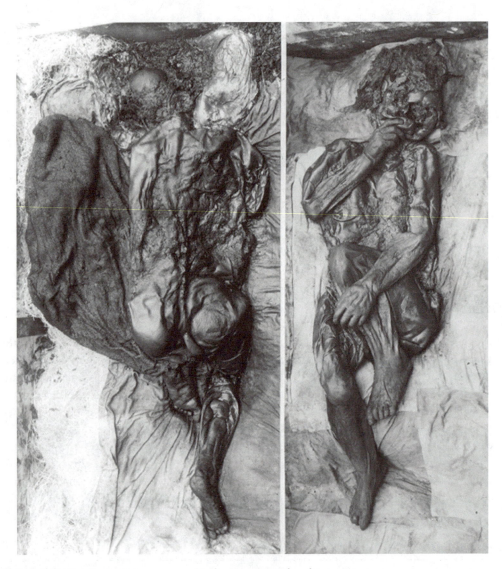

Figure 6.9 The Borre Fen woman, displaying severe head injuries.

In the case of pathology in general, surprisingly few bog bodies in the sample of 369 have been reported as showing anomalies. Eighteen males and eleven females, plus one of unknown gender, have been reported with some form of anomaly. As in the case of trauma, the pathology is mainly associated with fully adult individuals. There is a need to be aware of the possibility of pseudopathology in these human remains. In the case of the Huldremose woman, anomalous curvature of the bones of the forearm and femur was caused postmortem by decalcification and the pressure of wood within the peat (Figure 6.12).

Of the wide range of pathology that might potentially have been identified, it was only possible to divide the current evidence into five categories: Harris lines, arthropathy, oral pathology, miscellaneous, and congenital anomalies and endoparasites (helminths). The latter parasites were identified as worm eggs of the species *Trichuris trichiura* and

Figure 6.10 The head region of Tollund Man, with the rope still tight around the neck.

Figure 6.11 Scalp and skull injuries to the apex of Lindow Man's head.

Ascaris lumbricoides, one or both of which have been identified in seven peat bodies (Jones, 1986). Harris lines, an indication of some form of environmental stress, have been noted in only two individuals. Arthropathy, predominantly osteoarthritis, has been recorded so far in only six individuals, with Lindow II also displaying clear evidence of Schmorl's nodes in the lumbar region. Because radiological techniques are unlikely to pick up subclinical levels of infection, especially early periostitis, the eight cases of miscellaneous skeletal pathology must be seen as a minimum estimate. In fact, this category includes a case of sacral spina bifida and polydactyly. Oral pathology is the most commonly reported category, with eighteen individuals affected. In total, but excluding trauma, the pathology provides no evidence of the cause of death. This does not mean more pathology was not present in some of the bodies at death, but that taphonomic factors have since obscured the original changes.

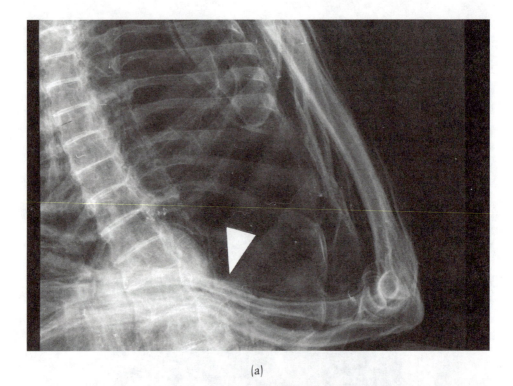

(a)

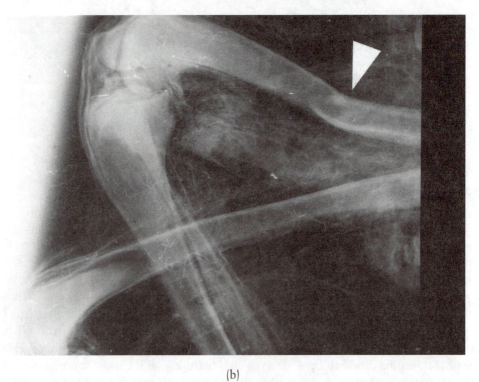

(b)

Figure 6.12 X-rays of the postmortem deformities to the forearm (a) and femur (b) of the Huldremose Woman.

References

Archibold, O.W.
    1995   *Ecology of World Vegetation*, Chapman & Hall, London.

Bell, L. S., M.F. Skinner, and S.J. Jones
    1996   The speed of post mortem change to the human skeleton and its taphonomic significance, *Forensic Science International* 82:129–140.

Brothwell, D.R.
    1996   European bog bodies: current state of research and preservation. In *Human Mummies: A Global Survey of Their Status and Techniques of Conservation,* edited by K. Spindler et al., pp. 161–172. Springer–Verlag, Vienna.

Brothwell, D. and J.B. Bourke
    1995   The human remains from Lindow Moss 1987–8. In *Bog Bodies, New Discoveries and New Perspectives*, edited by R. Turner and R. Scaife, pp. 52–58. British Museum Press, London.

Brothwell, D., D. Liversage, and B. Gottlieb
    1990   Radiographic and forensic aspects of the female Huldremose body. *Journal of Danish Archaeology* 9:157–178.

Brown, D.A.
    1995   Carbon cycling in peat and the implications for the rehabilitation of bogs. In *Wetlands Archaeology and Nature Conservation*, edited by M. Cox, V. Straker, and D. Taylor, pp. 99–107. HMSO, London.

Child, A. and M. Pollard
    1990   Microbial attack on collagen. *Archaeometry* 32:617–625.

Delaney, M. and R. O'Floinn
    1995   A bog body from Meenybraddan Bog, County Donegal, Ireland. In *Bog Bodies, New Discoveries and New Perspectives*, edited by R. Turner and R. Scaife, pp. 123–132. British Museum Press, London.

Evershed, R. and R. Connolly
    1988   Lipid preservation in Lindow Man. *Naturwissenschaften* 75:143–145.

Glob, P.V.
    1969   *The Bog People. Iron-Age Man Preserved*, Faber & Faber, London.

Helbaek, H.
    1958   Grauballemandens sidste måltid, *Kuml*, Aarhus, 83–116.

Holden, T.G.
    1986   Preliminary report on the detailed analysis of the macroscopic remains from the gut of Lindow Man. In *Lindow Man, The Body in the Bog*, edited by I. Stead, J. Bourke, and D. Brothwell, pp. 116–125. British Museum Press, London.

    1995   The last meals of the Lindow bog men. In *Bog Bodies, New Discoveries and New Perspectives*, edited by R. Turner and R. Scaife, pp. 76–82. British Museum Press, London.

Jones, A.K.
    1986   Parasitological investigations on Lindow Man. In *Lindow Man, The Body in the Bog*, edited by I. Stead, J. Bourke, and D. Brothwell, pp. 136–139. British Museum Press, London.

Landweer, G.J.
    1906   Twee Oud-Germaansche lijken uit Let Weerdingerveen, *Eigen Haard* 597–600.

O'Floinn, R.
    1995   Recent research into Irish bog bodies. In *Bog Bodies, New Discoveries and New Perspectives*, edited by R. Turner and R. Scaife, pp. 137–145. British Museum Press, London.

Painter, T.J.
  1991   Lindow Man, Tollund Man and other peat-bog bodies: the preservative and antimicrobial action of *Sphagnum*, a reactive glycuronoglycan with tanning and sequestering properties, *Carbohydrate Polymers* 15:123–142.

  1995   Chemical and microbiological aspects of the preservation process in *Sphagnum* peat. In *Bog Bodies, New Discoveries and New Perspectives*, edited by R. Turner and R. Scaife, pp. 88–99. British Museum Press, London.

Pyatt, F., E. Beaumont, P. Buckland, D. Lacy, and D. Storey
  1991a An examination of the mobilisation of elements from the skin and bone of the bog body Lindow II and a comparison with Lindow III, *Environmental Geochemistry and Health* 13:153–159.

Pyatt, F., E. Beaumont, D. Lacy, J. Magilton, and F. Buckland
  1991b Non isatis sed vitrum or, the color of Lindow Man *Oxford Journal of Archaeology* 10:61–73.

Reznek, R., M. Hallett, and M. Charlesworth
  1986   Computed tomography of Lindow Man. In *Lindow Man, the Body in the Bog*, edited by I.M. Stead, J. Bourke, and D. Brothwell, pp. 63–65. British Museum Press, London.

van der Sanden, W.A.B.
  1995   Bog bodies on the continent: developments since 1965, with special reference to The Netherlands. In *Bog Bodies, New Discoveries and New Perspectives*, edited by R. Turner and R. Scaife, pp. 146–165. British Museum Press, London.

West, I.E.
  1986   Forensic aspects of Lindow Man. In *Lindow Man, the Body in the Bog*, edited by I. M. Stead, J. Bourke, and D. Brothwell, pp. 77–80. British Museum Press, London.

The Effect of Cultivation on Buried Human Remains

7

WILLIAM D. HAGLUND
MELISSA CONNOR
DOUGLAS D. SCOTT

Contents

0-8493-1189-6/02/$0.00+$1.50
© 2002 by CRC Press LLC

Figure 7.1 Two-row moldboard plow.

Introduction

Archaeologists deal with sites in cultivated areas on a regular basis (Ammerman, 1978, 1985; Frink, 1984; Lewarch and O'Brien, 1981; Odell and Cowan, 1987; Roper, 1976; Yorston et al., 1990). In fact, plowing exposes subsurface archaeological sites by bringing remains to the surface. Because of this, archaeologists study how far material in an agricultural field is moved by cultivation activities and how deep the material is affected. This chapter outlines crop planting and other agricultural activities that affect buried material, discusses the relevant archaeological studies, and then presents a case study.

Machines for Power Farming

The tasks necessary to cultivate a field have been the same for millennia, although the technologies used to complete those tasks have grown increasingly powerful. The basic tasks are primary tillage (to aerate and loosen the soil), seedbed refining (breaking up lumps and clods), fertilizer application, planting and seeding, weed, insect and pest control, and harvesting (Stone and Gulvin, 1977). Some activities, such as primary tillage, affect subsurface remains more directly than others, such as harvesting. Other activities involve applying chemical substances to the soil, which may affect soil chemistry.

Primary Tillage

The purpose of primary tillage is to aerate and loosen the soil. This prepares a suitable seedbed, destroys competitive weeds, and improves the soil's physical condition (Smith and Wilkes, 1976). The implement most commonly used for tillage is the plow. There are moldboard plows, disc plows, subsoil plows, disc tiller plows, and rotary tillers. The most common plow for primary tillage is the single moldboard plow (Figure 7.1), which comes in two main groups that are relevant for this discussion. One-way plows throw the soil in one direction at all times. On two-way plows, the bottoms can be replaced with a set that turns the soil the opposite way. So at the end of the field, the tractor turns around,

Figure 7.2 Disc plow. When the plow is in use, the first set of discs (vertically oriented) come toward the viewer and align with discs on the bottom.

mechanically reverses the plow bottoms, and plows into the furrow made on the last traverse. Common furrows made by moldboard plows are 14 to 16 in. across, with a depth of less than half their width.

A double moldboard plow, also called a lister or middlebuster, does not turn the soil to the side, and so only forms ridges and furrows. It does not till all the soil, as the area between furrows is not turned over. The advantage is that a larger area of land can be prepared more quickly. For our purposes, it is worth noting that not all the soil in the plow zone is moved using this type of plow.

The disc plow (Figure 7.2) is becoming a competitor of the moldboard plow particularly in many areas of the United States. The blades on a disc plow are usually set at an angle, and it depends on the weight of the disc and the angle for soil penetration. The soil is cut and moved with a rolling action, mixing the soil. The disc plow can be used with scrapers which help to invert the soil, although seldom as well as with a moldboard plow. Disc plows, however, do work in adverse soil conditions where a moldboard plow may become bogged down.

Soil cultivated regularly over a number of years becomes very compact from the heavy machinery running over it. This can make some soils impervious to water below the plow zone. In these cases, heavy subsoil plows are used to break up the soil at a deeper level than the normal plow. Subsurface plows are designed to penetrate the soil as much as 20 to 36 in. (Figure 7.3). There are even deeper plows, called giant plows, designed to bring up soil from depths of as much as 2 to 6 ft (Smith and Wilkes, 1976:146). These are used in areas where fill or flood deposits have covered better soil. Use of the giant plow is infrequent.

Primary tillage is probably the major culprit in disturbing subsurface material. The common moldboard plow disturbs objects to a depth of 7 to 10 in. below the surface, inverting the soil, and moving it sideways from its original position. Subsurface plowing breaks up the soil at depths of 20 to 36 in. The plowing itself may not move material to the surface, but breaking up the soil makes objects in the soil subject to movement through the repeated freezing and thawing of moisture in the soil, as well as insect and rodent activity.

Figure 7.3 Subsurface chisel plow. Man and dog on right for scale.

Seedbed Refining

This is also called secondary tillage and basically consists of stirring the soil at shallow depths to further pulverize the soil, cut up crop residue, and destroy weeds on fallow lands. Harrows are a common implement for this step and can be divided into the descriptively named disc, spike-tooth, and spring-tooth harrows. The spike-tooth harrow has a series of teeth that resemble spikes and commonly stir the soil to a depth of about two in. Spring-tooth harrows have curved teeth that penetrate to a greater depth than spike-toothed harrows. The disc harrow is by far the most common. It cuts small furrows with the front edge of the concave disc cutting the soil and stalks with the back edge acting as a moldboard, throwing the soil to the side (Stone and Gulvin, 1977:192).

Pulverizers add the finishing touch to the seedbed, crushing lumps and compacting the soil after plowing or harrowing. The common V-shaped roller pulverizer consists of a number of wheels strung on a shaft commonly pulled behind the tractor. The wheels may have plain, wavy, or serrated edges, or have sprockets attached.

Fertilizer Application

Fertilizers come in the form of liquid, gases, and solids, and application methods are even more diverse. The machinery for spreading solid fertilizer commonly simply rolls over the soil spreading the fertilizer on the top and depending on water to move the nutrients into the roots and seeds.

Planting and Seeding

Planters deposit seeds evenly over the ground surface and cover each seed with soil. They may have a furrow opener, a hopper and drop mechanism for the seeds, and a furrow coverer (Figure 7.4). There are multiple types of furrow openers, depending on the seed and soil type. They can either plant at a constant depth throughout the field or at a variable depth, depending on the soil and the crop. The same is true for furrow coverers that can cover the seed with a light soil cover or a deeper one, depending on the soil and crop. Seeders may also have a fertilizer attachment that will sow fertilizer along with the seed. Finally, another attachment that also moves soil and material in the soil is a bar marker.

Figure 7.4 Planter. Note plastic hoppers for seeds and discs for furrow openers.

Figure 7.5 Cultivator. Arrow-shaped tillers followed by harrow teeth are moved between the crop rows to destroy the weeds.

These drop at the side of the seeder to mark the edge of the last row planted so that the tractor driver can easily follow the edge of the row back to the end of the field.

Planting and seeding devices operate a much shallower depth than plows. Their impact on bone and evidence in the soil mainly will be to subject material near the surface to yet another yearly instance of being pulverized, dragged, and compacted by heavy equipment.

Weed, Insect, and Pest Control

The war on weeds is carried out by cultivators that stir the soil, burning, chemicals, or laying plastic strips between the rows. The mechanical cultivator can be at the front or rear of the tractor and tills the ground between the crop rows (Figure 7.5). As with the seeders, there are various types of cultivators for different soils and crops, but they operate at a shallow depth relative to the plows.

Flame cultivators can also be mounted on a tractor, and consist of a fuel tank, feed lines, control valves, and burners. The concept is that the plants to be cultivated are larger and woodier than weeds, and the weeds will burn first. While this system doesn't move the soil it, too, could be detrimental to surficial bone and evidence by charring or burning either or both. Chemical measures to control weeds, insects, and pests are frequently applied by sprayers or dusters and do not mechanically impact material in the soil.

Harvesting

Harvesting equipment can be very crop specific: mowing machines, rakes, and balers for hay; the combine (harvester-thresher) for grains; specialized corn harvesters; cotton strippers; cotton pickers; sugar-cane harvesters; tobacco harvesting machines; and root crop (potato, sweet potato, beet, peanut) harvesters. Root crop harvesters are the machines with the most impact to the soil, usually having a blade running deep enough to scoop up the crop. They differ from other machinery in that they merely separate the crop from the soil.

Impact of Cultivation on Buried Materials

Soil in a cultivated field is plowed, pulverized, crushed, fertilized, aerated, compacted, burned, and thrown into a harvester. Overall, these activities have a high potential to be detrimental to the investigation of buried remains. Archaeologists have completed a number of studies on cultivation of archaeological sites and how it affects their ability to reconstruct past human activities at a site (Ammerman, 1978, 1985; Frink, 1984; Lewarch and O'Brien, 1981; Odell and Cowan, 1987; Roper, 1976; Yorston et al., 1990). As this is directly relevant to the ability to reconstruct the activities at a clandestine burial, these studies will be briefly summarized.

Chemical Changes

The local chemical environment is one of the major factors affecting the decomposition of human remains (Gill-King, 1997). Chemicals added to fields include fertilizers, pesticides, and herbicides. Commercial fertilizers are usually composed primarily of oxygen, nitrogen, and phosphorus with traces of a number of other elements. Organic fertilizers, such as manure, have high amounts of organic material and bacteria, as well. These are usually spread on, or near, the ground surface, and target the nutrients toward the level of the plant roots, where many are absorbed. The chemicals do penetrate further into the soil, usually as surface water moves through the soil into the groundwater. It is likely that many fertilizers accelerate the decomposition of soft tissue by providing nutrients for bacterial growth.

The chemical composition of pesticides and herbicides is widely variable with over 30 companies producing over 150 brand names of herbicide applications (Smith and Wilkes, 1976). The variability of these compounds makes it impossible to give a blanket statement about their effects on buried human remains. If any chemical tests are planned on the remains, then soil samples, as described below, should be collected.

Detailed chemical analyses of a number of these compounds, particularly pesticides, can be found on the Internet. The U.S. Department of Agriculture operates a web site (http://www.arsusda.gov/rsml/ppdb3) that lists pesticides and their molecular formulas, physical state (gas, solid, liquid), water solubility, and field dissipation half-life. Other web sites include ChemFinder (http://www.chemfinder.camsoft.cam/), EXTOXNET (http://www.ace.ace.orst.edu/info/extoxnet), and Spectrum (http://www.speclab.com/compound/chemabc.htm).

The interaction of soil and bone chemical constituents is a process called diagenesis. The chemical composition of bone reflects the diet of the individual; thus, archaeologists are interested in bone chemistry and the interaction of soil and bone chemistry. Much of this body of literature is summarized by Whitmore and others who include a summary table of postmortem impact on bone by various elements (Table 5.2, Whitmore et al., 1989:220–239). For forensic purposes, it is sufficient to note that, given a generally basic soil pH, bone can be found in soil after tens of thousands of years. Should the investigator wish to complete any chemical testing on the remains, samples of the soil adjacent to the body should be taken. These will give the chemists an idea of the postdepositional environment of the remains and potential diagenetic conflicts with the test results.

The first step in taking a soil sample is rinsing the implement (usually a trowel) with which the sample will be taken in water, preferably distilled water, in order to prevent contamination of the sample with other elements or soil. The first several millimeters of soil on the exposed surface are then scraped away, again in order to avoid contamination, and about 1.5 cups of soil placed in a clean plastic Ziploc™ bag. This bag is closed and placed in a second, labeled Ziploc™ bag. A piece of paper labeled with the provenience information can also be placed between the two plastic bags and provides the needed information if the labeling on the bag becomes smeared or wiped off. The location of the sample should be placed on the scene map. Two or three of these samples from different areas around the body will normally be sufficient. The sample should be stored in a refrigerator to prevent growth of molds or fungi.

Mechanical Changes

Plow zone studies follow three general lines of inquiry: (1) interpretation of surface collections and their relationships to their original locations; (2) displacement of artifacts both horizontally (lateral) and vertically; and (3) damage to the material from cultivation activities. These studies have been pursued through actual archaeological sites, experimental models, and computer simulations. Some authors concluded that the effects of cultivation are minimal (Odell and Cowan, 1987; Roper, 1976), while others contend this is a rather sanguine and complacent stance (Yorston et al., 1990). Nevertheless, cultivation can affect the site at the feature, artifact, or attribute level.

Surface Collections and Their Relationship to Subsurface Materials

Surface collections have long been used as a guide to locating subsurface materials and as a sample of what materials are at a site (Redman and Watson, 1970). Surface assessments are less expensive than excavation to carry out and, relative to excavation, require much less time and resource investment. Additionally, surface assessment minimizes disturbance to the site. Although the dislocation of artifacts moved by the plow disrupts spatial relationships of artifacts within the plow zone, Roper (1976:374) claims, "Archaeologists working in areas of intensive agricultural activity should be able to use surface scatter as a reliable indicator of subsurface distributions."

The relationship between surface artifacts and subsurface feature or artifact distribution is rarely straightforward (Yorston et al., 1990). Surface representation is subject to change from one bout of tillage to another and artifacts or bones recovered from the surface represent only a fraction of the subsurface assemblage (Ammerman, 1985). Lewarch and O'Brien (1981) originally estimated surface-to-subsurface assemblage ratios to represent 1 in 20. They later adjusted this estimate to less than 10% (1981). An elegant study (Odell and Cowan, 1987) confirmed a mean surface representation of 6.63%, close to the 1 to 20 figure given by Lowarch. Other estimates have ranged up to 15–16% (Reynolds, 1982), and 15% (Frink, 1984) of artifacts in the plow zone are seen on the surface. However, Reynold's experimental design has been criticized because of the lack of variability in the shape and size of artifacts collected. Additional findings suggest that artifacts within the plow zone have a probability of reappearing on the surface every 6 or 7 years.

Both experimental studies and archaeological materials studies suggest that the greatest concentration of surface material will be near the original site (Odell and Cowan, 1987; Redman and Watson, 1970; Yorston et al., 1990). Based on these studies, a potential investigative strategy used to look for a specific subsurface feature, such as a grave, is to mark all surface remains with a pin flag. Rain washes surface artifacts, making them more visible. A similar effect might be expected from irrigation. Intense summer light increases surface reflection and visibility of surface artifacts; however, it is best first to look at horizontal displacement of materials and excavate the area where the concentration is greatest.

More studies have been completed on the horizontal, rather than vertical, movement of artifacts in the plow zone. The dominant direction of displacement is in the direction of tillage activity (Nartov, 1979; Odell and Cowen, 1987). Movement is most prominent in first passes and artifacts are affected to a lesser degree with successive tillage; however, the directional change is cumulative. When the tillage pattern is reversed from year to year (i.e., the plow is used in the opposite direction), the artifact movement is reversed. There is relatively little transverse flow of materials across furrows (Nartov, 1979).

Spurious clusters can be created by lifting the plow or disc, thus either skipping artifacts or dropping all the artifacts rather than spreading them out. Differences in the topography of the field can also cause artifacts to cluster as they may be harder to drag upslope and may travel downhill with soil erosion. Potential displacement is greatest on slopes, where the downhill movement of material is assisted by rain and drainage. In a cultivated field, it is likely that part of the year there will be vegetation on the slope and part of the year there will not. Vegetation does inhibit downslope movement (Rick, 1976).

Vertical dislocation of material in the plow zone is less studied; however, it appears that larger artifacts are more abundantly represented at the surface relative to their proportion in the total population (Ammerman and Feldman, 1978). Over time, fragment size on the surface becomes more heterogeneous as the plow fractures breakable material. The distance that bones and artifacts are moved from the original location is influenced by the size of the element or artifact, the duration and direction of tillage, and the topography of the field.

Modification of Bone

As buried deposits are disrupted by tillage practices the material is subject to mechanical abrasion and breakage. Fresh bone breaks differently than older, dry bone and as bone dries out, it will be more subject to fracture. Compaction of the soil as heavy machinery rolls over subsurface, or surface, elements may lead to fracturing of elements. This will occur not only during the plowing, or primary field tillage, but any time that machinery is run over the field. After harvest, cows or other animals are frequently allowed to graze in fields, and this will subject the surficial elements to trampling as well as being run over by farm machinery.

Bones in the plow zone are subject to sharp and blunt force modification by machinery, which can result in simple breaks or, in very dry bone, splintering. Abrasion can also occur on bones through direct contact with the agricultural machinery, or through contact with other cultural or natural inclusions in the surrounding soil matrix as movement initiated by the machinery occurs.

Once exposed to the surface, the skeletal elements begin to weather; in other words, they are affected by the combination of sunlight, temperature differentials, and moisture. Exposure to the sun and heat from the sunlight will dry the bone and bleach it. As small fractures occur in the bone, moisture will seep into them and expand as the temperatures lower, causing weather "checking" or exfoliation of the material. These factors destabilize the bone and cause accelerated decomposition. Skeletal elements exposed to the surface for a greater period of time should have a lighter color, less grease (be dryer and lighter), and may show variations in, and exfoliation of, the periosteal material.

Impact of Cultivation on Recovering Buried or Surface Remains

Cultivation activities can displace skeletal elements and evidence vertically and horizontally from their original position. They can fracture bone into increasingly smaller pieces, hence increasing exposure that accelerates weathering and decomposition.

Plowing, tilling, and other cultivation activities may disperse remains within the plow zone from their primary resting places, and through repeated tillage episodes redistribute previously displaced materials. The plowing process may break up and mar bones. The overall impact of cultivation will depend upon the depth of the burial, the soil type, the crops grown, the cultivation strategy, and the number of episodes of cultivation that the land has undergone. It is also dependent upon the length of the postmortem interval and the condition of the remains.

Case Example

A four-person forensic team was deployed to Cyprus in 1997 to investigate a potential gravesite for the remains of an American of Greek-Cypriot ancestry. The man disappeared during the military events of August, 1974 when the Republic of Cyprus was torn by military conflict resulting in the partition of Cyprus into a Greek southern portion and a Turkish northern portion. During the military activity, the Turkish Army and Turkish Cypriot Militia arrested many Greek males ages 15 to 50. Turkish Cypriot militia units were given the responsibility of guarding the prisoners.

The missing person was a 17-year old American citizen of Greek-Cypriot descent who was arrested by two Turkish militiamen at his home August 20, 1974. Also arrested was his sister's 23-year-old fiancé, a Greek Cypriot. According to information gathered by investigators, the two men were taken to a detention camp situated near agricultural fields several kilometers from the nearest town. No trace of either man has been found since they were last seen at the camp.

On a humanitarian basis, the United States government, in 1981, supported the formation of a tripartite Committee on Missing Persons (CMP) under the auspices of the

Figure 7.6 View of site area to east. Excavations are over the area of the bone concentration. Trees on the right side of the photograph mark the small rise with the well in the center.

United Nations. The CMP, comprised of a Greek Cypriot, a Turkish Cypriot, and an international member, accumulated a great deal of information about the missing of 1974. United States Public Law 103-372 was passed October 1994 mandating "the investigation of the whereabouts of the United States citizens and others missing from Cyprus since 1974." Pursuant to the law, an investigative team under the direction of Ambassador Robert S. Dillon (retired) and Investigator Edward L. Lee II began work in 1995. Their report concluded that five Americans were missing from 1974. Four were elderly and probably dead (Dillon and Lee, 1995). The fifth man, the subject of this discussion, was 17 years old in 1974 and was considered missing and probably dead.

During the recent investigation, informants were interviewed. They were able to describe the location of the detention camp, the last place the missing man was known to be alive. Comparing this statement with previous interviews of two soldiers and other corroborating evidence, Ambassador Dillon's team felt the story was credible and recommended an effort to recover the remains. In 1997, the Turkish Cypriot Member of the CMP requested technical assistance from the U.S. government to locate the remains. The mission described here was the result.

The Site

When the technical team arrived they were told the site was purportedly near two wells and large bushes. The team was taken to the general area located in a microenvironment that matched the description. A large mound, built around a limestone cut-block well shaft and an island of vegetation which included a eucalyptus tree, very large yucca-type plants and large fern-type plants, marked the site area (Figure 7.6). A smaller mound between the well and the road consisted of straw-filled mud and probably marked the site of a former mud brick structure. A second well was approximately 100 m west of the first. Eucalyptus trees lined the road to the west of the well and a stand of approximately five olive trees lined the north side of the road to the west. Clothing, water bottles, and aluminum cans were hanging or placed in the trees, apparently by the field workers. A general scatter of trash had accumulated around the tree area. A variety of ceramics in the immediate area around the well and the tree area suggested that a relatively recent archaeological site was present as well.

The fields on either side of the road were planted in barley at the time of the investigation. The barley was in its early growth stage, and ground visibility in the fields was approximately 80%. The edges of the fields and the mound around the well were covered in a dense stand of clover and ground visibility was closer to 10% in those areas. The team gained better visibility by working on their hands and knees and either pulling the clover up or cutting it off at ground level.

Methods

The initial method of investigation was a visual observation of the site surface. The four-member forensic team lined up at approximately 1.5-m intervals and walked successive parallel transects in a north and south direction covering an area approximately 100 m north to south by 65 m east. As bones or other potential evidence were identified, each location was marked with a surveyor pin flag.

The visual inventory identified human tarsals on the surface in the first pass across the relatively flat agricultural field. Unassociated fragments of cloth and foot apparel were also found. The area immediately surrounding the well contained a moderately dense surface concentration of modern domestic trash, including ceramic shards, tin cans, aluminum foil, and other metallic debris. These items were undoubtedly associated with agricultural and pastoral activities conducted on the site.

The open well was examined by lowering team leader Haglund to the bottom on a stout rope. The well was dry and approximately 10 m deep. Skeletal remains of a domestic sheep were found as were tree branches and decomposing vegetation, but no human remains were observed.

After completing the visual inventory of the field, a metal detecting inventory was begun. The metal detecting effort, using a White's Classic SL with an 11.5-in. coil, was concentrated in an area measuring 25 m north to south by 30 m east to west and around the area where human bones were found. Sweeps were made in an east to west direction with overlapping transects to insure as complete a coverage as possible. The soils and rocks proved to contain minerals that affected the detector's sensitivity. The detector was tuned to eliminate the mineralized soil and rocks. The metal detecting identified approximately 30 additional surface and buried targets in the search area. Each target was flagged as it was identified. After completing the initial metal detector search the targets were excavated and examined.

The same metal detector was used to examine the targets. A smaller coil (4-in. diameter) was used to pinpoint the metal targets. Each target was dug with a 4-in. mason's pointing trowel by scraping away the earth until the object was encountered. Each target was examined and identified by an archaeologist. All metallic targets were domestic trash including tin cans, a large iron hook, and fragments of various metal containers. No bullets, cartridge cases, or other items potentially related to causes of death or identification were encountered.

Following the metal detector inventory, the pin flags marking human bone, shoes, or pieces of cloth were individually numbered or lettered, and the associated remains mapped and collected. An east–west baseline was established to facilitate mapping using standard

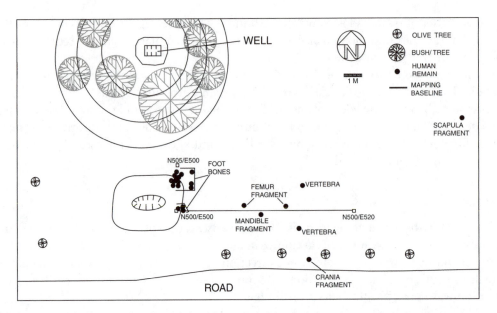

Figure 7.7 Site map showing distribution of recovered bones and bone fragments. (The rectangle and the oval within it mark the mound of a former mud brick structure.)

triangulation techniques. All flagged items were entered on the site map (Figure 7.7) and placed in a bag or envelope with the corresponding number or letter.

The surface distribution of skeletal elements suggested that it was most likely that the original grave was near the concentration of bone at the west side of the site (Figure 7.7). So, two team members established Excavation Unit 1 (initially 2 m wide and 4 m long) oriented along the axis of a concentrated distribution of human tarsals and metatarsals. The unit and all subsequent excavation units were excavated by hand using shovels, trowels, brushes, bamboo excavation tools, and other standard archaeological tools. All fill was screened through a 1.0 cm × 0.5 cm wire mesh screen. The units were excavated down to undisturbed sterile subsoil to insure no human bone, grave features, or other cultural manifestations were missed.

Approximately 11 m² around the bone concentration was hand excavated in the manner described above. Excavation extended below the plow zone so that the excavator could identify any discontinuities in the soil. Such a discontinuity could have indicated a grave. An additional 4 m², in two 2 m × 1 m strips, was shoveled past the depth of the soil disturbed by the plow to look for further remains and examine the soil for discontinuities. None were found.

At this point, the forensic team requested the use of a backhoe or front-end loader. The machine, a Massey-Ferguson tractor with backhoe and front-end loader, was provided. The entire area between the well and the road was graded well below the depth of soil disturbed by the plow. A cement floor, approximately 2 m × 3 m, was encountered at a depth of approximately 30 cm below the surface of a low earth mound. A few pieces of cut limestone and numerous pieces of unshaped limestone were laid over the edges of the cement floor. These formed a rock foundation for mud brick walls that had nearly completely eroded away. The feature may have been a small house, a pump house, or a capped well. The backhoe was used to remove the cement floor in an effort to ascertain if anything

Table 7.1   Inventory of Recovered Skeletal Remains

Skeletal Remains Collection Number	Element	Condition
1	Right calcaneus	Complete, stained
2	Left 3rd metatarsal	Complete
6	Femoral shaft fragment	Fragment
7	Right navicular and right proximal; 2nd phalange	
8	Right cuboid and right middle cuneiform	Complete
9	Right proximal 1st phalange	Bleached, surface erosion
	Femoral shaft fragment[a]	Fragment
11	Parietal bone fragment	Fragment
12b	Mandibular condyle	Fragment
13	Partial upper thoracic vertebra	Fragment
14	2nd cervical vertebra	Bleached, weathered, complete
10	Femoral shaft fragment[a]	Bleached, longitudinal cracks, spalled cortex
16	Left 4th metatarsal	Complete
17–20	Left middle phalanges 1–4 and left distal 1st phalanges	
	Complete	
21	Left 2nd metatarsal	Complete
22	Right 1st metatarsal	Complete
24	Left 1st metatarsal	Complete
25	Right talus	Complete
26	Right 2nd metatarsal	Complete
27	Left distal scapula fragment (inclusive of glenoid fossa, coracoid process, and distal inferior border)	Irregular fractured margins; bleached, longitudinal cracks; some spalling
16 and 23	Left 5th metatarsals	Distal ends missing
17–20	Left middle phalanges 2 through 5	Complete

[a] Femoral fragments 6 and 10 conjoined to form 23-cm length of lateral femoral shaft.
Note: Missing numbers were collected, nonskeletal materials.

was present below the structural feature; only natural clay soil was present. The grading continued around the south, east, and west sides of the well. An area 12 m east to west and 15 m north to south (between the road and the well) was excavated to depths ranging from 1 m to 2 m. No evidence of cultural features was noted. The unexcavated plowed field was also reinventoried and one additional human bone, a fragment of the glenoid region of a left scapula, was located, mapped, and collected.

In all, over two dozen human skeletal elements and fragmented bones were recovered (Table 7.1). Their distribution is shown in Figure 7.7. Except for undisturbed right and left foot elements found *in situ*, the majority of the bones and bone fragments were recovered from the surface. Elements of the upper body (crania, scapula, and vertebra) were furthest from undisturbed foot bones at the eastern extreme of the bone distribution.

Osteological Examination

Differential weathering of the skeletal elements collected from the surface suggests that they were exposed for varying lengths of time for intervening periods from 1974. The extremely weathered long bone shaft and scapular fragments lay exposed during several seasons, although, because of their small size and the irregularities of the ground surface, their exposure would not have been as total as complete bones. Elements of the right ankle were probably exposed during more recent cultivation activities. Other elements were found within the plow zone but were unexposed and probably most recently disturbed from a burial.

Morphologically, these skeletal remains represented the remains of a minimum of one individual of undetermined sex. The maturity of the remains suggested an individual of at least late adolescent to young adult age at time of death. Based on the size, articulation, and other common factors, the left and right tarsals and metatarsals were definitely from the same individual. Identification was based on mitochondrial DNA analysis. However, the remainder of the bones (6, 10, 11, 12b, 13, 14, and 27) could represent one or more additional individuals of approximately the same age and build.

Site Analysis

No soil discontinuity indicative of a grave was discovered. The human remains were scattered a maximum distance of 32 m east to west and 14 m north to south. The left and right foot elements were in a cluster less than 4 m in diameter, and in association were several fragments of simulated brown leather foot apparel. These shoe fragments are of lightweight construction consistent with a house slipper, although they were too fragmentary for definitive identification.

The remains were in, and adjacent to, a field sown in barley. The machines observed in the area cultivating the fields were medium-powered farm (60 to 75 horse power) tractors (Culpin, 1975:4–7). Some cultivation machinery was observed in operation and others were seen sitting at the edge of fields. No moldboard plows were observed, but harrows and discs were seen on several occasions. This was probably because the crop was past the stage of primary tillage. Six- to eight-row seed grain drills were observed that combined a small plow or subsoiler to cut the furrow, the device to drop the seed in the furrow, and harrows or discs to cover the seed to a uniform depth (Culpin, 1975:96). The machinery observed would turn the soil to a 7 to 10 in. depth, consistent with the depth of the plow zone observed in the excavations at the well site.

The linear distribution of the skull, vertebrae, scapula, and femur fragments was consistent with cultivation activities over a number of seasons. The disarticulation and mixing of the right and left foot elements were also consistent with disturbance from the primary burial context due to plowing and related activities. The presence of the broken and disarticulated human bones across the field suggested the original burial location was nearby and probably relatively shallow. The burial site was probably somewhere within the low mound south of the rock-lined well, and subsequent agricultural activities over the ensuing 23 years dispersed the remains and obliterated the grave itself.

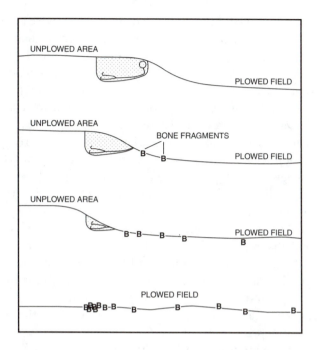

Figure 7.8 Model of burial destroyed by cultivation activities.

A model the authors propose for the distribution of the remains is described in Figure 7.8. The grave may originally have been shallow and outside the area then cultivated. Over time, possibly as the remnants of the deteriorated mud brick wall became plowable, the farmer expanded the area plowed and began to catch portions of the burial in the equipment. The larger bones were moved furthest and survived longest. The cranial vault was crushed into smaller pieces, one of which was pushed to the side of the field where we found it. Many of the smaller bones were probably pulverized in secondary tilling or cultivating. The feet were either deepest or furthest from the plowed area, but appear to have been the last elements brought to the surface.

Human Remains from Cultivated Areas: An Investigative Strategy

The burial of human remains within the depth of soil disturbed by the plow and other agricultural activities is not conducive to long-term preservation, or to the preservation of evidence to determine cause of death and identification. In the case example, the decedent was buried approximately 23 years before the investigation, and it is likely that no remains would have been found in another few years. The remains collected were not enough to determine cause of death. It was only luck, and access to extremely good DNA specialists, that allowed the investigators to collect remains from which DNA could be extracted and the identification made.

In this case example, due to political reasons, it was not possible to talk to the men who cultivated the land. However, a number of questions about the type of farming were relevant to the investigation. The type of crop grown, the type of plow and other field

equipment and fertilizer used, and the typical plowing pattern were agricultural information helpful to the investigation. The investigators had to rely on their own observations,
but it would have been much more informative to talk directly to the farmers.

During the first few months after burial, a depression is the best indicator of a grave
area, the sharpness of which may vary with the soil type. Postburial precipitation hastens
the formation of the depression. Rain, or irrigation, sufficient to dampen soil 2 to 3 ft
below the surface results in a depression. There should be visible cracks in the soil in the
grave depression that are wide (1 to 2 in.) and fairly deep (up to 10 in.), depending on
the soil type. Cultivation tends to mask the grave depression (Duncan, 1983:13). The best
chance of visually recognizing a depression in a cultivated area is directly after the area has
been plowed, disced, or harrowed. Subsoil may even have been inverted to the surface,
visually marking the disturbed area.

Talking to the field hands may determine whether they noticed a depression in the
field, or remembered that the wheels of the tractor sank into the ground at a certain
location (Duncan, 1983). Interviewing the field hands also would include outlining the
agricultural strategy. Hence, the number of inversions of the soil is important in determining the amount of potential disturbance. The pattern and direction of plowing are also
significant. Knowing the time since death and the cultivation usage the land has undergone
will focus the direction of searches.

The most successful search will be early in the growing season before the crop obscures
visibility. Rain washes the dust from objects on the surface and makes them easier to see,
so conducting the search directly after a rain also helps ensure success. Finally, the glare
from the sun is worst when it is directly overhead, and pieces in the ground are easiest to
see either early to mid-morning or mid-late afternoon.

The initial search in a plowed field should be conducted by a series of investigators
lined up shoulder-to-shoulder and walking the field in the direction of the furrows. Each
should carry surveyor pin flags and place one next to any potential piece of human remains
or evidence. Bone fragments are not easy to recognize in the dirt, and the search should
include an anthropologist or others with experience in recognizing dirty, fragmented bone
and determining whether it is human or animal.

When the investigators are sure all visible material has been flagged, a metal detector
should be used on the relevant area. This may lead to subsurface concentrations of material,
as well as to metal objects that were on the surface, but not spotted.

By this time, a pattern should be apparent in the placement of the pin flags. It will
probably be linear. There may be a concentration on one end of the line, as there was in
the case example. However, if the field has been plowed in different directions over the
years, the material may be more dispersed. The area with the greatest concentration of
materials should be hand excavated, as this suggests that it is the area closest to the original
subsurface feature. In any case, the soil should be removed below the depth disturbed by
the plow, in order to look for a soil disturbance consistent with a grave. Additional material
can be found by dividing the entire area containing remains into square units and shoveling
the soil, to the depth of the plow zone, through 1/4-in. hardware screen. Although
extremely laborious, this method will collect pieces of bone in the plow zone, but not
currently on the soil surface.

Conclusion

Recovery of human skeletal remains from areas that have been cultivated is enhanced by an understanding of cultivation practices and their potential impact on subsurface materials. Ideally, recovery strategy should involve interviews with those who participated in the cultivation activities. For disturbed graves, return site visits should be considered.

References

Ammerman, A.J.
   1985   Plow-zone experiments in Calabria, Italy, *Journal of Field Archaeology* 12:33–40.

Ammerman, A.J. and M.W. Feldman
   1978   Replicated collection of site surfaces, *American Antiquity* 43:734–740.

Culpin, C.
   1975   *Farm Machinery*, Granada Publishing, New York.

Dillon, R.S. and E.L. Lee
   1995   *The President's Report to Congress on the Investigation of the Whereabouts of the United States Citizens Who Have Been Missing from Cypress since 1974*, Office of Southern European Affairs, Department of State, Washington, D.C.

Duncan, J.
   1983   Excavation and Recovery, In *Handbook of Forensic Archaeology and Anthropology*, edited by D. Morse, J. Duncan, and J. Stoutamire, pp. 13–14. Rose Printing, Tallahassee, FL.

Frink, D.S.
   1984   Artifact behavior within the plow zone, *Journal of Field Archaeology* 11:356–363.

Gill-King, H.
   1997   Chemical and ultrastructural aspects of decomposition. In *Forensic Taphonomy: The Postmortem Fate of Human Remains*, edited by W.D. Haglund and M.H. Sorg, pp. 93–108. CRC Press, Boca Raton, FL.

Lewarch, D.E. and M.J. O'Brien
   1981   The expanding role of surface assemblages in archaeological research, *Advances in Archaeological Method and Theory* 4:297–342.

Nartov, P.S.
   1979   Movement of soil masses by working surfaces of spherical discs, *National Tillage Machinery Laboratory Report* NTML-WRG876, Auburn University, Alabama.

Odell, G.H. and F. Cowan
   1987   Estimating tillage effects on artifact distributions, *American Antiquity* 52:456–484.

Redman, C.L. and P.J. Watson
   1970   Systematic, intensive surface collection, *American Antiquity* 35:279–291.

Reynolds, P.J.
   1982   The plow zone, *Festschrift zum 100 Jahrigen Jubitaun der Abtelung der Naturhistorischen Gesellschaft*, Nürnberg. V. 315–341.

Rick, J.W.
   1976   Downslope movement and archaeological intrasite spatial analysis, *American Antiquity* 41:133–144.

Roper, D.
   1976   Lateral displacement of artifacts due to plowing, *American Antiquity* 41(3):372–375.

Smith, H.P. and L.H. Wilkes
   1976   *Farm Machinery and Equipment*, 6th ed., McGraw-Hill, New York.
Stone, A.A. and H.E. Gulvin
   1977   *Machines for Power Farming*, John Wiley & Sons, New York.
Whitmore, A.M. et al.
   1989   Stability or instability: the role of diffusion in trace element studies. In *Archaeological Method and Theory*, Vol. 1, edited by M.B. Schiffer, pp. 205–273. Academic Press, New York.
Yorston, R.M., V.L. Gaffney, and P.J. Reynolds
   1990   Simulation of artifact movement due to cultivation, *Journal of Archaeological Science* 17:67–83.

Detection and Recovery of Abducted and Murdered Children: Behavioral and Taphonomic Influences

8

ROBERT J. MORTON
WAYNE D. LORD

Contents

Introduction

Although child abduction/homicides comprise less than 1% of all murders (Hanfland et al., 1997), these cases are extremely high profile. Public and media attention is often overwhelming and national in scope. The value placed on children by families, communities, and entire societies often results in a greatly heightened public focus during child abduction cases. The overwhelming attention and concern generated when a child is abducted produce intense internal and external scrutiny during law enforcement investigations. Law enforcement agencies are routinely faced with strained resources, an immediate and intense demand for answers, and the seemingly insurmountable task of attempting to locate and safely return victims. In child abduction cases, the ability to rapidly locate, recover, and return victims to loved ones becomes crucial for the law enforcement community.

Child Abduction Prevalence

While the greatest number of child abduction cases (approximately 350,000) reported in the United States each year involve parental discord and custody disputes, approximately 100,000 attempted abductions by non-family members occur each year (Finkelhor et al., 1992). Most of these non-familial abductions are of short duration, are perpetrated by acquaintances, and involve varying degrees of sexual abuse. Fortunately, only about 200 to 300 non-family abductions involve the taking of the child for an extended period of time, the transportation of the child a significant distance from the place of contact, and the intent to keep, ransom, or kill the child. Annually within the United States, however, 40 to 150 children are abducted and killed by strangers (Hanfland et al., 1997). Homicide rates for infants and children (ages 0–4) have risen to their highest levels in 40 years. Finkelhor (1997) indicates that child homicides have risen 50% over the last 3 decades.

Child Abduction/Homicide Characteristics

Recently, two major studies have examined the characteristics of victims, offenders, and offenses in cases of child abduction and child homicide. Both studies revealed commonalities in the behaviors and methods employed by predators and their motivations.

In 1996, the FBI sponsored research into the epidemiology of child abduction and homicide, looking at 550 cases from 47 states, drawn from FBI files over a 10-year period (Boudreaux et al., 1999.) Cases in this study were drawn from the FBI's Violent Criminal Apprehension Program (VICAP), and the National Center for the Analysis (NCAVC). VICAP is a national database utilized by police agencies to link unsolved violent crimes. The NCAVC serves as the FBI's primary child abduction investigative and research entity. The parameters for case inclusion in the study were twofold. First, the victims were required to meet the federal definition of a child (0 to 17 years old). Second, cases were required to have been reported to the FBI as an abduction, suspected abduction, or murder with abduction originally suspected or reported. This study divided case data into four general categories: the offender, the victim, the offense, and remains disposal characteristics. The study categorized victims into seven age groups: neonates, infants, toddlers, preschool, elementary school, middle school, and high school. Offenses were divided into five motivations: sex, emotional, profit, infant replacement (maternal desire), and unknown motivation.

In 1997, The Washington State Attorney General's Office, working through a grant from the United States Department of Justice, Office of Juvenile Justice and Delinquency Prevention (OJJDP), published a Research Findings Report, titled "Case Management for Missing Children Homicide Investigation" (Hanfland et al.1997.) The study included 577 cases from 44 states, 621 victims, and 419 killers, including a mix of juvenile and adult victims. The study included cases involving adult victims only when they were part of serial crimes involving juvenile victims. Of the 621 victims, 562 were under 18 years of age. Cases were obtained through written requests sent to police departments nationwide. Case data were obtained through interviews conducted with police agencies having cases meeting the inclusion criteria. Case inclusion required the homicide of a victim (or victims) younger than 18 years old, that the case was worked by the police agency as an abduction, or that the case was a part of a homicide series in which at least one victim met the first two criteria. The study also compared features of all homicides to child abduction homicides.

Child Remains: Disposal, Discovery, and Distances

The results of both the FBI and Washington State studies included body disposal data concerning when, where, and how remains were disposed; the distances between the victim's residence, the abduction site, the murder site, and the body disposal site; and the degree and type of concealment.

In the FBI study, remains were disposed of in different scenarios depending upon the motivation of the offender and the age of the victim. These motivations had specific operational definitions. Infant replacement was defined as the abduction of a child with the intent of keeping the child. Emotional motivation included child abuse fatalities, child abuse fatalities resulting in parents claiming abduction (false allegation), revenge, retribution, and rage-based crimes. Sexual motivation required physical evidence of a sexual act, including visible trauma, and serology/DNA. Profit motivation included drug, robbery, and extortion cases. Unknown motivation included cases where the motivation was unclear or undetermined. (See Table 8.1).

In the neonate category (age 0–1 month), most of the victims were abducted for infant replacement reasons. This type of motivation comprised 79% of the cases. The offenders who were motivated by infant replacement were primarily female abductors. The victims were recovered alive in almost all the cases.

The remaining victims in neonate cases were killed for emotional reasons by biological parents. These victims were usually killed in their residences. They were disposed of 1 to 5 miles from their residences in 67% of the cases. The remainder of these victims were disposed of at their residences.

In the infant category (age 1–12 months), the victims were killed for emotional reasons in a majority of the cases. The offender was always a family member, usually the biological parents. The victims were typically killed in their residences and primarily disposed of within 5 miles (83%). The remaining victims were disposed of 5 to 10 miles from their residences (17%).

Table 8.1   Distance Between Victim's Residence and Body Disposal Site

Age of Child	Distance					
	< 100 yards	< 1 mile	1–5 miles	6–10 miles	11–30 miles	> 30 miles
0–1 month	—	—	67%	—	—	—
1–12 months	—	—	83%	—	—	—
13–36 months	—	56%	—	22%	—	—
3–5 years	58%	—	—	17%	25%	—
6–11 years	—	23%	18%	—	12%	16%
12–14 years	—	27%	—	6%	29%	15%
15–17 years	—	36%	42%	—	15%	—

In the toddler category (age 13–36 months), the offender motivation was again primarily emotional. This motivation comprised 90% of the cases. Family members were the primary offenders in 82% of the cases. Disposal of victims' remains was similar to infants; they were disposed of within 1 mile in 56% of cases, and 22% within 1 to 5 miles.

In the preschooler category (age 3–5 years), the motivations were divided among emotion based (54%), sex based (30%), and profit (16%). For all categories, victims were disposed of within 100 yards of the offense site in 58% of the cases, within 5 to 10 miles in 17% of the cases, and 10 to 30 miles in 25% of the cases.

In elementary age (6–11 years) victims, sex was the primary motivation, comprising 89% of the cases. Victims were disposed of within 1 mile of the abduction site in 23% of the cases, 1 to 5 miles in 18% of the cases, and over 10 miles away in 28% of the cases, with more than half of these over 30 miles away. For emotion-based cases, victims were disposed of within 100 yards in 73% of the cases, within 1 to 5 miles in 9% of the cases, and 10 to 30 miles in 18% of the cases.

In middle school age (12–14 years) victims, sex was the primary motivation (79%). Victims were disposed of within 1 mile in 27% of the cases, 5 to 10 miles in 6%, 10 to 30 miles in 29%, and over 30 miles in 15% of the cases.

In high school age (15–17 years) victims, motivation for offenders was divided between sex (52%), emotion based (25%), and profit (23%). The increase in emotion-based crimes for this age is attributed to boyfriend, ex-boyfriend relationships. Profit motivation primarily involved males. For victims of sex-motivated crimes, remains were disposed of at or within 1 mile of the abduction site 36% of the time, 1 to 5 miles in 42%, and over 10 miles in 15% of cases.

In the Washington State study, all the cases were homicides. The study revealed that in the disposal scenarios of victims, 52% were concealed to prevent discovery. Another 39% were deposited in a manner suggesting the offender was unconcerned as to discovery, and 9% were openly placed. Offenders in this study deliberately selected disposal sites in 49% of the cases, randomly chose sites in 37% of the cases, and were forced to dispose of the victim by circumstances in 14% of the cases. In 63% of the cases, the body recovery site was greater than 1.5 miles from the victim's home (see Table 8.1). As a general rule, the younger the victim, the closer to the victim's home the remains were found.

This study also divided the stages of the crime into the initial contact site, the murder site and the disposal site (see Table 8.2). The distances from initial contact site to the murder site, were from 0 to 199 feet in 31% of the cases, 200 feet to .25 mile in 16% of

Table 8.2   Distances Between Sites

	Initial Contact Site	Murder Site	Body Recovery Site
Last known location	< 200 feet (65%)	> .25 mile (55%)	> .25 mile (66%)
Initial contact site	—	> .25 mile (54%)	> .25 mile (63%)
Murder site	—	—	< 200 feet (72%)

the cases, .25 mile to 1.50 miles in 10% of the cases, 1.50 miles to 12 miles in 25% of the cases, and greater than 12 miles in 18% of the cases.

The distances from murder site to body recovery site were 0 to 199 feet in 72% of the cases, 200 feet to .25 mile in 6% of the cases, .25 mile to 1.50 miles in 4% of the cases, 1.50 miles to 12 miles in 10% of the cases, and greater than 12 miles in 8% of the cases.

In classifying the types of geographic areas in which initial contact took place, 51% were urban areas, 33% were suburban areas, and 16% were rural areas. The person who discovered the body was found to be a passer-by in 58.4% of the cases, the police in 23.1% of the cases, search party in 6.5% of the cases, relative or acquaintance of victim in 4.5% of the cases, the offender in 2.7% of the cases, witness to the death in 1.8%, and fire department/rescue personnel in 1.6% of the cases.

The FBI study revealed that several factors accounted for different disposal scenarios. These factors included the sex of the offender, sex of the victim, and the motivation for the abduction. Male offenders were the overwhelming perpetrators in the age groups from preschool through high school. Females were the primary victims of male offenders in 74% of all of the cases. Sex was the primary motivation for the abduction in 60% of all of the cases in the study, with emotion-based motives comprising 27%. Male offenders abducted their victims from inside the victim's residence in 31% of the cases, and from public streets inside and outside the victim's neighborhood in 37% of the cases. The male offenders were acquaintances of the victim in 41% and strangers in 40% of the cases. Male offenders lived at or within 1 mile of the abduction site in 46% of the cases. Victims were disposed of at the abduction site in 32% of the cases, transported less than a mile in 17% of the cases, 1 to 5 miles in 19% of the cases, 5 to 10 miles in 6% of the cases, and surprisingly, over 10 miles in 26% of the cases.

The Washington State study revealed that in most of the abduction/homicide cases, the body was concealed to prevent discovery. In a majority of cases, disposal was located greater than 1.5 miles from the victim's residence. The Washington State study also identified the importance of identifying the initial contact site, the murder site, and the disposal site. The murder site was the least found of the three sites identified in the study. Obviously, the murder site is very important in linking physical evidence between the offender and the victim. In this study, 75% of the murder sites are within 200 feet of the disposal sites. Search strategies should incorporate this fact, and it should be standard procedure to search in at least a 200-foot diameter around any child homicide crime scene. The discovery of the initial contact site is equally important. In this study, the case clearance rate dropped 40 percentage points below the average clearance rate if the initial contact site was not located. If the initial contact site was located, the clearance rate rose to 13 percentage points above the average clearance rate. In 80% of the cases in this study, the initial contact site was within .25 mile of the victim's last known location.

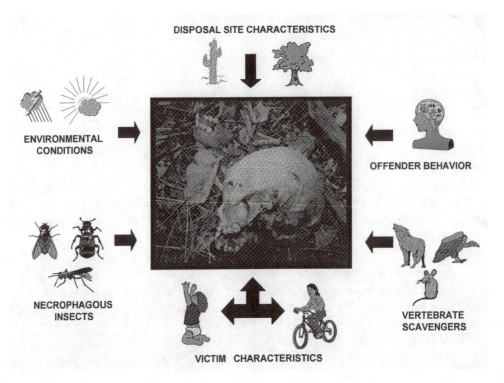

Figure 8.1 Diagrammatic summary of the major factors influencing taphonomic changes and decomposition rates in the remains of childhood victims of abduction and murder.

Issues of Decomposition and Child-Sized Remains

There have been very few studies conducted regarding environmental and taphonomic effects on child-sized remains during decomposition. Based on the findings of the few existing studies that have employed child-sized decomposition models and on reports from actual cases, child-sized remains appear to be "returned to nature" much more quickly than those of adults (Crist, 1997). A variety of influences, including environmental, behavioral and zoological factors, contribute to the rate of childhood taphonomy (Figure 8.1). In warm weather total skeletonization has been observed to occur in as little as 6 days (Morton et al., 1999). The quick reduction to skeletal remains can present serious recognition problems for untrained searchers who are looking for a "whole" child.

The differences in decomposition changes in child-sized remains vs. adult remains are quite logical. Child remains undergo decomposition processes in a shorter time interval than adult remains due, in part, to smaller size and greater surface-to-volume ratios. The smaller body size and lower weight of child remains contribute to the shorter interval. There is less flesh for arthropods to consume, and so the remains are reduced to skeletal elements more quickly. Size is also a factor in scavenging by feral animals. In larger remains, scavenging canids are forced to pull and tear at limbs and other extremities to remove them. Smaller size allows for easier disarticulation and removal of an entire corpse. Greater surface-to-volume ratios characteristic of child remains facilitate more rapid environmental degradation and arthropod consumption.

This quick return to nature when coupled with the small size of child victims and the disposal methods employed by offenders help contribute to the poor success of organized searches.

Animal (Swine) Model Research

In 1998, members of the FBI's National Center for the Analysis of Violent Crime (NCAVC) conducted a research project looking at the decomposition changes of child-sized remains. During the time period from late May 1998 through July 1998, remains of small pigs (less than 30 lb.) were deposited in a wooded area adjacent to a dirt road in a suburban area of Virginia. The sites were located between 40 and 80 feet from the shoulder of the road. The pigs were placed in a variety of scenarios, including surface deposit, no covering; surface deposit, covered with tree branches and deadfall; surface deposit, enclosed in a rolled up carpet; shallow burial (less than 1 foot); and suspended by rope from a tree approximately 2.5 feet above the ground. All the pigs were deposited in late May, and were environmentally exposed and monitored for a total of 75 days. The pigs were secured with wire mesh for the first 8 days, which was then removed. Environmental temperatures averaged from the 60s (lows), to 80s and 90s°F (high) for the entire 75-day time period.

The use of pigs as substitutes for human remains is an accepted standard in decomposition and taphonomic research, and has become routine in anthropological and entomological research. Although not a perfect substitute for human remains, pigs are an accepted comparative model. The decomposition process for pigs approximates decomposition for humans, and takes place in similar time frames (Payne, 1965; Haskell, 1989). The unique microenvironment created by the introduction of a pig carcass or human body into an existing habitat results in the attraction of a variety of scavengers and insects. Creation of a temporary food source, shelter, nursery, and the production of decomposition by-products alter normal flora and faunal communities, and produce observable and detectable changes.

A broad, multidisciplinary approach was employed during the collection and subsequent analysis of study data. The five sites included in this study were observed regularly to record various decomposition stages and taphonomic changes. Observations included stages of the decomposition process, activity of necrophagous arthropods, and the extent of remains scavenging and scattering by birds and mammals. Remains were monitored weekly to chart disarticulation and skeletal disposal. Site surveillance was conducted prior to approach to minimize impact on scavenger activity. Scavenging effects were photographed and examined in an effort to identify species of vertebrate predators. At the conclusion of the study, an archeological approach was used to recover the remains. Loose vegetation was raked and removed, and various skeletal components were located and charted. Remains from each site were collected, sorted and tabulated to identify missing skeletal components.

Carrion predators common to northern Virginia include the coyote (*Canis latrans*), stray domestic dogs (*Canis familiaris*), the red fox (*Vulpes vulpes*), both turkey (*Cathartes aura*) and black (*Coragyps atratus*) vultures, and a variety of scavenging rodents, including fox squirrels (*Sciurus niger*), gray squirrels (*Sciurus carolinensis*), deer mice (*Peromyscus maniculatus*), and voles (*Microtus pennsylvanicus*).

Figure 8.2 Photographic depiction of the surface deposit study site (site #1) characterized as a mixed eastern deciduous forest with prominent leaf and plant litter. The study animal (swine) was placed directly on top of the existing leaf fall.

Field Research Data

Five sites will be discussed individually and the observations will be described chronologically.

Site #1 (Figure 8.2)

This site was a surface deposit. The area was a mixed deciduous and evergreen forest. There was significant leaf and plant litter on the surface. The pig was deposited directly on the top of the leave litter. On the first day, adult necrophagous flies arrived within minutes and began laying eggs. Over the next 6 days the insect infestation continued unabated increasing in both species diversity and richness. By day 7, fly larvae (maggots) had consumed approximately 60% of the soft tissue. By day 12, the remains were totally skeletonized; the only tissues remaining were small bits of mummified integument. After 75 days, the skeletal elements were scattered in a small area approximately 14 feet long and 11 feet wide. There was very little carnivore/scavenger activity. A detailed search resulted in the recovery of all the skeletal elements from this site.

Site #2 (Figure 8.3)

This site contained a small pig placed within a rolled-up carpet, with the ends open. On the first day, necrophagous flies were very active and were laying eggs. The open carpet did little to inhibit access. The shelter produced by the carpet increased egg laying activity by adult flies, and consequently produced many more fly larvae (maggots). The increase in the numbers of maggots allowed for quicker consumption of the soft tissues. By day 6, fly larvae had invaded the entire carcass. After 12 days, the remains were completely skeletonized, and the maggots had migrated from the remains into the surrounding substrate to complete their development. After 75 days, approximately 60% of the skeletal elements

Figure 8.3 Photographic depiction of the rolled-carpet study site (site #2). The study animal (swine) was placed within the rolled residential carpet, which was then deposited on the ground surface.

were recovered, found mostly within the carpet. The skull, mandible, a rib, and several vertebrate were found within 6 feet of the carpet. These elements were removed from the carpet by scavengers, primarily turkey vultures.

Site #3 (Figure 8.4)

This site was a shallow burial. A small pig was placed in a shallow depression, approximately 2 feet deep, and covered with dirt. On the first day, there was insect activity but the burial prevented adult fly access. After 6 days, however, there was significant adult and larval insect infestation. After 12 days, the pig had been removed from the shallow grave by vertebrate scavengers and dragged 46 feet away. The head was missing and there were obvious signs of canid scavenging. After another week, the carcass of the pig was devoid of soft tissue and had been disarticulated. An area of soil discoloration and some small pieces of tissue, revealed where the pig had lain during early decomposition prior to being disarticulated by scavenging canids. The skeletal elements of the pig were scattered around the site. Several skeletal elements (ribs and vertebrate) were dispersed in an area approximately 15 feet wide and 9 feet long. Numerous skeletal elements were missing, primarily the skull and long bones. After 75 days, the scattering was distributed over a wider area. The furthest element recovered was located 89 feet from the burial site.

Site #4 (Figure 8.5)

This site had a hanging pig. The pig was secured by a rope and suspended approximately 2.5 feet above the ground. On the first day, carrion insect activity was observed almost immediately, with adult female flies beginning to oviposit within minutes. After 6 days, there was heavy insect infestation. Fly larvae (maggots) had eaten most of the soft tissue, particularly within the abdominal cavity. Fly larval infestation became so heavy that maggots were seen falling out of the pig to the ground below. These maggots were unable

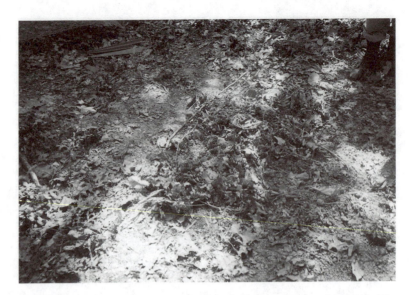

Figure 8.4 Photographic depiction of the shallow burial study site (site #3). The pig carcass was interred in a shallow depression, approximately 2 feet deep, and covered with dirt from the surrounding environment. This site displayed the most prominent vertebrate scavenger activity of all of the carrion study sites.

Figure 8.5 Photographic depiction of the suspended carrion study site (site #4). At this location a pig carcass was suspended by a small diameter rope at an approximate height of 2 feet above ground level. It should be noted that the study animal was deceased prior suspension.

Figure 8.6 Photographic depiction of the carrion study site (site #5) containing a pig carcass covered with deadfall vegetation and branches. Dead vegetation from the surrounding deciduous forest habitat was utilized to completely cover the study carcass.

to re-infest the suspended carcass and thus a complex community of carrion insects developed in the fluid stained soil beneath the hanging carrion. After 12 days, dry, windy environmental conditions had mummified the skin, creating a hard protective shell. No soft tissue remained. Several teeth had dislodged, as well as one rib, which was on the ground beneath the carcass. After 75 days, the carcass was still intact, but several more ribs had dislodged. The carcass appeared to remain intact for such a long period because the suspension of the carcass precluded vertebrate scavenging, limited insect colonization, and allowed the wind to rapidly desiccate the integument. This mummification process formed a protective leathery shell, securing the majority of the skeletal elements within the carcass.

Site #5 (Figure 8.6)

This site contained the pig covered with deadfall and branches. The deadfall completely covered the carcass. On the first day, there was pronounced insect activity. Adult flies were observed to gain carrion access through gaps in the covering. Fly oviposition and maggot population development, however, were less intense than that observed on more exposed carrion. After 6 days, the carcass of the pig had been dragged out of the deadfall and was lying approximately 3 feet from the original deposition site. After 12 days, almost all of the soft tissue had been consumed. The skeletal elements were still in close proximity, the furthest less than 13 feet. After 75 days, the skeletal elements were still in the immediate area of the deadfall, the furthest element being located about 15 feet away. Almost all of the skeletal elements were recovered at this site.

Observations conducted at the previously described study sites revealed that small pigs decompose within a short time interval. Each of the pigs, other than the hanging pig, was reduced to skeletal components (almost devoid of soft tissues) within 12 days. Skeletal components were most often recovered in the near vicinity of the original disposal site,

Table 8.3 Animal (Swine) Model Research: Remains Recovered

	Pig #1	Pig #2	Pig #3	Pig #5
Cranium	X	X	0	X
Mandible	X	X	X	X
Pelvis	X	*	*	*
Scapula	X	0	X	X
Humerus	X	X	0	*
Radius	X	X	*	X
Ulna	X	X	0	X
Femur	X	*	*	X
Fibula	X	*	*	X
Patella	X	0	0	*
Cervical vertebrae	X	*	0	*
Thoracic vertebrae	X	*	*	*
Lumbar vertebrae	X	*	*	*
Sacrum	X	*	0	*
Caudal	X	*	0	*
Ribs	X	*	*	*
Carpals	X	0	0	*
Metacarpals	X	*	*	*
Tarsals	X	*	0	*
Metatarsals	X	*	*	*
Phalanges	X	*	0	*

Note: X = all found, * = part found, 0 = none found.

with the majority located within 15 feet (Table 8.3). Disarticulated remains were scattered, and in some cases, difficult to see due to similarities in their appearance and the color of the environmental background on which they were located. The small size of many skeletal elements required careful and structured procedures to ensure recognition and recovery. Unexpectedly, remains interred in the shallow burial were subjected to greater vertebrate scattering than those that decomposed on the surface.

In this study, the vertebrates involved in scavenging were mostly canids (coyotes and fox) and turkey vultures. Scavenging activities by small rodents was limited to skeletal element gnawing with little actual remains movement noted. Coyotes are generally predaceous, but will readily participate in carrion scavenging activities. They hunt both singularly and in cooperation with other coyotes, are largely nocturnal, but are also active at dusk and dawn. Coyote diets include carrion, birds, rodents, and larger animals. Red foxes are also efficient predators who participate in carrion scavenging activities, are solitary hunters, and are primarily nocturnal. Common food items include carrion, mice, voles, rabbits, bird's eggs, large insects, and fruit. Turkey vultures are large raptors whose primary food source is carrion. They soar on wind currents and thermals and are able to detect dead animals at great distances. Squirrels, mice, and voles are primarily herbivores, but will scavenge bone for calcium.

There are several explanations for the differences observed in the taphonomic process characteristic of each of the pig carcasses. At site #1, the pig was laying on the surface. This allowed easy access for a wide variety of necrophagous insects. The adult insects and their offspring were able to rapidly colonize and consume the carcass. This carcass had the least amount of scavenging activity by larger predators, and the least scattering of skeletal elements. At site #2, the pig carcass was contained within the rolled-up carpet. The open, but narrow carpet ends allow easy access for colonizing insects, which again devoured carcass soft tissues rapidly. However, there was very little vertebrate scavenging observed at this site, as the carpet presented a formidable barrier to both birds and canids. Again, skeletal scattering was almost non-existent at this site. Site #3 was the shallow burial. There were noticeable increases in vertebrate activity and remains scavenging at this site. Research has shown that burial of bodies retards the decomposition process. Burial slows down bacterial putrefaction via cooler, more uniform temperatures and reduced oxygen availability. Burial also provides a soil layer, which prevents easy carrion detection and access by insects and, with sufficient depth, acts as a barrier to larger scavengers.

The carcass at site #3 was buried in a shallow grave that suppressed insect colonization, thus preserving the food source for larger scavengers. As a result, the carcass was dug out of the burial site, carried a greater distance, disarticulated more completely, and subsequently scattered to a greater extent than those at other sites. There was significant evidence (hair and scat) of scavenging by canids. Vultures also fed upon the remains after the carcass was disinterred. This was evidenced by the presence of beak injuries in the carrion and by fecal deposits and feathers in close proximity. This site had the most scavenging activity and the fewest number of skeletal elements recovered. Site #4 was the pig carcass that was suspended above the ground. This carcass had no evidence of bird or mammal scavenging activity. There was insect activity; however, the lack of access prevented re-infestation by maggots once they fell to the ground. The carcass exhibited drying by the wind. Mummification progressed until the skin became very hard and shell-like. This hardened skin allowed most of the skeletal components to remain in place. In the absence of insect infestation and vertebrate scavenging, less destructive decomposition processes (mummification) prevail. The last site was the deadfall covered carcass. This site allowed insect infestation, and the scavengers eventually dragged the carcass out of the deadfall. At this site, the scattering of skeletal elements was localized in a small area, and most of the skeletal elements were recovered. The deadfall covering resulted in both a moderation of insect infestation and vertebrate scavenging, perhaps indicating a more pronounced competition between vertebrate and invertebrate consumers.

The different patterns of decomposition and scattering exhibited at the five sites were based primarily on the physical and climatic conditions to which the remains were exposed and the differential impacts of vertebrate and invertebrate activity. Each site was characterized by different factors that dictated which populations of consumers had the competitive edge in carrion exploitation. Competition exhibited between vertebrates and invertebrates for a highly prized food source, the length of time the food source was available, and prevailing climatic conditions, all contribute to differing rates of decomposition and scattering of remains by scavengers. An understanding of these influences is crucial to the successful detection and recovery of child-sized remains.

Child Abduction Case Histories and Disposal Scenarios

Case Study #1

This case is presented because the offender transported the victim over 30 miles away from her residence and buried her in a remote area. The victim was a 6-year-old female, and the offender in this case was the victim's biological father.

This case first came to the attention of law enforcement after the father and stepmother reported the victim missing after she went out to play one morning. The police organized a large-scale search effort, continually expanding the boundaries to include numerous bodies of water. At one point, the search effort involved hundreds of police and volunteers.

Police became suspicious of the parents when they learned the father had been previously investigated by child protective services for being physically abusive to his daughter on at least three occasions. He had temporary custody of his daughter at the time of the homicide.

Case investigators were able to persuade the stepmother to cooperate during questioning. She eventually provided the details of the murder to the police. Additionally, she led police to the burial site. Once the body was discovered, the father confessed.

The evening before the victim was reported missing, the father stated he became angry with his daughter and lost his temper. He repeatedly hit and threw the victim against a wall, killing her. After she was killed, he wrapped her in a blanket, and attempted to dispose of the body. He drove to several locations, even visiting a friend with the body of the victim lying in the back seat next to the father's and stepmother's infant. The offender finally drove to a recreational area the young victim enjoyed visiting. The father buried her there, in a secluded location.

The facts in this case relate directly to the abduction research conducted by the FBI's NCAVC. This case was an emotion-based crime. In this age group, female children who are murdered for emotional reasons are disposed 10 to 30 miles from their residences. The victim was buried 30 miles away. The offender also disposed of the victim in an area familiar to him. Ironically, the disposal site was also one of the victim's favorite places to visit. The burial was unusual, and was used to conceal the victim to prevent discovery of her body.

The victim was buried in a deep, clandestine grave, approximately 3 feet deep. The body was in a moderate stage of decomposition with skin slippage, and bloating. There was no insect or scavenging activity because of the depth of the grave (see Table 8.4).

Case Study #2

This case is offered because of the unusual disposal scenario. This offender deposited the victim in a river, and the victim was transported several miles downstream before being discovered. The stream had a normal depth of less than 2 feet. The fluvial action of the river was possible because of several days of storms, which raised the water level well beyond normal.

An 11-year-old female disappeared while riding her bike from her residence to her aunt's apartment. The victim had been playing with friends at a nearby playground. The victim left the playground and went to her residence. No one was home, so a neighbor instructed the victim to go to her aunt's residence. She rode her bicycle toward her aunt's apartment. The victim was not seen alive again. After several hours, the family reported her missing. A search of the area was organized and the victim's bicycle was located in the storage area of the aunt's apartment.

The offender lived with the aunt in her residence. He advised that he was at the apartment that afternoon and had seen the victim. According to the offender, the victim sat in his vehicle and he talked with her for a few minutes. The offender stated he went to work and left the victim. He advised that he last saw the victim riding away on her bicycle.

Table 8.4   Case Characteristics and Disposal Method

	Case No.[a]						
	1	2	3	4a	4b	4c	4d
Locale[b]	SE	MW	W	NE	NE	NE	NE
Age in years	6	11	7	12	16	10	12
Sex	F	F	F	M	M	F	F
Height (inches)	45	66	48	64	62	54	60
Weight (pounds)	55	140	38	125	110	60	68
Cause of death[c]	BFT	MS	MS	LS	Unknown	Unknown	BFT2
Postmortem interval	1 wk	1 wk	1 wk	1 mo.	N/A	2 mo.	N/A
Disposal method[d]	DB	W	DLF	SB, RT	N/A	SB, ES	N/A
Decomposition type[e]	P	S, P	P, M	P, M	Unknown	P	Unknown
Month of death	Nov.	May	Aug.	Oct.	Nov.	Aug.	Aug.

[a] Victims #1–3 had different offenders; #4a–4d had the same offender.

[b] All victims from continental United States. NE = northeast, etc.

[c] MS = manual strangulation, LS = ligature strangulation, BFT = blunt force trauma, BFT2 = blunt force trauma according to offender version only.

[d] S = surface, SB = shallow burial <2 feet, DB = deep burial >2 feet, W = water deposit, DLF = body placed in trash bag in dumpster and buried in landfill, RT = rope around neck and attached to tree but not hanging, ES = skeletal elements scattered over 100 yards and many elements missing.

[e] P = putrefaction, S = saponification, M = mummification.

The offender related that after leaving the victim, he went to work and was there until the early evening hours. When the offender returned, he participated in the search for the victim.

Police questioned the offender and during a subsequent interview, he requested an attorney. The next day, the offender contacted the police and told them he was having visions concerning the victim. The offender voluntarily related that in his visions the victim was wet, cold, and in the immediate area. The search broadened, but the victim was not located.

After a week, the victim was discovered by a passerby in a small creek several miles away. The victim was clothed, and had duct tape around her mouth. The autopsy revealed the cause of death to be strangulation, although the victim had some water in her lungs. It is believed that she was strangled until unconsciousness by the offender, who thought she was dead. The victim was then dumped in the stream where she finally died. The location where she was found was .5 mile from the nearest road. A few miles upstream from this location was an area where the offender had spent a great deal of time several years earlier. This site was one of the few spots upstream from the recovery site that was readily accessible by a vehicle. The offender's residence and vehicle were searched, and some of the victim's blood was located on items in the back seat of the vehicle.

A review of the offender's action in this case revealed many characteristics common to the two abduction research studies discussed previously. The victim was taken from near her home, by an offender related to her. She was abducted from the site where she was last seen. The offender assaulted her in his vehicle. The offender disposed of the victim in an area with which he was very familiar. He concealed the victim by placing her in the shallow stream. The stream's usual depth was very shallow, less than 2 feet in the deepest portions. The stream meandered, and was not navigable through its length by a floating object, unless the water level was high due to storm activity. The body could only reach the area where it was recovered through fluvial action. The weather conditions consisted of severe thunderstorms during the week the victim was missing. The victim was found on a bank of the stream, in a location where she would have been carried by the action of the stream. The elevated water levels allowed the transport of the victim to the recovery location.

The remains were very decomposed and bloated, with evidence of saponification. There was evidence of scavenging by insects, but no evidence of activity by large scavengers (see Table 8.4).

Case Study #3

This case involved the abduction of a 7-year-old female, who disappeared on her way home. The offender was acquainted with the victim; his daughter was a friend of the victim. The disposal scenario in this case was unusual in that the offender hid the victim in a garbage bag, which he placed in a dumpster near his residence.

The victim left her residence and rode her scooter down the street to water her grandfather's vegetable garden. She was observed leaving the garden and was last seen heading toward her residence. However, she never returned to her home. She was reported missing within the hour, and a massive search of the neighborhood was undertaken. The majority of the searchers were volunteers, and they combed the immediate area around the residence and the neighborhood. The searchers even opened the dumpsters, and looked in, but never opened the garbage bags themselves.

The dumpsters were emptied the next day and transported to the landfill. The operator of the landfill isolated the garbage from the neighborhood from which the child had disappeared and stored it separately. He did this because he felt it might be helpful. A search of the garbage from the dumpsters was eventually conducted, and the victim and her scooter were located in garbage bags. The scooter had been taken apart and placed in separate bags.

The offender came to the attention of the police because his daughter and the victim were playmates. A check of his criminal record revealed that he had been previously convicted of a sexual offense. He was home the afternoon the victim disappeared; he had been babysitting his children at his residence. He told police he was home and had fallen asleep. He claimed he woke up when searchers knocked on his door, looking for the victim. He also participated in the search.

Once the victim was located, the offender admitted he had lured the victim into his residence, sexually assaulted her, and strangled her. He disposed of her in the dumpster because it was close and convenient. The victim was in an advanced state of decomposition. She was bloated and there was heavy insect infestation. The black plastic garbage bag she was placed in increased the temperatures to which the body was exposed. There was no evidence of scavenger activity. The lack of scavenging can be attributed to the placement of the victim in a dumpster, which was eventually deposited in a landfill. The victim was buried beneath numerous other bags of garbage.

The recovery of the victim in this case was due to the initiative taken by the landfill operator who isolated the trash. This allowed for a more comprehensive search of trash taken from the immediate area of the abduction. The fact that the dumpsters in the area were searched by volunteers should not preclude a more detailed search of the contents of garbage bags at a later time by law enforcement professionals (see Table 8.4).

Case Study #4

This case is offered because it involved a number of victims and disposal scenarios. There were five victims, one of whom was recovered alive. Of the four murdered victims, only two bodies were recovered. Two of the victims were killed in one state and disposed of in a different state. The victim recovered alive was the last victim in this series of abductions.

This offender was a serial child abductor/murderer who operated in two separate states. The offender came to the attention of law enforcement after he was arrested for the attempted abduction of a 12-year-old female. His vehicle was seized and his kidnap kit was recovered from the vehicle. Subsequent to his arrest, the offender confessed to the attempted abduction, the abduction and murder of a 12-year-old male and a 12-year-old female.

In the fall of early 1990, a 12-year-old male disappeared. He was last seen riding his bicycle in the parking lot of a strip mall adjacent to a major county road. A month later the victim's body was discovered by deer hunters in a wooded area approximately 200 miles away. The body was recovered on top of the ground, face down, completely nude, with a 7-foot length of clothesline tied around the neck. The other end of the clothesline was tied to a tree 5 feet from the ground, but was not a hanging attempt. The body was found approximately 200 feet from the closest access roadway and no attempt was made to conceal the body. The findings indicated the victim's arms and legs had been bound with tape but no bindings were found on the body. The tape bindings were recovered from the victim's clothing. Investigation indicates the victim walked into the crime scene wearing his sneakers. The victim's eyes and mouth were covered with duct tape, which was still in place when the body was found.

The victim's clothing was found 200 feet away from the body, further into the woods and away from the access road. The clothes included a tee shirt, a pair of jeans, underwear, sneakers, and socks. The tee shirt had been cut off in one piece to allow removal without removing the bindings. The Medical Examiner determined that the cause of death was ligature strangulation from the clothesline found around the victim's neck. No semen was found at the scene and no evidence of sexual assault was found.

The offender admitted that he was working near the strip mall where the victim was last seen. He lured the victim with the promise of money to help move furniture. The offender placed the victim and his bicycle in his van, drove to his apartment, and walked the victim into the residence. The offender attempted a sexual assault but could not perform sexually. At that point, the offender decided to kill the victim.

The following morning, the offender drove to an adjacent state to an area he was familiar with from his childhood. The offender told the victim he was going to release him in the woods. He tied the clothesline around the victim's neck and walked him into the woods. As they were walking, the offender tightened the ligature and the victim fell. He continued pulling the rope until the victim stopped struggling. The offender then tied the rope to a tree and kept pressure on the victim's neck to insure he would die. He removed the victim's clothing and cut his shirt off with his knife. The offender reported he removed the clothes to make it appear that a pedophile had killed the victim and to also insure the victim would die of hypothermia if the strangulation did not kill him. The offender removed all of the victim's clothes and deposited them in a puddle of water, to remove any trace evidence. The offender then drove home back to his residence. He later disposed of the victim's bicycle in a lake; police recovered it. The body had moderate decomposition because of the cool temperatures during the postmortem period. There was also extensive skin drying due to the position of the body.

Several years after the previous abduction, a 16-year-old male disappeared from the area of his residence. The victim suffered from a mental disability and his mental age was less than his chronological age. He was small and slightly built and appeared to be approximately 12 years old. He, too, was last seen riding his bicycle along a major county highway. Less than a week later, the victim's bicycle was found in a wooded area a short distance away. Crime scene investigation by police failed to locate any evidence on the bicycle.

The victim's body has never been found and the offender has denied any involvement in his abduction. Investigation by police after the offender's arrest determined that offender was in the same general area where the victim was last seen.

The next year, a 10-year-old female disappeared from a rural road in a neighboring area. A thorough search was conducted in the area where the victim was last known to be and her left sneaker was recovered along a secondary road. Two months later, the victim's skeletal remains were found by hunters in a heavily wooded area, approximately 16 miles from the abduction site and a short distance from a major county highway. Examination of the scene determined the victim's body decomposed on top of the ground and there was no attempt to conceal the body. The victim's shorts, tee shirt, and right sneaker were recovered in the same general area as the body. The remains were completely skeletonized and had been widely scattered throughout the area by animals. The disposal area was frequented by numerous large scavengers including coyotes, dogs, and foxes. Due to the extensive decomposition involved, the cause or manner of death or sexual assault could not be determined.

Two weeks after the previous abduction, a 12-year-old female disappeared from a country road in an adjacent state. Her bicycle was located on the side of the road but the victim's body has never been recovered. After the offender's arrest, he advised investigators that during the same time frame, he went for a ride along the same county highway previously mentioned, looking for vulnerable girls to kidnap. He turned off the county highway onto a rural road and he came upon a girl pushing a bicycle, and who was both vulnerable and sexually arousing to him. He pulled alongside the girl and jumped from his van with his knife. She tried to run but he grabbed her, threatened her with the knife, and forced her into the van. He duct-taped her hands and feet and quickly threw her bicycle and packages into the woods. The offender identified an unusual feature of the bicycle that had not been disclosed to the public prior to the confession.

The offender advised he drove the victim to a very sparsely populated area. He found a dirt road in an extremely remote area and pulled over. He climbed into the back of the van, removed the victim's clothes and vaginally raped her. He then forced her out of the van and instructed her to walk up a hill, away from the van. The offender claimed he then struck the victim in the back of the head with a large tree limb, killing her. He said that he buried the victim in a shallow grave, face down, digging the grave with a pick and shovel he had in the van. He then placed her clothes in a plastic bag and left the area. The offender disposed of the clothes in a dumpster, on his way back to his residence. He disposed of the pick and shovel the next morning near his residence.

Table 8.5 Distance from Residence to Various Sites in Case Studies

Case #[a]	Last Known Location (Verified Sighting)	Initial Contact (Verified Sighting)	Murder Site if Known	Body Recovery Site if Known
1	< 200 feet	< 200 feet	< 200 feet	> 30 miles
2	< 1 mile	< 1 mile	> 5 miles	> 15 miles
3	< 200 feet	< 200 feet	< 200 feet	> 15 miles
4a	> 5 miles	> 5 miles	< 200 feet	N/A
4b	< 200 feet	< 200 feet	Unknown	< 200 feet
4c	> 1 mile	> 1 mile	Unknown	> 15 miles
4d	< 1 mile	< 1 mile	> 50 miles	N/A

[a] Cases #1–3 had different offenders, #4a–4d had the same offender.

The offender provided investigators with a hand-drawn map indicating where the victim was supposedly buried. As a result of this information, a massive, methodical search was initiated by the police. The search continued throughout the winter in sub-zero temperatures and blizzard conditions. During the search, tons of snow and dirt were moved but the victim's body was never found.

A review of this offender's crimes reveals that he would use separate murder and disposal locations when committing his crimes (Table 8.5). He was responsible for possibly five victims, one of whom lived. Of the four homicides, only two of the bodies were recovered. Both of these victims were located accidentally by citizens, and not by organized searches by law enforcement personnel. In the case of the fourth victim, the offender provided a map to a location where he supposedly buried the victim. After an exhaustive search, no remains were located. The burial, however, falls outside the offender's usual pattern of surface disposal. The distance the suspect traveled to dispose of his victims varied greatly. One victim was located 16 miles from the abduction site, and the other 220 miles away, in a different state.

Multidisciplinary Approaches to Search/Recovery Strategies

The failure of law enforcement to locate child-sized remains is not because of lack of resources or technology. The biggest issues are twofold:

1. Recognition of the behaviors exhibited by offenders who abduct and murder children and the patterns inherent in their selections of remains' disposal methods and sites.
2. An understanding of the environmental influences that affect child-sized remains, the subsequent taphonomic changes that occur, and the impact that these have upon remains' recognition, detection, and recovery.

Taphonomic changes in child-sized remains present unique patterns and challenges to agencies and personnel involved in search and recovery operations. Judging from the literature available concerning child abduction/homicide scenarios, it is apparent that most search strategies employed by law enforcement in response to such cases are misdirected. Most law enforcement searches for missing children begin around the victim's residence, and then expand outward, usually terminating less than a mile from the alleged abduction site. Available research, however, suggests that abducted victims are often transported much farther than the traditional search parameters encompass. Disposal methods and scenarios also appear to differ with victim age and gender. These differences appear to be rooted in the motivation for the abduction/homicide, the spontaneity of the offense, and the relationship between the victim and the offender. This frequently translates into considerable distance between the abductions and recovery site. Hanfland et al. (1997) provide an excellent review of the important sites associated with child abduction /homicide cases, and strategies for intensive investigative efforts to locate and process these sites.

Because child-sized remains are rapidly recycled through the environment into which they are placed, and because of the lengthy time interval frequently preceding remains discovery, great care must be taken in the processing of child recovery sites. The cryptic and scattered nature of such remains requires a well-organized, pre-planned, team approach to both detection and recovery. A multidisciplinary team of experts including forensic pathologists, anthropologists, entomologists, botanists, soil scientists, geophysicists, serologists, trace evidence experts, canine search personnel, crime scene technicians, and behavioral scientists should be utilized to the fullest extent possible in cases of child abduction. Investigators must remain mindful of the fact that most child abduction/homicide cases are successfully resolved through thorough investigative efforts and the proper collection, preservation, documentation, and analysis of tiny items of trace evidence. Recognition of the role that invertebrate and vertebrate scavengers play in the recycling process, coupled with the ability to recognize and interpret signs of their activities is often crucial to successful detection and recovery. The development of a knowledgeable multidisciplinary team, prior to the onset of a child abduction case, will maximize the appropriate allocation of investigative resources early on in subsequent investigations and enhance the probability of successful case resolution. At the very least, law enforcement agencies should compile lists of qualified local experts who are willing to provide assistance in child abduction cases and establish and maintain continuing liaison with these individuals. Little people leave behind little things and special investigative insights and efforts are required to recognize and recover such evidence.

References

Boudreaux, M.C., W.D. Lord, and R.L. Dutra
    1999   Child abduction: aged-based analysis of offender, victim, and offense characteristics in 550 cases of alleged child disappearance, *Journal of Forensic Sciences*, 44(3):539–553.

Crist, T. A. J., A. Washburn, H. Park, I. Hood, and M. Hickey
    1997   Cranial bone displacement as a taphonomic process in potential child abuse cases. In *Forensic Taphonomy: The Postmortem Fate of Human Remains*, edited by W.D. Haglund and M.H. Sorg, pp. 319–336. CRC Press, Boca Raton, FL.

Finkelhor, D.
    1997   The homicides of children and youth: a developmental perspective. In *Out of the Darkness: Contemporary Perspectives on Family Violence*, edited by G.K. Kantor and J.L. Jasinski, pp. 17–34. Sage Publications, Thousand Oaks, CA. pp. 17–34.

Finkelhor, D., G.T. Hoatling, and A.J. Sedlak
    1992   The abduction of children by strangers and non-family members, *Journal of Interpersonal Violence* 7(2):226–243.

Haglund, W.D.

1991   Applications of Taphonomic Models to Forensic Investigations, Ph.D. dissertation, Department of Anthropology, University of Washington, Seattle. University Microfilms, Ann Arbor, MI.

1997   Dogs and coyotes: Postmortem involvement with human remains, In *Forensic Taphonomy: The Postmortem Fate of Human Remains,* edited by W.D. Haglund and M.H. Sorg, pp. 367–379. CRC Press, Boca Raton, FL.

Hanfland, K., R. Keppel, and J. Weis

1997   Case Management for Missing Children Homicide Investigation: Executive Summary. Christine O. Gregorie, Attorney General of Washington and United States Department of Justice, Office of Juvenile Justice and Delinquency Prevention, Office of Justice Programs, pp. ii, 5–92.

Haskell, N.H.

1989   Calliphoridae of Pig Carrion in Northwest Indiana: A Seasonal Comparative Study. Master's thesis, Purdue University, West Lafayette, IN.

Morton, R.J., W.D. Lord, and M.L. Goff

1999   Taphonomic effects on child sized remains located in surface deposit and shallow burial disposal sites, *Proceedings of the American Academy of Forensic Sciences 51st Annual Meeting,* American Academy of Forensic Sciences, Colorado Springs, CO.

Payne, J.A.

1965   A summer carrion study of the baby pig, *Sus scrofa* Linnaeus, *Ecology* 46:592–602.

Rodriguez, W.C.

1987   Postmortem Animal Activity: Recognition and Interpretation. Paper presented at the 39th Annual Meeting of the American Academy of Forensic Sciences, San Diego.

Insects Associated with the Body: Their Use and Analyses

GAIL S. ANDERSON
VALERIE J. CERVENKA

Contents

Introduction

After death, a body, whether human or animal, goes through many rapid changes, the most noticeable of which is the decomposition of the soft tissue. Decomposition is driven by many factors, but among the most important are bacterial and insect action. Insects can be primarily responsible for the removal of most of the soft tissue. As such, they provide an extremely important ecological role, recycling the biomass of an animal so that it can be re-utilized in the food chain. A human body is a valuable food resource to a large number of insects and becomes attractive to insects immediately after death (Anderson and VanLaerhoven, 1996; Dillon, 1997; Dillon and Anderson, 1995; 1996; Nuorteva, 1997; Smith, 1986). The body changes biologically, physically, and chemically as it decomposes, so the composition of the food resource modifies over time. However, insects are extraordinarily good at exploiting just about all food niches possible, and a changing sequence of insects will be attracted to the remains after death, until there is no more utilizable nourishment left. Insects are, therefore, a very noticeable part of the decomposition process.

Insects are not only of ecological importance in decomposition, but are extremely valuable in death investigations. Although used in Europe for nearly 150 years (Haskell et al., 1997; Smith, 1986) it is only in the last 30 years that insects have become commonly used in death investigations in North America (Catts and Haskell, 1990). Now, in most regions, the entomologist has become an accepted part of the death investigation team. Insect evidence is used to estimate time of death, as well as drug use before death, position and presence of wounds, and whether the body has been disturbed or moved since death (See Anderson, 1999a; Catts and Goff, 1992; Haskell et al., 1997 for reviews.)

There are two fundamental ways to use insects to estimate time of death. The first method, blow fly developmental rates, is used when the body is relatively fresh, i.e., in the first few hours, days, or weeks after death. The second method relies on the fact that insects colonize remains in a predictable sequence, and is used when the victim has been dead from weeks to months to years in some cases.

Blow flies are the large metallic-colored flies seen attracted to meat or food. They belong to the family Calliphoridae, in the order Diptera, or True Flies. They are the first arrivals, laying their eggs on the body very soon after death. Their development from egg to first, second, and third instar, to pupa, and to adult follows a predictable pattern and is most influenced by species and temperature. As the development rates are predictable, an analysis of the oldest insect stage on the body, together with the meteorological conditions and the micro-climatic conditions at the scene, can be used to estimate how long insects have been feeding on the body, and hence how long the victim has been dead. All stages of the blow fly developmental cycle can be used in the death investigation.

In the late postmortem interval, species composition of insects present on the body at the time of discovery, with the species composition of those that have already left the remains, can be used to estimate time since death. However, caution must be taken when analyzing insect succession as it is strongly impacted by geographical region, habitat, and season (Anderson and VanLaerhoven, 1996; Dillon, 1997; Dillon and Anderson, 1995, 1996; Hobischak, 1997; Hobischak and Anderson (in press); MacDonell and Anderson, 1997; VanLaerhoven, 1997; VanLaerhoven and Anderson, 1996, 1999).

The following briefly reviews how both of these techniques are used, emphasizing the use of each stage of blow fly development, and illustrates their use with a variety of case studies.

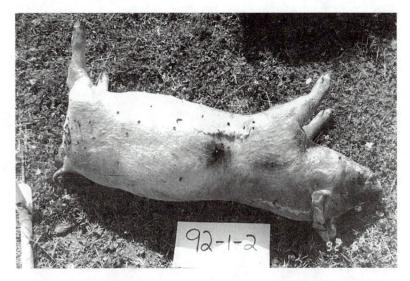

Figure 9.1 Large egg mass on pig (*Sus scrofa* (L.)) carcass, resulting from several female blow flies laying eggs. This egg mass was laid in under 5 min, as the carcass had previously been lying on the other side and had been turned over to collect insects from underneath the body. The wound is an exit wound from a .22 pistol. (Photograph taken by G.S. Anderson and S.L. VanLaerhoven. With permission.)

Blow Fly Eggs

Blow flies are the first insects to colonize remains, although the species will vary with geographical region and season. Some individuals will obtain a protein meal from the remains in order to develop their ovaries and testes (Erzinclioglu, 1996), but the majority of females are attracted to the body to lay their eggs. When the eggs hatch into first instar (first stage larvae), they are very small and vulnerable. They require a liquid protein meal but are unable to break skin (Smith, 1986). The female, therefore, ensures that she lays her eggs close to a wound site or a natural orifice that provides blood, body fluids, or a mucosal layer upon which it is easy to feed. Therefore, eggs are usually first found around these areas. If the wound is very wet, eggs and early instars may drown, so the female often lays her eggs extremely close to, but not actually in, a wound (Figure 9.1). The eggs are usually laid in large batches, up to 180 eggs at a time (Erzinclioglu, 1996). If one female has laid her eggs, many others become attracted to the same area and lay their eggs at the same site. Therefore, an egg mass may be several square centimeters in size and may contain many thousands of eggs. Eggs hatch after a predictable period of time, dependent on temperature and species, ranging from hours to days (see Table 9.1).

As time of death estimations using insect evidence are based on the age of the oldest insects on the body, eggs are only of value in the very early postmortem interval. In the later stages larvae or maggots are more important. Therefore, if the body already has maggots present, eggs are of little value. Blow flies will continue to lay their eggs on a body as long as it remains attractive to them. It is quite possible to find a body with extensive maggot activity from third instar, down through second and first instars, as well as freshly laid eggs; the third instars, then, would be of the most value. In fact, entomologists are usually involved in cases in which the decedent has been dead for 72 h or more. It is after

Table 9.1   Developmental Time for Two Species of Blow Fly under Varying Temperature Regimes

Temp. (°C)	Time for Eggs To Hatch (h)	
	Phaenicia (=Lucilia) sericata	*Phormia regina*
15.0	42.37	51.97
17.8	29.42	34.42
20.6	20.89	24.14
23.4	15.78	18.10
26.1	12.63	14.32
28.9	10.25	11.42
31.7	8.82	9.51
34.5	8.10	8.55
37.3	8.09	8.13
40.0	None hatched	8.70
42.8	None hatched	None hatched

Adapted from: Melvin, R., *Annals of the Entomological Society of America,* 27:406–410, 1934.

this time that medical parameters are of less use in estimating postmortem interval (Henssge et al., 1995), and insects may be better. However, as there are a tremendous number of variables involved in using medical parameters to determine time since death (Henssge et al., 1995), we have found that pathologists are calling entomologists into more and more cases of early postmortem interval for a second opinion.

Case Study #1

A young girl was found dead in late summer close to a riverbank in an urban area in western Canada. She was naked and face down. There were no wounds. The pathologist called to the scene called the entomologist (GSA). The victim had been found a few hours earlier, and had been rolled onto her back when examined. The only insect evidence on the remains consisted of unhatched insect eggs in the corners of the eyes and in one nostril. Half the eggs were preserved immediately for later court purposes, to prove that the exhibits had contained only eggs when collected. The remaining eggs were placed on a piece of fresh beef liver in a gallon glass jar and observed every hour until the majority had hatched. The eggs were received at 1030 h and the very first larva began to hatch at 1320 h later that day. Hatching in larger numbers began at 1750 h. The larvae were then reared through to adulthood in the forensic entomology lab at Simon Fraser University and identified as *Calliphora vicina* (Robineau-Desvoidy).

The duration of insect development stages decreases in a linear manner with increasing temperature (Chapman, 1980). Once maggots reach the third instar, large numbers together can generate heat and raise the body temperature considerably (Anderson and VanLaerhoven, 1996; Catts and Haskell, 1990; Dillon, 1997; Dillon and Anderson, 1995, 1996; Early and Goff, 1986; Greenberg, 1991). However, at the egg and early instar stages, development rates are entirely dependent on the ambient temperatures. Temperature data are available through Environment Canada throughout Canada, but hourly data could be obtained from only two Environment Canada weather stations in the area, both several kilometers from the death scene. On bright sunny days, there could be a great deal of variation between weather stations several kilometers from each other; however, the days including and preceding the discovery were overcast, which flattens out temperature variation. Thus, both stations would probably differ little from the crime scene temperatures (Webster, 1999). The mean temperature for the preceding 2 days was 17.4/17.9°C depending on which weather station was used. *Calliphora vicina* takes a minimum of 41.4 h to hatch at 15.8°C (Anderson, 2000); however, the scene temperature was warmer and fluctuated. Temperatures were converted to a thermal measure, accumulated degree hours (ADH), to allow for the warmer conditions. ADH were calculated for *C. vicina* by multiplying the developmental duration (in hours) for the time to hatch, by the rearing temperature. *C. vicina* would require a minimum of 654.12 ADH for eggs to hatch. The date and time of oviposition or egg laying are calculated by a simple reverse summation process. Table 9.2 shows the meteorological data from both Environment Canada Weather Stations and the summation of ADH.

The majority of larvae began to hatch at 1750 h on the day of collection (25th). As can be seen from Table 9.2, the weather stations indicated very similar temperatures and 654.12 ADH were accumulated by 0800 to 0900 h the previous day, whichever weather station is used. This means that at the temperatures the insects were exposed to, in order to hatch by 1750 h on the date of discovery, the eggs must have been laid by 0800 to 0900 h the previous day. Most blow flies do not oviposit at night. Although one study (Greenberg, 1990) indicated that some blow fly species will oviposit in small numbers on rat carcasses exposed at night near sodium vapor lamps in Chicago, it has never been observed in British Columbia (Anderson, unpublished data) nor was it observed in extensive studies in Indiana (Haskell et al., 1997). In fact, in a case in Manitoba, disemboweled and bloody bear cubs, shot at night at a garbage dump in the vicinity of large numbers of blow flies, were not colonized until the following morning (Anderson, 1999b). Therefore, the insect evidence indicated that the victim could have been killed any time during the evening of the 23rd or the night of 23/24th. The decedent could not have died during the day of the 23rd; otherwise, the eggs would already have hatched. Therefore, death occurred before 0800 to 0900 h the day prior to discovery and probably occurred the previous night. During the trial the defendant changed his plea and admitted to killing the victim in the night of 23/24th.

Collection and Handling of Eggs at a Crime Scene

Eggs should be carefully collected and observed in relatively fresh cases, in which no, or very little, maggot activity is present.

1. Look for egg masses in, or close to, wounds and natural orifices (e.g., inside nostrils and in and under eyelids). Eggs are usually laid in a mass, but more isolated eggs in eyelashes may look like insignificant cream-colored specks. Note position of egg masses.
2. Collect from each mass separately and keep each exhibit separate as site of oviposition may be of value later.
3. Collect using forceps and break a small piece of the egg mass away. The eggs appear glued together so breaking some off the main mass feels a bit like breaking a piece from a cookie. The forceps will invariably break some of the eggs but as such large numbers are usually collected, this is not a problem. The exhibit should be approximately a quarter the size of a dime (3 to 4 mm²). Do not collect from the very edge of the mass as eggs on the edge could well be desiccated and may not survive.

Table 9.2   Temperature Records and Accumulated Degree Hours (ADH) in Case Study 1

Time	Temperature Weather Station 1 (°C)	Temperature Weather Station 2 (°C)	ADH Weather Station 1	ADH Weather Station 2	
0700	14	15	674	667	
0800	16	16	660	652	*Oviposition began*
0900	18	17	644	636	
1000	19	18	626	619	
1100	20	18	607	601	
1200	21	17	587	583	
1300	20	18	566	566	
1400	20	18	546	548	
1500	20	18	526	530	
1600	20	18	506	512	
1700	19	18	486	494	
1800	18	18	467	476	
1900	18	18	449	458	
2000	17	17	431	440	
2100	17	17	414	423	
2200	17	17	397	406	
2300	17	17	380	389	
0000	17	17	363	372	
0100	17	17	346	355	
0200	17	17	329	338	
0300	16	17	312	321	
0400	15	17	296	304	
0500	14	16	281	287	
0600	14	16	267	271	
0700	15	17	253	255	
0800	15	16	238	238	
0900	17	17	223	222	
1000	18	17	206	205	
1100	18	18	188	188	
1200	26[a]	26[a]	170	170	
1300	24	24	144	144	*1st hatch*
1400	24	24	120	120	
1500	24	24	96	96	
1600	24	24	72	72	
1700	24	24	48	48	
1800	24	24	24	24	*Over 5% hatched*

[a] Temperatures from 1200 h August 25 are the temperatures at which the insects were maintained after collection and do not reflect temperatures from Environment Canada weather stations.

4. Each exhibit should be divided into two. One half should be immediately killed and preserved by placing in a vial with 75% alcohol (ETOH). The rest should be kept alive.

5. Place the live eggs in a vial with a piece of damp paper towel to prevent desiccation. Make a lid with dry paper towels, two layers thick, held in place with an elastic band to allow for air circulation. As soon as possible, a small piece of beef liver should be added.

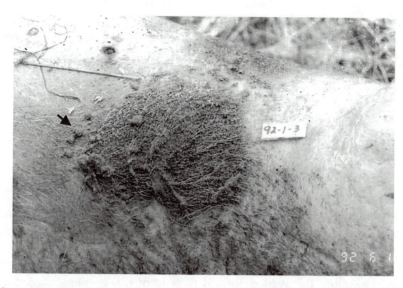

Figure 9.2 Small mass of first instar larvae on pig carcass. The mass is centered on a small wound in the skin, which is not visible under the maggots. Arrow indicates discarded chorions or egg shells. (Photograph taken by G.S. Anderson and S.L. VanLaerhoven. With permission.)

6. Place the vial with the live eggs in a protected area, out of direct sunlight. Observe the eggs every 30 to 60 minutes, noting any signs of hatch. Note also when first hatch occurs, then continue to monitor until all have hatched, approximating percentage hatch at each time.

7. Ensure that all vials are labeled with case number, collection site, date, time of collection/preservation, name, and phone number of collecting officer. Deliver to entomologist as soon as possible.

Blow Fly Larvae

Blow fly eggs hatch into the first of three separate stages of larvae (maggot). The first stage, or first instar, is a very tiny animal, about 1 to 2 mm in length. Figure 9.2 shows a mass of first instars around a small wound site. The cast chorions or egg shells can also be seen. The first instar feeds for a period of time, then molts into a second instar, which again feeds, then molts into a third instar. At each of these molts, the insect sheds its outer layer, as well as its internal cephalopharyngeal skeleton or mouthparts, and the lining of its tracheal system. Therefore, each new stage has a new set of spiracular slits and a new set of mouthparts. It is the mouthparts that contain the most diagnostic features for identification. During the third instar, the maggots may form large masses which can greatly increase the temperature of the body (Anderson and VanLaerhoven, 1996; Catts and Haskell, 1990; Deonier, 1940; Dillon and Anderson, 1995, 1996; Early and Goff, 1986; Greenberg, 1991; Haskell et al., 1997; Payne, 1965; Shean et al., 1993). During these feeding stages a bright red or brown crop or food storage organ is clearly visible. After a period of time in the third instar, the maggots enter a prepupal or wandering stage, leaving the body and searching for a safe, protected area in which to pupate. They will frequently burrow into soil, clothing, hair, or carpet. If the remains are on a hard floor, linoleum or

Table 9.3   Actual Temperatures Recorded at Environment Canada Weather Station and Scene Temperatures Predicted Using Regression Analysis, Case Study 2

Date	Environment Canada Weather Station (°C)	Predicted Scene Temperatures (°C)	
13th	17.5	21.6	*Victim last seen alive*
14th	18.0	22.2	
15th	17.8	22.0	
16th	18.3	22.5	
17th	21.8	26.4	*Victim found in morning*

concrete, for example, the larvae may travel great distances to find a suitable area, and may be found underneath boxes, flowerpots, etc. In extremely wet conditions, they have even been observed to climb the trunks of trees (Haskell et al., 1997). Some species such as *Protophormia terraenovae* (Robineau-Desvoidy) may stay close and pupate on the body (Erzinclioglu, 1996), but this is rare. Toward the end of this prepupal stage the maggots contract and broaden and become opaque. The time that the insect spends in each stage is dependent on temperature and species.

When large numbers of larvae are present on remains, large quantities of flesh may be consumed. Great care must be taken to determine whether any of the insects have entered the pupal stage. Failure to locate pupae will result in an underestimate of elapsed time since death. Conversely, if a thorough search for pupae is made, and none are found, then it can be safely concluded that the larvae are the oldest insects on the remains.

Case Study #2

Human remains with severe head trauma were found in a rural area of central Canada in summer. The head was colonized by larval blow flies. The victim was last seen alive on the 13th and was found on the 17th of the month. The remains were refrigerated overnight and the insects were sampled the following morning. The majority of insects collected from the remains were *Lucilia illustris* (Meigen) and the oldest specimens were in the third instar.

Weather records from Environment Canada indicated that the mean temperature for the area for the previous few days was between 17.5 and 21.8°C. A portable data logger (SmartReader®) was placed at the scene to determine whether the temperature at the scene was in general warmer, cooler, or similar to that recorded at the Environment Canada weather station. The logger recorded temperatures at the scene for 3 weeks and these were compared with data recorded at the Environment Canada weather station for the same time period. The data were compared visually and statistically using a regression analysis, which showed a good correlation between the two sets of data, with an R^2 of 0.69. The regression equation was used to predict the temperature at the scene, based on the temperatures recorded at the Environment Canada weather station. The results confirmed that the mean temperatures at the scene were warmer than those recorded at the Environment Canada weather station (as shown in Table 9.3), with mean temperatures ranging around 21 to 22°C, and rising to 26.4°C on the date of discovery and removal.

It is always preferable for a qualified forensic entomologist to attend both the crime scene and the autopsy to collect the insects. However, because Canada is an extremely large country, covering five time zones, this is often not possible. In these cases, identification (specialized crime scene police) officers (called Ident Officers) specifically trained in the collection of entomological evidence can be used. Entomologists frequently train police officers in insect collection, and a police training video has been developed for Canada (Royal Canadian Mounted Police "E" Division Training, 1997). The insects in this case were collected at the autopsy by a Royal Canadian Mounted Police (R.C.M.P.) Ident Officer. Half were killed and preserved immediately to stop the clock and the rest kept alive. If they are not killed, they will continue to develop and many more parameters, such as temperature during transit, will have to be taken into account. Moreover, such preserved specimens can be produced in court later if there is any question about their stage or identity. The rest of the specimens are kept alive to be reared to adulthood in the lab for identification. It is much easier to identify an adult fly than it is a maggot.

The entomologist (GSA) examined both live and preserved specimens. The majority of the preserved specimens were immature *Lucilia illustris* in the third instar, with some molting from second to third instar. As the live insects then took a further 6 days to pupate in the lab, it is probable that they were in the early stages of the third instar when collected. *L. illustris* takes a minimum of 93 h or 3.9 days to reach the third instar at a mean temperature of 21.2°C (Anderson, 2000). This is extremely close to the temperature of the death scene.

The remains were refrigerated for 11 h. Refrigeration of up to approximately 200 maggots at a time has been shown to stop development almost immediately (Johl and Anderson, 1996). However, as some maggot masses were present, the temperature in the remains probably will have dropped more slowly, possibly allowing some continued development. Maggot masses increase the temperature of the body, and when in large numbers and well advanced into the third instar, can maintain temperatures as high as 27 to 38°C for several hours within the refrigerator (Haskell et al., 1997). However, temperature does not rise significantly in a maggot mass until the maggots have entered the third instar. The insects in this case had only just entered this stage so it is probable that they did not have a major impact, although they may have increased the temperature of the remains slightly.

It would have been far preferable had the body been available for insect collection before refrigeration; however, this was not possible. So, as the insects were at the beginning of the third instar when collected at 0910 h on the 18th, they had either entered this stage just before refrigeration at 2142 h on the 17th, or had continued to develop briefly during refrigeration and entered this stage after 2142 h on the 17th, but before 0910 h on the 18th. The maggots would have begun to cool after they were refrigerated and development would probably have been arrested sometime between being placed in refrigeration and being removed from refrigeration. The oldest insects were a minimum of 93 h old when collected. Counting back from the time of refrigeration and the time of collection, eggs would have been laid between midnight the 13th and noon the following day, the 14th. Blow flies do not usually lay eggs at night in dark, rural areas; therefore, it is probable that the eggs were laid in the early morning of 14th, and that death could have occurred in the previous evening, 13th or in the night of the 13 to 14th. The victim must have been dead by the morning of the 14th. She was last seen alive the previous evening.

Case Study #3

In some cases, blow flies will colonize a person in life. This is called myiasis or the infestation of living vertebrate animals with dipteran larvae which, at least for a certain period of time, feed on the host's dead or living tissue, liquid body substances, or ingested food. This usually occurs in animals, when an injury or presence of excretory material makes the living animal attractive. It is a major problem in the sheep industry, resulting in blow fly strike and causing $100,000s of damage every year (Wall et al., 1992, 1995; Wardhaugh and Morton, 1990). When found in humans it is usually the result of neglect. There have been many reports worldwide of cases of accidental myiasis in humans (Bauch et al., 1984; Carpenter and Chastain, 1992; Deroo et al., 1990; Erzinclioglu and Whitmore, 1983; Fawzy, 1991; Fotedar et al., 1991; Greenberg, 1984; Hall et al., 1986; Kpea and Zywocinski, 1995; Lee and Yong, 1991; Miller et al., 1990; Morsy and Farrag, 1991; Nielsen, 1993; Richard and Gerrish, 1983). In most of these cases, the insects are colonizing a living person, and feeding on the dead organic matter, rather than on living tissue. In fact, this ability to remove dead tissue, cell for cell, while leaving the living tissue intact has been used in medical systems for centuries for debridement of wounds (Baer, 1931; Sherman and Pechter, 1988) and has recently been revisited as a viable option to surgery (King and Flynn, 1991; Kumar and Joshi, 1995; Pechter and Sherman, 1983; Sherman, 1998; Sherman and Pechter, 1988; Sherman et al., 1995, 1996).

From a forensic perspective, myiasis may cause confusion. It is generally assumed that the blow flies have colonized shortly after death; so postmortem interval estimation is based on this. For instance, if larvae are determined to be a minimum of 7 days old, then it is usually accepted that the victim has been dead for a minimum of 7 days. However, if the victim was colonized when alive, the insect evidence is indicating time of neglect or injury, rather than time of death (Goff et al., 1991). If the victim subsequently dies prior to discovery, this can result in an error in postmortem interval estimation.

In the following case, the victim was found prior to death. A man was found in spring in a major city in western Canada, unconscious with severe head injuries. He was lying down an embankment in partial shade. He was taken to hospital, but died 2 days later from his injuries. A large number of maggots were feeding in the head area, in the wounds, and in the mouth and throat. In fact, at the hospital, the victim appeared to be choking on the large numbers of maggots in his mouth and throat (Dillon, pers. comm.). The mean temperatures for the area ranged between 10.7 and 16.9°C, with highs ranging from 13.6 to 23.4°C. However, as the victim was alive and the insects were feeding in the wound, the temperature to which the maggots were exposed was probably considerably higher. Body temperature is 37°C, so the insects were probably at a temperature between the two.

Larval *Calliphora vomitoria* (L.) and *Phaenicia sericata* (Meigen) were collected from the wounds. These species normally colonize dead material, but will feed on dead organic matter on a living person. *C. vomitoria* is normally considered a more rural species, and its presence at this urban site is unusual, although *P. sericata* is a common urban species (Anderson, 1995).

At 29°C, *Calliphora vomitoria* takes a minimum of 45 h to reach the beginning of the third instar, and at 35°C, it takes a minimum of 42 h to reach the beginning of this stage (Greenberg and Tantawi, 1993). This is probably a reasonable temperature range as the insects would not have been at a temperature as high as body temperature, nor as low as ambient air temperature, but somewhere between. The oldest insects had already entered the 3rd instar, so were older than this, but had not yet reached the prepupal stage, which takes a further 88.8 h at 29°C and a further 44.4 h at 35°C (Greenberg and Tantawi, 1993). Therefore, these insects were probably at least 2 days old and could have been 3.6 or more days old. *Phaenicia sericata* takes a minimum of 50 h to reach the beginning of the third instar at 29°C, and spends a further 22 h in this stage before entering the prepupal stage

(Greenberg, 1991). Therefore, insects from this species were probably at least 2 days old and could have been almost 3 days old.

It is probable that the victim was injured but not colonized by insects for some days, especially if conscious. It is likely that the insects began to colonize the man when he started to lose consciousness. These species usually colonize dead victims or carrion animals; when found on living victims, they feed on the dead and infected tissue, not on the living tissue. Therefore, the insects would not have colonized until the wound reached a stage where infection and dead organic matter were present. This may have taken a few days. Therefore, the insects probably colonized the victim at least 2 to 3 days before discovery, but the injuries would have occurred some days before this.

If the victim in this case had died before discovery, an overestimate of time since death could have been made, without attention to the colonization, wounds, and general scenario. In cases involving myiasis, the forensic entomologist is determining time since injury or neglect, rather than time since death.

Collection of Blow Fly Larvae

1. Blow fly larvae may be found as 1st, 2nd, 3rd or prepupal (post feeding) maggots. The 1st to 3rd stages will be found on the remains. They may be first found close to wound sites and/or natural orifices, but as decomposition progresses, they will be found throughout the body. They may be found in small groups or in large masses. Prepupal larvae will have begun to move away from the body and may be found in the hair, clothing or first 3 to 5 cm of soil. They may wander as far as 50 m from the body (Haskell et al., 1997), but are usually found quite close to the remains, if suitable media are found nearby.

2. There may be several sites of maggot activity on the body. If so, collect and keep separately, as the actual location of the maggots may be important in wound determination later (Rodriguez and Bass, 1987). Note whether maggot masses are present and how large. If possible, carefully take the temperature of each mass. Mass temperature fluctuates diurnally, dropping at night (Anderson and VanLaerhoven, 1996; Dillon, 1997; Dillon and Anderson, 1995, 1996), so a temperature taken during the day will probably give the maximum mass temperature.

3. For each exhibit, approximately 100 to 200 larvae should be collected (insects have a very high mortality rate so more, within limits, is usually better). An ideal vial size is a 250-mL urinalysis vial (Figure 9.3).

4. Collect the larvae with forceps (gently); 50% of each exhibit should be preserved immediately at the scene. The larvae should be placed first in hot water for 5 min then placed in preservative, preferably 75% or higher ethanol. This is the best method because it prevents shrinkage and preserves the larvae very well (Tantawi and Greenberg, 1993). However, if hot water is not available, the larvae should be placed directly in preservative. It is extremely important to preserve the insects in the quickest manner at the scene for later forensic analysis. The vial should be clearly labeled with the time and date of preservation, location of collection, collecting officer's name, etc.

5. The other half of each exhibit should be kept alive for later rearing to adulthood, for identification purposes. The larvae should be placed in a vial (Figure 9.3) with no more than will cover the base in a single layer. In the past, samples have been sent to entomologists with the vial filled to the brim. Larvae are air breathers, and

Figure 9.3 Vials used in insect collection. The screw lid (on the right) should be used for insects in preservative, and the paper towels, held in place with an elastic band, used for live specimens. The paper towels allow the passage of air, but prevent insect escape. A piece of slightly damp paper towel prevents drowning or desiccation and increases surface area. A small piece of raw beef liver should be added as soon as possible. A full label should be placed on every vial. (Photograph taken by G.S. Anderson. With permission.)

when the vial is filled to the top, there is no air, and the majority, if not all, will die. So larvae should be placed in the vial no more than one layer deep. A piece of paper towel can be placed inside to increase the surface area. Care should also be taken to ensure that maggots collected from the remains do not drown. Maggots, particularly those in the third instar in masses, are often very wet from body fluids and the products of their own metabolism (Figure 9.4). When on the remains they are capable of moving away from very wet areas, but in a small vial, they can frequently drown. The paper towel helps prevent the insects from drowning. Conversely, if the larvae are very dry, perhaps from being in the soil, then the towel can be moistened slightly to prevent desiccation. The normal screw lid should be discarded and replaced by two layers of paper towel held in place by an elastic band, as shown in Figure 9.3. As soon as possible, the larvae should be fed a small piece of beef liver. Do not use the plastic lid pierced with holes. The holes will be either too small for adequate air circulation or large enough to allow escape.

6. Prepupal larvae should be treated in the same manner as above, but will be found away from the body. They do not require food, but a piece of damp paper towel will prevent desiccation.

7. See R.C.M.P. "E" Division Training (1997) for further details.

Blow Fly Pupae

Once the prepupal maggot has contracted, it will begin to pupate. It does not shed its third instar cuticle as was done in its previous molts, but rather loosens itself from the cuticle, and secretes a number of substances into this cuticle which then hardens and darkens to form the puparium. The pupa is a living insect and the outside pupal case or puparium is the non-living structure that encloses it (Erzinclioglu, 1996; Fraenkel and Bhaskaran, 1973). However, for simplicity's sake, the puparium, together with the internal, living pupa,

Figure 9.4 Maggots on human remains at autopsy. Note how wet the maggots are. Caution should be taken when collecting maggots from masses such as this as they may drown if placed directly into a vial. The addition of a small piece of paper towel will prevent this. (Photograph taken by C. Newell, B.C. Coroners Forensic Unit. With permission.)

will be referred to as the pupa, and the puparium as the pupal case, as these are terms usually used at crime scenes. At the onset of pupation, the pupa is a pale cream color which darkens over a few hours (Smith, 1986). Therefore, if a very pale-colored pupa is found, then it has only just begun to pupate and its age can be determined very precisely. If such pupae are found, they should be kept separate from other samples and it should be noted on the label that they were pale in color when collected, as they will continue to darken in transit and will be fully tanned by the time the entomologist receives them.

Once pupae are found at a scene, it is very important to continue to search to determine whether any have already reached the adult stage and left empty pupal cases behind. If such evidence is missed, then the determination of elapsed time since death will be an underestimate. Conversely, if a full search is made and only pupae are found, it is safe to assume that the pupae are the oldest stage.

Case Study #4

Human remains were found on large rocks beneath a cliff in western Canada in early summer. Insect evidence was collected from the remains and from the rocks beneath and below the body. Further evidence was collected at the autopsy. The remains were not skeletonized, and were dried in areas that were exposed to the sun.

Weather records for the area from Environment Canada indicated that the mean temperature for the previous 3 weeks was 15.2°C, with highs reaching into the twenties on occasion and a low down to 6.5°C. Three species of blow fly were collected from the remains:

Phormia regina (Meigen), *Protophormia terraenovae,* and *Calliphora vomitoria.* However, the vast majority were *P. regina.* The oldest specimens of *P. regina* were in the pupal stage, but few pupae were found, indicating that pupation probably had only just begun. This species takes a minimum of 18.4 days to reach the beginning of the pupal stage at 16.1°C or 296 accumulated degree days (ADD) (Anderson, 2000). These would have accumulated if eggs had been laid 20 days earlier. Other species collected were *P. terraenovae,* which develops at a similar rate to *P. regina* (Greenberg, 1996; Kamal, 1958) and *C. vomitoria,* which was in the third instar when collected and was younger. Therefore, the insects indicated that death had occurred 20 or more days prior to discovery. The victim was last seen alive late in the day, 21 days earlier.

Collection of Blow Fly Pupae

1. Search soil under and around body. Also search clothing, hair, and any other debris around scene. Prepupal larvae can migrate great distances, but usually stay within a meter or so of the body. Usually, the majority are found within the area that is gridded and screened. Therefore, no further work is being asked for, only that the investigator keep an eye out for pupae when looking for other evidence in soil as it is screened.
2. Pupae must NOT be put into preservative. They should be placed in a dry vial, with a piece of damp paper towel to cushion the insects and to prevent desiccation. If transport time will be less than 24 h and the vial is at least 250 mL, then the original screw lid can be used. Otherwise, a lid of paper towels should be used instead (Figure 9.3).
3. A small soil sample from close to, but not under, the body should also be placed in a separate container. Usually a coffee or paint can-type container is appropriate and should be half-filled with soil. The lid can then be placed securely on the can as the loose soil, together with the air space above, will allow enough air for any insects in the soil. Do not fill up to the top with soil, or use plastic bags, as this will not allow enough air.
4. See RCMP (Royal Canadian Mounted Police) "E" Division training video for further details.

In some cases forensically important insects may themselves be parasitized by other insects. This can also aid in determining time since death.

Case Study #5

The remains of an unidentified female were discovered in the underbrush near a cornfield by a deer hunter in mid-November. The body was clothed and almost entirely decomposed, with the head and feet skeletonized and disarticulated. During the postmortem exam 2 days later, VJC collected insect evidence, including the larvae of *Fannia canicularis* (L.), *F. manicata* (Meigen), *F. scalaris* F., *Piophila casei* (L.) and Heleomyzidae. *Fannia* species, also known as latrine flies, occur on bodies in a state of protein fermentation, arriving later in the successional colonization of the body. The timing of their arrival depends on geographic region but is usually about 2 months after death (Dillon, 1997; Dillon and Anderson, 1995, 1996) or more (Smith, 1986), although they can be found on buried bodies much earlier (VanLaerhoven, 1997; VanLaerhoven and Anderson, 1996, 1999). More importantly, however, large numbers of *Protophormia terraenovae* and *Phormia regina* (Meigen) puparia were collected, many eclosed, and some containing parasitoid emergence holes.

Figure 9.5 *Muscidifurax* sp. ovipositing egg in fly puparium. (Photograph taken by V.J. Cervenka. With permission).

In this case parasitoid were tiny wasps (Hymenoptera) that lay their eggs in the eggs or pupae of other insects, causing the host insect's death. The wasps belonged to the family Pteromalidae, which can lay single or multiple eggs. They sting or oviposit in the pupae of muscoid flies, including blow flies (Figure 9.5). The wasp eggs hatch, and the larvae feed on the fly developing within the puparium, or pupal case, killing it. The wasp larva pupates and emerges as an adult, still within the fly puparium. Once emerged, it chews a small, circular hole in the pupal case and climbs out, to repeat the process on another fly. Since the wasps will only oviposit on pupae of a certain age, they can be used to estimate postmortem interval. The wasp waits until the last larval skin has separated from the inside of the fly puperium before it deposits the egg. This generally occurs from 24 to 30 h of pupal age (Fraenkel and Bhaskeran, 1973).

One of the *Protophormia terraenovae* pupae collected from the remains contained a parasitoid, *Muscidifurax* species. *Muscidifurax* sp. lay their eggs in puparia that are at least 24 h old (see Figure 9.5). Pupae continue to be attractive to parasitoids until several days later (Moon, pers. comm.).

Muscidifurax has a developmental threshold or base temperature of 6°C (Moon, pers. comm.). At a constant temperature of 30.6°C, the wasp needs 344.4 ADD to reach adulthood. In order for *Muscidifurax* to complete its development, it would have had to lay its egg in the *Protophormia terraenovae* pupa around August 12, when the fly pupa would have been at least 24 h old. Since *P. terraenovae* needs 110 ADD to reach the pupal stage (Moon, pers. comm.), adding this amount to the 344 ADD that *Muscidifurax* needs brings the date of fly egg laying to sometime between August 2 and 3. Assuming flies had access to the remains soon after death, it is likely the woman was dead at the end of July at the earliest or around August 3 at the latest.

Empty Blow Fly Puparia and Newly Emerged Adult Flies

When the insect has completed its metamorphosis inside the pupal case, or puparium, the adult fly emerges. The fly breaks open the puparium by expanding and contracting a haemolymph (blood)-filled sac, or ptilinum, on its head (Erzinclioglu, 1996). This ptilinum

Figure 9.6 Empty puparia and ecdysial caps from *Calliphora vicina* left behind after the adult fly emerged. (Photograph taken by G.S. Anderson. With permission.)

forces the tip of the puparium, or operculum, off and the new adult emerges from the pupal case. As the operculum is broken off, it splits into two halves or caps (Figure 9.6). The upper cap still has the respiratory horns attached and the lower cap bears the mouthparts (Erzinclioglu, 1996). When the adult fly emerges, it is fairly unrecognizable as the bright, metallic-colored fly that it will become. The wings are crumpled, the legs spindly, and the body dull, dark, and puny. It cannot fly, but can run very fast, often leading investigators to mistake it for some other type of insect, or even a spider (Haskell et al., 1997). This can be likened to a butterfly emerging from the chrysalis, which also has crumpled wings and nothing of the splendor it will later achieve. The newly emerged blow fly crawls out of the soil or clothing in which it has secreted itself during the pupal period and orients itself toward the light, digging upward (Fraenkel, 1935). This positive phototropism is why adult flies often appear to be attracted to light bulbs later in life. The ptilinum is then withdrawn back into the head, and has no further use. During the following few hours, the adult pumps haemolymph into its wings and the rest of the body and the wings expand and the body begins to take on its usual metallic sheen. The fly may appear to be fully expanded and pigmented after a few hours, but it usually takes 24 h for the process to be completed (Erzinclioglu, 1996).

Newly emerged flies are of great forensic significance as they indicate that a complete blow fly life cycle has been completed on the body. If they are the first flies to emerge and the majority of other forensic evidence consists of complete pupae, then they can be used to determine the postmortem interval very precisely. However, they are extremely delicate and can be crushed easily. They are also very mobile and prefer to hide, presumably because they are so vulnerable at this stage. If found, such flies should be placed in a dry vial and not preserved. If killed at this stage, even if they have begun to expand their wings and attain color, they immediately crumple and lose all color if placed in preservative. This can make it extremely difficult to identify the species. The appearance of the fly when collected should be clearly noted because once it reaches the entomologist, it will have completed its expansion and will look like any other adult fly of that species. Adult blow flies are normally of little forensic value as there is usually no way to determine whether the fly has emerged from the body or has just arrived to feed, lay eggs, or mate. However, when newly emerged, non-expanded specimens are found, they cannot fly and are clearly associated with the remains.

It is quite rare to find newly emerged flies, but they leave behind the puparium or empty pupal case as evidence that this life cycle has taken place. These can be identified, but some species have few identifying characteristics. The scanning electron microscope has been used to identify more diagnostic criteria (Liu and Greenberg, 1989), but this is an expensive technique that is rarely available. Empty pupal cases are dark and fragile and are usually buried in a few centimeters of soil or hidden in the clothing seams, making them difficult to locate. They have also been confused with rat droppings (Haskell et al., 1997).

In addition to the puparium, the two parts of the ecdysial caps are also left behind. The third instar mouthparts are the main features used to identify the species of the larva, and are left behind after the fly emerges. In most cases, the ecdysial cap is broken away from the rest of the pupal case and, as it is so small and delicate, it is invariably lost. However, in some cases, particularly when the body has been protected or sheltered, such as in a vehicle or closet, the ecdysial caps may also be recovered. They are usually separate from the main puparium, but may, in some cases, remain attached. These are particularly valuable, as the mouthparts can be used to identify the puparium.

The presence of empty pupal cases indicates a minimum elapsed time since death. However, as the pupal case is made of chitin, it is very durable, and although an empty pupal case is fragile, in that it is easily crushed, in a protected environment it may last an extremely long time. In some cases they have been found in graves 130 to 160 years old (Gilbert and Bass, 1967). This usually occurs only in sheltered situations, as weathering from rain, wind, soil action, etc. usually breaks down the puparia. Most of the time it is possible to tell whether puparia are relatively fresh or have been exposed for a while from the level of deterioration, but it is not possible to tell whether a fly emerged a day, a week, a month, or more before discovery.

Case Study #6

The skeletonized and heavily scavenged remains of a young girl were found in summer in central Canada, in a forested area in complete shade. The victim had last been seen alive 38 days earlier, on June 5. The insect evidence collected included empty pupal cases which were identified as belonging to *Phormia regina* and *Protophormia terraenovae*, as well as pupae of *P. regina* and *P. terraenovae*, larval *Hydrotaea dentipes* and *H. houghii* (Diptera: Muscidae), larval Psychodidae, larval and adult Histeridae (*Hister depurator*; Coleoptera), larval Staphylinini (Coleoptera: Staphylinidae), larval Hydrophilidae (Coleoptera), and adult *Geotrupes semiopacus* (Coleoptera: Geotrupidae).

The empty pupal cases of *Phormia regina* and *Protophorma terraenovae* indicated that both species had completed an entire life cycle of egg to adult on the remains. The mean temperature for the previous 38 days recorded from the nearest Environment Canada weather station was $15.7 \pm 3.8°C$. Other Environment Canada weather stations in the vicinity showed means of 15.2°C and 15.3°C for this time period, indicating that the overall temperatures in the area were similar. However, the remains were found in a forested region and were shaded so the conditions there may have been somewhat cooler. Therefore, a portable SmartReader® data logger was placed at the scene which recorded the temperature every 30 minutes for 6 wks. These data were then compared statistically using a regression analysis, with data recorded for the same time period by Environment Canada. The cor-

Table 9.4 Comparison of Regression Analyses for Four Weather Stations in the Vicinity of the Crime Scene, Case Study 6

Weather Station	R^2	Significance	Regression Equation (Scene Temperature =)	Predicted Scene Mean Temperature (°C)
1	0.84	1.65^{-18}	Station 1 temp. × 1.060172 − 1.97833	14.7
2	0.82	4.44^{-17}	Station 2 temp. × 0.974563 + 0.092445	15.0
3	0.91	2.61^{-23}	Station 3 temp. × 1.069499 − 1.55617	14.8
4	0.90	3.11^{-22}	Station 4 temp. × 0.996069 − 1.508	14.7

relation between the two sets of data was extremely high, with an R^2 of 0.84; the significance of the relationship was 1.65^{-18}, extremely significant. The equation generated by this regression analysis was used to predict the temperature at the death scene, and was found to be a mean of 14.7°C for the 38 days that the victim had been missing, on average 1°C cooler than that at the weather station. Originally, the data used were those from the Environment Canada weather station that was closest to the crime scene and which also had the most similar habitat (station 1). However, defense counsel expressed concern that this station, despite being closest, might not actually be representative of the area. Therefore, the analysis was repeated using data for all four weather stations within a 100 km radius of the scene. Each weather station gave very similar results (Table 9.4). Overall, the temperature at the scene would have been slightly cooler than that at the weather stations, as would be expected in a forested, shaded region.

Phormia regina takes a minimum of 29.8 days (716.3 h) and a maximum of 36 days to complete development and emerge as an adult fly at 16.1°C (Anderson, 2000). The scene temperatures were cooler than this so development would have taken longer. *Protophormia terraenovae* takes 13.9 days to complete development at 23°C and 90.7 days to complete development at 12.5°C (Greenberg, 1991). No published data are available for this species at temperatures close to the death scene, but *P. terraenovae* has been reported to develop at the same rate as *P. regina* (Greenberg, 1996; Kamal, 1958) so it can be assumed that it also would have taken 29.8 to 36 days to complete development.

As the temperatures at the scene were slightly lower than 16.1°C, the data can be converted to accumulated degree days (ADD) to allow for the cooler temperatures. The use of ADD is based on the assumed linear relationship between temperature and development; however, although the relationship is linear over optimum temperature ranges and within small temperature ranges, it becomes more sigmoid at extremes of temperature. Therefore, ADD should only be used for situations in which developmental data are available that have been generated from temperatures close to those at which they will be applied. As the temperature gap becomes wider, the relationship between temperature and development rates becomes less linear. For instance, *Protophormia terraenovae* takes 13.9 days to complete development at 23°C or 319.7 ADD, and 10.9 days or 314.7 ADD at 29°C (Greenberg, 1991), showing that the relationship between development and temperature for these two temperatures is very close to linear, allowing for the accurate use of ADD to predict development times between these temperatures. However, at the much lower temperature of 12.5°C, this species takes 90.7 days or 1133.75 ADD to complete development; the relationship is more sigmoid than linear at this temperature.

If data generated at 16.1°C, very close to that of the death scene, are converted to ADD, it would take *Phormia regina* (and presumably *Protophormia terraenovae*) a minimum of 480.5 ADD and a maximum of 580 ADD to reach the adult stage (Anderson, 2000). Using the temperatures predicted for the crime scene by the regression analysis, 480.5 ADD would have been accumulated by June 5 and 580 ADD by June 11.

Other factors that must be considered include whether or not a maggot mass increased the temperature of the body, and so speeded up development. This is difficult to predict in most cases, when the insect colonization has gone beyond the maggot stage. However, in this case the entire scene was very carefully gridded, searched and screened and a total of only 20 puparia and 19 pupae were found. Even when exhaustive search methods such as this are used, it is quite possible that some pupae/puparia may have been missed, but even if only 10 to 20% were collected, there would still not have been nearly enough maggots to generate any significant increase in temperature. It could be argued that scavengers had moved the remains away from its original decomposition site, but this was not the case as decomposition had clearly occurred at the discovery site. Even when maggot masses are present, the lab data still appear to be representative of field data. This is possibly because the oldest prepupal maggots appear to leave before a maggot mass begins to generate heat when the remains are in shade (Dillon, 1997; Dillon and Anderson, 1996, 1998) or it may be because lab data still incorporate a measure of maggot mass activity as large numbers of maggots are raised together.

Field experiments with pig carcasses (*Sus scrofa* (L.)) in the northern interior region of British Columbia showed very similar developmental data for *Phormia regina* (Dillon, 1997; Dillon and Anderson, 1996). A large number of carcasses were placed at the research site and were monitored throughout decomposition. Insects were regularly collected from them in order to observe development and insect succession in a natural environment (Dillon, 1997; Dillon and Anderson, 1996). The research site had very similar weather conditions to those found at the scene in this case, and as temperature is the main governing force in blow fly development, these data are probably representative of those from the crime scene.

These similarities, of course, do not apply to successional data, as geographic differences have a great deal more influence on arrival times and species composition on later successional species. In the field research, the very first blow fly to emerge was observed 30 days after death (Dillon, 1997; Dillon and Anderson, 1996). After considerable searching of the remains and the soil nearby, only one empty pupal case was found, but within the next 5 days 200 pupal cases were found (Dillon, pers. comm.). This indicates that the very first flies emerged after 30 days and continued to emerge for several days. *Phormia regina* was the dominant species at this site, representing over 80% of the blow flies (Dillon, 1997; Dillon and Anderson, 1996).

The mean temperature at the research site was 15.4°C, very similar to that at the crime scene, with the mean maximum temperature at 22.2°C, slightly above that at the weather stations near the scene, and the mean minimum temperature was 8.6°C, slightly lower than the mean minimum temperatures at the weather stations (Dillon, pers. comm.; Dillon, 1997; Dillon and Anderson, 1996). So the weather conditions at the research site in British Columbia were very similar to those indicated for the death scene, using any or all of the weather station data.

Large maggot masses were present on the carcasses at the research site and they did raise the internal carcass temperature. The mean internal carcass temperature was 23.1°C, with a mean maximum of 27.6°C and a mean minimum of 18.7°C. The highest temperature reached was 44.8°C, and the lowest was 8.0°C. (Dillon, pers. comm.; Dillon, 1997; Dillon and Anderson, 1996). However, despite the increased heat generated by the maggots, the first insects still took 30 to 35 days to develop (Dillon, pers. comm.; Dillon, 1997; Dillon and Anderson, 1996), just the same as laboratory data indicated (Anderson, 2000). *P. regina* takes a minimum of 15.4 days to complete development at 23.0°C (Anderson, 2000). Had the mean carcass temperature of 23.1°C been used to determine developmental rates for the research carcasses, rather than ambient temperatures, death of the research pigs would have been predicted to have occurred 15.4 days postmortem, rather than the actual 30 days. Obviously, although maggot masses can raise the temperature of the carcass, development at these temperatures still appears to be very closely linked to ambient temperature, rather than maggot mass temperature. These field data (Dillon, pers. comm.; Dillon, 1997; Dillon and Anderson, 1996) completely support the laboratory data (Anderson, 2000).

These data also answer questions about the potential effect of constant vs. fluctuating temperatures. Frequently, there is a question in court as to whether data generated in a lab, at constant temperatures, can be applied to a field situation in which the insects are exposed to fluctuating temperatures. The proper use of degree days should eliminate some of this concern; however, it is possible that fluctuating temperatures could retard or increase developmental rates as is seen in some insect groups (Bradshaw, 1980; Hagstrum and Leach, 1972; Messenger, 1964, 1969; Richards and Suanraksa, 1962; Yeargan, 1980). Research on blow flies has shown that in most species there is no significant difference between development rates of insects raised at constant temperatures and those raised at a temperature that fluctuated around the mean (Dallwitz, 1984; Greenberg, 1991). This is supported by field research (Dillon, 1997; Dillon and Anderson, 1996) and lab data (Anderson, 2000). In some blow fly species, fluctuation in temperature slightly delayed development rate (Erzinclioglu, 1996; Greenberg, 1991), which means that in these cases, because forensic entomologists usually estimate a minimum elapsed time since death, any error generated by using data developed at constant temperatures will be conservative.

The estimate of 480.5 ADD, reached on June 5, is based on the minimum developmental time to reach the adult stage and assumes that the very first flies have only just emerged on the day of collection. The estimate of 580 ADD, reached on June 11, is based on the maximum time to reach the adult stage, and assumes that all the flies have eclosed. In this case, however, just over half the collected pupae and empty puparia consisted of puparia, indicating that approximately half the insects had already emerged. Therefore, these insects were probably oviposited midway between June 5 and 11, around June 8.

Another factor to be taken into account is the fact that *Phormia regina* is a species that is often not attracted to the remains for the first few days after death (Anderson and VanLaerhoven, 1996; Denno and Cothran, 1976; Goddard and Lago, 1985; Hall and Doisy, 1993; Lord and Burger, 1984), with the majority attracted 2 to 3 days after death. So it is possible that death occurred 2 to 3 days before oviposition, indicating that death probably occurred on June 5, the day the victim went missing.

Many other species of insects were associated with these remains, as well as blow flies, and were mostly those seen in later succession: days, weeks, or months after death. Blow flies are ubiquitous and most data used in their analyses are lab generated. Therefore, such data can be applied to any geographical area, as long as careful attention is made to local meteorological conditions, which are the main governing forces in blow fly development.

However, the successional colonization of remains by carrion insects depends heavily on geographic region and biogeoclimatic zone. Different species will be present in various geographic areas, and their arrival times and tenure on the body may change greatly from region to region (Anderson and VanLaerhoven, 1996; Dillon, 1997; Dillon and Anderson, 1995, 1996). Therefore, data generated from one geographic region should only be applied to another geographic region with utmost caution. No successional database existed at the time of this case for any region of central Canada, so the timing of arrival of the other species in this case could not be used to back up the estimation based on blow fly development. We have, however, begun an extensive set of experiments to develop a database of insect succession on carrion for the southern Manitoba region in the future (Gill et al., 1998/2000).

Collection of Puparia

1. Empty pupal cases will be found hidden, usually a few centimeters deep in the soil, or within clothing pockets, folds, and seams — see Collection of Blow Fly Pupae for full details.
2. Empty pupal cases look very similar to pupae, but as if the top has been cut off, a bit like a boiled egg with the top removed (Figure 9.6). They will be hollow inside. See Haskell et al. (1997).
3. Search for puparia but also for the tiny caps that have been pushed off, as these can be very diagnostically useful. The caps are tiny and very fragile (Figure 9.6).
4. Place in a dry vial and add a piece of tissue paper to cushion them in transit. No preservation is required as they are not alive.
5. A small soil sample should also be collected — see Collection of Blow Fly Pupae for details.

Successional Colonization of the Remains

Once blow flies have gone through an entire life cycle on the remains, they can be used only to indicate a minimum elapsed time since death. Additional analyses of the later colonizing species are useful in refining that estimate. This method usually is not as precise as using maggot development, but can estimate the postmortem interval up to a year or more after death. However, much more than blow fly development, the successional colonization of remains is very dependent on biogeoclimatic zone, habitat, and season. Therefore, databases of insect succession on carrion should be established for all areas, seasons, and habitats in which such analyses are being attempted.

Case Study #7

Human remains were found under the frame of a waterbed in northwestern Canada. The mattress was not present; the remains were completely enclosed by the frame, and the frame was covered with a plastic lining. The remains were partially mummified and fully clothed. The victim had last been seen alive the previous year, in March. The bed was in a basement bedroom of a house (the house had been continuously occupied). A number of different species were collected from the remains, including pupae and puparia from

Figure 9.7 Cast larval skins of dermestid beetles (Dermestidae: Coleoptera). (Photograph taken by G.S. Anderson. With permission.)

the families Fanniidae and Sphaeroceridae (Diptera), and cast larval skins of Dermestidae (Coleoptera) (Figure 9.7), together with large quantities of dermestid frass (excreta) and peritrophic membrane. Peritrophic membrane lines the gut of insects and is passed out when the insect defecates. Normally, it is lost, together with the delicate cast larval skins of beetles, due to the action of environmental conditions such as rain and wind; however, in sheltered conditions, peritrophic membrane associated with dermestid beetles (Coleoptera: Dermestidae) may build up and survive for a long period of time. It is often found years after death (Haskell et al., 1997; Voigt, 1965), but has been observed as early as 4 months after death (Haskell et al., 1997). Although the remains would have been highly unattractive to blow flies at the stage they had reached when discovered, some evidence of blow fly presence, such as empty pupal cases, would have been expected had they been present earlier. No Calliphoridae were found at any developmental stage, nor was there any evidence of past colonization. In fact, peritrophic membrane is usually found in cases in which fly activity has been minimal. (Haskell et al., 1997)

The remains were found in late May, a time when mean daily temperatures were in the single figures, and night time temperatures still commonly dropped below 0°C. It was too early for insects to have colonized the remains that season, so the remains must have been present the previous year. The large numbers of puparia and pupae of later colonizing insect species indicated the remains had been present in the room during an entire insect season. Since there was no reason blow flies could not have penetrated to the body, the complete lack of these first colonizers provided evidence that the victim did not die in the summer. A delay in colonization might have been expected due to the protected state of these remains, but no more than a matter of days. Clearly, the fact that the remains were under a waterbed frame did not prevent other insect families from colonizing.

When the insect season began in June, the remains would no longer have been attractive to blow flies, but would have been to later colonizers, such as Fanniidae, Sphaeroceridae, and Dermestidae. Their presence indicated that the victim had died during the wintertime, over a year previous to discovery. The victim must have died, and had time to become mummified before the insect season began. The defendant later admitted strangling the victim the previous March, and placing the victim under the bed.

Collection of Other Insect Evidence

1. Search the body, the clothing, and all the surrounding area for insects. They may be found on or under the body, above the body in the air, or in the soil or carpet.
2. Beetle adults and larvae move rapidly, so the collector must be ready to catch them. They can be placed in separate vials (evidence will eat evidence!) or in one vial filled with alcohol.
3. Small adult flies or larvae can be collected with a paint brush dampened with water. Adults can be placed in alcohol and larvae should be treated in a similar manner to blow fly larvae, with half preserved and half kept alive.
4. A sweep net can be used to collect flying insects, but care must be taken not to disturb other evidence.
5. Measure ambient and soil temperatures, and leave a data logger at the scene, if possible, for 3 to 4 weeks to record the temperatures. If the victim is buried, soil temperature at the depth of the victim should be recorded as this more approximates the body temperatures (VanLaerhoven, 1997; VanLaerhoven and Anderson, 1996, 1999).
6. The soil or area under and near the remains should be screened, and a small soil sample collected as before. See R.C.M.P. "E" Division Training (1997) for further details.

Conclusions

Insects can be extremely valuable in a forensic investigation, and can be used to determine time of death, from days to years after death. However, accurate collection is vital. If the insects are not collected properly at the scene, then little or no analysis can be completed. It is, therefore, vital that a trained specialist, preferably a Board Certified Forensic Entomologist (American Board of Forensic Entomology), is called to the scene. If time does not permit the presence of the entomologist at the scene, then officers should contact the entomologist to receive advice over the phone. Above all, a qualified forensic entomologist should be located and contacted long before such a case occurs so that he or she can be quickly contacted when the need arises. Insects collected by investigators should be hand delivered or sent by courier to the entomologist as soon as possible. A good collection should include collection at the scene and at the autopsy, when a more detailed examination of the remains can be made.

References

Anderson, G.S.

1995 The use of insects in death investigations: an analysis of forensic entomology cases in British Columbia over a five year period, *Canadian Society Forensic Sciences Journal* 28(4):277–292.

1999a Forensic entomology: the use of insects in death investigations. In *Case Studies in Forensic Anthropology*, edited by S. Fairgreave, pp. 303–325. Charles C Thomas, Toronto.

1999b Wildlife forensic entomology: determining time of death in two illegally killed black bear cubs, a case report, *Journal of Forensic Sciences* 44(4):856–859.

2000   Minimum and maximum development rates of some forensically important Calliphoridae (Diptera), *Journal of Forensic Sciences* 45(4):824–832.

Unpublished data, School of Criminology, Simon Fraser University, Burnaby, British Columbia.

Anderson, G.S. and S.L. VanLaerhoven
1996   Initial studies on insect succession on carrion in southwestern British Columbia, *Journal of Forensic Sciences* 41(4):617–625.

Baer, W.S.
1931   The treatment of chronic osteomyelitis with the maggot (larva of the blow fly), *Journal of Bone and Joint Surgery* 13:438–475.

Bauch, R., K. Ziesenhenn, and C. Groskoppf
1984   *Lucilia sericata* myiasis (Diptera: Calliphoridae) on a gangrene of the foot, *Angewandte Parasitologie* 25(3):167–169.

Bradshaw, W.E.
1980   Thermoperiodism and the thermal environment of the pitcher-plant mosquito, *Wyeomyia smithii, Oecologia* 46:13-1.

Carpenter, T.L. and D.O. Chastain
1992   Facultative myiasis by *Megaselia* sp. (Diptera: Phoridae) in Texas: a case report, *Journal of Medical Entomology* 29(3):561–563.

Catts, E.P. and M.L. Goff
1992   Forensic entomology in criminal investigations, *Annual Review of Entomology* 37:253–272.

Catts, E.P. and N.H.E. Haskell
1990   *Entomology and Death — A Procedural Guide*, Joyce's Print Shop, Inc., Clemson, SC.

Chapman, R.F.
1980   *The Insects, Structure and Function*, Hodder and Stoughton, London.

Dallwitz, R.
1984   The influence of constant and fluctuating temperatures on development and survival rate of pupae of the Australian sheep blow fly, *Lucilia cuprina, Entomologie Experimentalis et Applicata* 36:89–95.

Denno, R.F. and W.R. Cothran
1976   Competitive interaction and ecological strategies of sarcophagid and calliphorid flies inhabiting rabbit carrion, *Annals of the Entomological Society of America* 69:109–113.

Deonier, C.C.
1940   Carcass temperatures and their relation to winter blow fly activity in the Southwest, *Journal of Economic Entomology* 3:166–170.

Deroo, H. et al.
1990   Human cutaneous parasitosis: two cases of furuncular and creeping myiasis, *Dermatologica* 180(3):199–200.

Dillon, L.C.
1997   Insect succession on carrion in three biogeoclimatic zones in British Columbia, M.Sc. thesis, Simon Fraser University, Burnaby, B.C., p. 76.

Personal communication, Dept. of Biological Sciences, Simon Fraser University, presently Coroner, B.C. Coroners Service, Burnaby, B.C.

Dillon, L.C. and G.S. Anderson
1995   Forensic entomology: the use of insects in death investigations to determine elapsed time since death, Canadian Police Research Centre, Technical Report TR-05-95, Ottawa, Ontario.

1996   Forensic entomology: a database for insect succession on carrion in Northern and Interior B.C., Canadian Police Research Centre, Technical Report TR-04-96, Ottawa, Ontario.

1998   Insect Succession on carrion in three biogeoclimatic zones of British Columbia, American Academy of Forensic Sciences, San Francisco.

Early, M and M.L. Goff
1986   Arthropod succession patterns in exposed carrion on the island of Oahu, Hawaiian Islands, *Journal of Medical Entomology* 23:520–531.

Erzinclioglu, Y.Z. and R.P. Whitmore
1983   *Chrysomya albiceps* (Wiedemann) (Diptera: Calliphoridae) in dung and causing myiasis in Oman, *Entomologist's Monthly Magazine* 119:51–52.

Erzinclioglu, Z.
1996   *Blow Flies*, Richmond Publ., Slough.

Fawzy, A.F.
1991   Otitis media and aural myiasis, *Journal of the Egyptian Society of Parasitology* 21(3):883–885.

Fotedar, R., U. Banerjee, and A.K. Verma
1991   Human cutaneous myiasis due to mixed infestation in a drug addict, *Annals of Tropical Medicine and Parasitology* 85(3):339–340.

Fraenkel, G.
1935   Observations and experiments on the blow fly (*Calliphora erythrocephala*) during the first day after emergence, *Proceedings of the Zoological Society of London* 893–904.

Fraenkel, G., and G. Bhaskaran
1973   Pupariation and pupation in cyclorraphous flies (Diptera): terminology and interpretation, *Annals of the Entomological Society of America* 66:418–422.

Gilbert, B.M. and W.M. Bass
1967   Seasonal dating of burials from the presence of fly pupae, *American Antiquity* 32:534–535.

Gill, G. et al.
1998/2000 Dept. of Entomology, University of Manitoba, and School of Criminology, M.Sci. thesis in progress, Simon Fraser University.

Goddard, J. and P.K. Lago
1985   Notes on blow fly (Diptera: Calliphoridae) succession on carrion in Northern Mississippi, *Journal of Entomology Sciences* 20:312–317.

Goff, M.L., S. Charbonneau, and W. Sullivan
1991   Presence of fecal matter in diapers as a potential source of error in estimations of post-mortem intervals using arthropod development rates, *Journal of Forensic Sciences* 36(5):1603–1606.

Greenberg, B.
1984   Two cases of human myiasis caused by *Phaenicia sericata* (Diptera: Calliphoridae) in Chicago area hospitals, *Journal of Medical Entomology* 21:615.

1990   Nocturnal oviposition behavior of blow flies (Diptera: Calliphoridae), *Journal of Medical Entomology* 27:807–810.

1991   Flies as forensic indicators, *Journal of Medical Entomology* 28:565–577.

1996   Personal communication, University of Illinois, Chicago, IL.

Greenberg, B. and T.I. Tantawi
1993   Different developmental strategies in two boreal blow flies (Diptera: Calliphoridae), *Journal of Medical Entomology* 30(2):481–484.

Hagstrum, D.W. and C.E. Leach
   1972   Role of constant and fluctuating temperatures in determining developmental time and fecundity of three species of stored products Coleoptera. *Annals of the Entomological Society of America* 66:407–410.

Hall, R.D., P.C. Anderson, and D.P. Clark
   1986   A case of human myiasis caused by *Phormia regina* (Diptera: Calliphoridae) in Missouri, USA, *Journal of Medical Entomology* 23(5):578–579.

Hall, R.D. and K.E. Doisy
   1993   Length of time after death: effect on attraction and oviposition or larviposition of mid-summer blow flies (Diptera: Calliphoridae) and Flesh Flies (Diptera: Sarcophagidae) of medicolegal importance in Missouri, *Annals of the Entomological Society of America* 86(5):589–593.

Haskell, N.H. et al.
   1997   On the body: insects' life stage presence and their postmortem artifacts. In *Forensic Taphonomy: The Postmortem Fate of Human Remains,* edited by W.D. Haglund and M.H. Sorg, CRC Press, Boca Raton, FL, pp. 415–448.

Henssge, C. et al.
   1995   *The Estimation of the Time since Death in the Early Postmortem Period,* Arnold, Seven Oaks, CA.

Hobischak, N.R.
   1997   Freshwater invertebrate succession and decompositional studies on carrion in British Columbia, M.P.M. thesis, Simon Fraser University, Burnaby, B.C., p. 54.

Hobischak, N.R. and G.S. Anderson
   In press.   Time of submergence using aquatic invertebrate succession and decompositional changes, *Journal of Forensic Science.*

Johl, H.K. and G.S. Anderson
   1996   Effects of chilling on development of the blow fly *Calliphora vicina* Robineau-Desvoidy (Diptera) and their relationship to time of death, *Journal of the Entomological Society of British Columbia* 93:93–98.

Kamal, A.S.
   1958   Comparative study of thirteen species of sarcosaprophagous Calliphoridae and Sarcophagidae (Diptera). I. Bionomics. *Annals of the Entomological Society of America* 51:261–270.

King, A.B. and K.J. Flynn
   1991   Maggot therapy revisited: a case study, *Dermatology Nursing* 3:100–102.

Kpea, N. and C. Zywocinski
   1995   Flies in the flesh: a case report and review of cutaneous myiasis, *Cutis* 55(1):47–48.

Kumar, A. and B.P. Joshi
   1995   Studies on the clinical efficacy of ivermectin against cutaneous myiasis in domestic animals, *Indian Veterinary Journal* 72(3):277–280.

Lee, H.L. and Y.K. Yong
   1991   Human aural myiasis, *Southeast Asian Journal of Tropical Medicine and Public Health* 22(2):274–275.

Liu, D. and B. Greenberg
   1989   Immature stages of some flies of forensic importance, *Annals of the Entomological Society of America* 82:90–93.

Lord, W.D. and J.F. Burger
   1984   Arthropods associated with Herring Gull (*Larus argentatus*) and Great Black-Backed Gulls (*Larus marinus*) carrion on islands in the gulf of Maine, *Environmental Entomology* 13:1261–1268.

MacDonell, N.R. and G.S. Anderson
   1997   Aquatic forensics: determination of time since submergence using aquatic invertebrates, Canadian Police Research Centre, Technical Report TR-01-97, Ottawa, Ontario.

Melvin, R.
   1934   Incubation period of eggs of certain muscoid flies at different constant temperatures, *Annals of the Entomological Society of America* 27:406–410.

Messenger, P.S.
   1964   The influence of rhythmically fluctuating temperatures on the development and reproduction of the spotted alfalfa aphid, *Therioaphis maculata, Journal of Economic Entomology* 57:71–76.

   1969   Bioclimatic studies of the aphid parasite *Praon exsoletum.* 2. Thermal limits to development and occurrence of diapause, *Annals of the Entomological Society of America* 62:1026–1031.

Miller, K.B., L.J. Hribar, and L.J. Sanders
   1990   Human myiasis caused by *Phormia regina* in Pennsylvania, *Journal of the American Podiatrical Medicine Association* 80(11):600–602.

Moon, R.D.
   Personal communication, University of Minnesota, St. Paul.

Morsy, T.A. and A.M. Farrag
   1991   Two cases of human ophthalmomyiasis, *Journal of the Egyptian Society of Parasitology* 21(3):853–855.

Nielsen, B.O.
   1993   Cases of human myiasis from Denmark, *Entomologiske Meddelelser* 61(3):81–82.

Nuorteva, P.
   1977   Sarcosaprophagous insects as forensic indicators. In *Forensic Medicine: A Study in Trauma and Environmental Hazards,* Vol. II, edited by C.G. Tedeschi, W.G. Eckert, and L.G. Tedeschi, pp. 1072–1095. W.B. Saunders, Philadelphia.

Payne, J.A.
   1965   A summer carrion study of the baby pig *Sus scrofa* Linnaeus, *Ecology* 46:592–602.

Pechter, E.A. and R.A. Sherman
   1983   Maggot therapy: surgical metamorphosis, *Plastic and Reconstructive Surgery* 72:567–570.

Petersen, J.J. and B.M. Pawson
   1988   Early season dispersal of *Muscidifurax zaraptor* (Hymenoptera: Pteromalidae) utilizing freeze-killed housefly pupae as hosts, *Medical and Veterinary Entomology* 2:137–140.

Richard, R.D. and R.R. Gerrish
   1983   The first confirmed field case of myiasis produced by *Chrysomya* sp., (Diptera: Calliphondae) in the continental United States, *Journal of Medical Entomology* 30:685.

Richards, A.G. and S. Suanraksa
   1962   Energy expenditure during embryonic development under constant versus variable temperatures (*Oncopeltus fasciatus* (Dallas)), *Entomology Experimentalis et Applicata* 5:167–178.

Rodriguez, W.C. and W.M. Bass
   1987   Examination of badly decomposed or skeletonized remains — overlooked evidence. Thirty-ninth annual meeting American Academy of Forensic Sciences, San Diego.

Royal Canadian Mounted Police "E" Division Training
   1997   *Forensic Entomology,* Vancouver, B.C.

Shean, B.S., L. Messinger, and M. Papworth
   1993   Observations of differential decomposition on sun exposed v. shaded pig carrion in coastal Washington State, *Journal of Forensic Sciences* 38(4):938–949.

Sherman, R.A.
    1998   Maggot debridement in modern medicine, *Infections in Medicine* 15(9):651–656.

Sherman, R.A. and E.A. Pechter
    1988   Maggot therapy: a review of the therapeutic applications of fly larvae in human medicine, especially for treating osteomyelitis, *Medical and Veterinary Entomology* 2(3):225–230.

Sherman, R.A., J.M. Tran, and R. Sullivan
    1996   Maggot therapy for venous stasis ulcers, *Archives of Dermatology* 132:254–256.

Sherman, R.A., F.A. Wyle, and L. Thrupp
    1995   Effects of seven antibiotics on the growth and development of *Phaenicia sericata* (Diptera: Calliphoridae) larvae, *Journal of Medical Entomology* 32(5):646–649.

Smith, K.G.V.
    1986   *A Manual of Forensic Entomology,* Trustees of The British Museum (Nat. Hist.) and Cornell University Press, London.

Tantawi, T.I. and B. Greenberg
    1993   The effect of killing and preservative solutions on estimates of maggot age in forensic cases, *Journal of Forensic Sciences* 38(3):702–707.

VanLaerhoven, S.L.
    1997   Successional Biodiversity in Insect Species on Buried Carrion in the Vancouver and Cariboo Regions of British Columbia, M.P.M. Thesis, Dept. of Biological Sciences, Simon Fraser University, Burnaby, B.C., 60 pp.

VanLaerhoven, S.L. and G.S. Anderson
    1996   Forensic entomology. Determining Time of Death in Buried Homicide Victims Using Insect Succession. Canadian Police Research Centre, Technical Report TR-02-96, Ottawa, Ontario.

    1999   Insect succession on buried carrion in two biogeoclimatic zones of British Columbia, *Journal of Forensic Sciences* 44:31–41.

Voigt, J.
    1965   Specific postmortem changes produced by larder beetles, *Journal of Forensic Medicine* 12:76–80.

Wall, R., N. French, and K. Morgan
    1992   Blow fly species composition in sheep myiasis in Britain, *Medical and Veterinary Entomology* 6:177–178.

    1995   Population suppression for control of the blow fly *Lucilia sericata* and sheep blow fly strike, *Ecological Entomology* 20:91–97.

    1990   The incidence of flystrike in sheep in relation to weather conditions, sheep husbandry and the abundance of the Australian sheep blow fly *Lucilia cuprina* (Wiedmann) (Diptera: Calliphoridae), *Australian Journal of Agricultural Research* 41:1155–1167.

Webster, A.
    1999   Personal communication, Environment Canada, Pacific Region.

Yeargan, K.V.
    1980   Effects of temperature on developmental rate of *Telenomus podisi* (Hymenoptera: Scelionidae), *Annals of the Entomological Society of America* 73:339–342.

Human Remains in Water Environments

10

WILLIAM D. HAGLUND
MARCELLA H. SORG

Contents

0-8493-1189-6/02/$0.00+$1.50
© 2002 by CRC Press LLC

Table 10.1   Global Water Inventory

Reservoir	Volume (thousand km)	Volume (%)
Rivers	1	0.0001
Atmosphere	13	0.0010
Soil moisture	67	0.0049
Freshwater lakes	125	0.0092
Saline lakes and inland seas	104	0.0076
Groundwater (to 4-km depth)	8350	0.6149
Glacial ice	29,200	2.1504
Oceans	1,320,000	97.2118
Total	1,357,860	100.0001

Source: Adapted from Skinner and Porter (1987).

Introduction

Approximately 71% of the earth's surface is hydrosphere, i.e., covered with water. More than 97% of the earth's water resides in oceans and saltwater seas. Of the remaining 3%, 2% is distributed in snow and ice, and 1% is distributed in rivers, freshwater lakes and seas, groundwater, and water vapor (Table 10.1). The nature of these water accumulations varies tremendously in physical and chemical characteristics and biology. Variation between and within hydrospheric units depends on climate, depth and topography, underlying geochemistry, access to other bodies of water, and ecological relationship to the adjacent landforms. From a geological point of view, bodies of water and landforms are dynamic and interactive. Snow, ice, and water are part of a vast array of exogenous agents and processes constantly changing the earth's surface, and being changed by it.

Because humans are primarily terrestrial animals, from one taphonomic perspective they constitute allochthonous remains when found in water; that is, they are foreign remains derived from other biological communities. From another taphonomic perspective, however, because humans extend their activities near and into water, the natural distribution of their remains can be expected to extend there, too, particularly at the land–water interface.

Human remains in water are subject to many potential actions, dependent upon the remains themselves and the type and characteristics of the water environment (Table 10.2) (Parsons and Brett, 1991; Sorg et al., 1997). Oceans, rivers, lakes, and ponds may differ radically with respect to temperature, depth, salinity, oxygenation, or current. Features of shores, bottoms, and life forms are also variable. Dependent upon these and other microenvironmental factors, bodies entering water may initially float or sink, possibly to surface later, or remain submerged, or even be buried by accumulating sediment. They may be carried by currents, cast upon shores, caught up in jams of debris, or rafted with floating objects. They may be disarticulated, or consumed by scavengers, or become abraded, dissolved, or otherwise decomposed. Bodies in aqueous environments may also be stationary, i.e., burial in snow or ice, or terrestrial burial where groundwater is abundant.

Thus, bodies become modified due to their physical nature (an object that is transported), biochemical nature (a decomposing animal that becomes disarticulated and scattered), and biological nature (a source of food).

**Table 10.2 Factors of Environment and the Body Affecting
the Postmortem Fate of Remains Exposed to Aqueous
Environments**

Environment Factors	Body Factors
Temperature	Body covering
Depth	Body habitus
Currents	Submerged or floating
Fauna and flora	Type of joint
Obstruction and debris	Position of joint
Season	Amount of tissue surrounding joint
Water chemistry	Trauma: position and character
Sedimentation and geology	Adipocere presence

Significance of Aqueous Environments to Fossil and Forensic Assemblages

In the fossil record, as in forensic practice, hydraulic factors have played a significant role in transport, modification, and burial. Western (1985) studied the waterside deposition of East African samples of *Homo* and noted that the record is skewed toward more watered, axial areas of basins associated with the Eastern Rift. According to White (1988), 70% of all hominid specimens whose sedimentary envelope could be established were derived from sand or gravel sediments deposited by moving water. The potential for rapid burial, and hence for preservation, is enhanced in such settings. Some of the most remarkably complete fossil assemblages in the hominid record were water depositions, including the "First Family" of *Australopithecus afarensis* which may have died in a flash flood, and the Nariokoteme *Homo erectus* boy whose body was preserved in the marshy floodplain associated with the Omo River (Walker and Leakey, 1993). Extremely waterlogged soils, such as bogs, allow preservation of soft parts, even at the expense of bone (Brothwell, this volume).

Certain aqueous environmental settings (e.g., anoxia, rapid burying) associated with mass mortality have produced large concentrations of exceptionally preserved material, sometimes termed *lagerstätten* by taphonomists (Martin, 1999; Seilacher et al., 1985). Anoxia (usually associated with stagnation) inhibits necrolysis, scavenging, and disarticulation. When coupled with rapid burial (obrution), decaying carcasses will mineralize quite rapidly, sometimes even preserving soft parts (Martin, 1999); extremely alkaline environments in both fresh and saltwater will further enhance the likelihood of certain types of concretions (hence, preservation). Deep lacustrine environments are well-known to promote preservation of both soft tissue and skeletons (Allison and Briggs, 1991a,b).

In stark contrast, the forensic literature has, until quite recently, paid scant attention to cases from aqueous environments. When human remains are recovered from water, unique questions are posed regarding their origin (Ebbesmeyer and Haglund, 1994, this volume; O'Brien, 1997), postmortem history (Boyle et al., 1997; Brooks and Brooks, 1997; Haglund, 1993; London et al., 1997; Nawrocki et al., 1997; Sorg et al., 1995; 1997), identity (Rathbun and Rathbun, 1984), and injuries (Brooks and Brooks, 1997). For example, drifting bodies sometimes move long distances from where they entered the water (Ebbesmeyer and Haglund, 1994, and this volume). Giertsen and Morild (1989) discuss two bodies that traveled in excess of 300 miles. Modification of soft tissue, including adipocere formation, can interfere with postmortem interval estimates (Cotton et al., 1987; O'Brien, 1997; Simonsen, 1977) and interpretation of injuries (Dix, 1987). Disarticulation, resulting in loss of body parts and their dispersal, can confound identification and the re-attribution of parts to a single person (Haglund, 1993; Symes et al., this volume). Water environments can modify bones through encrustation, abrasion, bioerosion, and even dissolution (Sorg et al., 1997). Disasters such as floods (Charney and Wilber, 1980, 1984), ship tragedies (Berryman et al., 1988; Ebbesmeyer and Haglund, this volume; Timperman, 1991), and airplane disasters over water provide tremendous challenges to forensic investigators with regard to body recovery, identification, and scene reconstruction. Large losses of human life can be attributed to water. Pennsylvania's Johnstown Flood of May 31, 1889, accounted for over 2000 fatalities (McCullough, 1968). Current interest in the sinking of the passenger liner *Titanic* has revived awareness of the large number of its victims (Ebbesmeyer and Haglund, this volume).

Behavior of Carcasses in Bodies of Water: Sink or Float?

At the time a carcass enters the water it either sinks or floats. Archimedes' Principle asserts that an object in water will experience a buoyant force equal to the weight of the water it displaces. Body fat content affects buoyancy, such that bodies with relatively higher fat content have a greater tendency to float, while bodies of lower fat proportion sink (Schäfer, 1978). For animals, hair and feathers trap air and increase carcass buoyancy (Haynes, 1980). Density and viscosity of the surrounding water may alter the speed of changes in position and depth (Martin, 1999).

Four potential phases of movement have been suggested by Dilen (1984) for bodies in rivers. They may settle to the bottom, move along the bottom, ascend to the surface, or drift along the surface. These modes are generally applicable to non-riverine, current-driven bodies of water. Standard forensic references have provided various opinions with regard to the initial behavior of human remains in bodies of water. Simpson (1965) asserts that dead, unclothed bodies are heavier than water and, therefore, sink when immersed. Adelson (1974:563) states that because "specific gravity of the lifeless human body, regardless of cause of death, exceeds the specific gravity of fresh or sea water, any recently dead person always sinks to the ocean floor, river bed, lake, or pool bottom." Spitz (1980:360) points out that trapped air in clothing could cause a body to be buoyant. Buoyancy significantly increases with the build-up of decomposition gasses (Teather, 1994). Rafting on debris can also account for bodies floating (Haglund, 1993).

Donoghue and Minnigerode (1977) calculated specific gravity for living, nude men at functional, residual, and total lung capacity. In both seawater and fresh water, at total lung capacity, all 98 subjects floated. At functional residual capacity, approximately the lung volume of a dead body, 69% floated in seawater and 7% in fresh water. This relationship can be altered by body size and composition, clothing, flotation devices, weights, and decomposition gas.

As a body sinks, hydrostatic pressure increases 1 atm for every 10 m. This is a function of Boyle's Law. Snyder (1972) suggests that once a body begins to sink it goes directly to the bottom. Dilen (1984) claims bodies sink in incremental steps. Because pressure increases with depth, gas in tissue and air in the lungs are compressed, which in turn causes further sinking. These forces alternate until the bottom is reached. Adelson (1974:563) states that, as a body approaches the bottom, it floats in a head down position because the head has a higher specific gravity than the feet. This conclusion is based on observations of accentuated cephalad hypostasis of recovered remains. Once it reaches the floor of an ocean, riverbed, lake, or pool bottom, a body may become encumbered by irregularities

Figure 10.1 Floating position of fresh remains. (Adapted from *Spitz and Fisher's Medico Legal Investigation of Death,* 2nd ed., Charles C Thomas, Springfield, IL, 1993.)

of the substrate, entangled by vegetation or moved by currents. When movement at the bottom occurs, it is because forces of drag and lift overcome forces of gravity and friction.

Low temperatures may preclude or significantly inhibit decomposition gas build-up. Anaerobic waters of protected troughs are unfavorable for bacterial activity (Schäfer, 1978). If sufficient depth is reached, no amount of decomposition gas will overcome external water pressure. When temperature, depth pressure, and lack of encumbrance allow, decomposition gas may accumulate and expand the volume of body cavities to a point where internal pressure overcomes external water pressure, the body expands, and the body becomes buoyant. Some of the gas is trapped in body cavities, possibly contained by distention of the esophagus and anus (Schäfer, 1978). Interstitial spaces also confine significant gas build-up.

Behavior of Floating Carcasses: Position and Movement

If afloat, parts of a carcass are above the surface while others are submerged. This allows differential access to agents of destruction. Position of floating bodies relative to the water line may also affect the rate and sequence of soft tissue destruction and disarticulation of bones or body units. For instance, surfaced portions may be exposed to infestation by insects and devastation by other animals such as birds, while submerged portions are exposed to water life.

Mammals with grossly different conformations float in different positions. Fetal pigs float belly-up (Payne and King 1972). Fresh, nude, adult human remains generally float with the back exposed, and the majority of the head and limbs dangling below the water line (Figure 10.1). Such a position in shallow environments exposes these dangling body parts to mechanical abrasion from dragging along the bottom. Especially vulnerable are the forehead, toes, and volar aspects of the hands (Spitz, 1993). Once remains have decomposed with accompanying gas build up in the abdomen they may float face up.

The susceptibility of appendages to wave and current action is different from that of the torso. For example, extended appendages such as tails and limbs of terrestrial vertebrates are more vulnerable to being caught on obstructions. Marine mammals are protected from mechanical destruction by their barrel-shaped bodies (Schafer, 1978). This is no doubt enhanced by their diminutive limbs which do not protrude from the body in as exaggerated a fashion as those of terrestrial mammals.

Schäfer (1978) has provided several comments regarding the behavior of marine carcasses in the closed basin marine environment of the North Sea, where carcasses may drift for weeks on the surface. In such enclosed ocean basins, carcasses generally reach a beach before disintegration, to subsequently be refloated by high tides, or set adrift by backwashing surf. This beaching and refloating may occur many times.

Surf action separates, tumbles, and jumbles skeletal parts. Weigelt (1927:83–84) quotes Abel's description of the action of waves and river currents upon carcasses:

> A large carcass rolls along the swell, closer to the shore. It is a dead manatee, whose abdomen, blown up like a balloon by gases of decomposition, rises now and then above the surface. Then breakers shove the carcass into the sandy beach. It is already in an advanced stage of decay: the head hangs loosely on the trunk, and the lower jaw has long since fallen to the bottom of the sea.

Shipwreck literature is a virtually untapped source of information regarding behavior of human remains in water (Ebbysmeyer and Haglund, 1994; and this volume). Hydraulic and other oceanographic models may be used to track or predict trajectories of remains in large bodies of water. Potential applications for forensic death investigators include (1) setting geographic and time limits for searches; (2) estimating the likely origin of remains found floating or beached; (3) confirming correlative information regarding entry into the water and sightings of remains; and (4) estimating postmortem interval.

Decomposition of Carcasses in Water

For longitudinal observations of the rate and pattern of decomposing carcasses in water we must look to the experimental studies of Dodson (1973) and Payne and King (1972). Dodson examined decomposition of mouse (*Mus*) and frog (*Bufo*) in an aquarium of pond water. Deterioration of muscle was followed by skin, then tendon. Payne and King (1972) focused on decomposition and insect succession of previously frozen fetal pigs (*Sus scrofa*). The specimens were thawed and placed in wire baskets, which were suspended in tanks of water. Specimens were weighed at 4-hour intervals up to 20 hours. Insect succession was monitored. The process of decomposition was divided into six stages: submerged fresh, early floating, floating decay, bloated deterioration, floating remains and sunken remains.

In the initial fresh stage, the majority of pig carcasses sank. They bloated in 2 days in summer or 2 to 3 weeks in winter. In the early floating stage the distended abdomen was usually first to project above water. Eggs were laid on the exposed carcass surfaces by blowflies. Decomposition and insect scavenging took place in tandem. By the bloated deterioration stage most exposed flesh was gone. Maggots migrated from the body and many fed on the carcass below the water line with only spiracles extending above the surface. Head, shoulders, abdomen, and hindquarters had separated by this time. Thus, the body floated until it lost buoyancy and sank.

Payne and King and Dodson considered their observations to be affected by a complex interplay of variables, which included pH, pO_2, salinity, and temperature. They were critical of the artificiality of their decomposition experiments, particularly the agitation of the carcasses when the baskets in which they were suspended were removed for weighing and observation. Payne was of the opinion that moving the baskets was probably not unlike wave or surf action. His self-criticism included his use of previously frozen specimens. His use of fetal material might also have significantly affected his results. Protection from scavenger access is also an issue.

Table 10.3   Observations of Taphonomic Changes in 15 Remains from a Sequestered Environment Over a Period of 433 Days

Time since Death (Days)	Number of Bodies	Postmortem Changes
2	2	Washerwoman hands
25	3	Bloating, marbling, skin slippage
38	1	Bloating, skin slippage, dark gray-brown discoloration, focal adipocere, purge fluid in body cavities
68	2	Bloating, skin slippage, dark gray-brown discoloration, extensive subcutaneous adipocere, purge fluid in body cavities
109	3	Total saponification covered by a thin friable crust
433	4	Total saponification with thick friable crust and skeletonization

Source: Adapted from Kahana, T. et al., *Journal of Forensic Sciences*, 44(5), 897–901, 1999.

A recent comment on decomposition in water involves adipocere formation in a series of 15 bodies recovered from Belgian flag cargo ship, the *Mineral Dampier*, sunk in the East China Sea at a depth of 65 m in water that ranged from 10 to 12°C (Kahana et al., 1999). Thirteen of the remains were recovered over a period of 433 days from the same contained environment aboard the ship. A summary of taphonomic observations is shown in Table 10.3. The authors point to discrepancies between their data and other published accounts of the rate of adipocere formation, and conclude that the presence of adipocere formation is unreliable for estimating postmortem interval.

Disarticulation of Carcasses in Water

Disarticulation sequences have important ramifications for differential skeletal element survival and accumulation. One would expect differences in disarticulation pattern between bodies floating in water vs. those supported by a firm substrate. For example, the dangling appendages of carcasses floating in water are subject to constant movement, agitation, and potential transport.

Schäfer (1972) asserts that bones of drifting whale carcasses become largely separated prior to the skin rupturing. Once rupture of the hide occurs, bones fall one by one as if from a drifting sack. For seals, whales, and dolphins, the integument tears where tensile strength is particularly strong: above roof of skull, at outer rims of jaws, and above the shoulder, scapula, and tail section. He asserts that for drifting seals, drying of gum tissue results in teeth being pulled from gums. Phalanges and forelimbs are next to disarticulate. Commenting on disarticulation of cows from the Gulf Coast of the United States, Weigelt (1927) observed that the mandible separates first, then disarticulation proceeds from the extremities. Dodson (1973) noted the following disarticulation sequence: caudal vertebrate sections, femur from acetabulum, jaw from skull, and hand from arm. Eventually, disarticulated bony elements and carcass units separate from a carcass or the carcass loses buoyancy and settles to a new environment where it is subjected to different taphonomic circumstances.

In one study of the disappearance of soft tissue and the disarticulation of human remains recovered from aqueous environments in the Puget Sound area, bodies were scored for regional presence of soft tissue, exposure of bone, and loss of body parts to determine the general pattern of soft tissue loss and loss of body parts (Haglund, 1993). The following regions were scored: cranium, mandible, neck, hands, forearms, upper arms, feet, legs, pelvic girdle, and trunk. Initial disappearance of soft tissue, exposing underlying bones, occurred in areas thinly covered by soft tissue beginning with the head, hands, and anterior lower legs. For this small sample (11 individuals) disappearance of body parts followed a general sequence: bones of the hands and wrists, bones of the feet and ankles, and mandible and cranium. The lower legs, forearms, and upper arms are the next units to separate from the body.

Postmortem intervals for 6 of the 11 remains were known and ranged from 1.25 to 36 months. As seen from Table 10.4, when the cases were ordered using the above criteria, post-mortem interval could not be reliably estimated based on the condition of the body and time of recovery. As parts drop away from a floating carcass in large or current-driven bodies of water, they are often separated from the major body unit. This complicates both the recovery and the interpretation. Knowledge of disarticulation sequences allows more informed assessment of skeletal elements expected vs. recovered in the forensic context, and assists in the interpretation of artifacts and events produced by different disarticulating environments (Figure 10.2).

Fluvial Transport Studies and the Behavior of Single Bones

Nawrocki et al. (1997) point to three unit-phases of fluvial transport: (1) the body as a unit of transport, before significant disarticulation has occurred; (2) movement of disarticulated body parts; and (3) the movement of isolated bones. It is the third phase that has hitherto received most attention. Studies of bone sorting and movement in water have focused on single bones of animals (Behrensmeyer, 1982; Dechant-Boaz, 1982; Hanson, 1980; Voorhies, 1969). A major reason for the concentration on single bones is the assumption that fossil bone accumulations resulted from sheet-wash transport of previously disarticulated skeletal elements that had been deposited on flood plains. These experimental studies used artificial flumes (inclined channel with running water).

Voorhies (1969), in a now classic report, attempted to determine the process of bone accumulation in the Valentine Formation of northeastern Nebraska. He tested whether the relative differences of skeletal elements represented in this early Pliocene bone concentration could be due to current sorting. He used coyote and sheep bone in "stream table" experiments to determine the effect of current sorting of various bony elements. Condition of the bones was not indicated. The general conclusions were that bones, which tend to move by rolling, will become oriented transverse to the current and those with one end markedly heavier than the other will tend to move by sliding with their long axis parallel to the current. Exceptions arose in very shallow water, where the bone was partially submerged. Voorhies classified bones as falling into highly transportable, intermediate, and lag groups.

Boaz and Behrensmeyer (1976) provide the only direct observations of human bones in moving water. Using 35 human bone elements or parts and an artificial flume, different transport groups were achieved. Skeletal parts consisted of fragmentary and weathered material, as well as whole skulls. Behavior was characterized as (1) sliding, movement along the bed in which the bone material remains horizontal; (2) flipping, movement around the axis perpendicular to the current in which the piece turns over once; (3) rolling, successive tumbling of a skeletal part around an axis perpendicular to the current; (4) stable, where the piece lies flat on the bed and shows no movement; and (5) quasi-stable, where there is little or no component of longitudinal movement, but the piece is not flat on the bed or moves slightly in some direction. Orientation was defined as the relationship of

Table 10.4 Disappearance of Soft Tissue and Bone for Bodies Subjected to Aqueous Environments (in order of increasing tissue and body part loss scores)

Case	Mandible	Cranium	Hand	Lower Leg	Neck	Fore-arm	Feet	Upper Arm	Trunk	Upper Leg	Pelvic Girdle	Total	Post-mortem Interval
1	1	1	0	0	0	0	0	0	0	0	0	2	1.25
2	1	1	1	0	0	0	0	0	0	0	0	3	26
3	1	1	1	1	0	0	0	0	0	0	0	4	9
4	1	1	1	1	0	0	1	0	0	0	0	5	31
5	2	2	1	1	1	0	0	0	0	0	0	6	—
6	2	2	2	1	2	0	0	0	0	0	1	9	—
7	4	2	4	3	1	1	0	1	0	0	0	16	2.5
8	4	4	4	3	3	3	4	2	1	1	0	29	—
9	4	4	4	1	2	4	3	3	1	2	1	29	—
10	4	4	4	3	4	4	3	4	3	1	1	35	36
11	4	4	4	4	4	4	4	4	3	1	1	37	—
Total	28	28	26	18	17	16	15	14	8	5	4		

Note: 0 = soft tissue complete; 1 = partial exposure of bone; 2 = total exposure of bone; 3 = exposure of bone and partial absence of area; 4 = absence.

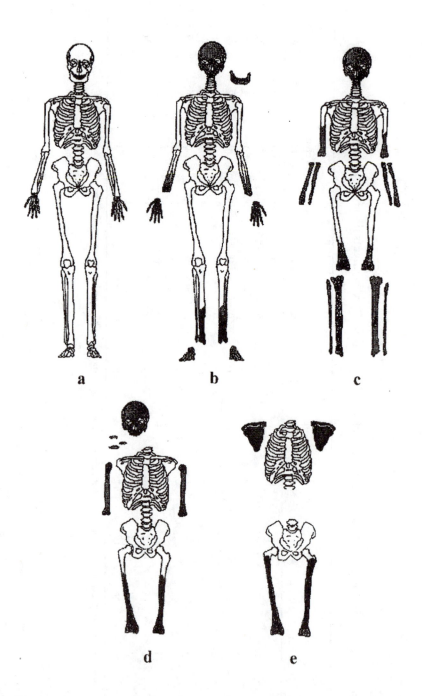

Figure 10.2 Schematic representation of disarticulation and bone exposure of floating bodies in aqueous environments (in order of increasing tissue and body part loss).

the long axis to the current. Orientation can be influenced by water depth, initial orientation of bone, size and shape (Hanson, 1980; Hill, 1975; Toots, 1965; Voorhies, 1969).

Dodson (1973) sought to determine the sequence of mouse bone movement. He reported the following sequence: large thoracic vertebrae, small thoracic vertebra, pelvis, caudal vertebrae, cervical vertebrae, tibia-fibula, femur, calcaneus, radius, ulna, jaw, incisor. Very low water velocities were sufficient to move any of these small bones.

Each of these experiments has shown the behavior of bones in current-driven water to be idiosyncratic for particular skeletal parts (Boaz and Behrensmeyer, 1976; Dodson, 1973; Voorhies, 1969). Initial placement did not seem to affect behavior. Elongate pieces, circular in cross section, roll in an arc around the smaller end, resulting in a quasi-stable orientation with the larger end of the piece pointing downstream. Samples could be divided into transportable and non-transportable groups. Flat or small skeletal parts lacking processes maintain stable or quasi-stable positions. Individual cranial and mandibular parts do not move (lag group), whereas complete crania are the fastest moving of single elements. Table 10.5 summarizes skeletal elements and their respective transport groups from the studies of Voorhies (1969) and Boaz and Behrensmeyer (1976).

Inconsistencies between these studies are explained, in part, by variations in experimental conditions (Table 10.6). Potts (1988) discusses commonalities in the experimental results: (1) mandibles in the lag category; (2) tibia and radius (proximal ends only for human bones) in the intermediate group; and (3) sacral vertebrae and sacrum in the highly transportable category. A major inconsistency was found for bones with high surface-to-volume ratios (e.g., ribs, sacrum, and scapula) placed in Voorhies group I, but in Boaz and Behrensmeyer's group III.

Hanson (1980) suggested that improvement is needed in attempts to define fluvial transport criteria. The experiments of Voorhies (1969) and Boaz and Behrensmeyer (1976) assumed ideal rather than natural conditions. Hanson suggested that further refinement needs to insure that (1) vertical distribution of fluid velocity is adequately described; (2) water depth is much greater than element height; (3) there is an insignificant amount of sediment in transport; (4) bones are not impeded, buried, or sheltered by bed features; and (5) the normal force between the bone and the bed is greater than zero and equal to the submerged weight of bone. He attempted to derive equations predictive of bone behavior in fluvial environments, pointing out that such schemes are applicable only if hydraulic transport is the only biasing agent and if three further conditions are addressed. First, skeletal elements should be completely disarticulated prior to the initial transport event. If this assumption is not met, the term *unit* rather than *skeletal element* should be used when referring to complete carcass or a physically connected portion of it. Second, predicted biases may not be apparent if the parent assemblage included only a narrow transportability spectrum of elements. Third, there should be no non-fluvial biases, for instance, a parent assemblage that is made up of bones that would be underrepresented in a fluvial transport assemblage.

Todd and Frison (1986) analyzed mammoth bones deposited in an arroyo bottom at the Colby Site. Their observations and conclusions underscore the idiosyncrasies of natural conditions, which create fluvial biases and may dictate dispersal, orientation, and accumulation of bones. The arroyo was narrow, steep-sided, and composed of bentonite that becomes extremely slick when wet. Movement of bones was constrained at the narrow channel bottom. Although long bones were aligned roughly parallel to the channel, they were aligned without regard to polarity, i.e., with their heavier ends pointing upstream and lighter ends downstream. In the constricted channel they had equal opportunity of sliding to its bottom with polarity in either direction. The narrowness of the stream further restricted dispersal. For instance, when a mandible or innominate lodged crossways at the bottom of the channel, it served to trap smaller elements coming downstream later.

As expected, bone density, size (weight), and morphology are major characteristics of bone invoked to explain flume study results. Factors that influence transport and accumu-

Table 10.5   Hydraulic Transport Groups Comparing Voorhies and Boaz and Behrensmeyer

Transport Group	Voorhies	Boas and Behrensmeyer
I (highly transportable)	Scapula[a]	Talus
	Phalanges[a]	Metatarsals I and IV
	Ulna[a]	Proximal ulna
	Ribs	Proximal humerus
	Vertebrae	Vertebra T12
	Sacrum	Acetabulum
	Sternum	Calcaneus
		Cuboid
		Sacrum
		Cranium
II (intermediate)	Femur	Mandible with teeth
	Tibia	Vertebra T1
	Humerus	Proximal tibia
	Metapodial	Proximal radius
	Pelvis	
	Radius	
	Scapula[a]	
	Ramus[a]	
	Phalanges[a]	
	Ulna[a]	
III (lag)	Skull	Cranial vault pieces
	Mandible	Hemi-mandible
	Ramus[a]	Mandible without teeth
		Molar
		Incisor
		Patella
		Proximal radius
		Distal radius
		Rib
		Atlas
		Proximal femur
		Scapular fragment
		Clavicle

[a]   Appears in more than one category.

Sources: Data from Voorhies, M., *Contributions to Geology,* 1969; Boaz, N.T. and Behrensmeyer, A.K., *American Journal of Physical Anthropology,* 45(1), 53–60, 1976.

lation of bone by water include the following: shape, breakage, orientation relative to flow, and irregularities of the substrate including vegetation (Potts, 1988). The condition of a bone or body unit and its effect on buoyancy are significant variables affecting the dispersal of bones in moving water (Dodson, 1973). Throughout the postmortem interval the density spectrum of body units and bones is affected by loss of soft tissue, loss of grease and moisture content, as well as the weathering state of a bone.

Flume experiments to date have assumed single bone transport, not the transport of whole carcasses or units of bones with varying amounts of soft tissue. Hence, they have little practical relevance for forensic cases with short postmortem intervals. The time of exposure between death and disarticulation plays a significant role in the fate of remains in water.

Table 10.6 Comparison of Experimental Conditions in Fluvial Transport Studies of Skeletal Elements

Experimental Conditions	Voorhies (1969)	Boaz and Behrensmeyer (1976)	Dodson (1973)
Stream table substrate	Fine sand	Coarse sand	Medium sand
Gradient	0.9 in./foot	31 cm/sec	6.35 in./sec
Time of bone placement	Before water	After water	Before water
Taxon	Coyote, sheep	Human	Mouse, toad, frog
State of bone	?	?	Fragmented, weathered
Number of trials	15/specimen	?	10/specimen

Sources: Data from Voorhies, M., *Contributions to Geology*, 1969; Boaz, N.T. and Behrensmeyer, A.K., *American Journal of Physical Anthropology*, 45(1), 53–60, 1976; Dodson, P., *Contributions to Geology*, 12(1), 15–19, 1973.

Bone Modifying Effects of Water Environments

Taphonomic factors in water environments include abrasion, disarticulation, bioerosion, dissolution, encrustation, fragmentation, spatial orientation, decomposition, and scavenging (Table 10.7) (Parsons and Brett, 1991; Sorg et al., 1997). Current-driven, sediment-laden water tends to abrade, or round off, projections of bone (e.g., muscle markings and articular ends). Abrasive modification of bone can result when bones are exposed to particles suspended in moving water or when the skeletons themselves are moved relative to other particles or objects (Parsons and Brett, 1991). The ability of sediments in energetic water flow to abrade or round off articular ends and muscle markings has also been noted by Potts (1988). Such transport or positional abrasion can be generalized or focal. Abrasion can play a significant role in interpretation of taphonomic history as reported by Brooks and Brooks (1997). Generalized sediment abrasion can obscure signs of trauma, such as gunshot or stab wounds.

High-energy currents or surf in conjunction with barriers, rocky bottoms, or rocky shores can cause bones to break apart along natural lines of weakness or produce defects from blunt or sharp force, possibly leading to fragmentation, dispersal, and loss (Brooks and Brooks, 1997; Nawrocki et al., 1997). When such damage occurs early in the postmortem period, the fracture or puncture margins may be impossible to differentiate from perimortem trauma.

In both forensic and archaeological settings, marine organisms are commonly seen encrusting bones. In general, these creatures settle on hard surfaces above the water-sediment line. When properly identified in the early postmortem period, barnacles can suggest, or at least confirm, the postmortem interval and location (Skinner et al., 1988; Sorg et al., 1997). Caution must be used, however, due to environmentally dependent variations in growth patterns, even within species. Other encrusting epifauna are coralline algae, foraminifera, coelenterates, surpulid worms, bryozoans, barnacles, and some mollusks (Parsons and Brett, 1991).

Corrosion or pitting of skeletal surfaces is termed dissolution. Such damage may occur in environments with high salinity, low temperature, or active bioturbation. These alterations have been observed in human remains recovered from near-coastal settings as early as during the first year after death (Sorg et al., 1997). Bioerosion results from boring, grazing, or shelter-seeking organisms and often co-occurs with dissolution (Parsons and Brett, 1991). Grazing fish can leave telltale scrape marks from their mouth plates. Radula scrapes of gastropods (sea snails), which are carrion feeders, can create significant damage, particularly to long bone ends. Although some radula signatures can be identified microscopically, the majority of gazing organisms simply grind away substrate without leaving characteristic signatures.

Table 10.7 Taphonomic Modification in Water Environments

Modification	Implications
Abrasion	Wearing-down of bone due to sediment action, particularly in high-energy settings.
Encrustation	The overgrowth of hard skeletal elements by other organisms. Indicates exposure above the sediment–water interface, encrustation can specify environment and may be an indicator of time passage.
Bioerosion	Corrosive processes by organisms. The most pervasive causes of degradation are boring or grazing. Bioerosion erases surface features, but leaves traces made by the organism. Patterns and processes of bioerosion vary among environments due to the distribution of bioeroders, energy levels, and other habitat differences.
Dissolution	Skeletal remains are often in equilibrium with surrounding waters, but changes in chemical conditions can cause skeletons to dissolve. Dissolution represents fluctuations in temperature, pH or PCO_2 in calcium carbonate skeletons.
Erosion	Broken edges of skeletons become rounded due to either dissolution or abrasion of the exposed surface. The processes that control edge erosion are not fully known, but are probably a combination of dissolution, abrasion, and bioerosion. Rounding may give a relative estimate of time since breaking.
Decomposition	Decomposition attracts scavengers in phases and increases the probability of soft tissue loss. Its presence generally signifies the presence of oxygen and above-freezing temperatures.
Disarticulation, fragmentation	Separation of body units increases the probability of transport and influences the type of transport possible. Dispersal resulting from disarticulation may change the accessibility of soft tissue or bone to other taphonomic processes.
Scavenging	Consumption by other organisms decreases the probability of preservation and may increase dispersal and fragmentation. The presence of some scavengers may attract others.
Spatial orientation	Position exposes particular surfaces to taphonomic agents and processes; it may enhance or impede transport by wave or current action.

Sources: Adapted from Parsons, K.M. and C.E. Brett, in *The Processes of Fossilization*, edited by S.K. Donovan, Columbia University Press, New York, 1991, pp. 22–65; Sorg, M.H. et al., in *Forensic Taphonomy: The Postmortem Fate of Human Remains*, edited by W.D. Haglund and M.H. Sorg, CRC Press, Boca Raton, FL, pp. 1–9.

Recovery Issues

Forensic remains from aqueous environments present significant challenges for both recovery and taphonomic interpretation. Most floating or beached remains are discovered by accident by people involved in fishing, boating, or shoreline activities (Boyle et al., 1997) and are frequently recovered by first responders, law enforcement, or forensic personnel. Many submerged remains, on the other hand, are discovered when they are recovered by accident in fishing nets (Sorg et al., 1995; 1997).

When recovery is done purposefully as part of a forensic investigation, divers or other recovery personnel should be instructed to gather data about the immediate surrounding, including exact location and depth, bottom type, water currents and, whenever possible, temperature and water chemistry. Flora and fauna associated with the remains should be recovered. Knowledge about the taphonomic setting will be useful in interpreting modification of soft tissue and bone and understanding distribution pattern, attrition of elements, scavenger changes, and differentiation from trauma.

Conclusion

The study of human remains in aqueous contexts offers enormous potential for exchange between forensic taphonomy and archaeology/paleontology. Water is perhaps the most ubiquitous taphonomic agent transporting, modifying, and accumulating remains. Yet, the hydrodynamics and chemistry of decomposing carcasses, carcass units, and bones in water are poorly understood for either archaeological or forensic assemblages. Actualistic observations of carcasses in water are rare. The majority of studies involving fluvial transport deal with behavior of single bones, studies which have sought to understand assemblages of fluvially accumulated skeletal elements. This represents an unfortunate lapse, because the depositional fate of the majority of forensic remains in water is inextricably bound to their hydraulic behavior as carcasses, their loss of soft tissue and subsequent disarticulation from the body, and the taphonomic environment in which these processes occur. Research gaps should be bridged not only by the use of animal proxies in experimental contexts, but also by careful documentation of data from forensic cases, particularly those in which details about the postmortem period become available.

Acknowledgment

We acknowledge the assistance of graphics artist Megan Abbott-Moore.

References

Adelson, L.
1974 *The Pathology of Homicide*, Charles C Thomas, Springfield, IL.

Allison, P.A. and D.E.G. Briggs
1991a The taphonomy of soft-bodied animals. In *The Processes of Fossilization*, edited by S.K. Donovan, pp. 120–140. Belhaven Press, London.
1991b Taphonomy of nonmineralized tissues. In *Taphonomy: Releasing the Data Locked in the Fossile Record*, edited by P.A. Allison and D.E.G. Briggs, pp. 25–70. Plenum Press, New York.

Behrensmeyer, A.K.
1982 Time resolution in fluvial vertebrate assemblages, *Paleobiology* 8:211–227.

Berryman, H.E., J.O. Potter, and S. Oliver
1988 The ill-fated passenger steamer *Sultana*: an inland maritime mass disaster of unparalleled magnitude, *Journal of Forensic Sciences* 33(3):842–850.

Boaz, N.T. and A.K. Behrensmeyer
1976 Hominid taphonomy: transport of human skeletal parts in an artificial fluviate environment, *American Journal of Physical Anthropology* 45(1):53–60.

Boyle, S., A. Galloway, and R.T. Mason
1997 Human aquatic taphonomy in Monterey Bay Area. In *Forensic Taphonomy: The Postmortem Fate of Human Remains*, edited by W.D. Haglund and M.H. Sorg, CRC Press, Boca Raton, FL, pp. 1–9.

Brooks, S. and R.H. Brooks
    1984   Effects on bone of abrasive contents in moving water. Abstract from the First International
    Conference on Bone Modification, Carson City, NV, August 1984.

    1997   The taphonomic effects of flood waters on bone. In *Forensic Taphonomy: The Postmorem Fate of
    Human Remains*, edited by W.D. Haglund and M.H. Sorg, pp. 553–558. CRC Press, Boca Raton, FL.

Charney, M. and C.G. Wilber
    1980   The Big Thompson flood. *American Journal of Forensic Medicine and Pathology* 1(2):139–1444.

    1984   The Big Thompson flood. In *Human Identification: Case Studies in Forensic Anthropology*,
    edited by T.A. Rathbun and J.E. Buikstra, pp. 107–112. Charles C Thomas, Springfield, IL.

Cotton, G.E, A.C. Aufderheide, and V.G. Golschmidt
    1987   Preservation of human tissue immersed for five years in fresh water of known temperature.
    Journal of Forensic Sciences 32(4)1027–1037.

Dechant-Boaz, D.
    1982   Modern Riverine Taphonomy: Its Relevance to the Interpretation of Plio-Pleistocene
    Hominid Paleoecology in the Omo Basin. Ph.D. dissertation, University of California, Berkeley.
    Ann Arbor University Microfilms (no. 8312762) (unpublished).

Dilen, D.R.
    1984   The motion of floating and submerged objects in the Chattahoochee River, Atlanta, GA.
    Journal of Forensic Sciences 29(4):1027–1037.

Dix, J.D,
    1987   Missouri's lakes and the disposal of homicide victims, *Journal of Forensic Sciences*
    32(3):806–809.

Dodson, P.
    1973   The significance of small bones in paleontological interpretation, *Contributions to Geology*
    12(1):15–19.

Donoghue, E.R. and S.C. Minnigerode
    1977   Human body buoyancy: a study of 98 men, *Journal of Forensic Sciences* 22(3):573–579.

Ebbesmeyer, C.C., J.M. Cox, and B.R. Salem
    1991   1875 Floatable wreckage driven inland through the Strait of Juan de Fuca. Proceedings of the
    Puget Sound Research Conference, 1:75–85. Puget Sound Water Control Authority, Washington.

Ebbesmeyer, C.C. et al.
    1991   Eddy induced beaching of floatable materials in the eastern Strait of Juan de Fuca. Pro-
    ceedings of the Puget Sound Research Conference, 1:76–98. Puget Sound Water Control Author-
    ity, Washington.

Ebbesmeyer. C.C. and W.D. Haglund
    1994   Drift trajectories of a floating human body simulated in a hydraulic model of Puget Sound,
    Journal of Forensic Sciences 39(1):231–240.

Giertsen, J.C. and I. Morild
    1989   Seafaring bodies, *American Journal of Forensic Medicine and Pathology* 10(1):25–27.

Haglund, W.D.
    1993   Disappearance of soft tissue and the disarticulation of human remains from aqueous
    environments, *Journal of Forensic Sciences* 38(4):806–815.

Hanson, B.C.
    1980   Fluvial taphonomic processes: models and experiments. In *Fossils in the Making: Vertebrate
    Taphonomy and Paleobiology*, edited by A.K. Behrensmeyer and A. Hill, pp. 156-181. University
    of Chicago Press, Chicago, IL.

Haynes, G.
  1980   Prey bones and predators: potential ecologic information from analysis of bone sites, *Ossa*
         7:75–97.

Hill, A.P.
  1975   Taphonomy of Contemporary and Late Cenozoic East African Vertebrates. Ph.D. disser-
         tation, University of London, U.K.

  1979   Disarticulation and scattering of mammal skeletons, *Paleobiology* 5(3):261–274.

Kahana, T. et al.
  1999   Marine taphonomy: adipocere formation in a series of bodies recovered from a single
         shipwreck, *Journal of Forensic Sciences* 44(5):897–901.

London, M.R., F.J. Krolikowski, and J. H. Davis
  1997   Burial at sea. In *Forensic Taphonomy: The Postmortem Fate of Human Remains*, edited by
         W.D. Haglund and M.H. Sorg, pp. 615–622. CPR Press, Boca Raton, FL.

Martin, R.E.
  1999   *Taphonomy: A Process Approach.* Cambridge University, Cambridge, U.K.

McCullough D.
  1968   *Johnstown Flood*, Simon & Schuster, New York.

Nawrocki, S.P., J.E. Pless, D.A., Hawley, and S.A. Wagner
  1997   Fluvial transport of human crania. In *Forensic Taphonomy: The Postmorem Fate of Human
         Remains*, edited by W.D. Haglund and M.H. Sorg, pp. 529–552. CRC Press, Boca Raton, FL.

O'Brien, T. G.
  1997   Movement of bodies in Lake Ontario. In *Forensic Taphonomy: The Postmortem Fate of Human
         Remains*, edited by W. D. Haglund and M.J. Sorg, pp. 559–565. CRC Press, Boca Raton, FL.

Parsons, K.M. and C.E. Brett
  1991   Taphonomic processes and biases in modern marine environments: an actualistic per-
         spective of fossil assemblage preservation. In *The Processes of Fossilization*, edited by S.K. Dono-
         van, pp. 22–65. Columbia University Press, New York.

Payne, J.A. and E.W. King
  1972   Insect succession and decomposition of pig carcasses in water, *Journal of the Georgia
         Entomological Society* 7:153–162.

Potts, R.
  1988   *Early Hominid Activities at Olduvai*, Aldine de Gruyter, New York.

Rathbun, T.A. and B.C. Rathbun
  1984   Human remains recovered from a shark's stomach in South Carolina, *Journal of Forensic
         Sciences* 29(1):269–272.

Schäfer, W.
  1972   *Ecology and Paleocology on Marine Environments*, edited by G. Craig and translated by I.
         Ortel, p. 22. University of Chicago Press, Chicago, IL.

Schafer, W.
  1978   *The Ecology and Paleoecology of Marine Environments*. University of Chicago Press, Chicago,
         IL.

Seilacher, A., W.E. Reit, and F. Westphal
  1985   Sedimentalogical, ecological and temporal patterns of fossil lagerstatten. In Extraordinary
         fossil biotas: Their ecological and evolutionary significance. Philosophical Transactions of the
         Royal Scoeity of London 311:5–23.

Simonsen, J.
  1977   Early formation of adipocere in temperate climate, *Medicine Science and Law* 17(1):53–55.

Simpson, K.
  1965   *Taylor's Principles and Practices of Medical Jurisprudence,* Vol. 1, 12th ed., Churchill Livingston, London, p. 379.

Skinner, J.B. and S.C. Porter
  1987   *Physical Geology,* p. 240. John Wiley & Sons, Inc., New York.

Skinner, M.F., J. Duffy, and D.B. Symes
  1988   Repeat identification of skeletonized human remains: A case study. *Journal of the Canadian Society of Forensic Sciences* 21(3): 138–141.

Snyder, L.
  1972   *Homicide Investigation,* 2nd ed., p. 218, Charles C Thomas, Springfield, IL.

Sorg, M.H., J.H. Dearborn, K.G. Sweeney, H.F. Ryan, and W. C. Rodriguez
  1995   Marine taphonomy of a case submerged for 32 years. Proceedings of the American Academy of Forensic Sciences 1:156–157.

Sorg, M.H. et al.
  1997   Forensic taphonomy in marine contexts. In *Forensic Taphonomy: The Postmortem Fate of Human Remains,* edited by W.D. Haglund and M.H. Sorg, pp. 1–9. CRC Press, Boca Raton, FL.

Spitz, W.U. (Ed.)
  1993   *Spitz and Fisher's Medicolegal Investigation of Death: Guidelines for the Application of Pathology to Crime Investigation,* 3rd ed. Charles C Thomas, Springfield, IL.

Spitz, W.U. and R.S. Fisher
  1980   *Medicolegal Investigation of Death: Guidelines for the Application of Pathology to Crime,* 2nd ed., p. 360, Charles C Thomas, Springfield, IL.

Teather, R.G.
  1994   *Encyclopedia of Underwater Investigations,* p. 6, Best Publishing, Flagstaff AZ.

Timperman, J.
  1991   How some medicolegal aspects of the Zeebrugge Ferry disaster apply to the investigation of mass disasters, *American Journal of Forensic Medicine and Pathology* 12(4):286–290.

Todd, L.L. and G.C. Frison
  1986   Taphonomic study of the Colby Site mammoth bones. In *The Colby Site Mammoth Bones,* pp. 27–90. Albuquerque, NM.

Toots, H.
  1965   Sequence of disarticulation in mammalian skeletons, *Contributions in Geology* 4(1) January: 37–39. University of Wyoming Press, WY.

Walker, A. and R. Leakey (Eds.)
  1993   The Nariokotome Homo Erectus Skeleton, Harvard University Press, Cambridge, MA.

Weigelt, J,
  1927   *Recent Vertebrate Carcasses and their Paleobiological Implications,* translated by Judith Schaefer, University of Chicago Press, Chicago, IL.

Western, J.
  1985   Discussions. In *L'environment des Hominides au Plio-Pleistocene,* pp. 402–405. Masson, Paris.

White, T.D.
  1988   The comparative biology of robust Australopithecus: clues from context. In *Evolutionary History of the Robust Australopithecines,* edited by F.E. Grine, pp. 449–483. Aldine de Gruyter, New York.

Voorhies, M.
  1969   Taphonomy and population dynamics of an early Pliocene vertebrae fauna, Knox County, Nebraska, *Contributions to Geology,* Spec. Paper, No. 1., pp. 1–69. University of Wyoming Press, WY.

Floating Remains on Pacific Northwest Waters *

11

CURTIS C. EBBESMEYER
WILLIAM D. HAGLUND

The dust on the sea is the grave of a ship. It is only a temporary marker,
but it is an indelible one to those who have seen it.
Dust on the Sea
Edward L. Beach (1972, p. 7)

Contents

---

* This chapter contains adaptations from three previously published papers: Ebbesmeyer et al. (1991a,b) and Ebbesmeyer and Haglund (1993).

Figure 11.1 Map of the waters of Juan de Fuca Strait and locations mentioned in text (adapted from Ebbesmeyer et al., 1991a). Illustration by Megan Abbott-Moore. With permission.

Introduction

A huge gap divides oceanography and forensics because specialists in these fields are rarely familiar with the other discipline. Consequently, little is known about where human bodies drift on the sea. This chapter seeks to bridge that gap and describes studies of the inland drift of bodies and debris after two maritime disasters in the vicinity of the Pacific Northwest's Juan de Fuca Strait. The incidents are the 1875 sinking of the steamer *Pacific* after it collided with the clipper *Orpheus*, and the 1904 sinking of the ferry *Clallam*. Both tragedies involved vessels carrying a large number of passengers and resulted in great loss of life. For weeks afterward searches were made for bodies and debris. The last three cases illustrate patterns of movement on two other areas of Puget Sound.

These five studies provide important scientific implications that deviate from traditional studies of floating objects for three reasons: (1) searches for objects floating at the sea surface are rarely done in oceanography because of the expense involved; (2) drifting objects tracked by satellite are tethered to underwater sails (drogues) usually placed at depth in the Strait, and thus do not necessarily represent the movement of water and bodies floating at the sea surface; and (3) recovery of drift bottles and cards may be influenced by population density along selected segments of the shoreline. The potential applications of this information for forensic death investigators include the ability to set geographic and time limits for searches; determine the potential origin of remains found floating or beached, and confirm and correlate information regarding entry into the water and sightings of remains.

Turned on its side, a map of the Pacific Northwest waters resembles a tree with its roots in the coastal Pacific Ocean (Figure 11.1). Its trunk is Juan de Fuca Strait, Georgia Strait is the northern foliage, and Puget Sound is the southern overhang. The eastern Strait is a junction between several estuarine reaches (Haro Strait, Rosario Strait, Admiralty Inlet, western Strait of Juan de Fuca). Each of these regions has distinctly different current patterns. Strong tidal eddies are present in a number of other junctions [off Alki Point, near The Narrows (see discussion of case 4, Figure 11.7), and the five-way junction south of Dana Passage].

Tale of Two Ferries

Historical accounts of maritime disasters can provide valuable insights into the fate of floating debris and human remains. The first ferry account in this chapter relates the collision between the paddle wheeler *Pacific* and the clipper *Orpheus* off the Washington State coast. It took place during the evening November 4, 1875, and demonstrates how storm-related reversed surface currents in Juan de Fuca Strait transported bodies and wreckage as far as 100 miles inland. In the second account, tidal eddies dispersed the debris from the ferry *Clallam*, sunk on January 8, 1904, by a violent storm off Victoria, Canada, to specific shorelines around the head of Juan de Fuca Strait.

Case #1: Collision of the Pacific and the Orpheus

The illustrious career of the steam-powered paddle wheeler *Pacific* began with her launching on September 24, 1850 in Buffalo, New York (Figure 11.2a). On her maiden voyage, the 226-foot long, 876-ton vessel logged 360 miles in 24 hours, a record run for a steamer at that time. In her 5th year of service, on a run between Nicaragua and New York, a cholera outbreak killed 45 of 800 passengers. On July 18, 1861, on a trip down the Columbia River from Portland to Astoria, the notoriously strong winds in the Columbia Gorge area grounded and sank the side-paddle wheeler near Coffin Rock. No casualties resulted and soon she was raised and repaired. By 1872, after 22 years of service, she quietly decayed for 3 years on the mud flats in San Francisco Bay (Bailey, 1967). However, in 1875, the new owners unwisely pressed the aged vessel back into service in order to ferry miners to San Francisco from the lucrative Cassiar gold fields of British Columbia.

November 4, 1875, found the *Pacific* southbound to San Francisco from Victoria with 250 to 300 passengers aboard. During the day the weather was moderate, although by evening, the wind had churned up the oncoming seas. Rounding Cape Flattery, at the northwestern corner of Washington Territory (now Washington State) the *Pacific*, in an apparently minor accident, collided with the northbound clipper ship *Orpheus*, and sank off the mouth of Juan de Fuca Strait.

The clipper *Orpheus* (Figure 11.2b) was 6 years newer than the *Pacific*. The Rice and Mitchell Company launched the medium clipper at Chelsea, Massachusetts on March 1, 1856. With an overall length of 200 feet, the 1272-ton clipper ship sailed the Pacific Ocean, setting record times. It was on her second trip to Puget Sound from San Francisco that the *Orpheus* collided with the *Pacific*, losing her foretop mast and main top gallant mast, with all starboard rigging. Her Captain, Sawyer, made for land but mistook the newly installed light on Cape Beale for the older light at Tatoosh Island. The clipper went aground, becoming a total wreck. The magnificent vessel, once valued at $20,000 to $30,000, was scrapped for $380.

Though the collision had damaged *Orpheus* only slightly, the *Pacific* sank within 20 minutes. Although carrying lifeboats for 160 persons, the ship sank so quickly that only one lifeboat with 15 women and 6 men could be launched. Unfortunately, it slammed against the steamer drowning most of those on board. The next day, a handful of survivors drifted on floating wreckage. Of these, passenger H.F. Jelly died of exposure a few days after being rescued. The other was quartermaster Neil Henley, a second survivor, a hardy Scotsman, who lived another 60 years, reaching the age of 85.

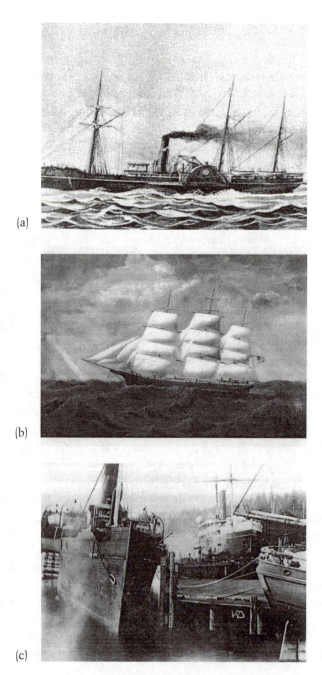

(a)

(b)

(c)

Figure 11.2 (a) The steamship *Pacific*. (b) The clipper *Orpheus* from painting. (c) The *Pacific* seen listing against Yesler Wharf. (Courtesy of the Museum of Industry and History, Seattle, WA.)

The massive effect of the slight collision might be attributed to the fact that the *Pacific* received the blow on her Achilles heel, near the buff of her bow, where the bracings were too far apart (~18 in.). In steamers, frames were separated from 12 to 20 in., whereas, in sailing vessels of the day, it was usually never more than 3 to 6 in.; the timbers of steamers were also smaller and their whole construction lighter, from the water mark up. According to other speculation, this seemingly minor collision may have just been the last in a cascade of events that lead to the sinking.

Despite intensive court trials, theories persist as to why the *Pacific* sank from a seemingly slight blow. One theory attributes the sinking to her instability in the water. In a photo taken in Seattle in the year of the collision, she can be seen listing against Yesler Wharf (Figure 11.2c). Shortly before departing Victoria on the day of the collision, water had been poured into the lifeboats in order to trim the overcrowded ship. This apparently occurred because more than 200 of the 600 tons of coal stored below deck had shifted.

A few months before her last voyage, the *Pacific* was thoroughly overhauled and critically inspected. A few days prior to sailing, she was in dry-dock to be cleaned. The inspector of hulls carefully examined her bottom and did not hesitate to say that she was in perfectly seaworthy condition. However, suspicions surrounded the premature retirement of the *Pacific* prior to the Cassiar gold fever, when the vessel had lain for years in the company's San Francisco "bone yard" (Bailey, 1967). According to carpenters who refurbished the ship in 1875, she had substantial dry rot and was structurally weak at the time of the collision. An explosion during her sinking, inferred by the scalded condition of one of the recovered bodies, coupled with dry-rotted wood, may explain the extensive debris. Parts of the *Pacific's* frame that came ashore at Foul Bay were so decayed that beachcombers picked them to pieces with their fingers, the wood about bolt heads was gone and bolts played in their sockets.

The most probable scenario for what happened after the collision is that water quickly poured in through the bow, destabilizing the *Pacific*. Afterward, she apparently broke in half, much like the *RMS Titanic*. Though a number of attempts have been made to salvage the estimated $178,000 in gold aboard the *Pacific*, accurate measures of the latitude and longitude of the collision remain speculative because oceanographic reconstructions of the winds and coastal currents have not yet been performed.

Official inquiries found that the clipper *Orpheus'* captain disregarded the universal rule of navigation in putting his helm to starboard, then to port, then to starboard again, and then again to port, repeatedly changing his course so that the steamer could not anticipate his movements and thereby avoid her. He countered, saying that the steamer had given, not received, a blow and no one aboard the clipper had any idea that damage had been done to the *Pacific*. The collision seemingly minor, the *Orpheus'* crew occupied themselves with repair of her riggings, and then sailed on 2 hours after the collision. It has been rumored that the *Orpheus'* Captain was the scapegoat in a cover-up that remains mysterious to this day. Some would lay the blame at the feet of the owners and inspectors of the *Pacific*. The condition of the recovered wreckage was at variance with the report of the Inspector of Hulls who stated that the Pacific "...was in perfectly seaworthy condition" (Annual Report of the Supervising Inspector of Hulls, 1876:39).

The time of the collision was shortly after 9:30 p.m., according to testimony from Captain Sawyer of the *Orpheus*. At the time of the accident, Captain Jefferson D. Howell, brother-in-law to Jefferson Davis, former president of the Confederate States during the Civil War, reckoned that his ship lay 15 to 20 miles offshore. Other accounts place the collision closer to shore. Testimony of H. F. Jelly and Neil Henley, confirmed by the watches found on two bodies, indicated that the *Pacific* sank within 20 to 30 min after the collision, carrying down with her all aboard except a few persons who floated off on wreckage.

Table 11.1   Chronological Order of Recoveries and Sightings of Survivors, Bodies, and Prominent Debris from the Steamship *Pacific*

Date 1875	Description of Sighting or Victims	Location of Sighting or Recovery
Nov. 6	Survivor Jelly and great amount of wreckage sighted	Rescued by vessel *Awkright*
Nov. 7	Body of unidentified woman[a] and great quantity of debris	Sighted off Neah Bay by vessel *Awkright*
Nov. 8	Bodies of Keller,[a] Vining,[a] and an unidentified steward[a]	Recovered in the vicinity of Neah Bay
Nov. 10	Large mass of debris	Sighted near Race Rock by vessel *Wolcott*
Nov. 11	Bucket rack	Found off Victoria
Nov. 12	Body of Jones[a] recovered	Recovered near Neah Bay
Nov. 13	Body (unidentified[a])	Sighted in the Eastern Strait
Nov. 13	Bodies of Crowley and unidentified Negro[a]	Recovered
Nov. 13	Part of a life boat	Found near Victoria
Nov. 13	Horse	Found floating off Slip Point
Nov. 13	Body of Helmut	Recovered floating 12 miles west of Race Rock at mid-channel
Nov. 14	Ceiling beam written on by passenger Moody and body (McIntyre[a])	Recovered between Sooke and Becher Bay
Nov. 14	Light wreckage	Sighted floating from Point Wilson to Freshwater Bay
Nov. 18	Bodies of Sullivan,[a] Farrell	Recovered
Nov. 19	Wreckage	Floating off Elwah River
Nov. 22	Body of Hastings	Recovered on Ediz Hook
Nov. 22	Rudder of SS *Pacific*	Found on Bentinck Island
Nov. 25	Body of Palmer	Recovered on San Juan Islands
Nov. 27	Some wreckage	Sighted just south of Cape Flattery
Nov. 29	Piece of bucket	Recovered at Fort Bellingham
	Body of (Chinese) and Timbers marked 30 and 41	Recovered at Neah Bay
Nov. 29	Wreckage	Sighted off Hoko River
Dec. 10	Trunk belonging to passenger Palmer	Found at Fort Dungeness

[a] Presence of life preserver according to newspaper account.

Note: Resulting from the November 4 collision between the SS *Pacific* and CS *Orpheus*. Locations are shown in Figure 11.3 by day of discovery in November of 1875 and December 10 (from reports published in the *Daily British Colonist* and supported by eight other Pacific Northwest newspapers of the time).

Source: Adapted from Ebbesmeyer, C.C. et al., Puget Sound Research '91 Proceedings, Puget Sound Water Quality Authority, Olympia, Washington, 1991.

Whereas the *Orpheus'* crew safely made it to land, all but one of those aboard the *Pacific* perished. She did not go down quietly, leaving an enormous floating debris field. Ironically, the currents carried the bodies and other debris back towards Victoria, her last port of call, strewing them along the shorelines for 100 miles as detailed in local newspaper accounts (Table 11.1 and Figure 11.3). The resulting debris field from the *Pacific* provides a dramatic example of bodies and debris driven inland by storms.

Case #2: The Ill-Fated *Clallam*

Whereas the *Pacific* wrecked in her third decade of service, the ferry *Clallam* perished in her maiden year (Figure 11.4a). In June 1903, at Tacoma, Washington, the 167-foot *Clallam*

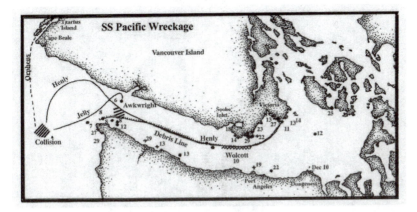

Figure 11.3 Location and date of recovery or sighting of the SS *Pacific* wreckage. Notation: hatching, offshore distance at time of collision between the SS Pacific and the clipper ship *Orpheus* (the north–south position of the wreck is considered to be speculative); dashed line, approximate track of the clipper ship Orpheus from the site of the collision to her grounding near Tzartus Island in Barkley Sound. Solid lines, approximate trajectories for the two survivors (Jelly and Henley). Parallel lines indicate sightings of the main mass of wreckage by the vessels *Awkwright* and *Wolcott*. Corkscrew indicates line of debris between Cape Flattery and Victoria reported by George Fox to George Davidson. Staircase pattern eastward from Port Angeles, scattered light wreckage. Dot, recovery of survivors or bodies; +, location of prominent debris; number with dot or +, date sighted or recovered in November 1875 (one sighting, December 10). (Illustration by Megan Abbott-Moore. With permission.)

slid broadside from Heath Shipyard's gangways, an ill-fated omen according to mariners witnessing the ship builder's daughter christening the new ferry.

Just 6 months later, at noon on Friday, January 8, 1904, the *Clallam* departed Port Townsend (on the U.S. side of Juan de Fuca Strait) for a routine 3-hour, 20-mile-run to Victoria on Canada's Vancouver Island. Shortly after departing, the *Clallam* encountered a 54-mile-per-hour gale. At mid-Strait, 10 miles from shore, she began taking on water through deadlights (portholes) located only 18 in. above the port-side waterline facing into the gale. Within 3 to 4 miles of journey's end, the crew managed to staunch the inflow of water entering the deadlights. Nevertheless, enough water flooded in to reach fireman Maddock's shoulders and snuff out the boilers. Without power, the pumps failed. At the mercy of currents, bucket brigades and hand pumps madly flailing, the *Clallam* drifted out of the sight of shore-bound onlookers who witnessed the mayhem.

Captain Roberts, thinking the *Clallam* likely to sink at any moment, ordered all women and children overboard in three lifeboats manned by carefully picked men to row them the short distance to shore. It was impossible to lower the remaining three lifeboats on the weather side of the ship. Men watched in horror as a few hundred yards away gigantic waves swamped the lifeboats, drowning the women and children. Survivors told later of their heartbreak. S.E. Bolton, for example, who was returning home from his honeymoon after just 10 days of marriage, watched his wife drown. Thomas Sullins, a mine owner, lost his wife and three children.

By this time, winds and tides had carried the *Clallam* east to a position off Trial Island near Clover Point, just 20 minutes from Victoria. Through the afternoon and evening, crew and passengers battled to keep the *Clallam* afloat by jettisoning 2 tons of coal, oilcakes,

(a)

(b)

Figure 11.4 (a) The steamer *Clallam*. (b) Steamer *Clallam's* top foredeck lying on the beach at Sidney Spit, Vancouver Island, British Columbia. (Courtesy of the Museum of Industry and History, Seattle, WA.)

and cargo. Finally, midway between Smith and San Juan islands, the tug *Holyoke* got a tow line on the *Clallam*. Nevertheless, in the darkness, the *Holyoke's* captain couldn't discern the *Clallam's* waterlogged condition. After 12 miles, the *Holyoke*, herself in peril, cut the towline. The *Clallam's* bow rose out of the water; the men remaining on board ran forward, clinging to the railings. Among them was Captain Robert, who along with others was swept overboard by a monstrous wave. On sinking, the upper two decks detached. Of the 89 aboard, at least 55 passengers and crew perished. Over the next 13 days, searchers recovered 32 bodies (Table 11.2) and wreckage including the whole foredeck (Figure 11.4b).

Storms Drive Debris Inland

The great loss of human life resulting from the sinkings of the *Pacific* and *Clallam* motivated intensive searches on both occasions. Results of these searches provide two rare instances in which the destinations of floating objects were intensively traced in inland waters. The *Pacific's* debris provides the only data on floatable objects driven inland by coastal storms through Juan de Fuca Strait. When combined, the *Clallam's* and *Pacific's* debris show that most of the bodies were found along only 10% of the 277 miles of the eastern Strait's

Table 11.2 Chronological Order of Sightings and Recovery of *Clallum* Passengers and Debris during January 1904

Date 1904	Victim No.	Description of Sighting or Victims[a]	Location of Sighting or Recovery
Jan. 9	1–5	Captain Livinston,[b] William Buchanan Gibbons,[b] W.H. Hicks,[b] unidentified elderly male,[b] unidentified male,[b]	Recovered 1/2 mile from floating pilot house near site of sinking
Jan. 10	6	Louise Harris[b,c,d]	Recovered from lifeboat 2 miles east of Clove Point, off Victoria
Jan. 10	7	Mrs. Thomas Sullins[b,c]	Recovered off Beacon Hill alongside life boat no. 1
Jan. 10	8	Miss Galletly[b,c]	Recovered, Clover Point
Jan. 10	9	Ethel Diprose[b]	Recovered, Beacon Hill
Jan. 10	10, 11	Alex Harvey,[b] unidentified female[b]	Recovered off Williams Head
Jan. 10	12–15	N. P. Shaw,[b] Miss Gill,[b] C. H. Joy,[b] Miss Minnie Murdock[b]	Recovered 1/2 mile from floating pilot house between Race Rock and Brochie Ledge by Tug Mary Reynolds
Jan. 10	16	Peter LaPlante[b]	Recovered between Victoria and New Westminster
Jan. 10	17–21	Captain Thomson,[b] W.B. Gibbons,[a,b] Eugene Hicks,[a,b] Archie Hudson,[a,b] C.F. Johnson[a,b]	Recovered near site of sinking (one body wedged between stanchions)
Jan. 12		Upper deck, and sacks of oilcakes[e] Wreckage[e]	Sighted as far as San Juan Island
Jan. 12	22	William Cherret[f]	Recovered off Clover Point
Jan. 13		Life boat no. 1[g]	Sighted, off Beacon Hill
Jan. 14		Wreckage[g]	Sighted, along north side of San Juan Island
Jan. 13	23	Col. Charles W. Thompson[h]	Recovered off D' Arcy Island Beach
Jan. 15	24	Harvey Sears[h]	Recovered near Brochie Ledge
Jan. 15	25	R. G. Campbell[h]	Recovered near Albert Head
Jan. 16	26–28	E. Lockwood,[h] Guy L. Daniels,[h] A.K. Prince[i]	Recovered, floated into Esquimalt Harbor
Jan. 17	29	W. F. Rocklidge[i]	Recovered at the end of Angeles spit
Jan. 17		Wreckage[i]	Sighted, near Port Angeles
Jan. 19	30	Homer S. Swaney[j]	Recovered 1 mile off Dungeness Light in the straits
Jan. 22	31	Unidentified female[k]	Recovered off Ediz Rock
??	32	Bruno Lehman	Recovered, location not stated

[a] Presence of life preserver according to newspaper account.
[b] *Seattle Post Intelligencer*, January 10, 1904.
[c] *Seattle Post Intelligencer*, January 11, 1904.
[d] *Seattle Times*, January 12, 1904.
[e] *Seattle Post Intelligencer*, January 13, 1904.
[f] *San Juan Islander*, January 14, 1904.
[g] *Seattle Times*, January 14, 1904.
[h] *Seattle Times*, January 16, 1904.
[i] *Seattle Times*, January 18, 1904.
[j] *Seattle Post Intelligencer*, January 20, 1904.
[k] *Seattle Post Intelligencer*, January 23, 1904.

shoreline. By identifying the pattern of floating bodies on particular shores, medical investigators may substantially narrow their searches for bodies and other floating forensic evidence.

Newspaper accounts provide most of what is known about the debris field and recovery of human remains from these two disasters. To ascertain the quantity and variety of wreckage from the *Pacific,* nine Pacific Northwest newspapers published between November 6 and December 10, 1875 were examined. According to their reports, the shores throughout Juan de Fuca Strait were thoroughly searched and hefty rewards were offered for the bodies of loved ones. Scant debris was reported outside the Strait, whereas extensive amounts were found inside. Despite diligent searches, only about 6% of the approximately 250 to 300 bodies were recovered. Judging from their well-preserved condition and that most of those who jumped from the ship wore life preservers, it is a fair assumption that they had been floating between the time of the collision and recovery.

As they clung to floating pieces of wreckage, two *Pacific* survivors realized that they drifted inland to the east rather than the expected northward trajectory along the Vancouver Island coast. Jelly, the wreck's survivor who died shortly after being recovered, drifted close to Cape Flattery, then within a mile of Vancouver Island, and was rescued off Port San Juan. Henley, the Scotsman, drifted within sight of the Cape Beale lighthouse, then close to Vancouver Island, and finally to mid-channel between Pillar Point and Sooke Inlet where he was rescued after 72 hours adrift in a wooden box (Lockley, 1926).

Normally, because of river discharge from Georgia Strait and Puget Sound, the sea surface stands higher in the eastern Strait than at the Strait's mouth to the Pacific Ocean. As a result, the surface water usually flows downhill from east to west. However, during winter storms, low atmospheric pressure and southerly winds along the Pacific Ocean coast often elevate the surface water at the mouth, effectively reversing the sea surface slope along the Strait, thereby pushing surface water counter to the usual direction. Statistical correlations with currents measured in the Strait revealed that coastal winds were of prime importance, with local winds in the Strait itself exerting small influence on the reversed currents (Holbrook et al., 1980). Because of the Earth's rotation, the water intruding from the coast (known as current reversals and oceanic intrusions) tends to flow inland along the Strait's southern shore.

Oceanographic measurements in the Strait during 1977–1981 showed that reversals may occur in any month (Holbrook et al., 1980, 1983). In winter, 2 to 3 reversals, each lasting 2 to 7 days, typically occur each month (Holbrook et al., 1983). Although most frequent during winter, intrusions also occur in summer, e.g., movements of surface drifters were observed when a low pressure cell lay off the Washington coast during August 23–25, 1978, and trajectories of several drifters abruptly reversed in the western Strait (Cox et al., 1978; Ebbesmeyer et al., 1979; Holbrook et al., 1980; Frisch et al., 1981).

The rate of intrusion (eastward surface current speed) was computed from Benjamin's (1968) equation for the hydraulic flow of a lens of lighter water drawn by gravity inland over denser sea water (Holbrook and Halpern, 1982; Holbrook et al., 1983). Subtracting an assumed mean westward estuarine current of 15 to 20 cm/sec from the theoretical intrusion speed yielded an eastward speed of 25 to 30 cm/sec (12 to 14 nautical miles/day).

Information reported in newspapers was sufficient to estimate the speed at which *Pacific* wreckage drifted inland. Wind drag on the wreckage was neglected because wind observations in the Strait were not available and windage on the wreckage could not be ascertained. Over an 11-day period the largest mass of wreckage drifted inland as reported at three places (Figure 11.3): (1) off Neah Bay during the afternoon of November 7 (vessel *Awkwright*); (2) north of Port Angeles in the afternoon of November 10 (vessel *Wolcott*); and (3) in the vicinity of Victoria during November 11 to 14 (many recoveries). These

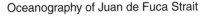

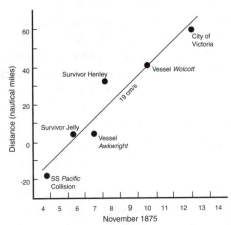

Figure 11.5 Distance in miles vs. time in days for sightings of selected wreckage and accounts of the two survivors from the SS *Pacific*. The straight line represents a linear regression fit to the observations, where r equals the regression coefficient and speed (19 cm/sec) corresponds to the slope of the regression. Notation: SS *Pacific* COLLISION, collision of vessels *Orpheus* and *Pacific*; JELLY AND HENLEY, the two survivors, AWKWRIGHT & WOOLCOTT, sightings of the main mass of wreckage by the vessels Awkwright and Wolcott; and VICTORIA, frequent reports in the vicinity of Victoria (adapted from Ebbesmeyer et al., 1991a). (Illustration by Megan Abbott-Moore. With permission.)

data, in addition to those of the collision itself and the rescue of the two survivors, were entered on a graph of distance vs. time, and a linear regression was computed (Figure 11.5). The regression slope, equivalent to the wreckage's average inland speed, explained 92% of the variance (19 cm/sec; 9 nautical miles/day). Some flotsam traveled inland more quickly than the average; on November 8, debris began appearing at Victoria, equivalent to 20 miles per day.

If the observations of *Pacific* wreckage are reliable, the inland speed derived from them should be comparable to speeds derived from modern oceanographic measurements. Floatable oil spilled from the *Nestucca* barge off Grays Harbor in 1989 and floated inland through Juan de Fuca Strait at 9 miles per day (U.S. Coast Guard, 1989). Reversals transported *Pacific* wreckage inland at 9 to 20 miles per day and surface drifters, during the summer intrusion of 1978, at 18 miles per day. We see that the intrusion speed derived from the *Pacific* wreckage is comparable to that derived from a model, an oil spill, and oceanographic field measurements.

Tidal Eddies Concentrate Wreckage

Observers aboard search vessels on Juan de Fuca Strait reported the *Pacific's* debris concentrated in well-defined trails and patches in open water and at specific locations along the shore. Survivor Henley had noticed a large patch as a current reversal carried him inland. George Fox (1910), in a letter to Professor George Davidson, wrote of a 60-mile-long line of debris, aimed at the southern end of Vancouver Island, coinciding with the many recoveries of bodies and wreckage.

Between 1875 and 1984, more than 16,000 drift objects were released in the waterways approaching eastern Juan de Fuca Strait, including the Pacific Coast, Georgia Strait, and

Puget Sound. The drifters found within the eastern Strait showed two striking patterns: (1) 73% of the recoveries came from the northern shores vs. 27% from the southern shores; (2) 50% of the recoveries were made in three specific locations totaling about 10% of the eastern Strait's shoreline (Victoria, San Juan Islands, Dungeness Spit) (Ebbesmeyer et al., 1991a,b). These results were insensitive to the type of drifter, or whether the drifters were actively sought out or were simply found by beach walkers happening upon them.

The tidal water volumes feeding the eastern Strait between mean high water and mean lower water are comprised of 76% from Georgia Strait and 24% from Puget Sound. These percentages are within one standard error of those associated with the north–south asymmetry (73% of recoveries on northern shores; 27% on southern shores). This explains why the eddies in the northern areas of the eastern Strait are larger and more vigorous than those in the south.

Overlaying the recoveries on maps of surface currents (derived from models and field studies) showed that the localized recovery areas coincided with tidal eddy currents directed onshore. Fourteen prominent tidal eddies in the eastern Strait have been documented with hydraulic and numerical models, as well as with oceanographic field observations (Figure 11.6). Each eddy was observed in the hydraulic model, and nine with field observations and the GF7 numerical model, Georgia Strait–Juan de Fuca version 7, numerical model utilizing 61 tidal constituents (Crean, pers. comm.) (Figure 11.6a). The eastern Strait wreckage reports can be explained by the strength and position of tidal eddies. In Figure 11.6b the ovals circumscribe the approximate extent of the net currents that circulate around the individual tidal eddies shown in Figure 11.6a.

Explanations for the observed asymmetries in drifter recovery were found by comparing the recoveries with positions of the tidal eddies (Figure 11.6b). The highest frequency occurred between eddies #2 and #3 in the vicinity of Victoria. The second highest frequency occurred along the outer half of Dungeness Spit in the vicinity of eddy #10. Between eddies #11 and #10 there is a net along-shore flow that sweeps floating objects, or drifters, to Dungeness Spit (Ebbesmeyer et al., 1979). A third concentration occurred between eddies #4 and #5. This comparison suggests that tidal eddies gather drifters and send them ashore where the currents are perpendicular to the beach.

Recoveries of individual releases are often said to be modified by winds. The releases reported herein represent a composite from many months, sites, and years. The agreement between recoveries and tidal characteristics further suggests that winds are of secondary importance to the recovery patterns in the eastern Strait.

Three Puget Sound Cases Involving Individuals

The following cases involve additional areas of Puget Sound: (1) the Georgia Strait where a passenger fell overboard from a ferry; (2) southern Puget Sound between Tacoma and Seattle Washington which was traversed by a jumper from the Tacoma Narrows Bridge; and (3) Deception Pass, a narrow slot between Fidalgo and Whidbey islands and the alleged disposal site of a homicide victim.

Case #3: An Accidental Fall from a Ferry in Georgia Strait

Late on Sunday night, July 25, 1993, Robert Lord, aged 42 years, boarded a Canadian ferry to travel across the southern end of Georgia Strait from Tsawassen (a suburb of Vancouver)

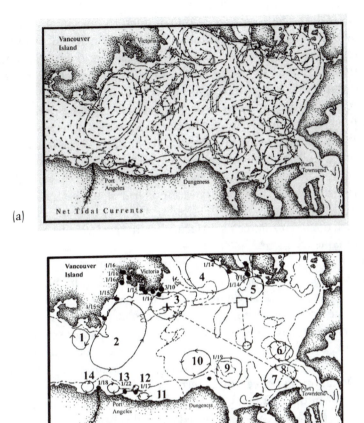

Figure 11.6 (a) Direction of net currents computed over a 30-day interval using Crean's (1983) numerical model. Dots indicate location of computation and sticks point in current direction without regard for speed. Outlines show tidal eddies. (b) Location and date of recovery or sighting of the steamer *Clallam* wreckage. Dashed lines connect last port of disembarkation at Port Townsend area of *Clallam's* initial distress (+), launching of lifeboats (□), and *Clallam's* sinking (○). Dot, recovery of survivors or bodies; +, location of prominent debris. Number with dot or +: date sighted or recovered in January 1904, with the exception that three bodies were recovered near Victoria on January 10 and 12 as noted in parentheses. * next to 'DECK' = top foredeck recovered. Ovals, areas of thirteen tidal eddies, where arrows show the rotation of the eddy currents. Numbers refer to tidal eddies at the following approximate locations: (1) Becher Bay; (2) Race Rocks; (3) Victoria; (4) San Juan Islands; (5) Lopez Island; (6) Partridge Point; (7) Point Wilson; (8) Diamond Point; (9, 10) Dungeness Spit; (11, 12) Ediz Hook; (13, 14) Elwah R. Delta. (Illustrations by Megan Abbott-Moore.)

to Sydney, British Columbia (on Vancouver Island). Reeling from severe nausea, Lord leaned out from an upper-deck window so as not to make a mess. But he leaned too far, and pitched overboard 25 feet into the water. Without a life jacket or survival suit, Lord, 6′4″ tall and weighing 240 lbs., survived adrift for the ensuing 8 hours.

Georgia Strait is a large coastal waterway connected to the Pacific Ocean by Juan de Fuca Strait to the south and Discovery Passage to the north. The tide and the plume of Fraser River drainage, which spreads out over much of southern Georgia Strait, dominate surface currents. Winds can be important in surface drift, but happened to be particularly light during Lord's ordeal. The combined effects of tides, rivers, winds, and ocean density were modeled by Jim Stronach, Sea Consult Marine Research Ltd., using GF9, a 3D hydrodynamic model implemented on a 2-km Cartesian grid for the entire Juan de Fuca–Georgia Strait-Puget Sound system. GF9 evolved from several decades of dedicated research and is summarized in a monograph by Crean (1983).

Tides and ocean density conditions were specified at the Pacific Ocean entrances, and river flow was prescribed from daily discharge measurements. Winds from 13 coastal stations provided the necessary stress data at the sea surface. To eliminate the transients that develop when complex computer models first begin running, GF9 was initialized on July 1 and spun up for 25 days prior to coupling with the surface spill simulator program (SPILLSIM). Turbulence in the tidal waters was modeled at 10-minute intervals with the release of 10,000 particles dispersing with an eddy viscosity of 8 m^2/sec in Monte Carlo fashion. The modeled currents agreed satisfactorily with surface currents measured with a SeaSonde high frequency radar.

The modeled drift also agreed well with the time and location where Lord was rescued. Throughout his grueling ordeal, Lord was conscious and aware of his position. After falling overboard at 11:15 p.m. Pacific Daylight Time (PDT used throughout this section) he drifted for 1.75 hours, coming within a few hundred meters of Galiano Island. After 3.5 hours (2:45 a.m. on July 26), a large southbound freighter passed close by Lord then floating a few miles offshore. By sunrise, near Orcas Island in the San Juan archipelago, Lord had drifted about 15 nautical miles (28 km). Finally, after 8 hours (7:15 a.m.) and 22 miles adrift (40 km), a vacationing police officer recovered him.

At a hospital some hours after being rescued, Lord's body temperature registered 93.2°F. Coast Guard officials told Lord that he survived the chilly waters longer than the expected 1 to 2 hours for two reasons. First, he drifted in an unusually warm current draining from the Fraser River. Second, Lord's windbreaker jacket acted as a flotation device by holding air in its shoulders.

How accurate was the computer simulation? The Monte Carlo simulation of tidal turbulence yields probabilities of target locations. In this case, Lord was rescued in the center of the high probability area spread over an elliptical region measuring approximately 10 × 20 nautical miles. A good simulation by oceanographic standards, it presents forensic investigators with the uncertainties associated with hundreds of square miles.

Case #4: Jumper from the Narrows Bridge, Southern Puget Sound

The case below represents a unique opportunity for high-resolution tracking with respect to the drift of human remains. The model showed that small changes in the time of a jump (± 30 min) from a high bridge made great differences in where the body drifted (± 30 miles; 48 km).

On Friday February 5, 1988, a 22-year-old male leapt from midspan of the Tacoma Narrows bridge that connects the city of Tacoma and the Olympic Peninsula (Figure 11.7a). Two friends, who were also at the site of the jump, later told police the time of the jump was 3:00 a.m. (Pacific Standard Time used throughout this section). They then proceeded to a predestinated location on the eastern shore of the Tacoma Narrows (approximately 1 km away), where they were to meet their friend when he swam to onshore. The two friends waited until 7:20 a.m. before reporting their friend missing to local police. According to these friends, the missing man was an experienced bridge jumper and leapt for sport.

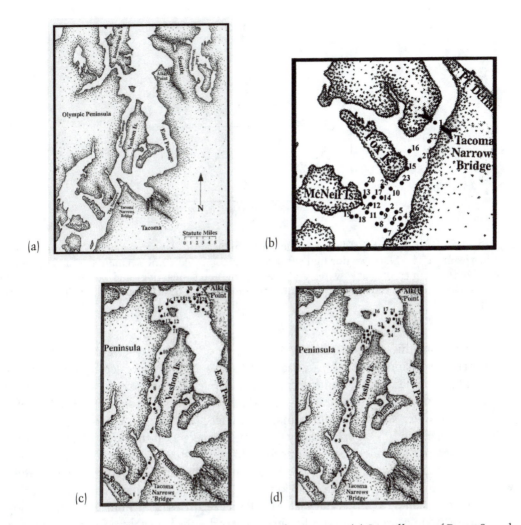

Figure 11.7 Model predictions for the Narrows Bridge remains. (a) Overall map of Puget Sound. (b) Using the Puget Sound hydraulic model, a trajectory of a bead released at approximately 0230 hours on February 5, 1988. Hour 1 corresponds to 0230 and numbers (bead counts) by dots thereafter are spaced at intervals of 2 hours. Note that after 48 hours (bead count = 25) the bead is still located south of the Tacoma Narrows Bridge. (c) A trajectory of a bead released at approximately 0300 hours on February 5, 1988. Hour 1 corresponds to 0300 and numbers (bead counts) by dots thereafter are spaced at intervals of two hours. Note that after two hours (bead count = 2) the bead is located off Fox Island, and that after 56 hours (bead count = 29) the bead is located near Alki Point. (d) A trajectory of a bead released at approximately 0330 hours on February 5, 1988. Hour 1 corresponds to 0330 and numbers (bead counts) by dots thereafter are spaced at intervals of two hours. Note that after a half hour (bead count = 1.5) the bead is located about a mile south of the Tacoma Narrows Bridge, and that after 48 hours (bead count = 25), the bead is located off the northern end of Vashon Island. (Illustrations by Megan Abbott-Moore.)

According to police reports, a fisherman sighted the body off Fox Island, approximately 6 km south of The Narrows, late in the afternoon of February 5 (Figure 11.7b). On February 7 at 11:25 a.m., after a higher high tide at 7:39 a.m., the deceased was recovered on the beach near Alki Point in Seattle approximately 20 miles north of the bridge (statute miles

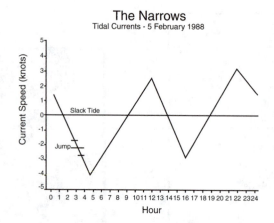

Figure 11.8 Tidal currents predicted by the National Oceanic and Atmospheric Administration at midstream in The Narrows during February 5, 1988. Straight line segments connect predictions given for times of slack water and maximum flood (negative) and ebb (positive) tidal currents. Dot and lines indicate ± 30 minutes before and after indicate jump from The Narrows Bridge.

used throughout this section; 32 km). At the time of recovery, the body was clad in a sweatshirt, sweat pants, boxer shorts, shoes, and socks. Autopsy revealed bilateral injuries to the lungs, liver, left kidney and spleen, as well as fractures of the right wrist and ribs.

According to construction drawings, the distance from the mid-span of the Narrows Bridge to the water surface is approximately 221 feet (67 meters). Hydrographic charts indicate a water depth of approximately 209 feet (64 meters) at the point of entry (Chart No. 1874) and mid-channel tidal currents for February 5, 1988, predicted by standard tidal current tables, are shown in Figure 11.8. At the time of the jump, currents in The Narrows were flowing south at approximately 2.3 knots (1.2 m/sec) (U.S. Department of Commerce Tidal Current Tables, 1988). Winds at Alki Point recorded at 3-hour intervals during October 5–7 were calm except for a few brief intervals when they were from the north at 3 to 8 knots. According to historic records, water temperature at this time of year is near its annual minimum of approximately 8°C (46°F) (Collias et al., 1974).

Fast tidal currents in The Narrows and Colvos Passage cause considerable turbulence and homogenize the water such that temperatures and densities near the sea floor are nearly the same as those of the sea surface. If the deceased were neutrally buoyant, his depth could have varied substantially. The fact that the body was clad and its movement, as shown later, agrees with that of surface currents in the hydraulic model, suggests that the body was at the sea surface most of the time between the jump and beaching. Clearly defined flow patterns and several other factors including the known time of entry into the water, the sighting south of the jump, and subsequent recovery of the body north of the bridge, make this case ideal for demonstrating the applicability of hydraulic models for correlation of oceanographic and forensic information.

Hydraulic models have been used successfully since the 1880s to perform simulations of the tidal currents in estuaries (Rouce and Ince, 1957). Concrete is often used to simulate the seafloor, where the vertical and horizontal scales are selected based on fluid dynamic principles. Water level in the models is made to rise and fall through the use of plungers and water pumps that are usually placed at the entrance to the estuaries, where the rates of flow are also scaled from physical equations governing tidal currents. They vary in size from areas covering several hundred square feet to several acres. Experience gained over a century has shown these concrete tidal hydraulic models often to be of considerable accuracy.

The hydraulic model of Puget Sound located at the School of Oceanography, University of Washington, was used to simulate the body's drift. The model was constructed in the early 1950s to study currents in Puget Sound (Collias and Andreeva, 1977; Rattray and Lincoln, 1955). For more than 40 years it has been in active use as a teaching aid for students, as well as being used in numerous engineering and environmental studies (Collias and Andreeva, 1977). Experience from many studies has shown that the water currents near the sea surface of the subject area are accurately represented, except close to the shore.

The design of the hydraulic model incorporates a number of physical characteristics, including simulation of tides that accurately reproduce predictions given in standard tidal (U.S. Department of Commerce Tide Tables, 1988) and current tables (U.S. Department of Commerce Tidal Current Tables, 1988) and approximate representation of the outflow of major rivers and the salinity in Puget Sound. For our purpose, simulation was simplified as wind effects could be neglected because local winds were mostly calm during the body's drift.

The model was programmed to simulate tidal currents at the reported time of the jump and was operated for 3 model-time days (a 24-hour day of model time equals approximately 70 seconds real time; 1 hour corresponds to approximately 2.9 seconds). To represent the body, a small floating bead with a diameter of 2 mm was used in three experimental runs. As the tidal and mean currents transported the bead, its location was videotaped and later mapped with a personal computer as shown in Figure 11.7.

Preliminary model runs (not shown) indicated that the correct jump time within a small tolerance is crucial in determining where the body might have traveled, because the tidal currents were changing rapidly at the time of the jump. Therefore, three simulations, a jump a little earlier than 3:00 a.m. (approximately 2:30), one close to 3:00 a.m., and another a little later than 3:00 a.m. (approximately 3:30), were investigated (Figures 11.7b, c, and d), respectively. Positions of the bead in the three model runs are shown at 2-hour intervals, with positions numbered consecutively, beginning with "1" at the time of jump.

By comparing the bead counts with times when the body was observed, the approximate time of the jump was judged to be a fraction of an hour earlier than given in the police reports. The first sighting of the body off Fox Island at approximately 4:00 p.m. on February 5 (about 13 hours after the jump) corresponds to a bead count of 7 to 8. The second sighting (i.e., recovery) at 11:25 a.m. on February 7 on Alki Point (about 56 hours after the jump) corresponds to a bead count of 29. However, as the winds were calm, it is likely that the body actually beached at high water prior to being discovered. For example, the body could have beached at approximately 6:53 p.m. during darkness on February 6, or at 7:39 a.m. on February 7. These times correspond to approximately 40 and 53 hours after the jump, or bead counts of 21 and 27 to 28, respectively. Therefore, the body could have beached at any time between bead counts 21 and 29.

We determined that the jump occurred earlier than 3:00 a.m. in the following manner: In the model simulation, the body was off Fox Island at the reported location at bead counts of 15 and 2, corresponding to jump times of 2:30 and 3:00 a.m. (Figures 11.7b and 7c, respectively). For a jump occurring at 3:30 a.m. the body did not reach Fox Island (Figure 11.7d). A bead count of 8 for the sighting off Fox Island corresponds to a model time approximately mid-way between counts of 2 and 15 (Figures 11.7b and 7c), or approximately 15 minutes before 3:00 a.m. The effect of a jump a little earlier than 3:00 a.m., as shown in Figure 11.7b, is to increase the bead count off Fox Island by 6 and to decrease it by 6 to 23 off Alki Point. The count of 23 nearly corresponds with the high water of February 6 mentioned earlier (count = 21). This correlation suggests that the body was in the vicinity of Alki Point shortly after darkness on February 6. Given the uncertainties with the model, it is possible that the body actually beached at Alki Point during the evening of February 6, but was not discovered until the morning of February 7. Also, it is possible that the body beached during the night then floated away for a time before again washing ashore.

In the three simulations (Figures 11.7b, c, and d) within 2 days after the jump, the beads were found as far south as 6 miles from The Narrows Bridge and as far north as 20 miles from The Narrows Bridge, off Alki Point. This wide dispersion occurred for jump times spanning 1 hour (2:30 to 3:30), thereby illustrating the sensitivity of the recovery to small changes in the jump time.

Case #5: Deception Pass: The Body in the Nylon Suitcase

The following case illustrates that currents sometimes display so much drift variability in time and space that where a body may float is not predictable.

In the early morning hours of May 17, 1993, Petty Officer Mark Allen Eby, 38, strangled his wife Teresa S. Eby, 26, at the Naval Air Station, Whidbey Island, Washington. Afterward he stuffed her 5′2″, 102-lb. body clad only in a nightshirt into a black nylon soft-sided suitcase measuring 33 × 24 × 10 inches. Shortly after the crime, Eby drove to the northernmost bridge span of the Deception Pass Bridge and dropped the suitcase into the tidal waters 180 feet below. At that time, which Naval investigators estimated to be 2:39 to 3:15 a.m., the tidal currents were flowing at 6.0 to 6.8 knots westward into Juan de Fuca Strait.

Divers searched extensively for 48 hours without success in the 42°F waters. Meanwhile, a 14-person ground party searched the shoreline. For ideas of where the suitcase could have drifted, divers released a surface float that quickly exited Deception Pass and snagged on the shore a few miles to the north. Naval investigators also considered the historical oceanographic measurements collected nearby for siting a nuclear power plant, an oil pipeline, and a floating fish farm. Without exception, floating markers placed immediately east of the bridge drifted within a few days into Juan de Fuca Strait. Overall, the average water movement from the sea surface to the bottom exited Deception Pass into Juan de Fuca Strait.

During one study in 1992, oceanographers dropped 250 postcard-sized wooden placards from a small aircraft flying at 500 feet altitude immediately east of the Deception Pass Bridge. Specifically, five drops of 50 cards each were made off Hoypus Point (48°24.75′N, 122°45.85′W) on the following dates: January 20, January 28, February 7, February 21, and February 29. The placards were painted with red nontoxic paint to aid beachcombers in finding them.

Figure 11.9 shows the location where drift cards were recovered through March 27, 1992. With two exceptions, the recoveries were generally west of the drop site. The recovery pattern is as expected from the other oceanographic studies because drift markers, despite the tides, moved toward and into Deception Pass in a day or two. Eby's body would be

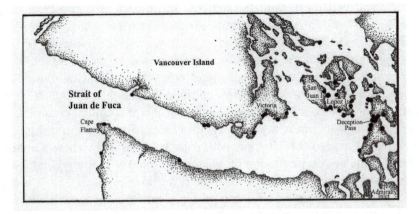

Figure 11.9 Locations where drift cards were recovered through March 27, 1992 are indicated by dots. The victim's body would be expected to drift out into Juan de Fuca Strait or beach within Deception Pass itself. (Illustrations by Megan Abbott-Moore.)

expected to drift out into Juan de Fuca Strait or beach within Deception Pass itself. Within about a month, beachcombers reported 35.2% (78) of the cards scattered along a thousand miles of shoreline westward to the Pacific Ocean over an area measuring roughly 50 by 100 miles.

Naval investigators concluded that it was virtually impossible to determine where the suitcase drifted once it hit the water due to the many variables involved: water in the victim's lungs, current speed and direction, water depth due to tide height variations, the condition of the body when it hit the water, whether the body remained in the suitcase after it hit the water, and the inability to determine exactly where the body was thrown off the bridge. Though the probability was high that Mrs. Eby's body drifted into Juan de Fuca Strait, searching this large water body was virtually impossible.

Not surprisingly, her body was never recovered. Nevertheless, based on his confession not long after the crime, in October 1993 a Naval court convicted Eby of first degree murder and sentenced him to life imprisonment.

Discussion

The previous accounts illustrate that given accurate tidal, wind, and river inputs, computer simulations can provide reliable predictions over hour to day-long intervals even in areas of fast, complex currents and strong turbulence.

Only a small number of observations are available with which to derive the inland movement of floatable materials. Conclusions from this study of the collision between the steamship *Pacific* and clipper *Orpheus* may be summarized as follows: (1) substantial amounts of floatable material can be transported from oceanic regimes through the Strait of Juan de Fuca to the entrances of Puget Sound and the Strait of Georgia (order of 100 miles inland); (2) the inland transport speed of the SS *Pacific* wreckage was comparable to that of surface drifters, an oil spill (Canadian Coast Guard Western Region Report, 1989) and a dynamic model; and (3) during episodes of reversed estuarine currents, extensive lines and patches of floatable material form, with significant amounts of the material tending to beach at specific locations in the eastern Strait.

A variety of oceanographic models may be utilized to demonstrate trajectories of floating human remains and to obtain the time required to arrive at certain locations. Some are physical, being constructed mostly of concrete covering substantial areas, and some are numerical, being run on electronic computers. Examples of physical or hydraulic models include the one described in this chapter for Puget Sound and models on display at the U.S. Army Corps of Engineers Waterways Experiment Station at Vicksburg, Mississippi.

Oceanographic models do not show with complete reliability where a floating object will travel under all environmental conditions for a number of reasons. Despite shortcomings, the models often predict probable trajectories the body could travel and indicate areas that the body is not likely to travel. By superposing oceanographic models with up-to-date field data, death investigators may set limits for searches, determine potential origins of floating or beached remains, and correlate information regarding points of water entry and sightings of remains.

Acknowledgments

My thanks to Brian Gisborne, owner-operator of the water taxi *Juan de Fuca Express*, Victoria, British Columbia, for locating photos of the *Pacific* and *Orpheus*; to Nick Hanson and Carolyn Marr, Museum of History and Industry, for reproducing photos of the *Pacific* and *Clallam*; to Jim Stronach, SeaConsult Marine Research Ltd. for simulating Bob Lord's drift; to Gary R. Miller, Trans Mountain Oil Pipe Line Corporation, for permission to use the drift card data for Deception Pass; and to Douglas A. Tomaso, Naval Criminal Investigative Service Field Office Puget Sound, for information regarding Mark Allen Eby.

References

Annual Reports of the Supervising Inspector of Hulls, First District
   1876   Annual Report of the Supervising Inspectors, San Francisco, CA.

Bailey, R.G.
   1967   British Columbians enraged at *Pacific–Orpheus* Disaster of 1875, *Marine Notebook*, 50:54–56.

Beach, E. L.
   1972   *Dust on the Sea*, Zebra Books, New York.

Benjamin, T. B.
   1968   Gravity currents and related phenomena, *Journal of Fluid Mechanics* 31(2):209–248.

Chart No. 1874, National Oceanic and Atmospheric Administration.

Collias, E.E. and S.I. Andreeva
   1977   *Puget Sound Marine Environment: An Annotated Bibliography*, Washington Sea Grant Program Publication Seattle, WA, WSG 77-2, 392 pp.

Collias, E.E., N. McGary, and C.A. Barnes,
   1974   *Atlas of Physical and Chemical Properties of Puget Sound and its Approaches*, Washington Sea Grant Publication, University of Washington Press, Seattle 235 pp.

Cox, J.M., C.C. Ebbesmeyer, and J.M. Helseth
    1978 Surface drift sheet movements observed in the inner Strait of Juan de Fuca, August. National Oceanic and Atmospheric Administration Technical Memorandum ERL MESA-35, Washington, D.C.

Crean, P.B.
    1983 The development of rotating, nonlinear numerical models (GF2, GF3) simulating barotropic mixed tides in a complex coastal system located between Vancouver Island and the mainland. Institute of Ocean Sciences, Dept. of Fisheries and Oceans, Canadian Tech. Dept. of Hydrography and Ocean Sciences No. 31, p. 65.

Ebbesmeyer, C.C. and W.J. Haglund
    1993 Drift trajectories of a floating human body simulated in a hydraulic model of Puget Sound, *Journal of Forensic Sciences* 39(1):231–240.

Ebbesmeyer, C.C. et al.
    1979 Dynamics of Port Angeles Harbor and approaches. U.S. Environmental Protection Agency Research Report EPA600/7-79-252, Washington, D.C.

    1991a 1875 Floatable wreckage driven inland through the Strait of San Juan de Fuca. Puget Sound Research '91 Proceedings, Puget Sound Water Quality Authority, Olympia, Washington, pp. 75–85.

    1991b Eddy induced beaching of floatable materials in the eastern Strait of Juan de Fuca. Puget Sound Research '91 Proceedings, Puget Sound Water Quality Authority, Olympia, Washington, pp. 86–98.

Fox, G.H.
    1910 Personal letter dated 23 September to George Davidson. George Davidson Papers, University of California, Berkeley, California.

Frisch, A.S., J. Holbrook, and A.B. Ages.
    1981 Observations of a summertime reversal in circulation in the Strait of Juan de Fuca. *Journal of Geophysical Research* 86(C3):2044–2048.

Holbrook, J.R. and D. Halpern
    1982 Wintertime near-surface currents in the Strait of Juan de Fuca, *Atmosphere–Ocean* 20(4):327–339.

Holbrook, J.R., G.A. Cannon, and D.G. Kachel
    1983 Two-year observations of coastal–fjord interactions in the Strait of Juan de Fuca. In *Coastal Oceanography,* edited by H. Gade, A. Edwards, and H. Svendsen, pp. 411–426. Plenum, New York.

Holbrook, J.R., R.D. Muench, and G.A. Cannon
    1980 Seasonal observations of low-frequency atmospheric forcing in the Strait of Juan de Fuca. In *Fjord Oceanography,* edited by H.J. Freeland, D.M. Farmer, and C.D. Levings, pp. 305–317. Plenum, New York.

Lockley, F.
    1926 Impressions and observations of the Journal man, *The Journal,* Portland, OR, April 6–9.

Rattray, M., Jr. and J.H. Lincoln
    1955 Operating characteristics of an oceanographic model of Puget Sound, *Transactions of the American Geophysical Union* 36, 251–261.

Rouse, H. and S. Ince
    1957 *History of Hydraulics,* Iowa Institute of Hydraulic Research, State University of Iowa.

U.S. Coast Guard
    1989 Oil sample analysis report. Marine Safety Office Puget Sound Case Number MP89000186, Oil Identification Laboratory Case Number 89-117.

U.S. Department of Commerce

Tide Tables 1988: High and Low Water Predictions, West Coast of North and South America including the Hawaiian Islands, National Oceanic and Atmospheric Administration, National Ocean Service.

Tidal Current Tables 1988: Pacific Coast of North America and Asia, National Oceanic and Atmospheric Administration, National Ocean Service.

U.S. Signal Office

1875   Bulletin of international meteorological observations, November and December.

Year Wind Observations, National Weather Service, personal communication, Robert Anderson, Chief, Seattle Ocean Service, Seattle, Washington.

Section 3

Mass Fatalities
and Mass Graves

Recent Mass Graves, An Introduction

12

WILLIAM D. HAGLUND

Contents

0-8493-1189-6/02/$0.00+$1.50
© 2002 by CRC Press LLC

Introduction

Under normal circumstances, burial of human remains is a common cultural means of disposal. Human burials also can result from natural phenomena such as animal caching, sheet wash, leaf fall, or various forms of mass wasting such as avalanches, slides, debris flows, and slumping (Skinner, 1987). As a criminal means of disposition of human remains, burial is relatively infrequent. Figures for U.S. State of Washington serve to illustrate. For the period 1981 through 1990, of the 1,960 murders for which deposition information is available, only 27 (1.38%) were recovered from burials (Homicide Information Tracking System (HITS)). Legally condoned, manmade mass burials occur only under extraordinary circumstances, when they are deemed necessary for humanitarian or sanitation purposes. Mass burials in the aftermath of the August 1999 earthquakes in Turkey are but one example (Thieren and Guitteau, 2000).

Tragically, burial is a commonplace, extra-legal expedient to cover up both human rights abuses and war crimes. The victims in contemporary clashes, to a large extent, are not combatants, but civilians. Hostilities fueling these killings range broadly, including declared wars between nations, nondeclared border clashes, struggles between ethnic or political entities within a country, or "dirty" wars of repression (Geiger and Cook-Deegan, 1993).

Although such mass graves are not necessarily a new phenomenon, it is only over the past two decades that their forensic investigation has been on the rise, beginning with Argentina, Guatemala, Iraqi Kurdistan, Ukraine, and El Salvador (Anderson, 1993; Bevan, 1994; Danner, 1993; Equipo de Anthropologia Forense de Guatemala, 1994; Joyce and Stover, 1991; Stover and Manuel, 1991). Rwanda, Croatia, Bosnia, Kosovo, and East Timor continue to supply the current surge of ongoing mass grave investigations (Ferllini, 1999; Jiménez, 1996; Koff, 1996; Stover, 1997; Stover and Peress, 1998). Less publicized mass grave investigations have been carried out in Somaliland, Indonesia, Sri Lanka, and Bangladesh in the past 5 years.

These investigations add new dimensions to the knowledge base of forensic taphonomy with respect to buried remains and mass graves. This chapter considers the definition of mass grave, briefly recaps seminal mass grave investigations, and borrows from recent experience to discuss the dynamics of mass graves, approaches to their exhumations, and issues encountered in their forensic investigations.

Defining Mass Grave

There is no agreement on the minimum number of individuals that comprise a mass grave (Haglund et al., 2000). Mant (1987) in his discussion of post-World War II exhumations defines a mass grave as containing two or more bodies that are in contact with each other. The UN Special Rapporteur interprets a mass grave as a location where three or more victims of extra-judicial, summary, or arbitrary executions, not having died in combat or armed confrontations are buried (International Criminal Tribunal for The Former Yugoslavia, 1996). Skinner (1987) suggests a mass grave contains at least half a dozen individuals.

It should be noted that each of these definitions introduces a qualifier that incorporates the particular interests of its author. Mant's stricture that the bodies must be in physical contact with each other incorporates his interest in variables that affect decomposition of buried remains. The burden of the Special Rapporteur's definition (above) that the grave occupants must be victims of a particular type (International Criminal Tribunal for The Former Yugoslavia, 1996) serves the Tribunal's legal concerns regarding how the grave occupants died (Haglund et al., 2000). Another qualifier, introduced by Skinner et al. (this volume), suggests a functional distinction between single graves, group graves in which bodies are laid out in parallel, and mass graves in which bodies are disordered. Although not meant as a precise definition, Skinner et al. (this volume) introduce the distinction of organized group graves, in which individuals lie parallel to one another, vs. mass graves in which placement of the dead is disorganized. Disorganization of buried victims, though not a strict rule for mass graves, reflects the lack of dignity given to disposal of mass grave occupants (Skinner, pers. comm.).

Mant's definition, while using the minimum number of individuals needed to comprise the mass grave, recognizes a salient taphonomic character of mass graves. A mass grave involves remains in contact with each other. It is this contact that creates the unique grave environment in which the rate and character of decomposition depart from patterns in graves containing a single individual. It is for that reason that this discussion revolves around graves containing a mass or aggregate of individuals, whether organized or disorganized.

Why Exhume Mass Graves? The Social Context

There are multiple rationales for the exhumation and investigation of contemporary mass graves. First, in the human rights context, is to collect narrative and physical evidence that will assist in establishing accountability for those responsible and bring them to justice. Second is the process of collecting evidence to identify the victims in order for their remains to be returned to their survivors. Third, the investigative process creates a document that should stand up to historical revisionists. Fourth is to expose atrocities to world opinion and to establish an international standard to prevent such crimes from occurring in the future. A fifth inducement for investigation of mass graves involves a basic dignity for the victims and for human life. If victims remain buried along with the secrets of their deaths, their deaths will have been in vain, threatening a similar fate for future generations. Exhumation of a particular mass grave may or may not address all of these objectives. Some mass grave exhumations are performed for purely humanitarian reasons with no goal of prosecutions in mind.

Selected Accounts of Mass Grave Exhumations

Even though experience with excavation of mass graves is on the ascent, little has appeared in peer-reviewed literature. Skinner's thoughtful 1987 paper, "Planning the Archeological Recovery of Evidence from Recent Mass Graves," reviewed relevant literature, considered logistical aspects, and advocated the use of archeologists. During the past 15 years much of the experience involving mass grave exhumations languishes in the respective reports of their investigations. Certainly, with the continued experience of the multitude of investigators now involved in international forensic investigations, we can expect more articles in the future dealing with issues of mass graves (Haglund, 2000; Haglund et al., 2000; Simmons, this volume; Skinner et al., this volume; Schmitt, this volume).

A few historical examples of reporting on mass grave investigations are in order. One intriguing case is the 1943 forensic investigation into the massacre of over 11,000 Polish prisoners in the Katyn Forest near Smolensk, in modern-day Russia (Abarinov, 1993; FitzGibbon, 1979). The victims were Polish soldiers, primarily officers, who had been held as prisoners of war by the Soviets. The executions took place in 1941. The graves were first brought to the attention of the public by the Germans in April of 1943. Earlier, in February of that year, German troops advancing through the Katyn Forest near Smolensk had discovered suspicious earth mounds planted over with young pine trees. Preliminary excavations confirmed the existence of mass graves. A concern of the Nazi government was that they would be blamed for the deaths, which occurred at a time when the region was under Russian occupation. In May of 1943, strategizing to counter future allegations that they had carried out the massacres, the Germans established an international medical mission composed of professors of forensic medicine from nine German-occupied European nations, Italy, and neutral Switzerland. The commission was to report manner, cause, time of death, and probable culpability in the deaths.

The report, edited and issued by German authorities, was released in April 1943. FitzGibbon (1977), citing from translations of the report, relates that 4143 bodies were exhumed and 2914 were identified on the basis of personal artifacts and documents recovered from the bodies. A majority of the victims had been shot in the head; 5% were found with their hands tied behind their backs with ropes. The report went on to comment that absence of insects, as well as the presence of documents, correspondence, diaries and newspapers in the grave, indicated that the deaths occurred in March, April, and May of 1940.

The Soviets reoccupied the area of Smolensk in September of 1943. They vigorously denied charges that they were responsible for the Katyn atrocities and began their own investigations that in turn laid blame on the Nazi German government for the executions. At the insistence of the Soviets and over the reluctance of the French, British, and American prosecutors, allegations of the massacre were included in count three of the indictment at the Nuremberg War Crimes Trial. Although the falsity of these indictments was strongly suspected by many, they were allowed to stand though they not mentioned in the verdict (Davidson, 1997; Taylor, 1992). It has become clear in recent years that the Soviets were responsible for these mass executions and popular accounts have since been published (Abarinov, 1993; FitzGibbon, 1977; Zawondy, 1962).

It was not until Mant's 1950 Doctoral Thesis in Medicine at London University that variables involved in the preservation of remains in mass graves were more systematically analyzed. He served in the British Army Royal Medical Corps as a pathologist during and after World War II. His primary mission was the identification of missing allied military personnel, especially fliers. The largest mass grave he reported held 40 bodies, and the total number of individual remains in his study was 150 (Mant, 1950).

Other World War II-associated mass graves have been investigated in Saipan (Russell and Flemming, 1991) and in the Ukraine (Bevan, 1994). The latter investigation was carried out by an Australian forensic team in June of 1990. From one grave they performed examinations on selected skulls of 553 individuals. The dead were alleged to be Jewish men, women, and children who had been rounded up from the area around the town of Serniki. Limited examinations were carried out at the graveside, with the goal of estimating age and sex and determining cause of death. This was part of an investigation by the Australian government into the case of Nazi Officer Ivan Polyukhovich who was indicted for his involvement in a massacre outside the town of Serniki in the fall of 1942.

Nineteen hundred ninety-six stands as a watershed year for launching large-scale mass grave exhumations. A primary influence was provided by the Boston-based organization,

Physicians for Human Rights (PHR). They provided the forensic expertise for the International Criminal Tribunals for Rwanda (ICTR) and The Former Yugoslavia (ICTY), fielding international teams of experts to exhume nearly 1200 individuals from seven sites on two continents. The 1996 work was launched in Rwanda where massacres had taken place in 1994. Nearly 500 individuals were exhumed and examined from the site of the Roman Catholic Church in Kibuye, a western Rwandan province. A second Rwandan site in the capital, Kigali, was also examined. The Rwandan investigations were followed by exhumations in The Former Yugoslavia at the Bosnian sites of Cerska, Lazete, Nova Kasava, Pilica, and finally the Ovcara grave in eastern Croatia. As of this writing, the ICTY continues seasonal exhumations.

Anatomy of a Mass Grave: Concepts and Terminology

Each mass grave is unique. A grave may consist of a simple trench in which bodies are arrayed with minimal contact with each other. In more complex graves, bodies may form a dense, contiguous aggregate known as a *body mass* (Figure 12.1). Within a body mass, individuals are in contact with each other, often extremely jumbled, contorted, and entangled (Figure 12.2). It is not unusual that individuals are in various stages of dress and undress. When exposed, such a body mass presents a jolting, chaotic vision that assaults all sensibilities. Some graves may contain more than one discrete body mass (Figure 12.1A and B). Not infrequently, there will be *satellite remains* that are not a part of the body mass.

Multiple body masses within the same grave indicate their entry into the grave at different times. Another indication of multiple bouts of entry into a grave is the presence of layers of remains interrupted by intervening fill (Figure 12.1B and Figure 12.3). This is a result of groups of individuals being deposited in successive events, each group covered by fill and then the next group of individuals added. In this type of grave the intervening layers of fill allow increased drainage that can drastically alter the decomposition dynamics. Such a grave is described by the Germans investigating in the Ukrainian area of Vinnytsia where graves were found to contain groups of 100 to 120 bodies separated by a layer of clothing and earth, followed by another group of bodies (Eher, 1944).

Regardless of its configuration, a large body mass presents a complex taphonomic environment affected by a multitude of variables (Table 12.1). Mant is truly the pioneer in systemizing observations affecting preservation of buried human remains including those in mass graves. Among his many contributions to the field of forensic investigation are his analyses of the various processes of body decomposition in different grave contexts and his demonstration that mass graves create their own micro-environment (Mant, 1950, 1957, 1987). Mant clearly showed that bodies decompose at different rates depending on their condition at burial, method of burial, and soil conditions in and around the grave. He also pointed out that bodies in the center of mass graves decompose more slowly than those on the outer edge of the body mass, thus creating a *feather edge effect*, which ran contrary to the general consensus of medical opinion at that time.

A major factor in determining of the state of a particular individual in a mass grave is its relative position in relation to the body mass. Satellite remains are least preserved. Peripheral bodies of the body mass are less preserved (Figure 12.4) than individuals within the core of the assemblage (Figure 12.5). This dynamic was noted in the 1943 report of the International Medical Commission that investigated the Katyn Forest Massacre.

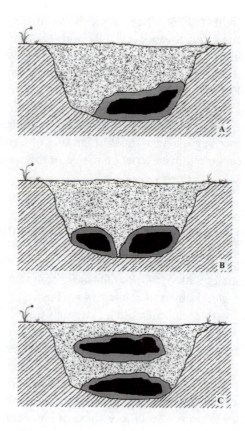

Figure 12.1 Three mass grave configurations in cross section: (A) single, contiguous body mass; (B) multiple discrete body masses in a single grave; and (C) multiple, layered configuration with intervening fill, indicative of separate bouts of entry. The body masses each consist of a core or *inner taphonomic zone*, an outer margin or *peripheral taphonomic zone*, and the outermost edge or the *mass/fill taphonomic interface*. ■ = core of the body mass or inner taphonomic zone; ▨ = margin of the body mass or peripheral taphonomic zone.

FitzGibbon (1977) relates the descriptions of the graves and the conditions of the remains as summarized by Dr. Buhtz, a professor of forensic medicine and criminology at Breslay (Wroclaw) University: Dr. Buhtz documents that the pits had been dug in stepped terraces in a hilly area and in sandy soil. In some places, they penetrated to underground water. He continues with observations on decomposition:

> The bodies were in various stages of decay. In a few cases mummification of the uncovered parts had taken place (bodies from the uppermost layers), but generally the formation of adipocere had started with the fat penetrating into the clothing. (p. 136)

> The stages of decay were found to vary in accordance with the position of the bodies in the pits. Whilst mummification had taken place on the top and at the sides of the mass of bodies, a humid process could be observed caused by the damp nearer the center. Adjacent bodies were stuck together with thick putrid liquid. The peculiar deformations due to pressure show that the bodies had remained in the position they had assumed when they were first thrown into the pits. (p. 142)

Figure 12.2 Large body mass with complex positioning of individuals, viewed from above. Postmortem interval is 1 year; same site as Figures 12.3 and 12.5. Note that portions of one individual may extend horizontally to be overlain by surrounding remains, or parts of an individual body may extend to higher or lower areas of the grave to be entrapped by other bodies. Decomposition and skeletonization are accelerated for individuals on the periphery. (Photograph courtesy of Gilles Peress.)

Figure 12.3 Portion of body mass viewed in cross section illustrating interrupted bouts of entry with further deposition of remains. Note layering of bodies with sediment and plants. Postmortem interval is 1 year; same site as Figures 12.2 and 12.5. (Photograph courtesy of Gilles Peress.)

**Table 12.1   Major Taphonomic Factors
Affecting the Condition of Remains
in Mass Graves**

Grave Characteristics
- Depth
- Compaction
- Inclusions
- Intervening fill

Temporal Factors
- Postmortem interval prior to burial
- Duration of burial
- Season

Body Characteristics
- State of decomposition
- Cause of death
- Body habitus
- Clothing or other wrapping

Soil Characteristics
- Ph
- Drainage
- Compaction
- Coarseness and type of soil
- Contaminants

Body Assemblage Characteristics
- Thickness and extent
- Position relative to core and perimeter

Other Characteristics
- Temperature during pre-burial period
- Moisture
- Post-burial exposure of remains to atmosphere
- Disturbance
- Oxygen content

Buhtz added that the accumulation of the initial products of decomposition in the surrounding soil had caused chemical changes that in turn affected the subsequent decomposition process.

Remains on the fringes of the body mass bridge two taphonomic interfaces: One is contact with other bodies, and the other is contact with fill or the surrounding matrix that forms the walls and floor of the grave. At the outer fringe they are affected by porosity and percolation characteristics of the surrounding substrate. Best preserved are remains within the interior of the body mass where they create their own synergistic environment, body on body. These remains, isolated from the grave substrate, trap moisture that originates from body fluids and the fluids of decomposition. For graves submerged beneath the water table or in areas susceptible to seasonal rains or flooding, additional moisture may be transported into the core of unsaturated body masses. Clothing may act as a wick.

The weight of the overburden or its method of compaction can compress bodies in the grave and reduce pore spaces between sedimentary particles. The overburden of schist in the grave at Kibuye, Rwanda, resulted in severely flattened remains that were often pressed into each other. Compaction will vary with respect to the weight of different

Figure 12.4 Three individuals in satellite position relative to larger body mass, illustrating the effect of relative position within the grave on preservation. Least preservation, in this case full skeletonization, is encountered for satellite individuals and for individuals located at the periphery of the body mass, especially those interfacing with the fill. Postmortem interval is 5 years. (Photograph courtesy of Gilles Peress.)

Figure 12.5 Bound hands of an individual found within the core of a body mass, illustrating the effect of relative position within the grave on preservation. Most preservation, in this case all of the soft tissue, is encountered for individuals located within the core of the body mass. Postmortem interval is 1 year; same site as Figures 12.2 and 12.3. (Photograph courtesy of Gilles Peress.)

soil/rock types and the depth of the fill. Coarser-grained sediments are more resistant to compaction due to the supporting effect of the grains and the lower water content (Briggs, 1990). Reduced porosity decreases permeability, the capacity to transmit fluids. Driving heavy machinery over the grave contributes to compaction. The degree of compaction and depth of burial will allow or dissuade encroachment of the grave by mammalian scavengers or necrophilous insects (Haskell et al., 1997; Rodriguez and Bass, 1985). For skeletal remains, compaction may also account for distortion of bone that can both mimic pathology and throw off statistical measurement. Nawrocki (1995) points out that subtle warping of cranial fragments is often not detected unless all fragments are present and incorporated into a reconstruction.

Under favorable conditions, a mass grave may yield partially to fully fleshed remains up to several years following the primary burial; for example, after 5 years of internment in the Ovcara Grave outside of Vukovar, Croatia, the majority of the 200 victims were fleshed remains, some retaining tattoos. On the other hand, the Bosnia-Herzegovina grave at Cerska, opened merely 12 months following burial, revealed 150 males in varying stages of advanced skeletonization.* The stark contrast of soft tissue preservation between these two examples can be attributed to several factors. The grave at Ovcara was relatively deep with clay soil that facilitated drainage from surrounding fields. The overburden had been firmly compacted. In locations of highest body density they had as many as eight bodies deep. Both the body mass and drainage conditions conspired to trap moisture. In contrast, bodies of the Cerska grave were deposited on a roadside embankment and had been covered by a relatively thin layer of loosely compacted gravel overburden. The lack of compaction and incline of the surface upon which the bodies rested did not allow moisture to be trapped. Drainage was transient and encouraged rinsing and draining of bodily fluids and products of decomposition from the area. Decomposition was accelerated further because the grave surface was fully exposed to the sun. This allowed warming of the overburden and the remains, some deposited as little as 50 cm below the surface. The moisture-trapping ability of the remains was lessened due to their low density. Throughout most of the grave, with the exception of the foot of the embankment where bodies had piled up against each other, the density of the remains tended to be only 1 to 3 bodies deep.

Approaches to Exhumation

Table 12.2 presents an overview of the steps involved in the exhumation of a mass grave. It can readily be seen that investigations of these graves necessitate an interdisciplinary effort. Once authority is granted for access to the site, the first priority ideally should be an on-the-ground assessment. For purposes of this chapter, only the steps of exposure, delineation and extraction of the remains (steps 6 to 8 in Table 12.2) will be addressed in detail.

---

* Some would advocate that the Cerska "grave" is not technically a grave. The bodies were simply deposited on the ground surface and covered with borrowed soil. No excavation or hole was made in which to deposit the remains. Regardless, preservation dynamics hold and are relevant to this discussion.

Table 12.2   Overview of the Exhumation Process for a Mass Grave

1. Assessment
2. Staging, equipment, supplies
3. Site preparation, surface evidence, and clearing of ground cover
4. Initial overview site mapping
5. Establishment of grave boundaries
6. Exposure and removal of overburden
7. Delineation in preparation for removal
8. Documentation: photography, mapping, completion of field forms
9. Extraction
10. Storage/transport to location of examination
11. Clean-up

Exposure and Delineation

The first step in actually preparing bodies for removal is their exposure. This requires removing fill that covers the topmost layer of the bodies and then cleaning the area so they can be clearly delineated. The presence of clothing can be beneficial on several counts. It provides protection to bodies from damage during excavation. Garments can be an asset in exposing remains as they can be very gently manipulated and shaken to dislodge soil. Done gently, this is less damaging to soft tissue and quicker than using tools. Clothing also serves as an envelope for the remains. As bodies are exposed, it is prudent to secure bags around unclothed hands, feet, and crania. This minimizes the potential for loss or displacement of teeth, bones, fingernails, and other remains or evidence (Haglund, 1988). If there is no clothing over exposed areas of soft tissue, often the hands and the face, great care is necessary so as not to damage the soft tissue of fleshed remains. Although soft materials, such as wooden chopsticks and brushes, are useful for many excavations, when one is working in damp soggy environments, brushes may prove next to useless. Soft adipose tissue, however, can be marred even by soft brushes. In these situations consideration should be given to more detailed cleaning at the time of postmortem examination.

Extraction of Fleshed Remains

Frequently, a single individual will not be completely exposed at the time the initial overburden is removed. Portions may extend horizontally to be overlain by surrounding remains or parts of the body may extend to lower areas of the grave to be entrapped by other bodies. This situation usually demands exposure of an area encompassing several surrounding individuals.

Fortunately, in larger, more recent graves, especially where moisture content has been trapped, groundwater is prevalent, or drainage poor, the remains may be well preserved, fleshed, and pliable. This flexibility allows adjacent remains to be rolled or lifted in order to facilitate freeing trapped body parts from their surroundings.

Extraction of a particular individual often requires manipulating several surrounding remains in order to remove the one that is potentially most free. When the majority of a body is visible, and perhaps a leg or an arm is still beneath surrounding remains, there is a tendency to want to pull it free. There is the danger that weakened articulations, especially the knee joint, ankles, wrists, or fingers, may separate, leaving the disarticulated body portion trapped beneath other remains. The level of the grave harboring the separated body part may not be reached for hours or days, thus increasing problems of reassociating body parts to appropriate individuals. Inability to reassociate such body parts can potentially confound the identification; for example, rings that could potentially lead to identification might stay on a finger that has been left behind. There is also the negative perception of not being able to repatriate the most complete remains once they have been identified.

Prioritizing remains for removal requires a good spatial sense. Where bodies are partly covered by another body, experience assists in determining which bodies should be manipulated next so they may be extracted. Care needs to be taken, however, that parts do not become detached while being manipulated. This might necessitate sliding an excavator's arm between bodies to the point where the end of the limb can be held and pushed gently back, freeing the limb from the mass. The excavator needs to ensure that all the digits at the end of the limb are held in place as this occurs, or those digits might be left behind when the limb is moved. Once hands or feet are exposed, if they are in any way disarticulated or vulnerable to disarticulation, they should be placed inside a bag tied to the nearest long bones, to ensure that the digits or phalanges do not detach when the body is moved. A bag might also be placed over the head, as the cervical vertebrae are frequently loose. This also ensures that hair and teeth are not lost during transport.

Documentation and Removal

Prior to removal, a case number is assigned and the documentation team can begin photographing, mapping, and describing the body. An overall photograph is taken showing the position of the body, as well as any detail shots deemed necessary. Close-ups might include tattoos, obvious trauma, or unusual clothing. The overall photograph is accompanied with a north arrow, scale and case number. The detail photograph also includes a scale, and the case number. All photographs are entered into a photograph log. At a minimum, the horizontal and vertical positions of the crania are plotted from a point usually taken from the top of the crania. The outlines of the body might also be plotted, depending on the detail of the map decided on by the investigator. The description of the body is brief. The purpose of the description is to gain enough information so that the remains will not be confused with others during transport to the morgue where a full description and postmortem are completed. Fleshed remains should be removed, as much as is possible, as intact units with minimal disturbance. This allows for proper inspection in the examination area and presents the remains in the best condition for postmortem examination.

Once photography, mapping, and other documentation are complete, the body is ready for removal. Minimally, the case number and date of removal are written on both ends of the body bag. The bag is unzipped, opened, and moved adjacent to the body. If the body is face up, the arms are moved close to the body and placed on the chest. The legs are lifted together. One excavator is positioned at the head, one in the middle of the body, and one at the legs. As these people lift, an additional person holds open the body bag and helps to slide it beneath the body. Once the body is inside, the bag is placed to the side while the team examines the soil underneath the body to ensure that no body parts or associated evidence are left behind. Any loose disassociated portions of the remains are separately bagged and included in the body bag. Remains lying face down often can be simply supported and rolled into the body bag. Finally, the bag is zipped and removed to a storage area.

Issues Involved in Mass Grave Investigations

Exhumation of mass graves is a complex process that requires the balancing of many simultaneous goals, issues, and activities. It also requires processing large numbers of bodies and volumes of evidence over a matter of days, weeks, or even months. This is a process that requires continual rechecking of procedures and data. Procedures of a field operation are frequently carried out in temporary or substandard facilities. Often, the exhumations and examinations are part of an evolutionary process and adaptation of procedures not only to address the goals of the mission, but also to generate pragmatic solutions to the many problems encountered, and to resource limitations. The following section explores some common issues encountered in the exhumation of mass graves and the examination of their victims.

Expert Assessment

Prior to exhumation, large graves should be assessed by personnel experienced in mass grave exhumations and attendant logistical needs. Such an on-site visit officially confirms the presence of human remains. Equipment and potential security concerns can be evaluated. Logical requirements of the work, such as transportation of remains, morgue facilities, and staff housing, are assessed at this time. The assessment phase typically entails notification of local authorities and determination of local cultural and religious sensitivities.

Levels of Examination and Documentation

A major question that arises in international investigations is what level of documentation and examination will satisfy both legal and professional standards? The United Nations Manual on the Effective Prevention and Investigation of Extra-Legal, Arbitrary and Summary Executions (1991) is often quoted as the benchmark by which investigations (including exhumations and examination of remains) should be judged. However, these are ideal standards and, as the guidelines caution, they may not be attainable for many reasons. For example, it is necessary to give recognition to the often-divergent perspectives of politics, religion and culture that pervade such investigations. Other impediments frequently encountered include lack of facilities, inadequate logistical support, limited financing, equipment and supplies, as well as inclement weather conditions, and security issues. Limitations and impediments leading to the relaxation of particular standards always should be disclosed in the final report.

Case Numbering and Removal Units

The term *removal unit* is used here to indicate remains or groups of remains that are packaged and numbered for removal from a particular site. Removal units may or may not bear a one-to-one correspondence to case numbers. A numbering system in which consecutive numbers are assigned to individuals is the most common approach when dealing with multiple fatality incidents such as mass graves. It would be ideal if each removal unit equated with a complete individual. Unfortunately, this frequently is not possible. What comprises a removal unit is dependent upon the condition of the remains. Under various circumstances a removal unit could consist of complete remains, partial remains or include the remains of more than one individual; for example, an infant hidden by its mother's swaddling clothing might be collected as one removal unit. A removal unit may receive one case number but be packaged separately. A single set of remains may end up distributed among multiple body bags when remains in advanced stages of decomposition are removed from an extremely muddy environment. Partial individuals may have been placed in the primary grave originally, or partial individuals can result from tampering, such as attempts to rob the grave.

Several operative concepts should be considered when assigning and numbering removal units. First among these is the need to enforce a uniform approach. This is critical when there is the potential of excavating multiple graves with parts of the same individuals distributed among them. It is necessary to be able to track removal units back to a relatively *in situ* location at particular sites. Attempts to allocate partial remains to a single individual should not be undertaken in the field, but are best accomplished under laboratory conditions with detailed supportive documentation regarding their recovery. This process may not be possible for weeks, months, or even years following the exhumations.

In addition to the problems imposed by condition or completeness of the remains or the grave, false totals of the number of individuals can arise at one of several junctures during the numbering, removal, and storage of remains. Error can occur in the initial assignment of numbers; for example, duplicate numbers may be given out or numbers may be skipped. Clerical errors can happen in writing numbers on body bags. Oversights can occur when placing individuals into body bags. These include placing parts of more than one individual in one body bag or the wrong body into a particular body bag. One staff member should be charged with giving out numbers for removal units. In any situation, the more staff involved in numbering and extracting of bodies, the higher the potential for error.

Another pitfall is to assign a number to a body or skeleton prematurely, before it is ready to be removed. This usually occurs when the availability of a body to be removed is misjudged. Inexperience is commonly at fault. A worker may request a number, assuming that a particular remains can be extracted, only to find upon trying to remove the remains that he or she cannot. This can happen when one misinterprets the position of one or more limbs, either assuming an unobservable limb would be no problem to extract or mistaking a freed and observable limb of a separate individual as belonging to the remains one wishes to remove. Such problems occur when a part of the body is trapped beneath other remains or debris. In these cases it is necessary to leave the "numbered" remains in the grave until additional bodies or overburden can be removed in order to free the trapped part. The final freeing of the remains may not occur for hours or days and result in reassigning a different number to the same remains at a later period.

An illustration of misnumbering is noted in the Argentine forensic report of the investigation into the 1981 El Mazote Massacre (Danner, 1993). At the end of the exhumation the tally of individuals was 119. During the examination phase of the investigation it was found that three skeletons (23, 61, and 72) had been miss-numbered (no skeletons matched those numbers) and two skeletons had been assigned one number (81). Hence, the final individual count was 117. Similar numbering problems were encountered in the 1996 exhumations of graves investigated under the International Tribunals; for example, although 154 numbers for body bags were given out during the exhumation of the Cerska site, only 150 individuals were exhumed. This discrepancy was attributed to clerical errors, numbers (21, 55, and, 56) being requested by team members but not immediately assigned to bodies or body bags. A fourth number, 93, was assigned to a remains, and these remains proved impossible to remove at that time. When the body was finally freed the next day, it was inadvertently re-photographed with a new number, body number 100.

These examples point out that when complicated graves are involved, it is imprudent to assume that the numbers allocated or number of body bags necessarily equates with the number of individuals. The calculation of the total number of individuals exhumed is best done after the postmortem examinations are completed and after commingling and reattribution of parts has been accomplished to the greatest extent possible. Prior to that point, comments about the numbers of bodies being removed should be presented as estimates only. This is especially germane in answering media demands regarding body counts.

There are various means of guarding against potential numbering errors. Organization of the removal process is essential. It is crucial to have a specific team member in charge of giving out numbers. Another strategy is to limit the numbers of team members involved in the body extraction processes. Fundamental to proper extraction is a full understanding of the relationship of bodies to other remains or features of the grave. The ability to judge the accessibility for removal of a remains needs to be a prerequisite for granting a number for its removal.

Identification of Victims

Although personal identification is the traditional goal of the recovery of human remains, the identification process is carried out at several levels: biological, anatomical, sociocultural affiliation (or circumstantial), and personal. Most elemental is to distinguish human from nonhuman remains. Assessment of an individual's biological characteristics (i.e., sex, age, stature, and ancestry) provides the groundwork for personal identification and constitutes the next level of identification. When multiple individuals are involved, their minimum number must be established. If body parts, individual bones or bone fragments are involved, efforts must be made to attribute them to the appropriate individual. Another level of identification is the assignment of an individual to a particular population segment such as a religious, cultural, or social affiliation. For example, associated artifacts or circumstances can aid in determination of individuals' military vs. civilian status, whether they were hospital patients, membership in a particular religious group, or whether they were rendered helpless at the time they were killed. Individualizing traits, such as dental characteristics, tattoos, osteological evidence of past injuries or life stresses may lead to a more specific level of identification and offer the greatest hope of unique personal identification. Geberth (1990:192) points out that in traditional homicide investigations:

> The identification of the victim is critical because in order to prove a charge of homicide, it must be established that a named or described person is in fact dead...furthermore, from an investigative point of view, identification provides a starting point and direction for the inquiry.

In part, the rationale for this dictum is that most homicide victims are killed by someone they know; a personal motive is involved in the killing. In upward of 75% of solved homicides, the victims were murdered by someone they knew. Hence, much investigative effort is expended to confirm personal identification of the victim. Fortunately, the potential to achieve personal identification is high in developed countries with infrastructures that allow sophisticated tracking of citizens, a level of health care that documents identifying features and, as a last resort, recourse to DNA technology. Stranger-on-stranger killings are most problematic for homicide investigators to solve.

By contrast, in the investigations of genocide and crimes against humanity involving mass graves there may be less emphasis placed on identifying the individuals who actually did the killing. Rather, the prosecutorial focus may be to identify those individuals in positions of authority who gave the commands to the killers. Actual killing may be carried out by anonymous persons remote from the chain of command. So with regard to mass graves and prosecutions involving war crimes, genocide, and crimes against humanity, personal identification of the victim(s) may not be a necessary starting point to the investigation. Particular persons became victims because of how they were perceived by the culture; for instance, they may have been singled out because of their religion or ethnicity. This categorization of the victim by the killers has consequences for the level of identification sought by investigators. It may be sufficient to be able to attribute categorical identification to the victims (such as ethnicity, religion, or political viewpoint) and to show that victims were killed because of attributes perceived by their killers. This is particularly true when indictments for killings are based on genocide: the deliberate intention to exterminate a national, ethnic, or religious group. For investigators, other categorical levels of identification could rest on whether or not the victims can be identified as civilians, women, children, or combatants. If military or civilians, for example, were they bound, blindfolded, or tortured?

The foregoing does not imply that personal identification would not lend a deeper level of support to indictments or to a tribunal's investigations, only that pursuit of positive personal identification of victims may not be a primary issue to the prosecution. Hence, there may be no resources allocated for that purpose. This legal aim does not necessarily satisfy the needs or desires of survivors to have their individual dead returned. But, in the context of current *ad hoc* tribunals, the efforts and funding for personal identification of victims often fall upon the shoulders of entities other than tribunal investigators.

A sad reality is that positive, personal identifications are often neither pragmatic nor even possible in poor nations and areas suffering from recent conflicts, where the infrastructure has been severely compromised or is nonexistent. Out of nearly 500 individuals examined from exhumations at Kibuye, Rwanda, evidence for identification could be established for only 17 persons; 6 carried identifying documents and 11 more had clothing or personal effects recognizable to acquaintances, none had hospital X-rays or dental records. For only two of these victims could surviving blood relatives be located (Haglund and Kirshner, 1997). In Bosnia-Herzegovina, there are currently 4420 body bags being stored, and awaiting identification (Knight and Rhode, 2001). Notably, the ICTY-investigated Croatian grave at Ovcara, with 200 remains, currently has approximately 150 individuals identified; the majority confirmed via DNA. This relatively high success rate of identification can be attributed to a concerted government effort to identify these victims, combined with the fact that the war left the country's infrastructure relatively unscathed, and there was a quality forensic community left to follow-up on identifications subsequent to tribunal examinations. Prior to the exhumations, however, 4 years were devoted to collection of antemortem data and there was local access to DNA technology.

Conclusions

Exhumation and examination of victims of a medium to large mass grave are huge undertakings in terms of resources for financing, staffing, expertise, logistical support, and often security. For both the exhumations and examinations, basic infrastructures that are taken for granted in industrialized countries, such as working facilities, storage for remains, water and electrical utilities, are often nonexistent. In areas plagued by war and civil disobedience, suitable equipment and supplies need to be ordered and shipped from other countries. Authority to carry out the work may depend upon changes of government or international will. These complexities translate into the necessity for careful and flexible planning. With the burgeoning amount of forensic experience in mass grave exhumation, we can expect more accounts of exhumations to appear in the peer-reviewed published literature. It is only through sharing of experience by mass grave investigators that we will learn how to better accomplish these investigations.

References

Abarinov, V.
   1993   *The Murderers of Katyn,* Hippocrene Books, New York.

Anderson, K.
   1993   *The Anfal Campaign in Iraqi Kurdistan: The Destruction of Koreme,* Human Rights Watch and Physicians for Human Rights, New York.

Bevan, D.
   1994   *A Case to Answer: The Story of Australia's First European War Crimes Prosecution,* Wakefield Printing, Kent Town, South Australia.

Briggs, D.E. G.
   1990   Flattening. In *Paleobiology: A Synthesis,* edited by D.E.G. Briggs and P.R. Crowther, Blackwell Scientific, Oxford, U.K.

Bulletin: International Criminal Tribunal for the Former Yugoslavia
   1996   Twin Tribunals ICTY/R, No. 9/10 14-VIII.

Danner, M.
   1993   *The Massacre at El Mazote,* Vintage Books, New York.

Davidson, E.
   1997   *The Trial of the Germans: An Account of the Twenty-Two Defendants before the International Military Tribunal at Nuremberg,* University of Missouri Press, Columbia, MO.

Eher, F.
   1944   German Government Report on Vinnytsia, 1944. Based on translation from the Forensic Medical Report prepared by Prof. Dr. Gerhard Schrader, Director of the Institute of Forensic Medicine and Criminal Investigation of the University of Halle-Wittenberg, Germany.

Equipo de Anthropologia Forense de Guatemala
   1994   *Las Massacres en Rbinal: Estudio Historico Anthropologico de las Massacres de Plan de Sanchez, Chichupak y Rio Negro.*

Ferllini, R
   1999   The role of anthropology in human rights issues. In *Forensic Osteological Analysis: A Book of Case Studies,* edited by S.I. Fairgrieve, Charles C Thomas, Springfield, IL.

FitzGibbon, L.
 1977 *Katyn Massacre*, Corgi Books, London.

Geberth, V.J.
 1990 *Practical Homicide Investigation: Tactics Procedures, and Forensic Techniques*, 2nd ed., Elsevier, New York.

Geiger, J. and R.M. Cook-Deegan
 1993 The role of physicians in conflicts and humanitarian crises: case studies from field missions of Physicians for Human Rights, *Journal of the American Medical Association* 270(5):616–620.

Haglund, W.D.
 2000 Archeology and forensic death investigations, *Historical Archeology* 35(1):26–56.

 1988 The scene and context: contributions of the forensic anthropologist. In *Forensic Osteology II*, edited by K. Reichs, Charles C Thomas, Springfield, IL.

Haglund, W.D. and R.H. Kirschner
 1997 Report: Investigations at Kibuye Roman Catholic Church: Kibuye, Rwanda. Prepared for the United Nation's *ad hoc* International Criminal Tribunal for Rwanda.

Haglund, W.D., M. Connor, and D. D. Scott,
 2000 The archeology of contemporary mass graves, *Historical Archeology* 35(1):57–69.

Haskell, N.H. et al.
 1997 On the body: insects' life stage presence, their postmortem artifacts. In *Forensic Taphonomy: The Fate of Human Remains*, edited by W.D. Haglund and M.H. Sorg, pp. 319–332. CRC Press, Boca Raton, FL.

HITS (Homicide Information Tracking System), Computer Database, Office of the Washington State Attorney General. Courtesy of Robert D. Keppel, Ph.D.

Jiménez, S.
 1996 Forensic anthropology in Bosnia-Herzegovina: the assembly-line approach, *The Connective Tissue* 12:7–11.

Joyce, C. and E. Stover
 1991 *Whiteness from and the Grave: Stories Bones Tell*, Little, Brown, Boston, MA.

Knight, G. and D. Rhode
 2001 Warehouse of death, *New York Times Magazine*, March 11, 2001, pp. 46–47.

Koff, C.
 1996 Have trowel, will travel: scratching the surface layer, *The Connective Tissue* 12:8–11.

Mant, A.K.
 1950 A Study of Exhumation Data. M.D. Thesis. University of London.

 1957 Adipocere: a review, *Journal of Forensic Medicine*. 4:18–35.

 1987 Knowledge acquired from post-war exhumations. In *Death Decay and Reconstruction: Approaches to Archeology and Forensic Science*, edited by A. Boddington, A.N. Garland, and R.C. Janaway, Manchester University Press, London.

Nawrocki, S.P.
 1995 Cemetery taphonomy. In *Bodies of Evidence: Reconstructing History through Skeletal Analysis*, edited by A. Grauer, Wiley-Liss, New York.

Rodriguez, W.C. and W.M. Bass
 1985 Decomposition of buried bodies and methods that may aid in their location, *Journal of Forensic Sciences* 30(3):836–852.

Russell, S. and M.A. Flemming
    1991   A bulwark in the Pacific: an example of World War II archaeology on Saipan. In *Archaeology Studies of World War II*, edited by W.R. Wood, pp. 13–28. Department of Anthropology, University of Missouri, Columbia, MO.

Scott, D.D.
    2000   Firearms identification in support of identifying a mass execution at El Mosote, El Salvador, *Historical Archaeology*, 35(1):79–86.

Skinner, M.
    1987   Planning the archeological recovery of evidence from recent mass graves, *Forensic Sciences International* 34:267–287.

Stover, E.
    1997   The grave at Vukovar, *Smithsonian* 27(12):7–25.

Stover, E. and A. Manuel
    1991   *Getting Away with Murder*, Americas Watch and Physicians for Human Rights, Human Rights Watch, New York.

Stover, E. and G. Peress
    1998   *The Graves: Srebrenica and Vukovar*, Scalo, New York.

Stover, E. and M. Ryan
    2001   Breaking bread with the dead, *Historical Archeology* 35(1):7–25.

Taylor, T.
    1992   *The Anatomy of the Nuremberg Trials*, Alfred A. Knopf, New York.

Thieren, M. and R. Guitteau
    2000   Identifying cadavers following disasters: why, *Disasters: Preparedness and Mitigation in the Americas* 80:1.

United Nations
    1997   Manual on the Effective Prevention and Investigation of Extra-Legal, Arbitrary and Summary Executions. United Nations, New York.

Washington State
    1990   HITS (Homicide Information Tracking System), Office of the Washington State Attorney General. Courtesy of Robert D. Keppel, Ph.D.

Zawodny, J. A.
    1962   *Death in the Forest: The Story of the Katyn Forest Massacre*, University of Notre Dame Press, South Bend, IN.

Taphonomy of a Karstic Cave Execution Site at Hrgar, Bosnia-Herzegovina

13

TAL SIMMONS

Contents

Introduction

Interpretation of postmortem, taphonomic processes in some outdoor scenes requires an understanding of geological processes and features. Geomorphologically induced microenvironments coupled with the taphonomic overprint of decomposition processes produce differential preservation, transport of body parts, and perimortem trauma. Remains deposited within vertical caves, in particular, are generally isolated from surface taphonomic processes such as weather and scavengers, but subjected to subsurface, geological taphonomy (Brain, 1975, 1981; Oliver, 1989). These variables provide limits and challenges to the interpretation of postmortem intervals, commingling, and evidence of the cause of death, as well as to the technical issues of scene processing and recovery of remains.

In the summer of 1992, early in the Balkan War, a cave in the Hrgar region of northwest Bosnia was used to dispose of approximately 70 individuals who had been executed on the ground surface near the vertical entrance shaft. After they were killed, their bodies were thrown down into the cave where they decomposed and were subject to taphonomic processes unique to this environment. The remains were discovered and exhumed 5 years later in 1997.

In 1996, just prior to the Hrgar region exhumation, the State Commission for Missing Persons (Bosniak Entity) had exhumed another vertical cave at Lanište. Nearly 200 individuals had been killed and deposited in two separate episodes, one of which was quite recent. Sand had been dumped on top of both sets of remains. The preservation of the bodies near the top (second deposition) was excellent, allowing visual identification of the victims by survivors in nearly all cases. The bodies lower in the cave (first deposition) were less well preserved and remain largely unidentified

It was this experience that the State Commission personnel brought to the exhumations at the cave at Hrgar. Excavators expected the same type of preservation and the ultimate recovery of relatively whole bodies. Unfortunately, however, differences between the modes of deposition and geomorphology resulted in much less soft tissue preservation at Hrgar. It is likely that the excellent preservation at Lanište was maintained by both the sand covering the bodies and because the cave was an old one, dry and no longer actively forming. Neither of these conditions was met at Hrgar. Not only was the cave there deeper, but it was still in the active formation phase, bringing excessive amounts of water into contact with the remains for a period of 5 years. Further, no attempt was made to cover the bodies dumped there.

The cave geology, including the cave type, the depth and width of the shaft, and the existence of the talus cone beneath the aven are key to understanding the taphonomy of the human remains deposited within it.

Cave Formation Geology

Geological features of karstic or dolomitic caves and their formation are relevant to a discussion of the taphonomy of the human remains thrown into the cave at Hrgar. C.K. Brain (1975, 1981) provided an early description of accumulated hominid remains in the South African australopithecine cave sites, in one case relating them to the feeding habits of leopards in trees hanging over these karstic avens. Karstic cave systems are part of

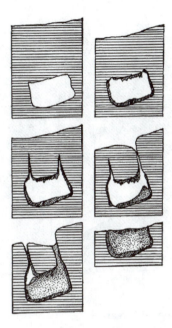

Figure 13.1 Stages of karstic cave formation, beginning from upper left: horizontal lines = dolomite; vertical lines = travertine; stippling = breccia. (Adapted from Brain, C.K., in *Archaeological Studies*, edited by A.T. Clason, North-Holland, Amsterdam; and Brain, C.K., *The Hunters or the Hunted? An Introduction to African Cave Taphonomy*, University of Chicago Press, Chicago, IL. With permission.)

limestone and/or dolomite rock formations. As Brain (1975, 1981) describes, their formations proceed in an ordered sequence.

While Brain describes six separate stages of formation (see Figure 13.1), only the first four are relevant to the cave at Hrgar. In Stage 1, a solution cavity is formed inside the rock strata. During Stage 2, the water level drops and the cavern becomes filled with air, which may be ventilated to the surface by distant and indirect means. Stalactites and stalagmites may begin to form during this period. The development of the aven (or vertical shaft to the surface) is the hallmark of Stage 3 and is caused by rainwater enlarging fissures in the rock. Brain (1981:7) notes that the passage of this water is accelerated by the presence of the cavern, since the water can drip freely from the roof of the cavern as it percolates down through the joint. Stage 4 witnesses the break-through of the aven to the surface, thus opening the cavern to the external environment. It is during Stages 3 and 4 that a depression may develop in the ground above the forming aven. Trees are plentiful in and around these depressions due to the abundance of water. The Stage 4 cavern begins to fill with debris from the surface and accumulating deposits form a talus cone on the floor beneath the aven.

Geologically, the northwest region of Bosnia is karstic with an abundance of both caves and actively forming sink-holes. If one travels along the north–south road connecting the cities of Ključ and Bihać (parallel to the border with Croatia), the area can be seen to exhibit wide expanses of grazing land where numerous shallow depressions mark the ground surface. These depressions are filled with trees. The site at Hrgar is located in a geologically similar, although more densely forested region.

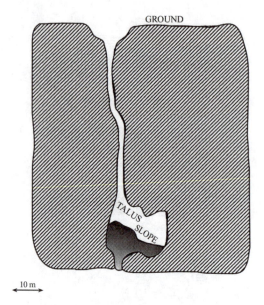

Figure 13.2 Cross section of cave at Hrgar.

Site History and Description

In June 1997, in the city of Bihać in northwestern Bosnia, preparations to exhume the remains of an unknown number of individuals from a karstic cave were begun. At this time, no site exploration had yet occurred, nor had local authorities defined with certainty which of three known cave shafts was the site identified by Serb informants as the mass grave. Local history asserts that on July 11, 1992 a number of prisoners from the nearby Ripać concentration camp were released by the Serbs. Those that remained interned, however, were never seen alive again. These individuals were believed to have been executed that same day at nearby Hrgar.

There was compelling evidence on the ground surrounding one of the cave shaft entrances to suggest that a large number of people had been killed at this location. Grenade pins and .762 cartridge casings littered the area. This cave was explored in early August by a Criminal Inspector from the Bihać police who is also an amateur speleologist. Descending into the shaft using a rope and harness, he photographed and videotaped the evidence within the cave. This visual record clearly documents the markings of explosives detonating along the length of the shaft itself as well as the presence of numerous human skeletal remains, remnants of clothing, and refuse on the cave floor. The cave was nicknamed Jama-Bezdan, or cave without daylight, because the shaft proved to be approximately 80 m in depth, and light adequate for exploration does not reach the cave floor (Figure 13.2).

Trees and other vegetation surround the broad entrance and grow along the shaft walls to a depth of approximately 10 m. At this point the aven narrows to a width of 2 to 3 m. The shaft is not completely straight and takes a slight bend about one third of the way down. Its walls are relatively dry in the upper half, but water runs freely down one side of the shaft from this point. One wall of the cave itself is continuously running with water and water drips heavily and steadily from other points in the cave ceiling. The floor of the cave (Figure 13.3) is roughly rectangular, and approximately 4 × 7 m in area, although one

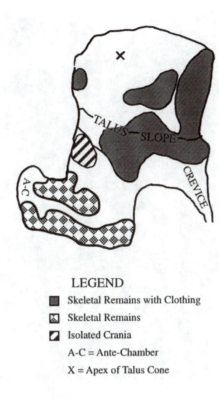

LEGEND

▣ Skeletal Remains with Clothing

▦ Skeletal Remains

◪ Isolated Crania

A-C = Ante-Chamber

X = Apex of Talus Cone

Figure 13.3 Plan view of cave at Hrgar.

narrow, tall crevice and one wide, low antechamber extend away from the main chamber. The ambient temperature inside the cave is a steady 3 to 4°C and the quality of the air is fresh and circulating.

In addition to containing commingled human remains, the cave also held quantities of refuse; it had been in use prior to the war as a municipal and police garbage dump. Once thrown down the shaft, the rubbish formed a talus cone of deposits ranging from 2.0 to 2.5 m higher than the floor of the cave. The area directly under the opening contained the deepest deposits of garbage and was the highest point on the cave floor. These accumulations consisted largely of tires and inner tubes, shattered glass bottles, plastic containers, animal carcasses, unassociated clothing and footwear, leather police belts and web gear, a variety of rusted firearms, old personal identity cards, and a vast quantity of vehicle license plates. The latter proved to be important in the taphonomy of the human remains.

The recently deposited corpses had, when thrown into the cave, dropped onto this talus cone and its coating of flat metal license plates (Figure 13.4). The license plates acted like sleds on the slope of the deposits to disperse the bodies, many of which were transported to the far edges of the cave floor with a layer of license plates often accompanying them. In addition, many bodies simply rolled down the slope and became lodged at its junction with the walls of the cave; bodies were frequently layered 4 to 5 deep in these areas as well as at the base of the talus cone.

The cave floor topography and differential moisture, along with the accumulating bodies themselves, acted to produce variable microenvironments (Figure 13.5). Bodies

Figure 13.4 License plates removed from the cave at Hrgar. They contributed to dispersion of remains.

exposed on the surface were less well preserved. Almost no articulated remains were found in the top layers. In several articulated bodies found on the slope, clothing and the skeletal remains within appeared stretched to an abnormal length from the effects of decomposition on the steep slope.

As decomposition continued in some individuals, the crania and other extremities separated from the trunk and subsequently rolled down the slope. This taphonomic progression was evidenced by the presence of scattered extremity elements in the lower and flatter portions of the cave floor. This area contained many crania that were clearly supernumerary to the complement of skeletonized individuals.

Nearly all the remains were completely skeletonized. It is likely that soft tissue decomposition was enhanced by the high moisture levels and dripping water within the cave during the 5 years since their deposition. The contributions of mammalian scavengers to the decomposition process were minimal as the depth of the shaft provided a protected environment. Although several mice and one frog were noted living in the cave shaft at the time of excavation, no evidence of rodent gnawing or carnivore chewing was noted on any of the remains. The activity of nematodes and other insects, however, clearly contributed greatly to the decomposition process. During the exhumation, the earthworm population of the cave was abundant and manifested robust health. A few bodies contained significant amounts of dry adipocere and, in some cases, recognizable muscle and skin tissue. Bodies exhibiting the best preservation were found in the shallow antechamber (see Figure 13.3) of the cave, where because of its greater distance from the aven it was a drier even more protected environment. Only one individual retained a desiccated brain while

Figure 13.5 The lower, flat portion of the cave floor during the first few days of the exhumation.

another retained some discernible organ structure (the diaphragm and intestinal mesentery). No detectable odor of decomposition was present during the exhumation.

Logistics of the Exhumation

During the course of 14 days in the second half of August, the site of Hrgar Jama-Bezdan was prepared for exhumation by the 5th Corps of the Bosnia-Herzegovina Army (Figure 13.6a). The area surrounding the cave entrance was assessed for de-mining; no mines were detected. All of the trees surrounding the shaft were bulldozed and an extensive, covered wooden platform was constructed over the opening in order to support and shelter the machinery necessary for descending into the cave (Figure 13.6b). The logging road which gave access to the site was regraded and new gravel roads were constructed in the site area itself. Canvas army tents were pitched and designated for specific purposes: housing the generators, storage for recovered remains, an autopsy area, changing areas, meeting areas, storage for identified remains, etc. Latrines were dug. A campfire kitchen and eating area was established. An ambulance and crew were always on site. An army and police checkpoint was established at the site entrance off the logging road. The exhumation began on September 1 and remains were recovered through September 12, 1997.

Descent into and ascent out of the cave were accomplished by means of an electrically driven winch and pulley system which raised and lowered a covered metal mining cage

Figure 13.6 (a) Hrgar cave opening prior to logistical preparations and removal of remains. (b) Entrance to Hrgar cave following logistical preparations. The wooden platform was constructed over the opening in order to support and shelter the machinery necessary for descending into the cave.

by means of a steel cable. This system was operated by a career army engineer who was in radio contact with members of the exhumation team during transport and as they worked in the cave. Other police officers, members of the exhumation team, were also in radio contact with the workers below. The geology often interfered with radio transmissions, however, but in these instances shouting would attract the attention of those on the platform above. The process of getting into and out of the cave took between 6 and 10 minutes in each direction. Four adults could squeeze into the mining cage at a time, and one of these was always the speleologist. His job was to maneuver the cage past the bend in the cave shaft by physically pushing it away from the walls. All   exhumation team members were equipped with warm clothing, rubber boots, Tyvek™ suits, rubber or latex gloves, hard hats, and battery packs connected to headlamps. Additional light was provided by one stationary and one mobile reflector lamp; however, the lighting was usually inadequate to the task. Any area of the cave not illuminated directly by the reflector lamps was extremely dark. The excavation of remains was accomplished using trowels and buckets to remove surrounding soil and debris. The garbage and dirt were placed into body bags which were rolled into a canvas tarpaulin. The tarp was then secured to the outside of the mining cage with ropes and taken to the surface with the speleologist inside the cage. All such material was sorted on the surface by other members of the exhumation team. Once remains were excavated, they reached the surface in the same manner. Between 1 and 14 body bags containing human remains were brought to the surface daily. Due to logistical constraints and level of documentation decisions made by the State Commission team (for example, lack of both mapping and body part inventories), subsequent resolution of issues relating to minimal numbers of individuals and the ability to re-attribute remains to particular individuals was severely hampered.

Differentiation and Exhumation of the Remains

Due to spatial constraints and the poor lighting quality, only a maximum of five or six members of the team could work in the cave at one time. Effective work time for any individual was also reduced by the cold temperatures and wet conditions to about 3 to 5 hours a day; for example, working along certain walls of the cave caused the Tyvek suits to become saturated with water in a matter of a few hours. Returning to the cave after a period of absence, with or without the work of another team having taken place between visits, was very disorienting. The poor light and pervasive mud made it very difficult to relocate and redefine characteristics of the work area, including individual bodies, clothing, and the relationships among them. Work thus proceeded slowly at the beginning of each group's shift.

A large quantity of cow and goat bones, as well as several decomposing animal hides, were present in the cave. All parts of the animals were represented, but terminal phalanges and hooves, caudal vertebrae, and horn cores (waste elements in food production) dominated the assemblage.

The first tasks of the exhumation team were to delimit individuals and to clear refuse away from the remains. Much of the garbage consisted of loose clothing, inner tubes, and leather belts, all of which had become entangled with the remains during deposition and decomposition. Defining and differentiating individuals were difficult due to poor light, water-saturated and mud-coated clothing, and the entangling garbage.

Commingling

The sliding and rolling taphonomic processes described above also contributed to the excavation complexity. Because most of the crania were shattered (see discussion below), cranial fragments could not be associated reliably with particular individuals. When skeletal remains with associated clothing were superimposed on one another, it was troublesome to distinguish where one body began and another ended. Similarly, when remains lacking clothing were overlain in this manner, the decomposition process had caused the bones of one individual to sink into the remains of the one below and become commingled. For example, bodies H-J 58 and H-J 59 found in the lower, antechamber part of the cave were both subadults of approximately the same epiphyseal age; separating these two individuals was difficult.

The positions that the bodies had assumed during decomposition made excavation problematic. Several individuals were thoroughly entangled with other bodies and webbing gear. In one instance the skeleton was supine with the knees bent upward. The entire individual from the proximal femora to the skull was free of surrounding mud, but the lower legs and feet were still covered by mud and the bodies of other individuals. The excavator had to choose either to slide a hand down the tibiae and fibulae in order to locate the feet, or to try to excavate the other bodies from over them first. In this instance, the excavator was able to determine that the bones of the feet were encased in socks and shoes, thus ensuring that all the elements would be recovered. She, therefore, opted to pry the legs and feet out from under the other bodies.

Isolated skeletal elements could not be reliably associated with a specific individual skeleton during the exhumation process. These elements, including isolated crania and halves of bodies that had decomposed on the slope, were collected in separate body bags. Positions and associations of remains were not mapped. During examination and analysis in the morgue, a few matching element pairs were identified. The majority of isolated elements, however, could not be reassociated with a particular body.

A total of 83 body bags (containing the remains of approximately 70 individuals) were recovered from the cave at Hrgar. The remains were examined on site by forensic anthropologists and pathologists during the 2.5 weeks following the exhumation. All the individuals were male and ranged in age from 16 to 65 years. In addition, a few fragmentary cranial and foot bones of a 3- to 5-year-old child of indeterminate sex were found associated with two small rubber boots and a red sock.

Perimortem Trauma

Although only one bullet was recovered from a body (H-J 56, lodged between the clothing and the sternum), perimortem injuries at Hrgar consisted primarily of gunshot wounds which were easily distinguished from taphonomic modifications. This finding is consistent with the presence cartridge casings on the surface of the site surrounding the entrance to the cave shaft. Forty-nine sets of remains exhibited gunshot wounds and the cause of death was attributed to either single or multiple gunshot wounds in 45 cases. Five bodies exhibited a combination of perimortem trauma, including gunshot wounds and blunt-force trauma, the latter always inflicted to the cranium. Three cases exhibited only blunt-force trauma

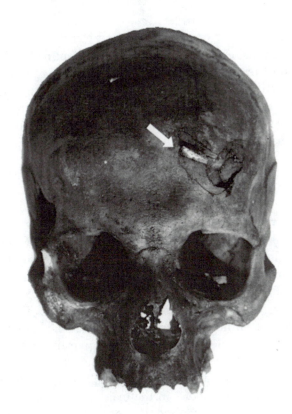

Figure 13.7 Blunt-force trauma to the frontal bone. The arrow indicates a piece of the instrument, a rock, still embedded in the cranium.

to the cranium. One case (H-J 52) exhibited penetrating sharp-force trauma to the cranium with an implement consistent with the size and shape of a screw driver. Ligatures of varied types (rope, wire, portions of a leather belt, etc.) were present on several, but not all of the bodies.

One of the greatest difficulties during autopsy was distinguishing deliberate, perimortem blunt-force trauma from injuries the corpse might have sustained from being thrown down the cave shaft; for example, there was a reasonably large portion of a jagged rock embedded in the frontal bone of one victim (Figure 13.7). It was determined that this was an example of deliberate blunt-force trauma; while many loose rocks of that type exist on the surface of the ground, none are to be found within the cave shaft, which is smooth-walled limestone. It was also difficult to reconstruct circumstances where a glancing impact with the cave shaft walls would have produced this type of focal trauma.

Most crania were fragmentary. Discriminating gunshot trauma from that due to impact with the walls and/or bottom of the cave required that the crania be reconstructed. This process revealed that most, if not all, of the trauma seen in the crania and other skeletal elements was patterned and had resulted from bullet impact. Likewise, the examiners found no evidence (such as impact or compression fractures to the legs or vertebrae) to support the contention that some of the victims had been thrown into the cave alive.

Identifications

Family members of the missing viewed the remains and identified their relatives primarily based on recognition of unique items of preserved clothing, in some cases a waistband mended in red thread, the pattern of a hand knit sweater, etc. In all, names were associated with 45 of the bodies recovered at the site of Hrgar, Jama-Bezdan. All the named individuals were males between the ages of 18 and 55 years at the time of their deaths in 1992. These individuals, as well as the remains of the unidentified, were buried on October 5, 1997.

Conclusions

Understanding the karstic cave formation processes, the role of flowing, seeping, and dripping water, and the constant temperatures deep in the ground are integral to the taphonomy of the human remains within the Hrgar, Jama Bezdan, cave. The transport and dispersal effects of the talus cone and the layer of license plates played a major role in the ultimate positioning of the bodies and separated elements. Taphonomic differences were produced by microenvironmental variation: whether the body lay nearer or farther from one of the wet walls; whether it was nearer the top or the bottom layer of bodies; or whether it decomposed on a flat surface or the talus slope. Remains on the talus slope and on the lower surface were completely skeletonized, while remains underneath these others often contained some adipocere. Bodies in the main cave chamber, exposed to constant moisture, were predominantly skeletonized. Bodies that had been deposited in the drier antechamber exhibited greater preservation, including some mummified skin and muscle, dry adipocere, and occasionally recognizable soft tissue structure.

Distinguishing deliberate perimortem trauma from circumstantial injury sustained by bodies in the depositional phase necessitated careful reconstruction of all fragmentary remains. Through this process at autopsy, the forensic anthropologists and pathologists were able to conclude that none of the perimortem fracture injuries could be clearly attributed to the depositional process itself, but resulted from gunshot wounds and/or deliberate blunt force trauma.

Acknowledgments

The exhumations at Hrgar were logistically challenging, physically taxing, and emotionally draining for all personnel involved. I would, therefore, like to express my appreciation to the members of the Bihac Expert Team, in particular to Kriminalni Inspektor Ermin Lipović, the amateur speleologist of the Bihać police. Thanks also to Dr. Šamira Mesic, Mr. Amor Maćović, Mr. Esad Bajramović, and Judge Adem Jakupović for fulfilling their roles at Hrgar. I am very grateful for the assistance of a rapidly and temporarily assembled Physicians for Human Rights team (Dr. Page Hudson, Dr. Onder Ozkalipci, and Ms. Ann Ross) during the autopsy phase. Finally, my gratitude is expressed to Mr. Zlaya Šabanović and Ms. Elvira Talurovič of Physicians for Human Rights in Tuzla, who ostensibly acted as my translators, but who, in reality, provided invaluable assistance throughout the exhumation and identification processes, respectively.

References

Brain, C.K.

  1975 An introduction to the South African australopithecine bone accumulations. In *Archaeological Studies*, edited by A.T. Clason, pp. 109–119. North-Holland, Amsterdam.

  1976 A reinterpretation of the Swartkrans site and its remains, *South African Journal of Science* 72:141–146.

  1981 *The Hunters or the Hunted? An Introduction to African Cave Taphonomy*, University of Chicago Press, Chicago, IL.

Oliver, J.S.

  1989 Analogues and site context: bone damages from Shield Trap Cave (24CB91), Carbon County, Montana, U.S.A. In *Bone Modification*, edited by R. Bonnichsen and M.H. Sorg, pp. 73–98. Center for the Study of the First Americans, Orono, ME.

Mass Graves and the Collection of Forensic Evidence: Genocide, War Crimes, and Crimes against Humanity

14

STEFAN SCHMITT

Contents

0-8493-1189-6/02/$0.00+$1.50
© 2002 by CRC Press LLC

Introduction

Individual responsibility is one of the cornerstones of international criminal law. Genocide, war crimes, or crimes against humanity, are all crimes for which an individual can be prosecuted. Legally, the concepts of war crimes and crimes against humanity had been established by the time the Nuremberg International Military Tribunal took up its work prosecuting Nazi war criminals in 1945 (Neier, 1998). The crime of genocide was first adopted by the United Nations General Assembly on December 9, 1948, in its Resolution 260 (III) (U.N.T.S., 1951). Articles II and III of the Convention on the Prevention and Punishment of the Crime of Genocide present a definition for genocide and which acts are punishable under this definition.

Since this time, war crimes and crimes against humanity have been further elaborated in the Geneva Conventions of 1949, which were expanded in 1977, adding among other things the phenomena of internal armed conflicts. These conventions are today generally accepted as customary international law (Neier, 1998).

Crimes against humanity encompass a broader spectrum than war crimes, which are restricted to crimes against combatants or nationals of a hostile power or an occupied territory. As Neier (1998:17) describes:

> In contrast, the concept of crimes against humanity applies only to crimes committed on a large scale. A defendant charged with crimes against humanity may be convicted only if the prosecution establishes the connection between the particular crime and a broad pattern and practice of the commission of such crimes for reasons of political, ethnic, or religious persecution. Accordingly the evidentiary burden on prosecutors is far greater when they prosecute a defendant for crimes against humanity than when they must demonstrate to a court the commission of a war crime.

These factors also apply to the crime of genocide, where the "intent to destroy, in whole or in part, a national, ethnical, racial or religious group…" (U.N.T.S., 1951) has to be demonstrated in order to support the accusation of genocide. Such an accusation implies organization on a higher level, such as would be provided by a government.

The concept of a "broad pattern and practice of the commission of such crimes for reasons of political, ethnic, or religious persecution" (Neier, 1998:17) also applies to the documentation and collection of evidence of what is generally termed as human rights violations. To prove the violation of human rights, which generally are committed by a government against its citizens, a pattern of such practices has to be documented. Since civilians are often the ones who commit such crimes, establishing a direct link to a government order might be difficult.

Defining "Mass Graves"

Before discussing how mass graves can provide evidence for war crimes and/or genocide, the term should be defined (also see Haglund, this volume). Some authors define it by the number of individuals; for example, Skinner (1987) suggests that a mass grave must contain at least six individuals. Mant (1987) limits the term to sites where two or more bodies physically touch each other. These definitions depend on the technical and physical characteristics of the grave itself. A more holistic definition is needed, however, which includes the anthropological context. It is this context that focuses and defines what evidence should be collected and which methods should be used to excavate. From this perspective, a mass grave can be defined as one that contains the remains of more than one victim who share some common trait connected with the cause and manner of death.

Using this definition emphasizes the importance of social context along with the forensic determination of manner of death. Some mass graves are the result of homicide; others, including many mass disasters, for example, are the result of an accident. Deaths from either may be examined forensically. In homicide-related mass graves the forensic investigation involves criminal wrongdoing. In some accident-related mass graves the forensic investigation may involve civil litigation, such as issues with insurance. Both are medicolegal, forensic types of scene investigation. In other, non-forensic, accident-related mass graves, the investigation may be purely archaeological; for example, the excavation of the volcano victims from Pompeii or the australopithecine "first family" group from the African Pliocene who may have been flash flood victims.

The putative manner of death and its social determinants form the core of the investigation and drive choices about the techniques and approaches to the excavation, including the types of evidence sought and methods for finding it. The forensic anthropologist, trained in linking cultural behavior, human biology, and archaeology, brings a holistic perspective to mass grave examination and analysis.

This chapter treats mass graves concerned with criminal or homicide-related mass murders due to war crimes or genocide. In these situations the victims share, or are perceived to share, some kind of common trait which justifies the homicides in the minds of the assassins. Therefore, a mass grave of this type is not so much defined by the number of individuals buried, but rather by the sharing of a common trait that led to their deaths.

Such criminal mass graves are frequently not secret. In Guatemala, for instance, mass graves of the 1980s military's anti-insurgency campaign are referred to as clandestine graves, implying that their locations are secret or unknown. The secrecy, however, lies not in their locations but in the repression of any acts that might commemorate the event that led to the mass fatality. That is, survivors often know very well where their loved ones lie; they are just not allowed to acknowledge the event that led to the death by performing religious ceremonies or decorating the grave site. The trauma caused by this proscription enhances the terror under which survivors live. They are constantly reminded of their subjugation by the fact that they cannot mourn their dead and openly acknowledge the injustice done to them.

Because of ongoing repression, perpetrators initially do not need to cover up their deed by burying the evidence. In fact, mass graves are often created by others, non-perpetrators, doing the clean-up work, rather than trying to hide the evidence of a crime. The reasoning behind this lies in the justification the perpetrators feel they have in killing the victims: in other words, "Why hide what is right?" As time passes and circumstances change, efforts may then be made to hide evidence, but generally not at the time the crime is committed.

To summarize then, criminal mass graves contain the remains of a group of individuals who share some common trait that justified their assassinations in the eyes of the perpetrators. Additionally, mass graves often are not secret in the sense that knowledge about them exists, even though the exact geographical location might still need to be determined scientifically. This two-point definition has methodological consequences when investigating what is assumed to be such a grave.

From a taphonomic standpoint it introduces the human as an agent of perimortem and postmortem changes. That is, the process from the selection of the victims to their killings and interments becomes evident taphonomically when exhuming such a mass grave with a holistic anthropological approach. Forensic anthropology then has to go beyond the mere investigation of the grave itself and also has to include the context in which the grave was produced. The following discussion and presentation of case examples elaborate this point.

Witness Testimony — Cornerstone of Mass Grave Forensic Analysis

The cornerstone of mass grave forensic investigation is witness testimony. As described above, a mass grave is seldom a secret. All of the mass graves in the present study were located with witness information. The witnesses were generally survivors of the massacres themselves who had managed to get away, or people who had helped bury the remains.

An example of the importance of witnesses is the mass grave discovered by forensic anthropologist Clyde Snow at the Ovcara farm which contained the victims from the Vukovar Hospital. He found the grave after listening to the story of one of the intended victims who managed to jump off the truck that was taking him and others from a farm equipment building, where they had been taken after being removed from the Vukovar Hospital to what was later confirmed to be a mass gravesite. The grave was exhumed by a forensic team from Physicians for Human Rights who were under contract to the United Nations International Tribunal for the former Yugoslavia in 1996 (Stover and Peress, 1998).

Witness testimony frequently leads investigators to the grave location, and may provide collaborative evidence about the circumstances that led to the fatality incident. Witness testimony also may provide the basis for the accusation that the massacre was part of an organized effort to eradicate, in whole or in part, such a group of people. The corroboration (and speaking in the objective language of science, the negation) of such testimony becomes the goal of the exhumation.

Approaches to Mass Grave Location and Evidence Collection

The exhumation of human remains from a mass grave uses archaeological techniques to test witness testimony. Such efforts occur in 5 phases: (1) the grave location and survey; (2) excavation; (3) collection and documentation of evidence; (4) analysis; and (5) reporting. This chapter focuses particularly on phases 1 and 3, including approaches to grave location, locating circumstantial evidence, labeling, estimating minimum numbers, and associating artifacts.

Location of Mass Graves by Trenching

The first step lies in determining if a mass grave actually exists at the suggested location. Eyewitnesses very rarely remember the exact location of a grave. In the best case, the grave may have been marked by people who buried the victims, but often this has not happened. Trenching can be used to find a grave, define its boundaries, and confirm that it contains human remains. Use of a probe is another method utilized to confirm the presence of decomposing tissue. All other methods, such as ground penetrating radar or cadaver dogs

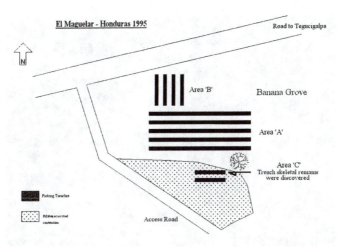

Figure 14.1 Site diagram for El Maguelar, Honduras (not to scale).

(trained to alert to the scent of buried, decomposing material) may indicate the presence of human remains, but they cannot rule out their absence. That is, one might use them, not get positive results, but still not be able to clear the site with a measurable degree of certainty.

Trenching is the most reliable method of locating a mass grave because it allows confirmation of the presence or absence of human remains in a specific area without a complete excavation. Trenches can be dug using either human or mechanical power, such as a backhoe in some cases. Traditional archaeologists may be reluctant to utilize untrained human power or a backhoe because of the risk of damaging evidence. However, due to limited resources and time, which are often extreme, this possibility has to be balanced against the risk of not undertaking or completing the excavation. The remedy is to document damage if it occurs. Postmortem trauma is usually distinguishable from perimortem trauma, particularly if the excavator notes that it occurred. The responsibility then lies with the forensic investigator to make sure that every step of the process of discovery is documented meticulously.

Example of Trenching: El Maguelar, Honduras

A good example of the use of trenching and untrained manual labor is the 1995 excavation at El Maguelar in Honduras. The investigation was carried out to determine whether two bodies found alongside the road leading to El Maguelar on April 18, 1988, were union leader Rolando Vindel and former vice president of the National Lottery, Gustavo Morales. Both reportedly had been kidnapped by the military on March 18, 1988 (Anon., 1995).

The discovery of the bodies in 1988 led to a semi-judicial inquiry with a minimal postmortem examination taking place beside the road where they were found. The judge decided to re-bury the bodies in the same location, a rather common practice in Honduras at the time.

Witness testimony pointed to the presence of this grave in an area of approximately 25 × 50 m (Figure 14.1). Since this constitutes an area of approximately half a football field, the task of trenching and clearing it of underbrush was considerable (Figures 14.2, 14.3, and 14.4). For this purpose the Special Human Rights Attorney of Honduras, Sonia

Figure 14.2 Beginning excavation utilizing trenching methods at El Maguelar, Honduras.

Figure 14.3 Completed excavation showing trenches at El Maguelar, Honduras.

Figure 14.4 Overview of banana grove including area 'e' trenches (covered with tarpaulin).

Dubón was asked to hire 30 people. They were hired from the surrounding area; most of them were farmers and thus used to hard, physical labor.

Reliable eyewitnesses did not become available for 3 days, during which excavation had commenced. It was decided to trench across the entire area pointed out by several villagers who claimed to have witnessed the burial of the bodies under supervision of the then Justice of the Peace. Each trench was separated by no more than 1.5 m, assuming this would not likely exceed the length of the disturbed area of the grave. The trenches were parallel and dug to a depth of 1.2 m where water was encountered and digging was impossible. Over the next 3 days, 5 major trenches were dug 30 m long, with 1.5 m separation between them (Figure 14.1, Area A) along with four minor trenches 9 m long with 1.0 m separation (Figure 14.1, Area B).

Before taking the next step of perpendicular trenches, dug in a checkerboard fashion, and thus definitely ruling out or finding the grave in the berms between the original trenches, early in the morning of the fourth day one of the workers uncovered one of two crania in one of the trenches of Area C (Figure 14.1). This area had been pointed out by the man who had actually buried the remains, a witness that appeared on the third day the dig was in progress. The crania were located at a depth of 2.20 m. As it turned out, an access road had been built and approximately 1 m of fill had been placed over the gravesite. The grave was located, outlined, and the skeletal remains of two individuals were exhumed (E.A.F.G./P.H.R., 1995).

Location of Mass Grave by Sniff Probe Method

Metal probes that are equipped with a T-bar on one end, measuring approximately 0.6 cm in diameter and 1 m in length, can be inserted into the ground in an area where one suspects the presence of a grave. The differences in subsurface resistance (i.e., the probe can be inserted easier in one area than in another, indicating disturbed soil) or the presence of the odor of decomposing flesh on the end of the probe when it is withdrawn might indicate the presence of buried human remains (Killam, 1990). Trenches are still necessary in order to confirm or rule out burials.

Example of Sniff Probe Burial Location Method: Pakracka Poljana, Croatia

Probes were used during the forensic exhumation in 1993 of several bodies near the town of Pakracka Poljana, Croatia. The area to be investigated consisted of several hundred meters of grassy field along a road. A backhoe was utilized to dig several trenches at intervals along the road. Probing was an additional technique utilized in locating the graves.

The bodies were suspected to have been buried in this area between August, 1991 and March, 1992. Considering they had been buried for a little over a year, one could assume that soft tissue was still likely to be present. The probe proved very successful in this case. A total of 19 individuals (16 males and 3 females) were exhumed from 9 separate graves, which were located this way (Report, Physicians for Human Rights, 1994).

Surface Evidence

Although the perpetrators may have left the scene of the crime quite some time ago, the grave is probably the best snapshot of what happened. That moment in time is in some way preserved, because the bodies have been isolated from further human manipulation by burial.

Some evidence may be located outside of the grave. This evidence is circumstantial, i.e., not directly associated with that evidence encountered in the grave; however, its location and the pattern it presents in conjunction with supporting witness testimony might indicate its relationship to the contents of the grave, and be critical to the reconstruction of events.

Example of Surface Evidence Collection: Koreme, Iraq

A good example of the pattern of evidence located outside of the grave proving to substantiate witness testimony is the incident investigated by the forensic team organized by Physicians for Human Rights and Human Rights Watch in 1992 at the village of Koreme in Kurdistan, northern Iraq. It involved the exhumation of two mass graves containing the skeletal remains of 27 men executed by the Iraqi military on August 28, 1988. Careful documentation and analysis of the spatial distribution of cartridge cases collected near the alleged execution site as well as an analysis of the firing pin patterns on each cartridge brass allowed reconstruction of the minimum number of weapons used, minimum number of shots fired, and the spatial relationship between the shooters and the victims (Scott and Connor, 1997). These details could then be compared with witness testimony.

Approaches to Documentation

Each grave is unique, and flexibility is essential to approaching an exhumation. Unlike a historical archaeological excavation, time and resources are usually more limited, having direct consequences as to which techniques are selected. In this way forensic mass grave excavation bears a strong resemblance to survey archaeology.

Features of the grave itself influence the techniques utilized to exhume them, particularly the extent of decomposition. It is important to ascertain the progress of disarticulation, as well as the preservation of outside coverings or clothing that may hold skeletal elements together. Preservation of soft tissue translates into the state of articulation of the remains, and, in turn, how recovery units need to be defined; for example, soft tissue preservation limits commingling.

Labeling, Inventory, and Determining Minimum Number of Individuals

The archaeological identification of remains and artifacts, as well as their labeling and inventory, are the first steps in determining what a mass grave contains. They are essential in determining the minimum number of individuals (MNI) present, especially if they are anatomically disassociated or commingled.

What the excavation team recovers, labels, and inventories ends up being analyzed as a unit by the team that carries out the postmortem examinations. The postmortem examination team frequently must revise the initial findings once the autopsy has been completed. A numbering system is needed which is flexible enough to allow revisions to be made without major complications, i.e., without having to relabel remains, containers, documentary photographs, and evidence lists.

With this in mind, the following labeling system seems to be the most appropriate. Each item bears a label including (1) a short acronym for the site, such as RN for Río Negro; (2) a roman numeral for each mass grave at the site; and (3) an Arabic number for each anatomically articulated or associated set of remains.

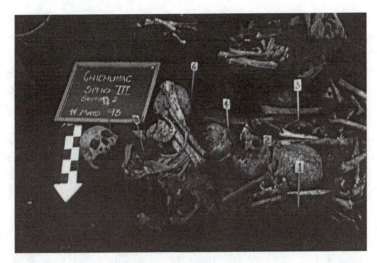

Figure 14.5 Grave III at Chichupac. Disturbed grave site with evidence of re-depositing of remains as can be seen from the long bone assembly.

Anatomically disassociated or partially associated remains present a problem. Although the emphasis at the excavation site is on keeping anatomic assemblages together, the set-of-remains number may not be correct in the final analysis. It is an arbitrary label based on the excavator's decision of association in the field.

Anatomically disassociated remains are numbered individually, but in such a way as to convey associative information. If the site is divided into arbitrary levels and quadrants, the disassociated skeletal remains can be labeled according to the quadrant and level from which they were extracted. This is more efficient than numbering each bone and then trying to document associations through photography alone. Individual element numbering, if necessary, can be reinstated later under laboratory conditions. For example, see Figure 14.5. This photograph of Grave III located close to the village of Chichupac in Guatemala shows one of the disturbed graves. It is apparent from the long bone assemblages that some type of re-depositing has occurred, something corroborated by the owner of the cornfield in which the graves were located. Utilizing the principle of numbering crania first, the skeletal assemblages and artifacts were numbered according to the crania they were closest to or according to the sector in which they were found.

It is recommended that any artifacts encountered in association with labeled remains be kept with them until the postmortem examination. Labeling of artifacts and remains must be done in the grave, prior to the actual exhumation. This is documented thoroughly by photographs and, if time permits, sketching and mapping.

The labeling has to be backed by an inventory. An inventory form is created for each label given, and these are filled out as the remains are extracted from the grave, requiring a preliminary determination of what is present. The remains then should be individually packaged and the bag marked with the appropriate label. At the end of an exhumation, one then should have a set of inventory forms to match each individual bag.

The inventory forms can be revised by the team carrying out the postmortem examinations, initially serving to confirm that a labeled bag contains no less than what it says it does. This is important for the exhumation team to keep in mind. Analysis of what is found is to be kept to a minimum by them, and items labeled only when reasonably sure of the finding. If a bag contains less than what it says it should, by virtue of a graveside identification error, it might suggest to the examination team or to the court that evidence was lost.

Obviously, a bag might very well contain more than what was initially inventoried by the exhumation team. This might simply happen due to breakage during transport, or because remains were not clearly visible at extraction.

An example of discrepancies between the exhumation team inventory and the examination team analysis is the many, partially decomposed and disassociated infant remains recovered by the forensic team for the International Criminal Tribunal for Rwanda at the mass grave in Kibuye, Rwanda, in 1996. They were so small, often enveloped in the mother's clothing, and encased in adipocere that often they were packaged with the remains of an adult without being inventoried. It was not realized until the postmortem examination.

The inventory form should not only provide insurance that no mistakes were made during the exhumation process, but also allow the possibility of revision by the postmortem team. Revision presents two possibilities: (1) there is less content in the bag than documented on the inventory form, or (2) there is more content in the bag than documented on the inventory form. In the first case, an investigation has to be launched to determine what error occurred along the line and then rectify and document it according to what is found. The second possibility often requires a change in labeling in order to adjust the inventory. If an extra set of remains, undocumented in the initial inventory is found, this can simply be corrected by creating a second identifier, based on the original one, such as adding a letter to the end of the original one and adding another inventory form to the records.

Minimum Number of Individuals: Examples from Plan de Sanchez, Guatemala, and Kibuye, Rwanda

The case of several mass graves in the village of Plan de Sanchez, Guatemala, investigated by the Guatemalan Forensic Anthropology Team/Equipo de Antropología Forense de Guatemala (E.A.F.G.) in 1994 demonstrates the importance of inventory keeping. Testimonial accounts stated that on Sunday, June 18, 1982, the military came to the small village of Plan de Sanchez where they blocked off the road. All the people who were returning from the market in the town of Rabinal, some 9 km away, were detained in a house alongside the road. Later in the day the military opened fire on the house and several grenade detonations were heard. Shots were also heard from 5:00 to 9:00 p.m., at which point the house with the bodies in it was set on fire.

The next day surviving family members put the fire out. Permission was asked of the military to bury the bodies. The charred remains were buried in several shallow graves. Several women who had been raped and then shot, but had not been burned, were buried separately. Based on interviews with surviving family members who were willing to come forward, at least 99 people lost their lives during this incident (E.A.F.G., 1995a).

At the time of exhumation, the remains ranged from complete to partial skeletons, commingled, charred, and fragmented. In order to determine the minimum number of individuals, an inventory was kept of all long bones, maxillae, and mandibles. Once the remains reached the laboratory for analysis, it became clear that a simple counting of bones was not sufficient. Many bones encountered were fragmented. This meant that potentially one might count the distal fragment and proximal fragment of the same right femur as two individuals. Hence, each long bone was divided into three units, each representing 33% of the bone. Over 50% of that third had to be present in order to be counted. A femoral head or a distal epiphysis of a long bone by itself was not counted, because most of the bone itself was missing and possibly could turn up somewhere else. The cranial vault, maxilla, and mandible were divided into the left and right halves, and the innominate was divided into its three components: left and right ilium, ischium, and pubis.

At Plan de Sanchez the element recorded with the highest frequency was the proximal third of the right femur, which appeared 84 times, suggesting a minimum of 84 people exhumed (E.A.F.G., 1995a).

This example demonstrates that an inventory starts out in the grave with the archaeological team and then is revised during the postmortem examination. The inventory depends very much on the condition of the remains. In the case of Plan de Sanchez, due to the burning, it was necessary to divide individual bones into separate analytical units in order to avoid duplication.

When recognition and identification of individual body parts or bones during exhumation are difficult due to commingling, partial decomposition, and presence of adipocere tissue, such as it was in the case in the mass grave in Kibuye, Rwanda, the inventory becomes even less precise. In this situation, we reverted to counting what appeared to be the most easily recognized feature (the cranium) to determine the minimum number exhumed.

Identification Issues: Examples from Chichupac, Guatemala, and Koreme, Iraq

Artifacts such as clothing, jewelry, and identification cards potentially shed light upon the identity of the human remains with which they are found. As indicated above, it is best to package these along with the associated human remains. At a later point their documentation can be completed through photography and inventory. They can be itemized separately from the remains by adding a distinguishing letter or number to the original identifier. For example, artifacts associated with remains XYZ-II-1, could be labeled as A-XYZ-II-1-a, b, c, etc. It must be underscored that just because an identifying artifact is found associated with a particular individual's remains, it does not necessarily mean it belongs to that individual or confirms their identity.

An example that points this out occurred in the case of the three mass graves exhumed in the small town of Chichupac in Guatemala by the Guatemalan Forensic Anthropology Team in 1993. During exhumations in Guatemala, it is customary for family members to watch the work in progress. Sometimes a family member might recognize a piece of clothing or other identifying artifact that is believed to belong to the loved one. In Chichupac this happened on several occasion. On one of these, the remains of CH-II-5 were identified by a family member as Francisco de Paz on the basis of clothing. As it turned out, Francisco was reported to be left-handed and a nonsmoker. Skeleton CH-II-5, however, appeared to be a right-handed individual with sufficient stains on his teeth to assume that he was a smoker. The identification based on the artifact was thus incorrect (E.A.F.G., 1993). There are several possible reasons for this mistake. One is that the family member's memory failed her as to the identification of clothing articles that had spent 11 years in the ground. Another might be that the clothing at some point was switched from one victim to another. This illustrates that associated artifacts are only circumstantial evidence.

For identification in a population lacking dental records, radiographs, and capacity for DNA testing, it is necessary that a pattern be found which elevates circumstantial evidence to the level of compelling circumstantial evidence.

Group patterns may also offer compelling evidence useful for forensic identification. The clothing worn by all 27 victims exhumed from the mass graves at Koreme were the traditional shirt and pants worn by Kurdish men (Middle East Watch and Physicians for Human Rights, 1993), distinguishing them as a distinct ethnic, religious, and in this case possibly even distinct political group from their executioners. This pattern can be considered compelling circumstantial evidence, even if no identifications of the remains themselves were made.

Mass Graves and Taphonomic Evidence: Illustration from Chichupac, Guatemala

Taphonomic evidence documented in the excavation and analysis of mass graves can be critical in the corroboration of witness testimony. This can be particularly useful in cases with a complex taphonomic history, including a sequence of events.

The massacre at Chichupac, Guatemala is an excellent example. On January 8, 1982, 32 men were pointed out to the military as subversives by 15 men of a neighboring village. They were then detained and taken to the small town hall where they were tortured. Later on they were led up a hill, executed, and buried in two shallow graves (E.A.F.G., 1993). Witness testimony reported that severed fingers, noses, and ears were found later by the villagers in the town hall.

One of the surviving widows reported that she and several other women went to the graves a week to 10 days later. Due to their shallow burial, many of the bodies were exposed and the smell was described as being unbearable. They decided to dig another pit into which they dragged several bodies with the help of their hoes.

Eleven years later, in May of 1993, the E.A.F.G. was asked to exhume the remains. At the time of the incident the area was forested. During the intervening years the hill had been deforested by slash and burn agriculture; the land had been under cultivation for 5 years. This traditional practice disturbs the top layer to a depth of about 1 m.

Trenching revealed the location of three graves on the sloping hillside. These were designated Sites I, II, and III (see Table 14.1). Numerous fragments of clothing were recovered from the surface throughout the cultivated area, suggesting that farming had disturbed the graves.

Excavation of the top 90 cm revealed that all three sites contained some partial skeletal remains in approximate anatomical order, some disassociated but arbitrarily grouped elements, and clothing. Between 90 and 125 cm in Site II 10 skeletons in anatomical order were also found, although in unnatural positions, with scavenger damage and one arm missing postmortem. Also found at this level were artifacts and personal effects such as machetes, carrying bags, wallets, and documents. Sites I and III had no remains below about 90 cm.

The three sites were arranged on a hillside, with Sites I and III about 1.5 m above Site II. Site I was disturbed by the cultivation in progress, which in Guatemala is done using large hoes with which the soil is aired and made to form mounds in which the corn is

Table 14.1   Comparison of three sites at Chichupac, Guatemala

	Site I	Site II (Secondary)	Site III
Surface	Clothing fragments	Clothing fragments	Clothing fragments
Upper excavated layer	1. Partial skeletal remains of three individuals in approx. anatomical order 2. Disassociated remains but belonging to the anatomically arranged individuals found in arbitrary groups, including few small bones 3. Clothing 4. Condition: some burned, most unburned	1. Partial skeletal remains in approx. anatomical order 2. Disassociated remains 3. Clothing	1. Partial skeletal remains not in anatomical order, including 14 crania concentrated in two areas 2. Disassociated remains found in arbitrary groups 3. Clothing
Below 90 cm		1. Ten skeletons in anatomical position, but some flexions not possible in life; one missing left arm postmortem; several with scavenger damage 2. Artifacts and personal effects	
Burial pit		2.70 × 1.35 cm	Approx. 1.30 × 1.80 m
Disturbance by cultivation in progress	Yes	No	No

planted. The mounds are occasionally reformed and secured to provide the necessary support for the corn to grow.

The condition of the remains suggested many bodies must have been interred superficially, i.e., within the top 90 cm, susceptible to damage by the agricultural processes. Even after the reburial and grave reinforcement by the widows, cultivation of the land had caused the fragmentation and disassociation of the remains and clothing found in all three sites. Several of the skeletal elements were found to have been burned, leading to the conclusion that they were on the surface when the land was made agriculturally useable by the slash and burn method used by Guatemalan peasants. In addition, the arbitrary groupings of mainly larger bones suggested they had been exposed during agriculture, recollected by the peasants (who may have easily missed or ignored the smaller bones), and reburied in the general area known to contain the original graves.

The condition of the remains in the deeper layer of Site II suggests they had minimal disturbance, but that burial had taken place after decomposition had loosened the articulations. The remains were in anatomical association, but in positions impossible prior to decomposition. Evidence of scavenger damage, including a missing left arm, supports the interpretation that this burial took place following a period of decomposition and exposure, especially in view of the fact that the body with the missing arm also was the one lowest in the grave, i.e., it must have been one of the first ones to be redeposited into Site II. It, therefore, must have come from a top layer of either Site I or Site III and, thus, was the one most exposed to any scavenging.

All of these factors combine to corroborate the witness testimony of initial shallow burial, exposure, and reburial of some of the partially decomposing remains 7 to 10 days later. This was followed by agricultural disturbance and reburial of the (by then) skeletonized remains. Site III presented the highest number of long bones grouped in arbitrary assemblages, along with a total of 14 crania found concentrated in two areas. It is probable that the peasants used this site more often than the one in which they would rebury remains they found on the surface while tilling the soil.

Another detail reported in a witness statement was the aftermath of torture in the town hall. Evidence of amputation of fingers was observed in skeletons CH-II-4 and CH-II-9, including perimortem fractures of several metacarpals and absence of phalanges. In the latter skeleton, several cut marks were observed on the fourth right metacarpal (E.A.F.G., 1993).

The taphonomic processes documented at Chichupac were essential in providing compelling circumstantial evidence to corroborate witness testimony. It also suggested that the farmer using the field did not attempt to erase the evidence, but made an effort to consolidate it.

Conclusions

The objective of exhuming mass graves is to provide evidence of war crimes, crimes against humanity, and genocide. The intent to destroy a particular group has to be demonstrated in order to prosecute these cases. Forensic investigation focuses on collecting data to reconstruct events in question.

The examples presented here show that archaeological techniques and taphonomic interpretation can provide evidence of such patterns. Witness testimony often provides critical information for grave location, identification of victims, and interpretation of perimortem trauma and postmortem sequences. Likewise, the forensic taphonomy analysis can corroborate witness reports. Data about time since death, scavenger modification of remains, disarticulation, and postmortem sequences can play a critical role in building a case.

Forensic anthropology and taphonomy of mass graves in this context are more than technical and isolated approaches to evidence collection and remains recovery. Anthropology in all of its facets, including law, cultural patterns, biological diversity, and archaeological interpretation of cultural patterns can and should be brought to bear in the investigation of genocide, war crimes, crimes against humanity, and human rights violations. The combination of taphonomic and anthropological expertise in the recovery and examination of forensic evidence provides the most effective approach.

References

Andino, L.

1995 Encontraron la primera osamenta en El Maguelar, *El Heraldo,* Tegucigalpa, Honduras, October 24.

Anonymous

1995 Los antropólogos iniciaron la busqueda de tres desaparecidos, *El Heraldo,* Tegucigalpa, Honduras, October 23.

Equipo de Antropología Forense de Guatemala

1993 Informe de Investigaciones Antropológico Forenses. Aldea Chichupac, Rabinal, Baja Verapaz. E.A.F.G., Guatemala City.

1995a Informe de Investigaciones Antropológico Forenses. Aldea Plan de Sánchez, Rabinal, Baja Verapaz. E.A.F.G., Guatemala City.

Equipo de Antropología Forense de Guatemala/Physicians for Human Rights

1995 Report to the Special Human Rights Prosecutor of Honduras on the Forensic Investigations Carried Out in October of 1995 at El Maguelar, Honduras. E.A.F.G., Guatemala City.

Haglund, W.D.

1997 *Report of the Exhumation and Examination of Remains from the Kibuye,* Physicians for Human Rights, Boston.

Killam, E.W.

1990 *The Detection of Human Remains,* Charles C Thomas, Springfield, IL.

Mant, A.K.

1987 Knowledge acquired from post-war exhumations. In *Death Decay and Reconstruction: Approaches to Archeology and Forensic Science,* edited by A. Boddington, A.N. Garland, and R.C. Janaway, Manchester University Press, London.

Middle East Watch and Physicians for Human Rights

1993 *The Anfal Campaign in Iraqi Kurdistan: The Destruction of Koreme,* Human Rights Watch, New York.

Neier, A.

1998 *War Crimes. Brutality, Genocide, Terror, and the Struggle for Justice,* Random House, New York.

Physicians for Human Rights

1994 *Report of a Preliminary Medicolegal Investigation of a Series of Clandestine Graves near Pakracka Poljana, Former Yugoslavia,* Physicians for Human Rights, Boston.

Scott, D.D. and M. Connor

1997 The Koreme execution site: a modern crime scene investigation using archaeological techniques. In *Forensic Taphonomy: The Postmortem Fate of Human Remains,* edited by W.D. Haglund and M.H. Sorg, pp. 34–38. CRC Press, Boca Raton, FL.

Skinner, M.

1987 Planning the archeological recovery of evidence from recent mass graves, *Forensic Sciences International* 34:267–287.

Stover, E. and G. Peress

1998 *The Graves: Srebrenica and Vukovar,* Scalo, New York.

United Nations

  1997   Manual on the Effective Prevention and Investigation of Extra-Legal, Arbitrary and Summary Executions, United Nations, New York.

U.N.T.S.

  1951   Convention on the Prevention and Punishment of the Crime of Genocide, Vol. 78, No. 1021, United Nations, New York.

Postburial Disturbance of Graves in Bosnia-Herzegovina

15

MARK F. SKINNER
HEATHER P. YORK
MELISSA A. CONNOR

Contents

0-8493-1189-6/02/$0.00+$1.50
© 2002 by CRC Press LLC

Introduction*

Much forensic taphonomic analysis is undertaken to elucidate the decay of evidence. In the case of clandestine removal of bodies from mass graves** the taphonomic data *are* the evidence (cf. Holland et al., 1997). Recent investigations undertaken by Physicians for Human Rights (PHR)*** and International Criminal Tribunal for the Former Yugoslavia (ICTY) suggest strongly that in the aftermath of hostilities in the former Yugoslavia, several mass graves were emptied and the remains disposed elsewhere. For example, on November 4, 1996, *Newsweek* quoted Dr. R. Kirschner, Director, International Forensic Program, PHR, as observing about the Lazete Site: "We have several bags of extra limbs and other body parts [which] indicates there has been tampering" (Sullivan, 1996). Similarly, a UN team found only 146 bodies along with miscellaneous unmatched limbs and appendages at the site of Pilica where up to 1200 Muslims died on July 6, 1995, according to Drazen Erdemovic, a confessed Serb executioner testifying at the Hague. Significantly, satellite photographs taken 3 months after interment showed heavy equipment returned to the site (Stover and Peress 1998). By contrast there was no evidence of tampering at the site of Nova Kosaba which yielded only 33 bodies when more than 600 were expected (Sullivan, 1996).

This report describes four additional sites in Bosnia-Herzegovina where tampering is suspected and compares them with other monitored sites in which prior, proper removal of bodies took place.

Background

Christian unity was sundered in 1054 AD by a schism between Rome and Constantinople. Historical interactions between the Catholic West and Orthodox Christian East have centered on the Balkans. Turkish occupation commencing in the 14th century converted many of the area's Slavic inhabitants to Islam. Three ethnicities based on religious differences coexisted more or less successfully as colonial subjects at the boundary between the Austro-Hungarian and Ottoman empires (Kaplan, 1996). Serbian nationalism emerged in the early part of the 20th century, contributing to the conflict that resulted in the First World War. Out of this conflict arose the nation of Yugoslavia (southern Slavs) dominated by Serbs.

At the outbreak of hostilities in the Second World War, a Nazi-dominated faction of disaffected Catholic Croats called Ustashe participated in barbaric acts of genocide directed at Jews, Gypsies, and Partisan Serbs, termed Chetniks, who fought a long guerrilla war of resistance (Kinzer, 1996). Memories of this conflict, particularly the infamous mass grave

---

* The views expressed here are those of the authors and should not be construed to reflect those of Physicians for Human Rights.
** This chapter is not concerned with the precise definition of a mass grave. Functionally, one may distinguish between single graves, group graves in which bodies are laid out in parallel, and mass graves in which bodies are disordered. All three site types were monitored in Bosnia-Herzegovina.
*** Physicians for Human Rights (PHR) is an organization of health professionals, scientists, and concerned citizens that use the knowledge and skills of the medical and forensic sciences to investigate and prevent violations of international human rights and humanitarian law. One component of PHR Bosnia Projects is the Forensic Monitoring Project, which monitors the exhumation of human remains, dating from the 1992–1995 conflict in the former Yugoslavia, by members of the State Commissions within and between entities. PHR issues Findings Reports, which provide a neutral source of information about the contents of such graves and their manner of formation and exhumation.

Figure 15.1 Map of Bosnia-Herzegovina within the boundaries of the former Yugoslavia showing location of four sites where clandestine removal of bodies is inferred.

of Serb dead at the Jasenovac death camp smoldered through the peaceful decades of communist rule under Tito and fueled the outbreak of ethnic violence in 1992.

The main conflict in post-communist Yugoslavia developed between Serbians in the east led by Slobodan Milosevic and Croats in the west led by Franjo Tudjman (Cohen, 1993). Both areas contained significant enclaves of Orthodox, Catholic, and Islamic communities. According to the 1991 census, of some 4.35 million inhabitants from the Bosnia-Herzegovina area, 48.0% were Muslim, 33.6% Serb, and 12.7% Croat (Tokaca, 1996). The term Bosniak, meaning people from Bosnia, is increasingly accepted as an alternate for designating a Muslim from Bosnia.

Bosniaks fared worst during the 1992–1995 war because they lacked large weaponry and geographical access to supportive European and Warsaw Pact nations (Dydynski, 1997). With the imposition of peace created by the Dayton Agreement in November 1995, there were approximately 16,806 missing Bosniak Muslims, 2503 missing Bosnian Serbs, and 704 missing Bosnian Croats registered with the International Committee for the Red Cross* (figures released January 9, 1998). Most of them are believed to be in mass graves scattered throughout Bosnia-Herzegovina. The war in Bosnia ended officially in December 1996 with the Dayton Accord in Paris. Bosnia-Herzegovina currently comprises the Serb Republic entity, covering 49% of the territory, and a more or less cooperating political body called the Croat-Bosniak Federation comprising 51% (Cohen, 1998) (Figure 15.1). Hence, there are two states (Federation and Republic) encompassing Bosnia-Herzegovina and three functional entities (Croat, Bosniak, Serb).**

An ICTY team sponsored by Physicians for Human Rights exhumed the mass grave of Ovcara near the Croatian city of Vukovar in December, 1992, leading to the indictment of three members of the Yugoslav People's Army in November of 1995. Commencing in

* Government sources in Sarajevo put the number of missing persons at 25,000 (Tokaca, 1996).
** Inter-entity exhumations require monitoring while intra-entity exhumations do not.

late 1996, Physicians for Human Rights, supported by the Office of the High Representative and the Stabilization Force organized by NATO to preserve the peace created by the Dayton Accord, have monitored the efforts of the local entities to locate and excavate many mass graves. Initially, efforts in 1997 were restricted primarily to intra-entity exhumations resulting in the monitored exhumations of approximately 99 bodies from 5 sites. In late 1997, PHR monitored inter-entity exhumations at 2 sites containing approximately 94 bodies. Commencing in 1998, inter-entity activities resulted in the exhumation of 1653 bodies from 374 sites (PHR, 1999), the majority of these being Bosniaks recovered from the Serb Republic.

Historical Propaganda and Mass Graves

It is an extreme irony that political manipulation of the historical existence of mass graves results in another generation of such graves. Bax (1997) concludes from an investigation of memorials created in Bosnia-Herzegovina to commemorate mass graves from the Second World War that such memorials functioned ritually to preserve and engender animosity and thus help explain the local sources of renewed conflict.

> During the appalling Serb–Croat combat last year, it [Jasenovac Memorial] was occupied for a while by Croatian forces. They methodically trashed the museum and the exhibits, and left only the huge, ominous mounds that mark the mass graves. (Hitchens cited in Denich, 1994).

In a remarkably prescient article, conceived before the outbreak of hostilities in the former Yugoslavia, Denich (1991) reasons that rival exhumations of Second World War dead were publicized to advance extreme nationalist political agendas. In order to offset the victim status of Serbs created by Ustashe-led events at Jasenovac, Croats deliberately publicized the existence of mass executions perpetrated in the immediate aftermath of the Second World War by Communist-led Partisan troops.

The publication of these revelations led to the discovery of actual burial sites. In June, 1990, word reached the Zagreb media of a cave called Jazovka. Like the pigeon-caves of massacred Serbs, its existence had been known to nearby villagers, who now revealed the secret. The media in Croatia published pictures of the 40-m-deep cavern, piled with killing field relics. A Croatian emigrant publication described the cave as "full of bones of innocent Croat postwar victims of Communist savagery" (Denich, 1994:378).

The Serbian media in turn emphasized the repatriation of Serbian World War II genocide victims from Croatia and Bosnia-Herzegovina:

> the exhumation of their collective graves, recovery of bones, and reinterment in village cemeteries with Orthodox burial rites. Such ceremonies increased in scale. In 1991, caves in Bosnia-Herzegovina were exhumed, and mass public burials were shown over television throughout Serbia. At one of these ceremonies, Radio Belgrade described the line of coffins as extending for 1.5 km (Denich, 1994:382).

Political and ethnic conflicts persist in Bosnia-Herzegovina. Even within political entities, there is an essential tension between those who wish to forget the past and only look forward vs. those who seek to right historical wrongs through analysis of what happened.

The internationally monitored exhumation of mass graves is potentially destabilizing. In the wake of national media reports of exhumations, there are frequent allegations of manipulated coverage ranging from misreporting of age and sex of victims to site names. Nevertheless, it is generally accepted by the local entities and the international community that documentation of mass graves and their contents is necessary for a lasting peace. Exhumations lend themselves to propaganda. Hence, the international forensic community has a significant responsibility to treat this problem as both a sociopolitical and forensic science issue with historical roots.

Varieties of Postburial Disturbance

In addition to the obvious political use to which mass graves can be put, there are other less obvious ploys. For example, there is the oft-voiced suspicion expressed at monitored exhumations that the continued removal of bodies, single or massed, from known cemeteries is a form of ongoing ethnic cleansing. This act has been characterized as killing the dead — the ultimate form of ethnic cleansing (Bax, 1997).

> In the Bosnian countryside the deceased continue to be part of their kinship group. Via them, their progeny can lay claim to the use of land and water and to the produce of fruit and olive trees. It is not until all the traces of their lives have been wiped out that these claims cease to exist (Bax, 1997:17).

A war-time Muslim burial in an orchard near Carakovo-Zeger appeared, from grave architecture and the widow's account, to have been a formally conducted affair; nevertheless, it contained the partial remains of a pig inserted under the traditional sloped wooden plank cover within the grave which serves to protect a body from the grave fill; these anomalous inclusions could be construed as having been added as a form of religious insult (field observation by MFS, 1998). According to a Serb forensic pathologist, rubbish had been heaped on a mass grave at Carevo Polje (nr. Jajce) (Savic, 1998). The rubbish consisted of small pile of dirt and bricks on a small area of the mass grave (field observation by MFS, 1998).

Evidence is presented below to substantiate the conclusion that some gravesites in Bosnia-Herzegovina have experienced the clandestine removal of bodies prior to monitored exhumations. However, there are several other situations that include the prior removal of bodies; these have to be differentiated forensically from improper activities. Clearly, one defense to the charge of clandestine removal of bodies from a mass grave would be to allege prior undocumented exhumation, which would affect the evidentiary properties of forensic observations made at a mandated exhumation.

Body Trading during the War

This is commonly alleged in Bosnia-Herzegovina and is a familiar practice in war. The first 16 bodies recovered in 1998 at the Muslim graveyard site of Balinovac in West Mostar were each contained in two body bags, rather than one. These bodies are alleged by representatives of the State Commission to be exhumed Bosniaks, from an unnamed site, returned in 1993 by Serbs to the Croat entity, in an apparent three-way trade (Skinner, 1999).

Similarly, 70 bodies from undesignated sites in the Mostar area were handed over by the Croatian Council for Defense (HVO) to the Bosniaks on March 29, 1994 after the local cessation of hostilities (pers. comm. April 9, 1998, President, State Commission on Missing Persons). One of these bodies was buried at Sarica Podharem designated as NN61; at autopsy an accompanying note sealed in plastic attested to the date the body trade occurred (Skinner, 1999). Also, unmonitored body trading took place in the immediate aftermath of cessation of hostilities in November 1995 (Silber, 1996).

Mandated Exhumations with Reburial during the War

Nine small graves in the vicinity of the execution site of Pakracka Poljana, Croatia suspected to contain Serb bodies were excavated in November, 1993 by personnel from Physicians for Human Rights. The remains of 19 exhumed individuals were re-interred in body bags with formaldehyde preservative at an UNPROFOR observation post (Physicians for Human Rights, 1996) pending full forensic examination which took place in late 1995; the bodies were re-buried as originally (Haglund, pers. comm. April 28, 1999).

Body Relocations

On the north side of the formal cemetery site of Medine, near Mostar, were some 20 or so numbered wooden T-shaped grave tablets plus 12 or so tablets strewn about dating primarily from 1993 which are alleged to mark remains of Bosnian Croat individuals who were previously autopsied at the Clinical Hospital in Split, Croatia (Skinner, 1999). Where they were previously interred/stored and why they were transferred to Medine is not known.

Similarly, it is alleged by the President of the State Commission on Missing Persons that Bosniak civilians were used by HVO forces as a human shield to protect defense lines in battles over Makljen and Crni Vrh on July 31, 1993 (Tokaca, 1996).

Those who died were buried, but disinterred later, possibly in 1995, and jointly re-interred at Lapsunj Village after the signing of the Dayton Agreement (ONASA, September 25, 1998). Twenty-one bodies were removed in a monitored exhumation of this site September 23–24, 1998 (Connor, 1998c).

Members of a Serbian family abandoning Sarajevo at the end of hostilities privately removed the body of a family member who died during the war (*New York Times*, February 16, 1996). This scene was probably repeated many times over throughout Bosnia-Herzegovina as families permanently relocated.

Unmonitored Intra-Entity Exhumations

The site of Miljkovici, south of Mostar, was alleged to have been excavated by unspecified persons 7 to 8 months prior to a monitored exhumation by the State Commission (Bosniak side) in April 1998 (pers. comm. to MFS, August 4, 1998, Police Representative, Federal Commission on Missing Persons). This site is mentioned as the burial place of individuals from the Heliodrome Concentration Camp (run by the HVO) who were allegedly taken out for forced labor and to act as human shields (Tokaca, 1996). The monitored exhumation yielded partial remains of two individuals plus four identity cards (Skinner, 1999).

Unmonitored Inter-Entity Exhumation

Allegedly, on August 4, 1997, 16 Serb bodies (civilians and soldiers) were exhumed at the cemetery site of Caprazlije by Bosnian Croat diggers in the presence of a Serb Republic crime technician; monitored exhumations of 36 remaining bodies occurred at this site in 1998 (Connor et al., 1998). Similarly, at the nearby site of Donja Rujani beside an Orthodox church, 82 bodies of soldiers were allegedly removed prior to monitored exhumations of the same ground in 1998 that yielded only fragments of clothing (Connor and York, 1998).

Removal of Grave fill with Continued Interment in Same Grave

This unusual situation observed in a Croatian cemetery developed during the war on the west side of a Catholic Seminary at Humac near Prozor. There are several east–west oriented rows of single, marked graves arrayed among a plum tree orchard. These bodies were buried in 1993 by the Army without family members present and without formal rites. The Humac priest stated that there had been a problem with vandalism of temporary grave markers in 1993, 1994, and 1997. There were numerous family members present at the exhumation on August 4, 1998. Some of them volunteered the information that they had previously opened particular graves to view the remains and confirm identification to their satisfaction. Several stated that they had placed objects in the graves to ensure proper identification in the future. Excavation revealed that Grave 5 contained a shallowly buried metal washbasin that an attending family member stated she had placed in the grave to mark it with certainty. Similarly, jars and plastic bags containing names written on pieces of paper were discovered at shallow depths in Graves 14, 18, and 19. Surgical gloves were observed in the grave fill from Graves 11, 12, 13, 14, 17, and 18. These observations are consistent with claims that these graves had been previously opened for examination of the remains (Skinner, 1998a).

Case Studies of Sites in Bosnia-Herzegovina Where Clandestine Removal of Bodies Is Inferred

Tasovcici

Tasovcici is located 2 km east of Capljina, Bosnia-Herzegovina. The site is on a hill called Modric, the location of a damaged memorial cemetery for Second World War Partisan soldiers (Figure 15.2). The State Commission on Missing Persons (Bosniak) investigated the site from April 24–27, 1998. Exhumations were monitored by Physicians for Human Rights.

Exposure of the bodies was accomplished by backhoe supplemented by shovels. Trowel work was undertaken by autopsy assistants supported by the pathologists and various members of the State Commission. Excavation revealed an unmarked, mass grave of 30 bodies arranged in 2 discontinuous east–west rows (Figure 15.3); bones on the surface represented 2 individuals (Skinner, 1998b). About 75% of the bodies were in body bags; the remainder were lying on remnants of canvas sheets. Of the entire series, most were clothed and, judging from the clothing, civilian. There were 12 males and 11 females, the remainder indeterminate. Virtually all individuals were skeletonized. Skeletally and dentally, the adults were relatively elderly with an average age of 66 years. Two of the Tasovcici

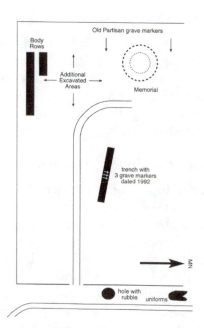

Figure 15.2 Sketch map of Tasovcici site.

remains were children who came from a cluster burial of several related women and children. The forensic pathologists determined that 20 of 22 sets of fairly complete remains showed hard tissue trauma. Nine individuals had experienced two or more wounding events. Most traumata were confined to the head and trunk; arms and legs were little affected. In nine instances, there was unequivocal evidence of gunshot wounds in the form of bullet holes or actual bullets. Deaths are said to have occurred in 1993. The total number of identifications obtained at Tasovcici was not stated.

Observations at the Site

Although, 30 bodies were exhumed, 9 were incomplete (TAS 6, 7, 8, 9, 12, 17, 19, 20, 30); also, there were obvious gaps in the rows of bodies. This is shown in Figure 15.3. There is a clear pattern in which bodies adjacent to gaps in the body row were damaged and incomplete. Five incomplete bodies bordered on four gaps in the southerly row of bodies. Also, at the west end of the southerly row and the east end of the northerly row, the bodies were incomplete suggesting prior removal of bodies in these areas, both of which were excavated in their entirety by the team.

The average distance between adjacent bodies was 0.75 m; thus the estimated number of missing bodies in the measured gaps is as follows: between TAS 5 and 6 — 1; between TAS 8 and 9 — 5; between TAS 11 and 12 — 4; between TAS 17 and 18 — 2; to east of TAS 30 at end of row — minimum of 1. In total, a minimum of 13 bodies may have been previously removed from this site. In other words, there is evidence of at least 43 bodies having been present at the Tasovcici site, which is still considerably less than the figure of 80 bodies alleged by the State Commission's investigators to have existed.

There is other evidence consistent with the allegation that prior removal of bodies has occurred at this site:

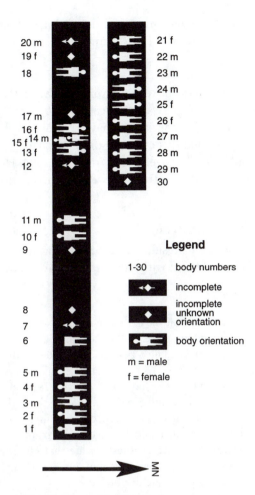

Figure 15.3 Distribution of bodies from Tasovcici site.

- During the grass removal, a number of pieces of clothing were encountered including a pair of running shoes, one of which had foot bones in it. These items were not found associated with other remains.
- Two fused neck vertebrae were found on the surface.
- Several rubber gloves were found on or close to the surface.
- A military document bearing an individual's name was found in the grave fill. It is not known whether this came from one of the identified individuals.
- In the gap between bodies 5 and 6 there were remnants of another body bag.
- At the west side of body 21, there was a shallowly buried blanket like those found wrapped around bodies at many other sites.
- In the dirt above bodies 21 and 22 (that is, at the west end of the row), two pieces of crumpled sheet metal from a coffin were encountered by the backhoe. One of the sheet metal pieces had remnants of a glass viewing window. These metal sheets can be accounted for in two ways: either they were used separately to carry bodies or they represent the remnants of a coffin from a disinterred body to the west of 21.

- Fragments of coffin wood with impressed design, unassociated with any observed body, were found in the excavated earth immediately west of the northerly row of bodies.

The observations summarized above are strong evidence that a prior exhumation occurred at this site. However, body parts can be scattered at the time of burial if the bodies are badly decomposing. Similarly, secondary burial may leave clothing and body parts on the surface. Also, it could be argued that evidence on or close to the surface (foot and neck bones, rubber gloves) could simply have been surface remains. However, it was possible to show at autopsy that the buried shoe from TAS 26 matched a shoe found on the surface (Skinner, 1999).

Prior Site Disturbance at Tasovcici

Before the start of exhumation, the President of the State Commission stated that 80 bodies were to be expected. This is consistent with the description of this site provided by Tokaca (1996:153):

> Already in June 1993, information on the existence of mass grave on the Modric hill near Tasovcici was known. That was the place of the Partisan Cemetery where from July 15, 1993, in evening hours, the bodies of killed persons were taken to the place in trucks (this is according to the witness statements). As the action of ethnic cleansing was in process in the region of this municipality between July 13/14 and 15, 1993, and the torture against population of the village in Dubrave and Stolac also was performed, and having in mind many cases of murders and taking of persons from Capljina concentration camps in unknown directions, the conclusion could be made that many persons from the area finished in that mass grave. Namely, eyewitnesses state that 60 corpses were driven on trucks on July 15, 1993 and that two days after that, on July 17 and 18, 1993, the mass grave was excavated with a dredging machine and the corpses were thrown in. The mass grave was not covered and that meant new corpses would be taken in. That was true and it lasted for another 20 days.

However, one wonders whether the full complement of 80 bodies was truly to be expected since a newspaper account dated March 28, 1996 claimed prior removal of 26 bodies:

> *Disputed delivery of victim's bodies from Modric Pit.*
> *IFOR blocks death site*
>
> After the recent delivery of 26 disputed bodies of Bosniaks from the Capljina and Stolac area removed from the Modric pit by the HVO entity, of which 15 are already identified and re-buried, it seems that disentanglement of this tragic story is in sight. Namely, after simultaneous public condemnation by several specific institutions of the delivery of these bodies without proper legal representatives plus information supplied by forensic pathology experts that remnant soil from four different, successive burial sites was found on the bodies, there is an unconfirmed report that IFOR used its strong influence to close the Modric burial pit for Bosniaks, located near Capljina beside the coast road to Stolac. After this demonstration of power by IFOR, chances are increased that international and legal institutions of Bosnia-Herzegovina will go to the site.
>
> With reference to the unidentified bodies from the above-mentioned delivery, these will be buried as NN assuming the approval of representatives of the State Commission

for Missing and Tracing Persons including the involvement of Mr. Amor Masovic. We should remember that there are 44 reported missing persons from the Capljina commune and 32 from Stolac. (G. Smajic, 1996)

In addition, part way through the monitored exhumation commencing on April 24, 1998 the Forensic Monitor was shown a video by the President of the State Commission alleged to have been taken in April 1997 at the Tasovcici site showing it recently dug over with bare earth, rocks and surgical gloves on the earth. He alleged that 26 bodies had already been removed from this site, taken to the Mostar Bridge in November 1996 and given without explanation to the Bosniaks. He insisted that there were still some 24 bodies missing and that these were improperly removed either prior to November 1996 or later in April 1997 as attested by the alleged date of the video.

Clearly, these are complex matters.* Nevertheless, it can be concluded that there is obvious postburial disturbance at this site.

Vojno

This area included a prison organized by HVO members at which numerous deaths are alleged to have occurred in the fall of 1993 with the victims being buried in nearby fields (Tokaca, 1996). A witness led the President of the State Commission to this site, claiming that several Bosniaks had been buried there and that at least some of the bodies had been subsequently removed (York, 1998).

The site is on a raised plateau, northwest of the highway that parallels the Neretva River. The exhumation team processed this site on May 21, 1998. After the laborers cleared thick, uniform vegetation from an area of approximately 25 × 8 m, 8 depressions of about 60 cm in depth became evident (Figure 15.4). There were approximately 40 cm between adjacent depressions. No surface remains were visible.

A backhoe was brought in to determine whether there were any graves outside of the area of the visible depressions. Finding nothing, the decision was made to use the backhoe to break up the soil in each of the depressions to search for remains.

Prior Site Disturbance at Vojno

The first depression (Figure 15.4A) yielded a large piece of blanket with a sheet of plastic beneath it. Some pieces of soft tissue were stuck to one side of the plastic. One laborer shoveled into the bottom of the depression while others sifted through the backdirt by

---

* Conceivably, these 26 bodies, given to the Bosniaks, were re-interred at Miljkovici, since, as noted, at the latter site there were 26 discarded blank T-shaped markers.

It is known that at the Miljkovici Site, which yielded no intact bodies, a Red Cross document was exhumed in 1998 bearing the name of an individual (A...C...) registered on March 18, 1993 (Skinner, 1999). Interestingly, an individual, with the same surname (C...) and purportedly part of a body exchange, was disinterred from Sarica Podharem (NN96) on May 6 or 7, 1998 in an unmonitored exhumation and autopsied that same day; significantly perhaps, as part of the Tasovcici series (field observation by MFS, 1998). He had some broken bones. Furthermore, a body known as Balinovac 104 exhumed on May 5, 1998 had the same surname but different first name (D...C...). At autopsy the next day it was determined that he had been shot in the head.

Two individuals (brothers) with the same names as noted above (A...C... and D...C...) were allegedly taken from the town of Capljina in early July 1993 to Rastanje Hill, used as a human shield and killed and buried in an unspecified mass grave, possibly the Tasovcici site (Tokaca, 1996). Thus, there may be a link between the missing bodies at Tasovcici and those removed from Miljkovici.

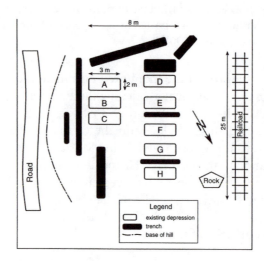

Figure 15.4 Distribution of pit features at Vojno.

hand and trowel, but no other remains were found. Shoveling in the depression to the west (Figure 15.4D) revealed a right mandibular ramus and an open and empty silver-colored body bag. A backhoe trench through the northeasternmost depression (Figure 15.4E) yielded a piece of clear plastic and an orange and white print blanket. A backhoe trench through a depression in the northwest corner of the site (Figure 15.4G) revealed a silver body bag but no human remains. Another trench through the adjacent depression at the northwestern limit of the plateau (Figure 15.4H) exposed another torn piece of a body bag. A small trench dug between these two depressions yielded one torn, short white sock.

Other backhoe trenches approximately 50 cm wide and 60 cm deep were dug around the perimeter and between some of the adjacent depressions (Figure 15.4, shaded areas), but no further remains or body bags were found. Behind a rock approximately 15 m to the west northwest and upslope of the depressions, crime technicians found a pair of military pants with cigarettes in the pocket, and a camouflage vest with a knife sheath and holster in another pocket.

Bijelo Polje

This site is located a few kilometers north of Mostar between the Neretva River and the highway to Sarajevo. The area to the north had been mined and unexploded ordinance was found throughout the site area (Connor, 1998b). The State Commission conducted monitored exhumations at this site on June 15, 1998. The site is in the vineyard and orchard of a destroyed house. Large areas of the site were trenched; however, evidence was recovered only from an obvious pit feature in the de-mined path.

Prior Site Disturbance at Bijelo Polje

The laborers found two hand bones and a bullet. A blanket was present at the bottom of the depression. The laborers unfolded the blanket and found two buttons stuck to the inside. One was a four-hole shirt button and the second a loop-back jacket button. The remains and evidence found were consistent with one set of remains previously removed from this location (Connor, 1998a).

Zaklopaca

The State Commission on Missing Persons conducted exhumations on June 22–24, 1998 at Zaklopaca, east of Vlasenica in the Srebrenica region. The grave was said to be that of the Bosniak residents of the village killed in their homes in 1992 and brought to the grave area on tractors. A witness said the grave was dug with a mechanical excavator and was so deep that only the scoop of the backhoe, rising out of the ground, could be seen from the informant's vantage point. The witness said the bodies of children were placed in the grave first, those of women and young boys next, and the adult males last. There were said to be 58 people of known identity in the grave. Attempts to locate the grave began around a pile of earth about 50 m long, 2 m wide, and less than 1 m high. The exhumations continued for 3 days with a small, and then much larger, backhoe (Connor, 1998a).

Prior Site Disturbance at Zaklopaca

Near the initial trench, a sock containing foot bones, ankle bones, and some cloth were found. The digging unearthed a tire rim; a portion of a child's cranium was found in the rim. Hair and clothing were also collected from the backdirt. Digging with the backhoe was stopped when a shoe, an adult cranial fragment, and several hand bones were seen in the profile of the trench. The deepest human material was about 2 m below the original ground surface. The shoe was bent back on itself. The partial remains found were isolated and no additional materials were found adjacent to them. The Forensic Monitor calculated that the area of disturbed soil was roughly 20 m in diameter.

It was concluded that there had been two episodes of soil disturbance; first, the actual digging of the grave, and second, the soil disturbance reflecting the digging to remove the bodies that resulted in the partial remains scattered in the disturbed soil.

Discussion

At two sites (Tasovcici and Vojno) informants stated that bodies had been taken away. Monitored exhumations suggest that a minimum of 13 individuals had been removed from Tasovcici and 8 from Vojno. It is not clear how many had been removed from the other two sites.

There is a variety of surface, grave fill, and buried evidence indicative, in these instances, of site disturbance. At all four sites incomplete remains represented by flesh and/or bone remnants were observed. Clothing fragments were observed at all four sites. Empty body containers, in the form of blankets, plastic, wood, and body bag fragments were observed at three sites (excluding Zaklopaca). Various artifacts supported the prior presence of human remains (bullet, plastic gloves, military document in grave fill). In one instance (Tasovcici) an association between surface and buried evidence could be shown. At two sites (Tasovcici and Vojno) military clothing was observed to one side of the site. At two of the sites (Vojno and Bijelo Polje) surface depressions containing partial human remains were observed. At one site (Tasovcici) spatial anomalies in the form of gaps in the row of bodies were observed. Also, at this site there was a clear association between gaps and damage to bodies on either side of the gap suggestive of crude body removal techniques. At Vojno, the digging appeared to have been selective and circumscribed; that is, there were no random trenches or holes and all holes were grave sized and no larger.

Conclusion

The women of Srebrenica seek to understand the whereabouts of their husbands and sons who disappeared in 1995; thousands disappeared — they ask, "Where are their graves?" (Stover and Peress, 1998). As we have seen, there are many reasons why bodies are removed from mass graves prior to monitored exhumations. Only one of these may be clandestine. The others include body trading, mandated wartime exhumations, post-war body removals and transport, and unmonitored post-war exhumations within and between geopolitical entities. Distinguishing among these will be difficult unless steps are taken to obtain the following:

- Informant accounts (full disclosure by various state commissions)
- Site topography, including artifact distribution, prior to excavation
- Mapping of all features
- Careful attention to stratigraphy especially grave cuts
- Screening or at least examination of grave fill

In order to remove bodies from a grave a hole has to be dug, usually with a backhoe. Consequently, it may be that apart from informants' accounts, the only way to differentiate between secret and public exhumation is the relative care given the exhumation. It is the careful integration of statements from local eyewitnesses and taphonomic experts which provides sufficient evidence to determine that a clandestine exhumation has occurred. In our opinion, it is essential that potentially disturbed site topography be recorded by neutral personnel with expertise in the processes of site formation.

While it is important to substantiate clandestine exhumations intended to hide evidence of war crimes, it is equally essential to keep in mind that mass graves can be used for a variety of political ends by competing entities. Both parties have vested interests, depending on site history, in the accurate determination of why bodies have been previously removed from a site. Most important for international organizations involved in the monitoring of exhumations is a means of keeping track of sites exhumed in the past including unmonitored, monitored, and what are ultimately determined to have been clandestine exhumations. Where clandestine removal of bodies and other evidence from mass graves is substantiated, it should be viewed as a serious breach of international humanitarian law as is inhuman treatment of protected persons (Physicians for Human Rights, 1996).

Mass graves are more than repositories of the dead. Unexcavated, they can function as political tools to intimidate survivors; scientifically excavated they are threats to the perpetrators. Clandestine efforts to remove the bodies inevitably leave taphonomic clues behind for forensic archaeologists and anthropologists to discover and interpret.

Acknowledgments

We thank the following organizations and key personnel for their support: PHR Boston (Len Rubenstein); PHR Bosnia Projects (Laurie Vollen, Brenda Kennedy); Office of the

High Representative (Agneta Johansson); International Commission on Missing Persons (Laura Bowman); State Commission on Missing Persons Bosniak Side (Amor Masovic); Federal Commission on Missing Persons Croat Side (Jerko Radic); and Republika Srpska State Commission on Missing Persons (Berislav Pusic and Jovo Rosic).

The authors also wish to thank particular individuals for their professional and personal kindnesses during our work in Bosnia-Herzegovina: Sime Andelinovic, Mujo Azic, Berislav Cvitanovic, Marija Definis-Gojanovic, Ilias Dobraca, Kemal Dragonovic, Doug Ford, Saudin Hrnjic, Page Hudson, Zeljko Karon, Roy Lausecker, Halil Maksumic, Huso Mehrimic, Muhamed Mujkic, Adnan Music, Jerko Radic, Adnan Rizvic, Elvira Tarhovic, Miroslav Tomic, Ismet Trebinjac, Werner Zofal, Gordana Zovko, and Hamza Zujo.

References

Bax, M.
1997   Mass graves, stagnating identification, and violence: a case study in the local sources of "The War" in Bosnia Herzegovina. *Anthropological Quarterly* 70(1):11–19.

Cohen, L.J.
1993.   *Broken Bonds. The Disintegration of Yugoslavia*, Westview Press, Boulder, CO.

1998   Whose Bosnia? The politics of nation building, *Current History* 97(617):103–112.

Connor, M.A.
1998a Forensic Monitoring Project Findings Report, Physicians for Human Rights, Exhumation Conducted by State Commission on Missing Persons at Zaklopaca, Bosnia I Herzegovina, June 22–24, 1998, Report Date: July, 1998.

1998b Forensic Monitoring Project Findings Report, Physicians for Human Rights, Exhumation Conducted by State Commission on Missing Persons at Bijelo Polje, Bosnia I Herzegovina, June 15, 1998, Report Date: August, 1998.

1998c Forensic Monitoring Project Findings Report, Physicians for Human Rights, Exhumation Conducted by State Commission on Missing Persons at Lapsunj, Bosnia I Herzegovina, September 23–24, 1998, Report Date: November, 1998.

Connor, M.A. and H.P. York
1998   Forensic Monitoring Project Findings Report, Physicians for Human Rights, Exhumation Conducted by Republika Srpska State Commission on Missing Persons at Donja Rujani, Bosnia I Herzegovina, June 11, 1998, Report Date: November, 1998.

Connor, M.A., H.P. York, and M. Skinner
1998   Forensic Monitoring Project Findings Report, Physicians for Human Rights, Exhumation Conducted by Republika Srpska State Commission on Missing Persons at Caprazlije Cemetery and Provo Surface Collection, Bosnia I Herzegovina, June 11, 1998, Report Date: November, 1998.

Denich, B.
1991   Unbury the victims: rival exhumations and nationalist revivals in Yugoslavia. Paper for the American Anthropological Association Annual Meeting, Chicago.

1994   Dismembering Yugoslavia: nationalist ideologies and the symbolic revival of genocide, *American Ethnologist* 21:367–390.

Dydynski, K.
1997   *Eastern Europe*, 4th ed., Lonely Planet Publications, Oakland, CA.

Holland, T.D., B.E. Anderson, and R.W. Mann
   1997   Human variables in the postmortem alteration of human bone: examples from U.S. war casualties. In *Forensic Taphonomy: The Postmortem Fate of Human Remains*, edited by W.D. Haglund and M.H. Sorg, pp. 263–274. CRC Press, Boca Raton, FL.

Kaplan, R.D.
   1996   *Balkan Ghosts*, Random House, New York.

Kinzer, S.
   1996   *When did the war begin? Atlas of War and Peace*, Macmillan, New York.

New York Times
   1996   Photo Agence France Presse, February 16, 1996.

Physicians for Human Rights
   1996   *War Crimes in the Balkans. Medicine under Siege in the Former Yugoslavia 1991–1995*. Boston.

   1999   Forensic Monitoring Project 1998 Joint Exhumation Process. Summary, March 23, 1999, PHR Bosnia Projects, Tuzla, Bosnia-Herzegovina.

Savic, V.
   1998   Their crosses were touching, *Reporter* May 21, 1998.

Silber, L.
   1996   Reconciliation means finding where the bodies lie, *The Financial Times*, October 14.

Skinner, M.F.
   1998a Forensic Monitoring Project Findings Report, Physicians for Human Rights, Bugojno Area Exhumations (Vucipolje, Rosulje, Causlije, Sultanovici, Humac), of Federal Commission on Missing Persons Croat Side, August 3–4, 1998, Report Date: November, 1998.

   1998b Forensic Monitoring Project Findings Report, Physicians for Human Rights, Capljina Area Exhumations (Tasovcici and Kapica) of State Commission on Missing Persons Bosniak Side, April 24–27, 1998, Report Date: November, 1998.

   1999   Forensic Monitoring Project Findings Report, Physicians for Human Rights, Mostar Area Exhumations (Balinovac, Bijeli Brijeg, Bijelo Polje, Blagajtusa, Donja Jasenica, Liska Park, Medine, Miljkovici, Podhum Mosque, Sarica Harem, Sipad, Soinovac, Zahum-Pijesak) of State Commission on Missing Persons, Bosniak Side, March 16–May 18, 1998, Draft Report Date: February 1999.

Smajic, G
   1996   IFOR blokirao stratiste. Newspaper report March 28, 1996.

Stover, E. and G. Peress
   1998   *The Graves. Srebrenica and Vukovar*, Scalo, Zurich.

Sullivan, S.
   1996   Genocide without corpses, *Newsweek* Nov. 4, p. 37.

Tokaca, M.
   1996   Missing Persons — Analysis of Causes and Circumstances in Territory of Bosnia and Herzegovina April 1992–December 1995, State Commission for Gathering Facts on War Crimes, Presidency Bosnia and Herzegovina, Sarajevo.

York, H.P.
   1998   Forensic Monitoring Project Findings Report, Physicians for Human Rights, Capljina Area Exhumations (Rastani and Vojno) of State Commission on Missing Persons, Bosniak Side, May 21–22, 1998, Report date: September, 1999.

Cannibalism or Violent Death Alone? Human Remains at a Small Anasazi Site

16

SALLY GRAVER
KRISTIN D. SOBOLIK
JOHN WHITTAKER

Contents

Introduction

It has been proposed that cannibalism was practiced by prehistoric populations in the southwestern United States for about 4 centuries, beginning around AD 900 (Turner and Turner, 1999). Evidence for cannibalism has centered along the Little Colorado River and in the Four Corners region at the Anasazi sites during the Pueblo III phase, approximately AD 1075 to 1300, although evidence for cannibalism is also claimed at a small number of sites dated earlier in time and located outside this region (Billman et al., 2000; Fagan, 1995; Turner and Turner, 1999; White, 1992). Although the existence of Anasazi cannibalism in the Southwest is widely accepted by many archaeologists (Billman et al., 2000; Preston, 1998; White, 1992), the issue is still highly controversial (Arens, 1979; Darling, 1999; Dongoske et al., 2000).

The human assemblage at the Grinnell Site, a small Anasazi ceremonial center dated to the late Pueblo II and early Pueblo III time periods (Luebben, 1983), has been considered by other researchers as evidence of cannibalized remains (Billman et al., 2000; LeBlanc, 2000; Turner and Turner, 1999; White, 1992). Although the human remains have been described previously (Luebben and Nickens, 1982), they have not been analyzed for many of the traits currently used to characterize cannibalized assemblages. This chapter reports results of a comprehensive reanalysis of the Grinnell Site human remains to assess the validity of claims made about the evidence of prehistoric cannibalism at the site, using criteria for recognizing cannibalism developed by Turner (1983) and Turner and Turner (1999).

The Grinnell Site

The Grinnell Site is situated 1.66 km southwest of Yucca House National Monument in southwestern Colorado (Figure 16.1). Structures there included a low ceremonial mound with steps and a ramp that overlays a small trapezoidal structure, a Mesa Verde type kiva (Kiva 1), an elaborate tunnel complex which linked Kiva 1 to a completely subterranean room and a circular tower, and a larger and older Mancos type kiva (Kiva 2) that underlay the eastern end of the passages and part of the tower (Figure 16.2). The mound was flanked along its north side by a masonry retaining wall that held back alluvium. Kiva 1 had burned completely and contained a large number of artifacts indicating habitation use of the kiva. Tree-ring dates obtained from Kiva 1 indicated that the timber was cut in 1244 A.D. No other living accommodation existed at the site.

In contrast, Kiva 2 contained few artifacts but yielded a mass burial. Bones of eight individuals were deposited in Cist 2, situated on the southern recess of Kiva 2. Some bones were in a corrugated pot that sat on top of and was surrounded by other bones. Outside the cist, additional bones were found on the recess surface adjacent to the cist and on the kiva floor between the kiva wall and deflector (Figure 16.2). The latter may have been dropped accidentally when bones were brought into the kiva and deposited in the cist. The human remains pre-date 1244 A.D., the date of an overlying Kiva 1 timber.

While the report by Luebben and Nickens (1982) claimed the mass burial provided evidence of brutality, it stopped short of suggesting cannibalism. In an earlier unpublished paper, however, Nickens (1979) concluded that the data indicated cannibalism. For the current authors, the nagging question persists. Had the individuals whose remains were found in the mass burial been both traumatized and cannibalized? To find a more definitive answer, the osteological assemblage from Kiva 2 was reexamined.

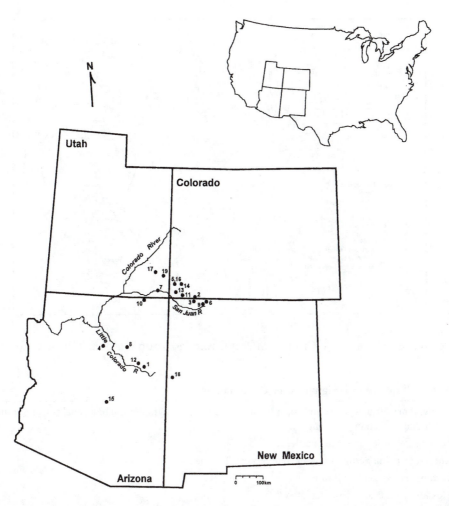

Figure 16.1 Location of the Grinnell Site (13) and other southwestern sites considered to provide evidence of cannibalism. 1 = Canyon Butte Ruin 3; 2 = La Plata 23; 3 = La Plata 41; 4 = Big Hawk Valley NA-682; 5 = Yellow Jacket Porter Pueblo 5MT-1; 6 = Sambrito Village LA-4195; 7 = Bluff; 8 = Polacca Wash NA-8502; 9 = Burnt Mesa LA-4528; 10 = Monument Valley; 11 = Mancos 5MTUMR-2346; 12 = Leroux Wash NA-12854; 13 = The Grinnell Site; 14 = Marshview Hamlet 5MT-2235; 15 = Ash Creek AZ:U:3:49; 16 = Yellow Jacket 5MT-3; 17 = Cottonwood Canyon; 18 = Fence Lake Area; and 19 = Verdure Canyon. (Modified from White, T.D., *Prehistoric Cannibalism at Mancos 5MTUMR-2346*, Princeton University Press, Princeton, 1992, p. 37. With permission.)

Methods

The criteria for cannibalism developed by Turner and Turner (1999) were applied to our data (Table 16.1). The first step of the reanalysis was to prepare an inventory to compare with that of Luebben and Nickens (1982) (Table 16.2). Initially, the bones were counted and recorded by element to determine a minimum number of individuals (MNI), and age and sex were evaluated where possible from skull, teeth, innominates, bone size, and epiphyseal fusion (Bass, 1987; Buikstra and Ubelaker, 1994).

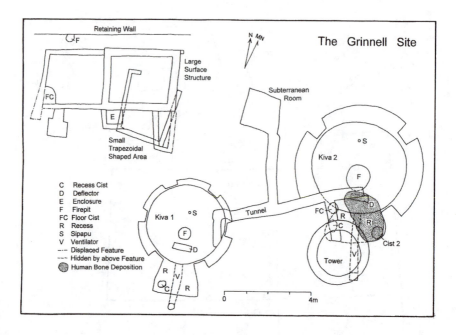

Figure 16.2 Site plan of the Grinnell Site, illustrating location of human bone deposition.

Table 16.1   Taphonomic Signature of Cannibalism

1. **Single, short-term depositional episode** (discerned from stratigraphy and bone quality), preventing bone weathering and animal scavenging.
2. **Bone preservation good to excellent.**
3. **Animal gnawing** occurs on fewer than 5% of all elements.
4. **Vertebrae** are usually **missing**.[a]
5. Most body parts are "**disarticulated**."[b]
6. **Perimortem breakage** occurs in 40 to 100% of skeletal elements.
7. Head, face, and long bone **breakage is universal**.[a]
8. Total bone **fragment counts** range between 400 and 3500 elements in a given episode. Body reconstruction is difficult due to a high rate of unaccounted for bone loss.
9. **Breakage** is by **percussion hammering** against some form of **anvil**, with **spiral and compression fracturing** very common.[a]
10. **Burning** after butchering and breaking is present in 2 to 35% of all elements.[a]
11. Butchering and skinning **cut marks** occur on 1 to 5% of bone elements, usually in appropriate locations for muscle tissue or scalp removal.[a]
12. Taphonomic **sequence** includes: (a) cutting; (b) breaking, and (c) burning (or, if evident, gnawing).
13. Pseudo-tools or **accidentals** made of human bone may occur in the frequency range of 1 per 10,000+ pieces.
14. The **frequency of alteration** in cannibalized bone lots is 95% for perimortem breakage, 20% for burning, 3% for cut marks, and 2% for possible gnawing or chewing.
15. Evidence of **pot polish** — the smooth polish that appears on the ends of bone that were cooked in prehistoric vessels — should be present.[a]

---

[a] Denotes Turner's six key, minimal taphonomic features of cannibalism.
[b] Term used by Turner to refer to bones out of anatomical order.

Source: Modified from Turner, C.G., II, in *Carnivores, Human Scavengers, and Human Predators: A Question of Bone Technology,* edited by G.M. LeMoine and A.S. MacEachern, 1983, pp. 233–244. With permission.

Table 16.2   Human Skeletal Fragmentation at the Grinnell Site

Element	Whole	Fragments
Frontal		8
Temporal		8
Parietal		3
Occipital	1	3
Maxilla	2	10
Zygoma		6
Mandible	4	
Tooth	29	
Unclassified vault fragment		136
Unclassified facial fragment		34
Vertebra	4	9
Clavicle	1	
Scapula		2
Humerus		
Radius		4
Ulna		4
Rib		2
Pelvis		1
Femur		7
Tibia		4
Fibula		2
Metacarpal		
Phalange	11	
Navicular	1	
Unclassified long bone fragment		68
Unknown		10
Total	374	

Next, each bone was thoroughly examined with a 10-power hand lens for human or animal modification and for antemortem, perimortem, and postmortem alteration using the taphonomic criteria listed in Table 16.1.

Results and Discussion

Most evidence for Anasazi cannibalism correlates with periods of environmental stress, the result of a severe drought that started in the area at about AD 1145 and continued to the end of the 12th century. During the Pueblo III phase, these environmental problems may have led to widespread agricultural failure and famine. Tree-ring records show severe drought co-occurring with depopulation of Chaco Canyon from AD 1145 to 1193 (Billman et al., 2000). A number of Anasazi sites, including Chaco Canyon and the Cowboy Wash areas, were abandoned. Some archaeologists propose that the resulting competition for resources may have triggered violence and cannibalism among the Anasazi (Billman et al., 2000; White, 1992).

The existence of cannibalism in the Southwest has been argued by a number of scholars for decades. The earliest published claim for cannibalism was made in 1902 by Hough, an anthropologist from the Smithsonian Institution. Hough based his conclusion on an assemblage of burnt and broken human bones that were uncovered at a small pueblo in northeastern Arizona, Canyon Butte 3 (Turner and Turner, 1999). However, when Morris first presented her hypothesized findings of cannibalized remains at Polacca Wash at the 1969 meeting of the Society for American Archaeology in Santa Fe, her views were not accepted by many participants (Turner and Turner, 1999). Opposition to Anasazi violence and cannibalism in the Southwest was strong due to popularly held conceptions of peaceful puebloan Native Americans. The controversy surrounding cannibalism still exists today (Dongoske et al., 2000).

While we believe that White and the Turners have made a convincing argument for the presence of cannibalism in the Southwest, the evidence is not equally good in all of the instances proposed. In his report on prehistoric cannibalism at Mancos 5MTUMR-2346, White (1992:37) cited 19 other sites where cannibalism occurred in the Southwest (Figure 16.1). In a more recent publication (Turner and Turner, 1999:55), they identify evidence of cannibalism based on the remains of 286 individuals in 38 sites. However, Billman et al. (2000:169) propose that there are only 18 well-documented and dated sites that exhibit cannibalism. The strength of these claims of cannibalism in the Southwest rely on their shared taphonomic and osteological features, including abundant evidence that these human remains were processed like game animals prepared for consumption.

Cannibalized human remains show a number of defining characteristics. Turner (1983) published a list of 15 taphonomic traits that he believed typified cannibalism in south-western sites (Table 16.1). More recently, Turner and Turner (1999) have proposed that a minimum of six critical perimortem effects must be present. These taphonomic signatures include breakage, cut marks, anvil abrasions, burning, many missing vertebrae, and pot polishing (Table 16.1).

The mass inhumation at the Grinnell Site included 374 bone fragments (Table 16.2) and contained remains of at least eight individuals, including three pre-teen children, two subadults 16 to 21 years old, and three adults: one female aged 21–25, a male aged 21–25, and a female aged 26+. These results differ from Nickens' previous study (Luebben and Nickens, 1982) by six bones and one individual. Our age assessments also differed.

Depositional Pattern

The most obvious taphonomic indicator of cannibalism in the archaeological record is the presence of a non-considerate burial. Non-considerate burials, specifically those of canni-balized remains, consist of one or more individuals with evidence of trauma and disartic-ulation usually deposited in a nonstandard and presumably discourteous manner. Sometimes type of burial is difficult to determine because many Anasazi considerate burials are bodies disposed of in trash middens and on the floors of abandoned rooms. Considerate burials, however, usually contain one or more complete skeletons in correct anatomical position, and may be associated with grave goods.

At sites with evidence of cannibalism, the osteological record demonstrates an absence of animal scavenging or bone weathering, indicating rapid interment of the remains. Similarly, bone preservation at these sites, with few exceptions, is unusually good, despite fragmentation of many of the bones. Weathering and animal gnawing are minimal, occur-ring on fewer than 5% of the bones. Turner and Turner (1999) attribute excellent preser-vation to a single, short-term disposal episode. The above characteristics closely resemble both damage patterns and depositional characteristics of the remains of large and small game animals taken for food.

Another important taphonomic signature of cannibalism is the absence of vertebrae in bone assemblages. Those that are present are out of order anatomically. Turner postulates the underrepresentation of vertebrae may be because they were broken and boiled to extract oily contents. However, human vertebrae may be missing in burials for the same reason animal vertebrae are at archaeological sites; namely, vertebrae are left behind at the kill site.

The commingled remains of eight individuals from the mass interment in Cist 2 and other parts of Kiva 2 are disorganized and highly fragmented, but well preserved. Most were deposited in Cist 2, inside, below, and around a corrugated jar. The presumably hasty manner in which this burial was prepared, including scattered remains, suggests that it is a non-considerate burial, a taphonomic indicator of violence and possibly of cannibalism. Bones found in the kiva fill may be attributed to later rodent activity (Luebben and Nickens, 1982).

The entire assemblage from Kiva 2 contains only four complete and nine fragmentary vertebrae. For a sample of eight individuals, these numbers are especially small. In addition, only two bones in the previous study were interpreted as having been gnawed (Luebben and Nickens, 1982:74); the present study recorded no gnawed bone. How much time elapsed between the death and mass burial of remains in Kiva 2 is not known. Evidence suggests that the humans were processed outside the kiva. Soon afterward, they were buried inside and abandoned, either carelessly deposited by the perpetrators, or hastily cleaned up by others.

Breakage Pattern

An important characteristic of cannibalized remains is the prevalence and character of bone breakage. The latter suggests a perimortem timeframe just before or fairly soon after the time of death in dry climates. Peri- and postmortem damage patterns can be distinct, particularly if the former occurs on "green" or "fresh" bones, and the latter occurs on dry bones. Postmortem, dry-bone damage due to impacts with dynamic loading often includes shatter with multiple, rectangular pieces of bone. Antemortem fractures, by contrast, are more likely to show bone reaction or healing, or signs of infection.

Human bones from cannibalized assemblages appear to have been processed like game animals. It is rare to find any whole bone, including the skull. Bones tend to be recovered in many small fragments with numerous pieces either missing or unidentifiable. Of the 374 human bone specimens from the Grinnell Site, only 24 are whole (most from crania), 321 are fragments, and 29 are teeth. The large proportion of fragments (93% of the sample) is indicative of perimortem bone processing (Table 16.3). Spiral fractures appear on most long bone fragments (Table 16.3; Figure 16.3). Spiral or compression fractures can result from percussion hammering against some form of anvil, although anvil abrasions, common at Anazasi cannibalism sites (Turner and Turner, 1999), were not observed in this sample.

Overall, skeletal indicators of blunt trauma and perimortem damage occur on 20% of all cranial elements (Table 16.3; Figure 16.4). First, the crania have been broken apart into many fragments; however, assessment of the number of individuals present in the assemblage was possible as a result of cranial reconstruction (Figure 16.5). Cranial injuries are more ambiguous than long bone anvil fractures and could result from opening the cranium to remove the brain, death by bludgeoning, or postmortem mutilation. Empty and damaged anterior sockets suggest the front teeth of most individuals have been knocked out (Figure 16.6).

Table 16.3   Taphonomic Factors Present on Human Remains (Number of Occurrences)

Element	Whole	Fragments / Side	Blunt Impact Depression or Other Defect	Spiral Fractures	Cutmarks	Burning
Maxilla	2	5L, 5R	7		23	
Mandible	4		4		10	
Frontal		4L, 1R, 3	8		23	
Parietal		3L	4		2	
Occipital	1	2R, 1	2		2	
Temporal		4R, 3L, 1	2		4	
Zygoma		6				
Teeth	29					
Cranial fragments		170	18		17	21
Cervical vertebrae	4		1			
Lumbar vertebrae		2				
Miscellaneous vertebrae		7	1			
Scapula		2L				
Clavicle	1L				1	
Ribs		2	2			
Radius		1LD, 1LP, 2RP		4	1	
Ulna		2LP, 2RP	1	4		
Phalange	11		2			
Navicular	1					
Pelvis		1R				
Femur		4+ 1D, 1DR, 1LP	2	6	7	
Tibia		3 + 1D	7	3	13	
Fibula		2		2		
Long bone fragments		68	1	61	23	
Unidentified		10				
Total = 374	53	321	62	80	126	21

Note: L = left; R = right; D = distal; P = proximal.

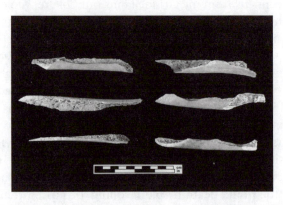

Figure 16.3 Photograph of spirally fractured long bone fragments from the Grinnell Site.

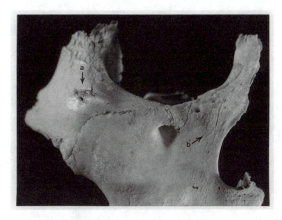

Figure 16.4 Photograph of the right maxilla of a subadult approximately 16 years of age, illustrating blunt trauma on the zygomatic process (a) and cut marks near the nasal bone (b).

Figure 16.5 Photograph of the reconstructed cranium of a male aged 21 to 25 years illustrating perimortem breakage.

Burning

According to Turner and Turner (1999), the presence of burned bone is another indicator of human remains being cannibalized (Table 16.1). Following butchering of animals for food, bone is often burnt during the cooking process when exposed directly to fire or not covered by a sufficient amount of flesh. Burning on human remains, Turner believes, is evidence of prehistoric cooking. He hypothesizes that burning should be evident in 2 to 35% of all elements in the cannibalized assemblage.

Remains from the Grinnell Site yielded very little evidence for burning: 10 burnt and 11 slightly charred cranial fragments, comprising 5.6% of the total sample, were burnt only on the exterior surface. Although this frequency falls within the range stipulated by Turner, it is significantly lower than that observed at other southwestern sites with evidence of cannibalism.

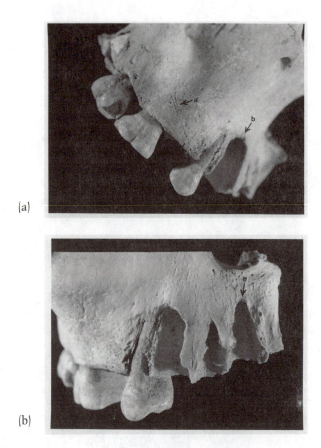

Figure 16.6 Photographs of the right maxilla of a subadult approximately 16 years of age illustrating cut marks near the alveolar ridge and incisors that have been evulsed.

Cut Marks

Cut marks constitute a ubiquitous signature on bones that have been processed for food. On game animals, cut marks usually appear either near joints from dismemberment, or on bone surfaces where defleshing took place. Cut marks around the joints indicate that bones were disarticulated prior to final deposition. A number of sites in the Southwest contain human skeletal remains with cut marks on both crania and long bones. Cut marks on the crania probably indicate scalping or facial flaying (Allen et al., 1985).

Cranial elements from the Grinnell Site exhibited 126 cut marks. Most of them were on the maxilla in the nasal area and above the teeth (Figures 16.4 and 16.6), on mandibles, and on the frontal bone above the orbits. Occasionally, cut marks were even observed inside the orbits, and one cut mark and one scrape were noted on the interior of a skull. Post-cranial elements exhibited 45 cut marks, including 7 chopper marks on a tibia fragment. All cut marks occurring on long bone fragments were near the proximal and distal ends of bones, suggesting disarticulation and butchering of meat.

Pot Polish

The last taphonomic signature in Turner's criteria is the presence of pot polish. Although not widely accepted (Bahn, 1992), pot polish is one of the main taphonomic indicators of cannibalism at Anasazi archaeological sites (Turner and Turner, 1999). "Pot polish" is a term used to describe a smooth polish that appears on the ends of bones that were cooked in prehistoric vessels to extract grease or oil. When cooked and stirred in a pot tempered with coarse sand, the gritty inner surface of the vessel causes the edges of bone to become smooth and polished. This polish is visible to the naked eye, and striations are clearly visible with a scanning electron microscope. The presence of polish on human bones cannot be attributed to deliberate polishing; no evidence for this practice exists on animal bones or elsewhere in the Southwest (Turner and Turner, 1999). Bone remains from the Grinnell Site do not exhibit evidence of pot polishing. This absence does not necessarily rule out that human remains were cooked or eaten; however, Turner (1983) claims that the presence of pot polish is necessary to support an argument for cannibalism (Table 16.1).

Conclusions

A reanalysis of the osteological data from the Grinnell Site provides evidence that eight individuals met a violent and traumatic end as indicated by extensive perimortem breakage patterns, including both blunt- and sharp-force trauma to crania and long bones. Although the Grinnell Site contains considerable evidence that Turner (1983), Turner and Turner (1999), and others have considered indicative of cannibalism, two main taphonomic criteria are missing: pot polishing and high frequency of burning. It is possible that cannibalism could have occurred without leaving these markers, but using Turner's criteria, the Grinnell Site remains should not be considered evidence of cannibalism.

A more conservative assessment nevertheless still indicates perimortem trauma. There is no evidence for the use of projectile or stabbing weapons, but such evidence could have perished with the soft parts and missing bones. Facial crushing and cranial fractures suggest that these individuals were beaten to death. While the bones were still high in fat and moisture, they were dismembered with stone tools. Their heads were mutilated or flayed, and probably broken up further. The limbs were defleshed enough that long bones could be extensively fragmented. Whether the Grinnell Site people were eaten or not, they were probably victims of the endemic violence and warfare for which evidence is accumulating in the prehistoric Southwest (Haas and Creamer, 1993; LeBlanc, 2000).

Acknowledgment

We would like to acknowledge Steve Bicknell for figures and photographs.

References

Allen, W.H., C.F. Merbs, and W.H. Birkby
    1985   Evidence for prehistoric scalping at Nuv Akwewtaqa (Chavez pass) and Grasshopper Ruin, Arizona. In *Health and Disease in the Prehistoric Southwest*, edited by C.F. Merbs and R.J. Miller, Anthropological Research Papers No. 34, Arizona State University, Tempe, AZ.

Arens, W.
    1979   *The Man-Eating Myth: Anthropology and Anthropophagy*, Oxford University Press, New York.

Bahn, P.
   1992   Ancestral cannibalism gives us food for thought, *New Scientist* 134(1816):40–41.

Bass, W.M.
   1987   *Human Osteology: A Laboratory and Field Manual*, 3rd ed., Special Publication No. 2, Missouri Archaeological Society, Columbia.

Billman, B.R., P.M. Lambert, and B.L. Leonard
   2000   Cannibalism, warfare, and drought in the Mesa Verde region during the twelfth century A.D., *American Antiquity* 65(1):145–178.

Buikstra, J.E. and D.H. Ubelaker, Editors
   1994   *Standards for Data Collection from Human Skeletal Remains*, Arkansas Archaeological Survey Research Series No. 44, Fayetteville.

Darling, J.A.
   1999   Mass inhumation and the execution of witches in the American southwest, *American Anthropologist* 100(3):732–752

Dongoske, K.E., D.L. Martin, and T.J. Ferguson
   2000   Critique of the claim of cannibalism at Cowboy Wash, *American Antiquity* 65(1):179–190.

Fagan, B.M.
   1995   *Ancient North America: The Archaeology of a Continent*, Thames & Hudson, New York.

Haas, J. and W. Creamer
   1993   *Stress and Warfare among the Kayenta Anasazi of the Thirteenth Century A.D.*, Fieldiana, Anthropology, Field Museum of Natural History, Chicago, IL.

Hough, W.
   1902   Ancient people of the petrified forest of Arizona, *Harper's Monthly*, 105:897–901.

LeBlanc, S.A.
   2000   *Prehistoric Warfare in the American Southwest*, The University of Utah Press, Salt Lake City.

Luebben, R.A
   1983   The Grinnell Site: a small ceremonial center near Yucca House, Colorado, *Journal of Intermountain Archaeology* II:1–26.

Luebben, R.A. and P.R. Nickens
   1982   A mass interment in an early Pueblo III kiva in southwestern Colorado, *Journal of Intermountain Archaeology* I:66–79.

Nickens, P. R.
   1979   Osteological Analysis of Human Skeletal Material from the Grinnell and Ismay Sites, Montezuma County, Southwestern Colorado. Manuscript in author's possession.

Preston, D.
   1998   Cannibals of the canyon, *The New Yorker* 74:76–89.

Turner, C.G., II
   1983 Taphonomic reconstructions of human violence and cannibalism based on mass burials in the American southwest. In *Carnivores, Human Scavengers, and Human Predators: A Question of Bone Technology*, edited by G.M. LeMoine and A.S. MacEachern, pp. 219–240. Archaeological Association, University of Calgary, Calgary.

Turner, C.G., II and J.A. Turner
   1999   *Man Corn: Cannibalism and Violence in the Prehistoric American Southwest*, The University of Utah Press, Salt Lake City.

White, T.D.
   1992   *Prehistoric Cannibalism at Mancos 5MTUMR-2346*, Princeton University Press, Princeton.

Damnum Fatale: The Taphonomic Fate of Human Remains in Mass Disasters

17

PAUL S. SLEDZIK
WILLIAM C. RODRIGUEZ, III

Contents

Table 17.1   Forensic Anthropological Skills for the Mass Fatality Incident (MFI)

At the Scene

- Set up grid system for search and recovery of remains
- Locate, recognize, and recover human remains, especially those burned and fragmented
- Document location of remains within grid units
- Devise search criteria based on size and scope of disaster

In the Morgue

- Assist in triage of remains
- Describe incomplete/fragmentary remains and conditions of remains
- Conduct forensic analysis to determine sex, age, race, stature, and distinguishing characteristics
- Separate commingled remains
- Obtain radiographs for age estimation and unique skeletal features
- Reassociate body parts based on biological profile and descriptions of missing parts
- Determine minimum number of individuals based on remains recovered
- Assist in organizing identification exclusion/inclusion matrix
- Compare antemortem and postmortem data (e.g., radiographs, skeletal information)
- Assist in age determination of complete remains/bodies
- Analysis of trauma patterns/evidence and crash-related injuries

Introduction

The public health and economic effects of natural and technological (manmade) disasters increased dramatically during this century. International public health agencies report that natural disasters disrupted the lives of 800 million people, caused more than $50 billion in property damage, and killed 3 million people in the past 2 decades (International Federation of Red Cross, 1993). With global population growth and the development of vulnerable areas, disasters will claim more lives and property in the future (Noji, 1994).

Disaster planners and emergency managers call a mass disaster involving a large number of deaths a mass fatality incident (MFI). MFI management has undergone significant change in the past decade, as a greater focus is placed on the search for, recovery of, and identification of human remains. The forensic anthropologist plays a key role in these areas. Forensic archeology, skeletal analysis, and other skills are invaluable to the MFI response (Sledzik, 1996a,b; 1998). Table 17.1 enumerates these and other forensic anthropological skills used in an MFI.

As the end result of the perimortem and postmortem factors affecting the human body during and after a disaster, disaster taphonomy can be viewed as a continuum, with survival and total disintegration of the body at opposite ends of the scale. Along the continuum, two groups of factors impact the human body: primary and secondary. Table 17.2 delineates these factors. Primary factors result directly from the disaster, and may be the cause of death. Secondary factors affect the body after death. For example, in an explosion, taphonomic changes may result from the actual blast (primary), the crushing effects of the collapsing structure, and burning from the ensuing fire. Primary and secondary effects may be indiscernible.

Because disaster forces are more variable in duration and intensity than those encountered during normal decomposition and skeletonization, predicting the taphonomic outcomes of

Table 17.2 Primary and Secondary Factors Affecting Human Preservation in Mass Disasters

Primary	Secondary
Explosion fragmentation	Burning
G-force impact fragmentation	Temperature and humidity effects
Burning	Water effects (warm, cold, salt, fresh)
Crushing (structure collapse)	Decomposition effects
Dismemberment (e.g., from flying debris)	Crushing (e.g., building collapse)
	Carnivore/rodent actions
	Freefall injuries
	Ground impact injuries

a specific disaster is difficult. The forensic anthropologist should understand these forces, how they influence taphonomy, and how they affect search, recovery, analysis, and identification. For example, disasters involving high speed and flammable products (e.g., an aircraft accident) leave human remains burned and highly fragmented. In these cases, fragmentation occurs before burning, resulting in remains that are unassociated, fragmented, and burned. In house fires, remains may be extremely burned, but they generally are not unassociated.

Literature Review

If disaster taphonomy is defined as the preservation of human remains in an MFI, few publications exist in the forensic anthropological literature. The paucity of published information is likely due to several factors: forensic anthropology's recent focus on taphonomy, the relatively recent inclusion of the forensic anthropologist into the MFI team, the focus on identification rather than taphonomy during MFI work, and restrictions on the use of MFI victim data for publication.

Some taphonomic information can be gleaned from forensic pathology or aerospace medicine publications. Aerospace pathology confines itself to the examination of injuries received in aircraft accidents, using the pattern of these injuries to help determine the cause of the accident. However, some of these publications mention taphonomic factors. Forensic pathology publications discuss taphonomic issues, but these are largely early postmortem changes or general discussions of fragmentation and burning. Taphonomic information can be extracted from the forensic reports of specific disasters (e.g., TWA 800 and KAL 801 reports on the National Transportation Safety Board web site, www.ntsb.gov).

T. Dale Stewart's edited volume *Personal Identification in Mass Disasters* (Stewart, 1970) is the earliest work examining forensic anthropology in disasters. One chapter in that volume, "Identification Involving Atrocities" by A. Keith Mant, discusses the appearance of remains from aircraft that "crashed, caught alight, and exploded." The remains were a few inches in size and the author presents his methods for determining the minimum number of individuals.

Because only a few publications by forensic anthropologists give insight into taphonomic issues in specific disaster situations, these publications will be referred to in the sections pertaining to specific disasters.

Table 17.3   Characteristics of Decelerative Crash Forces

Observation	G-force
Vertebral body compression	20–30
Fracture dislocation of C1/C2	20–40
Mandible fractures	40
Skull fractures	50+
Pelvic fractures	100–200
Total body fragmentation	350+

Disaster-Specific Taphonomy

The cause and outcome of every disaster are unique. The preservation of human remains in a disaster is unique as well. Generalities about taphonomic changes related to specific disasters are extractable from the working knowledge in the literature by forensic anthropologists. These changes are grouped below into categories based on disaster type. The taphonomic categories reflect the forces acting during and after the disaster.

Aircraft Accidents

Aircraft accidents involve a variety of forces: forces, fire, freefall, impact, and environmental effects. Impact g-forces cause fragmentation — the greater the g-force at impact, the greater degree of fragmentation. After a crash, a fire often ensues. The intensity and duration of the fire determine the degree of burning to the remains. When fragmentation and burning are combined, the degree of preservation of body parts and bone decreases. Other factors, such as water and freezing temperatures, also alter decomposition.

There are some consistencies in how remains are fragmented during a crash that are related to the forces experienced during the crash and anatomical structures (Hill, 1989; Wagner, 1990) (Table 17.3). Large joints (e.g., hip, knee, and ankle) are often recovered because numerous ligaments hold these joint areas together. The authors observed this preservation after several crashes, including the 1994 crashes of USAir 427 and American Eagle 4184. In addition, cranial bones fragment severely at impact, leaving little of the cranium intact because of the jelly-like actions of the brain within the cranial cavity (Hill, 1989). An estimate of the degree of fragmentation and tissue destruction can be made by comparing the total weight of recovered remains to the estimated total weight of passengers before the crash.

Slower impact crashes, such as a controlled flight into terrain or a ditching, exhibit a greater range of preservation. In the controlled crash of a United Airlines jet in Sioux City, Iowa, in 1989, 17 people survived the crash, and the 110 dead showed fragmentation and burning (Randall, 1991). A wide range of preservation, from calcined bone to complete bodies was documented in the crash of KAL 801 on Guam in 1997 (Saul and Saul, 1999).

The 1985 crash of Delta 191 at Dallas/Fort Worth International Airport was documented by Gilliland and co-workers (1986). The crash killed 137 people, including one on the ground. Intact bodies were flattened from front to back and incurred cranial damage at the level of the mouth. First-class passengers and the cabin crew suffered the most disruptive injuries; some were not recognizable as human. Most of the survivors were in the back of the plane, a finding mistakenly interpreted to mean that the safest seats on all aircraft are in the rear.

The 1989 crash of a Norwegian aircraft into the ocean revealed a pattern of trauma (Gregersen et al., 1995). Of the 48 bodies recovered (most of which were in complete condition), the most frequently observed fractures were of the ribs (100% of the victims), skull (96%), pelvis (88%), face and spine (83%), sternum (71%), lower leg (63%), thigh (58%), and upper arm (56%). Few fractures of the hand (19%) and foot (17%) were observed. The authors report that a small percentage of the fractures resulted from the midair breakup of the aircraft; a majority were caused by the impact.

Hinkes (1989) examined the role of forensic anthropology in resolving identification issues at the 1985 crash of a chartered DC-8 in Gander, Newfoundland, carrying 256 U.S. military personnel. She reported that the remains were incinerated and dismembered. Her work involved assessing age, sex, stature, and race, determining the minimum number of individuals, and reassociating remains, which were fragmented and shrunk due to post-crash burning. Of the 50 sets of remains she analyzed, four consisted of a lower torso (hip to mid-thigh), two were hemipelves with legs and feet, and one comprised a head and shoulders.

Explosions and breakups of aircraft in midair pose other taphonomic challenges. The bombing of Pan Am 103 over Lockerbie, Scotland, and the explosion of TWA 800 off Long Island, New York, and other similar accidents have been examined (Eckert, 1990.) In the Pan Am 103 case, the remains were subjected to high winds, flying debris, and impact. Eckert (1990) reported that none of the remains overtly showed evidence of the explosion. Of the 264 passengers killed, more than 160 were bodies that landed individually or in clusters.

If the conditions are right, the actions of humans may influence aircraft accident victim taphonomy. The U.S. Army Central Identification Laboratory, Hawaii (CILHI) recovers and identifies U.S. servicemen killed in Southeast Asia. CILHI's experience in examining highly fragmented, skeletonized remains that have been in soil for nearly 40 years is unique and important (Holland, Anderson, and Mann, 1997; Holland and Mann, 1996; Webster, 1999). Of particular note are remains removed by Southeast Asian residents and modified for use in the "bone trade."

Bombing and Explosions

An explosion creates direct and indirect forces that cause body fragmentation. A body impacted by a direct explosive force (e.g., landmine) is fragmented in large pieces. Indirect explosive forces impact the body after the initial explosion; for example, a body may be crushed in a building collapse caused by an explosion.

Marshall (1993) divides the injurious effects of explosions into six categories: complete disruption, explosive injury, injury by separate fragments, injury by falling masonry, burns, and blast. Complete disruption occurs when the body is in close contact to a large explosive. As the location of a victim moves away from the explosion, the amount of trauma will decrease. Victims within a meter of the explosion will be severely mangled, while those farther away will incur less damage. Falling structures cause nonspecific traumatic injuries that can be discerned from blast-related injuries.

Remains fragmented by an explosion can differ from fragmented remains from a high-speed plane crash. In a bombing, the fragmentation is a result of bomb construction, device detonation, and the presence of flying debris from the explosion. The explosive forces may not be applied in equal strength to the body as a whole. Severe fragmentation is often seen if the victim was near the detonation site. The farther the person is from the detonation site, the larger the body parts (e.g., foot and lower leg, entire arm, head) recovered.

Kahana and co-workers (1997) describe the methods used to identify remains from suicide bombings in Israel from 1993 to 1996. Many of these bombings took place in public places and involved cars, buses, or metallic objects used in the bombs. Of the 136 bodies examined, 17.4% of the victims showed total disruption of the body, 69.7% showed explosive injuries, 10.4% showed injuries from flying debris, and 2.3% showed injuries directly related to the blast.

Earthquakes

A majority of earthquake deaths are due to falling buildings, masonry, or engineering structures (Alexander, 1985). Studying the mortality following a 1985 earthquake in Chile, Ortiz et al. (1986) reported that of 145 documented deaths, 53 (36.6%) were the result of injury to the skull. Other causes included multiple trauma (52 cases), thorax crush injuries (12 cases), and myocardial infarction (10 cases).

Remains from earthquakes typically will be found crushed but complete inside collapsed structures. Although normal decomposition will occur, there may be some variation in the severity and extent of the trauma may occur. Fragmentation and burning of remains may not happen unless explosions and fires occur as a secondary effect of the earthquake.

Earthquakes have left bioarcheological evidence. The New Madrid earthquakes of 1811–1812 devastated large areas of western Tennessee and Kentucky, northeast Arkansas, and southeast Missouri. Prehistoric Native American burials at the Campbell site in Missouri were impacted by the quakes, causing disruption of skeletal elements and creating fissures cutting through skeletons (Chapman et al., 1955).

Fires

Fires can be the primary cause of death or may cause secondary effects. Heat-related shrinkage of the muscles results in the pugilistic position, often preserving the fingertips, which are useful for identification. In more severe fires the ends of the protruding long bones may become burned, while the shafts of the bone are less affected by burning. Blowout fractures of skull result from vapor pressure within the heated cranial vault.

Secondary effects of fire may be seen in aircraft accidents, bombings, and explosions and as a secondary effect can involve intact whole bodies or fragmented remains. The intensity of the fire may cause charring, burning, or calcination.

Ubelaker et al. (1995) reported on the taphonomy of the victims of the Branch Davidian fire in 1993. The data collection procedure for bone inventory allowed the authors to reconstruct the preservation of bones in body regions (e.g., head/neck, arm/shoulder, chest, etc.) and the completeness of major bones. They report that the more massive and better protected bones were more frequently preserved. Pelvic bones were most often found complete. The mandible and maxilla was least often preserved. Bones of anthropological interest that were most often preserved were the os coxae and femora.

Floods

Flash floods and hurricane storm surges are the most common flood events. About 90% of flash flood deaths are attributable to drowning (French et al., 1983). Debris in the floodwaters results in trauma and dismemberment to bodies. Large body sections with multiple fractures are often observed. Severe fragmentation resulting in small body parts is infrequent.

Charney and Wilber (1980) described their efforts to identify remains recovered from the 1976 Big Thompson flood in Colorado. They noted that all 139 bodies recovered after the flood were whole or partly fragmented. Bodies were difficult to locate because mud and silt camouflaged the remains. Many bodies showed evidence of multiple fractures, loss of extremities, bruises, abrasions, and avulsions, presumably from impact with stationary objects or floating debris.

Sledzik and Hunt (1997) reported on the processing and identification of skeletal and fleshed remains from a cemetery washed away during the 1993 midwestern United States floods. Thousands of skeletal elements and several hundred bodies in various states of preservation were recovered. The search and recovery methods and the size of the search area (more than 34,000 acres) resulted in the recovery of recognizable human remains (e.g., crania) and large bones (e.g., femora). No discernible pattern of preservation based on the length of internment was noted in either the complete bodies or partial remains.

To understand the taphonomy of a flood event, the anthropologist should examine the factors leading to the flood (e.g., flash flood, hurricane) and the location of the event (e.g., rural, urban). Knowledge of intervening factors such as the amount of debris the bodies may encounter aids in assessing taphonomic information.

Infectious Disease Outbreaks

Emerging and reemerging infectious diseases threaten public health worldwide. At present, deaths from these diseases that intersect with forensic identification are limited. Pathologists play an important role in identifying emerging diseases such as Hantavirus, but, at present, there has been no outbreak requiring identification of large numbers of fatalities.

The taphonomic aspects of an MFI involving a disease outbreak are speculative. Since most infectious diseases take time to cause death, there is the opportunity for the exposed person to seek medical care. In a mass exposure situation, local health care facilities would be overwhelmed by a large number of deaths. People may also die at home or in a quarantine facility. Once decomposition begins, the way the disease affects the body may alter the normal decomposition pattern; for example, purging of blood, vomit, or urine/feces from the body may cause more rapid decomposition.

Epidemiological issues are important in disease outbreaks. Forensic specialists should use typical crime scene documentation procedures in a disease-related MFI. Death scene documentation would supplement the pathological information to help understand disease etiology. In addition, information on the age, sex, and race of the individual is helpful in epidemiological analyses.

Landslides, Mudslides, and Avalanches

The effects of mudslides, landslides, and avalanches on the human body after death would presumably by similar to those seen in flood events — whole bodies showing some dismemberment. The degree of fragmentation would be a function of the force of the event, the distance traveled, and the amount of debris encountered during transport. The presence of a large amount of mud, earth, or snow may act to preserve bodies.

Mass Suicides

Mass suicide deaths caused by poison will not directly cause taphonomic changes of interest to the anthropologist. But, if the time from death to discovery is long, decomposition will occur. This happened after the mass suicide of over 900 members of a religious cult in Jonestown, Guyana, in 1978. The bodies were first examined 6 days after the event, and a range of decomposition was noted (Thompson, Manders, and Cowan, 1987).

Tornadoes and Hurricanes

Flash floods and the storm surges associated with hurricanes are the most common flood events. About 90% of hurricane deaths are due to drowning (Noji, 1993), and the same percentage is reported for flash floods (French et al., 1983). Bodies can be struck by debris, resulting in trauma and dismemberment. In general, large body sections are often seen and severe fragmentation resulting in small body parts is infrequent.

War-Related Deaths and Weapons of Mass Destruction

Wars can leave large numbers of combatants and noncombatants dead from a variety of causes. Bombs and gunfire are the common modern methods of wartime killing.

The most recent wave of concern among disaster managers is the potential for a chemical or biological weapon used against a civilian population, a so-called weapon of mass destruction (WMD). Although these two terms are often linked, the effects of chemical and biological weapons differ greatly, and are mostly in the area of onset time of symptoms (or incubation period of the pathogen) and the biological effects on the victim.

In a biological attack, days may pass before death occurs. Epidemiological tracking of disease symptoms and deaths is the only way to accurately assess if a biological weapon has been used (Franz et al., 1997). Most emergency managers and bioweapon experts believe that most bioweapon deaths will occur in hospitals. No resultant taphonomic effects will be observed in this situation. Conceivably, in the event of a large number of deaths or where the body is not recovered for a period of time, differential decomposition may occur, depending on the pathogen used. In some situations, certain animal "sentinels" may be the first to die. If the bioweapon kills carnivores, no dispersal of the body by this method would occur.

Deaths from chemical weapons are more rapid. Many chemical weapons affect the skin and internal organs, which may lead to differential decomposition. The effects on skeletonization are unknown.

Conclusion

Disasters are chaos in action. Taphonomy, like chaos, is characterized by being consistent only in its variability. The forensic anthropologist reassembles the human body after the chaos of a disaster takes it apart. In a sense, the forensic anthropologist continually fights the second law of thermodynamics.

In the realm of disasters, one cannot help but be impressed by how difficult it is to predict how the human body will be deposited in the environment. We have attempted to document our experiences and those of others, and do some extrapolating to help understand the taphonomic effects of disasters.

References

Alexander, D.
  1985   Death and injury in earthquakes, *Disasters* 9:57–60.

Chapman, C.H., L.O. Anderson, and R.F. Spier
  1955   The Campbell Site: a late Mississippi town site and cemetery in southeast Missouri, *Missouri Archaeologist* 17:3–140.

Charney, M. and C.G. Wilber
  1980   The Big Thompson flood, *American Journal of Forensic Medicine and Pathology* 1:139–144.

Eckert, W.G.
  1990   The Lockerbie disaster and other aircraft breakups in midair, *American Journal of Forensic Medicine and Pathology* 11:93–101.

Franz, D.R. et al.
  1997   Clinical recognition and management of patients exposed to biological warfare agents, *Journal of the American Medical Association* 278:399–411.

French, J. et al.
  1983   Mortality from flash floods: a review of national weather service reports, 1969–1981, *Public Health Reports* 98:584–588.

Gilliland, M.G.F. et al.
  1986   Disaster planning for air crashes: a retrospective analysis of Delta Airlines flight 191, *American Journal of Forensic Medicine and Pathology* 7:308–316.

Gregersen, M., S. Jensen, and P.J.T. Knudsen
  1995   The crash of the Partnair Convair 340/580 in the Skagerrak: traumatological aspects, *Aviation, Space, and Environmental Medicine* 66:152–157.

Hill, I.R.
  1989   Mechanism of injury in aircraft accidents — a theoretical approach, *Aviation, Space, and Environmental Medicine* 60(7, suppl.):A18–25.

Hinkes, M.J.
  1989   The role of forensic anthropology in mass disaster resolution, *Aviation, Space, and Environmental Medicine* 60(part 2):A60–A63.

Holland, T.D. and R.W. Mann
  1996   Forensic aviation archaeology: finding and recovering American MIA remains, *Cultural Resource Management* 19(10):29–31.

Holland, T.D., B.E. Anderson, and R.W. Mann
  1997   Human variables in the postmortem alteration of human bone: examples from U.S. war casualties. In *Forensic Taphonomy: The Postmortem Fate of Human Remains,* edited by W.D. Haglund and M.H. Sorg, pp. 263–274. CRC Press, Boca Raton, FL.

International Federation of the Red Cross and Red Crescent Societies
  1993   *World Disasters Report.* Martinus Nijhoff, Dordrecht, The Netherlands.

Kahana, T., M. Fruend, and J. Hiss
  1997   Suicidal terrorist bombings in Israel — identification of human remains, *Journal of Forensic Sciences* 42:260–264.

Mant, A.K.
  1970   Identification involving atrocities. In *Personal Identification in Mass Disasters,* edited by T.D. Stewart, pp. 11–18. Smithsonian Institution, Washington, D.C.

Marshall, T.K.
  1993   Violence and civil disturbances. In *The Pathology of Trauma,* 2nd ed., edited by J.K. Mason, pp. 71–85. Hodder and Stoughton, London.

Noji, E.K.

1993   Analysis of medical needs during disasters caused by tropical cyclones: anticipated injury patterns, *Journal of Tropical Medicine and Hygiene* 96:370–376.

1994   Progress in disaster management, *Lancet* 343:1239–1240.

Ortiz, M.R. et al.

1986   Brief description of the effects of the earthquake of 3rd March 1985, Chile, *Disasters* 10:125–140.

Randall, B.

1991   Body retrieval and morgue operations at the crash of United flight 232, *Journal of Forensic Sciences* 36:403–409.

Saul, F.P. and J.M. Saul

1999   The evolving role of the forensic anthropologist as seen in the identification of the victims of the Comair 7232 (Michigan) and KAL 801 (Guam) aircrashes, *Proceedings of the American Academy of Forensic Sciences* 5:222.

Sledzik, P.S.

1996a Physical anthropology's role in identification of disaster fatalities. In *Proceedings of the Second National Symposium on Dentistry's Role and Responsibility in Mass Disaster Identification,* pp. 62–64. American Dental Association, Chicago, IL.

1996b Federal resources in mass disaster response, *Cultural Resources Management* 19(10):19–20.

1998   Anthropology and mass fatality response. In *Proceedings of the International Symposium on Family and Victim Assistance for Transportation Disasters,* National Transportation Safety Board, September 28–29, 1998, Arlington, VA.

Sledzik, P.S. and D.R. Hunt

1997   Disaster and relief efforts at the Hardin Cemetery. In *In Remembrance: Archaeology and Death,* edited by D.A. Poirier and N.B. Bellantoni, pp. 185–198. Bergin and Garvey, Westport, CT.

Stewart, T.D., Editor

1970   *Personal Identification in Mass Disasters,* Smithsonian Institution, Washington, D.C.

Thompson, R.L., W.W. Manders, and W.R. Cowan

1987   Postmortem findings of the victims of the Jonestown tragedy, *Journal of Forensic Sciences* 32:433–443.

Ubelaker, D.H. et al.

1995   The role of forensic anthropology in the recovery and analysis of Branch Davidian Compound victims: recovery procedures and characteristics of the victims, *Journal of Forensic Sciences* 40:335–340.

Wagner, G.N.

1990   Aerospace pathology. In *Handbook of Forensic Pathology,* edited by R.C Froede, pp. 197–204. College of American Pathologists, Northfield, IL.

Wagner, G.N. and R.C. Froede

1993   Medicolegal investigation of mass disasters. In *Spitz and Fisher's Medicolegal Investigation of Death: Guidelines for the Application of Pathology to Crime Investigation,* edited by W.U. Spitz and R.S. Russell, pp. 567–584. Charles C Thomas, Springfield, IL.

Webster, A.D.

1999   Human taphonomy and its impact on forensic recovery operations in Vietnam, *Proceedings of the American Academy of Forensic Sciences* 5:211–212.

Approaches to the Study of Commingling in Human Skeletal Biology

18

DOUGLAS H. UBELAKER

Contents

0-8493-1189-6/02/$0.00+$1.50

Introduction

In forensic anthropology, commingling refers to the mixing together of remains of different origins. Usually the term applies to situations in which remains of more than one individual have become mixed together. The scientific problem is to determine if this has occurred, and, if so, what parts and what different individuals are represented. In the most general terms, commingling refers to the mixing of evidence in a manner that may require scientific study to differentiate the various components.

Although in recent years much has been written about many aspects of forensic anthropology, relatively little attention has been focused on issues of commingling. The topic is largely absent in a frequently cited text by Krogman (1962) and the revision by Krogman and Iscan (1986). Stewart's classic *Essentials of Forensic Anthropology* (1979) devotes only 2 of its 300 pages to the topic. Yet increasingly, forensic anthropologists must apply their scientific skills to issues of commingling.

As noted by Stewart (1979:38), commingling usually is not an issue in forensic anthropology analysis because many of the materials we examine are recovered in contexts suggesting the presence of a single, isolated individual. Even these, however, have to be screened for mixed-in nonhuman elements, including the remains of nonhuman animals that can closely resemble those of humans. This process is usually easy when whole bones are involved. Difficulties intensify when remains have been fragmented, burned, or otherwise altered. As noted by Stewart, this is largely a sorting problem.

The criteria used to sort human remains are mostly morphological. The first step is usually a detailed inventory listing bones by type and side. The presence of multiple bones from the same type and side (e.g., two left tibiae) indicates clear evidence of commingling. Lack of such evidence by itself does not preclude the possibility of commingling; it just does not confirm it. For example, if 15 human bones are recovered without anatomical duplication, commingling is not proven, but it is possible that as many as 15 individuals could be represented. If duplication among the 15 bones was confined to only the presence of 2 left tibiae, the evidence would establish that at least 2 individuals are present (minimum number) but would not establish the actual number represented.

The amount of detail recorded in the inventory should be guided by the problem, and the condition of the remains. Buikstra and Ubelaker (1994) provide an inventory system developed from input by practicing skeletal biologists. Because this system is widely utilized, it also offers the advantage of capturing data that can be compared broadly. This inventory is not exhaustive; rather, it captures information considered to be most important in comparative analysis. Bones of the skull are coded as complete (at least 75% present), partially complete (between 25% and 75% present), poorly preserved (present but less than 25%), or absent. The postcranial bones other than limb long bones are recorded in a similar manner, except that some components of these bones are recorded separately (e.g., the glenoid fossae of the scapulae). For limb long bones, the degree of preservation categories are applied to the proximal and distal epiphyses and three sections of the diaphyses. The advantage of this system over simpler systems for assessing commingling is the level of detail that can be used to detect part duplication.

To determine the number of individuals represented by commingled remains beyond duplication of bone type and side, it is useful to consider age at death, sex, general bone size, and other information as applicable. For the next layer of detail beyond bone type and side, many investigators turn to age at death. A simple sort of immature and mature can yield useful results, although the criteria for such determinations become important. For long bones, if epiphyseal union is employed as a criterion, it must be remembered that union occurs earlier in females than in males, the timing and rate of union differ for the different bones and considerable time can elapse between beginning and complete epiphyseal fusion (Ubelaker, 1989). For example, because it unites early, the distal tibia from an adolescent might appear to be mature whereas the sternal clavicle (uniting relatively late) from the same individual might appear to be immature.

Observations on the general morphology of bone fragments can be relevant in some situations. For example if some skeletal or dental evidence within fragmentary remains suggests that a young infant or fetus is present, then the additional presence of mature bone (as suggested by bone type, size, and/or shape) of a nature that could not be present in a younger individual would suggest commingling, even though the specific age of the more mature bone could not be determined.

If relatively few individuals are involved, it might be useful to attempt to assemble the remains into likely individuals, in consideration of not only bone type, side, and age at death, but also overall bone size and shape. This exercise can be especially revealing with fragmentary remains in which, for example, several left tibia fragments all could have originated from one bone. It also may be possible to observe the morphological relationship of bones that articulate and determine if multiple individuals are represented. This process has been termed "positive articulation" by Kerley (1972:355) and may provide important information, depending upon the skills of the observer and the nature of the evidence. More sophisticated sorting approaches can involve chemical or radiographic techniques.

Morphological Techniques

As early as 1972, Kerley emphasized the importance of experience in the ability to detect commingling and to sort out the respective individuals. He also emphasized the value of comparative morphology, with thoughtful evaluation of age at death, sex, and ancestry. He appropriately recommended caution in the interpretation of differences in coloration patterns because environmental factors that likely contribute to such differences frequently are not known in forensic analysis. Kerley also called attention to specific analytical techniques that offered some potential for analysis of commingling, namely, ultraviolet light analysis of fluorescence, radiographic approaches, blood-type study, and neutron activation analysis.

Rösing and Pischtschan (1995) also offer a review of approaches to the assessment of commingling. They provide excellent discussion of mathematical approaches, but recommend (beyond inventory) the use of sex, robusticity, age at death, bone color, surface preservation, and bone density.

Judgment and experience are usually required to assess the probabilities of articulating bones originating from the same individual. Such evaluations are best made in areas of the skeletal anatomy where the relationship between articulating bones is especially close. Examples are the vertebral articular facets (including the occipital condyles of the cranium) and femur/acetabulum articulation. London and Curran (1986) and London and Hunt (1998) have called attention to the value of the latter in contributing useful information for commingling evaluation. Their research suggests that a combination of observations and measurements facilitates evaluation of the femoral head and acetabulum relationship.

Buikstra and Gordon (1980) document how evaluation of the articular surfaces and general morphology of the cervical vertebrae can be useful in assessing commingling. Their study of the Smithsonian's Terry collection emphasizes the use of both measurements and observations of epiphyseal union in establishing the probabilities involved. In a later publication, Buikstra et al. (1984) provide more detail on how such an approach proved useful in a dispute regarding, in part, if cervical vertebrae found in one location originated from the same individual as other cervical vertebrae from another location. These two publications also present useful summaries of the literature (largely not duplicated here) relating to these issues.

Bone weight represents another variable that could be relevant in some commingling assessments. Much of the relevant data here stems from an early interest in the relationship between bone weight and body weight. As noted by Baker and Newman (1957), this correlation is only very general; however, within individuals the correlation of the relative weight of individual bones is substantial. Using data gathered from 125 skeletons of war dead examined in Kokura, Japan, at Army Graves Registration Service Headquarters, they produced regression equations that enable dry weight of individual bones to be predicted from another bone. For example, using their regression equations, the approximate weight of a tibia could be predicted from a femur of the same individual. Baker and Newman (1957) offer a more detailed procedure for evaluating commingling using weight and other data. Stewart (1979) critically evaluated this approach: "Given the limitation of the method to fat-free bones, I feel compelled to express doubt that the separation of commingled remains by this untested metrical means can be done any better than, if as well as, by eye. Also, most certainly the eye can do the job faster" (Stewart, 1979:225–226).

In spite of the difficulties of using bone weight as a specific indicator of body weight, extreme situations can support opinions in some circumstances. Murray and Rose (1993) describe a civil case involving the analysis of cremains, the residue of human cremation. In this case two sets of cremains were present. Both had been presented to a family as representing the cremains of a particular decedent. Analysis revealed differences between the two sets of cremains, indicating to the authors that they did not originate from the same individual. The combined weight of the two sets of cremains was larger than the weight expected by the authors from a single individual. The weight information contributed to the evaluation that more than one individual was represented.

As discussed above, duplication of skeletal parts offers positive evidence of commingling; however, the lack of duplication, by itself, does not prove that commingling did not occur. As noted by Snow and Folk (1965), in most forensic contexts, in the absence of duplicated bones, the likelihood of commingling diminishes with the increasing size of the sample. They provide a statistical procedure to evaluate the probabilities involved.

Snow and Luke (1970, 1984) further offer an example of how the statistical evaluation procedure (Snow and Folk, 1965) can be applied in an actual forensic case. In the 1960s two children disappeared from the Oklahoma City area. Skeletonized child remains were later recovered with no duplication of skeletal elements. The application of the mathematical approach to the recovered remains suggested a high likelihood that only one individual was present. This contributed to the case interpretation that only one individual had been recovered.

Fluorescence

McKern (1958) suggested that the fluorescence of human bone when viewed under short wave ultraviolet light can be useful in some situations to evaluate commingling. His test of this technique on a large sample of human remains suggested it might be useful at times for sorting remains of individuals.

The problem is not only the natural variation within a skeleton for fluorescence, but also how it is influenced by postmortem effects that may have operated differentially on the different bones represented. Eyman (1965) experimented with human bones from individuals from an archeological context using a modification of this approach. Eyman found that ultraviolet fluorescence was useful in indicating which bones originated from the same individual, but it was less successful in separating individuals from different archeological sites.

Trace Element Analysis

In 1970, Guinn called attention to the potential of trace element analysis, particularly neutron activation analysis, in forensic analysis. In short, this application assumes that if two specimens being tested share not only major-element components but also minor or trace element components, they likely originated from the same source. Guinn noted that the technique was then widely used on many materials recovered in a forensic context and had excellent potential when applied to hair or blood if contamination factors could be controlled.

In a 1986 test on human bone, Fulton et al. found that ratios of trace metal provided some useful information in sorting out commingling problems. The data were not precise enough to sort out individuals from large commingled mass graves, but offered useful data in resolving some specific commingling problems when used in conjunction with other techniques. In this experimental study, 21 elements were sampled from 54 sites on 30 human bones from 5 skeletons. The ratio of magnesium to zinc was the most useful in addressing commingling problems. More recent research by Finnegan (1988) and Finnegan and Chaudhuri (1990) suggests that trace elements and especially measurements of isotopic strontium show promise for commingling analysis.

Although chemical techniques continue to show great potential, contamination remains a critical problem. Most forensic cases originate not from museum anatomical collections but from environments that are closer to archeological contexts. In such situations, the opportunity for environmental chemical invasion of hard tissue is significant. Considerable attention has focused on this problem in the context of chemical dietary analysis from archeological bone and teeth (Ambrose and Norr, 1993; Katzenberg, 1992; Schwarcz and Schoeninger, 1991; Sillen and Kavanagh, 1982). For example, Klepinger et al. (1986) conducted chemical elemental analysis of archeologically recovered human bone from Sicily and experienced difficulty separating dietary indicators from the effects of diagenesis.

In recent years, the ability to relate commingled remains, especially those including soft tissue, has been greatly aided by molecular approaches. When resources are available to allow molecular analysis of recovered samples, difficult cases show high potential for resolution. The molecular literature is too large to be summarized here, but coupled with

Figure 18.1 Bone concentration within ossuary II, Maryland. (From Ubelaker, D.H., Reconstruction of Demographic Profiles from Ossuary Skeletal Samples: A Case Study from the Tidewater Potomac, Smithsonian Contributions to Anthropology 18, 1974, p. 23. With permission.)

more traditional techniques, these new approaches offer powerful new tools. A logical use of molecular analysis involves first proceeding with sorting and identification using the techniques discussed above. Molecular techniques potentially could be applied to remaining problems.

An Ossuary Example

Ossuaries represent communal deposits of skeletal remains from multiple individuals who were initially deposited elsewhere after death. Ossuaries from archeological contexts are well known from eastern North America, especially the areas of the mid-Atlantic and the Great Lakes. Here, ethnohistorical and archeological evidence suggests that Indian groups living in those areas went to great lengths to gather up all of their dead for communal burial. Archeological discovery of these ossuaries has revealed the expected large deposits of many individuals. In the mid-Atlantic area, the ossuaries that have been carefully excavated have produced individuals in various stages of articulation. Since the ossuary burial procedure calls for the mutual inclusion of all individuals who had died since the last burial ceremony, some individuals would have been included who had died relatively recently and were completely articulated. Others died earlier and were in more advanced stages of decomposition, allowing parts of the body to detach during the removal process. A final group died long before and were completely skeletonized. During ossuary burial the bones from this final group would completely disarticulate. Obviously, excavation and analysis of such an assemblage involve major assessment of commingling.

Table 18.1 Number of Individuals Represented by Each Type of Subadult Bone in Ossuary II

Bone	Left	Midline or Side Unknown	Right
Humerus	71		68
Radius	47		45
Ulna	58		54
Femur	89		82
Tibia	67		75
Fibula	35		35
Clavicle	47		49
Scapula	59		52
Temporal	81		84
Maxilla	49		49
Mandible	52		49
Gladiolus		10	
Manubrium		13	
Ilium	71		58
Ischium	43		48
Pubis	41		22
Patella	0		1
Rib		19 (494)[a]	
Vertebrae[b]		29 (775)[a]	
Sacrum		10	
Coccyx		1 (4)[a]	
Calcaneus	18		25
Talus		10 (20)[a]	
Other tarsals		3 (28)[a]	
Carpals		1 (10)[a]	
Metatarsals/metacarpals		16 (295)[a]	
Phalanges		6 (271)[a]	

[a] Numbers in parentheses indicate actual number of bones.

[b] Cervicals, thoracics, lumbars.

Source: From Ubelaker, D.H., Reconstruction of Demographic Profiles from Ossuary Skeletal Samples: A Case Study from the Tidewater Potomac, Smithsonian Contributions to Anthropology 18, 1974, p. 33. With permission.

In 1971 and 1972, T. Dale Stewart and I excavated such an ossuary (Figure 18.1) from a site in southern Maryland (Ubelaker, 1974). The site had been visited previously by Stewart, who supervised the excavation of a first ossuary there in 1953 and 1955. Although my involvement with the excavation dates back nearly 30 years, the experience offers an excellent example of the analysis of commingling.

Because most of the bone assemblage was secondary and lacked the articulations needed to relate bones to individuals, we conducted a skeletal inventory of bone and side, separated for immature and mature, to assess the minimum number of individuals. To examine cultural evidence of spatial variability within the ossuary, bones within artificially designated squares were first tabulated. These data then were merged to assess the overall representation. The inventory of immature remains was reported separately from that of mature individuals.

Table 18.2   Order of Representation of Subadults in Ossuary II as Indicated by Bone Types

Bone	Represented		Absent	
	No.	%	No.	%
Femur	89	100	0	0
Temporal	84	94	5	6
Tibia	75	84	14	16
Ilium	72	81	17	19
Humerus	71	80	18	20
Scapula	60	67	29	33
Ulna	58	65	31	35
Mandible	52	58	37	42
Maxilla	49	55	40	45
Ischium	49	55	40	45
Clavicle	49	55	40	45
Radius	47	53	42	48
Pubis	41	46	48	54
Fibula	35	39	54	61
Vertebrae	29	33	60	67
Calcaneus	25	28	65	72
Ribs	24	27	66	73
Metatarsals/metacarpals	16	18	73	82
Manubrium	13	15	76	85
Gladiolus	10	11	79	89
Talus	10	11	79	89
Phalanges	6	7	83	93
Other tarsals	3	3	86	97
Sacrum	3	3	86	97
Carpals	1	1	88	99
Patella	1	1	88	99

Source: From Ubelaker, D.H., Reconstruction of Demographic Profiles from Ossuary Skeletal Samples: A Case Study from the Tidewater Potomac, Smithsonian Contributions to Anthropology 18, 1974, p. 37. With permission.

Results of the immature remains inventory are provided in Table 18.1. The table reveals the variability of immature bone representation: 89 individuals were represented by left femora; at the other extreme, only 1 immature right patella was found. Table 18.2 presents these data arranged by bone type in order of maximum representation with an indication of the percentage of bones of this type that are not present as well.

Similar results were found for adults (Table 18.3). When these data are also arranged in order of greatest representation (Table 18.4), maximum counts come from the tibia, followed closely by the femur and humerus. At the other extreme, 96% of the second through the fifth distal foot phalanges was missing. The order of the bones present on both the adult and immature lists generally approximates their size. Since the ossuary was carefully excavated using fine hand tools, with backdirt screened, etc., and maximum care was provided after excavation in processing and storage, it seems likely that the differential representation results from events prior to excavation. Some small fragile bones that had been deposited in the ossuary possibly were not detected during excavation and analysis due to poor preservation. Because preservation of most bones was generally excellent, especially for the mature remains, loss due to this factor was likely minimal. Most of the variability in bone representation appeared to represent selection on the part of the Indians. Through either careful intentional selection of the parts buried or unintentional carelessness, not all of the remains had been transferred from their primary repository to the ossuary. Thus, as with many commingled bone assemblages found in archeological and forensic contexts, the final bone grouping represents the culmination of many factors, including human behavior.

In regard to the Maryland ossuary, the number of individuals represented by immature bones (at least 89 left femora) combined with the number of individuals represented by mature bones (at least 99 right mandibles) suggests the combined presence of at least 188 individuals. This represents the minimum number of individuals determined by the bone inventories. Of course, the actual number represented could be larger if some subadults were represented by bones other than the left femur and some adults by bones other than the right mandible. The minimum number represented perhaps could be determined more precisely by attempting to match pairs of bones, or arranging the immature bones by approximate age. Such additional analysis was complicated by the large size of the assemblage, but would be a recommended addition to smaller studies.

Portuguese Medieval Battle of Aljubarrota

Cunha and Silva (1997) chose a similar approach to examine the minimum number of individuals represented in their skeletal sample from a famous Medieval Period Portuguese battle. Victims of the 1385 battle had been commingled and placed in a communal ossuary. Careful inventory revealed that at least 400 individuals were represented by the right femur.

The Crow Creek Massacre Site

Selection of techniques to assess commingling and evaluate the individuals represented must be chosen on a case-by-case basis. Each problem and context should be assessed on its own merits. P. Willey reports (1990) an interesting example from the Great Plains of the United States. His excavation and analysis focused on a large prehistoric communal burial of American Indian origin. Archeological and skeletal findings suggested the individuals buried there were massacre victims who probably died at the hands of another hostile Indian group. Because of political complications stemming from contemporary American Indians (Ubelaker and Grant, 1989), the remains were available for analysis only for a relatively short period of time. Each "bag" of bones resulting from the excavation was analyzed separately. The contents of each were inventoried and then the numbers were totaled to obtain the maximum counts. This procedure recognized the possibility of some duplication of counts in the case of fragmented remains but also considered articulation data and observations on archeological context. The frequencies of the bones recovered suggest that 486 individuals were represented by right temporals, 477 by left temporals, 367 by left and right femora, 269 by right tibiae, and only 91 by left radii. Willey felt that scavenging activity of animals between death and burial as well as cultural selection of the parts to be buried likely produced most of the reported variability in the counts.

The Search for Father Bachelot

Smaller samples offer greater opportunities for refined analysis. Pietrusewsky and Willacker (1997) report their careful study of remains which were thought perhaps to represent an early Catholic missionary to the Hawaiian Islands. Father Bachelot was the leader of the first Catholic missionary group to the Hawaiian Islands between 1827 and 1837. In a search for the remains of this prominent figure in Hawaiian history, six sets of commingled remains were recovered. Father Bachelot was a male of French ancestry and 41 years of age at the time of his death.

Analysis involved sorting the remains by skeletal element, size and age at death. This procedure established that at least 10 individuals were present; 8 of the individuals could be eliminated from consideration as being those of the missionary because of their age at death, sex, and the likely presence of a disease (yaws) from which it was believed Father Bachelot did not suffer. The remaining two individuals showed evidence of Pohnpean ancestry rather than the French ancestry of the missionary. In addition, some artifacts of native (not French) manufacture were present with the remains. The authors concluded that the remains represented local inhabitants of the island and not the missionary. Theoretically, some of the bones present could have originated from the man and just happened to appear consistent with the other more identifiable remains. From the analysis conducted however, the probability of such commingling is low.

Taphonomic Factors in Commingling

Taphonomic factors are always present in commingled skeletal assemblages. The list of such factors is long and varied. It begins with the death of the individual and can extend to the time of analysis. Extensive discussion of the complex taphonomic factors that affect bone assemblages is available in the published literature (e.g., Binford, 1981,1984; Haglund and Sorg, 1997; Lyman, 1994). Human behavior plays a very important role in the process that leads to commingling in archeological assemblages (Binford, 1978) and especially in those of forensic contexts (Haglund and Sorg, 1997).

Although exotic explanations of commingled samples are not unexpected in forensic remains, they are less likely in most archeological assemblages. Brain (1976), for example, examined bone accumulations associated with Hottentot villages along the Kuiseb River in the Central Namib Desert. Bone refuse of goats was highly variable, reflecting human activity, animal chewing, and other preservation factors. Brain suggested that the bone distribution at the African Australopithecine site of Makapansgat could be explained by similar factors. This interpretation contrasted with more exotic explanations offered by others.

Many human activities can lead to incomplete skeletal representation and commingling. Burning of remains can lead to fragmentation and differential skeletal representation (Buikstra and Swegle, 1989; Heglar, 1984). Criminal behavior and/or mortuary practices can add complexity.

Willey (1997) studied human remains recovered from the Custer National Cemetery. The mixed preservation seemed to favor "larger, more proximal bones" over smaller distal ones (Willey, 1997:i). Such a preservation pattern reflected previous exhumation practice, in addition to other factors.

Table 18.3 Number of Individuals Represented by Each Type of Adult Bone in Ossuary II

Bone	Left	? or Midline	Right
Long			
Humerus	87		84
Radius	80		80
Ulna	88		86
Femur	82		85
Tibia	81		93
Fibula	74		81
Clavicle	70		72
Irregular			
Scapula	85		92
Temporal	92		91
Maxilla	86		81
Mandible	98		99
Gladiolus		56	
Manubrium		58	
Innominate	84		86
Patella	73		78
Rib		72 (1727)[a]	
Cervicals			
1		98	
2		97	
3–7		76 (389)	
Thoracics			
1–9		72 (645)[a]	
10		63	
11		80	
12		59	
10 or 11		37	
11 or 12		1	
10 or 11		11	
Lumbars 1–5		77 (385)[a]	
Sacrum		84	
Coccyx		9 (33)[a]	
Hand			
Navicular	59		63
Lunate	54		46
Triquetral	41		24
Pisiform		18 (35)[a]	
G. multangular	45		55
L. multangular	37		38
Capitate	69		58
Hamate	51		55
MC1	66		68
MC2	74		65
MC3	74		77
MC4	56		54
MC5	69		74
Hand phalanges			
Proximal 1		53 (106)[a]	
Proximal 2–5		66 (524)[a]	

Table 18.3 Number of Individuals Represented by Each Type
of Adult Bone in Ossuary II (cont.)

Bone	Left	? or Midline	Right
Middle		44 (348)[a]	
Distal 1		29 (57)[a]	
Distal 2–5		23 (181)[a]	
Foot			
Calcaneus	86		86
Talus	93		90
Cuboid	70		73
Navicular	69		80
Cuneiform 1	78		73
Cuneiform 2	73		68
Cuneiform 3	73		75
MT1	82		74
MT2	72		63
MT3	77		85
MT4	77		74
MT5	81		73
Foot phalanages			
Proximal 1		60 (125)[a]	
Proximal 2–5		46 (385)[a]	
Middle		19 (118)[a]	
Distal 1		45 (89)[a]	
Distal 2–5		9 (55)[a]	

[a] Numbers in parentheses indicate actual number of bones.

Source: From Ubelaker, D.H., Reconstruction of Demographic Profiles from
Ossuary Skeletal Samples: A Case Study from the Tidewater Potomac, Smithsonian
Contributions to Anthropology 18, 1974, p. 34. With permission.

In their analysis of archeologically recovered burials at the Larson Site in South Dakota,
Bass and Rucker (1976) discovered many graves with multiple individuals of varying
completeness. They felt this pattern reflected the Arikara's attempt to resolve the very
practical problem of how to bury their dead during the winter. During the freezing winter
months, the best site for burial was that of a previous burial in which the soil was less
compact. Articulation patterns and pit outlines noted during excavation provided the keys
to this interpretation.

Animal Chewing

Animal chewing is common on remains that are accessible. Animal activity can lead to
destruction of remains, dispersal, and even commingling. Much has been learned about the
effects of different animals on bone (Haglund and Sorg, 1997; Ubelaker, 1989). Animal
activity can affect bone counts and estimates of the minimal number of individuals in bone
assemblages. Marean and Spencer (1991) report an experiment with spotted hyenas suggesting that hyena activity is focused on the ends of the long bones. Thus, maximum bone
counts would come from the diaphyseal midshaft rather than the proximal or distal ends.

Hudson (1993) published a controlled study of faunal remains associated with the Aka
of the Central African Republic. In this community, domestic dogs played a major role in
dispersal of faunal remains. Hudson found that the smaller the animal, the greater the

Table 18.4   Order of Representation of Adults in Ossuary II as Indicated by Bone Types

Bones	Represented		Absent	
	No.	%	No.	%
Mandible	99	100	0	0
1st cervical	98	99	1	1
2nd cervical	97	98	2	2
Tibia	93	94	6	6
Talus	93	94	6	6
Scapula	92	93	7	7
Temporal	92	93	7	7
Ulna	88	89	11	11
Humerus	87	88	12	12
Innominate	86	87	13	13
Maxilla	86	87	13	13
Calcaneus	86	87	13	13
3rd metatarsal	85	86	14	14
Femur	85	86	14	14
10/11/12 thoracics	84	85	15	15
Sacrum	84	85	15	15
1st metatarsal	82	83	17	17
5th metatarsal	81	82	18	18
Fibula	81	82	18	18
Radius	80	81	19	19
Foot navicular	80	81	19	19
Patella	78	79	21	21
1st cuneiform	78	79	21	21
4th metatarsal	77	78	22	22
3rd metatarsal	77	78	22	22
Lumbars	77	78	22	22
3–7 cervicals	76	77	23	23
3rd cuneiform	75	76	24	24
5th metacarpal	74	75	25	25
2nd metacarpal	74	75	25	25
Cuboid	73	74	26	26
2nd cuneiform	73	74	26	26
2nd metatarsal	72	73	27	27
1–9 thoracics	72	73	27	27
Clavicle	72	73	27	27
Rib	72	73	27	27
Capitate	69	70	30	30
1st metacarpal	68	69	31	31
Prox. 2–5 hand phalanges	66	67	33	33
Hand navicular	63	64	36	36
1st prox. foot phalanx	60	61	39	39
Manubrium	58	59	41	41
Gladiolus	56	57	43	43
4th metacarpal	56	57	43	43
Greater multangular	55	56	44	44
Hamate	55	56	44	44
Lunate	54	55	45	45
1st prox. hand phalanx	53	54	46	46
2–5 distal foot phalanges	46	46	53	54
1st distal foot phalanx	45	45	54	55

**Table 18.4   Order of Representation of Adults in Ossuary II as
Indicated by Bone Types (cont.)**

Bones	Represented		Absent	
	No.	%	No.	%
Middle hand phalanges	44	44	55	56
Triquetral	41	41	58	59
Lesser multangular	38	38	61	62
1st distal hand phalanx	29	29	70	71
2–5 distal hand phalanges	23	23	76	77
Middle foot phalanges	19	19	80	81
Pisiform	18	18	81	82
Coccygeal vertebrae	9	9	90	91
2–5 distal foot phalanges	9	9	90	91

Source: From Ubelaker, D.H., Reconstruction of Demographic Profiles from Ossuary Skeletal Samples: A Case Study from the Tidewater Potomac, Smithsonian Contributions to Anthropology 18, 1974, p. 36. With permission.

probability of loss. Resulting bone counts accurately measured the presence of larger species but poorly accounted for smaller ones.

Bone Density

As noted by Lyman (1993), bone density can be an important factor in the survival of skeletal parts although animal chewing is not always correlated with density. Galloway et al. (1997) used a single photon absorptiometer to measure bone density in a modern forensic sample. Like others, they noted that density is a factor in postmortem preservation, but they also found that variation due to sex, handedness, and age may be influencing factors. The same group (Willey et al., 1997) found that bone density correlated with bone survival in the Crow Creek assemblage discussed earlier.

Age at death is closely linked with bone density in postmortem preservation issues. Guy et al. (1997) found that the low mineralization associated with infant bone contributes to poor preservation. Similar factors suggested to Walker et al. (1988) that age factors, especially the very young and very old, contribute to differential preservation. Again, low bone density in these age groups appears to be the key factor.

Preservation also relates to the many variables that are properties of the environment (Haglund and Sorg, 1997; Ubelaker, 1989). Gordon and Buikstra (1981) have demonstrated how soil acidity can affect bone preservation.

Excavation Factors

Excavation techniques can further alter the preservation of remains and lead to commingling. Bones that have been weakened by human or environmental factors are especially vulnerable to fragmentation during recovery. A hasty or incomplete excavation can alter the bone assemblage. Casteel (1972) demonstrated how a recovery technique such as mesh size used in screening can influence faunal samples. Similarly, Payne (1975) water-screened the backdirt of an excavation and found many smaller bones and bones of smaller species. Thus, recovery technique can influence the representation of species in faunal studies and of individual bones and ages in human studies.

Curation Practices

The final limitation placed on skeletal samples relates to storage and processing protocols operating on samples prior to analysis. The analyst may not be aware of what practices others have employed regarding the samples studied. This is especially a problem with older museum collections and forensic cases in which the forensic anthropologist may follow a long line of previous examiners.

Stewart (1937) describes an archeological project that sent 80 barrels of fragmentary human remains to the Smithsonian for curation. Stewart relates how lack of storage space forced curators to decide what aspects of the remains should be saved for analysis. Thus, storage facilities and curation policy can affect the final assemblage available for study.

Number of Individuals Represented by Bone Counts

As noted above, skeletal biologists and forensic anthropologists have utilized detailed bone inventories, coupled with observations on articulation, age at death, sex, joint congruence, and a variety of other factors to determine the minimum number of individuals represented by the assemblage. The related question of how many actual individuals are represented by the minimum number is rarely addressed. The mathematical approach advocated by Snow and associates (1970, 1984) reveals some information in this regard, but most anthropologists have been content to not estimate numbers beyond the minimum indicated, likely in recognition of the unknown variables involved.

Paleontologists and archaeozoologists working with faunal assemblages have struggled with the larger question of total individual representation for some time. Issues include anatomical defects as potential sources of error in individual counts (Steele and Parama, 1981), statistical procedures for sampling (Chapman, 1951), and general issues of the relationship between individual counts and the total number of individuals present (Allen and Guy, 1984; Casteel, 1977; Chase and Hagaman, 1987; Fieller and Turner, 1982; Gilbert et al., 1981; Gilbert and Singer, 1982; Grayson, 1973, 1978, 1981, 1984; Klein and Cruz-Uribe, 1984; Krantz, 1968; Lyman, 1987; Plug, 1984; Plug and Plug, 1990; Ringrose, 1993; Shotwell, 1995; Wild and Nichol, 1983; Winder, 1991). Specific techniques advocated include

A computer procedure to assist matching bones by size (Nichol and Creak, 1979)
Techniques modified from the mark-capture procedure in which a sample of a biological living population is captured, marked, and released, followed by the capturing of a new sample and observing the percentage that are marked (LeCren, 1965)
A sorting procedure that considers bone counts along with the size and age of the animal (Bökönyi, 1970)
The Lincoln Index based on matching pairs of bones (Winder, 1992)

As noted by Badgely (1986), Holtzman (1979), and Horton (1984), the selection of which methods to use depends upon the nature of the assemblage, problem orientation, and other factors. All of the methods make assumptions but offer a variety of approaches to estimating the size of the total population.

Although the issues discussed above have produced a voluminous and somewhat tedious discussion among archaeozoologists and paleontologists, physical anthropologists generally have remained on the sidelines. A notable exception is the work of Adams (1996)

who reviewed this literature and used one of the techniques, the Lincoln/Peterson Index, to assess the number of individuals represented in an archeologically recovered assemblage of human bone from South Dakota. The Lincoln/Peterson Index involves estimating the total population size by multiplying the number of bones of one side by the number of bones of the opposite side and dividing the product by the number of matched pairs of that bone. Adams applied this technique to the Larson village sample from the area of Mobridge, South Dakota, a sample that had previously been studied by others (Owsley and Bass, 1979; Owsley et al., 1977). In particular, the Owsley et al. (1977) work had obtained the minimum number of individuals by a straightforward count of right and left major bones. Adams' reanalysis of the material generally agreed with the Owsley et al. (1977) minimum number of individuals from the bone counts. His application of the Lincoln/Peterson Index then produced a slightly larger figure.

Summary

Although forensic anthropologists only occasionally deal with issues of skeletal commingling in their work, such cases can be challenging. As anthropologists become increasingly involved in mass disasters and other events leading to fragmentation and mixing of individuals, this work likely will grow.

Recent years have witnessed a gradual increase in the scientific tools available to study commingled cases. Although these developments are helpful, experience with skeletal morphology remains the principal requirement for skilled analysis.

References

Adams, B.J.
    1996 The use of the Lincoln/Peterson Index for quantification and interpretation of commingled human remains. Unpublished Master's Thesis, Department of Anthropology, University of Tennessee, Knoxville.

Allen, J. and J.B.M. Guy
    1984 Optimal estimations of individuals in archaeological faunal assemblages: How minimal is the MNI?, *Archaeology in Oceania* 19:41–47.

Ambrose, S.H. and L. Norr
    1993 Experimental evidence for the relationship of the carbon isotope ratios of whole diet and dietary protein to those of bone collagen and carbonate. In *Prehistoric Human Bone: Archeology at the Molecular Level,* edited by J.B. Lamber and G. Grupe, pp. 1–38. Springer-Verlag, Berlin.

Baker, P.T. and R.W. Newman
    1957 The use of bone weights for human identification, *American Journal of Physical Anthropology* 15:601–618.

Bass, W.M. and M.D. Rucker
    1976 Preliminary investigation of artifact association in an Arikara cemetery (Larson Site), Walworth County, South Dakota, National Geographic Research Reports, 1968 Projects, pp. 33–48.

Binford, L.R.
    1978 *Nunamiut Ethnoarchaeology,* Academic Press, New York.
    1981 *Bones: Ancient Men and Modern Myths,* Academic Press, New York.
    1984 *Faunal Remains from Klaises River Mouth,* Academic Press, New York.

Bladgley, C.
1986 Counting individuals in mammalian fossil assemblages from fluvial environments, *Palaios* 1:328–338.

Bökönyi, S.
1970 A new method for the determination of the number of individuals in animal bone material, *American Journal of Archaeology* 74:291–292.

Brain, C.K.
1976 Some principles in the interpretation of bone accumulations associated with man. In *Human Origins: Louis Leakey and the East African Evidence,* edited by G.L. Isaac and E.R. McGown, pp. 97–106. W.A. Benjamin, Menlo Park.

Buikstra, J.E. and C.C. Gordon
1980 Individuation in forensic science study: decapitation, *Journal of Forensic Sciences* 25:246–259.

Buikstra, J.E. and M. Swegle
1989 Bone modification due to burning: experimental evidence. In *Bone Modification,* edited by R. Bonnichsen and M. Sorg, pp. 247–258. Maine Center for the Study of the First Americans, Orono.

Buikstra, J.E. and D.H. Ubelaker, Eds.
1994 Standards for Data Collection from Human Skeletal Remains, Proceedings of a Seminar at the Field Museum of Natural History. Arkansas Archaeological Survey Research Series No. 44, Arkansas Archaeological Survey, Fayetteville.

Buikstra, J.E., C.C. Gordon, and L. St. Hoyme
1984 The case of the severed skull: Individuation in forensic anthropology. In *Human Identification: Case Studies in Forensic Anthropology,* edited by T.A. Rathbun and J.E. Buikstra, pp. 121–135. Charles C Thomas, Springfield, IL.

Casteel, R.W.
1972 Some biases in the recovery of archaeological faunal remains, *Proceedings of the Prehistoric Society* 38:382–388.

1977 Characterization of faunal assemblages and the minimum number of individuals determined from paired elements: continuing problems in archaeology, *Journal of Archaeological Science* 4:125–134.

Chapman, D.G.
1951 Some properties of the hypergeometric distribution with applications to zoological sample census, *University of California Publications in Statistics* 1:131–159.

Chase, P.G. and R.M. Hagaman
1987 Minimum number of individuals and its alternatives: a probability theory perspective, *OSSA* 13:75–86.

Cunha, E. and A.M. Silva
1997 War lesions from the famous Portuguese Medieval Battle of Aljubarrota, *International Journal of Osteoarcheology* 7:595–599.

Eyman, C.E.
1965 Ultraviolet fluorescence as a means of skeletal identification, *American Antiquity* 31:109–112.

Fieller, N.R.J. and A. Turner
1982 Number estimation in vertebrate samples, *Journal of Archaeological Science* 9:49–62.

Finnegan, M.
1988 Variation of trace elements within and between skeletons using multiple sample sites. Paper presented at the 15th Annual Meeting of the Paleopathology Association, Kansas City, MO.

Finnegan, M. and S. Chaudhuri
   1990   Identification of commingled skeletal remains using isotopic strontium. Paper presented at the 42nd Annual Meeting of the American Academy of Forensic Sciences, Cincinnati.

Fulton, B.A., C.E. Meloan, and M. Finnegan
   1986   Reassembling scattered and mixed human bones by trace element ratios. *Journal of Forensic Sciences,* 31(4):1455–1462.

Galloway, A., P. Willey, and L. Snyder
   1997   Human bone mineral densities and survival of bone elements: a contemporary sample. In *Forensic Taphonomy,* edited by W.D. Haglund and M.H. Sorg, pp. 295-317. CRC Press, Boca Raton, FL.

Gilbert, A.S. and B.H. Singer
   1982   Reassessing zooarchaeological quantification, *World Archaeology* 14:21–40.

Gilbert, A.S., B.H. Singer, and D. Perkins, Jr.
   1981   Quantification experiments on computer-simulated faunal collections, *OSSA* 8:79–94.

Gordon, C.G. and J.E. Buikstra
   1981   Soil pH, bone preservation, and sampling bias at mortuary sites, *American Antiquity* 46:566–571.

Grayson, D.K.
   1973   On the methodology of faunal analysis, *American Antiquity* 38:432–439.

   1978   Minimum numbers and sample size in vertebrate faunal analysis, *American Antiquity* 43:53–65.

   1981   A critical view of the use of archaeological vertebrates in paleoenvironmental reconstruction, *Journal of Ethnobiology* 1:28–38.

   1984   *Quantatative Zooarchaeology,* Academic Press, New York.

Guinn, V.P.
   1970   Forensic neutron activation analysis. In *Personal Identification in Mass Disasters,* edited by T.D. Stewart, pp. 25-35. Smithsonian Institution, Washington, D.C.

Guy, H., C. Masset, and C.-A. Baud
   1997   Infant taphonomy, *International Journal of Osteoarcheology* 7:221–229.

Haglund, W.D. and M.H. Sorg, Editors
   1997   *Forensic Taphonomy: The Postmortem Fate of Human Remains,* CRC Press, Boca Raton, FL.

Heglar, R.
   1984   Burned remains. In *Human Identification: Case Studies in Forensic Anthropology,* edited by T. Rathbun and J.E. Buikstra, pp. 148–158. Charles C Thomas, Springfield, IL.

Holtzman, R.C.
   1979   Maximum likelihood estimation of fossil assemblage composition, *Paleobiology* 5:77–89.

Horton, D.R.
   1984   Minimum numbers: a consideration, *Journal of Archaeological Science* 11:255–271.

Hudson, J.
   1993   The impacts of domestic dogs on bone in forager camps. In *From Bones to Behavior: Ethnoarchaeological and Experimental Contributions to the Interpretations of Faunal Remains,* edited by J. Hudson, pp. 301–323. Center for Archaeological Investigations, Carbondale.

Katzenberg, M.A.
   1992   Advances in stable isotope analysis of prehistoric bones. In *The Skeletal Biology of Past Peoples: Research Methods,* edited by S.R. Saunders and M.A. Katzenberg, pp. 105-120. Wiley-Liss, New York.

Kerley, E.R.
   1972   Special observations in skeletal identification, *Journal of Forensic Sciences* 17:349–357.

Klein, R.G. and K. Cruz-Uribe
   1984   *The Analysis of Animal Bones from Archeological Sites*, University of Chicago Press, Chicago, IL.

Klepinger, L.L., J.K. Kuhn, and W.S. Williams
   1986   An elemental analysis of archaeological bone from Sicily as a test of predictability of diagenetic change, *American Journal of Physical Anthropology* 70:325–331.

Krantz, G.S.
   1968   A new method of counting mammal bones, *American Journal of Archaeology* 72:286–288.

Krogman, W.M.
   1962   *The Human Skeleton in Forensic Medicine*, Charles C Thomas, Springfield, IL.

Krogman, W.M. and M.Y. Iscan
   1986   *The Human Skeleton in Forensic Medicine*, 2nd ed., Charles C. Thomas, Springfield, IL.

LeCren, E.D.
   1965   A note on the history of mark-recapture population estimates, *Journal of Animal Ecology* 34:453–454.

London, M.R. and B.K. Curran
   1986   The use of the hip joint in the separation of commingled remains (abstract), *American Journal of Physical Anthropology* 69:231.

London, M.R. and D.R. Hunt
   1998   Morphometric segregation of commingled remains using the femoral head and acetabulum (abstract), *American Journal of Physical Anthropology* 26 (suppl.):152.

Lyman, R.L.
   1987   Zooarchaeology and taphonomy: a general consideration. *Journal of Ethnobiology* 7:93–117.

   1993   Density-mediated attrition of bone assemblages: new insights. In *From Bones to Behavior*, edited by J. Hudson, pp. 324–341. Center for Archaeological Investigations, Carbondale.

   1994   *Vertebrate Taphonomy*, Cambridge University Press, Cambridge.

Marean, C.W. and L.M. Spencer
   1991   Impact of carnivore ravaging on zooarchaeological measures of element abundance, *American Antiquity* 56:645–658.

McKern, T.W.
   1958   The Use of Shortwave Ultraviolet Rays for the Segregation of Commingled Skeletal Remains. Environmental Protection Research and Developments Command, Quartermaster Research and Development Center Environmental Protection Research Division, Natick, MA.

Murray, K.A. and J.C. Rose
   1993   The analysis of cremains: a case study involving the inappropriate disposal of mortuary remains, *Journal of Forensic Sciences* 38:98–103.

Nichol, R.K. and G.A. Creak
   1979   Matched paired elements among archaeological bone remains: a computer procedure and some practical limitations, *Newsletter of Computer Archaeology* 14:6–16.

Owsley, D.W. and W.M. Bass
   1979   A demographic analysis of skeletons from the Larson site (39WW2) Walworth County, South Dakota: vital statistics, *American Journal of Physical Anthropology* 51:145–154.

Owsley, D.W., H.E. Berryman, and W.M. Bass
  1977   Demographic and osteological evidence for warfare at the Larson site, South Dakota, *Plains Anthropologist Memoir* 13:119–131.

Payne, S.
  1975   Partial recovery and sample bias. In *Archaeozoological Studies,* edited by A.T. Clason, pp. 7–17. American Elsevier, New York.

Pietrusewsky, M. and L.M. Willacker
  1997   The search for Father Bachelot: first Catholic missionary to the Hawaiian Islands (1827–1837), *Journal of Forensic Sciences* 42:208–212.

Plug, I.
  1984   MNI counts, pits and features, *Frontiers: Southern African Archaeology Today,* edited by M. Hall et al., British Archaeological Reports International Series, Oxford, 207:357–362.

Plug, C. and I. Plug
  1990   MNI counts as estimates of species abundance, *South African Archaeological Bulletin* 45:53–57.

Ringrose, T.J.
  1993   Bone counts and statistics: a critique. *Journal of Archaeological Science* 20:121–157.

Rösing, F.W. and E. Pischtschan
  1995   Re-individualisation of commingled skeletal remains, *Advances in Forensic Sciences,* edited by B. Jacob and W. Bonte, Verlag, Berlin, 7:38–41.

Schwarcz, H.P. and M.J. Schoeninger
  1991   Stable isotope analysis in human nutritional ecology, *Yearbook of Physical Anthropology* 34:283–322.

Shotwell, J.A.
  1995   An approach to the palaeoecology of mammals, *Ecology* 36:327–337.

Sillen, A. and M. Kavanagh
  1982   Strontium and paleodietary research: a review, *Yearbook of Physical Anthropology* 25:67–90.

Snow C.C. and E.D. Folk
  1965   Statistical assessment of commingled skeletal remains, *American Journal of Physical Anthropology* 32:423–427.

Snow, C.C. and J.L. Luke
  1970   The Oklahoma City child disappearances of 1967: forensic anthropology in the identification of skeletal remains, *Journal of Forensic Sciences* 15:125–153.

Snow, C.C. and J.L. Luke
  1984   The Oklahoma City child disappearances of 1967: forensic anthropology in the identification of skeletal remains. In *Human Identification: Case Studies in Forensic Anthropology,* edited by T.A. Rathbun and J.E. Buikstra, pp. 253-277. Charles C Thomas, Springfield, IL.

Steele, D.G. and W.D. Parama
  1981   Frequencies of dental anomalies and their potential effect on determining MNI counts, *Plains Anthropologist* 26(91):51–54.

Stewart, T.D.
  1937   The problem of the fragmentary human skeleton [abstract], *American Journal of Physical Anthropology* XXII(3, suppl. 1):7–8.

Stewart, T.D.
  1979   *Essentials of Forensic Anthropology,* Charles C Thomas, Springfield, IL.

Ubelaker, D.H.

1974 Reconstruction of Demographic Profiles from Ossuary Skeletal Samples: A Case Study from the Tidewater Potomac, Smithsonian Contributions to Anthropology 18.

1989 *Human Skeletal Remains: Excavation, Analysis, Interpretation,* 2nd ed., Taraxacum, Washington.

Ubelaker, D.H. and L.G. Grant

1989 Human skeletal remains: preservation or reburial?, *Yearbook of Physical Anthropology* 32:249–287.

Walker, P.L., J.R. Johnson, and P.M. Lambert

1988 Age and sex biases in the preservation of human skeletal remains, *American Journal of Physical Anthropology* 76:183–188.

Wild, L. and R. Nichol

1983 Estimation of the original number of individuals using estimators of the Krantz type, *Journal of Field Archeology* 10:337–344.

Willey, P.

1990 *Prehistoric Warfare on the Great Plains: Skeletal Analysis of the Crow Creek Massacre Victims,* Garland, New York.

1997 Osteological Analysis of Human Skeletons Excavated from the Custer National Cemetery. Midwest Archeological Center Technical Report No. 50, National Park Service, Lincoln, NE.

Willey, P., A. Galloway, and L. Snyder

1997 Bone mineral density and survival of elements and element portions in the bones of the Crow Creek Massacre victims, *American Journal of Physical Anthropology* 104:513–528.

Winder, N.P.

1991 How many bones make five? The art and science of guesstimation in archaeozoology, *International Journal of Osteoarcheology* 1:111–126.

1992 The removal estimator: a 'probable numbers' statistic that requires no matching, *International Journal of Osteoarcheology* 2:15–18.

Modification of Bones, Soft Tissue, and Associated Materials

Detecting the Postburial Fragmentation of Carpals, Tarsals, and Phalanges

19

CHRISTYANN M. DARWENT
R. LEE LYMAN

Contents

Introduction

During the past 30 years paleontologists and zooarchaeologists have displayed a serious interest in taphonomy, a term originally coined and defined by Russian paleontologist I.A. Efremov (1940) as the study of the transition of organic remains from the biosphere into the lithosphere. Weigelt (1927; English translation, 1989) had previously proposed the term *biostratinomy* and defined it as the effects on organic remains that take place between the time of an organism's death and the burial of its remains. Muller (1963) later proposed the term *diagenesis* to denote the effects on organic remains that take place between the time of their burial and their recovery by a paleontologist or zooarchaeologist. Taphonomy, therefore, concerns both the biostratinomic and diagenetic phases of what Efremov referred to as the science of the laws of embedding or burial.

The burst of interest in taphonomy during the past 30 years has resulted in a marked increase in the number of published articles on the formation of the geological record of past life, particularly zoological life (Donovan, 1991; Lyman, 1994c). In zooarchaeology, the literature has focused most closely on deciphering taphonomic traces that signify aspects of biostratinomy for two reasons. First, this phase of taphonomic history is the one during which hominid taphonomic agents have their most direct input to the accumulation, modification, and deposition of faunal remains and, thus, is the one of most concern to zooarchaeologists interested in past human behavior (e.g., Hudson, 1993). Second, the processes comprising the biostratinomic phase are much more readily studied in an actualistic context than the processes operating during the diagenetic phase.*

Literature concerning the digenetic phase of taphonomy has tended to be written largely by paleontologists who focus on fossilization processes, or those that maintain or alter the chemical composition of organic remains (e.g., Donovan, 1991). The few contributions by zooarchaeologist examining diagenetic processes center on recognizing what is often mislabeled as "postdepositional" fragmentation (e.g., Klein, 1989; Klein and Cruz-Uribe, 1984:69–75; Marean, 1991; Villa and Mahieu, 1991). We say mislabeled because although deposition can be coincident with burial, actualistic research indicates that deposition can also, and often does, precede burial by various, sometimes taphonomically significant, lengths of time (e.g., Behrensmeyer, 1978). Marean (1991:677) defined "postdepositional processes ... as including chemical and mechanical action on bones and teeth after the bones and teeth have entered the sediment and are no longer sources of food for mammals." Although we agree with this definition, we prefer the term *postburial* because it avoids potential confusion that may result from use of the term *postdepositional*, particularly when it is not defined.**

Researchers have attempted to discern the degree of fragmentation of faunal remains that is attributable to the weight of overburden and sedimentary compaction. It is suggested by some that the influence of these factors is greater on bones that have undergone chemical leaching and, therefore, are structurally weakened. Study of the degree of postburial fragmentation is important for several reasons. Most fundamentally, fragmentation influences identifiability and, hence, measures of abundance. An assemblage of broken bones and teeth

---

* Actualistic research comprises observation, in this case, of taphonomic processes, documentation of the effects of these processes, and use of the latter to infer that similar processes produced similar effects in the past.

** In the present context, burial need not be a result of intentional human behavior. It can simply be the result of natural geological processes involving deposition of sediment.

will produce higher NISP (number of identified specimens) counts than a taxonomically and skeletally identical assemblage of unbroken bones and teeth. Further, as individual skeletal elements become progressively more broken, the NISP value progressively decreases (Lyman, 1994b; Marshall and Pilgrim, 1993). This decrease occurs because smaller fragments are less likely to retain anatomically and taxonomically diagnostic landmarks.

In this chapter we examine and expand one proposed method for recognition of diagenetic or postburial fragmentation so that it might be distinguished from biostratinomic fragmentation. Much of what we discuss owes its presence in the taphonomist's analytical tool kit to the seminal work of others, and our contribution to the study of digenetic processes builds upon this research. We view our efforts here as another small step toward developing taphonomic methods that will allow paleontologists and zooarchaeologists (and perhaps forensic scientists) to decipher taphonomic histories of assemblages of bones and teeth, particularly the little-explored diagenetic phase of those histories.

Background

Several years ago zooarchaeologist Curtis Marean (1991:692) hypothesized that "a bone's resistance to postdepositional destruction is determined by its density, size and shape mediated by the postdepositional process involved (chemical or mechanical)." Marean did not evaluate this hypothesis, but instead described a method that he believed would allow analytical recognition of postburial fragmentation of bones. He discussed three prerequisites to his method: two concerned the skeletal elements used in the analysis and the other concerned quantification of bone specimens.* Skeletal remains to be used should, Marean reasoned, be those (a) that are seldom if ever broken by hominids or carnivores and (b) whose relative frequencies are not influenced by bone accumulation processes. Last, the unit of quantification should not be subject to inter-observer variation. The first and second requirements were met by using carpals and tarsals,** skeletal elements that Marean (1991) argued were seldom broken by hominids and carnivores and that all underwent similar transportation histories in actualistic contexts. He, therefore, reasoned that the relative frequencies of these skeletal elements would not be influenced by these processes, but perhaps would be by postburial processes.

Marean met his third requirement by using a "completeness index" to characterize the degree of fragmentation. The completeness index "is derived by estimating for each specimen the fraction of the original compact bone that is present, summing the values, and dividing that by the total number of specimens ascribed to that bone and taxon" (Marean, 1991:685). For example, if three specimens of the astragalus are present, and one is complete (1.0), one comprises half of an astragalus (0.5), and one comprises a quarter of an astragalus (0.25), then one solves the equation $[(1.0 + 0.5 + 0.25)/3] \times 100 = 58.3$ to derive a percent completeness index (CI%) for the astragalus. The CI% value is properly read as the average completeness of the specimens for the skeletal element under consideration, such that in the preceding equation the value denotes that these three astragali are, on average, 58.3% complete skeletal elements.

---

* A *skeletal element* is defined as "a single complete bone or tooth, a discrete, complete anatomical organ" (Lyman, 1994b:290). A *specimen* is "a discrete bone or tooth, or fragment thereof" (Lyman, 1994b:290).
** For purposes of brevity, we include the distal fibula, also known as the lateral malleolus, in the (artiodactyl) tarsal category.

Marean (1991) noted that under experimental conditions hyenas often ingested artic-ulated carpals and articulated tarsals: carpals seldom, if ever, displayed gnawing damage whereas among the tarsals only the calcaneum displayed such damage, and it did so only about half of the time. Both carpals and tarsals displayed corrosion subsequent to their ingestion and passage through the digestive tract. Marean reasoned that specimens dis-playing digestive corrosion should be omitted from calculation of the CI%. Similarly, he argued that specimens that had been burned should also be omitted because they are more brittle than unburned specimens (Stiner et al., 1995), and specimens that were heavily weathered (Behrensmeyer, 1978) should be omitted because of the possibility that cracks produced by subaerial weathering would result in greater fragmentation than unweathered specimens subsequent to burial. Finally, he indicated that carpals and tarsals displaying percussion damage should be omitted from specimens used to derive the CI% value because that value is meant to measure postburial fragmentation. The unnoted assumption underpinning the last is that percussion damage will result *only* from the impact of human-wielded hammerstones, an assumption we find untenable if the bones were recovered from a cave whose roof produces rock spalls that fall to the cave floor.

When comparing the assemblages of artiodactyl carpals and tarsals from two African cave sites, Marean (1991:687) concluded that one assemblage had undergone much more "postdepositional destruction" than the other largely because the CI% was consistently lower across different carpals and tarsals in one collection than in the other. He also noted that (a) larger skeletal elements such as the astragalus and naviculo-cubiod displayed the greatest differences in CI% between the two assemblages and thus would likely provide the most reliable indication of postburial fragmentation, and (b) taxonomic differences in body size indicated that (larger) skeletal elements of larger taxa had lower CI% values than homologous elements in smaller-bodied taxa. Both of these observations suggest that larger bones tend to be more prone to fragmentation, before or after burial, than smaller bones.

Expanding the Method

Marean (1991) suggested that collections with low CI% values indicate greater postburial fragmentation than those with high CI% values. Such an interpretation rests on a limited number of experiments and theoretical reasoning that suggest carpals and tarsals meet the criteria Marean specified for detecting postburial destruction. Actualistic research cited by Marean (1991), however, indicates that hominids do sometimes fracture carpals and the smaller tarsals. How, then, is fragmentation resulting from biostratinomic processes to be disentangled from fragmentation resulting from diagenetic processes? The theoretical rea-sons for analysis of carpals and tarsals relate to their mechanical properties as sedimentary particles and their value as food sources for predators relative to other skeletal elements. The former relates to Marean's hypothesis that postburial fragmentation is mediated by density, size, and shape. The food value, as we indicate below, is also influenced by their size and shape. Consideration of each of these factors suggests ways to evaluate and expand Marean's method for recognizing postburial fragmentation.

Mechanical and Nutritional Properties of Skeletal Elements

Carpals and tarsals are, by and large, compact skeletal elements. They tend to be structurally dense (Table 19.1), and they also tend to be spherical in shape (Figure 19.1). The notable

Table 19.1 Structural Density, Volume (ml), Marrow Utility, and Grease Utility Values of Artiodactyl Carpals, Tarsals, and Phalanges

Skeletal Element	Structural Density[a]	Volume	Marrow Utility Index[b]	Grease Utility Index[b]
Carpals			(1.0)	(36.47)[c]
Cuneiform (ulnar carpal)	0.72	2	1.0[d]	5.03[e]
Lunar (intermediate carpal)	0.83	3	1.0[d]	7.55[e]
Pisiform (accessory carpal)	—[f]	1	1.0[d]	2.51[e]
Scaphoid (radial carpal)	0.98	3.5	1.0[d]	8.80[e]
Trapezoid magnum (carpal 2 +3)	0.74	3	1.0[d]	7.55[e]
Unciform (fourth carpal)	0.78	2	1.0[d]	5.03[e]
Tarsals			(1.0)[c]	(29.87)[c]
Calcaneum	0.64	18	21.19	46.96
Astragalus	0.61	12	1.0	32.47
Naviculo-cuboid	0.62	8.3	1.0[d]	21.56[e]
Tarsal 2 + 3 (external cuneiform)	—[f]	2	1.0[d]	5.19[e]
Distal fibula (lateral malleolus)	0.52	1.2	1.0[d]	3.12[e]
Phalanges				
First phalanx	0.57	6	30.00	33.27
Second phalanx	0.35	4.3	22.15	24.77
Third phalanx	0.25	3.7	1.0	13.59

[a] Values are for deer (*Odocoileus* sp.) and are the greatest recorded of several taken for calcaneum, naviculo-cuboid, astragalus, first phalanx, and second phalanx. (From Lyman, R.L., *Vertebrate Taphonomy*, Cambridge University Press, Cambridge, U.K., 1994c, pp. 246–247.)

[b] From Binford, L.R., *Nunamuit Ethnoarchaeology*, Academic Press, New York, 1978, pp. 27, 33.

[c] Values in parentheses for all carpals as a single unit and, we assume, for the naviculo-cuboid, tarsal 2 + 3, and distal fibula as a single unit. (From Binford, L.R., *Nunamuit Ethnoarchaeology*, Academic Press, New York, 1978, pp. 27, 33.)

[d] Values assigned by Darwent and Lyman (see text for discussion).

[e] Values derived and assigned by Darwent and Lyman (see text for discussion).

[f] No data available.

exception to the latter is the calcaneum, a skeletal element that has a more rod-like shape. Artiodactyl carpals and tarsals all tend to have rather low nutritional values; they contain minimal amounts of grease and virtually no marrow, as indicated by Binford's (1978) grease and marrow utility indices (Table 19.1). The theoretically significant points here are two. First, the relatively high structural density (g/cc) of these elements means that they require a great deal of force to break (Currey, 1984). In combination with the fact that carpals and tarsals have minimal interstitial space containing grease and marrow, this suggests that these elements would seldom be broken by hominids in order to extract potential sources of nutrition because the cost — particularly using primitive technologies — may well outweigh the return. For example, Marean's (1991: 691) experiments prompted him to suggest "an extraordinary effort is required to break fresh compact bones by hammerstone percussion." Carnivores may extract nutrients by ingesting carpals and tarsals whole, as documented by Marean's (1991) experimental feeding of hyenas.

The second important point with respect to the mechanical properties of bones is that relatively solid spheres, particularly small ones, can withstand significant compression and other forces without deformation or fracture. Hollow spheres (such as crania), solid or hollow rods (such as long bones), or solid or hollow plate-like structures (such as innominates and scapulae) cannot withstand forces of similar magnitude (Currey, 1984:147–150),

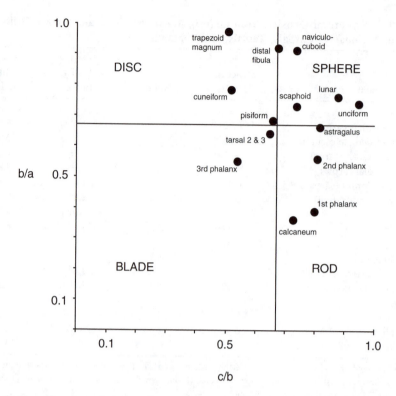

Figure 19.1 Classification of shape of carpals, tarsals, and phalanges.

particularly if their groundward surface is not uniformly in contact with the sediments on which they lie. Tarsals, with the exception of the calcaneum, and carpals are small and relatively spherical and thus their groundward surface is typically in uniform contact with the sediments on which they lie. Thus, they are unlikely to be regularly fractured by mere sediment overburden weight, which is not to say that they will *never* be broken by this taphonomic factor. For example, catastrophic burial, such as a roof-fall event within a cave, may not only bury bones, but fracture them as well (e.g., Thomas and Mayer, 1983). Chemical leaching no doubt weakens all bones, but we have no data to evaluate this diagenetic process and do not consider it further here.

If small spherical bones such as carpals and tarsals (except the calcaneum) are unlikely to be fractured except by diagenetic processes, then first and second phalanges should be more frequently broken than carpals and tarsals of the same taxon (Figure 19.1). This is because these phalanges contain more marrow and grease than carpals and tarsals (Table 19.1), and thus are more likely to be broken by predators (hominids or carnivores) during the biostratinomic phase. The second phalanx is also more likely to be broken than a carpal or tarsal because it is a hollow bone of rod-like shape, resulting in a greater probability of diagenetic fracture. First phalanges should be more broken than second phalanges because they are hollow rods and are longer than second phalanges, resulting in a greater probability of diagenetic fracture. For the same reason, the calcaneum, a relatively rod-like bone (Figure 19.1) with some marrow and grease (Table 19.1), should be relatively more broken than other tarsals and carpals as a result of both biostratinomic and diagenetic processes.

There are two assumptions underlying the statements in the preceding paragraph. First, we assume that during the biostratinomic phase, hominids and carnivores that are fracturing bones for purposes of grease/marrow extraction will break these bones in direct proportion to (a) their grease/marrow content and (b) ease of fracture (shape, size, and density related). Second, we assume that the probability that diagenetic processes will result in fragmentation decreases as skeletal element shape shifts from rod-like to sphere-like, and as skeletal elements increase in density (decrease in food utility) and decrease in size. Note what is said in the two immediately preceding sentences. Predators acting during the biostratinomic phase will break skeletal elements relative to the ease of element fracturing, and diagenetic processes will break skeletal elements relative to their shape, density, and size, or their ease of fracture. In other words, we suspect Marean's hypothesis that the fragmentation of skeletal elements will be mediated by the elements' shape, density, and size is correct, but that it is correct regardless of the fracture agent. This belief leads us to suggest an expansion to Marean's (1991) method.

Marean focused exclusively on bones he thought would most likely not be broken during the biostratinomic phase; in his view, these are the carpals and tarsals. He noted that the calcaneum has a "small marrow cavity that may entice predator fragmentation" and thus he thought it "best to exclude calcanea from any analysis of postdepositional [postburial] destruction" (Marean, 1991:681). The same argument could be made for the first and second phalanges. We think it unlikely, however, that postburial fragmentation and destruction will be limited to only those skeletal elements not broken during the biostratinomic phase. In particular, we suspect that there will be a continuum from a low to a high degree of fragmentation, and that this continuum will correlate directly with several variables: bone shape as it alters from spheroid to rod-like or blade-like; bone size as it alters from small to large; and marrow and grease utility as these alter from minimum to maximum values. We also suspect that the degree of fragmentation will correlate inversely (coefficients will be negative) with structural density because as density decreases, skeletal elements will be less strong structurally. We expand Marean's method and include phalanges and calcanea in our analyses below to evaluate our suspicions of a continuum of fragmentation. If statistically significant correlations are found between the degree of fragmentation and the food utility, shape, size, and density of skeletal elements, then it can be argued that the mere presence of fragmented carpals and tarsals is insufficient to indicate postburial fragmentation.

Quantification

Marean's (1991) CI% value was proposed as an improvement to other means of measuring the degree of fragmentation, particularly that proposed by Klein and Cruz-Uribe (1984), who suggested that a NISP:MNI or NISP:MNE* ratio would provide a measure of fragmentation. In proposing the CI% value, Marean (1991:680) was correctly concerned that inter-observer variation in both (a) how MNI and MNE values were calculated, and (b) which identified specimens were included in the calculations, would influence results. The first concern hinges on the fact that MNI and MNE values are derived rather than observational

---

* MNI values are derived from sets of all identified specimens and represent the minimum number of individual animals necessary to account for the specimens. MNE values are derived from sets of specimens of particular skeletal elements and represent the minimum number of skeletal elements necessary to account for the specimens.

and thus they can be determined in various ways (e.g., Grayson, 1984; Lyman, 1994a). We believe, however, that if the observer is consistent within an analysis, then the MNI and MNE values will be consistently derived. We also believe that variation in the inclusion of specimens can influence not only NISP:MNI and NISP:MNE ratios, but the CI% value because the latter also depends on which specimens are included in the tally. Therefore, although we understand Marean's concerns, we find them incompletely resolved by the use of the CI%.

Consistent application of criteria for inclusion of specimens in NISP tallies and for derivation of MNE and MNI values should circumvent the problems Marean identifies. Of course, there will always be variation between analysts in terms of what, for example, Lyman believes is identifiable and what Darwent does. In other words, inter-observer bias will always be a problem, regardless of which measure of fragmentation is used.

The NISP:MNE ratio is elsewhere termed the *intensity of fragmentation* (Lyman, 1994b:294). Lyman (1994b:294) suggested one could measure the *extent of fragmentation* as the "proportion of specimens [of a particular skeletal element] that are complete" or "%Whole," and that in conjunction with the intensity of fragmentation, these two measures would provide two indices of the degree of fragmentation. The extent of fragmentation is easily observed within a collection as long as what is tallied as a complete or whole specimen is consistent from specimen to specimen. Unlike the CI%, the NISP:MNE ratio depends on whether specimens overlap anatomically or not; that is, for the intensity of fragmentation, the distal half of two humeri, both from the same side, would be tallied as a ratio of 2:2 (reduced to 1:1), whereas the CI% would be 50%. The former ratio would be 2:1 if one proximal half and one distal half that did not overlap anatomically were represented, whereas the CI% would still be 50% in this case. Our point here is that the different indices — CI%, NISP:MNE, %Whole — measure different properties of a collection (Lyman, 1994a). Is one more correct than the other?

The only way that the preceding question can be answered is to agree on a variable that we wish to measure. The variable of interest in studies of postburial fragmentation is the *degree of fragmentation*, or what we define as a measure of how broken skeletal elements are. All three indices — CI%, NISP:MNE, %Whole — measure this variable. As we noted earlier, the CI% can be read as "the average completeness of specimens of element X." The NISP:MNE ratio, too, is a statement concerning the completeness of specimens because it expresses the average number of specimens per skeletal element.* The NISP:MNE ratio contains the same information as the CI%, but it also contains the additional information of specimen overlap as expressed by the MNE. The %Whole index indicates the proportion of all specimens that are anatomically complete or that comprise an entire skeletal element, thus its information content overlaps with, but is less than, the other two because it only indirectly accounts for specimens comprising incomplete skeletal elements. In one sense, then, the amount of information regarding fragmentation increases from %Whole (with the least information), to CI%, to NISP:MNE. Because of information overlap, the latter

---

* When Lyman (1994b:294) discussed the NISP:MNE index, he suggested that complete skeletal elements — whole bones — should not be included in the calculation. This suggestion was made there because the goal was to answer the two-part question, "How anatomically complete are the incomplete specimens, and how much anatomical overlap do incomplete specimens display?" The CI% merely asks, "How anatomically complete are *all* the specimens, on average?" Including anatomically complete specimens in the NISP:MNE ratio addressed the two-part question, "How anatomically complete are *all* specimens, on average, and how much anatomical overlap do the total specimens display?"

two should be inversely correlated (see also Marean, 1991:689–690); and, the %Whole and CI% should also be correlated when the former is large across multiple skeletal elements because when this occurs, the CI% will also be large.

The preceding suggests that Marean's (1991) method may be expanded to include three indices of fragmentation. Each index contains similar information, but each also contains unique information. Correlations between the various fragmentation indices, or lack thereof, and the structural density, size, or shape of the skeletal elements may reveal aspects of fragmentation not otherwise discernable were only one of them used during analysis. Incorporation of the size, structural density, and shape of the bones into the analysis addresses Marean's hypothesized relationship between these variables and the different aspects of the degree of fragmentation captured by the CI%, NISP:MNE, and %Whole indices.

Methods, Materials, and Caveats

We chose a sample of bones recovered from archaeological deposits in Moses Coulee Cave (45DO331) in eastern Washington State, to evaluate and expand on Marean's (1991) method. We chose this particular sample because (a) carpals, tarsals, and phalanges are abundant; (b) the majority of the specimens represent a single taxon; and (c) its postburial taphonomic history comprised a unique stage that potentially fragmented some of the specimens. Temporally diagnostic artifacts associated with the faunal remains span the last 10,000 years, and the bones we discuss here date to that entire time span. Finer temporal resolution is not possible because the site was not professionally excavated. Rather, the sediments within the cave and at the cave mouth were removed and redeposited several meters away from and in front of the cave in 1932 by a Fresno (Lyman, 1995).*

The relocated sediments, the "spoils pile," were screened and artifacts and faunal remains collected in 1988 and 1989 by avocational archaeologists. Lyman (1995) studied the faunal remains in 1993 and reported on the taxonomic composition of the collection. The majority of the bones from Moses Coulee Cave were readily identified as bighorn sheep (*Ovis canadensis*, NISP = 2190); a few represented deer (*Odocoileus* sp., NISP = 88), pronghorn antelope (*Antilocapra americana*, NISP = 19), wapiti (*Cervus elaphus*) NISP = 4, and bison (*Bison bison*) or domestic cow (*Bos taurus*, NISP bison + cow = 198) (bones modified into artifacts and isolated teeth were omitted).

We reexamined the carpals, tarsals, and phalanges of deer-sized artiodactyls for purposes of analyses discussed here. Specimens of bighorn sheep, deer, pronghorn antelope, and those deer-sized bones that could not be identified to species are included. The fact that multiple taxa are included should have minimal influence on analytical results. This is true for two reasons. First, the three taxa are similar in size and basic body plan, and their bones are similar in size, shape, and density, so taxonomic differences are unlikely to have contributed to variation in the taphonomic histories of individual specimens. Second, it is likely that the majority of the carpals, tarsals, and phalanges discussed here represent bighorn sheep. This is because the specimens of these elements that were sufficiently

* A Fresno is so-called because the Agricultural Works of Fresno, California, were a major manufacturer of them. A Fresno, also known as a buck scraper, is an earth digging and transporting device consisting of a crescent-shaped, bottomless bucket or scoop that is dragged along the ground. It has two runners upon which the scoop is lifted when it is filled.

Table 19.2 Frequencies (NISP) of Carpals, Tarsals, and Phalanges of Bighorn Sheep, Deer, Pronghorn Antelope, and Deer-Sized Specimens from Moses Coulee Cave

Skeletal Element	Bighorn Sheep	Deer	Pronghorn Antelope	Deer-Sized[a]
Cuneiform	58	1	—	4
Lunar	55	8	—	22
Pisiform	—	—	—	42
Scaphoid	72	6	—	15
Trapezoid magnum	94	2	—	22
Unciform	—	—	—	79
Calcaneum	63	—	—	184
Astragalus	—	—	—	325
Naviculo-cuboid	51	3	1	57
Tarsal 2 + 3	—	—	—	97
Distal fibula	—	—	—	74
First phalanx	203	1	1	265
Second phalanx	155	7	1	—
Third phalanx	106	7	—	—

[a] Counts differ from Lyman (1995) because some specimens could not be relocated, and some new specimens were identified.

anatomically complete to allow identification to species are dominated by bighorn sheep remains (Table 19.2). Thus, even if specimens of multiple taxa are included in NISP tallies, the few non-bighorn specimens will have minimal influence on these tallies and on analytical results.

We followed Marean's (1991) procedure and recorded various data for each specimen. The skeletal element represented, whether it was burned, excessively weathered, corroded as a result of digestion, displayed carnivore or rodent gnawing damage, displayed butchering marks such as chopping or percussion scars, were recorded.* Modern fractures were noted when the fracture surface was a lighter color than an unfractured surface of a specimen. We also noted if the proximal epiphysis of first and second phalanges were fused to the diaphysis, and if the tuberosity of the calcaneum was fused to the shaft. If a specimen was incomplete, we evaluated its completeness by superimposing it on a 2-mm grid and estimating the amount remaining relative to a complete specimen. To insure against inter-observer variation, Darwent recorded all data discussed here.**

Faunal remains recovered from Moses Coulee Cave included specimens representing five genera and at least six species of carnivore. These include the gray wolf (*Canis lupus*, NISP =1); dog (*C. familiaris*) or coyote (*C. latrans*) (NISP = 38); red fox (*Vulpes vulpes*,

---

* A number of carpals and tarsals have cut marks, but we do not consider them here. Similarly, few specimens display modern damage such as may have resulted from the 1932 mechanical movement by the Fresno of the sediment and bones; if present, such damage is superficial.
** To test for inter-observer bias in estimating specimen completeness, Darwent selected a sample of 10 first phalanx specimens and 10 naviculo-cuboid specimens. Lyman then estimated the completeness of each specimen and calculated the CI% for both samples. For the phalanges, Lyman's CI% was 31.5% and Darwent's was 34%; for the naviculo-cuboid, Lyman's CI% was 42.5% and Darwent's was 44.0%. This small test suggests inter-observer variation may influence CI% values.

NISP = 7); long-tailed weasel (*Mustela frenata*, NISP = 1); badger (*Taxida taxus*, NISP = 4); and bobcat (*Lynx rufus*, NISP = 1). Of these, the canids and badger are the most likely to have created the gnawing and digestive corrosion damage evident on some of the carpals, tarsals, and phalanges (Lyman, 1995)

In his experiments, Marean (1991) found that when metapodials were laid on an anvil and broken with a hammerstone, surfaces of carpals and tarsals articulated with the metapodials lacked percussion scars. He reasoned that the latter occurred because the carpals and tarsals "are encased in a thick and resistant ligament and tendon mass that cushions them from hammerstone blows" (Marean 1991:681). He also found that when carpals and tarsals are intentionally broken with a hammerstone, "the force needed to break a compact bone is so great that the hammerstone/anvil impact marks on the compact bone are extremely prominent and easily recognized" (Marean, 1991:681). Marean referenced Blumenschine and Selvaggio (1988) as illustrating the kinds of impact marks he found, and we consulted this paper, as well as a related one (Blumenschine and Selvaggio, 1991).

To insure that we knew the kinds of attributes to look for when searching for percussion damage and to be able to recognize them, we experimentally broke carpals, tarsals, and phalanges of domestic pig (*Sus scrofa*) with a hammerstone. All specimens had been defleshed by boiling, and we chose specimens that were still greasy to replicate possible prehistoric conditions. We laid individual skeletal elements on a smooth hard surface (anvil), and struck them with a quartzite cobble. After fragmentation, we collected all fragments and inspected them for evidence of impact damage.

In light of Marean's statements, our observations are rather disconcerting. Percussion damage to some specimens was minimal; refitting fragments sometimes made it easier to detect the damage such as when an articular surface of adjacent fragments did not match up smoothly across two refit specimens. Further, some phalanges were broken, yet none of the resulting specimens displayed what we could unambiguously term percussion damage. The shaft or diaphysis was simply broken. No crushing of what a lithic technologist calls the platform or point of impact was observable. The same applied to some carpals and tarsals; a few of these simply broke or split into pieces. Finally, some specimens of all elements did not display percussion damage of any kind; for example, the 10 astragali we broke produced a total of 70 fragments (individual astragali produced 3 to 16 pieces). Of those 70 fragments, only 12 (17%) clearly displayed percussion damage; 2 astragali, 1 that broke into 3 pieces and another that broke into 7 pieces, produced no specimens with impact damage.

Our observations have, we believe, extremely significant implications. They suggest that omitting specimens with percussion damage from derivations of fragmentation indices will not eliminate all specimens that were produced by hammerstone-generated fracturing. Because we as yet do not know how to account for this fact, we largely ignore it in our analysis. Further, we are unsure of the reason behind our results apparently not mimicking Marean's. Perhaps it is because we did not precisely replicate his experimental protocol. We do not know, for example, if the carpals and tarsals he broke were defleshed, nor do we know the precise kinds of percussion damage he sought and found to be "extremely prominent and easily recognized." And, Marean does not say that *every* specimen of carpal and tarsal generated by his breaking bones with a hammerstone retained percussion damage. Clearly, there is a need for more rigorous experimental fracturing of carpals, tarsals, and phalanges and more rigorous documentation of such, but we caution that all such experiments may be of more or less limited utility because of the particular historical contingencies of every instance of fragmentation.* With that caveat in mind, we turn to our analysis of the Moses Coulee Cave specimens.

Results

The taxonomic and skeletal composition of the assemblage of carpals, tarsals, and phalanges we examined is summarized in Table 19.2. In this section, we ignore taxonomic distinctions and summarize other data we recorded for this collection and describe our analyses of these data. Because many of our analyses involve calculating the degree of correlation between certain variable pairs, we describe these variables and note their significance before turning to detailed analyses.

Skeletal Element Frequencies

There are a number of reasons why the frequencies of the different skeletal elements we consider here may vary. Given our analytical focus on fragmentation, two of the reasons are important in the present context. First, smaller specimens (especially fragments) may have been less often recovered than large specimens. To explore recovery bias, we correlated the frequency of complete specimens of each skeletal element with the average maximum dimension and also with the average minimum dimension of each. Our reasoning in doing so is simple. If recovery methods resulted in a biased collection, the smallest specimens would be the ones most likely to be overlooked and not recovered (e.g., Schaeffer, 1992; Watson, 1972), irrespective of whether a specimen represented a complete skeletal element. Recovery bias would, therefore, be reflected by a positive correlation between specimen size and frequency. Rather than measure each individual specimen, we used the maximum and minimum dimensions of complete skeletal elements as the measure of size. Our assumption was that handpicking specimens from sediments would depend on their maximum size, and recovering specimens from screens would depend on their minimum size.

Relevant data are given in Table 19.3. There is no significant correlation between the minimum dimension and the number of whole skeletal elements (Spearman's rho = $-.244$, $p =. 4$) nor between maximum dimension and the number of whole skeletal elements (rho $= -.407, p = .15$). These statistics, in conjunction with the facts that some specimens included in the NISP counts are less than 1 cm³ in size, and that .25-in. mesh screens were used to recover the remains (Lyman, 1995), suggest that recovery methods did not result in failure to collect small fragments of the skeletal elements under study here.

The second reason specimen counts may be biased is that skeletal elements of lower structural density may have been more frequently destroyed by biostratinomic or diagenetic processes. One way to detect such destruction is to determine if the structural density of each skeletal element is inversely correlated with the NISP of each skeletal element. Our reasoning here is that skeletal elements of low structural density should be more fragmented (perhaps to the point of destruction or analytical invisibility) and thus have higher NISP

---

* Although a machine could be built to precisely replicate the amount of force applied and the point of force application in test after test, microstructural variation in, say, each astragalus broken in conjunction with variation in amounts of adhering soft tissue and grease content would undoubtedly result in variation in fracturing and percussion damage.

Table 19.3   Number of Whole Specimens, Average Minimum Dimension, and Average Maximum Dimension for Each Skeletal Element

Skeletal Element	Number Whole[a]	Minimum Dimension[b]	Middle Dimension[b]	Maximum Dimension[b]
Cuneiform	44	10.2	19.5	25.0
Lunar	56	15.5	17.7	23.3
Pisiform	22	8.4	12.8	18.8
Scaphoid	59	12.7	17.2	23.6
Trapezoid magnum	75	10.5	20.8	21.4
Unciform	53	13.3	14.6	19.6
Calcaneum	12	22.3	30.4	84.5
Astragalus	60	21.4	26.0	39.4
Naviculo-cuboid	27	20.8	28.1	30.8
Tarsal 2+3	67	8.6	13.2	20.7
Distal fibula	48	12.0	17.5	19.0
First phalanx	10	16.5	20.5	52.7
Second phalanx	38	14.8	18.1	32.5
Third phalanx	25	11.7	21.7	39.3

[a] Includes all complete specimens regardless of whether specimen is burned.
[b] Average of five specimens; all measurements are in millimeters.

values than elements of high structural density. The structural density of each skeletal element is given in Table 19.1, and the NISP values are given in Table 19.2; we summed the latter because we suspected taxonomic variation in structural density of the elements is minimal. The two variables are not correlated (rho $= -.371$, $p = .236$), suggesting that the overall NISP frequencies are not a function of density-mediated fragmentation and destruction. The bivariate scatterplot of these data, however, suggests that the NISP of phalanges, astragali, and calcanea may in part be a function of density-mediated processes, whereas the NISP of carpals, naviculo-cuboids, and distal fibulae are not (Figure 19.2). We return to this potentiality in our discussion of the influences of skeletal element shape on taphonomic history.

Sphericity

As indicated earlier, we suspect that as specimens approach perfect spheres in shape, they are less likely to be crushed or fragmented by sediment-overburden weight. This is because in part spheres have low surface-to-volume ratios. We used a method developed by sedimentologists (Zingg, 1935) to estimate the sphericity of the skeletal elements we studied. Sphericity is defined by the equation $[(bc/a^2)^{0.33}]$ where a is the maximum dimension (length), b is the middle-magnitude dimension (width), and c is the minimum dimension (thickness). These three measurements are taken at mutually perpendicular axes and are not related to the anatomical orientation of the bones but rather to the bone's shape. We measured these three dimensions on five complete specimens of each carpal, tarsal, and phalanx (Table 19.3), and then used the average of each dimension to calculate sphericity. Sphericity values for all elements are listed in Table 19.4. The higher the value, the greater the sphericity of the element.

Sedimentologists also use the minimum, middle-magnitude, and maximum dimensions to plot specimens on a graph to ascertain shape (Figure 19.1). Four nominal shape categories are recognized on the graph; spherical or "equant" shapes fall in the upper right

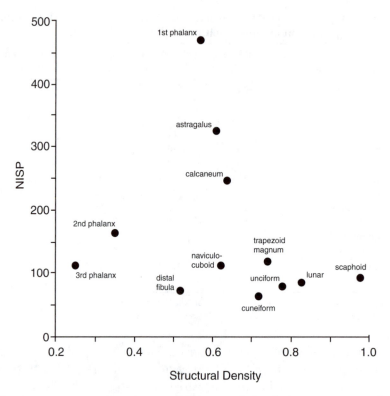

Figure 19.2 Bivariate scatterplot of NISP values per skeletal element against the structural density of each skeletal element.

quadrant; disc or "oblate" shapes fall in the upper left quadrant; blade shapes in the lower left quadrant; and rod or "prolate" shapes in the lower right quadrant (terms in quotes from Waters, 1992:27). Figure 19.1 suggests most carpals and some tarsals could be categorized as spheres whereas the calcaneum and first and second phalanges comprise rods. The third phalanx is the only blade-shaped element, and the trapezoid magnum and cuneiform are the only discs.

Recall from our discussion of skeletal element frequencies that as the structural density of phalanges, astragali, and calcanea increased, it appeared that their respective frequencies increased whereas the frequencies of carpals, distal fibulae, and naviculo-cuboids displayed no relationship to their structural density (Figure 19.2). We suspect the reason for this is that the sphericity of the latter group of elements is greater than that of the former group. As indicated in Table 19.4, skeletal elements comprising the first group are the four least spherical elements, plus the seventh least spherical element (astragalus); skeletal elements comprising the other group include the six most spherical elements plus the eighth least spherical element (cuneiform). This observation suggests that the reason for the lack of relationship between the NISP frequencies of carpals, distal fibulae, and naviculo-cuboids and their structural densities, and the apparent relationship between the NISP frequencies of phalanges, calcanea, and astragali and their structural densities, may reside in differences in the degree to which they are fragmented. As we argued earlier, we expect skeletal elements that more closely approximate spheres to be less fragmented. In other words, are phalanges,

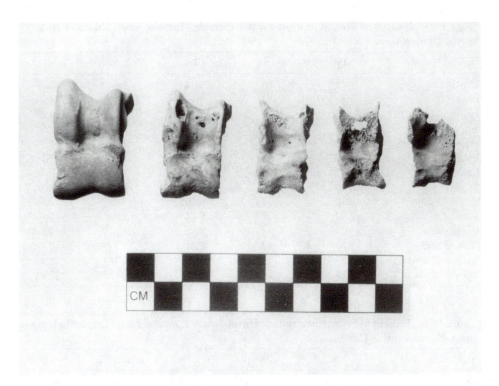

Figure 19.3 Bighorn sheep astragali from Moses Coulee Cave. The specimen on the left is complete and undigested; the other four specimens, from left to right, display progressively greater degrees of digestive corrosion yet appear to have been ingested when complete.

Table 19.4   Sphericity Values for Skeletal Elements Examined in This Study

Skeletal Element	Sphericity
Calcaneum	0.460
First phalanx	0.499
Third phalanx	0.551
Second phalanx	0.636
Tarsal 2 + 3	0.646
Pisiform	0.676
Cuneiform	0.685
Astragalus	0.713
Scaphoid	0.735
Trapezoid magnum	0.784
Unciform	0.799
Lunar	0.800
Distal fibula	0.836
Naviculo-cuboid	0.852

calcanea, and astragali more susceptible to fragmentation because they are less spherical in shape whereas carpals, distal fibulae, and naviculo-cuboids are less susceptible to fragmentation because they are more spherical? This is the topic we turn to next.

Table 19.5   Indices of Fragmentation for All Carpals, Tarsals, and Phalanges from Moses Coulee Cave

Skeletal Element	NISP	MNE	CI%	NISP:MNE	%Whole
Cuneiform	63	63	91.4	1	80.7
Lunar	85	82	90.8	1.04	74.7
Pisiform	42	42	93.4	1	64.7
Scaphoid	93	92	90.1	1.05	72.8
Trapezoid magnum	118	118	86.9	1	71.4
Unciform	79	78	92.2	1.08	79.1
Calcaneum	247	66	32.3	3.74	7.7
Astragalus	325	230	60.6	1.41	22.3
Naviculo-cuboid	112	91	66.0	1.23	27.3
Tarsal 2 + 3	97	97	96.4	1	80.7
Distal fibula	74	74	90.5	1	64.9
First phalanx	470	197	29.4	2.39	2.1
Second phalanx	163	119	58.2	1.37	21.3
Third phalanx	113	102	57.8	1.11	22.1

Table 19.6   Indices of Fragmentation for Unmodified[a] Carpals, Tarsals, and Phalanges from Moses Coulee Cave

Skeletal Element	NISP	MNE	CI%	NISP:MNE	%Whole
Cuneiform	51	51	92.9	1	82.3
Lunar	58	57	89.3	1.02	72.4
Pisiform	27	27	94.8	1	66.7
Scaphoid	55	55	95.7	1	85.5
Trapezoid magnum	78	78	70.6	1	74.7
Unciform	59	59	93.3	1	78.3
Calcaneum	59	26	43.4	2.27	20.3
Astragalus	107	91	80.1	1.17	35.3
Naviculo-cuboid	53	50	78.2	1.06	38.2
Tarsal 2 + 3	69	69	97.7	1	84.1
Distal fibula	45	45	90.2	1	66.7
First phalanx	325	159	29.7	2.04	2.8
Second phalanx	103	71	53.2	1.45	22.3
Third phalanx	76	67	59.3	1.13	23.7

[a]   Burned, gnawed, digested, and freshly broken specimens, and specimens with percussion damage, omitted.

Fragmentation

For analytical purposes, we define *modified specimens* as those that display attributes of burning, digestive corrosion, rodent or carnivore gnawing, percussion damage, or some combination of these traces of (with the possible exception of percussion) biostratinomic damage. *Unmodified specimens* are those that display none of these attributes. The three indices of fragmentation for modified and unmodified specimens combined are listed in Table 19.5. Fragmentation index values for unmodified specimens are given in Table 19.6. The CI% and %Whole values tend to increase when modified specimens are omitted, as Marean's (1991) analysis suggested they should. The majority of the NISP:MNE ratios, however, either do not change (five values) or they decrease only a small amount (six values). The single exception is the calcaneum, the NISP:MNE ratio for which decreases

Table 19.7   Absolute and Relative Abundances of Carnivore Gnawed, Digested, Rodent Gnawed, and Burned Specimens from Moses Coulee Cave[a]

Skeletal Element	Total NISP	NISP Carnivore Gnawed	NISP Digested	NISP Rodent Gnawed	NISP Burned	NISP with Percussion
Cuneiform	63	2 (3.2)	3 (4.8)	1 (1.6)	6 (9.5)	0
Lunar	85	0	10 (11.8)	0	17 (20.0)	0
Pisiform[b]	42	4 (9.5)	4 (9.5)	1 (2.4)	7 (16.7)	0
Scaphoid[b]	93	6 (6.5)	6 (6.5)	1 (1.1)	26 (28.0)	0
Trapezoid magnum	118	6 (5.1)	7 (5.9)	0	26 (22.0)	1 (0.8)
Unciform	79	7 (8.9)	5 (6.3)	0	8 (10.1)	0
Calcaneum	247	90 (36.4)	0	1 (0.4)	96 (38.9)	1 (0.4)
Astragalus	325	51 (15.7)	6 (1.8)	0	152 (46.7)	9 (2.8)
Naviculo-cuboid[b]	112	9 (8.0)	10 (8.9)	1 (0.9)	38 (33.9)	2 (1.8)
Tarsal 2 + 3	97	7 (7.2)	7 (7.2)	0	14 (14.4)	0
Distal fibula[c]	74	0	4 (5.4)	0	27 (36.5)	0
First phalanx[d]	470	10 (2.1)	33 (7.0)	9 (1.9)	88 (18.7)	13 (2.8)
Second phalanx	163	4 (2.5)	25 (15.3)	6 (3.7)	25 (15.3)	0
Third phalanx[e]	113	5 (4.4)	3 (2.7)	15 (13.3)	21 (18.6)	0

[a] Values in parentheses are relative (%) abundance of specimens with the indicated modification.
[b] One specimen displays more than one kind of modification.
[c] Two specimens display more than one kind of modification.
[d] Eight specimens display more than one kind of modification.
[e] Seven specimens display more than one kind of modification.

54% ($[3.74 − 2.27] + [3.74 − 1]$). This suggests that the calcaneum, the largest (Table 19.3) and also most rod-like (Figure 19.1) element, was the most prone to be fragmented if it was modified by burning, carnivore gnawing, and the like.

Thirteen first phalanx specimens, nine astragali, two naviculo-cuboids, one trapezoid magnum, and one calcaneum display percussion damage, suggesting they were broken by human predators wielding hammerstones, by roof-fall, or by a combination of the two (Table 19.7). We had intended to correlate the number of specimens displaying percussion scars with marrow and grease utility values (see below) under the assumption that larger proportions of elements with higher utility values would display such modification than elements with lower utility values if the percussion scars were the result of human tapho-nomic agents. The low number of specimens with percussion scars precluded calculating a coefficient, but we note that the calcaneum and first phalanx have the greatest marrow and grease values (Table 19.1), suggesting that they may have been broken for that reason. However, we also note that these are the two most rod-like elements and thus are, we suspect, the most prone to diagenetic fragmentation. Diagenetic fragmentation could account for the fact that identical relative abundances of first phalanx and astragalus specimens display percussion damage. But so could biostratonomic fragmentation account for the relative frequencies of specimens displaying percussion damage because the navic-ulo-cuboid, with the third highest grease utility value, has the third greatest proportion of specimens with percussion damage.

Gnawing damage by rodents may have obliterated some flake scars, though only a few specimens display such damage (Table 19.7). Part of the analytical difficulty we encountered is that some specimens were variously chewed and gnawed by carnivores, and the resulting damage could either have obliterated evidence of percussion scars or been confused with percussion scars. Also, modern damage to bones which may have resulted from mechanical movement (the 1932 Fresno) of the sediments possibly obliterated percussion damage, though we think this unlikely given that such damage is very superficial and does not occur on many specimens. Perhaps most importantly, as we noted when we experimentally broke pig carpals, tarsals, and phalanges, not all hammerstone-broken specimens can be expected to display obvious percussion damage.

There is no statistically significant relationship between the minimum or maximum dimension of the elements (Table 19.3) and the proportion of carnivore gnawed or proportion of digested specimens ($p > .2$ for all tests); however, more than 18% of all tarsals display evidence of carnivore gnawing whereas only 5.2% of all carpals and 2.5% of all phalanges display such damage. This rank ordering is exactly the reverse for digestive corrosion: 8.2% of all phalanges, 7.3% of all carpals, and 3.2% of all tarsal specimens display digestive corrosion. It seems reasonable to suppose that larger elements are more prone to display evidence of gnawing whereas smaller elements are prone to display digestive corrosion, granting the assumption that larger elements are more difficult to ingest than smaller ones. However, as shown in Figure 19.3, astragali, the second largest skeletal element under consideration (Table 19.3), were at least occasionally ingested whole by Moses Coulee Cave carnivores and underwent various degrees of corrosive destruction as a result. This prompts us to wonder if there is a relationship between carnivore gnawing and digestive corrosion, and the food utility of the elements.

Grease and Marrow Utility

Binford (1978) determined the food value of many skeletal elements of two artiodactyls species. We chose to use caribou (*Rangifer tarandus*) index values for our analysis because this species is similar in body size and shape to the three taxa under consideration. Binford derived a grease utility value and a marrow utility value for all carpals as an articulated mass; the naviculo-cuboid, tarsal 2 + 3, and distal fibula (we believe) as an articulated mass; the isolated calcaneum; the isolated astragalus; the first phalanx; the second phalanx; and the third phalanx. We did two things to derive the marrow and grease utility values given in Table 19.1 for each isolated skeletal element. First, because all carpals, the naviculo-cuboid, tarsal 2 + 3, and distal fibula are compact bones with no marrow cavity, it is reasonable to assign them a marrow utility value of 1, which is identical to the value Binford assigned to the astragalus, a compact bone with no marrow cavity. Second, we determined the volume (via water displacement) for several complete specimens of each element and calculated the average. This was used to calculate a grease utility index value for the naviculo-cuboid, tarsals 2 + 3, distal fibula, and isolated carpals. For the three indicated tarsals, we multiplied the percent of the total volume of the three as represented by one element by the grease utility index for all three (29.87). For the six carpals, we multiplied the percent of the total volume of all six as represented by one element by the grease utility index for all six (36.47). These calculations produced the grease utility values for each individual carpal, naviculo-cuboid, tarsal 2 + 3, and distal fibula (Table 19.1).

The proportion of carnivore-gnawed specimens per skeletal element is not correlated with either the marrow utility values or the grease utility values ($p > .5$ for both). Similarly, the proportion of digested specimens per skeletal element is not correlated with these food utility values ($p > .5$ for both). Finally, we note that the correlation between the simple sum of the two utility indices and the simple sum of the proportions of gnawed and digested

Table 19.8   Correlation Coefficients (Spearman's rho) Between Fragmentation Indices and the Summed Grease and Marrow Utility Indices

Fragmentation Index	Modified and Unmodified		Unmodified Only	
	Rho	p	Rho	p
CI%	−.833	< .0001	−.773	.001
NISP:MNE	.898	< .0001	.906	< .0001
%Whole	−.749	.0021	−.688	.0065

specimens is statistically insignificant ($p = .3$). In other words, it does not seem that Moses Coulee Cave carnivores were exploiting the carpals, tarsals, and phalanges of deer-sized artiodactyls at intensities commensurate with the food value of those elements. Do the food indices have any relationship to the degree of fragmentation? In fact, they do. All three fragmentation indices, whether derived from modified plus unmodified specimens or from only unmodified specimens, are significantly correlated with the sum of the marrow and grease utility values (Table 19.8). Why might this be the case? In short, we believe this is a function of the size, shape, and density of the skeletal elements.

What Mediates Fragmentation?

According to Marean (1991:691), postburial fragmentation of bones will be indicated by small CI% values, particularly if those values are for the astragalus and naviculo-cuboid. Marean noted that he could not answer the question of how small "small" CI% values should be to unambiguously indicate postburial fragmentation. He focused on the fragmentation of what he considered to be "small, compact bones" and hypothesized that the density, size, and shape of skeletal elements would mediate their postburial fragmentation. To evaluate the influence of density on fragmentation, we correlated the three indices of fragmentation with the structural density of each skeletal element. Resulting coefficients are given in Table 19.9. If all modified and unmodified specimens (Table 19.5) are included, only the correlations between CI% and density, and between %Whole and density are significant. If only unmodified specimens (Table 19.6) are included, then all three coefficients can be considered significant ($p < .085$). This tends to corroborate Marean's suggestion that inclusion of modified specimens will skew measures of fragmentation. More importantly, the coefficients suggest that the structural density of skeletal elements mediates their fragmentation irrespective of agent and process of fragmentation.

To evaluate the influences of bone shape on fragmentation, we correlated the three indices of fragmentation with element sphericity (Table 19.4). Resulting coefficients are listed in Table 19.9. If all modified and unmodified specimens (Table 19.5) are included, only the correlation between %Whole and sphericity might be considered significant. If only unmodified specimens (Table 19.6) are included, then two coefficients, for %Whole and NISP:MNE, can be considered significant ($p < .08$). This also corroborates Marean's suggestion that inclusion of modified specimens will skew results. Focusing then on the coefficients for unmodified specimens only, the most spherical specimens tend to be least fragmented whereas the least spherical specimens tend to be most fragmented, just as we predicted. We note that this would not be apparent were only the CI% values used as measures of fragmentation.

Table 19.9 Correlation Coefficients (Spearman's rho) between Fragmentation Indices and Structural Density, Sphericity, and Size of Skeletal Elements

Fragmentation Index	Modified and Unmodified		Unmodified Only	
	Rho	p	Rho	p
		Density		
CI%	.608	.036	.601	.039
NISP:MNE	−.366	.242	−.522	.082
%Whole	.692	.013	.727	.007
		Sphericity		
CI%	.446	.11	.411	.144
NISP:MNE	−.425	.13	−.542	.045
%Whole	.513	.06	.488	.076
		Size		
CI%	−.868	< .0001	−.754	.0018
NISP:MNE	.852	.0001	.885	< .0001
%Whole	− .689	.0065	−.673	.008

Finally, to ascertain the influence of bone size on fragmentation, we correlated the three indices of fragmentation with the maximum dimension (Table 19.3) of each skeletal element. All indices of fragmentation regardless of whether unmodified and modified, or only unmodified specimens are included, correlate strongly with the skeletal element's maximum dimension (Table 19.9). In other words, larger skeletal elements tend to display higher degrees of fragmentation than smaller specimens, regardless of the measure of fragmentation. This, too, corroborates Marean's hypothesis that fragmentation is mediated by skeletal element size.

To insure that the sets of correlations in Table 19.9 are not the result of relationships between size, density, and sphericity, we correlated all possible pairs of these three variables. Only size and sphericity are correlated (rho = −.556, p = .04); density and sphericity are not correlated (rho = .35, p = .265) nor are size and density (rho = −.42; p = .174). These coefficients suggest that each variable — size, density, shape — influences fragmentation largely independently of the other two variables.

Correlation coefficients in Table 19.8 indicate that as food utility (measured as the sum of the grease and marrow utility values) of a skeletal element increases, its degree of fragmentation increases. Does the food utility of a skeletal element correlate with its size, shape, or density? As might be expected, food utility and skeletal element size are directly correlated, whether the maximum dimension (rho = .923, p < .0001) or minimum dimension (rho = .775, p = .0011) is used. In other words, as the size of a skeletal element increases, so does its food utility. The food utility of a skeletal element and its sphericity, on the other hand, are weakly and inversely correlated (rho = −.482, p = .081). This is understandable because as skeletal elements become more rod-like and less spherical in shape, their food utility increases. Finally, the food utility and structural density of skeletal elements are not correlated (rho = −.344, p = .274). We believe this results because those elements with the greatest food utility also have marrow cavities and some of the lowest structural densities.

Discussion and Conclusions

Ascertaining the effects of diagenetic fragmentation on collections of faunal remains is critical for a number of reasons. Postburial fragmentation may, as Marean (1991:677) indicates, "confound interpretations of the bone fragmenting behavior of the [bone] collector." Also, as we noted earlier, it may variously reduce the identifiability of a collection thereby influencing the NISP tallies for collections that have undergone different degrees of diagenetic fragmentation. A significant analytical hurdle for taphonomists, then, is identifying if and to what degree a collection of bones has undergone postburial fragmentation. Recognizing this fact, taphonomists have attempted to design methods for recognizing such fragmentation. Marean's (1991) efforts are the most detailed in this respect, and they are important.

Marean hypothesized that the fragmentation of skeletal elements would be mediated or influenced by their shape, size, and density. Statistically significant correlations we found between these three variables and three fragmentation indices for a single collection corroborate Marean's (1991) hypothesis. Our analysis indicates that as skeletal elements decrease in sphericity and increase in size they will also increase in food utility and, at least among the Moses Coulee Cave materials, they will have a greater tendency to be broken. It also indicates that among the carpals, tarsals, and phalanges, an element's structural density does not influence the relationship between the element's food utility and its degree of fragmentation. The significant implication in the present context, then, is that the Moses Coulee Cave bones might have been broken during the biostratinomic phase, given the correlation between the fragmentation indices and food utility (Table 19.8). The densest, most spherical, and smallest bones tend to be the least broken (Table 19.9), suggesting that if diagenetic fragmentation occurred, it was mediated by those variables.

The preceding suggests that humans seeking to extract grease and marrow broke the bones during the biostratinomic phase. Many of the Moses Coulee Cave specimens comprising fragments of carpals, tarsals, and phalanges, however, display no obvious percussion damage. But recall that when we experimentally broke carpals, tarsals, and phalanges, we found minimal percussion damage. Perhaps, then it *was* a hammerstone-wielding human who broke the Moses Coulee Cave bones, but that is not in any sense unambiguously demonstrable because the correlations we calculated indicate that there is a continuum of degrees of fragmentation among the Moses Coulee Cave assemblage of carpals, tarsals, and phalanges. Perhaps this is the result of the early twentieth century mechanical movement, mixing, and redeposition of the sediments and bones, but we find that unlikely because few of the specimens we examined display modern breaks that might be attributed to that event. Instead, we think it much more likely that the specimens we describe were fractured by both biostratinomic and diagenetic processes. The effects of biostratinomic fragmentation, in other words, were exacerbated by diagenetic fragmentation, as fragmentation during both phases was, as Marean hypothesized, mediated by the size, shape, and density of the elements.

The fragmentation continuum among the Moses Coulee Cave carpals, tarsals, and phalanges that we have documented is predictable because the skeletal elements are of varying shape, size, and density. Fragmentation also correlates with food utility, which in turn is correlated with the size and shape of the skeletal elements. Together, these observations suggest it will be no easy matter to detect postburial fragmentation because its traces mimic those of biostratinomic fragmentation. Sorting out percussion-damaged specimens will not increase resolution because not all percussion-broken specimens display percussion damage. We conclude, therefore, that analytical efforts to sort out diagenetic and biostratinomic fragmentation must comprise more than measuring the degree of fragmentation. This does not mean that measuring the intensity and extent of fragmentation is not worthwhile. As we noted in the introduction, fragmentation influences identifiability. We would not recommend comparing taxonomic abundances of collections that were differentially fragmented. To detect differential fragmentation, fragmentation must be measured.

Acknowledgments

We thank the earlier researchers who examined the diagenetic phase of taphonomy, especially Curtis Marean for writing his intriguing paper (and for his comment that large samples are indeed required to detect postburial fragmentation); J. Darwent, S. Stout, and S. Wolverton for discussion and comments on an early draft, and Marci Sorg for asking us to contribute to this volume.

References

Behrensmeyer, A.K.
  1978 Taphonomic and ecologic information from bone weathering, *Paleobiology* 4:150–162.

Binford, L. R.
  1978 *Nunamuit Ethnoarchaeology*, Academic Press, New York.

Blumenschine, R. J. and M. M. Selvaggio
  1988 Percussion marks on bone surfaces as a new diagnostic of hominid behaviour. *Nature* 333:763–765.

  1991 On the marks of marrow bone processing by hammerstone and hyenas: their anatomical patterning and archaeological implications. In *Cultural Beginnings: Approaches to Understanding Early Hominid Life-Ways in the African Savanna*, edited by J.D. Clark, pp. 17–32. Union Internationale des Sciences Prehistoriques et Protohistoriques, Mongraphien, Band 19, Bonn.

Currey, J.
  1984 *The Mechanical Adaptations of Bones*, Princeton University Press, Princeton.

Donovan, S.K., Editor
  1991 *The Processes of Fossilization*, Columbia University Press, New York.

Efremov, I.A.
  1940 Taphonomy: a new branch of paleontology, *Pan-American Geologist* 74:81–93.

Grayson, D.K.
  1984 *Quantitative Zooarchaeology: Topics in the Analysis of Archaeological Faunas*, Academic Press, Orlando, FL.

Hudson, J., Editor
  1993 *From Bones to Behavior: Ethnoarchaeological and Experimental Contributions to the Interpretation of Faunal Remains*, Center for Archaeological Investigations, Occasional Paper No. 21, Southern Illinois University, Carbondale.

Klein, R.G.
  1989 Why does skeletal part representation differ between smaller and larger bovids at Klasies River Mouth and other archaeological sites?, *Journal of Archaeological Science* 16:363–381.

Klein, R.G. and K. Cruz-Uribe

  1984   *The Analysis of Animal Bones from Archaeological Sites,* University of Chicago Press, Chicago, IL.

Lyman, R.L.

  1994a Quantitative units and terminology in zooarchaeology, *American Antiquity* 59:36–71.

  1994b Relative abundances of skeletal specimens and taphonomic analysis of vertebrate remains, *Palaios* 9:288–298.

  1994c *Vertebrate Taphonomy,* Cambridge University Press, Cambridge.

  1995   Zooarchaeology of the Moses Coulee Cave (45DO331) spoils pile, *Northwest Anthropological Research Notes* 29:141–176.

Marean, C.W.

  1991   Measuring the post-depositional destruction of bone in archaeological assemblages, *Journal of Archaeological Science* 18:677–694.

Marshall, F. and T. Pilgrim

  1993   NISP vs. MNI in quantification of body-part representation, *American Antiquity* 58:261–269.

Muller, A.H.

  1963   *Lehrbuch de Palazoologie, Band I, Allgemeine Grundlagen,* Gustav Fischer Verlag, Jena.

Schaeffer, B.S.

  1992   Quarter-inch screening: understanding biases in recovery of vertebrate faunal remains, *American Antiquity* 57:129–136.

Stiner, M. C., S. L. Kuhn, S. Weiner, and O. Bar-Yosef

  1995   Differential burning, recrystallization, and fragmentation of archaeological bone, *Journal of Archaeological Science* 22:223–237.

Thomas, D.H. and D. Mayer

  1983   Behavioral faunal analysis of selected horizons. In *The Archaeology of Monitor Valley 2: Gatecliff Shelter,* edited by D. H. Thomas, pp. 353–391. American Museum of Natural History Anthropological Papers 59(1), New York.

Villa, P. and E. Mahieu

  1991   Breakage patterns of human long bones, *Journal of Human Evolution* 21:27–48.

Waters, M.R.

  1992   *Principles of Geoarchaeology,* University of Arizona Press, Tucson.

Watson, P.J.N.

  1972   Fragmentation analysis of animal bone samples from archaeological sites, *Archaeometry* 14:221–228.

Weigelt, J.

  1927   *Rezente Wirbeltierleichen und Ihre Palaobiologische Bedeutung,* Max Weg Verlag, Leipzig.

  1989   *Recent Vertebrate Carcasses and Their Paleobiological Significance,* University of Chicago Press, Chicago.

Zingg, T.

  1935   Beitrage zur schatteranalyse, *Schweizerische Mineralogische und Petrographische Mitteilungen* 15:39-140.

Degradation of Clothing and Other Dress Materials Associated with Buried Bodies of Archaeological and Forensic Interest

20

R.C. JANAWAY

Contents

0-8493-1189-6/02/$0.00+$1.50
© 2002 by CRC Press LLC

Introduction

The recovery of evidence of clothing and associated materials on buried bodies is essential to both forensic and archaeological investigations. In criminal cases clothing will frequently be intact, but may be disturbed by taphonomic processes. Recent experimental work has been conducted on pig cadavers to assess the effect of maggot masses in disturbing the position of clothing; such disturbance could be confused with evidence of sexual assault (Komar and Beattie, 1998). The correct identification of dress items can aid in the correlation of clothing with details in missing persons files. In the case of bodies recovered from war zones the presence of distinctive clothing or equipment can be used to distinguish between military personnel and civilians, or in the case of unmarked battlefield graves between the deceased from different armies or units. The specifications of military clothing very often require durability under taxing conditions, often with the selection of dyes and special finishes to resist biodeterioration. War zone graves may be investigated after longer time intervals than many forensic cases, and for this reason it is important to understand the resistance to biodeterioration of military dress under different soil conditions over many decades. In the last few years bodies have been exhumed and identifications attempted from graves associated with every major conflict of the 20th century, including World War I.

In archaeology, the reconstruction of how bodies were clothed and graves furnished is important to establish the nature of burial ritual. In burial traditions where the bodies were clothed, well-preserved burials can indicate details of dress and personal adornment and furnish models for forensic contexts. Of course, great care must be taken in extrapolation from the dress of the dead to that of the living. Not all burials investigated by archaeologists have been interred in soil. Recent archaeological investigations of intramural burials of the 18th and 19th centuries have revealed a wealth of information concerning burial ritual as well as funerary practice (Cox, 1998; Reeve and Adams, 1993). In particular, it has been demonstrated that there was more variation in the clothing and personal items included in the burials than implied by the documentary records (Janaway, 1998).

In order to contextualize this information it is important to understand the taphonomic processes at work, and especially the differential loss of vulnerable materials. This is particularly important with textiles, which under most burial conditions will be lost over archaeological timescales. Over shorter burial intervals associated with many forensic investigations, textile materials will be subject to differential decay depending on composition, dyes, surface finishes, and treatments such as rotproofing. There has been considerable archaeological interest in the interaction of corroding metal artifacts placed in graves and in contact with textile and other organic materials (Janaway and Scott, 1989).

Degradation of the Body and Its Effect on Clothing and Other Materials

As the soft tissue of the body decays it will create heat, gradually liquefy, and change the chemical environment of the immediate area (Janaway, 1987). Textile materials such as cotton will easily absorb water, and swell. If the body is wrapped in an impermeable material or is in a container such as a coffin, semi-liquid decomposition products will collect in the bottom. Under the liquid, low redox conditions are likely and until the bottom seal breaks and while there is a substantial tissue mass, there will be reducing conditions underneath the body. This has been demonstrated using small animal cadavers and metal coins (Janaway, 1987). Further work is required to investigate the precise relationship between the chemistry of the body decomposition products and associated textile materials. When a number of coffins were opened during the Christchurch Spitalfields project, semi-liquid decomposition products suggestive of a high ammonia content were observed (smelled). The wool textiles from these were in poor condition with a high degree of scale loss and fibrillation, which would be an expected reaction with a strongly alkaline solution. However, not all semi-liquid bodies had this strong ammonia smell and further analysis of the coffin liquor was not possible due to health and safety constraints.

Degradation of Textile Materials

Under the majority of soil conditions, textile materials do not survive long-term burial. Natural fibers are readily degraded by the action of microorganisms over a comparatively short period of time unless the burial conditions inhibit biodegradation. Desiccation, freezing, and the presence of metal ions such as chromium or copper will considerably retard microbial action. Waterlogged soils with anoxic or low oxygen concentrations will exclude aerobic fungi, although anaerobic bacteria may still flourish. Under these conditions, soil pH is a major factor in the differential preservation of textiles. The absorption of clay particles by biological molecules will retard microbial attack (Hopkins, 1998). In acidic conditions, proteinic fibers (wool, animal hair, and silk) are favored, while cellulosic-based materials (cotton and linen) degrade rapidly. Under the much more unusual anaerobic alkaline conditions, cellulosic-based material is favored; for instance, certain lake bed deposits in the Alps have preserved flax plants and linen textiles dating to the Neolithic.

Degradation of Wool

Wool has a long history as a textile fiber, with the earliest evidence for use in textiles dating from c. 3000 B.C. in northeast Iraq. Until the rise of cotton use in the 19th century, woolen textiles predominated in Europe for clothing, furnishings, and bedding. Into the 20th century wool was still an important textile material to produce hard-wearing, warm clothing, both as woven cloth and knitted garments; however, since World War II, 100% wool garments have lost market share to wool mixtures and synthetic fabrics. Wool serge was used as the basis of military combat dress by both British and German forces during World War II. Some specialist fabric mixes were used; for instance, the underwear used by the Luftwaffe was made from mixed fibers (40% rabbit hair, 30% merino wool, 30% rayon staple fiber). Rabbit wool is particularly prone to moth attack and was proofed with Eulan CNA before use. This was the only mothproofed material used in service uniforms by the Germans (Moncreiff, 1952:31–32).

Ninety-nine percent of a wool fiber is formed from the protein keratin with 1% or less minor compounds such as fats, sterols, lipids, as well as a very small mineral and phosphorous content (Ryder and Stephenson, 1968). The primary structure of keratin is in the form of a polypeptide chain of 18 different amino acids. All amino acids have the common basic structure of an amine and carbonyl groups, but are distinguished by different side chains. The secondary structure of keratin twists the primary chain into an alpha-helix. It is held in this position by a number of bonds: weak cross-links may be formed between ionized COOH and NH_2 groups as well as hydrogen bonds between groups, while disulfide bridges form much stronger structural reinforcement of the helix. When compared to other proteins, keratin has a relatively high proportion of cystine (Ryder and Stephenson, 1968). This molecule is capable of forming peptide links at either end, and thus has an important function in forming di-sulfide bridges which form a cross link joining two keratin chains or between different parts of the same chain. Three molecular chains of keratin twist together to form protofibrils, and possibly 11 protofibrils group together to form the microfibril which forms the principle structural unit of wool. The center of the fiber consists of longitudinal corticule cells, formed from microfibrils embedded in an amorphous matrix. The exterior is covered in overlapping cuticular scales also formed from keratinaceous microfibrils.

Thus, keratin is in two forms in the fiber: crystalline and amorphous (α-keratin and β-keratin). The crystalline fraction has well-ordered, three-dimensionally intermolecularly bonded chains that are regularly placed with respect to each other, while the amorphous fraction has more randomly arranged, sporadically linked, poorly packed chains. The proportion of crystalline microfibrils to amorphous material is low, which makes wool a relatively weak fiber (Sibley and Jakes, 1984).

The degradation of wool occurs in a number of stages, with the amorphous fraction being attacked much more readily than the crystalline fraction. The ion–ion and hydrogen bonds are easily broken, while the peptide and disulfide bonds are much more resistant.

Wool is susceptible to alkaline attack, affecting not only the weaker bonds but also the disulfide bonds and the peptide links. As temperature and pH increase, the extent of the damage increases. The ion–ion forces between the carboxyl group of one amino acid and the amine of another will be easily disrupted by the removal of a proton by the alkali. Thus, the amorphous areas, which rely more heavily on these weak bonding forces to retain structure (compared to the crystalline regions with a higher proportion of disulfide bridges), will be readily attacked by weak alkalis. Disulfide bridges react with weak alkali to form a new cross-link based on a single sulfur atom, the lanthionine link, allowing little weakening of the fibers (Sibley and Jakes, 1984). If wool is subject to higher concentrations of alkali or with higher temperature, then the lanthionine link is also broken, and if the conditions are severe enough, the peptide bonds can be broken. Wool is much more resistant to acids than alkalis (Cook, 1988). Weak acids will cause limited damage while stronger acids can hydrolyze the peptide links, disrupt the ion–ion bonds, and hydrolyze some amine groups. However, because the disulfide links are resistant to acid attack above about pH 2, and although the peptide chains are shortened by acid hydrolysis (Sibley and Jakes, 1984), wool in all but the most aggressive acid environment will retain structural integrity although weakened.

Wool is subject to attack by fungi and bacteria that involves enzymous attack of the disulfide bond followed by hydrolysis of the peptide links (Sibley and Jakes, 1984) attacking the crystalline and amorphous zones of the fiber (Cook, 1988). Bacterial attack on wool includes *Bacillus mesentericus, B. substilis, B. cereus,* and *B. putrificus,* while fungal agents include *Penicillium* sp., *Aspergillus* sp., and a number of Actinomycetes (Cook, 1988). Jain and Agrawal (1980) tested 34 fungi from 13 different genera for their ability to degrade keratin. There are three stages in the fungal degradation of wool when exposed to *Aspergillus* and *Penicillium* spp. First, there is an erosion of the surface structure; second, swelling and production of spindle-shaped cortical cell bundles; and third, the separation of cortical cells (Watanabe and Miyazaki, 1980). However, it should be noted that fibers can still retain cuticular scales, while the cortex has broken down to separating cellular units.

Degradation of Silk

Silk fibers are secreted from the larvae of wild or the oriental domestic species of silk moth, *Bombx mori*. After the silk moth caterpillar has grown to its full size, it envelopes itself in a cocoon of silk prior to pupation. This silk (a protein fibroin) is generated as two continuous fibers and is cemented together by silk glue or sericin. The basis of sericulture is to place the cocoons in nearly boiling water, so that the sericin is softened and the silk can be reeled off. Mythology places the origins of sericulture to China in 2640 B.C. (Feltwell, 1990), with the earliest direct archaeological evidence of silk dating to the Chinese Neolithic (Barber, 1991). The art of sericulture remained in the Far East for many centuries, and silk was traded to western Europe long before silk culture was introduced to Spain in the 8th century A.D.

Silk fibers are extremely light and strong. An undegraded silk fiber is equal in strength to steel of comparable diameter (Cowan and Jungerman, 1969). The fiber is highly hygroscopic, making it a comfortable fabric for high humidity applications. In the past it has been used for parachute cloth, hosiery, and of course luxury garments. In the 1940s silk's utilitarian uses were replaced by synthetics such as nylon. Despite its cost and the availability of synthetic fibers, it is still used for applications such as thermal underwear. Silk survives under similar archaeological conditions as wool although it is slightly less resistant to decay. In archaeological sites it is usually found in waterlogged anoxic conditions, where, like wool, it has usually turned a dark honey-brown color.

Degradation of Cotton

The earliest evidence for cotton cloth in the Old World comes from the Indus Valley (Marshall, 1931). By 3000 B.C. it had reached the Levant (Betts et al., 1994) and was a thriving industry in England by 1641. Cotton spinning and weaving were some of the key components in the industrialization of Britain during the 18th century. With the European colonization of North America, especially after the invention of the cotton gin (patented in 1794), cotton fabric assumed worldwide importance.

The cotton fiber is a seed hair formed by the elongation of a single epidermal cell of the cotton seed. During initial growth, the cell wall consists of a cuticular envelope. When elongation is almost complete, the cell wall is thickened by a secondary wall of cellulose being laid down on the inner side of the cuticle. When ripe the cotton boll bursts, and the hairs dry, collapse, and twist, taking the form of convoluted flattened tubes, open at the base and closed at the tip. The collapsed nature of the cell is particularly clear in the areas where it is most kinked. The principle component of cotton is cellulose, the bulk of which (95%) is located in the secondary wall (Bailey et al., 1963). The proportion of cellulose to other biomolecules in vegetable-based textile fibers, such as cotton and flax, is much higher than in many other plant-derived materials. For instance, cellulose comprises 90 to 99% of cotton and flax, while wood, with significant amounts of hemicellulose and lignin, has only around a 45% cellulose content.

Cellulose is a polysaccharide formed from about 14,000 glucose residues, held together by oxygen bridges with β-1,4-glucosidic bonding. Cellulose molecules combine in bundles of some 2000 molecules to form microfibrils (Esau, 1965). The stability of cellulose in terms of insolubility and mechanical strength indicates that it is unlikely to be a single-chain structure and that the chains must be interconnected in such a way that the hydrophilic groups (CH_2OH and OH) are masked. These groups take part in inter- and intramolecular hydrogen bonding. The orientation of the microfibrils is different between each layer of the primary and secondary walls (Berkley, 1948).

In an acid environment, cellulose molecules are highly susceptible to hydrolysis of the glycosidic link. This results in a shortening of the cellulose chains and a structural weakening of the fiber (Cardamone et al., 1991). In addition, cellulose can oxidize at the sites of the hydroxyl groups on C_2, C_3, and C_6 to form oxycellulose. It should be noted that these oxidative reactions can take place without hydrolysis of the glycosidic link, in which case the chain will remain intact (Cardamone et al., 1991). The effect of oxycellulose formation is to disrupt the hydrogen-bonded molecular network, thus reducing fiber strength and opening the fiber up to further degradation.

In addition to purely chemical degradation, cellulose is readily attacked by the cellulolytic enzymes of microorganisms. The enzymatic cleavage of cellulose is catalyzed by cellulase, which in fungi consists of at least three enzymes. First, endo-β-1,4-glucanases break the β-1,4 bonds, then exo-β-1,4-glucanases remove cellobiose units from the chain ends (cellobiose consists of two glucose units linked by a glycosidic link). Finally, β-glucosidases break the glycosidic link in cellobiose to form glucose (Schlegel, 1986). Some fungi do not produce endo-β-1,4-glucanases and can only degrade modified cellulose, which has already been subject to chain scission by other microorganisms or acid hydrolysis. In well-aerated soils, cellulose is degraded by fungi, myxobacteria, and eubacteria, while under anaerobic conditions it is bacteria of the genus *Clostridia* that predominate.

Cotton fibers are extremely absorbent. When exposed to water, the fiber will swell and lengthen. Cotton is highly susceptible to acids and, being almost pure cellulose, is very easily degraded by a range of microorganisms. In soil, cotton will not survive acidic burial or any conditions that are the least favorable to microorganisms. Untreated, undyed cotton will usually show active decay by 60 days in biologically active soil. For this reason, cotton textiles will usually only survive archaeologically under desiccated, frozen, or anoxic waterlogged conditions that also have a high pH.

Degradation of Linen

Plant stem (bast) fibers are probably the first textile materials to be used, with flax fibers identified from Nahal Hemar in the Judaean Desert dating from the 7th millennium B.C., and from Catal Huyuk in Anatolia dating to c. 5000 B.C. (Barber, 1991). While there is good evidence for the use of other bast fibers in antiquity, such as hemp and nettle (Barber, 1991; Hald, 1942), linen textiles have been used throughout the Middle East and Europe from the Neolithic onwards (Barber, 1991). In northern Europe linen was important as a textile for cloth worn next to the skin, often with woolen outer-garments, until the increase in cotton production during the 19th century. Throughout the 19th and early part of the 20th century, important centers of production remained in Europe. During the early 1950s linen suffered a decline due to the popularity of synthetic fibers that were more crease resistant.

Bast fibers, obtained from the stems of dicotyledonous plants, consist of elongated, thick-walled single cells with tapering closed tips. These cell (ultimates) are cemented together end-to-end and side-to-side, forming bundles along the stem of the plant. The number of fiber bundles in each stem range from 15 to 40, with each bundle containing 12 to 40 ultimate fibers (Textile Institute, 1970). They are accessed by the processes of retting, a process of partial maceration to weaken and then remove the non-fibrous stem material by combing. The cell walls have extensive secondary thickening, which in flax accounts for 90% of the cross-sectional area (Esau, 1965). Unlike cotton, whose cell walls are composed of over 95% cellulose, flax has significant amounts of hemicellulose (c. 15.4 to 16.7%), pectin (1.8 to 3.8%), and lignin (2.0 to 2.5%), as well as 68.6% cellulose (Florian, 1987). The flax cell wall is composed of three layers in which the cellulose microfibrils are laid down in a spiral, which is reversed for each layer (Roelofsen, 1951). The fibrils in flax are more orientated in relation to the fiber axis than is the case with cotton, which confers higher strength and rigidity on the bast fiber (Cardamone et al., 1991). Flax microfibrils are embedded in a matrix of hemicellulose, pectin, and lignin.

Morphological changes that occur in degraded flax fibers include a break up of the gross structure into individual fibrils (Cook, 1988). Linen is a hygroscopic fiber and, like cotton, will easily absorb water. Chemically, linen is slightly more resistant to acid and more reactive to alkalis than cotton. It is easily attacked by microorganisms. Like cotton, linen will degrade under most burial conditions. It will survive if desiccated or frozen. Most waterlogged, anoxic sites are not sufficiently alkaline for it to survive long. For this reason, despite the fact that it was probably a common fabric in prehistoric and medieval Europe, finds of woolen textiles from waterlogged sites are much more common than linen. While linen is of great interest to Old World archaeologists, it is of limited forensic interest.

Case Studies

Case #1: Waterlogged Site 1

The archaeological excavations at Christchurch Cork provide a good example of the type of textile preservation encountered on a non-funerary site with waterlogged anoxic deposits (Wincott et al., 1997). Of course, the main taphonomic differences between the textiles here and at a burial site are the absence of a body, the lack of modification of the burial conditions during soft tissue decomposition, and the fact that in burial the textiles tend to be complete and are deliberately placed in the grave. The textiles from Cork are refuse; their incorporation into the deposits is by discard, and the majority were probably rags at this stage. One large fragment of coarse woolen cloth found in a ball was heavily impregnated with tree resin and had probably been used in caulking ship timbers. The waterlogged medieval deposits and post-medieval pits yielded a range of organic material, including timber, straw, and leather, as well as textiles and animal hair. With the exception of a single post-medieval cloth fragment of bast fiber (possibly linen), the bulk of the textile and fiber materials are derived from wool, animal hair, or silk. The preponderance of proteinic fiber at this type of waterlogged site and the absence of more vulnerable plant fibers are repeated regularly on other sites.

Case #2: Waterlogged Site 2

In 1973 a log coffin was revealed by a mechanical excavator on an area of exposed moorland at Quernmore near Lancaster, U.K. (Glover, 1990). The burial was embedded in clay beneath peat; the acidic, anoxic conditions had preserved a wooden coffin and woolen cloth shroud. The coffin, made from two halves of a single tree trunk, was dated by radiocarbon to 525 to 745 A.D. Nothing remained of the body except the hair and finger and toe nails. These, like the wool of the shroud, are composed of keratin and are, therefore, resistant to decay in the acid bog water. The shroud is of plain woven wool, now a dark brown color. Archaeological textiles from waterlogged sites are usually colored brown, golden-brown to black. This does not reflect the original color, or whether the textiles were originally dyed or undyed. Natural dyes will usually degrade under these conditions, although residues are sometimes discernible by chromatography (Taylor, 1983).

Case #3: Dry Site

Near the monastery of Kasr-el-Yahud in the Jordan Valley, the site of an ancient mass grave was discovered. The site is on a desert alluvial soil, 1167 feet below sea level. The climate is arid with an annual temperature of 23 to 25°C and a mean annual rainfall of only 100 m. The grave most probably dates to a massacre that took place during spring of 614 A.D. The grave was unfortunately disturbed by a bulldozer and only 34 bodies were left *in situ*, and these had to excavated with great speed. The bodies were skeletonized and laid on top of each other in an East/West alignment (Joe Zias, pers. comm., 1989). The skeletal remains were still clothed in substantial textile remains, including a number of recognizable garments. In common with observations from other sites, the parts of the textiles covering the limbs were best preserved while the areas around and especially below the body cavity were in the worst condition.

Two hundred and thirty-seven textile samples were recovered, mostly undyed linen or cotton. Only three samples contained any wool. One consisted of a loose wool weft (?) that appeared to have unraveled owing to the differential destruction of the warp (?). This was probably due to microbial inhibition afforded by the use of a metal mordant in dyeing the weft (Shamir and Janaway, 1995). The largest textile fragments recovered come from the sleeve, shoulder, neck region, and the lower skirt of long-sleeved ankle-length tunics which appear to be the principle garments worn. There are a number of very large fragments (e.g., 550 × 1550 mm, 1550 × 1190 mm). There is no pattern of differential preservation between cotton and linen. In addition to microbial attack some of the textiles have been holed by fly larvae attacking the flesh of the body. These are characterized by small circular holes between 2 and 6 mm in diameter. Documentary evidence relating to this massacre indicates that the bodies had been attacked by jackals prior to burial, which was confirmed by the presence of fecal pellets in the grave that contained cloth and bone fragments.

Despite the fact that alkaline environments are damaging to wool, the ratio of wool to cellulosic fabrics probably largely reflects the fabrics in use, rather than differential preservation. Other dry sites have produced wool as well as linen. The site of Nahal Mishmar (Cave of Treasure) produced 97 linen fragments and 23 wool, dating from Chalcolithic (4000 to 3000 B.C.) to the early 2nd century A.D. (Bar-Adon, 1980).

Case #4: Intramural Burials

The church of Christchurch Spitalfields (London) was consecrated in 1729, and between 1729 and 1859 at least 1000 individuals were interred in the vaults. The western part of these vaults was excavated between 1984 and 1986 and over 500 textile finds were recovered. These came from a number of different types of burial, with different preservation conditions. At one extreme were the intact, sealed lead coffins, fully anaerobic with well-preserved soft tissue and associated textiles, to wooden coffins where the bodies had naturally mummified, to fully skeletonized individuals with little or no textile finds (Janaway, 1993). The exterior of the coffins was mainly covered with dyed wool baize. These textiles, not in contact with the body and generally dry, survived well and represent the largest category of textiles recovered from the site.

Inside the coffins textiles of cotton, wool, linen, and silk were present. Certain patterns of preservations were evident (Janaway, 1993). Cotton was generally only preserved in fully anaerobic sealed lead coffins (with extensive soft tissue preservation) or in a desiccated condition. Wool was represented in both lead and wooden coffins in anaerobic damp and dry conditions. The only category of burial where cotton was more frequently represented than wool was in nine wooden coffins that were dry with extensive mummified soft tissue. This small group may not represent a taphonomic pattern so much as a burial practice. Linen bast was poorly represented, but this was only used as clothing (shirts, etc.), while cotton was used for everyday clothing and for shrouds, as well as coffin linings provided by the funeral trade in the later burials. Linen garments that were recovered show a characteristic pattern of decay. The fabric was severely weakened or absent underneath the body, while the areas that remained relatively dry during the soft tissue decomposition were in better condition. Cloth covering the body cavity was generally in worse condition than sleeves or the lower portion of long garments that covered the legs. The most common silk items were ribbons used as ties; these were generally in good condition in most burial categories. One silk item recovered was the lining of an 18th-century man's waistcoat, only the silk remained and there was no indication as to what material made up the outer layer.

Experimental Investigation of Degradation

Soil burial has long been recognized as a particularly aggressive environment for textile materials and the soil burial test has been an essential component of a series of tests for resistance to rotting (Lloyd, 1968). However, it has also been noted that even with the use of standard procedures it is often difficult to obtain totally reproducible results (Turner, 1972). In this context, it is self-evident that to establish general trends a large number of replicates are needed. Extrapolation from case evidence to test resistance requires great caution.

British Standard BS6085 defines methods for determining the resistance of textiles to microbiological deterioration. The soil burial procedure is described as "most severe" and is used to test materials such as sandbags, tarpaulins, and cloth treated with fungicides. The soil bed is kept at an incubator temperature of $28 \pm 1°C$; it has a moisture content between 20 and 30% based on dry mass and a pH of 5.5 to 7. Of course, it must be pesticide free. Standard strips of test textile (150×25 mm) are buried along with undyed cotton control. After 7 days they are removed and loss of tensile strength is determined.

The soil burial test has been used to assess the effectiveness of rotproofing treatments of textile materials for military use (Turner, 1972). One test, developed by Defence Standards Laboratory, Department of Supply, Commonwealth of Australia, consisted of burying textile samples in a matured compost of loam, grass clippings, and stable manure. They were incubated for 14 days at $30 \pm 2°C$ at 95 to 100 % R.H. At the end of this period the textile samples were collected, sterilized in methanol and the breaking load was compared with unburied specimens (Turner, 1972). The fabric used was cotton duck treated with 0.95% pentachlorophenyl laurate (PCPL).

**Table 20.1 Expected Minimal Exposure of
Buried Death Scene Materials (in months)**

	Acid	Alkaline
Number of trenches	6	1
pH	4.4–6.5	7.5
Rayon	1	2
Paper	5	1
Cotton (treated)	10	7
Silk	15	7
Wool	15	5
Cotton/polyester	25	25
Nylon	X	X
Triacetate	X	X
Acrylic	X	X
Leather (shoe upper)	X	X
Plastic (sheet polyester)	X	X

Note: X = material in good condition after 48 months.

Source: Adapted from Morse, D. et al., *Handbook of Forensic
Archaeology and Anthropology,* Rose Printing, Tallahassee,
FL, 1983, p. 143.

A series of experiments was conducted to demonstrate the degree of reproducibility
of these tests. It is important to note that in these highly controlled conditions it was not
possible to fully replicate the results between experiments and between operators independently using a common technique (Turner, 1972). The aim of this work is to define loss
of functional strength, whereas from an archaeological or forensic point of view the ability
to identify morphologically recognizable textile fragments is the key issue.

Florida Experiments

In the late 1970s a set of field experiments was set up in Florida to study the rate of
degradation of associated death scene materials (Morse et al., 1983) (Table 20.1). The
materials selected were chosen because of their applicability to forensic investigations.
These included textiles with modern dyes and surface finishes. Samples were buried in six
locations with an acid pH, while only one site was used with an alkaline pH.

This work illustrates some general trends that have been borne out by the examination
of both forensic and archaeological data. Compared to natural fibers, wood, and wood
products, most synthetic materials show resistance to decay over forensic timescales. The
degradation of synthetic textiles has been discussed in detail by Rowe (1997). Modern
leather shows considerable resistance to decay and is discussed in more detail below. Under
moist burial conditions, the proteinic natural fibers, wool and silk, generally are much
more robust than fibers composed of cellulose. Seven different types of cotton, with
different dyes and surface finishes, were used in the Morse et al. (1983) experiments.
Deterioration started to become readily apparent between 2 weeks and 10 months, with
total destruction usual between 5 and 10 months. However, in some burial locations this
could have happened within the first month because of the large populations of cellulose-
decomposing organisms in most soils.

Prior to the 20th century, textile raw materials were derived from a number of plant
and animal sources, but during the last 100 years increasing use has been made of synthetic

fiber. Rayons are manufactured from regenerated cellulose, and as such tend to be vulnerable to soil burial. Viscose rayon, as used in the Florida experiments, was first patented in 1892. It swells in the presence of water and its reaction is similar to cotton, being totally destroyed within 1 month of burial. It can be dyed by the same dyestuffs as cotton. Cross-linked cellulosic fibers such as cellulose acetate or triacetate are also highly vulnerable to degradation in soils burial (Rowe, 1997).

Nylon is a manufactured fiber composed of a long-chain polyamide with recurring amide groups. Its first commercial use was in 1938 with a range of functions: World War II parachutes, towropes, nets, tents, and clothing. From this date it rapidly replaced cotton and silk for women's hosiery. It is highly resistant to decay in burials and there are examples from forensic investigations in which nylon hose have held the decomposing tissue together. Polyesters are manufactured from long-chain synthetic polymers composed at least 85% by weight of an ester of dihydric alcohol and terphalic acid (P–HOOC–C_6H_4–COOH). Discovered in 1941 and developed after World War II, these fibers have low water absorbency and are often used in fabrics of wool/polyester or cotton/polyester mixtures. In normal use they are not attacked by moth larvae and mildew does not grow on polyester.

Acrylics are manufactured from long-chain synthetic polymers composed of at least 85% by weight of acrylontrile units. In normal use they are highly resistant to chemical degradation and show little reaction to water. The fiber is moth resistant on its own, but in a wool–acrylic mixture moth larvae will attack through the acrylic to get to wool. Acrylics are naturally resistant to mildew and fungi. This is reflected in soil burial tests (Rowe, 1997). The fiber originally known as Spandex™ is manufactured from long-chain synthetic polymers comprised of at least 85% of a segmented polyurethane. In 1959 the name was changed to Lycra™. Commercial production started in 1960 to 1961. In recent years it has been used extensively for stretch, casual, and sports clothing. Unfortunately, it was not included in the experiments of Northrop, Singer, and Rowe (Rowe, 1997).

The Experimental Earthworks Project

In the United Kingdom there has been a long-term soil burial program, set up by archaeologists and natural scientists, which has relevance to the degradation of textiles, leather, wood, bone, and much else. The Experimental Earthworks Project was conceived between 1958 and 1960 (Jewel, 1963; Lawson et al., 2000). The first earthwork was constructed on Overton Down, Wiltshire in 1960, followed by a second near Wareham, Dorset in 1963 (Bell et al., 1996). Each experiment consists of a linear bank and ditch, with 8 sets of buried materials incorporated at intervals within the bank. Sections are cut, and buried material is to be recovered at intervals of 1, 2, 4, 8, 16, 32, 64, and 128 years. To date the experiment has progressed up to the 32-year section. The Overton earthwork was constructed on a chalk down, while the Wareham earthwork is on heathland overlying an acidic podsol. Within each earthwork buried materials were placed in a turf stack at the base of the bank, and within the bank itself (chalk at Overton, sand at Wareham). The burial environments can be summarized as follows in Tables 20.2 and 20.3.

From these experiments a number of conclusions can be made. First, the presence of metal ions in the cotton mineral khaki (iron/chromium), woolen gabardine (iron/copper mordant), and the black-dyed weft of the woolen contrast cloth (Cr mordant) have provided some degree of resistance to microbial degradation (Janaway, 1996). The cellulosic

Table 20.2   Survival of Buried Materials from Both Experimental Earthworks

| | Overton | | | | | | | | | | Wareham | | | | | | | | | | | |
| | Chalk | | | | | Turf | | | | | Sand | | | | | | Turf | | | | | |
Year	2	4	8	16	32	2	4	8	16	32	1	2	5	9	17	33	1	2	5	9	17	33
Cotton plain	3	2	0	0	0	0	0	0	0	0	3	3	3	3	2	1						
Cotton mineral khaki	4	4	3	3	3	0	0	0	0	0	3	3	2	3	3	3						
Woolen contrast	3	3	3	2	2	2	1	3	2	0	3	3	3	2	1	0	3	3	3	3	2	2
Worsted gabardine	4	2	3	3	2	2	1	3	0	0	3	3	2	3	3	3	3	3	2	2	2	2
Linen	4	3	3	2	3	1	0	0	0	0	1	1	1	1	1	0	3			1	1	0
Leather	4	4	4	4	4	4	4	4	4	4	4	4	4	4	4	4	4	4	4	4	4	4

Note: 0 = no trace; 1 = traces only; 2 = general degradation; 3 = local degradation; 4 = well preserved. Note that Wareham data relate to part of samples not in direct contact with copper coins or steel discs

Source: After Bell, M. et al., The Experimental Earthwork Project 1960–1992, Council for British Archaeology, York, 1996, p. 239. With permission.

Table 20.3 Environmental Context of Site in Experimental Earthworks Project

	pH	General Observations
Overton turf stack	4.8–5.3	Aggressive environment for textiles
Overton chalk bank	7.5	Biologically less active than turf environment
Wareham turf stack	—	Better general preservation organics
Wareham sand bank	—	Free-draining, well-aerated, most aggressive environment for most organics

materials generally decayed rapidly, although it is probable that in the nitrogen-deficient environments the initial rate of degradation was retarded. Of course, this is one of the principal differences between soil burial with and without a body. The detailed microbiological work carried out in association with the 33-year excavation at Wareham (Lawson et al., 2000) confirmed that the bulk of microbial activity had probably occurred when the materials were first buried and there was an excess of carbon. Although both the wool samples confirm the general pattern of keratin being more robust across a range of burial environments compared to cotton or linen, the effect of dyes and mordants must be borne in mind.

Dyes

It is clear that the effect of textile dyes and, in particular, metal mordants will significantly affect the resistance of textile fiber to microbial decay. Prior to the mid-19th century all dyes were natural dyes derived directly from plant or animal sources. Certain dyestuffs require the presence of metal ions to enable them to bond effectively to the fibers. These are referred to as mordant dyes, and common mordants have been iron, copper, and chromium. Of these, copper and chromium are of interest as they are toxic to microorganisms in sufficient concentrations.

From 1830 European chemists started to investigate these natural products. By the second half of the 19th century, synthetic aniline dyes were being produced. Throughout the late 19th century a mixture of synthetic and natural dyes was used. By the 1960s over 3500 dyes stuffs were in use (Hardie and Pratt, 1966). What effect each of these has on the degradation of textile materials during soil burial is in need of investigation. From the examination of archaeological samples, it is clear that the presence of certain dyes, and their associated mordants, will either promote or retard degradation. This is especially clear where cloth has been patterned by the use of different colored yarns. The limited set of textiles used in the Overton Down experiment discussed above supports this case for dyes having a modifying effect on the degradation of buried textiles.

Bradford Experiments

To investigate this further a provisional series of experiments were set up in Bradford (Terry, 1996) comparing dyed and undyed plain-woven cotton and a sample of blue-dyed cotton denim. Denim is a hard-wearing cotton twill fabric traditionally made with a blue warp and gray filling. The blue was traditionally natural indigo but has, since the mid-20th century, been dyed with a synthetic vat dye, Indanthran Blue RS® also known as C.I. Vat Blue 4, a synthetic blue developed in 1901 as an alternative to indigo. This is an insoluble

Table 20.4   Differential Environment Characteristics in Bradford Experiment

	pH	Initial Moisture (%)	2nd Moisture (%)	Organic Content (%)
Garden	6.8	24.1	28.3	19.30
Moors	6.3	33.6	36.9	21.30
Cellar	8.8	29.1	27.8	12.70

Source: Derived from Terry, J., Unpublished dissertation, University of Bradford, U.K., 1996. With permission.

dye formed by the fusion of 2-anthraquinone, which is light fast and low cost (Shore, 1995). Both the natural and synthetic indigos are vat dyes, the dyestuff being introduced from aqueous solution as leuco or reduced compounds formed by the reduction of the dye by alkalis. Once the dye has penetrated the material it can be oxidized to form the insoluble dye once more.

The Bradford experiments compared a standard fabric (plain-weave cotton) undyed, dyed with natural indigo and with Indranthan Blue. In addition, commercial denim fabric was used, taken from worn jeans. This fabric was of a different weave (a typical twill fabric) and as such is not directly comparable. Samples were buried for 70 and 140 days in three contrasting environments: garden soil, moorland, and under the floor of a cellar. Table 20.4 gives details of moisture content (weight loss on drying), organic content (weight loss on ignition), and pH.

Of the three environments, the cellar was the most aggressive with the total loss of most samples in 140 days. The next most aggressive was the garden soil. The relative decay of textiles can be assessed in a number of ways, including loss in strength, morphological changes to fibers, fungal colonization, and molecular changes documented by FTIR microscopy. However, in a forensic context, perhaps the most relevant is the amount of the original material that is recoverable in a morphologically identifiable state. In this case, a simple 5-point score based on area of original material recovered may be used. These results are summarized in Table 20.5.

The relative decay rates across the range of environments can be summarized as follows. The commercial denim was most resistant across all environments, including the cellar. The next most resistant was the Vat Blue 4-dyed sample, then the natural indigo-dyed sample. The most vulnerable was, as expected, the undyed cotton. Although the commercial denim and the samples prepared in the laboratory are not strictly comparable, these results do emphasize the need for caution when comparing relative decay rates of textiles dyed and finished differently.

Rotproofing and Mothproofing

During the 20th century there has been considerable development of agents to prevent damage by fungi and bacteria under damp conditions, as well as preventing insect attack. Under the current British Standard (2087, part 1, 1992), class A treatments are defined as having "found general acceptance by textile proofers and finishers and the specifying authorities." Of course, agents that may have been found effective in the past may have been dropped from current use due to health or environmental concerns. When considering the

Table 20.5 Preservation of Morphologically Identifiable Textiles in Bradford Experiments

Sample No.	Burial Environment	Dye	Days	Condition Score
1, 2, 3	Moors	Vat blue 4	70	1, 1, 1
4, 5, 6	Moors	Indigo	70	1, 1, 1
7, 8, 9	Moors	Undyed	70	1, 1, 1
10, 11, 12	Moors	Denim	70	0, 0, 0
13, 14, 15	Garden	Vat blue 4	70	1, 1, 1
17, 17, 18	Garden	Indigo	70	2, 2, 2
19, 20, 21	Garden	Undyed	70	3, 4, 4
22, 23, 24	Garden	Denim	70	1, 1, 1
25, 26, 27	Garden	Vat blue 4	140	5, 4, 5
28, 29, 30	Garden	Indigo	140	5, 4, 5
31, 32, 33	Garden	Undyed	140	5, 4, 5
34, 35, 36	Garden	Denim	140	3, 4, 4
37, 38, 39	Moors	Vat blue 4	140	1, 1, 1
40, 41, 42	Moors	Indigo	140	1, 1, 1
43, 44, 45	Moors	Undyed	140	1, 1, 1
46, 47, 48	Garden	Denim	140	0, 0, 0
49, 50, 51, 52	Cellar	Vat blue 4	140	5, 5, 5, 5
53, 54, 55, 56	Cellar	Indigo	140	5, 5, 5, 5
57, 58, 59, 60	Cellar	Undyed	140	5, 5, 5, 5
61, 62, 63, 64	Cellar	Denim	140	0, 0, 0, 0

Note: Scores for general condition on recovery: 0 = no discernible loss of fabric; 1 = loss of up to 30% fabric area; 2 = loss of up to 60% fabric area; 3 = loss of up to 90% fabric area; 4 = loss of over 90% fabric area; 5 = total loss.

Source: Derived from Terry, J., Unpublished dissertation, University of Bradford, U.K., 1996.

degradation of textile materials that have been used in the past, earlier treatments should be considered. For instance, in the current list (British Standard 2087, part 1, 1992) pentachlorophenyl laurate is not recommended for apparel, while in the earlier 1981 version it was suggested for use in hospital textiles, mattress covers, and woolen textiles in general. (See Table 20.6.)

From the Overton Down data it is known that mineral khaki, which according to these data only provided low microbial resistance, considerably affects the survival of buried cotton fabric (Jewel, 1963). There is need for further investigation into the effects of these treatments on the survival of buried textiles over forensic timescales.

In the past when there was a higher reliance on wool fabrics, moth damage both to raw wool fabric in storage and to clothes in storage was a major problem (Moncreiff, 1952). Bayer Co. in Germany discovered that fluorinated inorganic compounds would mothproof wool (Moncreiff, 1952). Eulan M™ was first marketed in 1920, followed by Eulan F™ in 1921. Both these treatments were fluoride based, but were unsuccessful and later withdrawn. Eulan Extra™, a double fluoride of aluminum and ammonia, was introduced in 1924 (Moncreiff, 1952). The main problem with fluoride is that it often powders off and easily washes out. Eulan Extra™ was not even fast in cold water. The uses of acid fluorides, e.g., potassium bifluoride, are more substantive. Just how resistant these compounds would be in long-term use and soil burial is debatable.

Table 20.6   Textile Treatments and Resistance to Degradation

Preservative Agent	Amount	Use	Microbial Resistance	Resistance to Leaching
Zinc naphthenate	0.8–1.2% Zn	Ropes, cordage, canvases, cotton duck	Fair to medium	Fair to good
Copper naphthenate	0.5–1.2%Cu	Cotton canvas, tarpaulins, webbing	High	Fairly good
Cuprammonium processes	1.0–1.5% Cu	Cotton and flax fabrics (e.g., tarpaulins)	High	Fair
Mineral khaki	0.4–2.0% Cr	Cotton and flax either alone or with vat dye	Low	Excellent
Pentachlorophenyl laurate (PCPL)	1.0–3.5% PCPL	Industrial textiles, not for clothing or furnishings	High	Fairly good
Copper 8 process	0.03–0.12% Cu	Heavy canvas, cotton duck, cordage, webbing, etc.	High	Good
Dichlorophen process	0.6–2.0%	Industrial textiles not used for clothing	High	Fairly good
Halogenated diphenylurea derivative process (HDUD)	>0.56% or >0.8% HDUD	Wool and animal fibers from insect damage, resistant to washing; used in uniforms	Nill	Good
Halogenated diphenylurea derivative process (DTMDU)	>0.12% DTMDU	Working life protection of wool and woolen blends against insect damage	Effective against gram-positive bacteria	Good

Source: Data collated from British Standard 2087, part 1, 1992.

Lowe's process, first specified in 1934, uses chromium fluoride. It is claimed that the chromium compounds are permanently fixed on the fibers (chromium oxides have a long history as mordants for the application of dyestuffs to wool). The amount of chromium fluoride applied in specification given by Lowe is much greater than would normally be used in chrome dyeing (Moncreiff, 1952) and as such may well have an effect on such fabrics. Wool dyed jungle green for use in the East during World War II was impregnated with chromium oxide in the combined form, but had to be used substantially free from uncombined chromium salts owing to toxic effects (Moncreiff, 1952). This impregnation with combined chromium was found in practice to give good microbial resistance compared to untreated wool.

It is clear that a number of mothproofing treatments are easily washed from the fibers and as such are unlikely to remain in sufficient concentrations to be toxic in soil burial. However, treatments that used sufficient amounts of chromium or copper may well be of significance and require further research.

Mothproofing agents used in the 1960s included final dry-cleaning baths based on DDT, naphthalene, and paradichlorobenzene (Cowan and Jungerman, 1969). In forensic investigations the key issues relating to mothproofing are whether the presence of the mothproofing agents in the concentrations first applied will have an appreciable inhibiting effect on microbial attack; second, whether those concentrations will be reduced to a significant degree by wear and laundering; and third, whether the mothproofing agents themselves will survive soil burial. It is clear that a number of mothproofing agents are

Table 20.7 Leather Sample Types Used at Overton Down

Sample Type	Comment
Oak-bark-tanned sole leather	Whole thickness of unsplit ox hide
Modern extract-tanned sole leather	Whole thickness of unsplit oxhide (note that this has a higher ratio of tan:protein than in the vegetable-tanned sample)
Modern upper leather of semi-chrome type	Chrome tannage applied after initial vegetable tan
Modern heavy upper leather	Chrome tanned
Modern upper leather of chrome retanned type	Vegetable tannage applied after initial chrome

known to resist biodegradation, e.g., DDT, and the biocidic effects of high chromium levels in textiles are well documented. It is clear further research is required.

Degradation of Leather

The experimental earthworks programs at Overton Down and Morden Bog have demonstrated the resistance of modern tanned leather to a range of soil burial conditions. The survival of leather items (shoes, belts) is well attested in forensic investigations. In the case of Stephen Jennings (Hunter et al., 1996), the only surviving clothing of a 3-year-old boy, excavated in a skeletonized state after being buried for 26 years, was the sandals. According to the murder confession by the boy's father, he had been wrapped in a sack of unknown composition. Modern leathers are generally more resistant to decay than the vegetable-tanned leather used in antiquity. This is borne out by the data from the experimental earthworks program (Edwards, 1996). At Overton Down, five different leathers were buried (Jewell, 1963) (Table 20.7).

Only one of these leathers (the oak-bark tan) is equivalent to leather used in antiquity; the rest were included to investigate the long-term stability of modern leathers. So far, 32 years of burial have resulted in very little deterioration of the samples and there are no consistent changes in either environment. The survival of leather over archaeological timescales is usually confined to dry sites, where the relative humidity is less than 50%, and waterlogged anoxic deposits (Cronyn, 1990). Dry leather is characterized by shrinkage, cracks, and exfoliation. If the moisture content rises, the leather will degrade to a black syrup that will dry to a resinous lump. Waterlogged leather is generally in good condition after many centuries of burial. There are extensive collections of Roman and Medieval leather items recovered from excavations in northern Europe (Cronyn, 1990). Small fragments of leather are often found in medieval graves attached to copper alloy buckles. Although the bulk of the belt has decayed, the area in direct contact with the corroding metal will have been protected from microbial decay.

Corrosion of Metals

Metal items are often included in graves in the form of jewelry, dress fasteners, buckles, etc. In forensic investigations, metal zippers or rivets from denim jeans may be recovered from clandestine burials.

The rate of metallic corrosion depends on a number of different factors, including the composition and structure of the metal artifact, the chemical nature of the burial environment,

Table 20.8   Metal Types and Corrosibility

1. Corrosion-resistant metals, e.g., gold (also surgical steel used in body-piercing studs).
2. Metals that after initial rapid corrosion form a layer of stable corrosion products and thus become resistant to further attack. In most burial environments these will have an extensive metallic core even after burial over archaeological timescales, e.g., copper.
3. Metals that corrode rapidly, but do not form a layer of protective corrosion products. Over archaeological timescales these may be either totally lost from the burial environment, or characterized by a mass of corrosion which may cover a much reduced metallic core, e.g., iron.

and the duration of burial. In simple terms, metals can be divided into three groups according to their susceptibility to corrosion in the burial environment (see Table 20.8).

The stability of buried metals largely depends on a combination of pH and redox (Edwards, 1998). The redox potential of a solution is a measure of its ability to donate or remove electrons from other substances. Under high redox values (oxidizing conditions) most metals will easily corrode, while under low redox values (reducing conditions) they will tend to remain uncorroded. In addition, acidic conditions (low pH) will assist corrosion, while alkaline conditions will tend to result in the formation of a stable corrosion matrix in most metals.

In a well-drained acidic, sand, or gravel site, all metals, except the most inert (e.g., gold), will corrode rapidly and extensively. If the conditions are sufficiently aggressive, ferrous objects may be totally lost, or at least be in the form of a massive corrosion matrix covering little or no metallic core. In this type of site even copper alloys will exhibit considerable loss of metal to the core. However, under most other burial conditions, most metal will be capable of recovery, albeit in a corroded state even after many centuries (Cronyn, 1990).

The Interaction of Corroding Metals with Organic Materials

In the vast majority of burial conditions organic materials do not survive over archaeological timescales. However, corroding metallic artifacts can preserve traces of organic materials with which they are in immediate contact. These are usually referred to as Mineral Preserved Organics (MPOs) or sometimes pseudomorphs. Both these terms are misleading because, depending on the materials concerned, either the actual organic material is preserved or the corrosion products have formed casts reflecting surface morphology. In the United Kingdom this type of material has been documented since the early nineteenth century with the examination by Michael Faraday (1836) of metal objects from Bartlow, in Ashdon, Essex. Interest was revived in the 1960s at the Ancient Monuments Laboratory of the Ministry of Public Buildings and Works, where the routine examination of corroded metal artifacts for traces of leather, textile, wood, etc. was established (Biek, 1963). The study of organic material preserved in metallic corrosion products has become routine, with Anglo-Saxon inhumation cemetery reports not being complete without a section on the textile and other remains.

Research into the mechanisms of metal corrosion deposition and the subsequent mineralization of fibers has included detailed study of archaeological remains as well as laboratory simulation (Barford, 1979; Edwards, 1974; Gillard et al., 1994; Keepax, 1975). At the second experimental earthwork at Wareham, copper alloy coins and steel discs were placed on top of textile, leather, and rope samples. SEM study by Janaway (1979, 1984), coupled with the study of archaeological assemblages, identified a critical issue — the formation of metal-preserved organic materials was favored by burial environments that resulted in the rapid corrosion of the associated metal, with extensive transport and deposition of corrosion products onto the organic material. In particular, well-aerated, acidic sites such as Mucking and Christchurch X-17 (Janaway, 1987) have produced a range of metal-preserved organics, while experimental observations (e.g., Janaway, 1984) have indicated that the critical time for their formation rests in the years immediately after deposition.

It is generally accepted that there are two distinct mechanisms at work in the formation of metal-preserved organics. On copper alloys, the copper ions are transported into and onto the organic material where, provided a high enough ion concentration develops, they act as a biocide, inhibiting microbial decay of the organic material. In practice, this critical level of copper ion concentration is only reached in areas of organic material in direct contact with the metal, as clearly demonstrated in the archaeological record. Cellulose-based materials (e.g., linen cloth), which readily absorb water and dissolved cations, are the most frequent group of materials preserved in association with copper.

Analysis of archaeological organic materials preserved in association with copper has shown that the cellulose is largely intact, with little degradation. Ferrous corrosion products do not have a biocidic effect; however, iron corrosion tends to form a much more extensive and encapsulating matrix. This corrosion matrix, which is principally formed of iron oxides, hydroxides, and soil mineral grains, will encapsulate any organic materials. Fine surface detail is preserved in the form of a negative cast provided that the primary layer of corrosion product has been laid down prior to any extensive degradation of the organic material. Because the iron corrosion will not inhibit degradation of the organic material, all that is usually left over archaeological timescales is the hollow casts. Generally, the most detailed corrosion-preserved organic structures associated with ferrous artifacts are derived from proteinic fibers, such as wool, goat hair, or leather, which have some resistance to decay in aerated, neutral-to-acid burial conditions. Because the critical period for the formation of these structures is within the first few years of burial, the approaches adopted by archaeological conservators in maximizing the amount of information derived from corroded metal artifacts are equally applicable to forensic investigations. Recently, a cor-roded watch was brought into the author's laboratory from the investigation of a suspicious death. From the condition of the body it was estimated the person had been dead some years and probably stored in a well-ventilated attic or loft. In addition, confirming the nature and type of the watch (cheap petrol station electronic), it was possible to confirm that the deceased had been wearing a cotton twill weave shirt and acrylic sweater (traces of the cuff and sweater fibers were preserved in the corrosion).

A recent experimental study (McGrath, 1999) examined differences in rates of biode-terioration of a range of commercial denim fabrics. These experiments utilized both new fabrics and used clothing that had been subject to repeated wear and laundering cycles. Both laboratory and field burial tests were used. While the results of this preliminary study were not conclusive, a number of general trends were observed. First, identical indigo dyed denim samples decayed at different rates in two superficially similar burial media (different batches of John Innes potting soil no. 1 from the same supplier). This extreme variability in burial media causes many problems of reproducibility within controlled trials and will have an even greater effect when considering the larger number of variables within real

Table 20.9   Gross Condition of Textile Samples after 24 Months

	Decay of Pig	Sample Position	Dyed Polyester	Undyed Wool	Undyed Cotton	Indigo Denim
Pig A	Largely skeletalized	Above	0	2	5	5
Pig A	Largely skeletalized	Below	0	0	5	5
Pig B	Some adipocere	Above	0	2–3	5	2
Pig B	Extensive adipocere	Below	0	0	2–3	0
Control	—	Above	0	5	5	5
Control	—	Below	0	5	5	5

Note: Average condition for all replicates; condition scores same as Table 20.5.

crime scenes. However, despite this, McGrath's work does indicate an underlying trend: different denim fabrics decayed at different rates when buried in soil. This sounds an important note of caution; even within a single class of material, in this case denim jeans, decay rates may be quite variable.

In addition to variability caused by fabric type and the non-heterogeneous nature of soils within a single burial location, the decay of a body causes major modification of the burial conditions during active soft tissue decay. In a recent series of experiments conducted in the Bradford region, pig cadavers have been buried with a range of highly replicated textile and hair samples (Janaway et al., in prep). Results from a preliminary set of experiments with a burial interval of 2 years have clearly demonstrated decomposing soft tissue will modify the decay rate of associated textiles. In this experiment three graves were dug; the control graves contained the textile samples but no pig, while a pig was placed in the remaining two. Pig A was subject to a longer postmortem interval between death and burial as well as a scavenging episode by foxes. Although this did not cause much physical disturbance of the grave, it did result in increased aeration. The result was that after 2 years burial pig A was in a more advanced state of decomposition than pig B. Textile samples were placed directly over and underneath the pigs or at the equivalent depth in the control grave. Table 20.9 summarizes some key observations.

As would be expected, the most robust fabric type over this period of burial is the polyester, which shows no gross morphological or color changes irrespective of burial conditions. The undyed cotton is the most vulnerable and only survived at all under the actively decomposing pig, where it is covered by semi-liquid soft tissue. The commercial indigo-dyed denim is more robust than the undyed cotton, but is still lost from burial environments that are not associated with active cadaveric decay. The wool samples from underneath both pigs are largely intact, while the wool samples from above the pigs are much more decayed. By contrast, wool samples were not recovered from the control grave.

The actively decomposing soft tissue forms a semi-liquid, anaerobic environment within which only a very specialized microflora can operate. This has the effect of retarding the degradation of a number of textile fabrics.

Summary

To conclude, the degradation of textiles, buried in the ground or buried in inhumation graves, is subject to a wide range of intrinsic and extrinsic factors resulting in differential loss or preservation. It is not possible to produce simple predictive models for universally applicable decay rates. Even within a single burial site considerable variation in the decay of a single textile fabric will exist due to differences in soil microenvironments. These differences will be exacerbated by the presence of an actively decomposing body. It is essential to take into account the effects of wear, laundering, dyes, and finishes on a textile's response to specific burial conditions. Despite these problems, well-controlled, well-replicated experiments are starting to confirm some general trends in textile decay that may assist in designing search strategies or reconstructing the circumstances of burial.

References

Bailey, T.L.W., V.W. Tripp, and A.T. Moore
  1963 Cotton and other vegetable fibres. In *Fibre Structure*, edited by J.W.S. Hearle and R.H. Peters), pp. 422–454. Butterworths for The Textile Institute, Manchester, U.K.

Bar-Adon, P.
  1980 *The Cave of Treasure: The Finds from the Caves in Nahal Mishmar*, The Israel Exploration Society, Jerusalem.

Barber, E.J.W
  1991 *Prehistoric Textiles: The Development of Cloth in the Neolithic and Bronze Ages with Special Reference to the Aegean*, Princetown University Press, Princetown NJ.

Barford, P.M.
  1979 Mineral Pseudomorphs of Organic Materials: A Study in Burial Environments, unpublished dissertation, Institute of Archaeology, University of London, U.K.

Bell, M., P.J. Fowler, and S.W. Hillson
  1996 *The Experimental Earthwork Project 1960–1992*, Council for British Archaeology Research Report No. 100, Council for British Archaeology, York.

Betts, A. et al.
  1994 Early cotton in northern Arabia, *Journal of Archaeological Science* 21:489–499.

Berkley, E.E.
  1948 Cotton – a versatile textile fibre, *Textile Research Journal* 18(2):71–88.

Biek, L.
  1963 *Archaeology and the Microscope: The Scientific Examination of Archaeological Evidence*, Lutterworth, London.

British Standard
  1992 2087, part 1.

Cardamone, J.M., K.M. Keister, and A.H. Osareh
  1991 Degradation and conservation of cellulosics and esters. In *Polymers in Conservation*, edited by N.S. Allen, M. Edge, and C.V. Horie, pp. 108–124. Royal Society of Chemistry, London.

Cook, B.
  1988 Fibre damage in archaeological textiles. In *Archaeological Textiles*, edited by S.A. O'Connor and M.M. Brooks, pp. 5–15. UKIC Occasional Papers No. 10, United Kingdom Institute for Conservation, London.

Cowan, M.L. and M.E. Jungerman.
  1969 *Introduction to Textiles*, 2nd ed., Appleton-Century-Crofts, New York.

Cox, M., Editor
  1998 *Grave Concerns: Death and Burial in England 1700–1850*, Council for British Archaeology Research Report No. 113, Council for British Archaeology, York.

Cronyn, J.M.
1990 *Elements of Archaeological Conservation*, Routledge, London.

Edwards, G.
1974 The Preservation of Textiles in Archaeological Contexts, unpublished diploma dissertation, Institute of Archaeology, University of London.

1996 Leather samples. In *The Experimental Earthwork Project 1960–1992*, edited by M.Bell, P.J. Fowler, and S.W. Hillson, pp. 176–177. Council for British Archaeology Research Report No. 100, Council for British Archaeology, York.

Edwards, R.
1998 The effect of changes in groundwater geochemistry on the survival of buried metal artefacts. In *Preserving Archaeological Remains in Situ*, edited by M. Corfield, P. Hinton, T. Nixon, and M. Pollard, pp. 86–92. Museum of London Archaeology Service, London.

Esau, K.
1965 *Plant Anatomy*, 2nd ed., Wiley, New York

Faraday, M.
1836 Letter on "recent discovery of Roman sepulchral relics in one of the greater barrows at Bartlow, in Ashdon, Essex," *Archaeologia* XXVI:30–31

Feltwell, J.
1990 *The Story of Silk*, Allan Sutton, Stroud, Gloucestershire.

Florian, M.L.E.
1987 Deterioration of organic material other than wood. In *The Conservation of Marine Archaeological Objects*, edited by C. Pearson. Butterworths, London.

Gillard, R.D. et al.
1994 The mineralisation of fibres in burial environments, *Studies in Conservation* 39:132–140.

Glover, J.M.
1990 The conservation of medieval and later shrouds from burials in north west England. In *Archaeological Textiles*, edited by S.A. O'Connor and M.M. Brooks. UKIC Occasional Papers No. 10, United Kingdom Institute for Conservation, London.

Hald, M.
1942 The nettle as a culture plant, *Folk-Liv* 6:28–49.

Hardie, D.W.F. and J.D. Pratt
1966 *A History of the Modern British Chemical Industry*, Pergamon Press, New York.

Hopkins, D.W.
1998 The biology of the burial environment. In *Preserving Archaeological Remains in Situ*, edited by M. Corfield, P. Hinton, T. Nixon, and M. Pollard, pp. 73–85. Museum of London Archaeology Service, London.

Hunter, J., C. Roberts, and A. Martin, Editors
1996 *Studies in Crime: An Introduction to Forensic Archaeology*, Batsford, London,

Jain, P.C. and S.C. Agrawal
1980 A note on the keratin decomposing capability of some fungi, *Transactions of the Mycological Society of Japan* 21:513–517.

Janaway, R.C.
1979 A pilot study of the examination and scanning electron microscopy of metal preserved textile fibers. Unpublished dissertation. University College, Cardiff.

1983 Textile fibre characteristics preserved by metal corrosion: the potential of SEM studies, *The Conservator* 7:48–52.

1987 The preservation of organic materials in association with metal artefacts deposited in inhumation graves. In *Death Decay and Reconstruction: Approaches to Archaeology and Forensic Sciences,* edited by A. Boddington, A.N. Garland, and R.C., Janaway, pp. 127–148. Manchester University Press, Manchester, U.K.

1993 The textiles. In *The Spitalfields Project.* Vol. 1. *The Archaeology,* edited by J. Reeve and M. Adams, pp. 93–119. Council for British Archaeology Research Report No. 85, Council for British Archaeology, York.

1996 Textiles. In *The Experimental Earthwork Project 1960–1992,* edited by M. Bell, P.W. Fowler, and S.W. Hilson, pp. 160–168. Council for British Archaeology Research Report No. 100, Council for British Archaeology, York.

1998 An introductory guide to textiles from 18th and 19th century burials. In *Grave Concerns: Death and Burial in England 1700–1850,* edited by M. Cox, pp. 17–32. Council for British Archaeology Research Report No. 113, Council for British Archaeology, York.

Janaway, R.C. and B. Scott, Editors
1989 *Evidence Preserved in Corrosion Products: New Fields in Artifact Studies,* UKIC Occasional Paper 8, United Kingdom Institute for Conservation, London.

Janaway, R.C. et al.
(in prep) Degradation of textiles and hair from inhumation burials: a preliminary study utilising pig cadavers as human body analogues.

Jewell, P.A., Editor
1963 *The Experimental Earthwork on Overton Down, Wiltshire 1960,* The British Association for the Advancement of Science, London.

Keepax, C.
1975 Scanning electron microscopy of wood replaced by iron corrosion products, *Journal of Archaeological Science* 2, 145–151.

Komar, D. and O. Beattie
1998 Postmortem insect activity may mimic perimortem sexual assault clothing patterns, *Journal of Forensic Sciences* 43(4):792–796.

Lawson, T. et al.
2000 The experimental earthwork at Wareham, Dorset after 33 years: interaction of soil organisms with buried materials, *Journal of Archaeological Science* 27:273–285.

Lloyd, A.O.
1968 The evaluation of rot resistance of cellulosic textiles. In *Biodeterioration of Materials: Microbiological and Allied Aspects,* edited by A.H. Walters and J.J. Elphick, pp. 170–177. Elsevier, Amsterdam.

Marshall, J.
1931 *Mohenjo-Daro and the Indus Civilisation,* Arthur Probsthain, London.

McGrath, C.
1999 Bideterioration of Cotton Denim in Soil Burial Environments, unpublished dissertation, Department of Archaeological Sciences, University of Bradford, U.K.

Moncreiff, R.W.
1952 *Mothproofing,* Leonard Hill, London.

Morse, D., J. Duncan, and J.W. Stoutamire
1983 *Handbook of Forensic Archaeology and Anthropology,* Rose Printing, Tallahassee, FL.

Reeve, J. and Adams, M., Editors
   1993   *The Spitalfields Project.* Vol. 1. *The Archaeology,* Council for British Archaeology Research
   Report No. 85, Council for British Archaeology, York.

Roelofsen, P.A.
   1951   Contradictory data on spiral structures in the secondary cell wall of fibres of flax, hemp
   and ramie, *Textile Research Journal* 21(6):412–418.

Rowe, W.F.
   1997   Biodegradation of hairs and fibers. In *Forensic Taphonomy: The Postmortem Fate of Human
   Remains,* edited by W.D. Haglund and M.H. Sorg. CRC Press, Boca Raton, FL.

Ryder, M.L. and S.K. Stephenson
   1968   *Wool Growth,* Academic Press, London.

Schlegel, H.G.
   1986   *General Microscopy,* Cambridge University Press, Cambridge, U.K.

Shamir, O. and R.C. Janaway
   1995   Unpublished Catalogue of Textiles from Kasyr-el-Yyahud, Israel Antiquities Authority,
   Jerusalem.

Shore, J., Editor
   1995   *Cellulosic Dyeing,* The Alden Press, Oxford, U.K.

Sibley, L. R. and K. A. Jakes
   1984   Survival of protein fibers in archaeological contexts, *Science and Archaeology* 26:17-27.

Taylor, G.W.
   1983   Detection and identification of dyes on Anglo-Scandinavian textiles, *Studies in Conservation* 28:153–160

Terry, J.
   1996   A Study to Investigate the Rate and Extent of Cotton Samples in Forensic Contexts
   Applicable to West Yorkshire, unpublished final year dissertation, Department of Archaeological
   Sciences, University of Bradford, U.K.

Textile Institute
   1970   *Identification of Textile Materials,* 6th ed., Butterworths for The Textile Institute, Manchester, U.K.

Turner, P.L.
   1972   Important factors in the soil burial test applied to rotproofed textiles. In *Biodeterioration
   of Materials,* Vol. 2, edited by A.H. Walters and E.H. Hueck-Van Der Plas, pp. 218–226. Applied
   Science Publishers, London.

Walton, P.
   1989   *Textiles, Cordage and Raw Fibres from 16-22 Coppergate,* The Archaeology of York: The
   Small Finds 17/5, York Archaeological Trust/Council for British Archaeology, York.

Watanabe, T. and K. Miyazaki
   1980   Morphological deterioration of acetate, acrylic, polyamide and polyester textiles by microorganisms, *Aspergillus* spp. and *Penicillium* spp., *Sen-I Gakkaishi* 36:409–415.

Wincott, H.E. and R.C. Janaway
   1997   Textiles, animal hair and fibres. In *Skiddy's Castle and Christchurch, Cork: Excavations
   1974–77,* edited by R.M. Cleary, M.F. Hurley, and E. Shee Twohig, D.C. Twohig Cork Corporation, Cork.

Taphonomic Context of Sharp-Force Trauma in Suspected Cases of Human Mutilation and Dismemberment

21

STEVEN A. SYMES
JOHN A. WILLIAMS
ELIZABETH A. MURRAY
J. MICHAEL HOFFMAN
THOMAS D. HOLLAND
JULIE M. SAUL
FRANK P. SAUL
ELAYNE J. POPE

Contents

Introduction

As we begin the new millennium, forensic anthropologists are enjoying unprecedented public popularity, developing innovative research techniques, and exploring new areas of inquiry. They are also the target of heightened scrutiny from other physical anthropologists and fellow professionals. Some physical anthropologists have labeled forensic anthropology as a non-theoretical specialty that lacks scientific methods and evolutionary theory so critical to the field as a whole. On the other hand non-anthropological forensic specialists have been slow or reluctant to recognize anthropologists for their potential contributions in the forensic sciences (Smith et al., 1990; Symes and Smith, 1998). These are criticisms that come at a time when the public and our legal system demands state-of-the-art techniques and irrefutable arguments in a court of law.

Recent developments in forensic anthropology suggest that these criticisms are far from justified. Three promising areas of research include accumulation of a modern forensic data bank and its analysis using FORDISC (Jantz, 1999, 2000; Moore-Jansen et al., 1994); a proliferation of studies in taphonomy (see Haglund and Sorg, 1997) and a new emphasis on the recognition of bone trauma, as evidenced in research with autopsy material (Berryman et al., 1991; Smith et al., 1991; Symes et al., 1991, 1996); and edited volumes introducing new research (Galloway, 2000; Reichs, 1998). These new research areas continue to substantiate forensic anthropology as a true subfield of anthropology and identify anthropologists as forensic scientists. These areas not only influence the recovery of human remains, but they also direct medical personnel toward answers concerning victim identity and cause and manner of death. While this chapter deals only with the area of bone trauma, specifically sharp-force trauma, these analyses will be defined and scrutinized using important taphonomic controls. In particular, the concept of context will be emphasized for bone trauma analysis and shown to contribute immeasurably to solving initial mysteries surrounding human deaths.

Sharp-Force Bone Trauma

Sharp-force trauma can be best recognized as the result of violent antemortem/perimortem confrontations that maim or kill victims, or the result of postmortem acts of dismemberment and mutilation. The former commonly involves a knife, while the latter may involve a multiplicity of tools, although these tools are commonly classified as knives and/or saws.

While the process of gathering evidence regarding human dismemberment and mutilation forces the forensic scientist to deal with a grisly side of human nature, such actions provide potentially valuable clues to crimes. Dismemberment of a victim has been identified as the product of (1) making a body more manageable for transport, (2) obscuring or hindering positive identification of the remains, or (3) a symbolic or savage expression or total disregard or loathing of a human body (Symes et al., 1992). Forensic examiners must quickly identify the value of cut mark characteristics in bone and the potential to provide additional information concerning a criminal act, whether perimortem or postmortem (Reichs, 1998).

Saw marks involve repetitive movements, generally reserved for situations of postmortem dismemberment and mutilation. The presence of saw marks in bone is rare and until recently was considered of little use in forensics (see Andahl, 1978; Bonte, 1975; Symes,

1992). Saw marks were seldom given more notice than a presence or absence assessment by the forensic examiner. Lethal knife wounds, on the other hand, are second only to gunshot wounds as a cause of homicidal deaths (see Martin, 1999:1–2) and as such have received ample recognition in the forensic literature (DiMaio and DiMaio, 1993:191; Spitz, 1993:252).

Unfortunately, knife wound analysis has also been demonstrably ignored or inadequate, e.g., utilizing meaningless categories such as "sharp" or "single-edged," as well as other misleading or errant descriptive terminology (Symes et al., 1999). "Hesitation mark," for example, is extensively used and is defined as superficial cuts or saw marks (DiMaio and DiMaio, 1993:183–184: Spitz, 1993:271). DiMaio and DiMaio go so far as to state that hesitation marks are almost always present in incised wound suicides. This terminology is considered potentially dangerous by the first author, because a particular behavior is easily suggested strictly from this wound description. It would be a logical defense for a trial lawyer to label any superficially incised wounds on a homicide victim as hesitation cuts (as commonly described in suicides), and to suggest that these superficial wounds represent a defendant's lack of intent in attempting to commit murder. Proper documentation and analysis of knife and saw marks do have the potential to contribute significantly to the interpretation of criminal acts.

Taphonomy and Sharp-Force Trauma

Forensic anthropologists have actively embraced taphonomy for many reasons; among them is its utility and potential for explaining variables and constants that were never considered 20 years ago. The clarification and analysis of intertwined taphonomic variables have been shown to be relevant to questions concerning circumstances of death and postmortem interval (Dirkmaat et al., 1997).

One must, however, consider the initial hazards of adding taphonomic variables to an investigation. It requires much more attention to the crime scene context and to aspects of that context which have not been routinely considered in the past. If scene context is confusing or misunderstood, the potential for error increases drastically. Taphonomic context also becomes increasingly complex as the interval between the victim's "last seen" and "found dead" times increases. In fact, the addition of new, taphonomic information increases the complexity of issues surrounding death and can initially muddy interpretations. Investigative researchers must be prepared to process these additional data. In the following pages we will demonstrate that this effort is worthwhile. Accurate and conservative interpretation of contextual taphonomic data ultimately reduces confusion by simplifying key variables and eventually clarifying evidence regarding cause and manner of death.

Confusion concerning perimortem and postmortem timeframe concepts often occurs when anthropologists consult in a medical examiner setting. Forensic pathologists sometimes assign clear temporal significance (i.e., antemortem versus postmortem) to traits that the anthropologist might, from a strictly taphonomic perspective, consider to be simply perimortem. For example, forensic pathologists might differentiate traits in two types of sharp-force trauma: stab wounds are evaluated as antemortem and sharp-force dismemberment and mutilation as postmortem. These types of wounds are differentiated medically on the basis of the presence of vital reaction in soft tissue, but also categorically, because victims are rarely stabbed following death, and dismemberment is not usually chosen as a method of murder.

Differences in sharp-force trauma evaluation between medical examiner/coroners and anthropologists result from their roles and training. The burden of cause-of-death judgments falls on medical doctors. Medical decisions are based upon what is known about the living organism's physiology and behavior. Taphonomic assessments, on the other hand, are more likely to focus on the material, organic, and ecological properties of human remains (Sorg and Haglund, this volume). Thus, medical personnel, working closely with law enforcement, can assess dismemberment as postmortem. In fact, it is not unusual for those anthropologists employed in a medical examiner setting to assist in medical as opposed to anthropological taphonomic assessments.

Anthropologists, when examining sharp-force trauma in bone, look for evidence of vital reaction (i.e., remodeled bone due to healing). When evidence is absent, they attempt to assess injuries in bone taphonomically as those occurring before or after advanced decomposition (specifically, bone elasticity loss). Although dismemberment cuts logically indicate postmortem activity, anthropologists using a taphonomic approach would consider these to be perimortem, unless it could be demonstrated that the bone was traumatically altered after it had decomposed beyond a fresh or green state during which elastic properties disappear. Thus, standard medical and taphonomic approaches differ in their theoretical base (e.g., soft tissue vital reaction vs. material/mechanical properties of bone) and in their definitions of common terms, such as perimortem. Evaluations of perimortem and postmortem trauma may differ, depending upon which profession makes the call (Nawrocki, pers. comm.).

While this treatment does not interpret trauma in a strictly anthropological framework, it does place taphonomic theory in a framework that combines efforts of anthropologists/scientists and medical examiners/coroners. Anthropologists are often required to operate as scientists within medical examiner/coroner settings. It is critical that anthropologists are aware of differences between anthropological and medical language and theory and how these differences affect process and outcome in a legal setting.

This chapter presents cases that have recently occurred in different environments and situations in various parts of the United States. Each case required anthropologists to use and analyze the particular contextual information to simplify and clarify their interpretations. With each case, a "Table of Context" illustrates the initial investigative/medical interpretations, followed by the initial anthropological/taphonomic assessment. Finally, a description of the tool mark and contextual information leads to an appropriate conclusion. This type of presentation is meant to simulate the investigative process, starting with an undeveloped story maturing with time and research. It also demonstrates how close examination of sharp-force trauma combined with taphonomic data may initially confuse issues, but later becomes critical for accurate anthropological interpretation of sharp-force trauma.

Definitions and Methods

Knives and Knife-Cut Wounds

Sharp-force trauma can involve a variety of weapons and tools. Any tool with a sharp edge can produce incised wounds. Most incised wounds are created by some class of knife and these wounds are recognized as sharp-force trauma. This wound is commonly termed a knife-stab wound (KSW). The term KSW is often misused, particularly by anthropologists, since most wounds they examine are without skin and soft tissue. Many of these wounds to bone are knife-incised (cut) wounds, but are not necessarily due to stabbing. Using the term knife-cut (incised) wound (KCW) instead of knife-stab wound (KSW) is more accurate and inclusive of many actions, i.e., incise/slash, flick, tear, chop/hack (Department of the Army, 1992). Incised wounds are defined medically as those where the length is greater than its depth (DiMaio and DiMaio, 1993:191; Spitz, 1993:252). A KCW in bone is indicated when a sharp-edged tool superficially incises bone while traversing over the surface of the bone. While a non-stabbing KCW often follows the contour of a bone, a stab will puncture, nick, or gouge a bone as it enters the body, externally to internally. If cut marks follow the contour of a bone onto different surfaces, it is more likely an act of dismemberment rather than an attempt to kill the victim.

Other Blades and Their Wounds

Confusion often occurs when trying to identify the weapon class associated with blade and knife wounds. Knives can be separated from other blades, in that knives are tools with a thin blade that sometimes terminate in a point. Knives commonly have blade bevel (blade tapering) but always have at least one area of edge bevel (sharpened edge) on the blade. Tools such as box cutters, razor blades, obsidian knives, or machetes can be classified as knives. This definition excludes other blades in machinery like airplane and boat propellers, grain augers, bush hogs, and tree chippers, because these blades do not combine the traits of a thin blade with edge beveling. Blades listed above have been known (in the experience of the first author) to cause lacerations mainly in soft tissue. While they may also produce incised bone, more commonly the resulting injuries can be characterized as scraping wounds terminating into classic tension/compression bone fractures.

The complexity of classifying knife blade wounding is demonstrated by examining a knife-cut wound to the chest. If a single-edged blade progresses externally to internally between two ribs, it is likely that two ribs will be wounded. Examination of the cut wound in bone reveals defects in each of the ribs. These defects differ in appearance, i.e., an incised wound is created in one rib by a thin blade with edge bevel while the other rib has a shaved defect, the result of a blade spine or back forced against bone. The spine of the knife is part of the blade, but it has no edge beveling. The production of a thinly channeled injury that shaves the bone is possible, even though that side of the blade has no sharp edge. Microscopic examination of this defect will reveal that it is due to blade shaving rather than incising. If shaving occurs, bladed weapons can only be suspected. Well-defined incised wounds, on the other hand, almost certainly have been created by a blade with an edge bevel, i.e., a weapon with a knife design. Therefore, examination of the two concurrently cut ribs would produce two different morphological results. The rib defect attributed to the spine of the knife cannot be classified conclusively as a wound created by a knife as defined; however, the incised wound in the other rib can. Because the proximity of the wounds conservatively suggests a single weapon, this knife can be described as a blade with only one edge that has edge bevel, or a single-edged knife. It is also essential to remember that a knife stab wound is simply blunt trauma (slow velocity) with a sharp object. A knife's cutting edge with applied energy simply incises material until that capability ends, then it is simply a blunt object impacting and pushing through bone (Symes et al., 1999). Knife-stab wounds can and do create blunt-force (tension/compression) fractures of bone.

Saws and Saw-Cut Wounds

Saws can be separated from knives again by edge bevel. While saws have teeth, the design of a saw would be defeated with a blade or edge bevel design. Except for true crosscut saws (which are becoming rare with mass production) and some Japanese carpenter saws, most saws cut with a flat-edged tooth, such that the saw cut is actually chiseling (shaving) rather than cutting the material. True crosscut saws have consecutive teeth filed at opposing angles (usually 70°). This filing creates a tooth that terminates in a point and essentially takes on the shape of a sharpened blade that cuts material rather than chisels (Cunningham and Holtrop, 1974; Jackson and Day, 1978; Lanz, 1985). Saw chiseling can be distinguished from knife incising since chiseling leaves a squared cross-section kerf floor. Filed crosscut (sharpened) saw blades create a kerf floor that resembles a "W," while beveled-edge blades used as a saw create a V-shaped kerf floor, whether there are teeth manufactured in the blade or not (Symes, 1992).

It is important to understand a few basic concepts about saws and saw blade action before attempting to interpret saw marks in bone. All saws have teeth. As saw teeth cut into bone, a groove or kerf is formed. Saw mark analysis basically involves examination of saw cut kerfs. A kerf can be defined as the walls and floor of a cut. Examination of floor variation includes false starts and, occasionally, breakaway spurs. Kerf floors offer the most information about saw type by revealing the relationship of the teeth to each other. This information includes the set and number of teeth per inch (TPI). Kerf walls offer information about the sides of the teeth. Wall striae commonly represent only those teeth set to that particular side, while shape, depth, and frequency of these striae may represent the shape of the blade, the amount of energy transferred to the material, and the motion in which the blade travels to cut bone. The object of saw mark analysis is to recognize characteristics on kerf walls and floors that may accurately reveal dimensions, shape of the blade and teeth of a saw, and how a tool was used to cut bone. Saw class (not type) characteristics facilitate the narrowing of potential saws utilized (Symes, 1992).

Establishing direction of cut on bones is feasible and contributes to crime scene investigation. However, "direction" may be misleading unless clearly defined. Direction of cut indicates two separate saw actions: the direction of blade progress, and the direction of blade stroke. Indicators of direction of saw progress center on the false start and breakaway spur. Initial cuts are commonly accompanied by false starts, where individual teeth strike and chisel material, or where actual kerfs are abandoned for another cut. The plane formed between the false start and the breakaway spur or notch usually gives the precise direction of saw progress. Direction of blade progress is essentially perpendicular to stroke and tooth striae. Direction of cutting and passive stroke is essentially the direction of the saw tooth striations.

Knife-blade wounding and knife and saw dismemberment and mutilation identification and classification are key to tool mark identification. Unfortunately, this often requires not only knowledge of how these tools are manufactured, but also how these tools react in bone when used maliciously. The cases presented below will demonstrate how the scene and initial investigative/medical and the anthropologic/scientific indicators may be confusing, especially without meticulous contextual information. This is where tool mark analysis combined with contextual data can provide enough taphonomic information to clarify the circumstances of death, rule out alternative hypotheses, and allow conservative forensic assessments concerning the tools used and the associated criminal behavior.

Cases

Case 1: Sharp Trauma vs. Rodent Modification

In the summer of 1997, a hiker discovered a human cranium just off a popular hiking trail that ascends 14,110 feet of Pike's Peak in Colorado's Front Range. Local law enforcement officials recovered the cranium but found no additional skeletal material after several days of searching. Dental records provided a positive identification: a white male, 32 years old at the time of his disappearance in November, 1992. Attached to the cranial base by dried ligamentous tissue were a nearly complete first cervical vertebra and a partial second cervical vertebra. Additional mummified tissue adhered to the zygomatic arches, cranial base, and areas of the cranial vault. The left posterior vault was weathered to a light gray color, while the remainder of the cranium and vertebrae was soil-stained dark brown. A mild odor of decomposition was present prior to cleaning.

Damage was present on the lateral rim of the left orbit and left zygomatic arch, the medial walls of both orbits, the tips of the nasal bones and adjacent areas of the nasal aperture, the right maxilla, the posterior hard palate, and the inferior occipital near the foramen magnum. Several teeth were also chipped or broken. This damage was consistent with carnivore scavenging, including transport over rough, steep terrain.

Both cervical vertebrae also suffered apparent postmortem damage. The transverse processes and a part of the right inferior articular surface of the first cervical vertebra were missing. The more heavily damaged second cervical vertebra was comprised of only the odontoid process, the left 2/3 of the body, and a portion of the left neural arch. The majority of the damage to both bones also appeared consistent with carnivore scavenging with what appeared to be large carnivore canine punctures.

Close examination by one of the authors (JMH) did reveal bone defects that were problematic in origin. The posterior portion of the bony rim of the left transverse foramen appeared to be cleanly shaved from the first cervical vertebra (Figure 21.1). Similarly, the left transverse foramen of the second cervical vertebra appeared to have been cut through the middle of the vertebral artery foramen to the area immediately posterior to where the inferior articular process begins (Figure 21.2). On each bone, immediately adjacent to the cuts, were several very small and fine superficial cut marks and larger scoring of the bone. Additionally, the color of the cut surfaces matched the surrounding bone. This indicates that the damage happened before or at the same time the soft tissue associated with these bones had decomposed, not after the bone was exposed from decomposition. Upon initial inspection these cut marks appeared to be due to the action of a sharp-bladed instrument. At this point the remains were transported to another co-author (SAS) for microscopic examination.

Closer examination of the suspect cut surface of the first cervical vertebra revealed additional information about the suspected incised surface (Figure 21.1C). The smooth area consisted of slightly scooped out grooved surfaces marked by fine striations running parallel to these grooved out surfaces. While these grooves were shallow and appeared to combine to create a very deceptively smooth surface, closer examination revealed that the grooves were not completely parallel to each other. Therefore, this suspect area was not created from a single action, but rather from a series of scraping actions that appear to be focused in the same direction; thus, this area appeared to be created by minute scraping rather than incising.

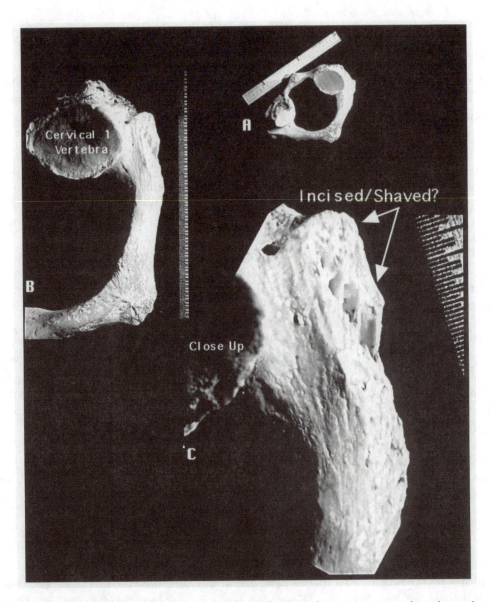

Figure 21.1 Case 1: Inferior surface of the cervical 1 vertebra is represented in three photographs with an illustration of the complete vertebra (A), and two magnified illustrations (B and C). The left transverse process appears suspiciously incised or shaved (arrows) (scale = 0.01 in.).

The suspect cut mark to the second cervical vertebra also had shallow groves that are the result of shaving actions. The two cut marks inferior to this surface (Figure 21.2B) begin as V-shaped cuts, but eventually fan into broad, smooth-bottomed troughs with longitudinal striations that are similar to the grooves mentioned above. This can be interpreted as the result of two scrapes from an edge that is rotated relative to a flat scraping surface (like a rodent tooth). Next to the suspect sharp cut/scrape marks are scores across the surface of bone where a large pointed object, such as a tooth, likely scratched the bone (Figure 21.2B).

As Table 21.1 indicates, a simple case of a missing suicide victim turns complicated after the initial anthropological examination of partial recovered remains revealed what

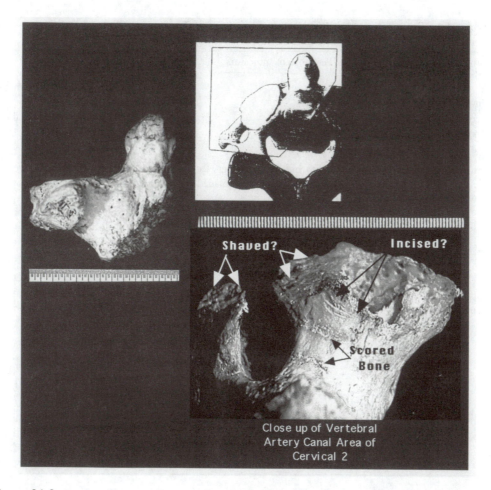

Figure 21.2 Case 1: Illustrates two views of the second vertebra, with a posterior view (left) and a close up of the left vertebral artery canal area (lower right) revealing an incised/shaved area with associated suspicious score and incised marks. The artist's rendition assists orientation for the close-up view (scale = 0.01 in.).

might be sharp-force trauma to a suspicious area. Microscopic examination of the suspect area allowed the tool examiner to rule out incised wounding and to recognize these defects as scraping marks of nonhuman animal origin.

A long postmortem interval (PMI) and rough terrain are two important taphonomic factors that provide the context that can explain rodent and large carnivore disruption and allow for cranial fractures to fragile areas of the skull. A combination of the context and microscopic examination removes doubts of foul play and takes the investigation back to original assumptions.

Case 2: Sharp Trauma vs. Carnivore Modification

In January 1994, a pathologist acting on behalf of the Hawaii County Police Department submitted partial human remains to the U.S. Army Central Identification Laboratory, Hawaii (CILHI) for analysis and identification by a co-author (TDH). The remains had

Table 21.1   Perimortem and Postmortem Indicators of Trauma on Skeletal Remains Demonstrating an Investigation that Matures with Age and Research

Investigative Stage	Perimortem Indicators	Postmortem Indicators
Scene and initial investigation of recovered skull and vertebrae		• Found exposed to elements in rough terrain • Probable postmortem damage due to scavenging • Partial recovery
Initial anthropological examination	• Clean shearing damage to cervical vertebrae suggesting sharp-bladed instrument • Superficial cut marks in neck area, including adjacent areas of C1 and C2 • No differential color in cut and uncut bone	• Typical postmortem damage from scavenger transport indicated by terrain and location of defects • Defects similar to large carnivore tooth scoring are evident

Application of taphonomic approach including microscopic examinations	• No color differences in cut and uncut bone	• Smooth defects follow along with typical modification pattern of rodent tooth marks:
		     Scrape marks
		     Wide grooves
		     Grooves not parallel
		     Parallel striae within grooves
		     Scoring in the same area

Conclusions	• Long interval between victim disappearance and recovery explains lack of color differences • Recovery minimal	• Rodent modification accounts for all defects that appeared to be due to sharp-force trauma • Damage due to scavenger transport

been found on a beach near the Waipio Valley on the Big Island of Hawaii and were held together by soft tissue in an advanced stage of decomposition

The remains consisted of one rib, lower vertebrae, pelvis, and upper legs. This pattern of decomposition fit the expected configuration of decomposition in water environments (Haglund, 1993). After macerating the remains, it was determined that they belonged to a white male, 19 to 20 years of age, who stood approximately 166 to 174 cm (65.5 to 68.5 in.) tall. Most conspicuous, however, were numerous cut marks to virtually every element (Figure 21.3). Cut marks to certain elements exhibited a pattern indicative of a sharp, serrated instrument (Figure 21.4, arrows). There appeared to be no recognizable pattern to the sharp-force and associated blunt-force trauma.

Microscopic examination of the purported cut marks revealed numerous contextual clues. Examination of the right femoral fragment revealed the presence of recognizable striations and a 1-mm long fragment of what appeared to be tooth tip embedded in the bone (Figure 21.4, arrow). Scanning electron microscopy confirmed that the patterned marks were incised striations to bone and that the imbedded fragment was indeed the tip of a tooth (Figure 21.5A, B). This evidence lead to the interpretation that the damage was in fact tooth marks and chewing trauma left by a large shark (Table 21.2).

Based on the anthropological analysis, the pathologist was able to associate the remains with a 19-year-old white male who had disappeared several weeks before while surfing

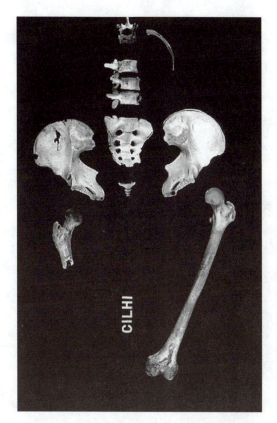

Figure 21.3 Case 2: Illustrates the processed remains submitted by the Hawaii County Police Department, after maceration. Most conspicuous were numerous cut marks to virtually every recovered element and numerous blunt-force fractures to the bones.

near the Waipio Valley on the Big Island. Predation or scavenging by a shark was consistent with the location in which this individual was lost.

Shark experts at Sea Life Park in Hawaii and at the Florida Museum of Natural History examined casts made of the serrated tooth marks and concluded that the shark was either a Great White or a Tiger shark in the 8-ft range. Great White sharks (*Carcharodon carcharias*) have been known to frequent the waters off of the Big Island in the winter months, and Tiger sharks (*Galeocerdo cuvieri*) are ubiquitous around all of the islands. Examination of shark teeth from several species, including the tiger shark, reveals a serrated morphology (Figure 21.5C) that can be reflected in the bite marks in bone.

Case 3: Sharp Trauma vs. Forensic Processing

In mid-October 1997, a burned car was found in an abandoned gravel pit in central Nevada. A severely burned human head and torso were discovered in the trunk. The remains were positively identified through dental records as those of the 39-year-old female owner of the car. It was learned that her death and discovery had occurred 17 hours after a domestic dispute. A cursory autopsy revealed no indication of cause of death. Approximately 1 month later the torso was transported to the University of North Dakota, where it was cleaned and examined by a co-author (JAW).

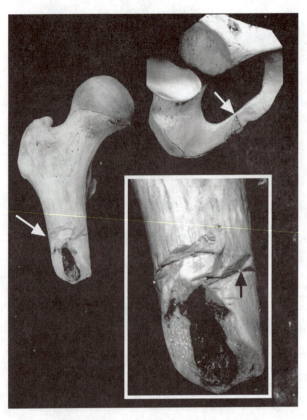

Figure 21.4 Case 2: Cut marks to the pelvis and right femora exhibit a serrated pattern indicative of a toothed instrument (arrows). There appears to be no recognizable configuration to the frequent sharp- and blunt-force trauma.

The skeleton presented a mixture of burned and unburned bone (Figure 21.6A). With the exception of protected areas, bone preservation was poor; exposed bone was generally burned to charred or complete calcination. The pattern of burning was consistent with a supine position with the head lying on its right side. The degree of burning corresponded to Levels 4 and 5 of the Crow and Glassman (1996) burn injury scale, where the body shows extensive thermal destruction. The skull and upper legs displayed the greatest range of variation from unburned to cremated. Charring and some delamination were observed on the left side of the vertebral bodies and adjacent spinous and transverse processes of all but the lumbar vertebrae. The cervical vertebrae were not as protected and suffered more damage, including partial loss of the lamina on the first through fourth cervical vertebrae.

Because charred flesh and soot remained, cleaning was a prerequisite for even the most cursory surface examination. To minimize processing damage on burned areas, dissection was used to remove burned tissue and to disarticulate bones. The articulated vertebral column required extensive use of the scalpel to separate the individual vertebra. The cleaned and processed bones were for the most part unremarkable and consistent in appearance with burn-induced damage. The exception to this was the first cervical vertebra where a suspicious puncture was found on the anterior right internal surface during processing (Figure 21.6B, C).

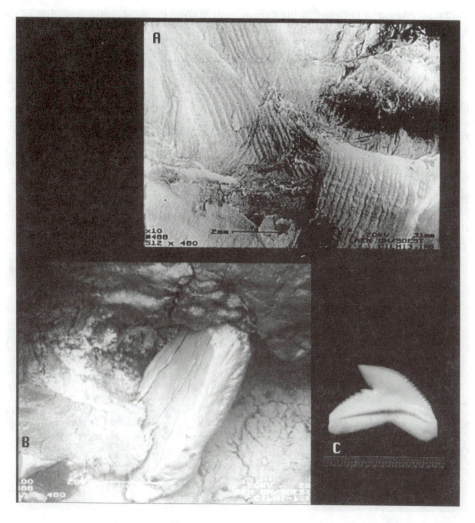

Figure 21.5 Case 2: Two microradiographs of the right femur. The top image (A) illustrates the serrated cut pattern to bone while the lower image (B) reveals a foreign object imbedded in the bone. This object was confirmed to be a shark tooth fragment. (C) A serrated shark tooth is illustrated.

The discovery of this unexpected sharp defect led to a thorough microscopic examination of the entire vertebral column. Sixty-three additional sharp-force trauma defects were tallied (Table 21.3). These were found on 18 vertebrae and appeared in the form of small nicks in the bone surface. These defects were short, less than .5 cm in length (0.02 in.), and very shallow. The most common location was on the right pedicle, accounting for nearly half of the total number of defects. Some marks were singular, while others were multiple.

The common appearance of KCWs corresponds with the use of a fine instrument (scalpel) in shallow repetitive strokes. They fit a pattern of inadvertent nicks from a sharp blade, as might be expected during laboratory processing of the remains. Nicks in the bone can also be identified as processing cuts when they are consistent with the dimensions of the cut and location. Figure 21.7 illustrates the fine nature of a cut and the size of the blade as the spine of the blade becomes trapped in bone. This is consistent in dimensions with

Table 21.2   Process of Differentiating Perimortem Marine Predator/Scavenger Modification from Normal Taphonomic Changes.

Investigative Stage	Perimortem Indicators	Postmortem Indicators
Scene and initial investigation (law enforcement and medical) of partial remains		• Recovery from ocean environment (beach) • Incomplete remains consistent with water environment decomposition
Initial anthropological examination	• Serrated cut marks • Fractured bones	• No recognizable patterning
Application of taphonomic approach including microscopic examinations	• Shark tooth found imbedded in bone • Consulted with shark expert regarding shark anatomy and behavior • Research regarding common fauna for that region of ocean • Physical comparison of a (serrated) shark tooth with defects in bone • Pattern of damage consistent with shark attack morphology • All blunt-force trauma is associated with sharp-force trauma • Pattern of damage consistent with shark	
Conclusions	• All defects consistent with shark modification (remember: an impact with a sharp object like teeth is simply a blunt impact with a sharp object)	• Difficult to determine predation or scavenging

a scalpel no. 21 blade. These interpretations are strengthened by the location of most of these cut marks on the internal surface of the pedicle. These areas would only be accessible after tissue was removed from around the vertebrae and, therefore, could only have occurred during postmortem laboratory dissection. This fits an effort to cut away connective tissue with a fine-bladed instrument. The general absence of connective tissue on the burned left side of the vertebral column explains the predominance of nicks on the right side.

The tenth thoracic vertebra had far more defects than any other affected vertebra. An explanation for this lies with the action of the pathologist who, in order to make the torso easier for transport, had earlier divided the spine into two pieces at the tenth thoracic vertebra.

Compounding the initial interpretation of the stab wound was the presence of a square-sided groove located on the inferior left lamina of the first cervical vertebra. Repetitive passes of a fine instrument produced a trough in the bone. The inferior left lamina had been scorched, and the instrument producing this groove disturbed the surface discoloration and exposed unburned bone. This groove is clearly postmortem in origin and corresponds in general size and shape to a no. 21 scalpel blade. The alignment of this defect

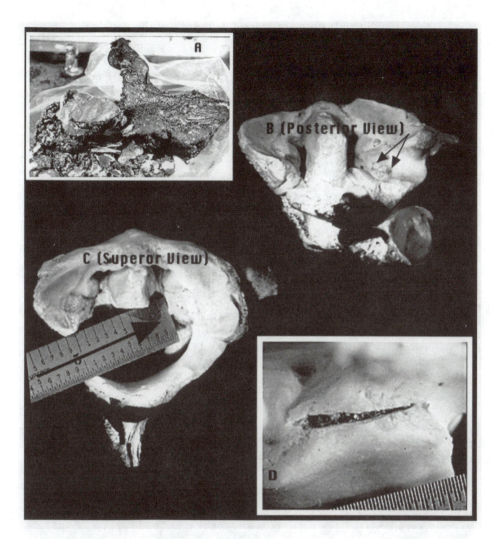

Figure 21.6 Case 3: The burned victim (A), and closer examinations of cervical 1 and 2 (B, C) and the sharp trauma defect in cervical 1 (D) on the right internal surface (scale = 0.01 in.).

on the inferior left lamina of the first cervical vertebra suggests that it, too, is dissection damage.

The suspicious triangular defect in question is immediately superior to the internal aspect of the inferior articular facet of cervical 1. The defect shows a definite taper from anterior to posterior, measuring 8.4 mm (0.33 in.) long, approximately 5.1 mm (0.20 in.) deep, and 0.9 mm (0.035 in.) at its widest point. This shape corresponds to a blade that is single edged and pointed at the tip. Microfractures found around the perimeter of the opening of the KCW were likely caused by a blade being wedged into the bone.

Even though the suspicious defect was associated with processing cuts, several features of the stab wound point to a perimortem context (Table 21.4). First, the area of the first cervical vertebra between the superior and inferior articular surfaces is dense and designed to withstand the weight and force of the head. Burning did not compromise the area. Puncturing this bone would require extreme force, equivalent to a horizontal stabbing

Table 21.3   Sharp Instrument Processing Defects of the Vertebral Column Found after Processing

Vertebra	Location	Number of Processing Cuts
Cervical 1	See text	3
Cervical 2	See text	6
Cervical 3	Right pedicle	5
Cervical 4	Right pedicle	5
Cervical 5	Left pedicle	2
Cervical 6	Right pedicle	4
Thoracic 1	Right pedicle	4
Thoracic 2	Right pedicle	3
Thoracic 3	Right superior articular facet	1
Thoracic 5	Right pedicle, left superior articular facet	7
Thoracic 6	Right pedicle	3
Thoracic 7	Right pedicle	2
Thoracic 8	Left pedicle	1
Thoracic 9	Right and left pedicle	3
Thoracic 10	Right and left pedicle, right superior articular facet	8
Thoracic 12	Right and left superior articular facet	4
Lumbar 1	Left pedicle	1
Lumbar 2	Left pedicle	1

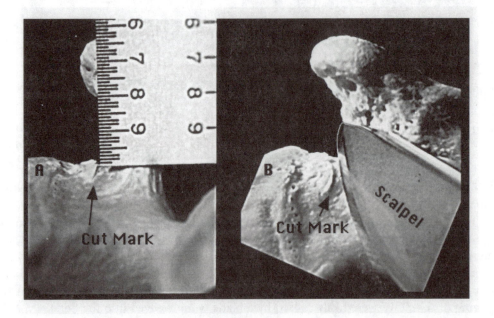

Figure 21.7 Case 4: Fine cut mark found in a vertebra (A). Close examination of this defect indicates that a standard scalpel blade is consistent with the defect (B). This conclusion is supported by the fine nature of the cut, as well as by the restricted area allowing only the tip of the blade into this location of the bone (scale = 0.01 in.).

Table 21.4   Process of Differentiating Multiple Perimortem Sharp Force Modification Patterns

Investigative Stage	Perimortem Indicators	Postmortem Indicators
Scene and initial investigation (law enforcement and medical) of burned remains	• No trauma found initially	• Severe postmortem burning • Pathologist dissected and separated remains at T10
Initial anthropological examination	• Cannot examine for trauma until body is macerated for visualization • Suspect KSW to internal C1 found after processing	• Overall pattern of burning on skull and limbs as expected • Skeleton processed with scalpel producing processing KCWs to all 18 vertebrae • KCWs location consistent with processing: Cuts shallow, short, and repetitive; cuts very fine and consistent with scalpel
Application of taphonomic approach including microscopic examinations	• C1 KSW could not be done with scalpel due to size and blade design • Single-edged pointed knife blade • KSW is stained suggesting hemorrhage	• Processing cuts are identified and inventoried, 63 total cuts, unstained • KSW location consistent with processing
Conclusions	• C1 KSW is perimortem	• KCWs are postprocessing

thrust left to right, posterior to anterior; this is not consistent with accidental nicking or prying of the scalpel blade. Scalpel blades are thin and likely would fail if such force were applied. Measurements of reinforced no. 21 scalpel blades show that their size and shape are inconsistent with the KCW defect. Scalpel blades have a uniformly thin cross sectional shape, tapering only at the cutting edge. At the knife point the blade often tapers from the non-cutting to the cutting edge the same as in the KCW defect.

Finally, the internal surface of the first cervical vertebra exposed at the stab defect was stained. While not definitive, this suggests that the wound was present prior to burning, thus allowing hemorrhage and decomposition fluids to stain the vertebra. In contrast, the scalpel nicks are clean.

This case illustrates the difficulties that can arise when examining badly burned remains. In this situation, a lethal KCW went unnoticed until dissection, processing, and careful examination occurred. Knowledge of where processing cuts are more likely to occur, the shape and the size of these defects, dimensions of scalpel blades, and the potential of such a blade to puncture dense bone differentiates processing cut marks from perimortem and potentially fatal wounds.

Case 4: Sharp Trauma Forms Used in Dismemberment

In August of 1996, two boys fishing at a lake in Butler County, Ohio, found a human cranium at the water's edge. The City of Hamilton Police Department and the Butler County Coroner's Office began an investigation. Divers searched the lake for additional remains and evidence but were unsuccessful. An examination and autopsy of the skull by

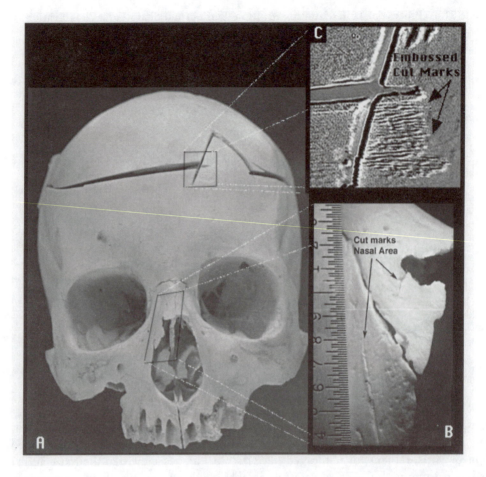

Figure 21.8 Case 4: Autopsied cranium with no teeth visible (A). Fine cut marks were visible on the face (B) and vault (C) (scale = 0.01 in.).

the coroner's office revealed limited soft tissue (Figure 21.8A), including adipocere and shrunken brain matter present within the cranium. Initial assessments suggested that the mandible and all maxillary dentition were lost postmortem. The cranial vault revealed sharp-force trauma near the vault apex (Figure 21.9).

Subsequent anthropological examination of the cranium by a co-author (EAM) demonstrated innumerable tool marks, including not only the large chop mark to the vault apex, but also hundreds of tiny cut marks and scrapes around the face (Figure 21.8B) and vault regions. Also observed were several puncture marks, including one to the left temporal region (Figure 21.10 A, B) and another to the left orbit. Marks on the occipital condyles suggested the possibility of decapitation.

An examination of the alveolar region showed a great deal of bone fracturing associated with the tooth sockets (Figures 21.8 and 21.10A). Damage to the right molar area was extensive and extended well into the walls of the maxillary sinus. A broken tooth root was evident in the socket for the left second molar (Figure 21.11A, B). The only complete teeth discovered were two impacted maxillary third molars. Anthropological analysis confirmed that the skull was most likely that of a young, white female, and that there appeared to

Table 21.5 Lists of Perimortem and Postmortem Indicators of Trauma on the Skull Demonstrating an Investigation that Matures with Age and Research

Investigative Stage	Perimortem Indicators	Postmortem Indicators
Scene and initial investigation (law enforcement and medical) of recovered skull	• Linear penetrating sharp-force wound to skull apex	• Limited soft tissues, adipocere, and shrunken brain • Mandible missing • Maxilla teeth missing • Incomplete recovery
Initial anthropological examination	• Chop wound to head • Fine KCWs to the face, vault sides, and occipital condyles • Punctures wounds • Alveolar bone damage where teeth are missing	• Saw mark consistent with autopsy procedure • Probable post-recovery processing by medical examiner • No evidence supporting postmortem tooth loss
Application of taphonomic approach including microscopic examinations	• Multiple tooth loss due to avulsion, leaving tool marks in bone • Broken tooth roots visible • Five tool mark classes	• Minute patterned striations are consistent with autopsy saw skips on bone
Conclusions	• Alteration of remains included defleshing, dismemberment, tooth removal, and other mutilation • Chop to vault with striations not matching suspect heavy-bladed weapon • Tools indicated besides autopsy saw include pointed knife blade, serrated knife, pliers, and heavy, broad blade with edge bevel and curved edge at point • Confession also confirmed location of remains, saw dismemberment, defleshing, and mutilation	• Scavenger damage and normal postmortem tooth loss ruled out • Other remains recovered after confession

have been a deliberate attempt to preclude identification through destructive removal of soft tissues and dentition.

In the meantime, detectives from the Hamilton Police Department became aware of a missing person who fit the biological profile of this individual. A 21-year-old white female had been reported missing in June of 1996, and her common-law husband was the prime suspect. Law enforcement officials began investigating leads and attempting to procure antemortem records relative to the missing person's report. Due to the extensive nature of the tool marks in this case, plans were made to forward the cranium to the Regional Forensic Center in Memphis, Tennessee, for further analysis. The co-author (EAM) preliminarily suggested that at least three different weapons might have been used in this dismemberment/mutilation. A first co-author (SAS) was requested to confirm initial analysis results.

Clearly, the damage to the upper jaw was inconsistent with any normal taphonomic pattern of postmortem tooth loss, and it became obvious that the teeth had been deliberately

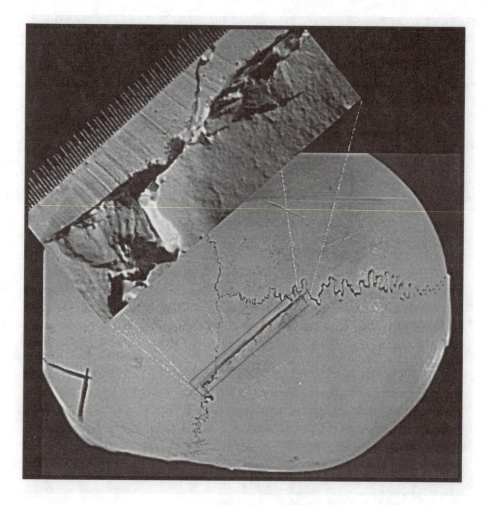

Figure 21.9 Case 4: Superior vault of discovered cranium. Most prominent chop mark (enlarged) produced with a sharp instrument (scale = 0.01 in.).

avulsed. It seemed likely that the perpetrator was unaware of the unerupted third molars, thus explaining their solitary postmortem presence. Detectives working on the case had confiscated several implements from the suspect's residence, including a knife and pliers, which they also forwarded for comparison.

Tool mark analysis (SAS) revealed a total of five tool mark classes evident in the bone. First and most obvious were the postmortem electric autopsy saw cuts. Various stray mechanical saw cuts occurred across the sectioned vault, and were not to be confused with parallel knife cuts in bone (Figure 21.8C). The second type of tool mark included the prominent wound to the vault apex, which could be termed a chopping wound due to striae oriented perpendicular to the contour of the bone (Figure 21.9). There were non-patterned defects deep in the bone that were created by irregularities in the cutting edge, thus suggesting a heavy non-serrated blade. There also appeared to be a slight curvature in the anterior portion of the defect floor. These characteristics indicated a weapon that had at least one beveled, non-serrated edge, curved at one end, broad, and heavy-bladed enough to penetrate the outer and inner cortex of bone and to leave a gaping wound.

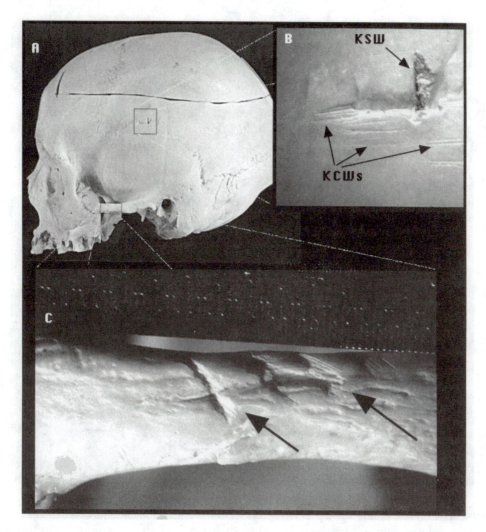

Figure 21.10 Case 4: Left lateral view of cranium (A) with enlargements of KCWs and KSW (B). The superior zygomatic arch (C) reveals chicken track striation patterns (arrows) (scale = 0.01 in.).

Comparisons between striations from a confiscated heavy knife and the chop mark to the vault apex failed to demonstrate any similarities.

The third and forth class of cuts included fine KSWs and KCWs in the skull. The KSW or puncture to the left parietal suggested a weapon that was single edged at the point and approximately 0.08 cm (0.03 in.) in breadth at 0.25 to 0.33 cm (0.10 to 0.13 in.) from the knife tip. No serrations were indicated at the tip. KCWs occurred with regular frequency over the whole skull with the only void occurring in the posterior parietal and occipital areas. The two co-authors concluded that these incised cuts likely represented a defleshing activity with a high frequency of cuts occurring on the mastoids, zygomatic arches, and occipital condyles. Some cuts were parallel and similar in length, occurring down the sides of the skull and suggesting a serrated knife that essentially skips across a hard surface. Although commonly difficult to prove, a serrated knife was positively indicated on the left

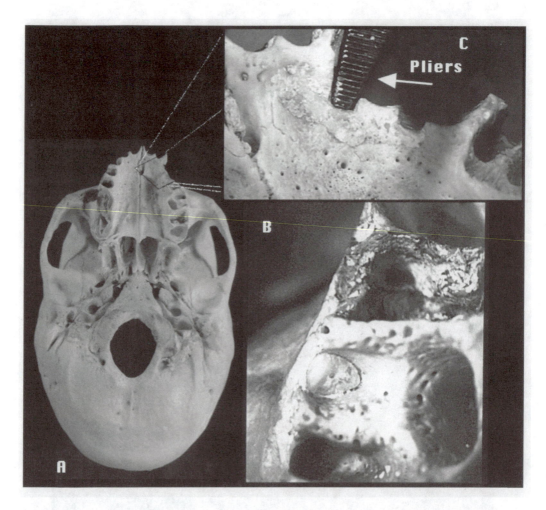

Figure 21.11 Case 4: Inferior aspect of the cranium (A) with enlargements of a damaged tooth socket illustrating broken tooth root (B), and an enlargement of the left mouth roof illustrating alveolus damage. Notice patterned defects with superimposed image of needle-nosed pliers (C).

lateral zygomatic arch (Figure 21.10C), where numerous teeth marks radiated out of a common kerf forming a chicken track wound (Symes et al., 1999). This wound pattern suggested a knife with manufactured teeth where each tooth mark combines to create a fan of striations.

Last, indications of perimortem dentition removal were evident in the two punched-out alveolar bone defects that were tapered with squared ends (Figure 21.11). This shape appeared consistent with the confiscated pliers and three different brands of exemplar needle-nosed pliers bought at a local hardware store. Superimposing these pliers over the bony defects (Figure 21.11C) revealed that all (including the suspect tool) were consistent with the bone damage with the exception of one of the purchased pliers that had an apparent nose defect.

A surgical bore attached to a standard power drill was used to extract cores of bone for DNA analysis, so as to do the least amount of damage possible to the skull for evidentiary purposes. The occipital region was selected due to its thickness and lack of cut marks, and the cores obtained produced a successful DNA result (a previous attempt utilizing the two third molars had been unsuccessful). At this point, the common-law husband of the decedent was arrested for her death. He confessed and revealed the details of her slaying, which included "accidentally" slitting her throat with his fishing knife, placing her in the bathtub, and then obtaining some knives and a meat cleaver.

A quote from his statement: "I started taking her apart. I cut off her head, her arms, her hands, everything. I skinned her whole body while it was in the bathtub. Some of the skin and stuff I flushed down the toilet, and some of it with the organs, I put in the bags that I used to get rid of the body. After I cut (her) head off, I used the meat cleaver and tried to split the head in half before I got the hacksaw out. I used a hacksaw to cut up the body. I know that (she) was dead when I pulled her teeth, because when (her) teeth were pulled, I had already cut her head off. I used a pair of pliers and pulled out her teeth. The teeth I put in bags and are with the body parts." The common law husband stated that he took two large plastic garbage bags containing the postcranial remains out to the local sewage treatment plant property and dumped them in a field. Then he threw the skull in a lake, approximately 1.5 miles from the sewage treatment facility.

At the sewage plant, a single tattered bag was located amidst a scatter of human bones. Although there was limited animal activity on the postcranial remains, the extent of the dismemberment was obvious. The marks of an additional weapon, a hacksaw, were apparent in numerous bones recovered, including the long bones, lumbar vertebrae, and sacrum. The typical kerf, striations, and characteristic break away spurs from the hacksaw damage were apparent on several of the long bones. Knife marks were also evident, particularly around articular surfaces of all long bones and on numerous smaller elements. Not a single bone recovered was without cut marks, including carpals, metacarpals, and phalanges. It became clear that a great deal of painstaking work had gone into this dismemberment. In fact, many of the cuts seemed to defy what would be necessitated to disarticulate elements. It is reasonable to suspect that perhaps the majority of these insults had nothing to do with thwarting identification or assisting in the transport of the victim. Perhaps they had more to do with the savagery of the perpetrator of this crime (the third rule of dismemberment).

In this case, a recovered cranium initially appeared to be part of a complete body that had decomposed and disarticulated naturally in a water environment (Table 21.5). The only initial trauma evidenced was sharp-force trauma to the top of the head. Anthropological examination was hindered due to a limited understanding of the recovery, the whereabouts of the postcranial remains, and post-recovery autopsy and processing. Upon closer examination, however, autopsy marks were eliminated as suspect perimortem trauma while many defects on the cranium appeared to fit a dismemberment/mutilation pattern. Taphonomic information and microscopic examination assisted in the substantiation of these assessments and contributed to a clearer picture of suspected disarticulation and mutilation. One or two knives (at least one serrated), a heavy-bladed sharp instrument, and a tool resembling needle-nosed pliers were listed as perpetrator tools. At the same time, a confiscated heavy-bladed knife was shown to be inconsistent with wounds. Subsequent confessions substantiated many of the findings.

Case 5: Sharp Trauma Forms Used in Dismemberment

In April of 1996, a fully fleshed partial torso wrapped in a plastic bag was found on the bank of the southernmost point of Lake Erie near Huron, Ohio, and sent to the Lucas

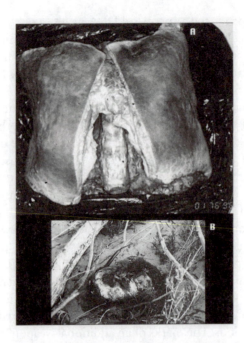

Figure 21.12 Case 5: Torso found floating in Lake Erie. Evisceration and longitudinal cut were performed at autopsy. The fully fleshed partial torso was wrapped in a plastic bag (B) and was found on the bank of the southernmost point of Lake Erie near Huron, Ohio.

County Coroner's Office in Toledo for autopsy. The autopsy report noted a shotgun wound to the left chest that had shattered the anterior end of the left second rib. Also present was a healed fracture on the right 8th rib located 6.5 mm (0.26 in.) from the sternal end. Skeletal analysis suggested these were the remains of an older teenager of unknown ancestry. Eventual DNA testing revealed the torso to be a male.

The severing cut (Cut A) on the upper torso penetrated the chest horizontally just above the nipples, passing clearly between the fourth and fifth thoracic vertebral bodies. Corresponding cut marks were present on portions of right ribs 1 through 5 and left ribs 1 through 4. Both right and left scapulae had been amputated above the epiphysis of the inferior angle. Positioning of the incisions indicated to the authors (JMS, FPS) that the arms were in a raised position when this cut was made. An additional cut (Cut B) on the lower torso was at the level of the umbilicus, penetrating through the body of the third lumbar vertebra. Figure 21.12A illustrates the recovered chest portion after autopsy and removal of chest organs. Since there were numerous bones with incised marks present, all cut bones were sent to the first author (SAS) for closer analysis.

In May of the same year, another fleshed piece appeared on the shore 5 miles west of the first location (Figure 21.12B). It consisted of a left hemi-pelvis and proximal left thigh of a male based on genitalia. Age at death was estimated from morphological features and epiphyseal union to be in the mid to late teens. The left hipbone had cuts to the midline, a left femur was sectioned 26.5 cm from the proximal end (Cut C), and fragments were cut from the left sides of the sacrum and lower lumbar vertebrae. There was no duplication of skeletal elements and the biological profiles for both sets of human remains were similar.

Additional remains were eventually recovered from surrounding areas. In the same month as the initial discovery, a fleshed partial right leg clad in part of a pant leg, a sock,

Victim last seen December 1, 1995

(1) April 12, 1996   Partial right leg
(2) April 13, 1996   Partial torso
(3) May 30, 1996   Left hemi-pelvis and thigh
(4) June 11, 1996   Upper torso, head and arms
(5) September 28, 1996   Left lower leg

Figure 21.13 Case 5: Map of the western end of Lake Erie illustrates the location of various body parts of dismembered victim from Detroit. (Illustration by Matthew J. Naujock. With permission.)

and a shoe was taken from the Detroit River. The driver's license of a teenage black male was found in the right rear pocket. The following June, an upper torso with head and arms (armpits and above with hands removed) of a black male was recovered from the Detroit River near Detroit, Michigan. Both body parts were sent to the Wayne County Medical Examiner's Office for autopsy. The medical examiner reported clusters of shotgun pellets in the upper torso, the right lower face and neck, and another below the clavicle in the left upper chest. Postmortem dental radiographs were compared with antemortem radiographs in order to provide a positive identification of the upper torso. That September, Canadian police in Ontario recovered a left lower leg from a male. The unusual distribution pattern of recovered remains from this single victim is illustrated in Figure 21.13. All recovered remains were consistent with a black teenage male, who was subsequently identified with DNA as a missing juvenile from Detroit last seen in December of 1995.

Analysis of cut marks on the chest, abdomen, and left upper leg conservatively indicated the use of a single class of saw and a complete absence of KCWs. Dismemberment Cut A (upper chest) involved 13 bones and appears to be the result of a single saw cut. Ribs, thoracic vertebrae, and scapulae indicated that direction of blade progress (direction a saw progresses through material) was left to right. Direction of cutting stroke (tooth striae on cut surfaces) was anterior to posterior. Such a blade must be considered large enough to cut through a torso measuring 94 cm (37 in.) in circumference. Many cuts to the ribs and, in particular, right rib 4 (Figure 21.14) indicated conspicuous, fine uniform striae, which are a characteristic of mechanically powered saws.

Dismemberment Cut B (lower chest), unlike A, reveals numerous deep cuts from different directions (Figure 21.15A, directions indicated by arrows). A minimum of four directions appear on this bone, suggesting rotation of either the saw blade or the remains. Cuts into

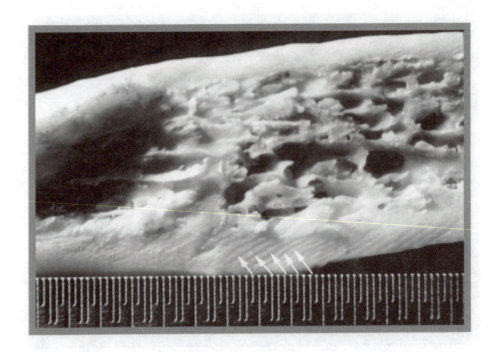

Figure 21.14 Case 5: Right rib 4, illustrating fine uniform saw striae (arrows), a characteristic of mechanically powered saws (scale = 0.01 in.).

lumbar vertebra 3 measure 0.13 to 0.15 cm (0.05 to 0.06 in.) in width (Figure 21.15B) and up to 3.8 cm (1.5 in.) in depth. Prominent wide blade indicators and deep false starts demonstrate an ease of cut and suggest a power saw. Dismemberment C reveals a cut with false starts and an irregular cut surface. Unlike the other cuts, Cut C is worn smooth, thus erasing many cut characteristics. Poor preservation of cut marks on the femur may be dependent upon the length of time until recovery, and protection from wave action provided by soft tissues or artificial wrapping intended to hide the remains. Interestingly enough, there appeared to be embedded metal particles in the cut surface (Figure 21.16). The origin of these particles could be attributed to numerous taphonomical influences, although it would seem likely that these were the result of high energy transfer, such as that produced by a powered cutting blade impacting metal artifacts in association with the leg during the dismemberment. This metal could conceivably be associated with items in the front pants pockets.

While no experimental saw characteristics matched perfectly with the suspect saw, the closest match was to a band saw (Table 21.6). Certain models of band saws would be capable of sectioning a human body. The section of body produced by cuts A–B (vertebrae still articulated) measures approximately 28 cm (11 in.) in length after moderate processing. A Butcher Boy Model B12 has 29 cm (11.5 in.) of cutting width and 42 cm (16.5 in.) of cutting height clearance. Therefore, this class of saw would facilitate a continuous cut through the upper torso and yet be consistent with lower torso cuts, as well as with the sectioned femur. The pattern of cut is also consistent with feeding a body through a saw.

Since two specimens of human remains that exhibited numerous differences in appearance were found separately in Lake Erie, there was a question of whether the bones were

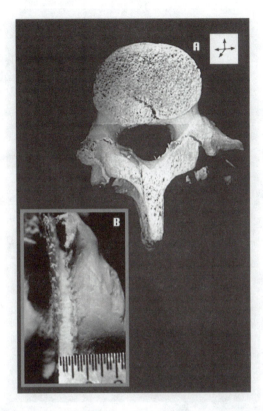

Figure 21.15 Case 5: Inferior view of dismembered lumbar vertebra 3 (A). Arrows represent detectable directions of blade progress produced by numerous cuts to bone. Also shown is a lateral view of a deep false start in the same vertebra (B) (scale = 0.01 in.).

cut with the same instrument. Existing characteristics appeared consistent with the same class of saw for specimens subjected to differing water environments and time since death. No knife stabs or cut wounds were evident on the bone. While this case is unsolved, this combined effort analysis was able to piece together evidence of a widely dispersed victim (Table 21.7). This evidence revealed an overkill situation and eventual dismemberment with at least one unusual type of tool.

Conclusion

Forensic anthropologists have been challenged to contribute to death investigation by using new tools and new standards (Smith et al., 1990; Symes and Smith, 1998). This challenge has been met with a variety of theoretical and experimental efforts, ranging from the development of modern forensic databases to the application of taphonomy and archaeological approaches to body recovery and interpretation of postmortem processes. An understanding of the biomechanics of bone trauma and its application to victims of violence constitutes a third frontier that opens new arenas of contribution to medicolegal death investigation.

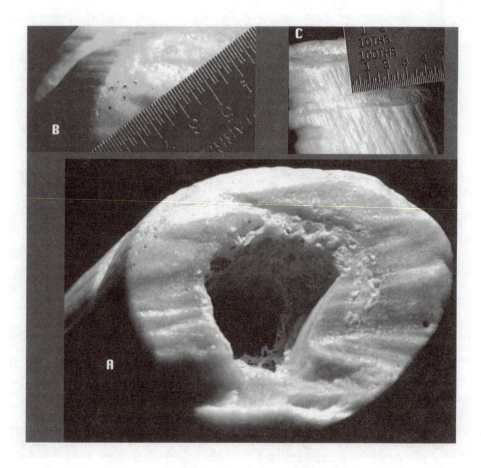

Figure 21.16 Case 5: Sectioned left femur recovered with hemi-pelvis in Lake Erie. (A) Cross-section of the dismembered femur midshaft. (B) Magnified section of this cut. Photograph illustrates imbedded metal fragments, possibly from a power saw impacting artifacts in pants pockets during dismemberment. (C) False starts to the femur shaft (scale = 0.01 in.).

The accounts presented above illustrate the development and evolution of cases as the anthropologist closely examines the facts and bases conservative estimates of trauma on data dependent upon context. Understanding the taphonomical context of each situation assists in determining the differences between environmental, faunal, and criminal activity to skeletal remains. Contextual assessment combined with a comprehensive sharp-trauma analysis leads the examiner to a more complete set of facts contributing to a feasible conclusion. From rodents to sharks, tissue processing (perimortem to postautopsy) to perpetrator dismemberment, the anthropologist's decision-making process must rely on all available information in order to make an accurate and conservative legal assessment.

Acknowledgments

For their editing comments, the first author is indebted to Jennifer Love, Regional Forensic Center, Memphis; Anne Kroman, Kansas University; Deb Kroman, Kansas City; Natalie

Table 21.6 Major Characteristics Describing the Class of Saw

Blade (Saw) Name	Type	KerfWidth Min.	Tooth Width	Between Teeth	Teeth Per Inch	Set of Teeth	Tooth Type	Cut Direction	Blade Cut Length
Suspect saw in this case	Power	0.05–0.06	0.02–0.30	0.22–0.26	3.8–4.5	ALT[a]	Chisel	Continuous	Large
Crosscut saw (standard)	Hand	0.060	0.030	0.14	6-7	ALT	Chisel	Reciprocate	26
Rip saw	Hand	0.050	0.035	0.23	4.5	ALT	Chisel	Reciprocate	26
Backed saw (premium)	Hand	0.055	0.030	0.09	11	ALT	Chisel	Reciprocate	10
Dovetail saw (premium)	Hand	0.035	0.020	0.07	14	ALT	Chisel	Reciprocate	10
Arched Pruning (peg toothed)	Hand	0.075	0.055	0.14	7	ALT	Cut	Reciprocate	ARC 13
Hack (alternating)	Hand	0.030	0.020	0.06	18	ALT	Chisel	Reciprocate	10
Hack (raker)	Hand	0.040	0.030	0.06	18	Raker	Chisel	Reciprocate	10
Hack (wavy)	Hand	0.030	0.020	0.04	24	Wave .13	Chisel	Reciprocate	10
Hack (wavy)	Hand	0.030	0.030	0.03	32	Wave .11	Chisel	Reciprocate	10
Chef (standard)	Hand	0.050	0.020	0.10	10	ALT	Chisel	Reciprocate	14
Meat (premium)	Hand	0.035	0.020	0.10	10	ALT	Chisel	Reciprocate	14
Serrated steak knife	Hand	0.030	0.020	0.13	8	None	Cut	Reciprocate	5
Japanese Ryoba (crosscut)	Hand	0.045	0.030	0.07	15	ALT	Cut	Reciprocate	9
Circular (piranha carbide)	Power	0.110	0.075	2.26	0.8	ALT	Chisel	Continuous	2–3
Circular (framer carbide)	Power	0.090	0.085	2.22	1		Chisel	Continuous	2–3
Circular (plywood)	Power	0.080	0.040	0.16	6	ALT	Chisel	Continuous	2–3
Circular (combination)	Power	0.110	0.055	0.56	1.6	ALT	Chisel	Continuous	2–3
Band (skip tooth)	Power	0.040	0.020	0.25	4	ALT	Chisel	Continuous	16.5
Reciprocal (alternating)	Power	0.080	0.045	0.14	7	ALT	Chisel	Reciprocate	5
Reciprocal (alternating)	Power	0.060	0.030	0.10	10	ALT	Chisel	Reciprocate	5
Reciprocal (wavy)	Power	0.045	0.030	0.06	18	Wave	Chisel	Reciprocate	5

Note: Suspect saw used in the dismemberment of the chest, abdomen, and left leg. Characteristics of other saws are also listed for comparative purposes. While no experimental saw characteristics matched perfectly with the suspect saw, the closest match was band saws. All linear measurements are in inches.

[a] ALT = Alternating set teeth.

Table 21.7   Perimortem and Postmortem Indicators of Trauma on Skeletal Remains Demonstrating an Investigation that Matures with Age and Research

Investigative Stage	Perimortem Indicators	Postmortem Indicators
Scene and initial investigation (law enforcement and medical) of recovered tissues	• Dismemberment of upper chest and abdomen • Dismemberment of left pelvis and femur • Shotgun wound to chest	• Discolored skin • Shotgun pellets recovered in tissues • Incomplete recovery
Initial anthropological examination	• Saw cut sections a chest with a circumference of 94 cm (37 in.)	• Embedded sand • Aquatic environment decomposition
Application of taphonomic approach including microscopic examinations	• One complete saw cut to chest • Saw large enough to cut through torso in a continuous motion • Abdominal cut from numerous directions • Likely a power saw with narrow blade	• Chest and abdomen tool mark preservation is excellent • Water action smoothed saw striations in femur
Conclusions	• Recovered body parts are eventually linked based on comparison of sharp-force trauma, biological, DNA, and taphonomic data • Sharp-force trauma analysis suggests a saw class consistent with a band saw	• Chest tool marks protected by soft tissues and plastic bag • Femur probably had less protection and longer exposure to aquatic environments

Langley, LSU, Baton Rouge; and as always, O.C. Smith, University of Tennessee, Memphis. For their expertise, assistance and cooperation, Julie and Frank Saul are indebted to S.A. Symes, Ph.D., Forensic Anthropologist, Memphis Regional Forensic Center; C.S. Beisser, M.D., Deputy Coroner of Lucas County, OH; T.J. Nesgoda, M.D., Coroner of Erie County, OH; S. Kanluen, M.D., Chief Medical Examiner of Wayne County, MI; A.J. Warmick, D.D.S., Chief Forensic Dental Consultant for Wayne County Medical Examiner's Office; and P.F. Ernst, D.D.S., Investigator for the Erie County Coroner.

For their expertise, and assistance, Tom Holland is indebted to Bruce Anderson and Tony Manoukian.

Elizabeth Murray would like to gratefully acknowledge Richard Burkhardt, M.D. and his staff at the Butler County Coroner's Office. I further thank Detectives Jim Nugent and Ed Buns of the Hamilton Police Department for their expert assistance. I am also grateful to the numerous enthusiastic students who assisted in the field recovery.

And finally, all authors would like to express their gratitude to the editors of this book, Marci Sorg and Bill Haglund. Their abilities, along with their patience and persistence, have been remarkable.

References

Andahl, R.O.
  1978   The examination of saw marks, *Journal of the Forensic Sciences* 18:31–46.

Berryman, H.E. et al.
  1991   Bone fracture. II: Gross examination of fractures. Paper presented to the 43rd Annual Meeting of the American Academy of Forensic Sciences, Anaheim, CA.

Bonte, W.
  1975   Tool marks in bones and cartilage, *Journal of Forensic Sciences* 20:315–325.

Cunningham, B.M. and W.F. Holtrop
  1974   *Woodshop Tool Maintenance,* Chas. A. Bennett Co., Peoria, IL.

Department of the Army
  1992   Combatives. Headquarters, Field Manual FM 21-150, Washington, D.C.

DiMaio, D. and V. DiMaio
  1993   *Forensic Pathology,* CRC Press, Boca Raton, FL.

Dirkmaat, D.C. and J.M. Adovasio
  1997   The role of archaeology in the recovery and interpretation of human remains from an outdoor forensic setting. In *Forensic Taphonomy: The Postmortem Fate of Human Remains,* edited by W.D. Haglund and M.H. Sorg, pp. 13–26. CRC Press, Boca Raton, FL.

Galloway, A.
  2000   *Broken Bones: An Anthropological Analysis of Blunt Force Trauma,* Charles C Thomas, Springfield, IL.

Crow, R., and D. Glassman
  1996   Standardization model for describing the extent of burn to human remains, *Journal of Forensic Sciences* 41(1):152–154.

Haglund, W.D.
  1993   Disappearance of soft tissue and the disarticulation of human remains from aqueous environments, *Journal of Forensic Sciences* 38:806–815.

Haglund, W.D. and M.H. Sorg
  1997   Introduction to forensic taphonomy. In *Forensic Taphonomy: The Postmortem Fate of Human Remains,* edited by W.D. Haglund and M.H. Sorg, pp. 13–26. CRC Press, Boca Raton, FL.

Jackson, A. and D. Day
  1978   *Tools and How to Use Them,* Alfred A. Knopf, New York.

Jantz, R.
  1999   Secular change and ancestry estimation. Paper presented to the 30th Anniversary Edition of the *T. D. Stewart Personal Identification in Mass Disasters.* Sponsored by the Central Identification Laboratory, Hawaii and the Smithsonian Institution.

  2000   Cranial change in Americans 1850–1975, *Proceedings of the American Academy of Forensic Sciences* 6:227.

Lanz, H.
  1985   *Japanese Woodworking Tools,* Sterling Publishing, New York.

Martin, J.R.
  1999   Identifying Osseous Cut Mark Morphology for Common Serrated Knives. Thesis presented for the Master of Arts degree, Department of Anthropology, University of Tennessee, Knoxville.

Moore-Jansen, P., S. Ousley, and R. Jantz
    1994   *Data Collection Procedure for Forensic Skeletal Material Report Investigations*, 3rd ed., The University of Tennessee, Knoxville.

Nawrocki, S.
    2000   Personal communication.

Reichs, K J.
    1998   *Forensic Osteology*, 2nd ed., Charles C Thomas, Springfield, IL.

Smith, O.C., H.E. Berryman, and S.A. Symes
    1990   Changing role for the forensic anthropologist. Paper presented to the 42nd Annual Meeting of the American Academy of Forensic Sciences, Cincinnati, OH.

Smith, O.C., H.E. Berryman, S.A. Symes, and S.J. Moore
    1991   Bone fracture. I: The physics of fractures. Paper presented to the 43rd Annual Meeting of the American Academy of Forensic Sciences, Anaheim, CA.

Spitz, W.
    1993   Sharp force injuries. In *Medicolegal Investigations of Death*, 3rd ed., edited by W. Spitz and R. Fisher, Charles C Thomas, Springfield, IL.

Symes, S.A.
    1992   Morphology of Saw Marks in Human Bone: Identification of Class Characteristics. Ph.D. dissertation, The University of Tennessee, Knoxville.

Symes, S.A. and O.C. Smith
    1998   It takes two: combining disciplines of pathology and physical anthropology to get the rest of the story, *Proceedings of the American Academy of Forensic Sciences* 4:208.

Symes, S.A. et al.
    1991   Bone fracture. III: Microscopic fracture analysis of bone. Paper presented to the 43rd Annual Meeting of the American Academy of Forensic Sciences, Anaheim, CA.

    1992   Saw dismemberment of human bone: characteristics indicative of saw class and type. Paper presented to the 44th Annual Meeting of the American Academy of Forensic Sciences, New Orleans, LA.

    1996   Bones: Bullets, Burns, Bludgeons, Blunderers, and Why. Bone Trauma Workshop presented to the 48th Annual Meeting of the American Academy of Forensic Sciences, Nashville, TN.

    1998   Saw marks in bone: introduction and examination of residual kerf contour. In *Forensic Osteology*, 2nd ed., edited by K.J. Reichs. Charles C Thomas, Springfield, IL.

    1999   Anthropological and pathological analyses of sharp trauma in autopsy. *Proceedings of the American Academy of Forensic Sciences* 5:177-178.

A Critical Look at Methods for Recovering, Evaluating, and Interpreting Cremated Human Remains

PAMELA MAYNE CORREIA
OWEN BEATTIE

22

Contents

Introduction

The number of case studies for cremated remains available for review by the forensic sciences community is slowly increasing through the presentation of brief reports at conferences (Manhein, 1991; Maples, 1988; Murray et al., 1991) and in publications (Dirkmaat, this volume; Fairgrieve and Molto, 1994; Owsley, 1993). Case studies provide a real world reflection of experimentally derived models of how bone reacts to fire and the fire environment, while also highlighting the need for future research through descriptions of challenges encountered during each case. This chapter adds to the resources of case studies by concentrating on the processes of successful recovery and subsequent analysis, and is intended for professional forensic investigators and students with little or no background in physical anthropology or the analysis of cremated human remains.

Physical anthropology is the subdiscipline of anthropology that deals with the study and understanding of past and modern human physical variation. When dealing with recent human death investigation within a medicolegal context, physical anthropologists having a strong background in human and comparative anatomy, and taphonomy can provide critical information that can assist in the resolution of an investigation. This application of physical anthropology is commonly referred to as forensic anthropology. The strengths of the forensic anthropologist rest in an ability to recognize and interpret minute anatomical detail in found human remains, and to evaluate the effects of natural and human interaction with these remains. Cases involving cremation with extreme fragmentation often present the most demanding challenges to investigators, and the role of the forensic anthropologist in such cases can be significant.

The recovery issues reviewed in this chapter are represented by a series of guidelines for dealing with scenes involving fire and human victims, and are supported anecdotally through our comments and evaluations of three cases involving burned human remains. These issues are

1. Scene evaluation: the development of a viable recovery plan
2. Scene access and exploration: minimizing damage prior to recovery
3. Scene and evidence documentation: mapping, photography, data recording
4. Evidence recovery: excavation, handling, recording and cataloguing
5. Bone and dentition evidence transportation: handling, packaging
6. Bone and dentition evidence preparation for analysis: handling, preservation
7. Bone and dentition analysis

The following three cases of cremation were selected from the files of the Office of the Chief Medical Examiner (Edmonton) and were chosen because they reflect very different fire situations and environments, each demanding scene-specific recovery, handling, and analysis strategies.

General Overview of the Cases

Case 1

This case involves a single individual whose remains were discovered after an intense fire in a two-story wood frame house located approximately 200 km east of Edmonton, Alberta.

The house was situated in a remote rural setting serviced by a volunteer fire department. Passersby noticed the fire at 2:30 AM. The volunteer fire department was notified, and immediately responded. When the call was made, the fire was already well advanced, and after two water trucks emptied their payloads into the fire with no effect, there remained no option but to let it burn out (Dowling, 1989). It was several days before the site could be examined. All flammable components of the house had collapsed onto the bare earth basement floor, forming a debris layer averaging an estimated 30 cm in depth. Police suspected that a male in his 60s was in the house at the time of the fire, and as soon as conditions allowed, police officers and a fire investigator searched for remains. This initial search was unsuccessful; however, during a second search, police raked the basement area and located a number of bone fragments suspected of being human. Following these discoveries, a team from the Office of the Chief Medical Examiner (including a forensic anthropologist) attended and processed the scene. Analysis of the recovered cremated remains provided a positive identification of the missing male, who was the owner of the house. There had been a witnessed altercation between this man and two other individuals in the days before the fire. This information, along with the discovered human remains, provided a foundation for the search for evidence of foul play.

Case 2

A witness to the disposal of the remains of a young woman on a farm located approximately 30 km northeast of Edmonton, Alberta, and who also was a witness to the description of the homicide of this individual made by two males, notified the police of the location of her remains. According to this witness, the victim had been stabbed and then shot. In an attempt to dispose of the remains, the suspects had wrapped her body in a carpet, which was then placed on creosote-soaked railway ties and ignited. The fire was maintained for 3 days. The fire debris containing the remains was then scooped up with the bucket of a front-end loader and scattered in a plowed field and over the partially buried, incompletely disassembled and burned-out frame of the victim's vehicle. Over a 4-day period a team from the Office of the Chief Medical Examiner (including a forensic anthropologist) collected the remains from the scene. Analysis of the remains resulted in the identification of the suspected victim (Dowling and Beattie, 1988).

Case 3

The third case represents a scene with multiple deaths (Pounder, 1986; Stratton and Beattie, 1999). On February 8, 1986, a freight train and a passenger train collided near Hinton, Alberta, resulting in the deaths of 23 people. The freight train had been carrying large quantities of sulfur and grain. The collision caused the mixing and ignition of spilled diesel fuel and these other materials. The resulting fire burned for a number of days, hampering the recovery of some of the victims' remains. Of the 23 individuals who perished in the accident, only one could be visually identified. The remaining 22 victims were identified using a combination of survivors' recollections of where victims were last seen prior to the accident (and linked to the recovery process), evaluation and matching of ante- and postmortem dental and medical information, and the use of other circumstantial evidence such as the association of personal effects with remains. The conditions of the remains varied from unburned to incompletely cremated. Limbs were frequently separated from the bodies and highly fragmented, while torsos were almost always intact. This scene was processed by a large number of individuals from the RCMP, the railway company's police staff, a team from the Office of the Chief Medical Examiner (OCME), and accident investigators from various agencies and companies. Anthropologists did not attend the scene of the accident, but were subsequently involved in the identification process in the morgue at the OCME's Edmonton facility.

Commentary on the Scene and Recovery

Scene Characteristics

Each of the above described cases represents unique circumstances requiring the use of different methods of searching for and collecting the human remains and associated items. Factors such as safety considerations for investigators, weather conditions, prior disturbance of the remains, the real time need for law enforcement and suspect apprehension, and scene complexity all require consideration during the planning stages for recovery. The goals for the anthropologist at the scene are to minimize loss of information during recovery, to document thoroughly the recovery process, and to transport the remains safely for subsequent analysis at an appropriate facility.

In Case 1, a number of police and fire department personnel had searched through the site prior to the arrival of the OCME team: the scene was disturbed first by the fire fighters, then the fire investigator, and then the police agency prior to the arrival of the ME's team. These disturbances were deemed necessary to extinguish the fire and to determine its cause, and to assess whether human remains were present (there were suspects at large). The search for remains included the removal of larger pieces of incompletely burned and surviving nonflammable objects and the raking of the remaining debris on the basement floor into two large piles. These investigators did not locate human remains in their initial search, but in a second search, the police did locate remains thought to be human. They were collected, and a selection was taken to the OCME in Edmonton where they were verified as being human. It was at this stage of the investigation that the team from the OCME arrived. As there had already been extensive disturbance of the scene, a recovery strategy involving gridding and the collection of exact provenience information for items was seen as having no value, and was not applied. As an alternative, the basement floor was divided into zones, with the focal areas being the two piles of materials. These were measured in relation to identifiable parts of the cement foundation and chimney structure, and plotted on a floor plan of the house. Investigators who were involved in the raking and initial searches indicated that the debris pile which eventually yielded the majority of bone and tooth fragments also marked the location where the initial concentration of remains was discovered. Few bones were noted to have come from the remaining areas of the floor raked into the other pile. During the next 4 hours the OCME staff excavated and screened all of the material from each pile. Bone and tooth fragments were placed in plastic evidence bags and labeled as to which pile they were from. Six-hundred and thirty-three bone fragments were recovered of which 304 were identifiable as to exact anatomical location within the skeleton. Two bones were nonhuman. Fragments ranged in size from 0.2 cm × 0.2 cm up to 27.0 cm long (a femur fragment with attached charred tissue). In hindsight, it was determined that the 1/4″ screen was insufficient for recovery of materials of such a fragmentary nature, especially for tooth fragments.

In Case 2, three locations on the property were identified by the witness as probably containing remains from the victim: the primary burn site near a trailer home, a 45-gal drum adjacent to the burn site and used by the resident of the trailer home for burning garbage, and the partially buried vehicle. The OCME team began its search for remains using these identified locations as starting points. A systematic foot search of the scene was able to locate bone fragments on the soil surface. When plotted, clear limits to the bone distribution were noted which closely approximated the witness's statements. A hands and knees search and recovery of surface remains followed the determination of the bone distribution limits. Discovered bone fragments were mapped *in situ* before removal. Hand troweling of these areas indicated that almost all of the remaining recoverable material was located in and on the soil that had been piled onto the partially buried vehicle. Further systematic hand troweling completed the recovery process. Screening was not used. The recovered remains consisted of 142 bone fragments ranging in size from 1.7×1.2 cm to 4.5×0.8 cm.

In Case 3 the remains of the 23 victims were dispersed throughout a very complex accident scene covering a huge area (see Stratton and Beattie (1999) for a detailed description of the disaster). At the initial stages of the recovery process a number of locations were still burning, and in some locations recovery had to wait for heavy equipment to remove large pieces of wreckage. Logically, those victims immediately accessible to the recovery team were removed first. Once access to other parts of the scene was secured, the search for and recovery of those victims covered by debris or located in hot areas began. A number of the victims were only partially cremated, and recovery was straightforward and uncomplicated; however, the condition and extensive dispersal of the incompletely cremated and commingled victims were such that an alternate collection strategy was required. Particularly challenging was the need to search through the tons of spilled grain, which contained many thousands of bone fragments. To deal with this huge volume of material a system was set up whereby hand-shoveled buckets of grain were dumped onto a slow moving engine-driven conveyer belt approximately 4 m long. As the belt transported this material toward a screen, the larger pieces of nonhuman debris and potential remains were collected. Further materials were revealed as the material passed through the screens. All materials either identified as bone, or suspected as being bone, were packaged in clear plastic bags of varying sizes, each labeled as to its original location in the accident scene. Temperatures in February in this region are rarely above −10°C; during some periods of the recovery process, temperatures were reported to have fallen below −20°C. Dealing with these conditions was a significant and additional challenge for the recovery team. The recovery process at the scene was completed in 9 days (Pounder, 1986).

Packaging and Transport Considerations

The key to the extraction of the maximum amount of information from recovered evidence is the meticulous collection, thorough documenting, and careful handling of this evidence. Handling includes the manner in which materials are extracted from the scene, packaged, and transported, and can be a weak link in the maintenance of the physical integrity of the evidence. Standard collection practices include the placing of recovered items in evidence bags made of plastic or paper. An appropriate form of catalogue or identification numbers and other scene and investigator information are written on each bag. It is common to group the more robust fragments from an identified unit in one bag, and to treat more fragile items individually. Most recovery scenes will generate a large number of evidence bags, and often these are further packaged in larger containers, even body bags. Each handling step, combined with the failings of the different types of containment materials to offer adequate protection, can put fragile burned bone at risk for further physical damage.

Preplanning the manner in which evidence is transported back to a laboratory facility is a critical aspect of the preparations for the on-site collection of that evidence. In one case (#3), a nearly complete ulna shaft was photographed *in situ*. Unfortunately, the collection methods could not provide complete protection of this bone, and by the time it was returned to the OCME, it had separated into a number of fragments which had commingled during transport with other bone fragments found in the same recovery unit. Additional time was required in the reconstruction of the ulna, and if not for the scene photography, it would have appeared that due to the apparent extensive fragmentation, there were larger and more complex forces experienced in this location of the accident scene than had actually occurred. Here the photo documentation was critical in establishing the original scene condition of the fragments. Other observations made during the process of recovery in this case highlighted the success in evidence protection provided by placing extremely fragile facial bone fragments into plastic bags lightly inflated with air, and then sealing with tape.

The use of individual containers, such as disposable foam coffee cups, hard plastic boxes, small cardboard boxes, or specimen jars can provide significant protection to the burned bone fragments. Containers can be padded with a variety of materials, such as cotton or synthetic batting, bathroom tissue, or crumpled acid-free paper to maximize the stability of the bone. Obviously, if the bone fragment is further damaged during transport to the morgue, information is lost and the analysis will be more incomplete. Some forethought prior to attending the scene can save many hours of repair and reconstruction after the return to the morgue. During the recovery phase and preparation for transport, efforts to speed up these processes (in other words, "This is taking too long, so move it!") must be discouraged. Time saved at the recovery scene all too often increases time needed to unpack, repair, and analyze remains at the morgue — and deal with the knowledge that valuable information has probably been lost.

Once the remains are packaged in the above manner, transportation should be successful. The remains will be secure, well labeled, and easily stacked or packed within the protective plastic container or cardboard box.

Post-Collection Handling and Preservation Considerations

Upon arrival at the morgue, the level of care invested in packaging and transport must be continued. Though at the scene there can be opportunities to use different means of physically stabilizing fragile materials, the time required to complete this task can negatively affect the other components of the scene investigation. It can best be accomplished at the morgue.

Various chemical solutions have been used to stabilize cremated remains. In Cases 1 and 2, after the remains were sorted by anatomical location, pieces that were identified and determined to be most important in the identification process were individually soaked for 1 minute in a solution of white (PVC) carpenters' glue and water (1 part glue to 4 parts water) and left to dry on a stainless steel table. It is interesting to note that some of these materials were retained and archived as evidence, and are in as good a condition today, after more than a decade. For Case 2, two of the most significant pieces relating to establishing identity, and preserved by this method, easily withstood being reproduced in a silicon mold. The materials deemed of less importance during the identification phase maintained their physical integrity during this process, and were not treated in these cases. Few of the remains in Case 3 were treated in this manner due in part to the presence of substantial amounts of soft tissue and the immediacy of the release of the remains to families following identification.

The decision to apply a preservative is always a difficult one, and often relates to the period of time anticipated for the identification process to take. If identification is going to be a lengthy process, then preservative action will be necessary; if the remains can be identified within a day and released to the family, then it will not be necessary except for materials retained as evidence. The choice of preservatives available is excellent, but it may not be necessary to use the more exotic preservatives over the PVC solution. Case 1 was analyzed over a 5-day period and there was substantial reconstruction completed on the remains; therefore, it was important to stabilize the bone to safeguard the physical survival of the evidence. Significant portions of the remains in Case 2 were retained by the Medical Examiner's Office, and were treated in the PVC solution.

Once the condition of the remains has been assessed and dealt with, the detailed examination can proceed. This should be well-planned in advance, and again the goal is to minimize the handling of the remains. One systematic approach is to use two or more tables/autopsy gurneys: one for the unpacking of the remains; the other for sorting, analysis, and identification. If a sheet marked with the life-size outline of an human body is placed on this second table, the identification process is greatly enhanced, and handling is minimized. On the first table, items are removed from their packaging, examined, and identified as to anatomical location and then placed on the second table in relation to its true location within the body outline. Fragments initially determined to be unidentifiable are placed at the foot end of the table for later examination. Following this procedure through until all recovered materials are placed either in anatomical locations or separated as unidentifiable eliminates repetitive and potentially damaging handling. Often provenience information is linked to individual items. Various forms of tagging can be used to maintain this information on the second table (for example, and depending on the condition of the bone, adhesive tags of various colors, and small, labeled containers, etc.). This can be very informative, as the movement of the bone during or after the fire may be significant in detailing the position of the body prior to the fire or the movement of the remains during or after the cremation process. Such information may identify a primary burn site in cases where the material has been moved. Sorting and placing the remains on an outline of a human body also simplify the detection of one or more additional victims. If this is established, more tables with body outlines can be set up. In multiple individual cases, the distribution of the remains may suggest the relationship of some of the bones, which would otherwise be unidentifiable.

Soft tissue remnants can be dissected and examined by the pathologist, and fluid or undamaged muscle tissue can often be recovered from which serological data and DNA may be collected and toxicological examination completed. After X-rays have been taken, it is advisable to dissect out the bone from such tissue if the remains must be stored for an extended period of time.

Other Considerations

As with any unforeseen event, there may be unique issues that need to be dealt with when approaching a recovery and investigation. For example, in the case of a suspected homicide or suspicious death, the needs of agencies may take initial precedence over the more focused priorities of remains recovery and examination — a reality which must be recognized and accepted. The anthropologists' experiences in the three cases demonstrated that the time allotted to the recovery process is dictated by the weather, the number of individuals involved in the recovery process, the number of individuals recovered, the security of the scene, the physical nature of the scene itself, and the demands of the police investigation. In Case 3, debris had to be removed from the scene to permit access to the remains and although in most instances, the human remains were not disturbed by this process, the safety of the recovery team had to take precedence over the removal of bodies.

One way of partially bridging these potentially competing priorities and unavoidable conditions is through the compilation of an accurate and comprehensive photo record during each phase of the investigation. As this record may be completed by other investigators, communication among the various agencies is essential. Copies of scene photos can be of critical importance when made available to the anthropologist.

Commentary on Analysis

Separating Human from Nonhuman Remains

In the cases presented here, nonhuman bones present in the assemblages were easily distinguished from the human material. As with unburned remains, the characteristics typical of burned animal bone can be recognized and separated from the human remains. In Case 1, one animal bone exhibiting saw marks was associated with the remains, and was interpreted to be kitchen refuse. Case 2 had the potential for significant amounts of commingled nonhuman remains with the human remains, as the owner of the property (a hunter) disposed of food refuse in a pit immediately adjacent to the area where the body was burned; however, no mixing had taken place during the cremation of the victim. In Case 3, though no nonhuman materials were identified, melted insulation from within the train cars acquired the gross appearance of bone, particularly cancellous bone. On close examination by a forensic anthropologist, this material was quickly recognized as lacking identifiable human or nonhuman morphological characteristics, though often it required the use of a 10× hand lens to establish that it was not bone. In the field, investigators unfamiliar with the variety of bone characteristics were not able to distinguish this material from bone, resulting in the collection of significant quantities of insulation material, a situation that was encouraged for obvious reasons.

The scene is not the location to make decisions on the more subtle aspects of materials collection, especially for individuals lacking osteological experience. It is far better to discard nonrelevant materials in the lab at a later date than to learn of materials that may have been overlooked, and have to return to the scene and rescreen the search area again — if this is even possible.

Estimating the Number of Individuals

The commingling of remains from more than one individual must always be considered as a possibility in fire scenes. The literature dealing with commingled human remains is not extensive (see Ubelaker, this volume). Procedures for evaluating the numbers of individuals represented in a scene invariably revolve around the identification of duplicated

Table 22.1   Classification of Cremation for Individuals in the Three Cases

Type	Subtype	Number of Individuals
Unburned	No thermal trauma	3[a]
Charred (CGS #1[b])	Only minor thermal trauma	0
Partially cremated[c] (CGS #2)	Internal organs present and some of the limbs	5
(CGS #3 and #4)	Internal organs present and calcined limb fragments	9
	Internal organs present, but mainly calcined skeletal tissue	1
Incompletely cremated (CGS #5)	Calcined skeletal tissue	7
Completely cremated	Only ashes remaining	0

[a] These specimens are not referred to in the discussions of osteobiographical information.
[b] Crow-Glassman Scale (Glassman and Crow, 1995).
[c] This type of cremation is divided into three subtypes depending on the amount of limb or soft tissue remaining. The internal organs may be present only as desiccated material identifiable as muscle, kidney, liver, etc.

anatomical features, the establishment of morphological consistency or inconsistency among the bones, and the identification of age and sex criteria. In Cases 1 and 2, sorting of the remains revealed no duplication of any bones, there was relatively even representation from all regions of the bodies, and there was morphological consistency among all fragments. In Case 3, two groupings of bones contained the commingled remains of two or more individuals. In each grouping the obvious disparity in bone sizes that were observed, and the presence of duplicated elements, clearly indicated that more than one individual was represented. In one grouping an older male and female were commingled and initially verified by the presence of 2 right patellae. The second grouping included 3 females (ages 71, 64, 53), which were separated through X-ray comparison of pelvic and lumbar regions and the comparison of dental characteristics.

For cases that do not relate to crematory remains, the use of weight of recovered material is of marginal value, and usually ineffective in establishing the number of individuals present. Published research is available which presents the average weight for males and females after cremation (McKinley, 1993; Murad, 1998), but these assume full recovery under optimal conditions. In a field situation, this is rarely possible as taphonomic processes act to alter the condition and placement of the bone remains, in contrast to the more closed environment of a crematory urn.

Classification of Cremation

The most obvious inconsistency found in the records for the three cases was the manner in which cremation was described. A number of nonstandard terms were used to describe the degree of cremation. "Partially incinerated remains," "naturally cremated," "severely charred," "extensive fire destruction of body," and "severe postmortem destruction," are just a few of the phrases used in the reports to describe remains that were all of a similar condition.

If a consistent terminology is used to describe a burned body, there is more likelihood of generating some understanding of what the material represents and might prevent the use of phrases like "naturally cremated" or "partially incinerated," neither of which make much sense in the context. Table 22.1 provides terminology that can be used to classify the remains more consistently, and further to this issue, listing the components that are present removes any doubt of the condition. In the three cases presented here, the classification of the condition of the remains can be broken down into the following categories (Table 22.1): unburned, charred, partially cremated, incompletely cremated, and completely cremated.

Estimating Sex

It is common practice, and usually most effective, to use the pelvis and skull to interpret the sex of the individual (Stewart, 1979; Ubelaker, 1989). In Case 1 the sex of the individual was established through the use of observable features located on cranial fragments, including the size and shape of the mastoid process (large), the presence and degree of development of the external occipital protuberance (prominent), the degree of sharpness of the supraorbital rim for the left orbit (rounded), and the size of the brow ridges (moderate). The remains of the pelvis, after reconstruction, yielded a sciatic notch that was ambiguous in its characterization (moderately wide). There was no pre-auricular sulcus, but there was a well-formed piriformis muscle attachment tubercle. The conclusion drawn, from the observations of these components, was that the individual was male. The pubic symphyses were not recovered for this case and the fragmentation of the pelvis made any further observations impossible. The calotte was reconstructed, but the face and base remained highly fragmented, so again overall robustness or gracility was not interpreted for the estimation of sex.

In the second case, the paucity of skeletal remains made the identification of sex more tentative. Fortuitously, one small fragment of the right frontal bone exhibited a sharp rim and no brow ridge. There was no pelvic material that could be used to estimate the sex. The long bone fragments were gracile, but so fragmented that any concrete assessment would have been impossible.

For those individuals in Case 3 where soft tissue was present, sex was established through observation of the genitalia, but for those individuals incompletely cremated (5 in total), the bone morphology was used. Humeral head size and overall robustness of the bones were used for the identification of the males, while the females were interpreted based upon the presence of pre-auricular sulci and/or widely flared sciatic notch.

The remains of one female were found commingled with a large male. Survivors of the accident indicated they had witnessed a married couple sitting together just prior to the collision. Medical records provided the evidence which established their identities. In these instances, it was not essential to establish the sex as other indicators were used to narrow the profile for the remains. The traditional osteobiographical sketch was not completed for these cases, but as soon as enough information was available to identify positively the remains, the analysis was concluded and the remains were released to waiting families. This limitation on the analysis will be discussed below, but it should be mentioned here that the identifications were the first priority, with any completion of an entire osteobiographical sketch secondary in importance.

Estimation of Age at Time of Death

For the male in Case 1, age estimation was straightforward. Although there were no pubic symphyses, rib ends suggested an age of 54 to 65+, and the auricular surface one of 60+. Other indicators including deep Pacchionian pits, parietal thinning, and osteoarthritic lipping of the knee, vertebrae, and shoulder as well as endocranial suture closure all supported the conclusion of an adult, probably 60+. The resident of the house was 67 years old.

The individual in Case 2 was assessed for age using cranial sutures, osteophytic lipping, and epiphyseal fusion. These indicators suggested a young adult, over 25 and less than 35 years. Again, in this case, there were no pubic bones and the teeth were too fragmentary to be used for any age assessment. Further to the value of teeth in cases involving cremated remains, if these cases are used for comparison, the survival of teeth was minimal; if they did survive, then only root fragments or separated crown fragments were available for analysis.

For one of the females in Case 3, the ischium showed no exostoses, the cranial sutures were open, and the thoracic vertebral epiphyseal rings appeared recently fused. The pubic symphysis was present and demonstrated no lipping on the dorsal rim, no parturition scars, and a billowed symphyseal face. As the two remaining females to identify were either under 20 or over 30 years old, it was concluded that this individual was more consistent with the former.

A denture and a partial denture were associated with two other females, and were consistent with the presence in two older women. These women were represented by minimal skeletal remains. Of the 23 victims in Case 3, investigation of only 7 utilized dental morphology and comparative dental X-rays for positive identification.

The degree of epiphyseal fusion is easily distinguished from postmortem changes resulting from the fire, and is very useful in establishing the age of the individual when incompletely fused.

Estimation of Ancestry

Opinions on the ancestry were not given for any of the individuals, as the condition of the remains did not allow such determinations. Facial bones were too damaged in all cases where skeletal material was being assessed, and overall cranial characteristics were not possible to observe. In the recovered dentition, the enamel had been destroyed, leaving only the underlying dentin, eliminating the possibility of examining cusp characteristics.

Estimation of Stature

Due to the significant degree of long bone fragmentation, and the preemptive positive identification of most of the victims in the three cases, stature estimations were not completed or used in the identification process for the materials in these cases. A stature estimate based on the incomplete femur in Case 1 was not a consideration relating to the identification of this victim.

Personally Unique Features

The most important information in establishing the identification of the human remains in these cases was that relating to the discovery and recognition of unique features in the skeleton. Individualizing features, by definition, are often completely unique to a single individual, or shared by very few individuals in a population. Forensic odontologists have long been using points of comparison in the dentition to establish identity, and the uniqueness of trabecular bone patterning and bone morphology has been established for comparison with medical X-rays (Angyal and Derczy, 1998; Kahana et al., 1997).

Individualizing features are by far the most important for providing a foundation for determining identity. The expertise of the investigators in finding and describing unique characteristics and the ability to compare these discoveries with antemortem X-rays and dental information are critical to the identification process. When looking at extremely fragmented, calcined bone a skill for identification of the fragment, as well as the ability to recognize something unusual about it, can make all the difference in leading to a positive identification.

In Case 1, the identification of a clavicle with a decades-old healed mid-body fracture was easily correlated with an antemortem medical X-ray taken a few months prior to death. The mastoid process was recovered from the fire scene, and the sinus pattern was convincingly matched to a recent antemortem X-ray. The recovered external occipital protuberance possessed asymmetrical characteristics, and two bone spicules that were successfully matched with a recent antemortem X-ray.

Pathology was also used in Case 2 to establish the identification of the victim. A small fragment of bone found during the scene search, and measuring 3 cm × 1.2 cm × 1.5 cm, was recognized as an osteochondroma, and was matched to an osteochondroma visible in an antemortem X-ray of the left femur of the suspected victim. Other materials providing support for the identification included a small fragment of maxillary bone that demonstrated healed antemortem tooth loss of the left canine and left second premolar. This fragment was compared to the antemortem dental X-ray of the suspected victim that recorded the canine extraction 4 years previously. There was also a photograph of this individual smiling, exposing the maxillary dentition with missing canine and premolar.

Dental X-ray comparison was used for seven of the individuals in Case 3 and medical X-rays were used to establish the positive identification in another seven instances. Only two of the incompletely cremated individuals were identified using dental comparisons and in one case this was a denture; the other individuals were partially cremated. Of the medical X-rays the sacroiliac joint was most often used and, in one instance, cervical vertebrae were compared. Pathology and degenerative disease were used for five of the individuals. It is important to note that fire does not produce characteristics that can be interpreted as disease (Kühl, 1980). Bone does not swell, but shrinks and fractures when heated. Bone spicules (enthesophytes) do not develop, nor do arthritic pits appear during the cremation process. The presence of a pathology, however, can have an effect on the bone during cremation, as in the production of the dense areas of bone associated with a fracture callus that can help preserve bone in a fire.

Cause and Manner of Death

The scene and witness testimony were used to establish the manner of death in these cases, while the cause of death was not provided by the skeletal analysis. In Case 1, the individual was suspected of having been shot, but no evidence from the remains supported this conclusion and an undetermined cause of death was recorded. The second case, in which witnesses said the individual had been stabbed and shot, did not produce any skeletal evidence to support this assertion.

Many of the individuals in the third case exhibited evidence of multiple traumas. Soft tissue and bones only minimally heat damaged could be assessed for sharp and blunt trauma. Of the individuals that were incompletely cremated, no perimortem trauma was distinguished from the heat trauma.

Lessons and Conclusions

Collection Priorities and Bone Preservation

The experience provided by these three cases allows us to make some specific recommendations for individuals who anticipate being involved in recovery of human remains from a fire scene. Time is the most important factor that dictates how you approach any given scene containing cremated human remains. Most scenes will be populated by members of various investigative agencies asking for immediate answers. Some must be addressed (e.g., "No, that area of the scene is not clear, and I suspect more remains will be found there."), while others can be delayed for a reasonable time ("I will be able to tell you how many individuals are represented only after proper examination in the morgue."). Other police matters may also dictate your approach to the scene or whether you attend the scene at all.

It may be impossible to attend the scene, as many forensic anthropologists have commitments to full-time positions elsewhere, or are not considered necessary by the agencies controlling the recovery process. Working with the crime scene officers, the medical investigators and others prior to a situation may not only result in better collection techniques by them, but also may encourage them to contact the individual who will be doing the analysis. Preparing those who may be involved in the collection process and making them aware of the different collection procedures and how these procedures will benefit the analysis and produce a more expedient conclusion are good approaches.

The team approach is more efficient than a one-person show. The type of cooperation that can develop between agencies (including police, medical, archaeological/historical) can result in a more productive investigation and analysis.

The team approach to analyzing cremated remains is extremely effective. Experience gained from these cases and others has shown that at least 3 or 4 people working through the remains will produce very good results.

Field photography can help to reassociate fragments that become commingled. Small diameter screens (.25 in. or smaller) can greatly increase the recovery of tooth fragments.

The use of white glue and water over cyanoacrilate is preferred for reconstructions, because with gentle soaking the cremated bone can be separated if needed. Cyanoacrilate glues do have solvents that can aid in separation of glued fragments, but with very thin and/or fragile bone, it usually requires the bone be broken. The white glue can be used to join fragments, but also to soak the entire fragment for stabilization. Cremated bone, depending on the amount of burning, may not need to be stabilized at all. If the bone is only carbonized it will withstand normal handling, whereas calcined bone can crumble under very little pressure. The decision to coat the bone should be made in each case, depending on whether the remains must be retained for a long period. The argument for reconstruction must be assessed given the amount of fragmentation and the potential use in the reconstructed fragments.

Limitations

There should not be an obligation to allocate all the recovered remains to an individual in cases where multiple victims have been commingled. Unless there is very good reason to conclude that the material belongs to one individual vs. another, the only decision that can be made is to leave these remains as unidentified.

In many human death investigations the teeth provide the evidence for identity, but for cremated human remains, they have a reduced value. Once the soft tissue has been burned away and the crowns are exposed to the intense heat they are unable to retain their structure. The crowns then commonly split away from the roots and the roots separate from the alveoli. It is possible, if enough is recovered, to reconstruct teeth for the purposes of comparison with antemortem dental records.

For the two cases presented here where the determination of the cause of death was an important aspect of the investigation, there was no evidence in the skeletal material to verify the injuries. In the train crash, the cause of death was obvious and attributed to multiple trauma. Although finding evidence for cause of death is less likely on cremated remains, evidence from a weapon will not be obliterated by cremation if the piece of bone is recovered.

Cautions

The interpretation of the color of the bone fragments as an indicator of fire temperature is not reliable (Mayne, 1990). In all the cremation cases above, the remains demonstrated bone with each of the recognized colors. The availability of oxygen and the insulating effects of muscle mass each play more of a role in the calcination process than does the temperature. Any suggestion of fire temperature based on bone color should be considered only an approximation.

Other cautionary notes relate to the collection of the data and how it is recorded. In reviewing the above cases, the lack of consistency in recordkeeping was most notable. Information on the amount and type of bone recovered, the bone condition, available antemortem records, identification criteria, and photo documentation would result in a more complete record, rather than only recording the identification criteria.

Given the push for standardization in other areas of forensic anthropology, it is surprising that, as yet, there has been no demand for consistency in data collection for cremated remains.

Each scene must be assessed individually, and procedures for collection and recovery must be adapted for each situation. This flexibility should permit circumstances to be exploited to the best advantage.

In conclusion, this chapter has provided anecdotal reviews of three cremation scenes with very different characteristics. It is hoped that the description of these cases, along with the authors' personal commentary on specific aspects of the issues relating to recovery and analysis, will stimulate further discussion of individual experiences that investigators have had with this difficult type of case.

Acknowledgments

We would like to thank the Office of the Chief Medical Examiner (Northern Region), Edmonton, and Cyril Chan, radiographer and forensic photographer at the same facility.

References

Angyal, M. and K. Derczy
1998 Personal identification on the basis of antemortem and postmortem radiographs, *Journal of Forensic Sciences* 43(5):1089–1093.

Beattie, O.B.
1986 Descriptions of identifications made on human skeletal remains from the Hinton/Via rail train disaster of February 8, 1986. Report on file, Office of the Chief Medical Examiner, Edmonton.

Dowling, G.
1989 Autopsy Report 8196-0-89 on file at the Office of the Chief Medical Examiner, Edmonton.

Dowling, G., and O.B. Beattie
1988 Autopsy Report 7841-8-88 on file at the Office of the Chief Medical Examiner, Edmonton.

Fairgrieve, S.I. and E. Molto
1994 Burning point: Canadian case studies of intentionally cremated human remains. In *Strength in Diversity: A Reader in Physical Anthropology*, edited by A. Herring and L. Chan. Canadian Scholars' Press, Toronto.

Glassman, D.M. and R.M. Crow
1995 Standardization model for describing the extent of burn injury to human remains, *Journal of Forensic Sciences* 41(1):152–154.

Kahana, T., J.A. Ravioli, C.L. Urroz, and J. Hiss
1997 Radiographic identification of fragmentary human remains from a mass disaster, *American Journal Forensic Medicine and Pathology* 18(1):40–44

Kühl, I.
1980 Harris's lines and their occurrences also in bones of prehistoric cremations, *OSSA* 7:129–171

Manhein, M.H.
1991 Explosions in the petrochemical industry: forensic anthropologists' role. In *Abstracts of the American Academy of Forensic Sciences 43th Annual Meeting*. American Academy of Forensic Sciences, Colorado Springs, CO.

Maples, W.R.
1988 Identification of the cremated remains in the Meek/Jennings case. In *Abstracts of the American Academy of Forensic Sciences 40th Annual Meeting*. American Academy of Forensic Sciences, Colorado Springs, CO.

Mayne, P.M.
1990 The Identification of Precremation Trauma in Cremated Remains. Unpublished Master's Thesis, University of Alberta, Edmonton, Canada.

McKinley, J.I.
1993 Bone fragment size and weights of bone from modern British cremations and the implications for the interpretation of archaeological cremations, *International Journal of Osteoarchaeology* 3:283–287.

Murad, T.A.
1998 The growing popularity of cremation versus inhumation: some forensic implications. In *Forensic Osteology: Advances in the Identification of Human Remains*, 2nd ed., edited by K. Reichs, pp. 86–105. Charles C Thomas, Springfield, IL.

Murray, E.A., H.J. Bonnell, and A.J. Perzigian
  1991 Cremation in a chicken coop: self-incineration or fowl play? In *Abstracts of the American Academy of Forensic Sciences 43th Annual Meeting*. American Academy of Forensic Sciences, Colorado Springs, CO.

Owsley, D.W.
  1993 Identification of the fragmentary, burned remains of two U.S. journalists seven years after their disappearance in Guatemala, *Journal of Forensic Sciences* 38(6):1372–1382.

Pounder, D.
  1986 Autopsy Reports 7595-86 to 7600-86, 7602-86 to 7608-86, and 7611-86 to 7620-86 on file at the Office of the Chief Medical Examiner, Edmonton.

Stewart, T.D.
  1979 *Essentials of Forensic Anthropology*, pp. 85–127, Charles C Thomas, Springfield, IL.

Stratton, S. and O. Beattie
  1999 Mass disasters: Comments and discussion regarding the Hinton Train Collision of 1986, *Forensic Osteological Analysis*, edited by S.I. Fairgreave, pp. 267–286. Charles C Thomas, Springfield, IL.

Ubelaker, D.H.
  1989 *Human Skeletal Remains: Excavation, Analysis, Interpretation*, Taraxacum, Washington, D.C., pp. 74–84.

Recovery and Interpretation of the Fatal Fire Victim: The Role of Forensic Anthropology

23

DENNIS C. DIRKMAAT

Contents

0-8493-1189-6/02/$0.00+$1.50
© 2002 by CRC Press LLC

Introduction

There has been renewed discussion with respect to expanding the role of forensic anthropologists in the criminal investigation of partially to fully decomposed remains from outdoor contexts (Dirkmaat, 1998a; Dirkmaat and Adovasio, 1997). An important part of this expanded role is an early entrance in the investigative sequence; that is, during the search and recovery of remains and during the postmortem examination. This expanded approach will lead to a more comprehensive recovery of contextual and associational data and information relevant to taphonomic reconstructions, and thereby allow for more accurate reconstructions of victim identity, issues related to manner of death, and circumstances surrounding the death event. Field recoveries of forensic evidence are most effective and efficient when contemporary archaeological recovery methods and interpretations are utilized (Dirkmaat and Adovasio, 1997; Hochrein, 1997, 1998; Morse et al., 1983; Nawrocki, 1998; Skinner and Lazenby, 1983). In what follows, it will be argued that similar benefits to event reconstruction can also be attained in contexts involving human remains partially or wholly destroyed by fire when the anthropologist is involved in the recovery of the remains in their initial undisturbed context (e.g., Bass, 1984; Dirkmaat, 1991) as well as during the postmortem examination (Dirkmaat, 1998b).

The Forensic Anthropologist and the Fire Investigation

During most forensic investigations involving human remains, including those associated with fire-related deaths, there exist three relatively discrete data collection phases or episodes (Dirkmaat, 1998b). The first data collection opportunity (described here as Level I) occurs during the location, documentation, and recovery of the body at the scene. The primary focus at this level is on the association of the body to other physical evidence and the scene. Level II data collection occurs during the postmortem examination, where the focus is upon soft tissue structures, and to a lesser degree on the skeletal system. The last phase (Level III) primarily involves the laboratory analysis of the physical evidence (for anthropologists, skeletal remains) and includes the interpretation of the results.

Forensic anthropologists frequently enter the investigation of suspicious deaths involving fire after the field recovery of remains and the postmortem examination by the forensic pathologist. This delayed laboratory-based role (Level III data collection) generally involves an attempt to provide or corroborate a presumptive personal identification via osteological parameters following unsuccessful forensic odontological efforts. On occasion, the forensic anthropologist will be called upon to differentiate perimortem trauma from the postmortem effects of heat damage to the bones. Although the forensic anthropologist can be very effective at this level of investigation, a case will be made here that a more significant role in the fire investigation during the postmortem examination (Level II data collection), and especially during the field recovery (Level I), serves to maximize contextual and associational data collection and subsequently provides more accurate event reconstruction along with other significant residual benefits to the forensic investigation. In what follows the potential role and benefits of forensic anthropological methodologies during the laboratory analysis, postmortem examination, and field recovery phases of the fire investigation will be described and illustrated via six forensic cases.

Level III Data Collection: Laboratory
Analysis of Heat-Altered Human Remains

As has been extensively reviewed recently (Mayne Corriea, 1997), laboratory-based forensic anthropological methods (i.e., skeletal analysis) have been used quite effectively in the determination of a wide range of skeletally based parameters from even highly fragmentary and friable burned remains. The unique skills of forensic anthropologists in the interpretation of heat-altered remains are well documented experimentally (Mayne Corriea, 1997) and as applied to fatal fire victims and commercial cremations (Maples, 1997a). A brief review of these benefits is provided below.

Element Identification and Determination of Significance

The expertise that forensic anthropologists can bring to the recognition and identification of severely fragmented and heat-modified bone is unique within the forensic sciences and ensures all bone associated with the fire incident is properly identified (Bass, 1984; Heglar, 1984). Skeletal inventories are often produced which allow for the analysis of body portions represented (i.e., specific bone presence/absence patterns) and a minimum number of individual (MNI) estimates (Ubelaker, 1989). This osteological expertise is especially useful in situations in which extreme temperatures have significantly altered the form and appearance of non-osseous materials associated with the fire (e.g., glass, wood, leather, insulation, etc.). Following exposure to fire, some of these materials possess secondary characteristics, which may cause them to be mistaken for bone by nonexperts.

Occasionally, household pets, domesticated animals, and even undesirable taxa (e.g., rats, mice, skunks) associated with human dwellings are caught and destroyed in fires. Forensic anthropologists can uniquely differentiate burned and fragmented human bones from those of animals.

Research conducted on heat-altered human bones has identified sequences of color changes in bone that indirectly provide evidence of fire temperature or fire duration (Shipman et al., 1984; Ubelaker, 1989) and even whether the body was burned in the flesh or in the dry state (i.e., devoid of soft tissue) (Baby, 1954; Buikstra and Swegle, 1987; Thurman and Wilmore, 1980).

Personal Identification

In many cases, the identity of the victim represented by burned human remains cannot be conclusively determined via traditional methods (especially odontology). These cases often involve commercially processed cremains (Maples, 1997a), very young individuals (no dental records), melted and/or missing dental amalgams, and significant destruction of dental structures (the result of heat affecting enamel). The coroner/medical examiner may then turn to the forensic anthropologist for aid in providing at least presumptive identification via osteological parameters. As is well documented, the forensic anthropologist is highly skilled in providing assessments of basic biological parameters (e.g., age, sex, stature, and ancestry) for even the most fragmentary specimens (Bass, 1995; Stewart, 1979; Ubelaker, 1989). Forensic anthropologists are also familiar with the range of skeletal non-metric variation (evident in gross examination and radiographically), enabling them to isolate unique and/or idiosyncratic features of the remains, which may ultimately lead to a positive identification (Krogman and Iscan, 1986; Ubelaker, 1989).

Trauma Analysis

Another important benefit of forensic anthropological analytical perspectives in the analysis of heat-altered human remains is the interpretation of trauma affecting skeletal tissues. Particularly significant is determining the timing of traumatic events, specifically differentiating perimortem from postmortem (i.e., fire-related) skeletal trauma. Criteria and methods utilized to accomplish this level of analysis are fully described in the forensic anthropological literature (e.g., Berryman and Symes, 1998; Maples, 1986; Rhine and Curran, 1990; Sauer, 1984).

Level II Data Collection: The Postmortem Examination

The opportunity for the second level of data collection occurs during the postmortem examination. The forensic autopsy is very similar to an archaeological excavation; in both cases, the process alters and/or destroys relationships and associations of primary evidence. In order to enhance interpretation, it is suggested that the forensic anthropologist work closely with the forensic pathologist during the autopsy (Symes and Smith, 1998), especially in cases involving severely burned human remains. It is important to document the condition and original disposition of the body (i.e., context), clothing associated with the body, and non-fire trauma of the soft tissue (e.g., bite marks [Stimson and Mertz, 1997]) and skeletal tissue, prior to the autopsy. During the autopsy, information such as collection and transport methods and burn patterns on the body can be gathered, allowing for more accurate reconstruction of manner of death and events surrounding the death. Further, as described above, the anthropologist can provide unique perspectives at the autopsy table with respect to identification and inventory of elements, differentiation of human from animal remains, provision of radiographic determinations of age and sex, identification of unique skeletal structures potentially useful for positive identification, and differentiation of postmortem from perimortem trauma.

Forensic Anthropology and Mass-Fatality Incidents

A strong case can be made for the side-by-side postmortem examination of victims conducted by the forensic anthropologist and pathologist during the documentation phase of most mass-fatality incidents. For example, many of the victims of the recent Korean Airline (KAL) Flight 801 crash on the island of Guam were severely burned. Documentation of even basic biological parameters (via examination of soft tissue) for many of the more complete bodies was hampered by the burned state of the remains. Through excision and gross examination of specific skeletal regions of the body (e.g., pubic symphyses, auricular areas, and sternal end of clavicle) and radiographic examination, forensic anthropologists were able to provide skeletal age, sex, stature, and ancestry information, and in some cases, establish personal identification through the recognition of unique skeletal features.

In some fire-related forensic cases, the context is sufficiently obvious that both identity, and cause and manner of death can be accurately reconstructed by the forensic anthropologist, pathologist, and dentist who are not involved directly in the recovery of the remains. Such an instance is illustrated in Case 1 described below.

Figure 23.1 View of the fire victim (in classic pugilistic pose) situated in the passenger seat of a burned automobile.

Case 1: Forensic Anthropological Contributions to Identity and Trauma Analysis of the Fire Victim at Autopsy

In the pre-dawn hours of a late January morning, a trucker traveling south on a major interstate in northwestern Pennsylvania noticed a burning car by the side of the road and notified the state police. After the fire was extinguished, fire investigators noted a charred human in the passenger seat (Figure 23.1). At his feet was a gasoline container. Fortunately, the VIN number of the vehicle was not destroyed and ownership of the car was traced to an orthodontist living in Detroit. The forensic pathologist called the forensic anthropologist to the autopsy for consultation. The postmortem examination revealed a nearly intact dentition, though surrounded by charred tissue which obscured details. As expected, the cranium was significantly damaged by the fire and highly fragmented, and it was not possible to determine at the autopsy table whether perimortem trauma was represented. The destruction of the femur–tibia joints was initially interpreted as perimortem damage, until examination by the forensic anthropologist led to reinterpretation as postmortem fire damage. The only perimortem skeletal trauma noted on the postcranium was exhibited by two cervical vertebrae (Figure 23.2, left). The damage was linear in nature and initial hypotheses suggested that the defects resulted from a knife or screwdriver driven through the neck of the victim.

The cervical vertebrae, cranium, and mandible were removed from the body and taken to the forensic anthropology laboratory for detailed skeletal trauma analysis. Following removal of soft tissue debris, the dentition revealed a relatively unique dental apparatus and, in conjunction with radiographic comparisons, allowed the forensic odontologist to provide a positive identification. The reconstruction of the two fragmented cervical vertebrae (Figure 23.2, right) clearly showed impact from a gunshot projectile. The bone-beveling pattern provided determinations of entrance and exit defects as well as direction of gunshot in three planes. Defect diameter provided a rough estimate of the caliber of the bullet (presented in the form of an upper size limit and a best-guess range). The

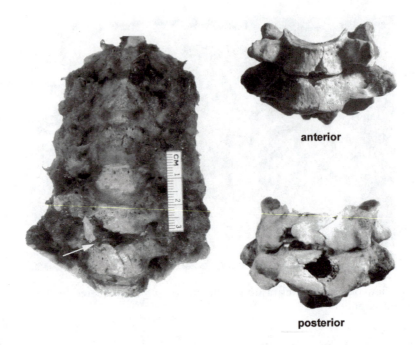

Figure 23.2 Left: ventral view of excised cervical vertebrae of fire victim at autopsy exhibiting potential undefined perimortem damage to cervical vertebrae 5 and 6 (arrow). Right: ventral (anterior) and dorsal (posterior) views of C5 and C6 following maceration and conjoining of all fragments. Note roughly circular defect indicating entrance wound in anterior view and roughly circular defect indicating exit wound in posterior view.

investigators interviewed suspects, who provided a description of the events surrounding the death, which closely matched the interpretive results of the forensic anthropological analysis. The case was solved in 3 days even though the body was transported over 2 state lines and was severely burned.

This case illustrates another benefit of including the forensic anthropologist during the postmortem examination: namely, that the anthropologist has techniques that permit safe and effective removal of charred soft tissue that often obscures morphological details (Maples, 1997b). This, in turn, facilitates: (1) odontological analysis (dental structures are more accurately documented if devoid of flesh and the mandible and maxilla are separated) a process which does not require resection/excision of dental remains (Morlang, 1997; Sperber, 1997), resulting in significant bone destruction; (2) refitting of bone fragments associated with perimortem skeletal trauma, permitting an extremely accurate trauma pattern reconstruction; and (3) courtroom presentation of the evidence in the form of skeletal material which is more palatable and presentable to a jury than those containing injured soft tissue.

In many other fire-related forensic cases, however, especially those involving bodies in houses or outdoor contexts, data relevant to determining manner of death and circumstances surrounding the death are simply not available. Their absence is due to the improper, ineffectual, or even destructive nature of the collection, documentation, and preservation of physical evidence and contextual data. This common situation is illustrated in Case 2 below.

Figure 23.3 Close-up of fire-damaged human remains within house structure.

Case 2: Loss of Information Due to Recovery and Preservation Methods

A call to the local municipal police in a rural town of northwestern Pennsylvania regarding the disappearance of an estranged husband led authorities to an isolated cabin recently purchased by the missing man. The police found the small cabin totally destroyed by fire. A search of the premises revealed a highly charred set of human remains in the middle of the cabin (Figure 23.3). The scene and remains were photographed and the body placed in a body bag for transport to the morgue for a postmortem examination the next morning. The pathologist notified the forensic anthropologist of the nature of the case and requested his presence during the autopsy. The circumstances surrounding the case (i.e., recent purchase, then destruction, of the isolated cabin; cabin owner a known drug dealer) indicated that extreme caution and care should be taken in the identification of the remains as well as reconstruction of circumstances of death.

During the postmortem examination, wire from an underwire bra associated with the remains was recovered. However, the nature of the association (worn by the individual at the time of death?) was indeterminable, because the *in situ* location of the artifact was not noted during recovery. Further, the gracility of the bones and individual skeletal features initially led to the suggestion that the individual represented a female and not the male owner of the cabin. The manner of death would quickly turn to an assignment of homicide rather than suicide or accidental. It was decided that a detailed forensic anthropological analysis of the remains was required.

The osteological analysis concluded that the individual recovered from the burned cabin was a gracile male. Although significantly fragmented from the intensity of the fire, careful sieving of the burned debris (using geological sieves) led to the recovery of significant portions of the dentition, which, given sufficient (even minimal) antemortem records or radiographs, could provide a positive identification of the individual. However, no dental records were ever found and identification remains presumptive.

The final questions to be addressed are cause and manner of death. Attempts to reconstruct the cranium produced only the cranial base and approximately 25% of the inferior portion of the cranial vault. Examination of the scene photographs showed that the skull, though missing much of the superior portion in its *in situ* position, was much more complete than the final laboratory reconstruction. The large number of very small cranial elements that could not be conjoined to the main cranium portion resulted from both the recovery methods (one of the deputy coroners reported, "The skull just crumbled in my hands.") and the placement and transport of the remains in a flexible body bag that allowed significant additional fragmentation of extremely friable/fragile bone elements. Further, the ultimate disposition of the body (orientation of the body, position of the arms and legs, etc.) was neither carefully noted at the scene nor obtainable from the scene photographs. The cause and manner of death of this individual remain undetermined.

Level I Data Collection: *In Situ* Recovery of Remains at Fire Scenes

As described above, non-archaeological recovery methods commonly employed almost invariably lead to loss of both osteological material (due to non-recognition of burned and modified human bones as well as a lack of sieving techniques) and contextual data including associated physical evidence, environmental setting, and body position and orientation).

When the recovery consists of overhauling or removing all debris from a room, often by tossing it out the closest window (Barracato, 1979) or bulldozing the scene (King and King, 1989), contextual information is destroyed. However, most fire investigators today realize that evidence must be carefully recovered and documented and have likened the process to an archaeological investigation: "Like an archaeologist, we fit together a complicated collection of clues that give a general impression and explanation of what happened before and during the fire" (King and King, 1989:72). Removal of fire debris over the remains of the fire victim should be conducted carefully and systematically level by level and be accompanied by comprehensive documentation (written, photographic, and videographic) of the process. This will allow the investigator to "observe, identify, and uncover patterns to form an idea of their relationships and the total picture" (King and King, 1989:72).

Nature of the Physical Evidence at the Fatal Fire Scene

When human remains are encountered at a fire scene, special consideration must be given to rather unique physical evidence associated with the burned body in order to insure that this evidence is carefully documented *in situ*. If a well-trained and experienced fire and arson investigator is not available during this phase of the investigation, the forensic anthropologist must be well acquainted with the scientific and anecdotally based literature regarding (1) the approximation of the intensity (temperature and duration) of the fire in the immediate vicinity of the victim, drawn primarily from descriptions of burning and melting temperatures of various materials (e.g., Redsicker and O'Connor, 1996); (2) fire behavior (e.g., burn paths) derived from charring and melting patterns of various artifacts such as wood, light bulbs, window pane glass (e.g., Brannigen et al., 1980); and (3) fire victim behavior (e.g., location of body in the structure, consideration of clothing apparel relative to time of day and season, examination of medicine cabinets for medicines possibly taken by the victim, locations of small children in closets or under beds, or victim orientation and proximity to windows or other possible escape routes (e.g., Battle and Weston, 1978; King and King, 1989).

Additionally, forensic anthropologists must be well versed in recognizing and providing initial interpretations during the recovery exercise of the effects of heat and direct flame exposure on the human body. Patterns of body and tissue alteration/destruction due to exposure to heat, smoke, and fire are well documented in the literature (e.g., Bass, 1984; Knight, 1991; Redsicker and O'Connor, 1996; Richards, 1977). In some cases, the recognition of unusual relationships (e.g., orientation of body relative to fire patterns) *in situ*, which would not be identifiable once the body was removed from the scene, may be crucial to final interpretation of death events. These observations can then be addressed more fully during the postmortem examination.

Another increasingly important consideration is the proper and appropriate recovery of DNA from a variety of contexts and tissues (Diefenbach, 1998; Weedn, 1997). The forensic anthropologist must be trained in the collection and preservation of this type of material.

Fatal Fire Scene Documentation

There are two key elements to the recovery process of the fatal fire scene: (1) the initial recognition and identification of potentially significant physical evidence and (2) the comprehensive documentation of contextual and associational relationships of the body (biological remains) relative to other physical evidence directly related to the death and the environmental setting (i.e., fire-altered debris).

Context and association are interrelated. As discussed in Dirkmaat and Adovasio (1997), the methodological underpinnings of these concepts, detailed in the archaeological literature, can be applied directly to forensic death scenes. The goal in both is to provide the most accurate possible reconstruction of past events.

Context relates to the theoretical establishment of a particular place at a particular time in the past, whether dealing with the ancient or recent past. Establishing *association* of two or more objects requires that they arrived at the same place at the same time *through the same set of depositional agents* (i.e., as a result of the same set of activities or actions). "If associated, these objects may be considered direct rather than circumstantial indications or reflections of a particular procession event in the past" (Dirkmaat and Adovasio, 1997:40), which is vitally important in both archaeological and forensic interpretations.

In most significant structural fires, debris overlies the victim. This debris is usually deposited in a predicable manner: from upper levels to lower levels, primarily in a horizontal orientation, and in a series of layers (strata) reflecting sequential emplacement events that mirror the original vertical relationships of the structure itself (e.g., basement, upper floor(s), ceiling, and roof). Through the careful uncovering of the structural debris layers, it is possible to more accurately determine the initial location of the body, and possibly even plot the course and sequence of burning events of the structure.

Comprehensive forensic archaeological documentation of the scene involves (1) extensive note taking, (e.g., descriptions of the scene, personnel involved, conditions encountered, and all other details that may be relevant during the reconstruction of the death event), as well as completion of a variety of standardized forms describing these relationships; (2) extensive 35-mm photography (bracketed exposures on color slide and black-and-white print formats) complete with written descriptions (on standardized forms) of the camera, film, and lens used, image photographed, direction of shot, and details of the camera settings (F-stop and speed); (3) videography (sound off) with associated written notes of video sequence and timing; and (4) the drawing of precisely measured plan view and profile maps of the scenes illustrating the orientation and location of the body and other biological materials relative to associated physical evidence (Dirkmaat, 1996). *Only* this level of data collection will allow for the unequivocal reconstruction of context and association of the scene and its contents such that all physical evidence directly related (i.e., in association) to the death event are fully described.

The final stage of the recovery process involves the careful removal of the body and associated physical evidence from the scene. The biological remains are placed in clean white sheets in a body bag containing a solid, flat, and broad underlayment, which should limit damage to the often friable, charred material during transport from the scene.

Site Visitation Following Initial Recovery

If the forensic anthropologist is not called during the initial recovery, especially in suspicious deaths, it is extremely beneficial to visit a fatal fire scene, even after the remains have been collected by law enforcement officials (including the coroner/medical examiner's office), and conduct a search for additional remains (Bass, 1984) or study contextual relationships not originally noted by law or fire officials.

As is illustrated by Case 3, the employment of standard archaeological methodologies during the recovery of burned human remains can produce unique and significant benefits to the forensic investigation even in cases requiring only establishment of identity. Cases 4 and 5, described below, illustrate the benefits of *in situ* recovery to all three of the main issues addressed by forensic anthropologists: (1) identity, (2) manner of death, and especially, (3) reconstruction of taphonomic events surrounding the death.

Case 3: How Many Victims?

This rather uncomplicated issue is very well illustrated by a case in which a tractor-trailer veered off an interstate highway, crashed into the woods, and burned. The cab and occupant(s) were totally destroyed. Company records indicated that the driver was alone; anecdotal evidence, however, suggested that a passenger may have been aboard. The forensic archaeological recovery team carefully excavated the charred debris for identifiable remains, which were provenienced in the field. All of the ash and cremains were taken back to the laboratory for processing through geological sieves. The subsequent analysis provided a biological profile, and even a dental identification, while the lack of duplicated skeletal elements conclusively showed that the driver was indeed alone at the time of the accident.

Case 4: House Fire Victims — Homicide or Accident?

A couple living in rural south-central Pennsylvania awoke late one morning to find their two-story frame house filled with smoke and fire. The husband had finished third shift at the local factory and his wife was napping on the couch. The smoke was so thick in the house that the couple collided in the hall in a frantic search for their two 3-year-old boys. Calls for the boys were not returned and the parents went outside, hoping to find them playing in the woods behind the house. They were not outside and their bodies were found later inside their bedroom closet (Figure 23.4). Reconstruction of the initial fire location pinpointed the boys'

Figure 23.4 View of fire-damaged closet containing the remains of two young fire victims.

bedroom. The father had attempted to re-enter the burning house but could not get into the upper floor due to the heat, fire, and smoke. State police interviews of the mother, however, indicated a suspicious detachment from the event. The remains were not disturbed and the coroner's office called the forensic anthropologist for assistance in the recovery.

The *in situ* recovery consisted of removing a number of layers of burnt rubble from atop the two victims. Following exposure of the bodies, a plan view map was made of the scene, including the position and orientation of the victims and the associated physical evidence (Figure 23.5). The individual farthest from the closet door was on his side while the other boy was lying on his back. The remains were carefully removed from the scene, placed on clean white sheets, and then put into new body bags. In order to limit further damage to the remains, a 2 ft × 4 ft plywood board was placed in each bag beneath the charred remains.

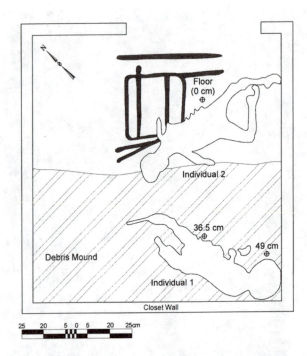

Figure 23.5 Plan-view map showing fire victim location and orientation relative to other physical evidence within the closet.

Radiographs of the entire set of charred remains taken during the postmortem examination revealed a healed fracture of the left distal tibia of one of the boys. These images were compared to an antemortem radiograph of a fractured left tibia suffered by the youngest boy the previous year (Figure 23.6). The location and morphology of the fractures matched.

The boys' tracheae were soot-filled, providing evidence that the boys were still alive when the fire began. The lack of perimortem trauma (aside from fire-related damage) in combination with the contextual reconstruction (including the final position and orientation of the boys) strongly suggested that the manner of death was accidental. The boys may have been playing with matches in their room and, rather than calling their parents when a fire started, panicked and hid in the closet.

Case 5: Homicide and Fire — Attempts To Destroy Evidence

Early on a rather chilly school day in May in south-central Pennsylvania, a woman called the state police when she noticed that a 6-year-old neighbor boy was riding his bicycle without a coat and shoes. The state trooper who responded to the call was told by the boy that his mother never made it home the previous night. Upon entering the dwelling, the police found that the woman, indeed, was not home; her bedroom, however, was awash in blood and the bed sheets and curtains were missing. When the officers made a trip to the house of the estranged husband to notify him of the disappearance, they found him in the backyard tending to a roaring fire in his burn pile. Suspiciously, blood, hair, and bone fragments were found in the bed of his truck, which led to his immediate arrest. The next day, after the fire was out, homicide investigations found a clump of charred tissue and

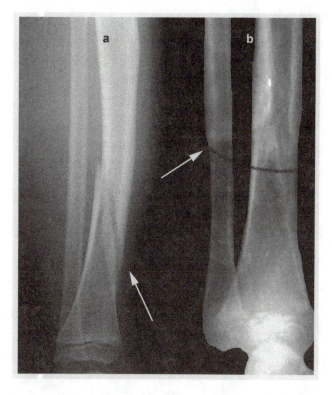

Figure 23.6 Comparison of postmortem (a) and antemortem (b) radiographs of fire victim. Comparison of fracture location and configuration (arrows) allowed for positive identification.

Figure 23.7 General view of fire pit and associated fire-damaged debris located at the back of suspect's house.

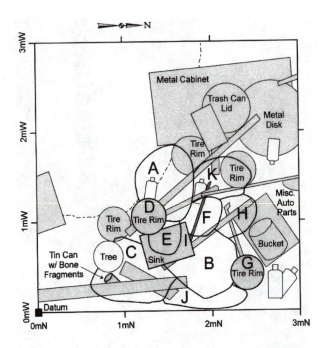

Figure 23.8 Plan-view map of fire-pit scene showing location of each excavation unit.

bone on the edge of the fire feature. The specimen was identified by the forensic anthropologist as a portion of the cervical region of a human. It was suggested that an archaeological recovery would maximize the information associated with the burning event.

The fire feature consisted of a garbage dump in which wood, brush, tires, appliances, glass, food debris, and other items were burned together (Figure 23.7). A north–south excavation baseline was established on the edge of the fire feature. The irregular nature of the feature surface, however, did not allow for the placement of 2 m × 2 m (6.6 ft × 6.6 ft) unit markers. Given the nature of the scene, the burn pile was divided into a series of irregularly shaped excavation units whose dimensions and locations were based on the different substrates present at the scene (Figure 23.8). For example, ash and debris situated on and in a horizontally oriented tire were assigned a unique unit designation different from an adjacent area of the feature that was 6 in. lower. Identifiable bone fragments were plotted *in situ* relative to the baseline and all of the ash and debris associated with a given arbitrary unit were collected in cardboard boxes. This material was taken back to the laboratory where it was sifted carefully through geological sieves, and all bone and teeth fragments collected, preserved, labeled (provenience relative to unit), and catalogued (Figure 23.9).

Subsequent identification and analysis of the entire assemblage of skeletal elements revealed the following information: (1) the coloration of the bones (most were calcined) suggested an intense high-temperature fire of long duration; (2) the fragmentation pattern of the bone, including bone surface cracking, strongly suggested burning of a fleshed victim; (3) only one human individual was represented (no elements duplicated); and (4) the entire skeleton was represented (from cranial elements to hand and feet phalanges). The random distribution of the elements within the fire feature (e.g., cranial elements were identified in 7 of 10 units) strongly suggested that the remains were disturbed (i.e., intentionally fragmented

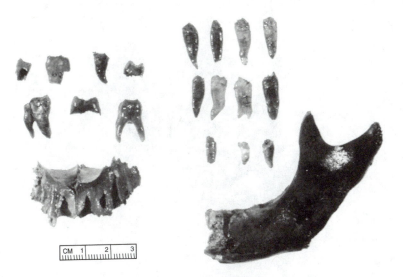

Figure 23.9 Dental, maxillary, and mandibular remains recovered from fire pit.

and scattered) during the intense burning episode. More detailed analysis of the skeletal elements revealed that (5) the victim was middle-aged (based on third molar root development, limited cranial suture fusion patterns, appendicular element epiphyseal-diaphyseal fusion patterns, and especially the fused nature of the sternal clavicular epiphysis); (6) the victim was a female, as indicated by a suite of cranial and pelvic features; and (7) the suggested ancestry was Caucasoid on the basis of mid-facial characteristics. This skeletally based biological profile was consistent with the description of the missing woman. The charred tissue initially recovered by the state police as well as charred bone samples and blood collected from the victim's house and the suspect's truck were submitted to a laboratory for DNA analysis. The results showed no incongruities between the missing woman's DNA structure and the DNA collected from both scenes.

Radiographs of the remaining dentition (tooth root and mandibular alveolar socket morphologies) were compared to antemortem radiographs from the woman's dentist. Interpretation of the results of the comparison between these two data sets differed, however, between anthropologist and the odontologist and the identity remained controversial. A trial date was set for early autumn. A renewed search for additional evidence later in the summer revealed that a number of bone fragments originally collected at the victim's house had not been analyzed. These fragments were identified as cranial elements and one (occipital) was conjoined with the reconstructed cranium recovered from the fire feature (Figure 23.10). Two days before the trial, the suspect pled guilty.

Special Issue: The Role of Heavy Machinery in the Fatal Fire Recovery

In many cases, fires resulting in extensive damage of a multiple-story structure are processed by law enforcement and fire officials via the use of heavy machinery (bulldozers or backhoes), often with the intent to get to the lowest reaches of the scene, assuming that evidence has settled to the bottom of the fire scene (King and King, 1989). Commonly,

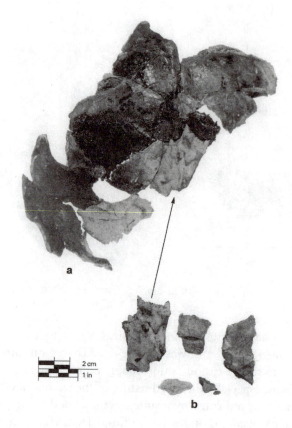

Figure 23.10 Posterior view of reconstructed posterior cranium of fire victim (a) cranial fragments (b) recovered from death scene (victim's bedroom). Note articulation of occipital fragment found in bedroom with the cranial remains found within the suspect's fire pit (arrow).

success in finding human victims is only realized when identifiable human remains are found in the scoop-bucket. Obviously, at that stage of the investigation, the remains have been significantly disturbed from their original context and information loss is significant.

There are cases, however, when the expedient use of heavy machinery in both archaeological (Dirkmaat et al., 1991) and fatal fire scenes (King and King, 1989) is extremely useful. In these special cases, a skilled and experienced machine operator must be combined with careful monitoring of the operation by a trained forensic professional (with a high degree of osteological expertise) in order to ensure success. An example of such a situation is described below in Case 6.

Case 6: Forensic Archaeology and Evidence
Recovery 22 Years after the Crime

In June of 1987, Pennsylvania State Police officials and the author visited a suspected crime scene in western Pennsylvania that was thought to contain the remains of a 16-year-old female victim. The house that formerly stood at the site was suspected to have been the scene of a homicide in 1965. The site was overgrown with brush, grass, and fallen tree branches; all that was visible above the present surface were a few large foundation stones, bricks, and window pane glass. Informant information suggested the victim had been

Figure 23.11 Early stages of forensic archaeological excavation of fire-damaged house structure. Note excavation grid and extensive debris associated with the structure.

cremated in the house and that the structure was burned to the ground shortly thereafter by the suspect. It was concluded that a standard archaeological excavation was required in order to obtain the maximum amount of information.

The excavation and removal of artifactual material from the house structure was accomplished over the course of 4 days by a 4-person recovery crew. On the first day of the project, the general vicinity of the house foundation was photographed and all surface vegetation removed in order to determine ground surface topography (Figure 23.11). A permanent datum point was established and the entire site sectioned into a grid system of 5 ft × 5 ft units. Each unit was photographed and a map of the surface contour and features produced. Excavations of two units on one edge of the site were conducted to (1) establish the location of the wall(s) of the former structure, and (2) determine the depth of the basement floor below the present-day ground surface (thought to be only 1 to 2 ft).

A large quantity of debris (bricks, glass, and foundation stone) was encountered during the excavation of these two units, and it was determined that the basement lay instead 4 to 5 ft below the ground surface. Further, the land owner at the time had bulldozed dirt and burned debris into the open pit of the burned structure for safety purposes. The depth of this disturbed fill, as well as the time constraints placed on the excavations suggested that the use of heavy machinery (i.e., a backhoe) was necessary to economically remove the upper 3 to 4 ft of debris and fill.

The experience and skill of the backhoe operator allowed removal of fill in approximately 6- to 10-in. horizontal levels. The excavated fill was carefully monitored for artifacts during removal as well as during placement of that material outside of the excavation units. Backhoe operation was terminated when 1.5 ft of material above the basement floor remained. At that point, shovels and trowels were utilized.

One area on the basement floor (labeled as Feature 4) contained highly fragmented and burned human skeletal elements (Figure 23.12). Due to the friability and small size of the bones, the need to maximize recovery, and impending adverse weather conditions,

Figure 23.12 Late stages of forensic archaeological excavation of fire-damaged house structure. Note the bed frame and unexcavated matrix at the center of the basement floor (Feature 4) containing concentration of fire-damaged human remains, prior to removal.

it was decided that the feature would be removed intact from the scene and excavated in the laboratory under better conditions. The fill was carefully searched for bone and keep remains, and potentially significant distribution patterns noted within the feature. Finally, the fill was dry-sieved through a series of geological sieves (4-mm, 2-mm, and 1-mm sieves).

A total of 420 identifiable human fragments representing all areas of the body were recovered from Feature 4; no elements were duplicated. No discernible distributional pattern with regard to anatomical position was noted. Features of the pelvic and cranial fragments indicated a female individual, while the developmental patterns evident in the dental remains suggested a mean skeletal age of 16 to 17 years (range of 15 to 20 years). Presentation of the forensic anthropologic recovery and analysis to the defense attorney and suspect resulted in a guilty plea.

Discussion/Overview

Fire investigation, as well as all forensic investigations of death, requires a multidisciplinary effort in order to provide the most informed and accurate interpretation of the events surrounding the death. Fire and law enforcement officials and jurisprudence and forensic specialists must work together to maximize data collection at each of three data collection levels of the investigation, namely, at the scene, at autopsy, and in the laboratory.

Most forensic investigations involving fire victims, however, do not include a forensic anthropologist specifically trained in the archaeological methods of recovery in the early stages. Law enforcement officials conduct data collection efforts at the scene. The forensic pathologist for determination of cause of death takes the remains to the morgue for postmortem examination, while the forensic odontologist is often called upon to corroborate or establish an identification of the victim. If the remains cannot be positively identified at autopsy or via odontology, osteological analysis may be requested, almost exclusively for identification. In rare cases the forensic anthropologist may be included in the investigation at this point to more fully document skeletal trauma related to cause of death.

The manner of death requires input from a variety of specialists from law enforcement through the forensic pathologist and a host of analytical specialists. This multidisciplinary effort revolves around a comprehensive and accurate reconstruction of events surrounding the death. However, at this point of a typical fatal fire investigation, data necessary for the interpretation of context and association of the remains (i.e., body location and orientation) relative to other physical evidence and the scene have been significantly disrupted or destroyed by (1) the lack of comprehensive scene documentation, (2) improper recovery and transport methods, (3) the postmortem examination, and (4) the odontological examination. The primary result is that the reconstruction of manner of death suffers, relying primarily on anecdotal or poorly documented descriptions of the scene.

The full-blown forensic anthropological analysis, including taphonomic analysis of depositional and associative data at the scene, can add information regarding not only victim identity but also cause of death, manner of death, and reconstruction of events surrounding the death. Archaeological methods to document, preserve, and recover physical evidence at the scene as well as anthropological analysis at autopsy and in the laboratory significantly benefit fire scene investigation.

References

Baby, R.S.
    1954 *Hopewell Cremation Practices,* Ohio Historical Society, Papers in Archaeology, No. 1, Columbus, OH.

Barracato, J.S.
    1979 *Fire … Is it Arson?* The Aetna Casualty and Surety Co., Hartford, CT.

Bass, W.M.
    1984 Is it possible to consume a body completely in a fire? In *Human Identification: Case Studies in Forensic Anthropology,* edited by T. Rathbun and J.E. Buikstra, pp. 159–167. Charles C Thomas, Springfield, IL.
    1995 *Human Osteology: A Laboratory and Field Manual,* 4th Ed. Missouri Archaeological Society, Special Publication No. 2, Columbia, MO.

Battle, B.P. and P.B. Weston
    1978 *Arson: Detection and Investigation,* Arco Publishing Company, New York.

Berryman, H.E. and S.A. Symes
    1998 Recognizing gunshot and blunt cranial trauma through fracture interpretation. In *Forensic Osteology II: Advances in the Identification of Human Remains,* edited by K.J. Reichs, pp. 333–352. Charles C Thomas, Springfield, IL.

Brannigan, F.L., R.G. Bright, and N.H. Jason
    1978 Fire Investigation Handbook. National Bureau of Standards Handbook No. 134, U.S. Department of Commerce, Washington, D.C.

Buikstra, J.E., and M. Swegle
    1987 Bone modification due to burning: experimental evidence. In *Bone Modification,* edited by R. Bonnichsen and M.H. Sorg, pp. 247–258. Center for the Study of the First Americans, Orono, ME.

Diefenbach, C.A.

1998   DNA in the Forensic Setting: Collection and Preservation Methodologies. Paper presented at the 50th Annual Meeting of the American Academy of Forensic Sciences, San Francisco, CA.

Dirkmaat, D.C.

1991   Applications of Forensic Anthropology: The Recovery and Analysis of Cremated Remains. Paper presented at the 43rd Annual Meeting of the American Academy of Forensic Sciences, Anaheim, CA.

Dirkmaat, D.C., compiler

1996   *Field and Laboratory Methods in the Location, Recovery, and Analysis of Human Remains in a Rural Setting,* Manual prepared for Forensic Archaeology Short Course, Mercyhurst College, Erie, PA.

1998a Reconsidering the Scope of Forensic Anthropology: Data Collection Methodologies Prior to the Laboratory. Paper presented at the 50th Annual Meeting of the American Academy of Forensic Sciences, San Francisco, CA.

1998b Forensic Anthropological Recovery and Interpretation of the Fire Victim. Paper presented at the 50th Annual Meeting of the American Academy of Forensic Sciences, San Francisco, CA.

Dirkmaat, D.C. and J.M. Adovasio

1997   The role of archaeology in the recovery and interpretation of human remains from an outdoor forensic setting. In *Forensic Taphonomy: The Postmortem Fate of Human Remains,* edited by W.D. Haglund and M.H. Sorg, pp. 39–64. CRC Press, Boca Raton, FL.

Dirkmaat, D.C., B. Gundy, and E. Siemon

1991   Notes regarding the mechanical excavation of archaeological sites containing human remains. Paper presented at the 31st Meeting of the Northeast Anthropological Association, Waterloo, Ontario.

Heglar, R.

1984   Burned remains. In *Human Identification: Case Studies in Forensic Anthropology,* edited by T. Rathbun and J.E. Buikstra, pp. 148–158. Charles C Thomas, Springfield, IL.

Hochrein, M. J.

1997   Buried crime scene evidence: the application of forensic geotaphonomy in forensic archaeology. In *Forensic Dentistry,* edited by P.G. Stimson and C.A. Mertz, pp. 83–99. CRC Press, Boca Raton, FL.

1998   An Autopsy of the Grave: The Preservation of Forensic Geotaphonomic Evidence. Paper presented at the 50th Annual Meeting of the American Academy of Forensic Sciences, San Francisco, CA.

King, C.G. and S. King

1989   The archaeology of fire investigation, *Fire Engineering* 142(6):70–74.

Knight, B.

1991   *Forensic Pathology,* University Press, New York.

Krogman, W.M., and M.Y. Iscan

1986   *The Human Skeleton in Forensic Medicine,* 2nd ed. Charles C Thomas, Springfield, IL.

Maples, W.R.

1986   Trauma analysis by the forensic anthropologist. In *Forensic Osteology: Advances in the Identification of Human Remains,* edited by K.J. Reichs, pp. 218–228. Charles C Thomas, Springfield, IL.

1997a Forensic anthropology. In *Forensic Dentistry,* edited by P.G. Stimson and C.A. Mertz, pp. 65–81. CRC Press, Boca Raton, FL.

1997b Forensic anthropology. In *Medicolegal Death Investigation: Treatises in the Forensic Sciences,* edited by Y.H. Caplan, pp. 160–175. Forensic Sciences Foundation Press, Colorado Springs, CO.

Mayne Correia, P.M.
1997   Fire modification of bone: a review of the literature. In *Forensic Taphonomy: The Postmortem Fate of Human Remains*, edited by W.D. Haglund and M.H. Sorg, pp. 275–294. CRC Press, Boca Raton, FL.

Morlang, W.M.
1997   Mass disaster management. In *Forensic Dentistry*, edited by P.G. Stimson and C.A. Mertz, pp. 185–236. CRC Press, Boca Raton, FL.

Morse, D., J. Duncan, and J. Stoutamire
1983   *Handbook of Forensic Archaeology and Anthropology*, Rose Printing, Tallahassee, FL.

Nawrocki, S.P.
1998   Excavation and Analysis of Human Remains from the Fox Hollow Serial Homicide Site, Hamilton County, Indiana. Paper presented at the 50th Annual Meeting of the American Academy of Forensic Sciences, San Francisco, CA.

Redsicker, D.R. and J.J. O'Connor
1996   *Practical Fire and Arson Investigation*, 2nd ed. CRC Press, Boca Raton, FL.

Rhine, J.S. and B. Curran
1990   Multiple gunshot wounds of the head: an anthropological view, *Journal of Forensic Sciences* 35(5):1236–1245.

Richards, A.F.
1977   Fire investigation — destruction of corpses, *Medicine, Science and the Law* 17(2):79–82.

Sauer, N. J.
1984   Manner of death: skeletal evidence of blunt and sharp instrument wounds. In *Human Identification: Case Studies in Forensic Anthropology*, edited by T. Rathbun and J.E. Buikstra, pp. 176–184. Charles C Thomas, Springfield, IL.

Shipman, P., G. Foster, and M. Schoeninger
1984   Burnt bones and teeth: an experimental study of color, morphology, crystal structure and shrinkage. *Journal of Archaeological Science* 2:307-325.

Skinner, M. and R.A. Lazenby
1983   *Found! Human Remains: A Field Manual for the Recovery of the Recent Human Skeleton*, Archaeology Press, Simon Fraser University, Burnaby, B.C.

Sperber, N.
1997   Forensic odontology (dentistry). In *Medicolegal Death Investigation: Treatises in the Forensic Sciences*, edited by Y.H. Caplan, pp.176–195. Forensic Sciences Foundation Press, Colorado Springs, CO.

Stewart, T.D.
1979   *Essentials of Forensic Anthropology: Especially as Developed in the United States*, Charles C Thomas, Springfield, IL.

Stimson, P.G. and C.A. Mertz
1997   Bite mark techniques and terminology. In *Forensic Dentistry*, edited by P.G. Stimson and C.A. Mertz, pp. 137–159. CRC Press, Boca Raton, FL.

Symes S.A. and O.C. Smith
1998   It Takes Two: Combining Disciplines of Pathology and Physical Anthropology to Get the Rest of the Story. Paper presented at the 50th Annual Meeting of the American Academy of Forensic Sciences, San Francisco, CA.

Thurman, M.D. and L.J. Wilmore
1980   Replicative cremation experiment, *North American Archaeology* 2:275–283.

Ubelaker, D.H.
    1989   *Human Skeletal Remains: Excavation, Analysis, Interpretation*, 2nd ed. Taraxacum, Washington, D.C.
Weedn, V.W.
    1997   DNA identification. In *Forensic Dentistry*, edited by P.G. Stimson and C.A. Mertz, pp. 37–46. CRC Press, Boca Raton, FL.

The Use of DNA in the Identification of Postmortem Remains

24

MICHELE HARVEY
MARY-CLAIRE KING

Contents

Introduction

Genetic analysis has become a fundamental component of the identification of postmortem remains. With technical advances in biotechnology and an increase in our understanding of the human genome, applications of human molecular genetics have impacted the fields of archeology (Brown and Brown, 1994; Foley, 1998; Hagelberg et al., 1991), evolutionary biology (Krings et al., 1997; von Haesler, 1996; Handt et al., 1996), medical sciences (Bucket, 1998; Elles, 1997; Lupski, 1998; White, 1996), and, of most importance for this readership, the forensic sciences (for review, see Alford, 1994; Benecke, 1997; NRC, 1992; 1996; Raymond, 1989). The use of current genetic techniques can determine individual identity with minute amounts of biological material, allowing for unprecedented accuracy and versatility.

The aim of this chapter is to provide a summary of techniques and approaches that laboratories have chosen for the genetic analysis of postmortem remains. Since many publications, including one in the first edition of this text (Parsons and Weedn, 1997), have thoroughly described the structure and function of DNA (Strachan and Read, 1999), genetic technology (Benecke, 1997; Decorte, 1993), and particular concerns of forensic genetic techniques (Lee et al., 1994, 1998), we do not present such information in this chapter. We instead explain the different approaches available for the genetic analysis of postmortem remains, as well as advantages and disadvantages of each approach. We provide case studies to illustrate each approach.

In the last decade, multiple genetic approaches have been developed for the identification of postmortem remains and missing persons. All genomic approaches involve the comparison of the genetic composition of one sample (the remains) to another (a potential biological relative). Autosomal, or nuclear, DNA methods include HLA typing (Di Leonardo et al., 1984; Lee, 1982), Y-chromosome genotypes (Foster et al., 1998; Underhill et al., 2000), and repeat loci (Parsons et al., 1997). Because one of two autosomal chromosomes is inherited from each parent, autosomal DNA comparison between a child and a parent will reveal 50% identical sequences. That is, a genetic screen comparison of parent and child should show one of every two alleles to be identical. This concept is fundamental to paternity testing. The most frequently used non-autosomal DNA method is mitochondrial DNA sequencing. The mitochondrial genome and Y-chromosome are inherited from the mother and father, respectively. Genetic analysis of mitochondrial sequence or Y-chromosomal markers, therefore, reveals maternal and paternal lineages.

Genetic markers used in forensic genetic analysis are chosen by their degree of variability. Regions of the genome with greater variability in the general population will have an increased chance of being different in two unrelated individuals. Inherent in this premise is that if two individuals have the same sequence in these variable regions, they are more likely to be biologically related. This approach is not unlike that established over a century ago for the use of fingerprints. After proving that in a large sampling of the population each had a unique fingerprint, criminal investigators were able to use fingerprints as a legally accepted means of verifying identity. Similarly, in the forensic postmortem identification, DNA from sets of remains (soft tissue, tooth, or bone) is compared to DNA from blood or tissue samples of putative relatives.

Autosomal markers have been the most widely used tools for identifications. As a result of the human genome project, thousands of sequences have been mapped and their variability in the general population calculated; see http://www.ncbi.nlm. nih.gov/UniGene/Hs.Home.html or http://www.cephb.fr/cgibin/wdb/ceph/system/form.

Microsatellite markers are, at the moment, used most widely in the forensic community because they can be analyzed with technical ease and display a high degree of variability. Automation of specific sets of microsatellites facilitates analysis, storage, quality control, and data networking. The latter has been particularly important in establishing national and international databases for the purpose of tracing serial criminals (Dabbs et al., 1988).

The use of mitochondrial DNA (mtDNA) has become increasingly important in forensic analysis (Ginther et al., 1992). A unique feature of mtDNA is its maternal inheritance pattern (Giles et al., 1980); that is, an individual will have the same mitochondrial sequence as that of his or her mother, maternal grandmother, maternal aunt and uncles, etc. Therefore, in those cases where immediate relatives are not available to give blood samples for comparison, mitochondrial DNA is a potential tool for determining identity. The mitochondrial genome, composed of 16,569 base pairs (bp) (Anderson, 1991), also harbors one of the most variable segments of the human genome, the hypervariable region (HVR). The extreme variability of this 1200 base-pair region can distinguish most maternal families (Stoneking et al., 1991). Finally, the mitochondrial genome is inherited only through one parent, the mother, which simplifies statistical analysis of the result.

Y-chromosomal analysis is also becoming an important tool for anthropological, historical, and forensic purposes (De Knijff et al., 1997; Jobling et al., 1997; Kayser et al., 1997; Underhill et al., 2000). The Y-chromosome also has a uni-parental inheritance pattern although it is paternally inherited. This type of analysis is particularly important for cases in which only distant male relatives are available for reference samples. Since the Y-chromosome is only inherited through the paternal lineage, it (like mtDNA) is haploid. Therefore, the analysis of the genetic results is simplified. For identification purposes, combinations of markers that distinguish different regions of the chromosome are available and used to distinguish specific genotypes.

In the cases where only distant relatives are available for reference samples (maternal or paternal), autosomal markers are not as useful for determining identity. An individual inherits one copy of every chromosome from each of his/her parents. Therefore, apart from monozygotic twins, the closest genetic relationship is between a child and a parent. Barring mutations, 50% of the alleles of a child would be identical to a parent. The next closest genetic relationship is that of full siblings who would share, on average, half of all alleles. They may also, though, lack any shared alleles in up to 25% of all loci (Ballantyne, 1997). As the relationship distance increases, the probability of the two individuals having the same alleles decreases. The Y-chromosome of father and son and of full brothers would be identical. The mitochondrial genome between mother and child, and of full siblings would also be identical.

There is an inherent weakness in the use of Y-chromosomal genotypes and mitochondrial DNA sequence for identification. Because the analyses determine paternal and maternal lineage, respectively, they are not able to distinguish between relatives of the same family. For example, if a mother and daughter are to be identified, the use of mitochondrial DNA sequence could determine that they are from the same biological family. The sequence would not distinguish which is the mother and which is the daughter. Obviously, Y-chromosomal analysis in this case would be futile as only males carry the Y-chromosome. However, classical forensic methods and nuclear marker information, combined with the mitochondrial DNA sequence information would differentiate the two individuals from each other and from other victims.

The following text describes the advantages and disadvantages of using particular genetic approaches for identification purposes. Included with each method is a case study that illustrates how each technique has been used. It is our expectation that this combination of descriptions and case studies will provide the reader with a fundamental understanding of the variety of approaches that can be used for genetic identification in forensic cases.

HLA Typing

For over 20 years, serologically based HLA typing has been recognized as a means of identifying individuals and determining relationship (Di Leonardo et al., 1984; Lee, 1982). The HLA genes are a subset of the genes within the major histocompatibility complex (MHC), which spans approximately 4,000,000 base pairs on the short arm of chromosome 6. The HLA genes are, therefore, autosomal genes. The MHC molecules are divided into three classes (I, II, and III) according to structure, alloreactivity, and function (Doherty and Nepom, 1990). Most importantly for identification purposes, two MHC class II molecules have been useful: HLA-DRB1 and HLA-DQ. The advantages of HLA typing are the amount of population information that is available, the reliability of the method, the high degree of variability of the HLA haplotypes, the ease of the techniques, and the large numbers of laboratories capable of HLA typing.

Since HLA haplotype information is important both medically and anthropologically, most of the world's populations have been genotyped for multiple HLA loci. Public databases have been established to allow access to worldwide HLA haplotype information (http://www.swmed.edu/home_pages/ASHI/sequences/; Teraski and Gjertson, 1997). HLA-DQ has been used in judicial cases worldwide as a means of identification (Decorte, 1994) and, therefore, is recognized in numerous legal systems. On the other hand, HLA-DRB1 is one of the most variable HLA genes with over 112 known alleles, and is, therefore, one of the most informative nuclear markers available (Doherty and Nepom, 1990). Initially, HLA typing was a serological test and an investigator needed 20 or 30 ml of fresh blood for the protein-based analytical techniques. With the introduction of polymerase chain reaction (PCR), analysis of the HLA locus could be performed with minute quantities of biological material. PCR-based kits for HLA haplotype determinations were widely marketed, allowing for systematic and routine analysis (Decorte, 1994).

The informative nature of the HLA locus for identification purposes is illustrated in the following case study.

Case Study

During the military dictatorship between 1975 and 1983 in Argentina, security forces kidnapped, tortured, and murdered approximately 8800* people, now referred to as the "Disappeared" (Amnesty International, 1995). A number of those kidnapped were children and pregnant women. Most of the pregnant women were kept alive until they gave birth, after which they were killed. The babies were trafficked. At least 250 children were kidnapped and kept or sold by military personnel. A group of grandmothers, the Abuelas de la Plaza de Mayo, organized themselves to protest the disappearances and to demand the

---

* The number of documented kidnapped individuals is 8800. Human rights organizations believe the number of individuals is closer to 15,000.

whereabouts of their children and grandchildren. Various types of evidence, falsified birth certificates, testimonies from released abductees, or statements from neighbors who noticed an unforeseen child in a household, led the Abuelas to believe that many of the grandchildren were still alive. It was immediately obvious to the Abuelas and to the scientific community, that nontraditional means of identification were necessary to identify the missing grandchildren. Genetic techniques and statistical formulations were created to establish the relationship between the grandchild and the grandparent, without the availability of the genetic material of the parents.

On February 5, 1977, when trying to obtain their passports, Stella Maris Gallichio and her 8-month-old daughter, Ximena, were detained at the federal police department. Stella has not been seen since. Eight years later, through an anonymous tip regarding clandestine adoptions, the Abuelas located a girl approximately 8 years old. The child was registered (under a different name) as the daughter of an orphanage worker. Because of circumstantial evidence and the child's physical similarity to Stella Maris Gallichio, it was hypothesized that the child could be Ximena. Blood samples were obtained from her and from the maternal grandmother of Ximena. HLA testing revealed that this girl was the daughter of Stella Mans Gallichio, to a 99.82% probability (King, 1991; Penchaszadeh, 1992, 1997).

Since the inception of efforts to find the children of the Disappeared of Argentina, HLA typing and mitochondrial DNA sequencing (see below) have successfully identified 63 of the estimated 250 kidnapped children.

Minisatellite and Microsatellite Markers

Autosomal markers for the identification of postmortem remains have been used routinely in the last decade. The first documented case of the isolation, amplification and analysis of DNA from bone of a murder victim was by Hagelberg in 1991 (Hagelberg et al., 1991). There are two types of nuclear markers frequently used for identification purposes: VNTR loci (*variable number of tandem repeats* or minisatellite markers), and microsatellite markers. VNTR loci are regions in the genome that vary in size as a result of having varying numbers of tandem repeat sequences. For analysis, the sequences are cleaved by specific restriction endonucleases (enzymes) to produce fragments of different lengths; these are visualized using Southern blotting and probe techniques. Microsatellite sequences are intermediately sized regions (0.1 to 2.0 kb long), interspersed throughout the genome, composed of short, tandemly repeating units, most often between 1 and 4 bases (Strachan and Read, 1999). Identifications require analyses of multiple minisatellites. For forensic purposes, microsatellites present several advantages: (1) they can be typed using PCR; (2) single base changes can be visualized because the genomic fragments are relatively small; (3) also, because the genomic fragments are small, typing is possible on particularly deteriorated samples.

Thousands of mini- and microsatellite markers have been documented. There is public access to these databases, and to multiple parameters of specific loci: http://www.cephb.fr/cgi-bin/wdb/ceph.fr/cgi-bin/wdb/ceph/system/form, and http://www.ncbi.nlm.nih.gov/UniGene/Hs.Home.html. Several particular markers, though, are used most frequently in the forensic community due to automation and technological ease. A commonly used set of markers is D3S1358, vWA, FGA, Amelogenin (for determination of sex), D8S1179, D21S11, D18S51, D5S818. D13S317, D7S820. Although any one of these markers would not provide sufficient specificity to make an identification, the combination of markers can provide a high probability. It should be noted, however, that many other markers are available for establishing identity. As the following case study will reveal, as long as the markers are internally consistent and have a high degree of variability in the population being studied, they may be sufficient for identification.

Case Study

On August 29, 1996, a Tupolev 154 aircraft carrying 128 passengers and 13 crew members crashed into the Opera Mountain. All 64 Russian and 77 Ukrainian citizens on board were killed. Because of the lack of particularly informative antemortem data, it was decided that DNA analysis was to be a main component of the identification effort. In total, 257 fragments of remains were collected and 182 reference samples were obtained from relatives. Of the 141 victims, reference samples were obtained for 139. Of these 139, 109 had only one reference sample (from a parent or a sibling). The remaining 30 cases had two or three reference samples.

To identify the victims, Olaisen et al. (1997) chose eight nuclear markers. The amelogenin marker was used for sex determination, three microsatellite loci (HUMACTBP2, IRJMAPOAI1, and Dl1S554) and five minisatellite loci (D2S44, D7S21, D7S22, D11S12, and D5S110) were used for further individual identification. Complete DNA profiles were obtained from the reference samples and all body fragments. Multiple fragments from the same body could be matched if they had an identical DNA profile. None of the 141 victims shared the same DNA profile. Genetic data were compiled in a spreadsheet format, and searches were carried out to match the parent/sibling and sibling/sibling pairs by comparing the DNA profile of the relative with those of the victims. Of the 145 relations, 141 matched at all loci. The four remaining relations were matched, although seven of the eight alleles were shared. These differences could be attributed to mutational changes to the divergent one allele, confirming the observed mutation frequency of approximately 0.004 per locus.

This particular case is noteworthy as the genetic identifications were made extremely quickly, accurately and inexpensively, setting a precedent for the use of genetic identification techniques when antemortem information is not available. Within 22 days of the accident, all of the bodies had been identified, their relations notified, and the bodies returned to Russia and the Ukraine. The genetic identification probabilities ranged between 1 in 491 to 1 in 1012. The cost of the DNA investigation was approximately 3 to 5% of the total cost of the whole identification effort. It is interesting to note that solely through external examination and genetic identification the bodies could not have been identified (Olaisen et al., 1997). Therefore, it may be of benefit for rapid action mass disaster forensic teams to incorporate genetic techniques in their repertoire.

Y-Chromosome

Recently, with increased knowledge of the human genome, Y-chromosomal analysis has become an important tool for male-specific identifications. The unique feature of the Y-chromosome is its paternal inheritance pattern, allowing paternal lineages to be identified and traced. This unilateral inheritance pattern also makes the analysis of genotypes simpler than autosomal chromosomal markers. In identifying a paternal lineage, a number of Y-chromosomal markers are used, as one marker is not sufficiently variable to determine identity.

Bi-allelic, minisatellite, and microsatellite markers on the Y-chromosome have been used in population-based studies (Cavalli-Sforza, 1998; De Knijff et al., 1997, Pierez-Lezaun et al., 1997), anthropology studies (De Knijff et al., 1997; Heyer et al., 1997), and for identification purposes (Jobling et al., 1997). The most studied polymorphic markers studied to date are DYS19, DYS288, DYS285, DYS388, DYS389I/II, DYS390, DYS391, DYS392, DYS393, YCAI, YCAII, YCAIII, and DXYS156Y, which have been used in a multicenter study (Kayser et al., 1997). Although the databases available for statistical analysis do not yet contain the quantity of data that the mitochondrial or nuclear marker databases do, they are sufficient to determine the probable paternal lineage of an individual as shown in the following case study.

Case Study

In 1802, President Thomas Jefferson was accused of fathering a child by Sally Hemings, one of his slaves. Various pieces of information were presented as evidence for this accusation. First, several of Sally Hemings' children (she had five) bore a physical resemblance to Jefferson. Second, one of Hemings' sons testified that Hemings had identified Jefferson as the father of her children. Finally, Jefferson was in the same residence as Hemings at the time of conception of each child. Many historians claimed the likely father was a maternal cousin.

In order to resolve this controversy, geneticists in England and The Netherlands gathered blood samples from multiple male-line descendants of Sally Hemings: her last son, Eston; her first son, Thomas Woodson; Thomas Jefferson's paternal uncle, Field Jefferson; and John Carr, the grandfather of the maternal cousin who was claimed to have fathered the children. Nineteen polymorphic markers on the Y-chromosome were analyzed. Four of the five undisputed descendants of Jefferson shared the same genotype. The fifth differed by a single repetitive unit at one locus, which indicated that the genotype was most likely the same nine generations ago and a small genetic change had occurred since that time. Of the descendants of Thomas Woodson, four of the five male descendants shared the same genotype and the fifth differed considerably from the others, indicating nonpaternity at some time in that line. Two of the three descendants of John Carr matched each other genetically; the third differed by one repetitive unit at one locus, indicating all three descendants were most likely descendants of one paternal line. Finally, the descendant of Eston Hemings was identical to that of the Field Jefferson descendants and different from the descendants of John Carr. These results indicate that President Jefferson could have fathered Eston Hemings.

The genotypes were then compared to databases composed of Y-chromosome microsatellite genotypes (1200 men, 670 of whom are European) and minisatellite genotypes (690 men, 308 of whom are European). The frequency of the Jefferson genotype is less than 0.1%, and is, therefore, considered rare. It should be noted, though, that Y-chromosomal analysis could not distinguish Thomas Jefferson from his brothers or paternal uncles. It also cannot completely rule out that Jefferson was not the father of Sally Hemings' other children, e.g., Thomas Woodson, as nonpaternity in any generation would introduce new Y-chromosomal genotypes in the male lineage (Foster, 1998; Lander and Ellis, 1998). As shown by this example, Y-chromosome analysis can be particularly informative for the determination of paternal relationships and will be useful for establishing identity in those cases where only distant paternal relations are available.

Mitochondrial DNA

Mitochondrial DNA (mtDNA) is used often in most forensic laboratories as a means of establishing identity in cases where nuclear DNA is too degraded, or in such low quantities that nuclear markers cannot be used (Ginther et al, 1992). MtDNA can also be used in cases in which distant maternal relatives are the only source of reference samples (Butler, 1998). Identification of skeletal remains from mass graves has been particularly successful using mitochondrial DNA sequencing (Boles et al., 1995; Primorac et al., 1996; pers. res.).

There are several unique features of mtDNA that make this genome particularly useful in the identification of postmortem remains. One of the most informative sequences in the human genome is the replication region of mitochondrial DNA (hypervariable region, HRV). Also, mitochondrial DNA is maternally inherited (Giles et al., 1980). Thus, an individual will have the same mtDNA sequence as his or her siblings, mother, maternal grandmother, or any other relative in the maternal lineage (e.g., mother's brother). Therefore, one need not sequence from multiple relatives to identify the family of the victim. Mitochondria are severalfold more plentiful than nuclei; therefore, mtDNA is more abundant per cell than nuclear DNA. This is particularly relevant for remains with a long postmortem interval or that are in very poor condition. The mitochondrial genome has been an important tool for anthropological studies, especially those concerning human evolution (Cavalli-Sforza, 1998; Howell et al., 1996; Vigilant et al., 1989; von Haesler, 1996) Therefore, the genome has been well characterized and frequencies of sequence variants are known for many populations (http://www.gen.emory.edu/mitomap.html).

Heteroplasmy

In the case of mitochondrial DNA, analysis may be confounded by heteroplasmy, i.e., the presence of two or more mitochondrial DNA molecule variants in a single cell or organism. In any one cell, hundreds of thousands of copies of the mitochondrial genome exist. Mutations in this genome occur more frequently than in nuclear DNA, most likely due to the high replication rate. A mitochondrial mutation may originate in one of the hundreds of copies of mtDNA in the cell. Heteroplasmy is identified as two bands of an autoradiogram (or peaks of an electropherogram) thereby confounding sequence determination. In all documented cases of heteroplasmy, only one single base-pair difference is seen (Lightowlers et al., 1997; Paabo, 1996; Parsons et al., 1997). To account for the high mutation rate, laboratories mandate more than one difference between the sequences of two individuals for an exclusion to be made.

The use of mtDNA for the identification of postmortem remains involves, as with nuclear DNA markers, a comparison of DNA sequence between a relative of the missing individual and, typically, a bone or tooth sample from the set of remains (Ginther et al., 1992; Hagelberg, 1991). The 1200 base-pair hypervariable region is PCR amplified (either as a single segment or in multiple segments), sequenced, and a comparison made between the sequences of the two samples. At this point, three outcomes are possible:

1. The two sequences match identically. In this case, the forensic sample could belong to a relative of the family. The probability that a match reflects biological relationship rather than chance is calculated for each case using likelihood methods (King, 1991; McKusick et al., 1992).

2. One difference exists between the forensic sample and the potential relative. Additional physical evidence should be reviewed and further genetic analysis must be undertaken before identity can be established.

3. More than one difference exists between the reference sample and the forensic sample. In this case, the set of remains does not belong to the maternal family to whom the reference sample belongs.

The following case studies illustrate the uses of mitochondrial DNA in forensic investigations.

Identification of Remains from the Vukavar/Ovcara Mass Grave in Croatia

On November 19, 1991, Serbian troops took siege of the town of Vukavar, Croatia, after 3 months of bombing and killing civilians. It was soon learned that hours before a special envoy was going to be sent to evacuate hundreds of patients from a city hospital, Serb forces had stormed the hospital, removed patients and staff, and executed them in a nearby farm outside of the city. Exhumation of the mass grave found in a field of the Ovcara farm, near Vukavar, was undertaken in 1995. Approximately 200 bodies were exhumed. We received tooth and bone samples from 68 of these cases chosen by their tentative identifications in the field. We were also sent 263 blood samples from probable relatives of the victims and 65 population control samples.

We sequenced the mtDNA hypervariable region for all of these samples. By comparing each of the sequences from the tooth samples with the database of the 263 sequences from the potential relatives, we were able to identify 44 of the victims. Nineteen of the victim samples contained mtDNA whose sequence did not match any person in the database of potential relatives, because a blood sample from the maternal lineage of every victim was not available. DNA could not be obtained from three of the forensic samples. The genetic evidence for this Ovcara massacre was combined with the physical evidence and used by the UN War Crimes Tribunal for the trial of the mayor of Vukavar for the murders.

Identification of the Romanov Family

Analysis of postmortem remains using mtDNA has provided identifications since the l980s. One case that received considerable public attention was the identification of the remains of the Romanov family. It was documented that the Bolshevik Army murdered this Russian royal family (the tsar, his wife, four daughters, and one son) on the night of July 16, 1918. Their bodies were later disposed of in an open grave, doused with sulfuric acid, and covered with earth. A mass grave containing 9 sets of remains was located using historical documents. Extensive analysis of the remains led to the possibility that 5 sets of these remains belonged to the Romanov family. MtDNA analysis was undertaken to establish the relationship and possibly the identity of the remains (Gill, 1994).

Bone extracts were obtained and two sections of the mitochondrial genome hypervariable region were sequenced for all samples. A total of 740 nucleotides were determined. Six different sequences were found in the nine samples through pairwise comparison of the nucleotides. The sequences differed, on average, at six bases. Four of the sequences were identical, which corresponded with the putative Tsarina and her three children. A maternal relative of the Tsarina, HRH Prince Philip, the Duke of Edinburgh, provided a blood sample as a reference sample. The comparison of the two sequences, which were identical, led to the conclusion that the remains did, in fact, belong to the Tsarina and her children.

Two maternal relatives of the Tsar were sequenced and used for comparison. One of the sequences from a male skeleton, the putative remains of the Tsar, matched those of the two maternal relatives except at one base pair. Further sequence analysis demonstrated that the single base-pair difference was a result of heteroplasmy. This single base-pair difference, therefore, did not exclude the set of remains belonging to the Tsar (Gill, 1994).

Statistical Analysis

If the genetic composition between the sample from the potential relative and the forensic sample differs, one can firmly conclude that they are not from the same biological family. For example, if a child has several alleles that neither putative parent has, firm conclusions of parental exclusion can be drawn. If all of the loci from the child are also seen in a hypothetical parent, the likelihood ratio must be calculated. This ratio describes the likelihood that two individuals are truly related biologically as opposed to having similar DNA sequences simply by chance. This calculation requires knowing the frequency of each sequence or allele within the relevant population. Choosing a marker with a high degree of variation within a population is extremely relevant at this point. With a greater degree of polymorphism, or variation, at a particular locus within a population, there is less likelihood of a chance match between unrelated individuals and, therefore, also a greater chance of a match between related individuals (King, 1991; McKusick et al., 1992; NRC, 1996).

Public databases (cited above) allow access to worldwide population data for mtDNA sequences, HLA polymorphisms, and different autosomal loci. The frequency of each allele in the relevant population provides the denominator for the likelihood ratio. If the frequencies of a particular locus or haplotype are known, then the expected frequencies can be calculated. In general, the estimate of gene and genotype frequencies improves as the number of population samples examined grows larger (Gaensslen, 1984; McKusick et al., 1992; NRC, 1996).

In the case of a mitochondrial sequence, a simple calculation of the frequency of the sequence in the relevant population can be performed and this estimate provides the likelihood ratio. For Y-chromosomal genotypes, the frequencies of each of the loci must be estimated from the population data. The probability of each can then be calculated, after which each probability is multiplied, yielding the overall probability that such a genotype is found in the population. The likelihood ratio can then be calculated from this probability. The same approach is used for the determination of the likelihood ratio for autosomal genotypes. As more loci are analyzed and when the amount of polymorphism of each locus is great, the derived statistical probability value increases.

Conclusion

The field of genetics is making advances at a tremendous speed. Technological and methodological innovations are advancing, along with our knowledge about the human genome.

One application of this knowledge is to the field of forensics, which has undergone an enormous wave of technological improvements. The genetic approach taken by a forensic investigator clearly depends on the state of the remains, the types of available reference samples, and the facility with which other identification methods can be applied. The explanations of the various approaches, along with case studies as examples, hopefully have provided the reader with a fundamental understanding of how to approach genetic identification of postmortem remains.

References

Alford, R.L. and C.T. Caskey
1994   DNA analysis in forensics, disease and animal/plant identification, *Current Opinion in Biotechnology* 5(1):29–33.

Amnesty International
1995   Argentina: the right to the full truth. Al Index: AMR 13/03/95.

Anderson, C.
1991   DNA fingerprinting discord, *Nature* 354(6354):500.

Anderson, S. et al.
1981   Sequence and organization of the human mitochondrial genome, *Nature* 290:457–470.

Ballantyne, J.
1997   Mass disaster genetic, *Nature Genetics* 15:329–331.

Benecke, M.
1997   DNA typing in forensic medicine and in criminal investigations: a current survey, *Naturwissenschaften* 84:181–l88.

Boles, T.C., C. Snow, and E. Stover
1995   Forensic DNA testing on skeletal remains from mass graves: a pilot project in Guatemala, *Journal of Forensic Sciences* 40(3):349–355.

Brown, T.A. and K.A. Brown
1994   Ancient DNA: using molecular biology to explore the past, *Bioessays* 16(10):719–726.

Bucket, P.
1998   Toward a new natural medicine, *Naturwissenschaften* 85(4):155–163.

Butler, J.M. and B.C. Levin
1998   Forensic applications of mitochondrial DNA, *Trends in Biotechnology* 16(4):158–162.

Cavalli-Sforza, L.L.
1998   The DNA revolution in population genetics, *Trends in Genetics* 14(2):60–65.

Commission on Life Sciences
1992   DNA technology in forensic science, National Research Council, National Academy Press, Washington, D.C.

Committee on DNA Forensic Science
1996   The Evaluation of Forensic DNA Evidence, National Research Council, National Academy Press, Washington, D.C.

Corach, D.A. et al.
1997   Additional approaches to DNA typing of skeletal remains: the search for missing persons killed during the last dictatorship in Argentina. *Electrophoresis* 18:1608–1612.

Dabbs D., P.D. Cornwell, and D.K. Wiecking
  1988 The use of DNA profiling in linking serial murders, *Medical Legal Bulletin* 37(6):1–10.

De Knijff, P. et al.
  1997 Chromosome Y microsatellites: population genetic and evolutionary aspects, *International Journal of Legal Medicine* 110:134–140.

Decorte, R. and J.J. Cassiman
  1993 Forensic medicine and the polymerase chains reaction technique, *Journal of Medical Genetics* 31(11):625–633.

Decorte, R. et al.
  1994 Identification of internal variation in the pseudoautosomal VNTR DXYS17, with nonrandom distribution of the alleles on the X and the Y chromosomes, *American Journal of Human Genetics* 54(3):506-515.

Di Leonardo, A.M. et al.
  1984 Human genetics and human rights: identifying the families of kidnapped children, *American Journal of Forensic Medicine and Pathology* 5(4):339–347.

Doherty, D.G. and G.T. Nepom
  1990 The human major histocompatibility complex and disease susceptibility. In *Principles and Practice of Medical Genetics,* 2nd ed., edited by A.E.H. Emery and D.L. Rimoin, Churchill Livingston, New York.

Elles, R.
  1997 An overview of clinical molecular genetics, *Molecular Biotechnology* 8(2):95–104.

Foley, R.
  1998 The context of human genetic evolution, *Genome Research* 8(4):339–347.

Foster, E.A. et al.
  1998 Jefferson fathered slave's last child, *Nature* 396:27–28.

Gaensslen, R.E.
  1984 Sourcebook in Forensic Serology, Immunology, and Biochemistry. U.S. Department of Justice, National Institute of Justice, Washington, D.C.

Giles, R.E. et al.
  1980 Maternal inheritance of human mitochondrial DNA, *Proceedings of the National Academy of Sciences USA* 77:6715–6719.

Gill, P. et al.
  1994 Identification of the remains of the Romanov family by DNA analysis, *Nature Genetics* 6:130–135.

Ginther, C., L. Issel-Tarver, and M.C. King
  1992 Identifying individuals by sequencing mitochondrial DNA from teeth, *Nature Genetics* 2:135–138.

Hagelberg, E. and J.B. Clegg
  1991 Isolation and characterization of DNA from archaeological bone, *Proceedings of the Royal Society of London: Biological Sciences* 244(1309):45–50.

Hagelberg, E. et al.
  1991 Analysis of ancient bone DNA: Techniques and applications, *Philosophical Transactions of the Royal Society of London, Series B: Biological Sciences* 333(1268):399–407.

Hagelberg, E., I.C. Gray, and A.J. Jeffreys
  1991 Identification of the skeletal remains of a murder victim by DNA analysis, *Nature* 352:427–429.

Handt, O. et al.
  1996 The retrieval of ancient human DNA sequences, *American Journal of Human Genetics* 59:368–376.

Heyer, E.J. et al.
  1997 Estimating Y-chromosome specific microsatellite mutation frequencies using deep rooting pedigrees, *Human Molecular Genetics* 6(5):799–803.

Howell, N., I. Kubacka, and D.A. Mackey
  1996 How rapidly does the human mitochondrial genome evolve? *American Journal of Human Genetics* 59:501–509.

Jobling, M.A., A. Pandya, and C. Tyler-Smith
  1997 The Y chromosome in forensic analysis and paternity testing, *International Journal of Legal Medicine* 110:118–124.

Kayser, M. et al.
  1997 Evaluation of Y-chromosomal STRs: a multicenter study, *International Journal of Legal Medicine* 110:125–133.

King, M.C.
  1991 An application of DNA sequencing to a human rights problem, *Molecular Genetic Medicine* 1:117–131.

Krings, M. et al.
  1997 Neanderthal DNA sequences and the origin of modern humans, *Cell* 90:19–30.

Lander, E.S. and J.J. Ellis
  1998 Founding father, *Nature* 396:13–14.

Lee, H.
  1982 Identification and grouping of blood stains. In *Forensic Science Review*, edited by Saferstein R., pp. 267–337. Prentice-Hall, Englewood Cliffs, NJ.

Lee, H. et al.
  1994 DNA typing in forensic science. Part 1: Theory and background, *American Journal of Forensic Medicine and Pathology* 15(4):269–282.

  1998 Forensic applications of DNA typing. Part 2: Collection and preservation of DNA evidence, *American Journal of Forensic Medicine and Pathology* 19(1):10–18.

Lightowlers, R.N. et al.
  1997 Mammalian mitochondrial genetics: heredity, heteroplasmy, and disease, *Trends in Genetics* 13(11):450–455.

Lupski, J.R.
  1998 Genomic disorders: structural features of the genome can lead to DNA rearrangements and human disease traits, *Trends in Genetics* 14(10):417–422.

McKusick V.A. et al.
  1992 *DNA Technology in Forensic Science*, Commission on Life Sciences, National Research Council, National Academy Press, Washington, D.C.

Olaisen, B., M. Stenersen, and B. Mevag
  1997 Identification by DNA analysis of the victims of the August, 1996 Spitsbergen civil aircraft disaster, *Nature Genetics* 15(4):402–405.

Paabo, S.
  1996 Mutational hot-spots in the mitochondrial microcosm, *American Journal of Human Genetics* 59(3):493–496.

Parsons T.J. and V. Weedn
    1997   Preservation and recovery of DNA in postmortem specimens and trace samples. In *Forensic Taphonomy: The Postmortem Fate of Human Remains*, edited by W.D. Haglund, and M.H. Sorg, pp. 109–138. CRC Press, Boca Raton, FL.

Parsons, T.J. et al.
    1997   A high observed substitution rate in the human mitochondrial DNA control region, *Nature Genetics* 15(4):363–368.

Penchaszadeh, V.
    1992   Abduction of children of political dissidents in Argentina and the role of human genetics in their restitution, *Journal of Public Health Policy* 13(3):291–305.

    1997   Genetic identification of children of the disappeared in Argentina, *JAMWA* 52:16–21.

Pierez-Lezaun, A. et al.
    1997   Population genetics of Y-chromosome short tandem repeats in humans, *Journal of Molecular Evolution* 45(3):265–270.

Primorac D. et al.
    1996   Identification of war victims from mass graves in Croatia, Bosnia, and Herzegovina by the use of standard forensic methods and DNA typing, *Journal of Forensic Sciences* 41(5):891–894.

Raymond, C.
    1989   Forensics experts tackle task of identifying thousands of 'disappeared' victims, *JAMA*, 26:1388–1389.

Stoneking, M. et al.
    1991   Population variation of human mtDNA control region sequences detected by enzymatic amplification and sequence-specific oligonucleotide probes, *American Journal of Human Genetics* 48:370–382.

Strachan, T. and A.P. Read
    1999   *Human Molecular Genetics*, John Wiley and Sons, New York.

Teraski P. and D.W. Gjertson
    1997   HLA 1997. UCLA Tissue Typing Laboratory, The Regents of the University of California, Los Angeles, CA.

Underhill, P.A. et al.
    2000   Y chromosome secquence variation and the history of human populations, *Nature Genetics*, 26:358–361.

Vigilant, L. et al.
    1989   Mitochondrial DNA sequences in single hairs from a southern African population, *Proceedings of the National Academy of Sciences USA* 86:9350–9354.

von Haesler, A., A. Sajantila, and S. Paabo
    1995   The genetical archaeology of the human genome, *Nature Genetics* 14:135–140.

Weir, B.
    1996   The second National Research Council report on forensic DNA evidence, *American Journal of Human Genetics* 59:497–500.

White, T.J.
    1996   The future of PCR technology: diversification of technologies and applications, *Trends in Biotechnology* 14(12):478–483.

Disarticulation Pattern and Tooth Mark Artifacts Associated with Pig Scavenging of Human Remains: A Case Study

25

HUGH E. BERRYMAN

Contents

Introduction

Taphonomy as a tool of the forensic anthropologist has grown considerably over the past decade as evidenced by increases in published material on the subject (Haglund and Sorg, 1997). Completeness of recovery and accuracy of forensic anthropological interpretation depend upon familiarity with perimortem and postmortem activities affecting forensic remains. The importance of differentiating perimortem trauma from perimortem damage by scavengers has been presented by Rodriguez (1984) and Sorg (1986). Hill (1979a,b) and Willey and Snyder (1989) discussed the disarticulation pattern and scatter of mammal skeletons relative to the estimation of time since death, while Haglund et al. (1989) described canid scavenging and disarticulation sequence of human remains. Haynes (1983) described the effects of trampling and wallowing by hoofed animals and scavenging by bear. Scavenging by dogs, pigs, rodents, vultures, crows, hawks, raccoons, opossum, crabs, turtles, fish, deer, and sheep has been reported by Morse et al. (1983) and Sutcliffe (1971), along with the specific bony artifacts produced by some of these animals. The present study describes the taphonomic characteristics of domestic pig scavenger activity and tooth mark artifacts on human remains as seen in one forensic anthropology case.

Case Report

The human remains were discovered by a hunter in a wooded area of rural western Tennessee approximately 50 yards from the single-room house of a 75-year-old, Caucasian male (Mr. X) described as a recluse. Clothing, location, and the fact that Mr. X was missing (last seen 10 days prior) made him the primary suspect. Unfortunately, he had no dental records, and no medical records remained of his only medical treatment, administered 35 years earlier. The remains were found between the house and public road, west of a path in a well-worn area that appeared to have been used as an outdoor toilet.

Although no positive identification could be made, all circumstantial evidence supported the remains being those of Mr. X. Although race could not be determined, age, sex, stature, clothing, possessions, and condition of the remains were consistent with those of the suspect. The pants contained a .25-caliber, 2-shot chrome derringer with white handles; .25-caliber bullets; Mammoth Cave brand, twist-type chewing tobacco; and an empty Mushroom Burger wrapper. Mr. X was known to carry such a derringer, chewed Mammoth Cave brand tobacco, and often purchased this type burger at a nearby convenience store.

In a scene report provided by a Special Agent with the Tennessee Bureau of Investigation, it was noted that there was an active hog pen nearby from which the hogs were free ranging. The report also indicated that animal feces containing hair was found in association with the remains, and chickens were seen feeding on the insects around them.

Disarticulation Pattern

The remains were found in deciduous woods with both mature and immature trees, brush, and weeds. The body was lying on its back with the knees flexed and separated as though the individual had been in a squatting position (Figure 25.1). Clothing on the remains included pants with a knotted rope belt and boots, while a shirt lay on the ground beside

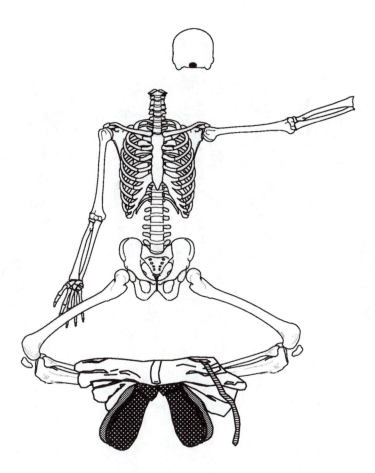

Figure 25.1 Position of the body at the scene indicated that the individual was on his back, knees flexed and separated, and the pants were around the lower legs. Most of the bones were in appropriate anatomic articulation. (Graphics application from LifeART™ Collections, 1993.)

the remains and a blue cap was nearby. The pants were still on the body, but were between the knees and ankles. Most of the bones, with the exception of the skull and left hand, were in appropriate anatomic articulation.

The remains were in the oily stage of decomposition, with the bones superior to the knees exposed. Beetle and fly larvae were present in large quantity and the odor was extreme. Most of the bones were present. Missing bones included those of the face, the mandible, cervical vertebrae 3 through 6, both pubic bones, most of the bones of the left hand and wrist, the proximal row phalange of the right thumb, two middle row phalanges of the right hand, and the distal row phalanges 2 through 5 of the right hand. Facial bones were fractured from the vault and missing, and the ribs and pubic bones exhibited fracturing due to scavenger activity.

Neither natural cover nor clothing protected the body from insect or scavenger activity. Bone fractures indicated that most of the scavenger activity was concentrated on the anterior, midline of the body (Figure 25.2). The bones of the face were fractured away from the vault, leaving it intact. Fractures occurred at the base of the zygomatic process of the right temporal bone, along the suture of the left zygomatic arch, and along both

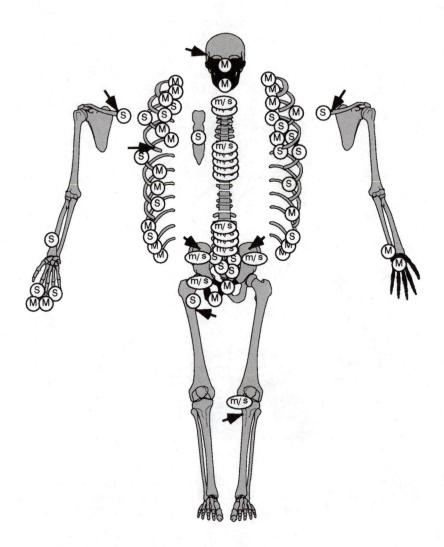

Ⓢ = Fractures related to scavenger activity

(m/s) = Fractures related to scavenger activity with some missing bone

Ⓜ = Fractures related to scavenger activity with major areas of missing bone

➤ = Broad scoring produced by anterior pig teeth

Figure 25.2 Scavenger damage to the bone indicates that the viscera, face, and hands were primary targets. The ilia show the greatest concentration of scoring produced by the pig's anterior, mandibular teeth. (Graphics application from LifeART™ Collections, 1993.)

zygomaticofrontal sutures. Both nasal bones were fractured with 25% of the free end missing, and the right and left maxillofrontal processes were fractured near the lacrimal duct. The anterior portion of the sphenoid was separated from the vault by fractures through both pterygoid processes and the anterior sphenoid body. The roof of the eye orbits were intact as was the cribriform plate, while both right and left ethmoid sinuses were exposed. The styloid processes were fractured and missing, and the base of the right mastoid process was fractured, exposing air cells. The mandible was not recovered and presumably had been removed from the scene by scavengers.

Fractures to the bones of the torso indicated that scavengers opened the body along the midline to feed on the viscera. Fractures were present at the medial ends of both clavicles and between costal facets 3 and 4 of the sternum. Seventeen of the 24 ribs had sternal end fractures, and 9 had fractures to the vertebral ends. The sternal ends exhibited direct evidence of scavenger activity (i.e., crushing), while fractures to the vertebral ends were produced largely by the indirect action of the scavenger, as the ribs were forced outward to provide access to the viscera. Fractures to the vertebrae appeared on the anterior body and transverse processes, and cervical vertebrae 3 through 6 were missing. All vertebrae, with the exception of thoracic vertebra 6 through lumbar vertebra 1, were affected. Of the bones of the pelvis, scavenger activity was evident to the sacrum, coccyx, and both pubic bones. The right pubic bone and most of the left were missing. The pubic rami had irregular fractures with crushing and depressed bone fragments. The sacral promontory was fractured away and there was crushing to the superior left ala and the internal surface of the sacrum. The most caudal vertebrae of the coccyx were missing.

Of the extremities, the left ulna and right radius exhibited scavenger activity with only minor damage to the distal ends. The bones of the hands showed more damage, and were incompletely represented. Four of the phalanges present had evidence of crushing and puncture defects. The right femur had bone missing from the inferior margin of the head, and the lesser trochanter had some crushing posteriorly. The left tibia had cortical bone missing along the margin of the medial condyle with associated crushing and depressed bone fragments.

Willey and Snyder (1989:896) described the dismemberment pattern of a deer carcass by wolves as follows:

> Initially, meaty sections such as the hindquarters are consumed, the thoracic cavity is opened, and the ribs are eaten. Often the throat is torn open, and the nose is eaten. Disarticulation of one or more limbs commonly occurs within 24 to 48 h, usually the forelimb before the hind limb. Following consumption of meaty parts, there is extensive destruction of limb bone ends, the vertebral column and the associated rib heads. Remnants of the vertebral column and hide are the last portions consumed, usually in four to seven days.

Haglund et al. (1989:589) examined canid scavenging of 30 sets of human remains discovered in forensic contexts and defined five sequential stages:

0 = Removal of soft tissue with no disarticulation.
1 = Destruction of the ventral thorax characterized by absence of the sternum and damage to distal ribs, accompanied by evisceration and removal of one or both upper extremities, including scapulae and partial or complete removal of clavicles.
2 = Fully or partially separated and removed lower extremities.
3 = Nearly complete disarticulation with only segments of vertebral column articulated.
4 = Total disarticulation and scattering, with only cranium and assorted skeletal elements or fragments recovered.

Galdikas (1978:69) described scavenging of a wild orangutan by Bornean bearded pigs (*Sus barbatus*):

The corpse was probably less that 12 hours old… The face, head, neck, all fingers and toes, and both legs and arms remained intact but the entire contents of the body cavity had been devoured, leaving the vertebral column, scapulae, clavicles, and pelvis exposed.

The pig-scavenged orangutan described by Galdikas (1978) was most similar to stage 1 of the canid-scavenged human remains described by Haglund et al. (1989). The visceral contents seemed to be the primary target for both canids (wolves, dogs, coyotes) and Bornean bearded pigs. Likewise, the viscera seemed to be a primary target for the domestic pigs associated with this case as can be more clearly demonstrated by the location of pig tooth mark artifacts on the bone.

Tooth Mark Artifacts

For carnivores, Binford (1981) identified four types of tooth mark artifacts (i.e., punctures, pits, scoring, and furrows), and Haglund et al. (1988), in an examination of 37 human skeletal remains, discussed the nature of tooth mark artifacts. Although not directly observed in the present case study, there was evidence of both canid and pig scavenging. Typical puncture defects were present on a number of the bones, indicating the presence of scavengers such as dogs, coyotes, or opossum. The characteristics associated with pig scavenging are most similar to a modified definition of Binford's "scoring."

Binford (1981:46) described scoring as "…the result of either turning the bone against the teeth or dragging the teeth across relatively compact bone… ." Characteristics specifically associated with pig scavenging consist of elongated and, often multiple, parallel scoring. The scoring was more obvious on flatter surfaces such as the skull and pelvis, but was also present on bones of the thorax and legs. Areas of bone modification showing scoring attributed to pig scavenger activity included (Figure 25.2) the following:

1. Skull. Scoring was present on the right temporal bone, right side of the frontal bone inferior to the temporal line, and right side of the sphenoid on the base of the cranium.
2. Thorax. Scoring was present on the posterior surface of the medial end of both clavicles. The head of right rib 4 was missing, and a thin score mark was present approximately 2.5 cm from the sternal end on the external rib surface.
3. Pelvis. The right innominate (Figure 25.3) was missing the pubic bone, and the internal surface of the ilium exhibited a 3.6 × 2 cm area of missing cortical bone with bone fragments displaced into the trabeculae. This finding is not typical of canids and was likely produced by the feeding action of the pigs. Multiple curvilinear scoring was present on the body of the ilium from superior to the greater sciatic notch to both the superior and inferior anterior iliac spines. The left innominate was missing the superior 75% of the pubic bone, and there was crushing of both rami. The internal surface of the ilium exhibited a 5.3 × 2.5 cm area of shattered and missing cortical bone. A few linear scoring marks were present on the internal surface superior to the greater sciatic notch.
4. Legs. The left tibia had an area of missing cortical bone along the margin of the medial condyle, and a 1.8 × 1.0 cm area of depressed and crushed bone 2.5 cm inferior to the medial condyle. The posterior surface of the proximal end of the tibia contained an area of linear scoring.

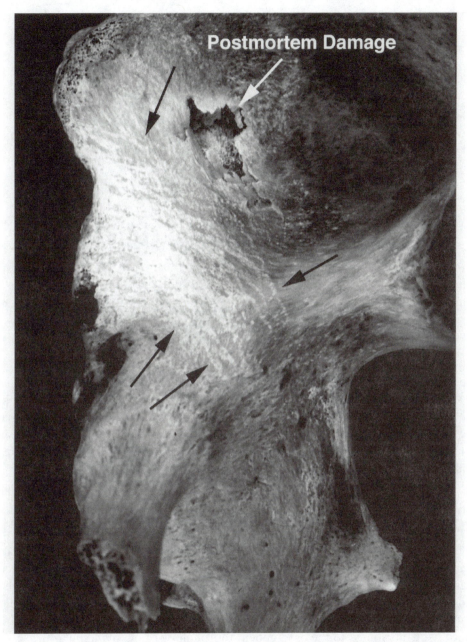

Figure 25.3 The right innominate exhibits an area of multiple curvilinear scoring (indicated by the black arrows) that extends from superior to the greater sciatic notch to both the superior and inferior anterior iliac spines. Also, a 3.6 × 2.0 cm area of missing cortical bone (indicated by the white arrow) represents an area of postmortem damage likely produced by pig scavenging.

Haglund et al. (1988:986) noted that "...tooth morphology, jaw mechanics, and strength relative to the bone have bearing on the amount of damage animals can produce." These also have a bearing of the type of damage imparted to the bone. The scoring in this case was produced by the mandibular incisors of the pig with their characteristically procumbent orientation (Figure 25.4). Pigs use the lower incisors in a rooting action to strip or

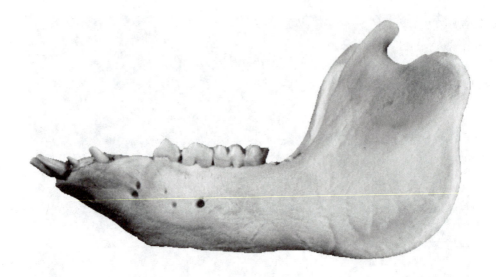

Figure 25.4 A lateral view of the pig mandible reveals procumbent incisors. This morphology along with the rooting action of the pig results in the production of the multiple scoring on the bone.

scrape the soft tissue from the bone surface. The scoring morphology presented in this case study differs from that described by Binford (1981) in that the floor of the individual score marks was broader as compared with the more V-shaped floor of canine drag marks. Also, there were areas of parallel scores that appeared to have been produced by a single action with multiple teeth contacting the bone surface as opposed to redundant or repetitive scoring from a single tooth.

Conclusion

The human remains were those of an adult male, dead less than 10 days in the relative warmth and humidity of a Tennessee September. Access to the body was not protected by clothing, and the surrounding vegetation was relatively open. The body was scavenged by canids and domestic pigs. Broad, parallel scores produced by a single action with multiple teeth contacting the bone surface, as well as repetitive scoring from a single tooth, are characteristics attributed to the procumbent morphology of pig mandibular incisors and the rooting action during feeding. Additionally, areas of missing cortical bone on the internal surface of the ilia bodies appear to have been produced by these incisors. Tooth mark artifact location indicates that the domestic pigs in this case focused primarily on the viscera, throat, and face as opposed to the meaty areas of the appendages.

Acknowledgments

To Dr. David L. Armbruster, University of Tennessee Memphis, for his critical review of the manuscript.

References

Binford, L.R.
 1981 *Bones: Ancient Men and Modern Myths*, Academic Press, New York.

Galdikas, B.M.F.
 1978 Orangutan death and scavenging by pigs, *Science* 200:68–70.

Haglund, W.D. and M.H. Sorg, Editors
 1997 *Forensic Taphonomy: The Postmortem Fate of Human Remains*, CRC Press, Boca Raton, FL.

Haglund, W.D., D.T. Reay, and D.R. Swindler
 1988 Tooth mark artifacts and survival of bones in animal scavenged human skeletons, *Journal of Forensic Sciences*, 33(4):985–997.

 1989 Canid scavenging/disarticulation sequence of human remains in the Pacific northwest, *Journal of Forensic Sciences*, 34(3):587–606.

Haynes, G.
 1983 Frequencies of spiral and green-bone fractures on ungulate limb bones in modern surface assemblages, *American Antiquity* 48(1):102.

Hill, A.
 1979a Butchering and natural disarticulation: an investigatory technique, *American Antiquity* 44(4):739–744.

 1979b Disarticulation and scattering of mammal skeletons, *Paleobiology* 5(3):261–274.

LifeART™ Collections
 1993 *Professional Medical Computer Graphics*, TechPool Corp., Cleveland, OH.

Morse, D., J. Duncan, and J.W. Stoutamire
 1983 *Handbook of Forensic Archaeology and Anthropology*, Rose Printing Co., Tallahassee, FL.

Rodriguez, W.C.
 1984 Postmortem Animal Activity: Recognition and Interpretation. Paper presented at the 39th Annual Meeting of the American Academy of Forensic Sciences, Anaheim, CA.

Sorg, M.H.
 1986 Scavenger Modifications of Human Skeletal Remains in Forensic Anthropology. Paper presented at the 38th Annual Meeting of the American Academy of Forensic Sciences, New Orleans.

Sutcliffe, A.J.
 1971 Similarity of bones and antlers gnawed by deer to human artifacts, *Nature* 246(5433):428–430.

Willey, P. and L.M. Snyder.
 1989 Canid modification of human remains: implications for time-since-death estimations, *Journal of Forensic Sciences* 34(4):894–901.

Index

A

Abduction. *See* Child abduction/homicides

Acrylics, degradation, 389

Actualistic research, 14–15

Adipocere formation, 207, 286

Age at time of death, 444–445

Agricultural cultivation
bones and, 140–141
buried materials and, 138–141
case histories, 141–149
cultivators, 137–138
fertilizer application, 136
harvesting equipment, 138
planting and seeding, 136–138
primary tillage, 134–136
secondary tillage, 136
seedbed refining, 136
weed control, 137–138

Aircraft accidents, 323, 324–325, 454, 478

American Indians. *See* Native Americans

Amplitude of movement, postdepositional, 103

Anasazi, cannibalism, 310–319

Animal turbation, 79–82
animal chewing, 342, 344
burrowing animals, 54, 55
carnivore modification, 411–413
commingling, 342, 344
predators, 157–163
pseudopathology and pseudotrauma and, 81–82
rodent modification, 409–411
scavenging by pigs, 488–494

Antemortem taphonomic period, 7, 9

Anthropologist, working with forensic taphonomist, 73–79

Aquatic settings. *See* Water environments

Argentina, "disappeared" children, 476–477

Arteries, impressions misinterpreted as cut marks, 82–84

Arthropathy, in human remains, 129

Articulation, 15, 103–104. *See also* Disarticulation

Autosomal DNA analysis, 474, 475, 477–478, 482

Avalanches, human remains from, 327

B

Battle of Aljubarrota (Portugal), 339

Bi-allelic markers, 479

Bijelo Polje grave (Bosnia-Herzegovina), 304–305

Biodeterioration. *See* Leather degradation; Textile degradation

Biological weapons, 328

Biostratinomy, 356

Bioturbation. *See* Animal turbation; Faunal turbation; Floral turbation

Blade wounds, 407

Blood vessels, 79, 82–84

Blow flies, 174
adult flies, 187–193
carcasses in water, 207–208
case histories, 176–177, 180–183, 185–187, 189–194
eggs, 174, 175–179
larvae, 179–184
myiasis, 181–182
pupae, 184–188, 193

Blunt-force trauma, contemporary mass graves, 272–273

Body surface, bog bodies, 122–124

Bog bodies, 17–18, 120–130
body surface, 122–124
connective tissue preservation, 125–126
dating of, 120–121
preservation of, 121–122
tissues and organs, 124–127

Bombings, human remains from, 325–326

Bone counts, 345–346

Bone density, 344

Bone fractures
agricultural cultivation and, 140–141
cannibalism and, 315
plant root trauma differentiated from, 79

Bones. *See also* Human remains; Skeletal elements
agricultural cultivation and, 140–141
animal chewing, 81–82, 342, 344
blunt-force trauma, 272–273